GEORGIE

PONTUS Trapesus
Trebisonde

AMAZONES

ARM

ASI

Thermodon fl.

Cyrus fluvius

Casalmac
Iris fl.

Erzeron

Araxes fl.

PADOCI

Mouratchai

Araxes fl. Aras R.

HIR

I A Euphrates
Eugrate

ASIATIQUE

Euphrates nunc

ATROPATENA

Gelæ seu Cadusii
GHILAN

Fons Tigridis

Gabris Tauris

ADERBI JANE

Fer
T.
TH
Ta

Pile

Adiabene

Montes Gordiæi

MEDIA

Rhages
Rhey ruine

Sochos
Vacchæ
Antioche

ASSYRIA
Soada Mtes

Gordiene

COURDISTAN

Echatana

Amadan

Tabas Sava

Berrhœa
Alep

Ninus
Mosul

Gaugamela
Arbela

I R A C A G E M I

Nisæus
Campus

Tarium

Tapsacus

MESOPOTAMIA

Nizus
Capro Irbil

Niphates M.

Celonæ

A S I

Cossæi

SYRI
SYRIE

DIARBEC

Euphrates flavius

Tigris Fluvius

Slambana

Bagistane

Pa
P

Damascus
Damas

Tigre Riv

Bagdad

Sitacene

Memnum sub
Fons Bituminis
Leth R.

Bab

Mon
Hella

Seu
Satrapene

Aspadan
Ispahan

bes Campestres

Bedouins

Bursia

Batana
Cara
Pag

Opis

BABILONIA
Chaldæi

Susa
Souster

U.

IRACARABI

A R A B I A D E S E R T A

Urbs ab Alexandro
condita

SU
CHU

SSIANA
SISTAN

Euphrates fl.

Basora
Diridotus
Vicu Bassora

RÆA

Eulæus fl.
Caron R.

A R A · B I E

SINUS

A R A B I A   F E L I X

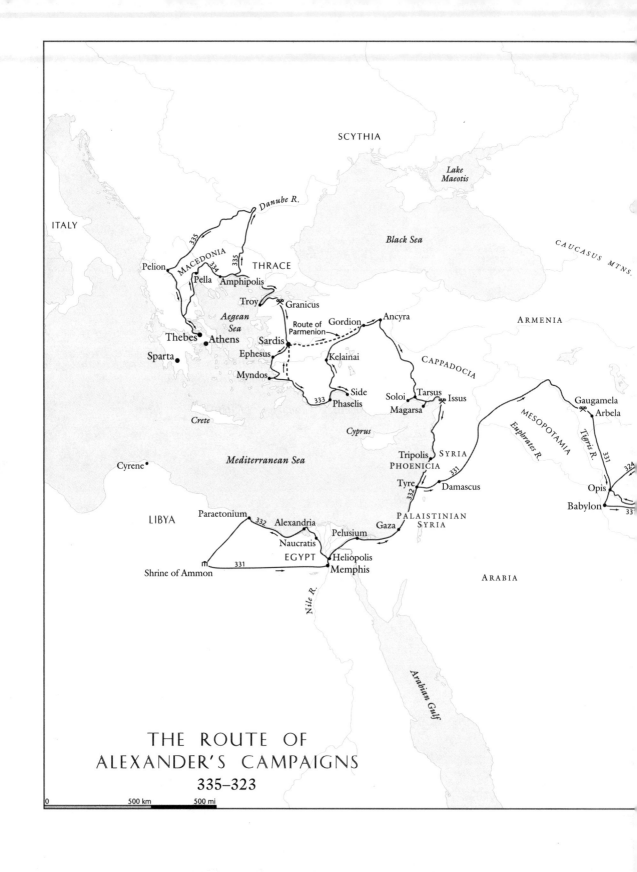

SCYTHIA

Lake Maeotis

ITALY

Danube R.

Black Sea

CAUCASUS MTNS.

335

MACEDONIA

Pelion

334

Pella

Amphipolis

335

THRACE

Troy

Granicus

ARMENIA

Route of Parmenion

Gordion

Ancyra

Aegean Sea

Thebes

Athens

Sardis

Ephesus

Kelainai

CAPPADOCIA

Sparta

Myndos

333

Side

Soloi

Tarsus

Gaugamela

Issus

Arbela

Phaselis

Magarsa

MESOPOTAMIA

Crete

Cyprus

Euphrates R.

Tigris R.

331

Mediterranean Sea

Tripolis

SYRIA

Cyrene

224

PHOENICIA

331

Opis

Tyre

Damascus

33

332

Babylon

LIBYA

Paraetonium

332

Alexandria

PALAISTINIAN SYRIA

Pelusium

Gaza

Naucratis

EGYPT

Heliopolis

331

Memphis

ARABIA

Shrine of Ammon

Nile R.

Arabian Gulf

THE ROUTE OF ALEXANDER'S CAMPAIGNS
335–323

0   500 km   500 mi

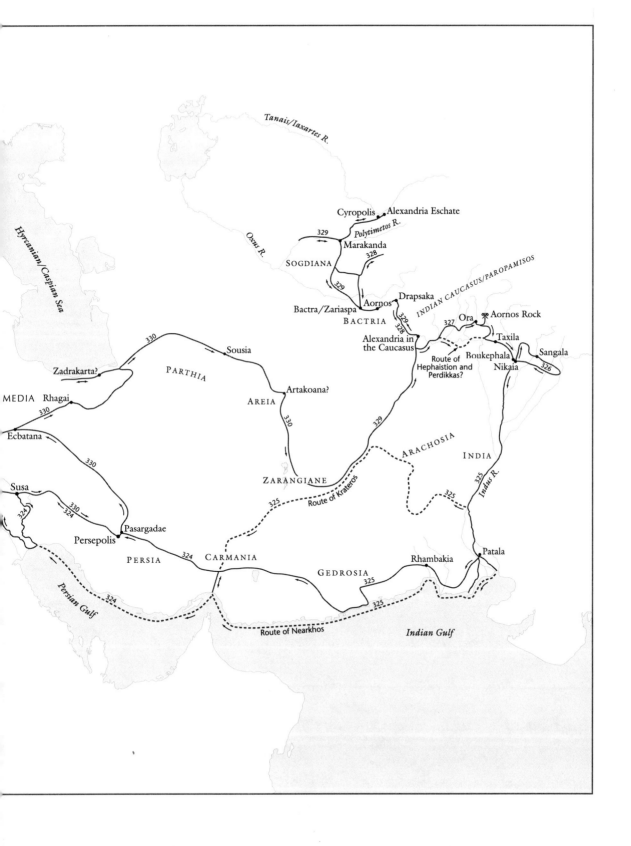

THE LANDMARK ARRIAN

THE LANDMARK
ARRIAN

THE CAMPAIGNS OF ALEXANDER

Anabasis Alexandrou

A New Translation by Pamela Mensch
with Maps, Annotations, Appendices, and Encyclopedic Index

Edited by James Romm

Series Editor Robert B. Strassler

With an Introduction by Paul Cartledge

PANTHEON BOOKS • NEW YORK

Frontispiece: fourth-century ivory bust usually assumed to represent Alexander as a young man, found in Tomb II of the royal burial complex at Aigeai.

Library of Congress Cataloging-in-Publication Data

Arrian.
[Anabasis. English]
The Landmark Arrian : the campaigns of Alexander : a new translation / by Pamela Mensch ; with maps, annotations, appendices, and encyclopedic index ; edited by James Romm ; with an introduction by Paul Cartledge.
   p. cm.
Includes bibliographical references and index.
ISBN 978–0–375–42346–8
1. Alexander, the Great, 356–323 B.C. 2. Alexander, the Great, 356–323 B.C.—Military leadership.
3. Greece—History—Macedonian Expansion, 359–323 B.C. 4. Greece—Kings and rulers—Biography.
5. Generals—Greece—Biography. I. Mensch, Pamela, 1956– II. Romm, James S. III. Title.
IV. Title: Campaigns of Alexander.
DF234.A77313 2010 938'.07—dc22 2010029650

Designed by Kim Llewellyn
Maps by Beehive Mapping
Photo research by Ingrid MacGillis
Index by Cohen Carruth, Inc.

www.pantheonbooks.com

Printed in the United States of America

First Edition

9 8 7 6 5 4 3 2 1

FOR MY DAD,
ALAN ROMM

CONTENTS

INTRODUCTION

Paul Cartledge

Arrian's Literary Models

§1.1. The book you are about to read is a history of the career—especially the expedition to conquer the Persian empire—of Alexander III, king of Macedonia, who became known posthumously and inseparably as "the Great" (b. 356, r. 336–323). The author was a second-century C.E. historian whom we call Arrian but whose given name was Lucius (or Aulus) Flavius Arrianus. Although he was an ethnic Greek from Nicomedia, in Bithynia in northwest Asia Minor, he was also—proudly and successfully—a Roman citizen. Indeed, he achieved the very rare double distinction of attaining the top office of the consulship at Rome and being appointed an archon (a member of the chief board of officials, a purely honorific appointment by this time) at Athens.[a] Both attainments bespeak high imperial favor, and indeed Arrian enjoyed that of the strongly philhellenic emperor Hadrian (r. 117–138 C.E.)—a Roman of Italian descent from colonial Spain and so principally a Latin speaker by upbringing, whereas Arrian was a native Hellenophone for whom Latin was a second language. Like all good high-ranking Romans, Arrian was given three names—a forename, a family name (which he shared with a former imperial dynasty, that of Vespasian and his sons, emperors from 69 to 96 C.E.), and an aftername. However, on top of those three, he seems to have greedily added a fourth—a very personal choice, and by no means an obvious one: Xenophon. This he took in homage to one particular Greek forerunner and adopted role model: Xenophon of Athens (c. 428–c. 354).

§1.2. Why did Arrian choose to make a history of Alexander the Great the object of his principal literary work? We shall never know for sure, since he didn't write an autobiography or even, despite his philosophical bent, a philosophical reflection in autobiographical form, like the *Meditations* of his younger contemporary emperor Marcus Aurelius (r. 161–180 C.E.). But the adopted name Xenophon is a rather heavy clue. Arrian flourished in the midst of a remarkable Hellenic liter-

---

NOTE: All dates in this volume are B.C.E. (Before the Common Era), unless otherwise specified. Most locations mentioned in the Introduction can be found in the Reference Maps section.

Intro.1.1a For more detail on Arrian's background, see Appendix R, Arrian's Life and Works.

ary efflorescence under the high Roman empire, a period or movement known as the Second Sophistic.[a] (It was so named because it resembled the flowering of rhetoric and philosophy that Athens had experienced in the fifth and fourth centuries, when intellectuals known as Sophists broke new ground in many schools of thought.) Xenophon was an almost exact contemporary of Plato's, nearly as well off as he (though less nobly born), and a fellow citizen of Athens. Like Plato, too, he had both the call and the leisure during his adolescence to attach himself to Socrates as a pupil or at least a follower. Xenophon's and Plato's adult careers took radically different paths, but both retained a deep and deeply spiritual fondness for their common mentor, and both took it upon themselves to write an imaginary *Apology* (defense speech) on his behalf; both used these speeches to express their doubts about the competence of the *demos*, the citizen body of democratic Athens, which condemned Socrates to death in 399 on a double capital charge of impiety and pedagogic/political subversion. But whereas Plato stuck pretty narrowly to writing what he may have been the first to label "philosophy," Xenophon—while never losing sight of philosophy, especially ethics, in a broad sense—indulged himself with literary forays into all the then-recognized genres of prose writing: history, memoir, encomium, technical treatise, and political pamphlet.

§1.3. Arrian, by no means a slavish follower of his Classical Greek model, combined the title of one of Xenophon's works, the *Anabasis*, with the subject matter of no fewer than three others: narrative history, memoir, and encomium. Xenophon's *Anabasis* was probably a riposte to another account of the same subject matter: the experiences of some thirteen thousand Greek mercenaries who were recruited under Spartan auspices to support the attempt in 401 of the Persian pretender Cyrus the Younger to overthrow and replace the reigning Persian emperor, Artaxerxes II, his older full brother. The attempt was a failure, because Cyrus was killed in a major battle near Babylon, one of the nerve centers of the Persian empire, but the Greek hired lances did themselves credit—too much so indeed for the taste of one of Artaxerxes' principal lieutenants, the satrap (viceroy) Tissaphernes, who treacherously arranged for the cold-blooded murder of all their principal commanders. Into the breach stepped, among others, Xenophon, and it was thanks largely to his leadership—if his own account may be trusted—that the surviving ten thousand or so struggled their weary way back in winter through what is now Iraq, Armenia, and eastern Turkey eventually to the southern shore of the Black Sea and so back to the pale of Greek civilization.[a] Xenophon had thus seen for himself vast stretches of the Persian empire that Alexander was to terminate some seventy years later. But he was also—as I suspect Arrian was, too—fascinated by the Persian empire as such, the largest and most multinational empire known to the West at that date, and it was onto Cyrus the Younger's ancestor and namesake Cyrus II the Great, the empire's founder, that

Intro.1.2a T. Whitmarsh, *Ancient Greek Literature* (Cambridge and Malden, MA: Polity Press, 2004), 146–148.

Intro.1.3a J. I. W. Lee, *A Greek Army on the March: Soldiers and Survival in Xenophon's* Anabasis

(Cambridge and New York: Cambridge University Press, 2007).

Xenophon projected a supposedly historical but in fact pedagogic account of ideal leadership, the *Cyropaedia*, or *Education of Cyrus*. Arrian might thus have been similarly inspired to follow and write up the career of the Persian empire's conqueror—or, rather, as Alexander projected himself, its new founder. The combination of politics, philosophy, and military history that Xenophon practiced was very much to Arrian's liking. As a student, he had sat at the feet of the Stoic sage and ex-slave Epictetus, much as Xenophon had at the probably rather smelly ones of Socrates. As an adult, Arrian fought and commanded in a wide range of theaters, mainly in the eastern, Greek half of the Roman empire. Above all, like Xenophon, he was a compulsive writer. Philosophical works, works on military tactics, memoirs—all flowed from his prolific stylus at various points between the 120s and 140s C.E.

§1.4. On top of those personal motives, however, there was the zeitgeist to impel Arrian in the same direction. It is a very striking fact that all the main narrative accounts of Alexander that survive come not from in or near his lifetime but from three hundred and more years later, from the high Roman imperial period—the last century B.C.E. and the first two C.E. Within that period, first the rival Roman magnates Pompey and Caesar sought to emulate Alexander's deeds and, no less, fame; then the Roman emperors, more than half of whose subjects belonged to the Greek-speaking eastern half of their empire, sought to borrow bits and pieces of Alexander's deportment and aura to modulate or bolster their own often rather shaky rule.[a] Arrian therefore, in choosing Alexander for his subject, had also a kind of captive audience to whom he could address himself. It is of course a huge tribute to him that it is his work and not another Roman Alexander historian's that we have chosen to include in the Landmark Histories series, and below I shall try to suggest some of the reasons his work remains important and eminently worth reading. But it has to be stated firmly at the outset that one of those reasons is not because his *Anabasis Alexandrou* is in any sense definitive (if indeed any work of history may properly be so called). Indeed, his work is as difficult and paradoxical, in its own ways, as any of the other Alexander histories.

Arrian's Sources[a]

§2.1. A distinguished scholar of Macedonia and Alexander, the Cambridge historian G. T. Griffith, once observed with a certain amount of frustration: "It is one of the paradoxes of history (and of historiography) that this king . . . should have been handed down finally in history as an enigma."[a] Alexander had gone to the lengths of appointing an official historian, Kallisthenes, setting a dangerous precedent; and he always took immense care that his image—understood in the literal, physical sense as well as metaphorically—should be disseminated as widely as possible throughout his empire in the forms that he personally had authorized and approved.[b] Yet a

Intro.1.4a D. Spencer, *The Roman Alexander: Reading a Cultural Myth* (Exeter and Chicago: University of Exeter Press, 2002).
Intro.2a For a lengthier discussion of the subject, see Appendix A, Arrian's Sources and Reliability.
Intro.2.1a G. T. Griffith, introduction, in Griffith (ed.), *Alexander the Great: The Main Problems* (Cambridge: Heffer, 1966), 425.
Intro.2.1b A. F. Stewart, *Faces of Power: Alexander's Image and Hellenistic Politics* (California and London: University of California Press, 1993).

fertile combination of the nonsurvival of the contemporary primary literary sources, the survival of a relatively small number of contemporary official and unofficial documents, and the immense controversies that his career generated both during and long after his lifetime has ensured that attempting to reconstruct the historical Alexander is almost as problematic as trying to reconstruct the historical Jesus. Actually, every reconstruction is a construction: every historian has an Alexander of his or her own, one that to some extent is a projection of the author's own fancies or fantasies. Arrian himself (7.30.1) sagely warns historians and other students of Alexander against seeking to drag him down to their own, humble level. Thus not only is it often impossible to say exactly what Alexander did, let alone why he did it, but it is also often impossible to place a particular event or episode within a convincing, coherent overall pattern. To take just two examples: we can never be sure how or why Kallisthenes died in 327, nor why Alexander paid his remarkable visit to the oracular shrine of the Egyptian god Ammon (Amun) in the far distant Siwa oasis in 332.[c]

The extant sources may be divided into five categories:

Eyewitnesses

§2.2. These survive either only in fragmentary form (quotations or allusions in other surviving writers, such as Strabo, a Greek geographer and historian of the later first century B.C.E.) or not at all. Kallisthenes of Olynthos was a relative of Aristotle's and probably was recommended to Alexander by his kinsman, who had tutored the teenaged Alexander at Mieza in Macedonia in the late 340s. Eumenes of Kardia in the Hellespont was Alexander's personal secretary, responsible for keeping his *Journals* (see §2.8). Khares of Mytilene on Lesbos was a courtier of Alexander's and, as his chamberlain, an indispensable functionary as Alexander developed an unprecedentedly—for a Greek monarch—elaborate court that fused Greek, Macedonian, and Persian personnel and protocols. He was privy to much gossip, which is what it seems he chose chiefly to purvey in his memoirs. Nearkhos was a Greek from Crete, privileged to be educated by Aristotle with Alexander at Mieza. Alexander elevated him to the position of admiral of the fleet—one for which kings of Macedon had hitherto had no use, as Macedon had had no fleet. Nearkhos wrote up his experiences with Alexander, no doubt with a certain amount of self-justification as well as self-promotion, since his missions along the coast from western India to southern Iran were by no means entirely successful. Arrian's *Indika* (*Indian History*) draws heavily on Nearkhos. Onesikritos, another Greek islander (from Aegean Astypalaia), brought a philosophical dimension to his memoir of his time with Alexander, being an adept of the Cynic school of philosophy and not above casting Alexander as a heroic king in a Cynic mold.

Intro.2.1c   On both, see P. Cartledge, *Alexander the Great: The Hunt for a New Past* (New York and London: MacMillan, 2004), Appendix, 267–294.

§2.3. The remaining two eyewitness writers have a special importance for us, as they are self-confessedly the sources of choice upon whom Arrian explicitly relied. Ptolemy (in Macedonian Greek, Ptolemaios) son of Lagos was another graduate of the Aristotelian Mieza school, but his tastes and aptitudes remained firmly terrestrial. Thanks to his military command capabilities and his unswerving loyalty, he rose to assume the status of a marshal of Alexander's entire empire by the time of his sovereign's death. After the rapid posthumous carve-up of that briefly unitary empire, Ptolemy chose for himself the province of Egypt, where, for example, he had played a prominent role in the expedition to the Siwa oracle (3.3–4). When in 306 his rival "Successors" claimed for themselves the title of king, in imitation of Alexander, Ptolemy trumped them by becoming also pharaoh—and it was as a new god-king that he thus founded the Ptolemaic dynasty named after him. This lasted remarkably until the death by suicide of Cleopatra VII, the famous—or notorious—Cleopatra, in 30 B.C.E. The founding Ptolemy reigned into a ripe old age, until 285, and it was as an old man, toward the end of his reign, that he composed the work of memoir-history on which Arrian chose to rely—on the rather odd grounds that Ptolemy, being a king, could not afford to lie (or, we might rather think, afford to be caught out in telling one; see Preface 2 and n. Pref.2a). Actually, what Arrian—himself an old soldier—probably appreciated most about Ptolemy's version of Alexander's campaign was its attention to military detail and incomparable firsthand knowledge of the high command strategy and tactics.

§2.4. Aristoboulos was a man and a writer of a very different stamp. He was a Greek by origin who later settled in a city in Macedonia founded after Alexander's death, Kassandreia, thereby declaring his continued allegiance to the Macedonian cause. He was by profession or avocation a designer of some sort—possibly also an architect or engineer. As such, he was ordered, for example, by Alexander in 324 to take charge of the restoration of Cyrus the Great's desecrated tomb at Pasargadae in southern Iran, the original capital of the Achaemenid Persian empire (6.29.4–10). But he had an interest also in natural history, in the flora and fauna of Asia, that appealed to the tastes of his Macedonian master. His chief drawback—as it might seem to us, but this was no deterrent to Arrian—is that he was one of several writers to attract the derogatory label of "flatterer." That is, he was a courtier who saw it as his duty to place the best possible construction on what critics considered to be major flaws in Alexander's character or behavior. For example, there seems little reason to doubt that on occasion Alexander would drink alcohol to excess—though whether that makes him a clinical alcoholic is quite a different matter.[a] For Aristoboulos, however, Alexander drank only in a social sense, as a polite way of improving relations with friends, and never binged. Flatterer, indeed.

Intro.2.4a Alcoholism is asserted most strongly by J. M. O'Brien, *Alexander the Great: The Invisible Enemy, A Biography* (London and New York: Routledge, 1992).

The Vulgate Tradition

§2.5. One of the greatest achievements of nineteenth-century philological scholarship was to sort out the complex "tradition" of ancient Alexander literature: that is, to draw a sharp distinction between what I have called the eyewitnesses and those writers who not only were not themselves eyewitnesses but preferred to base their accounts on an ultimate source who neither was an eyewitness (though he was a near-contemporary) nor was basically pro-Alexander. That source was the Greek Kleitarkhos, whose account was probably also written at Alexandria—indeed, King Ptolemy's was very likely a response to its challenge. Kleitarkhos could in principle have drawn heavily, as did Thucydides' account of the Peloponnesian War, on close cross-questioning of participants in the Alexander campaign, but actually he did not rise to anywhere near such a level of historiographical conscientiousness. What interested Kleitarkhos most, apparently, as it appealed most to his followers, was a ripping good story, rather heavily romanticized and laced with scandal. This is not of course to say that it is therefore no more historically worthwhile than the so-called Pseudo-Kallisthenes' *Historia Alexandri Magni*, the *Alexander Romance*, which, though it was developed at Alexandria in the last centuries B.C.E. and first centuries C.E., survives in versions written in a number of ancient languages besides Greek.[a] But it does mean that, even if for different reasons, one has to be no less wary of the vulgate tradition than of its rival, what is sometimes called the official tradition, stemming from Kallisthenes, of which Arrian's *Anabasis Alexandrou* is the prime extant witness.

§2.6. Diodorus Siculus was a Sicilian Greek active at Rome in the latter part of the last century B.C.E. His magnum opus was an oddly titled *Library of History*, a title that not only indicates his debt to the works of others but also implies the claim that all you needed to know about the ancient world in annalistic (year-by-year) narrative form could be found within his pages or, rather, scrolls. In what we know as Book 16 he dealt with the reign of Alexander's father, Philip (r. 359–336), and in Book 17 that of Alexander, though unfortunately Book 17 has not come down to us complete. Diodorus' usual technique for each topic (in this case a reign) was, it seems, to fasten on one principal predecessor as his main source, to fillet that source so as to yield a streamlined chronological narrative, and then to embellish that skeleton with flesh drawn from a number of other writers. In the case of Book 17, thanks partly to its incomplete survival, it's not possible to identify his main source with certainty. Contemporary with Diodorus the Greek was an account in Latin by a romanized Gaul named Pompeius Trogus; this work, however, survives only in an epitome done by a writer we know for short as Justin, working around 200 C.E. Finally, the vulgate tradition is represented most extensively and most engagingly by the first-century C.E. Roman writer Quintus Curtius Rufus, although the first two books of his ten-book work have been lost. Overly

Intro.2.5a For the *Alexander Romance*, see R. Stoneman, *Alexander the Great: A Life in Legend* (New Haven and London: Yale University Press, 2008). Also see Appendix L, The *Alexander Romance*.

rhetorical to our taste Curtius may well be, but what survives often has real substance, not least because Curtius was not above drawing on the "official" tradition too.

Plutarch

§2.7. In a category all by itself is Plutarch's biography or biographical history of Alexander.[a] Plutarch prefaces his life of Alexander with a ringing declaration that he writes "lives" and not "histories"—his "Alexander" was in fact one of his *Parallel Lives*, paired biographies comparing Greek figures with Romans, fifty in all (Alexander is paired with Julius Caesar). But his ethical conception of biography—the ultimate aim being to exemplify virtue and vice, providing a series of models for his readers to imitate or avoid—allowed for a lavish interest in history too, as that subject was generally then understood (Plutarch flourished in the decades on either side of 100 C.E.): namely, as an account of a people's or person's public, usually more or less political actions. The interest of the "Alexander," therefore, is enhanced rather than diminished by Plutarch's eye for the telling anecdote—or physical or character trait—that might not have struck a less subtle commentator in the same way, if at all. Not only that, but in his work Plutarch parades a vast array of previous Alexander-writers, his "sources," going back ultimately to eyewitness accounts, such as that of Khares the chamberlain, mentioned above.

Documents

§2.8. Historiography today is ideally based on documents. Documents illustrating Alexander's career, whether real or supposed, include the following. The *hypomnemata*, or "notebooks," referred to once by Diodorus (18.4), may have contained Alexander's own most intimate thoughts and plans, though it's more likely that they did not. The *Ephemerides*, or *Royal Journals*, were kept by Eumenes, Alexander's personal secretary, who later rose to be a major player in his own right and the subject of an extant biography by Plutarch. They would surely have thrown light on Alexander's last days, had they survived—and been reliable. The various letters attributed to Alexander, scattered liberally through Plutarch's "Alexander," for instance, are probably all—or almost all—spurious, pleasing though it would be to feel one had direct access to, say, exactly what propaganda Alexander conveyed to Darius before he had finally defeated him.[a] There are no official (or unofficial) Persian accounts certainly extant, and documents from the Persian side tend to be formulaic in any case. However, Darius was able right up to the final battle of Gaugamela to recruit huge numbers of Greek mercenary soldiers (see §3.4). From their circles there has been identified a "mercenaries source," but its value is dubious and limited. Contemporary documentary inscriptions from the Greek side include, for example, texts from Mytilene and Tegea bearing on the consequences of

Intro.2.7a J. R. Hamilton's *Plutarch: Alexander: A Commentary* (Oxford: Clarendon Press, 1969) deserves special mention; see also J. Mossman, "Tragedy and Epic in Plutarch's *Life of Alexander*" (1988), reprinted in B. Scardigli (ed.), *Essays on Plutarch's Lives* (Oxford: Clarendon Press, 1995).

Intro.2.8a Hamilton, *Plutarch*, lix–lxx.

Alexander's "Exiles' Decree" of 324, but between them they don't amount to a very tall hill of beans.[b]

Visual and Material Sources

§2.9. Finally, all sorts and conditions of visual and material sources are available, both contemporary and noncontemporary, that together can form the basis of a substantial book or two. One might single out the images in various media of Alexander himself[a]—"faces of power," as they have been nicely called—put about not only by Alexander himself, of course, but also by those after him seeking to tap into his aura and charisma.

Cultural Identity in the *Anabasis*

§3.1. Identity both personal and collective, especially ethnic, is one of today's most gripping historical and historiographical issues. As it happens, a fierce and seemingly interminable debate rages today over the meaning and reference of "Macedonia" as a political marker. The modern state of Greece and the modern Republic of Macedonia—or the former Yugoslav Republic of Macedonia, as Greece prefers it—are at loggerheads over the matter, and the dispute has strong resonances as far afield as the United States and Australia, exacerbated as it has been especially by murderous deeds in the south Balkan peninsula in the 1990s. One important dimension of the modern dispute, as is often, even perhaps usually, the case in issues of disputed nationalism and national identity, is the appeal to antiquity, and Alexander the Great stands firmly at the heart of this hotly contested appeal. I shall not get into the dispute here, but the question of in what sense Alexander and/or his Macedonian subjects were (also) Greeks—Hellenes—is very pertinent to our reading of Arrian.

§3.2. It was an issue at least by the early fifth century B.C.E., when Macedon was under the rule of Alexander I (c. 498–452). This Alexander, a direct ancestor of Alexander III's, acquired the sobriquet "the Philhellene." Clearly, this was meant to be flattering, even though in itself the title would seem to imply that he was not himself a Hellene but, rather, one who favored the Hellenes. The thinking behind the label seems to have been roughly as follows: On the one hand, he was a vassal ruler within the Persian empire, with links by marriage to the Persian royal family. On the other, when the crunch time came for him to decide between Persia and Greece during the invasion of Xerxes in 480, without formally defecting from his Persian suzerain he nevertheless did what he could for the cause of the Greeks. Herodotus, the main source as always, is cannily instructive. He details the Macedonian royal house's supposed southern Greek ancestry (the Argeads claimed to

Intro.2.8b A. J. Heisserer, *Alexander the Great and the Greeks: The Epigraphic Evidence* (Norman: University of Oklahoma Press, 1981).
Intro.2.9a R. Lane Fox's *The Search for Alexander* (London: Allen Lane, 1980) gives a good conspectus. It accompanied an exhibition of the same title (catalog published by Little, Brown: Boston, 1980) at the National Gallery of Art, Washington, D.C. See also Stewart, *Faces of Power*.

have migrated north from Argos). He notes that the authorities who decided such matters permitted Alexander I to participate, in the Greeks-only Olympic Games, then declares himself satisfied that on these criteria of descent and public ethnic classification Alexander I was indeed a Greek (*Histories* 5.22). But that did not mean that he thought any other Macedonians were, and he makes it quite plain that he considered Alexander I to be, though Greek, a really rather poor specimen.

§3.3. The issue resurfaced in a big way in the reign of Philip, Alexander the Great's father, and again a Panhellenic religious festival was involved, this time the Pythian Games of Delphi. Though Greeks such as Demosthenes condemned the Macedonians in general, and even Philip, as barbarian, Philip took up arms in 352 against the Phocians in a "Sacred" War over the control of Apollo's shrine at Delphi. Pointedly, he had his troops go into the battle of the Crocus Field in Thessaly wearing Apollo's hallmark laurel wreath, as if making a holy sacrifice to and on behalf of the god. When that war was concluded finally, in 346, Philip attempted to stamp his claim to Hellenicity (Greek ethnic identity) by presiding over the quadrennial Pythian Games, which conveniently happened to fall due that year. It was possibly also in that same year that Philip first conceived his Grand Project, again a peculiarly Panhellenic matter, since he explicitly framed his intended anti-Persian campaign as one of justified if delayed Hellenic revenge for Persian sacrilege committed during Xerxes' invasion of Greece in 480–479. Alexander, as he often did, followed where Philip had led. Arrian takes the full Panhellenic measure of such actions of Alexander's as the destruction of Thebes (and sparing of Pindar's house, 1.9.10) in 335 and the inscription accompanying his dedication at Athens of spoils from his first major battles at the Granicus River in 334 ("Alexander, son of Philip, and the Greeks . . . ," 1.16.7). But it is in his account of Alexander's second major battle, at Issus in 333, that he allows the undercurrent of contention over the issue of the Macedonians' Greekness to rise to the surface.[a]

§3.4. At 2.10.7 Arrian speaks of the *philotimia*—rivalrous ambition and contention—that had existed for some time between the Hellenic and Macedonian *genē* (roughly, "races") that is, he treats "Greeks and Macedonians" as members of two distinct ethnic groups, rather than the Macedonians as a subdivision of the Hellenic *genos*. And he says that this preexisting *philotimia* exacerbated the fighting at Issus, which—far from being a clear-cut issue between Greeks on one side and non-Greeks on the other—was among other things a battle of Greeks against Greeks, with more of them on the side of Darius than on that of Alexander. This was because Greeks had signed up in droves under Darius' flag as mercenaries, some for political or ideological reasons but the overwhelming majority for economic ones: Persians were traditionally better employers, not least better payers, than Greeks.[a] And that continued to be the case right down to and including the battle

---

Intro.3.3a For modern views on this issue, see Appendix B, Greek and Macedonian Ethnicity.

Intro.3.4a P. A. Brunt, *Arrian: Anabasis of Alexander and Indica*, 2 vols. (Cambridge, MA: Loeb Classical Library, 1976–1983), vol. I:

xxxv–xlv ("The Macedonians"), at xxxvii n. 33. These two volumes are far more than merely a translation; they constitute also a (superb) edition and commentary on the *Anabasis Alexandrou*.

of Gaugamela: more Greeks fought against Alexander than fought on his side, despite his "Panhellenic" propaganda vigorously promoted through all available channels.

Humans and Gods in the *Anabasis*

§4.1. Arrian concluded his work, as we shall see below, on a note of piety. There was, he found himself forced to infer, something more than merely mortal about Alexander's birth, as was similarly indicated to him by the oracles, dreams, and apparitions reported at the time of Alexander's death (7.30.2). However, there was for Arrian a very big difference between being divinely favored and inspired and being a divinity oneself. Throughout, Arrian draws attention to Alexander's piety—what we might be tempted to call his superstition or religiosity. The role of Aristandros of Telmessos, Alexander's favorite interpreter of omens and portents, is constantly highlighted (nine references to him are made). As Alexander's career progresses, Arrian registers the king's changing preferences for the gods and goddesses to whom he devoted special favor and attention, most obviously and in some ways above all to Egyptian Ammon, with whom he had communed in that extraordinary side trip to the Siwa oasis in 332, undertaken in response to one of his irresistible cravings (*pothos*, 3.3.1), and to whom he allegedly sent envoys after his beloved Hephaistion's death for advice on how to properly revere his friend (7.14.7).

§4.2. That sort of piety was one thing, perfectly within the reasonable bounds of accepted "normality" for Arrian. But that Alexander might actually have considered himself to be a god and therefore have demanded worship of himself as such during his lifetime from Greeks as well as barbarians, some of whom (the Egyptians, conspicuously) had traditionally worshiped their kings as living gods—that was quite another matter. Arrian, who could be a subtle writer and by no means only the bluff military narrator, makes his view quite clear to careful readers in his account of a Greek embassy sent to Alexander at Babylon very shortly before his death (7.23.2).

> Embassies from Greece also arrived at that time. The ambassadors, wearing golden crowns, approached Alexander and placed golden crowns on his head as well, really as though they had come to pay honor to a god. But as it turned out, Alexander's end was not far off.

§4.3. *But as it turned out*—the irony, though understated, is nonetheless savage. Gods, true gods, were by definition *a-thanatoi*, "un-dying," congenitally incapable of death. So much for these Greeks' flattery of Alexander—the event of his death all too soon proved it hollow and false. Arrian did not himself comment here on

Alexander's claim to divinity, either in the sense of his making such a claim or in the sense of his being thought worthy of it. He did not need to, since in a very remarkable passage of eight chapters in Book 4 (4.7.4–4.15.1) he had already made plain his view of that matter. For him, such a claim would have been the ultimate excess of the vice that we may summarize as "orientalism."

§4.4. Arrian, like Xenophon, conceived his work as a consecutive narrative. But at 4.7.3, which deals with an event within the timespan of the years 329–328, he abruptly abandons narrative sequence and continues a single train of thought that encompasses events extending well over a year. The connecting thread is Alexander's excessive orientalism, his undue aping of oriental, specifically Persian, modes of regalia and rule.[a] First, Arrian reports how Alexander ordered the noble Persian pretender Bessos, who after murdering Darius III had presumed to occupy his place as Great King, to be humiliatingly punished in a specifically non-Greek way—by facial mutilation—before he is executed. Whereupon Arrian plunges into a torrent of first-person statements, condemning in succession Alexander's adoption of Median as well as Persian dress, his slaughter of Black Kleitos at Marakanda (modern Samarkand)—though he praises his remorse for the drunken deed—and his execution of Kallisthenes for his alleged treason in opposing Alexander's demand that his Greek as well as his Persian courtiers make full ceremonial obeisance (*proskynesis*) to him, a typically Persian court custom. Associated with Kallisthenes' disobedience was an alleged plot hatched by the royal pages, led by one Hermolaos: noncommittally and with a great parade of his reading in the disparate sources, Arrian nevertheless tellingly allows the criticisms of Alexander already rehearsed to be repeated in a cumulatively damning way. At the end of 4.14 Arrian makes a slight acknowledgment that he has departed from his usual narrative practice, justifying that departure on the grounds of the essential connection between Kallisthenes' execution and "the story of Alexander and Kleitos." But he does not also attempt to account for or justify the earlier postulated linkage—between the Kleitos affair and his own condemnation of Alexander's decadence and despotism.[b]

Arrian on Alexander's Generalship

§5.1. Alexander has been called a military Midas—everything he touched on every kind of battlefield or scene of combat turned to gold. He was never defeated in person—though he failed to complete a siege at Halicarnassus in 334 (see 1.23.5–6) and troops of his elsewhere suffered reverses. And he won in every conceivable scenario and mode: the pitched battle from set premises (Gaugamela, River Hydaspes), from unforeseen premises (Issus), and from a mixture of the foreseen and unseen (River Granicus); the siege (Tyre, Aornos Rock); the guerrilla campaign in Bactria (a region mostly comprising modern Afghanistan) from 330 to 327; against scythed battle chariots (Gaugamela) and specially trained Indian war

Intro.4.4a   For a fuller discussion of Alexander's adoption of Persian dress and court ritual, see Appendix K, Alexander's Policy of Perso-Macedonian Fusion.

Intro.4.4b   Brunt, *Arrian*, Appendix XV.

elephants. His only "defeats"—that is, major setbacks—were either mutinies (River Hyphasis, Opis) or unambiguously self-inflicted (the Gedrosian desert march). Arrian is by far the best of our extant sources for all of these, thanks to his reliance on Ptolemy's account.

§5.2 Arrian, who himself served under a great military leader, Trajan, and who supervised defense of Rome's frontier in what is now eastern Turkey, had a keen interest in Alexander's generalship, though his understanding of it was often not very thorough. For all of Alexander's major battles, Arian carefully describes the lineup of troop units on both sides, allowing his readers to follow the shrewd tactical moves made by the commanders in the crucial prebattle phase. Once the action has begun, though, Arrian's narrative often becomes obscure and incomplete. Doubtless this comes from following eyewitness sources like Ptolemy, whose memory of prebattle movements was much sharper and more complete than that of actual combat; no soldier who takes part in battle can observe more than a small portion of the action, and memories of even that part become easily distorted after the fact. Arrian did not have access, as his forerunners Herodotus and Thucydides did, to multiple eyewitnesses whose accounts could be collated and compared to form a more complete picture. And he does not seem to have analyzed very closely the sources he did use, so as to make inferences about Alexander's intentions and strategic plans. Mostly he is content to show, as Ptolemy's narrative undoubtedly did, that Alexander had won personal glory in each battle by leading the decisive attack, often at great risk to his own safety. As a result, the battle scenes of the *Anabasis*, though staged as moments of high drama, often disappoint the reader who seeks a full understanding of how the action played out and why the Macedonians were always victorious.

§5.3 In the realm of military ethics, Arrian is determined to portray Alexander as restrained and humane rather than brutal and bloodthirsty, at least in the first half of his narrative. He insists that Alexander did not choose to begin the attack on rebellious Thebes but had it forced upon him (1.8.1–5), and that after the city fell, he did not order or lead the massacre of the inhabitants (1.8.8). He omits reports found in other authors about exemplary punishment of prisoners of war (see n. 2.24.4a) or of defeated leaders (see n. 2.27.7a). He recounts tonelessly and briefly the massacre of thousands of Greek mercenaries after the battle of the Granicus, as if this were an unremarkable event (1.16.2). As the *Anabasis* progresses, though, Arrian becomes more concerned about what he considers Alexander's growing cruelty toward enemies, starting from the mutilation of the captured Bessos at 4.7.3 (though even here he omits mention of the horrible form of execution inflicted on Bessos, variously reported by other sources). In his account of Alexander's Indian campaign (Books 5 and the first half of 6), Arrian gives a frank and unvarnished account of several massacres, including the killing of refugees, civilians, and enemy wounded, but without commentary on the ethical choices involved. He seems to have wanted to strike a balance between two competing portrayals of Alexander: that of a wise and just king, whose power was moderated by the enlightened principles of Greek humanism, and that of a fearsome warrior who brooked no challenge or self-assertion by any enemy or subject nation. The attempt to harmonize these two portrayals is not always very successful.

§5.4. But Arrian was more than just a military historian of high skill. He could also be a psychologist of considerable acuity. Commenting on the way Alexander was roused to a pitch of excitement by the prospect of combat, he observed that battle was to him as physical pleasure was to others—which raises the issue of Alexander's sex life.

Arrian's Treatment of Alexander's Sexuality[a]

§6.1. To suggest that Alexander was gay might provoke outrage or cheers from those who feel the need to categorize his sexual identity in one way or the other. Even to say he was bisexual is for many such to go too far. Actually, I agree with the critics that both labels are wrong—but that is because they are anachronistically misconceived. Homosexuality construed as a personal identity, as a lifestyle choice, is a thoroughly modern—that is, late-nineteenth-century—invention: think Oscar Wilde. There were indeed some ancient Greek men whose sexual preferences were exclusively homoerotic, some of whom lived in male-male cohabiting relationships. Alexander clearly was not among these, but it is likely that at some point in his life he did have male-male erotic experiences; for a Greek man of his class and standing in that period it would have been considered odd if he had *not* had any. But Alexander may yet have been eccentric in that his only certainly documented homosexual experience was with not merely a "barbarian" (Persian) but a barbarian eunuch, Bagoas.[a] I say "only certainly documented" because it is not absolutely certain that his relationship with his Macedonian friend from childhood, the noble Hephaistion, was ever actively sexual. For me, however, it is more likely than not that it was so at one time, and that would have been in Alexander's teens, the only slightly unconventional aspect of it being that Hephaistion was just a year or two older rather than the five years or more that was usual for a pederastic relationship in Greece to the south. The thoroughly conventional second-century C.E. Greek Arrian presumably found Alexander's relationship with Bagoas distasteful since he omits all reference to it, and about any sexual relationship of Alexander with his bosom buddy Hephaistion Arrian likewise kept a discreet silence.

The Philotas Conspiracy

§7.1. Ernst Badian, one of the most distinguished living Alexander historians, wrote a powerful article on the "loneliness of power" experienced by Alexander.[a] As

Intro.6a For more on Alexander's sexuality, see Appendix C, Alexander the Man (and God?), §8.
Intro.6.1a Plutarch, *Parallel Lives* "Alexander" 67; not confirmed by other ancient sources.

Intro.7.1a E. Badian, "Alexander the Great and the Loneliness of Power" (1962), reprinted in his *Studies in Greek and Roman History* (Oxford: Blackwell, 1964), 192–205.

with other absolute rulers—one thinks of the Roman emperor Augustus or the Russian czars—this feeling stemmed from the nature of his rule as (to borrow Count Münster's nice phrase about the czars' regime) "absolutism tempered by assassination." Some scholars have wished to believe that a Macedonian king was a kind of constitutional monarch. The evidence of repeated assassinations or assassination attempts, most conspicuously successful during the 390s, argues otherwise. Of course, no theoretically absolute monarch—that is, one technically above any constraining laws—is actually absolutely free to impose his will as and when and how he wishes. In the case of the Macedonian kings, there were the views of the most influential courtiers at Pella and, before Philip II unified the kingdom, the views of potentially independent-minded robber barons from upper, western Macedonia to take into account—or to contend with. No less important than they was the Macedonian army (indeed, sometimes it could be used against those courtiers and barons on the king's behalf), especially after it became conspicuously successful far and wide under Philip's reorganization, manipulation, and direction. It seems that formal approval by an assembly of the army had become a part of the official process of enthronement, at least by the time of Alexander's accession in 336. It was therefore prudent to have the approval of the army and to take proactive steps to ensure that it was maintained, not least by controlling the high command structure.

§7.2. This is the true context of "the conspiracy of Philotas" in 330.[a] Alexander suffered, or affected to claim that he suffered, from conspiracies of different kinds throughout his reign, all with the same aim of replacing him as king-emperor. The most serious of them all, apparently, was that allegedly mounted by Philotas, although if truth be told, like the alleged plot of Sejanus against the Roman emperor Tiberius, the conspiracy of Philotas seems to have been more a conspiracy against him than a conspiracy by him against Alexander. The affair unraveled in the year after the final decisive pitched-battle victory at Gaugamela. The issue behind it was—who rules? Alexander had inherited from his father a leading general, Parmenion, whom Philip had sent on ahead to Asia in 336, one of his last acts before he was assassinated at Aigeai. Parmenion was still there in Asia Minor, having established the required bridgehead, when Alexander himself arrived in 334. For the next four years the sources represent the relationship between the senior man (more than three times as old as Alexander) and the youthful king as one of uneasy cooperation. A recurrent motif in the pro-Alexander sources is the pitting of Parmenion's strategic and tactical caution against Alexander's risky and impetuous but in the event justified boldness of conception. But such officers'-mess banter pales in significance before the structural fact of the embeddedness of Parmenion and his immediate family members and their further marital and other connections in the uppermost reaches of the high command.

Intro.7.2a See further Appendix E, Alexander's Inner
   Circle, §6.

§7.3. Philotas, Parmenion's eldest son, was sole commander in chief of the premier force in the entire Macedonian army, the elite Companion cavalry. He was also the likely chief obstacle to Alexander's being able to dominate military decision-making for the foreseeable future. After the discovery of his alleged treason and execution—on remarkably flimsy grounds—Alexander, whether or not he had deliberately engineered this scenario, took two crucial decisions. The first was to order the murder (without even the façade of a show trial) of Parmenion. The second was to divide the overall command of the Companion cavalry into two, thereby elevating, on no obviously good evidence, his special friend Hephaistion to the highest rank, but taking care to appease any resentment on the part of the old guard by making the hugely experienced and respected Kleitos ("the Black") his co–commander in chief. It is a notable weakness of Arrian's that in 326, after citing Aristoboulos as well as Ptolemy, he thereafter relies for his account of Philotas' trial and execution and of the murder of Parmenion solely on Ptolemy—a deeply compromised witness, or rather propagandist, who benefited directly from the outcome of the affair. On the other hand, it is Arrian's utterly correct interest in the function and effect of the high command structure that leads him to preserve a compelling account of Alexander's management of men at the highest military level.

Arrian on the Alexander Legend

§8.1. Arrian ends the *Anabasis Alexandrou* with a review of Alexander's qualities, both positive and negative: on the one side, personal beauty, endurance, intellect, courage, religiosity, military genius, generosity; on the other, arrogance, excessive hunger for fame, lack of temperance. But the latter are explained away or excused. Arrian's conclusion (7.30.3) is clear:

> Though I have myself had occasion to find fault with some of Alexander's deeds in the course of my history of them, I am not ashamed to admire Alexander himself. If I have condemned certain acts of his, I did so out of my own regard for truth and also for the benefit of mankind. That, after all, was my purpose in embarking on this history, and I, too, have been favored with help from god.

§8.2. Just before that value judgment he had remarked, quite factually, on "the honor in which Alexander has to this day been held by mankind" (7.30.2), honor extending as far as religious worship, as had been the case in Alexander's own day (§4). In fact, Alexander is one of the most famous individuals who has ever walked the planet—celebrated and commemorated in the literature of more than eighty nations, and in Islamic and Hebrew writings as well as in Christian visual art. The shade of Arrian, if pressed, would surely confess that among ancient literary works his book has had less effect in establishing and maintaining Alexander's fame than, say, the *Alexander Romance*, a work without high historiographical pretensions to "truth" or the benefit of mankind. But those of us who are more concerned with—and impressed by—such things see and appreciate in Arrian's *Anabasis Alexandrou* a noble predecessor and even, perhaps, a little bit of a model.

Paul Cartledge
A. G. Leventis Professor of Greek Culture
Faculty of Classics
University of Cambridge
Cambridge, UK

EDITOR'S PREFACE

James Romm

§1. There are many reasons for a modern reader to be interested in Arrian's *Anabasis*, but by far the primary one is Alexander. The campaigns of this intensely compelling warrior-king can be followed by way of four ancient and dozens of modern narratives, but Arrian's holds the unique appeal of being both reasonably reliable and exceptionally well told. There are omissions and exaggerations, to be sure, and the cautious reader must be alert to many instances where Arrian's account differs from those of Plutarch, Quintus Curtius, Diodorus, and Justin. But Arrian succeeds better than these other authors in making the campaign a real event, and in making Alexander a real, if remote and inscrutable, human being. Arrian's text is the starting point for all modern research on Alexander, and in recent years has been the subject of a monumental work of historical scholarship, *A Historical Commentary on Arrian's History of Alexander*, by A. Brian Bosworth (volumes 1 and 2, Oxford, 1980 and 1995; the third volume is in preparation at the time of this writing). Though Bosworth often takes issue with Arrian's information and finds him too strongly supportive of Alexander, it is hard to imagine that he, or any scholar, would choose to make any other Alexander historian the focus of a three-decade-long investigation.

§2. Arrian's narrative has wonderful economy and drive, but for the modern reader it often stands in need of elucidation. To take only the first of countless instances, Arrian begins by telling us that Alexander succeeded his father, Philip, on the throne, but does not trouble to specify what throne this was or why it had become vacant. The widely-used translation of Aubrey de Selincourt clarifies by rendering "Philip" as "Philip of Macedon," but for some readers this may only create confusion, especially if they have become accustomed to thinking of Alexander as a Greek. Was Macedon a part of Greece? If not, what was the relationship between the two places? Already the questions raised by the text have gone far beyond what most English-language editions are able to answer. *The Landmark Arrian*, I hope, will give readers the resources they need—in particular, detailed footnotes at the bottom of each page and a set of in-depth appendices at the end of the volume—to resolve sources of confusion and pursue all questions of general interest, as well as quite a few more particular ones. My assumption has been that, no matter how compelling Alexander's story may be in its human dimensions, it becomes richer the better we understand the world in which Alexander lived, the army in which he fought, and the ideas on which he based his remarkable project of global transformation.

§3. The bodies of information to which Arrian's *Anabasis* gives access are extremely wide-ranging, deriving as they do from regions as diverse as the southern Balkans and the mountains of the Hindu Kush in modern Pakistan. Some previous editors have elected to deal with this enormous range by way of a multiplicity of appendices. (P. A. Brunt in his 1976–1983 edition of the *Anabasis* and another Arrian work, the *Indica* for the Loeb Classical Library ran 28 appendices occupying more than 200 pages). I have leaned more toward an approach that deals with questions as they arise in the text, by way of footnotes that serve as running commentary—a scaled-down version for nonspecialists of what Bosworth has provided for scholars reading Arrian in Greek (and what Francesco Sisti and Andrea Zambrini did in their 2001–2004 two-volume Italian edition of the *Anabasis*). The appendices in the current edition are designed to supply important background to the text, provide overviews of broad segments, or give supplementary information derived from recent archaeological finds. Three appendices are correlated with particular episodes of the text: H, which deals with Arrian's uniquely problematic account of the burning of the Persian palace complex at Persepolis, and O and P, which follow different approaches into the complex question of the death of Alexander. The Epilogue and Appendix L (on the *Alexander Romance*) are provided so readers can track the history of Alexander's empire, and the legend of Alexander himself, past the point at which Arrian rather abruptly terminates his narrative, on the afternoon of June 11, 323.

§4. In addition to giving insight into a wide variety of matters arising from Alexander's campaigns, *The Landmark Arrian* allows readers to follow the progress of those campaigns closely on land and sea, by using the mapping system common to all the Landmark editions (explained by its designer, Series Editor Robert Strassler, in the preface that follows this one). The maps, however, require a cautionary preface. The location of many peoples and places mentioned by Arrian cannot always be exactly determined. In some cases—for example, Alexander's voyage down the Indus to the sea (6.1–20)—efforts to trace his path are frustrated by changes in the courses of rivers and the configuration of coastlines over millennia of geologic activity. Our maps necessarily incorporate a certain amount of speculation and hypothesis. Moreover they are based on Arrian alone, without reference to any other historical sources. They are intended as illustrations of the text rather than as reconstructions of where Alexander actually went, though it is hoped that these two objectives do not often diverge (where they do, that divergence is discussed in the footnotes).

§5. The area maps characteristic of all Landmark editions have been supplemented in this volume by route maps at the opening of each of Arrian's seven books, illustrating the progress of Alexander's army during that section of text. These maps bear shaded relief to indicate degrees of elevation, another feature new to the Landmark series, and more urgently needed here than in the preceding volumes. Alexander's route through Asia was determined to a large degree by topography, and his choices and tactics (not to mention the travails endured by his army) can only be fully appreciated by way of a relief map. However, shaded relief produces a more legible image on large-scale maps than on more detailed ones, and so the smaller maps within each book do not include it. Two larger route maps in the Reference Maps section show the entirety of Alexander's route against the background first of the ancient world and second, in a unique conception first proposed by translator Pamela Mensch, of the modern world with its politically determined boundaries. Two conceptual maps (Reference Maps 8a and 8b) illustrate geographic notions of Alexander that are important for understanding sections of the *Anabasis* dealing with his plans for future conquests and for the internal development of his empire. Taken together, the map package contained in *The Landmark Arrian* present the fullest, clearest depiction of the Alexander campaign available to English readers for a very long time, perhaps ever.

§6. Also new to the Landmark series in this volume are battle diagrams illustrating six of Alexander's major engagements: the sieges of Thebes and Tyre and the open-field battles at the Granicus River, the plain of Issus, Gaugamela, and the Hydaspes River. The problems encountered in constructing such diagrams are far greater than those of geographic maps, and most commentators and historians who deal with the Alexander period do not attempt them. Apart from the difficulty of depicting troops in motion—an inherent problem in all battle diagrams—the Alexander engagements present further uncertainties: the sequences of events are described differently by the different ancient sources, and none of the descriptions is complete enough to satisfy historians that they know just what took place. Arrian's descriptions are thought by some to be so flawed, particularly in the case of the battle of the Granicus, as to be incoherent. But they are also in most cases the most detailed descriptions we possess; what is more, they were written by a general who, unlike modern scholars, had firsthand experience of ancient open-field combat. With some trepidation, the editors and cartographers of the *The Landmark Arrian* decided that these descriptions deserve to be illustrated despite their flaws and gaps, for the battle scenes of the *Anabasis* are hard to visualize without them. We also decided to illustrate only what Arrian describes, despite the flaws and gaps in his depictions of these battles. We have not, as many other cartographers have, imported information from other Alexander sources to fill gaps or smooth out improbabilities. Our goal was to elucidate Arrian's text rather than to construct a hypothesis as to how the action played out, and we preface the whole set of battle diagrams with the qualification that they are only illustrations of Arrian rather than a definitive reconstruction of what actually took place.

§7. The existence of multiple and divergent sources of information, not only for the battles but for the entire story Arrian tells, poses a problem for any editor of the *Anabasis*. The authors previously dealt with in the Landmark series, Herodotus, Thucydides, and Xenophon, had far fewer rivals than Arrian had. In the case of Xenophon, for example, it was possible to include the two main alternate sources for the period covered by the *Hellenika*—portions of Books 13–16 of Diodorus Siculus and portions of the fragmentary *Hellenica Oxyrhynchia*—allowing readers to make their own comparisons. In Arrian's case, such appendices would have more than quadrupled the length of the volume. Since it was not possible to print even one of the four competing Alexander narratives in its entirety, and since including only selections from any or all of them would be a highly tendentious undertaking, it was decided to offer no appendices of this kind at all but to use the footnotes to inform readers of instances where Arrian's account varies significantly from those of Diodorus, Quintus Curtius, Justin, or Plutarch. Even here I have had to be selective, limiting such footnotes to only the most consequential variations, for including all of them would overwhelm the *Anabasis* itself. But I have tried to give a fair hearing to the four alternative sources, since they often present a less admirable picture of Alexander than Arrian does. In particular I have called attention to the many events recounted by these authors that are missing from Arrian's narrative, some of them widely believed to be omissions by Arrian, others more likely inventions or fables to which Arrian, along with many modern scholars, did not give credence.

§8. The team that produced the *The Landmark Arrian* wrestled with numerous problems of translation, spelling, and orthography. Arrian was a military man writing about a military campaign, and his terminology often reflects the specialized usage of an army in the field. But Arrian is also frustratingly inconsistent in his use of such terminology ("phalanx," for instance, in some cases refers to the phalanx proper, but in other cases to the array of all infantry forces, including the shield-bearers, and in a few cases to the entire line of battle). We have followed Arrian's usage even where it is misleading or confusing but have used footnotes to try to sort out the difficulties. The translation uses rough English equivalents for Greek military terms wherever possible, for example, rendering *taxis* as "battalion" and *ile* as "squadron" (the principal units into which infantry and cavalry, respectively, were divided). However, two frequently recurring terms that could not be translated, and thus are written in italics, are *agema*, an elite unit of either cavalry or infantry that fought in close proximity to the king, and *sarisa*, the long (sixteen- to eighteen-foot) thrusting spear wielded by Alexander's infantrymen. The rarer term *asthetairoi* (designating a special class of infantry) is of uncertain meaning and is also kept in italics. The Greek word *proskynesis*, denoting the gesture of reverence practiced by Persian courtiers when greeting their monarch, has been translated "ritual bow" within the text but retained in transliterated form in notes and appendices.

§9. Terms that designate both a type of soldier and a military unit, like shield-bearers (our translation of the Greek term *hypaspists*), are written in lowercase, while terms that refer to units alone, like Scouts (*prodromoi*), are capitalized. The term bodyguard (*somatophylax*) is capitalized when it refers to the seven-man personal staff made up of Alexander's closest associates but kept lowercase when it designates the thousand-man cadre of shield-bearers, sometimes called the royal shield-bearers, who were charged with protecting the king's safety. The ubiquitous term companion (*hetairos*) is capitalized when it designates the official rank conferred by Alexander on his closest political and military officers; it is capitalized in the unit name Companion cavalry on the grounds that many of its members were Companions, but not in the term infantry companions, a more general term describing those who manned the phalanx. The word "king" is capitalized when it refers to the ruler of the Achaemenid Persian empire, a figure the Greeks considered so exemplary of monarchy that they often referred to him simply as "the King," with no further qualification.

§10. Personal names in *The Landmark Arrian* appear in the spellings typical of direct transliteration from Greek, rather than by way of latinization; thus Krateros is found here where other editions often use Craterus, Parmenion instead of Parmenio, Mazaios instead of Mazaeus, and so on. A few very familiar names have been retained in the form in which they are widely known in English: Alexander, first and foremost, who would otherwise be *Alexandros*, as well as Ptolemy, Darius, Philip, and a few others. Names of peoples and places follow the spellings used in the *Barrington Atlas of the Greek and Roman World*, as explained by Robert Strassler in the Series Editor's Preface. Again, very familiar names, such as Athens, Persia, and Greece, are printed in forms that are neither Greek nor Latin but English adaptations.

§11. In two instances, ancient toponyms that are totally unfamiliar to modern readers, unlike the very familiar bodies of water they designate, were replaced in our translation by modern English equivalents. Thus the River Istros here appears as the Danube, and the Pontus or Euxine is here the Black Sea. It was felt that these two cases deserved special treatment, in that they involve bodies of water that many readers can make use of to get their bearings. It does little damage to a reader's comprehension to come across a river in Bactria whose ancient name is profoundly different from the modern, if that river is unknown to him or her under either name. But in the case of the Danube and the Black Sea, which moreover loom large in the narrative in its very first stages, the potential loss of orientation was considered too great to justify using the more authentic Greek names. In most other cases, we have faithfully adhered to these names while supplying more familiar equivalents for selected place-names in the footnotes. In a few cases where Arrian's spelling of toponyms is only slightly at variance with the standard form found in the *Barrington Atlas*—Parapamisos in place of Paropamisos, or Akesines in place of Akesinos, for instance—we have altered the spelling in the text to avoid confusing readers who are consulting that or other geographical reference works. In cases where Arrian's variant spelling has been altered to a more standard Greek one, the change is signaled in the notes, but no such signal is given where a Greek place-name has been replaced by a more familiar Latinate or anglicized form, such as Egypt in place of Aiguptos, or Parthia in place of Parthyaia. In two cases, we have standardized names for which Arrian uses two different spellings, so that Zarangians and Tapourians always appear here in these forms, although Arrian sometimes calls them Drangians and Topeirians.

§12. A word should be said about the very fine translation produced for this edition by Pamela Mensch, based on the Greek text of Brunt's Loeb edition (with variants indicated in the footnotes). This translation aims above all for clarity but also for a certain fidelity to Arrian's style, for he wrote in a sober, elevated, and austere style that lends a certain grandeur to his story. Unlike the other Alexander chroniclers, but more in the manner of his great forerunners Herodotus and Xenophon, Arrian establishes an authorial persona or voice and is not timid about using it to make first-person interventions into the narrative. It is to the great credit of the Mensch translation that it captures the qualities of this voice: its self-assertiveness and severity, its reverence toward soldiers who sacrifice themselves in battle and above all toward Alexander. The opening and closing paragraphs of the text, in which Arrian speaks most directly to his readers, amply demonstrate the power both of Arrian's voice and of Pam Mensch's translation.

§13. The verdicts passed on Arrian and his *Anabasis* by modern scholars has often been harsh. P. A. Brunt, for example, concluded his discussion of Arrian in the introduction to the Loeb edition: "He was a simple, honest soul, but no historian" (vol. 1, p. xxxiv). Even if both these statements were accepted as true—and there is certainly room for debate about the first—the *Anabasis* would still be very much worth reading today. Arrian had the simple, honest man's eye for a great story, and there is none greater in the annals of ancient history than that of Alexander's campaigns. Arrian felt that, even four centuries after it took place, Alexander's story had not yet been adequately told, and so he decided to tell it himself. We might well wish that a Herodotus or a Thucydides had filled that historiographical gap, but we would also be very much poorer had Arrian not done so. The *Anabasis* is a stirring and important work that now takes its rightful place in an important series of publications, the Landmark editions of ancient history.

James Romm

SERIES EDITOR'S PREFACE

Robert B. Strassler

This Landmark edition of Arrian's *Anabasis Alexandrou* follows the publication of three other Landmark editions, Thucydides' *The History of the Peloponnesian War* (1996), Herodotus' *Histories* (2007), and Xenophon's *Hellenika* (2009). One might, therefore, expect that many readers would be familiar with the Landmark format and features. However, since it cannot be assumed that all readers will be thus informed, and because there are a couple of new wrinkles in the features of this volume not found in the others, I shall give a full explanation of them in this preface.

This edition of Arrian's *Anabasis* contains the full array of features that have become standard in the Landmark series: Introduction, maps, side notes, footnotes, explanatory appendices, tables, illustrations, bibliography, and a thorough index. First and foremost among those features are the maps.

A large array of maps have been provided to support every episode of the narrative, most of them located amid or adjacent to the part of the narrative episodes they support. Virtually every city, town, shrine, river, mountain, or other geographic feature that is mentioned in the text as part of Alexander's campaign is referenced by a footnote to a nearby map. Even places mentioned only incidentally, as for example in phrases like "Aristandros of Telmessos," can be located in the Reference Maps section at the end of the book. Maps that display many labels employ a simple coordinate system to help readers find a particular site, and with a few exceptions in the interest of clarity, each map displays the names of only those features that appear in the surrounding text. If the location of a place is unknown, the footnote says so. If we moderns are not sure of a site's location, our uncertainty is mentioned in the footnote and indicated on the map with a question mark.

Although a number of maps are single images, most are double and a few are triple, arranged in telescoping format from small scale (wide scope) to large scale (detailed scope). On the page, the reader will find that if there is more than one map, the scale of the maps increases from the top down. The first and topmost map is usually called a locator, covering the widest and most easily recognized area. It is framed by a thin black border. Within the locator map a dark and slightly thicker rectangular outline may identify the location and boundaries of the main map. Occasionally, when the main map is of sufficient scope to be easily recognizable itself, the locator map is dispensed with and the main map becomes the topmost map. A few of the main maps contain a thick, light gray rectangular outline indicating, in turn, the location and edges of larger-scale inset maps. These maps (always with light gray borders) show areas of particular narrative interest in greater detail. All maps display simple distance scales in miles and kilometers at the bottom left corner.

Following cartographic convention, water and other natural features such as islands and peninsulas are labeled with italics to distinguish them from cultural features, labeled with roman type. Centers of population are indicated using small dots and upper- and lowercase letters designed to approximate their relative sizes and degrees of importance at the time. Elevation, a feature not previously illustrated in the Landmark series, is shown by shaded relief on the route maps depicting Alexander's route that precede each of the seven books into which Arrian's work is divided, and sometimes also by caret-shaped mountains on the maps within the books. A **Key to Maps**, located just before the beginning of Arrian's text, contains a complete legend of typography and symbols used and an illustration of the map border-frame system.

Take, for example, the sample map to the right, Map 1.12 (from Book 1, chapter 12). The locator map at the top stretches over 1,000 miles, from Sicily to central Anatolia. The main map in the center extends a bit more than 300 miles, centered on the Aegean Sea. And the inset map covers less than 100 miles, for detail of the Hellespont (modern Dardanelles).

Footnotes that cite labels found on the locator map show the word "locator." Footnotes citing labels on main maps will show no other designation except for the coordinates (if the map has coordinates) indicating the quadrant of the map in which the reader will find the site. All footnotes referring to a site located on an inset map will use the word "inset." The sample footnotes below, referring to Map 1.12, illustrate those rules.

> 1.12.8a   Lydia; Ionia: Map 1.12, locator.
> 1.12.7a   Apollonia: Map 1.12.
> 1.12.6b   Lampsacus: Map 1.12, inset.

On rare occasions, a main map will have two different inset maps, in which case each is referred to in notes by the name of the primary area it covers, such as "India inset."

To assist the reader who wishes to rapidly locate a particular place, a **Reference Maps** section with a place-name **Directory** can be found in the final pages of this volume, along with ten reference maps. The Directory shows the map by number and the coordinates where the site can be located. Even minor sites mentioned only once in the text are included in the Directory, but if they are not shown on the

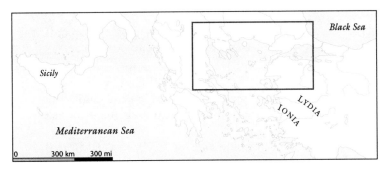

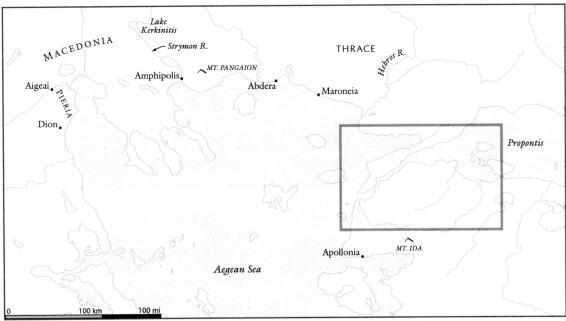

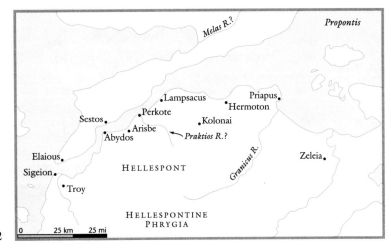

SAMPLE MAP 1.12

Reference Maps for reasons of clarity and lack of space, the reader will be referred to a map within the text where they can be found. Sites mentioned in the appendices but not in Arrian's text are not displayed on any maps of this volume.

The authority for all the maps in this volume is the *Barrington Atlas of the Greek and Roman World*, edited by Richard J. Talbert and published by Princeton University Press in 2000. Readers who would seek larger, more precise, and more detailed maps of any regions depicted in this edition should seek them in that atlas.

In order to help those readers who do turn to the *Barrington Atlas*, all labels that appear on the maps of this volume are spelled exactly as they are in the atlas, so that no one seeking to find Clazomenae or Cythnos in one volume will be confronted by Klazomenai or Kythnos in the index of the other. Since the *Barrington Atlas* covers both the Greek and Roman periods, it employs a hybrid orthographic system in which names of places and peoples appear in either Greek or Latin versions, depending on which is judged to be more familiar. The resulting system, in which some tribal names, for example, appear with -ai or -oi (Greek) endings and others with -ae or -i (Latin), is carried over into the maps of this volume to facilitate use of the *Barrington Atlas* as a reference tool. Where it seemed useful to do so for reasons of either clarity or euphony, we have also sometimes employed the English ending -ans for tribal names, for example "Assakanians" where the *Barrington Atlas* has "Assakanoi."

In the usual Landmark format, **running heads** are found at the top of each page of text. They provide at a glance the dates and locations (if known and applicable) of the action found in the first complete chapter on the page, and a brief description of that action. The sample running head below is typical.

BOOK SIX Winter 326/5		MALLOI TERRITORY	*Malloi are killed as they flee*

Side notes are found on the outside page margins at the beginning of the chapters into which the text was divided long ago by Alexandrian scholars. The first line of the side note displays the book, chapter, and section number (or numbers if the paragraph covers more than one section). The second line often shows the season and year of our calendar in which the events described take place (all dates that appear in this volume are B.C.E. unless otherwise noted). In contrast to earlier Landmark editions, dates are not shown by every side note but roughly once per two-page spread. In cases where the date shown in the sidenote falls in winter, the notation will take the form "326/5," indicating which two years of the Julian calendar are straddled by that winter. The third line of the sidenote shows in capital letters the location where the action takes place, if the chapter contains action that can be located. Finally, there is a brief description of the contents of the chapter of that section of text. The side note below, drawn from Book 6, is typical.

6.6.4–5	Book/Chapter/Section(s)
Winter 326/5	Date
MALLOI TERRITORY	Location
Perdikkas is sent to guard a nearby Mallian city to prevent word of Alexander's approach from spreading. Meanwhile, Alexander assaults the undefended walls; they are captured, and the Malloi within are killed en masse as they flee.	Summary of action

On those few occasions where Arrian's narrative breaks away from its normal direct temporal sequence and flashes forward to another time period, the dates displayed on the accompanying sidenotes are written in italics (see 4.8–14).

The original Greek units of distance (stade, plethron, foot, etc.) have been translated into common English miles and feet, as was done in the Landmark editions of Thucydides and Herodotus. We are not sure, however, of the precise value for many of the ancient units cited; there were different "standard" stade and cubit units in use in the ancient Greek world. Moreover the measurements cited by Arrian, for example distances marched by Alexander's army, were presumably estimates to begin with, based on the personal experience of Arrian's principal sources, Ptolemy and Aristoboulos. We have therefore used an admittedly rough conversion formula of eight Greek stades to one English mile, and rounded off to the half-mile where appropriate. A more precise measure of the Attic stade in the classical period yields 583 English feet.

To assist the reader who wishes to locate passages or subjects within the text, this edition offers the most thorough and complete **Index** that can be found in any English translation of the text. There is, in addition, a short **Bibliography** of both ancient sources and modern works, which is specifically designed for the general reader who might wish to read more about Alexander or his world.

The book also contains a number of **illustrations**. These are not intended to be attractive ornaments but have been chosen specifically to enhance the reader's sense of the historicity of the text. For example, Figure 3.15 (located in Book 3, by chapter 15) depicts a Babylonian cuneiform clay tablet which on one side records the battle of Gaugamela and fixes (for us) its date, and on the other side describes Alexander's proclamations to the Babylonians upon his entry into the city.

I want to mention how much I enjoyed working with James Romm on this book, to thank him for his patience with me on my first effort as a Series Editor, and to express my admiration for his many and fine skills as a scholar, historian, and writer. I think the product of his labors in *The Landmark Arrian: Campaigns of Alexander* fully live up to the standards of previous Landmark editions, and I am proud to add it to the list of Landmark History publications. I hope my efforts have been of some assistance to him. I would also like to express my personal admiration and gratitude to four other key collaborators on this volume: to Kim Llewellyn, our indefatigable and marvelous art director, designer, and pinch-hitting editor, whose efforts make the book a triumph of clarity and art; to Jonathan Wyss and Kelly Sandefer of Beehive Mapping, whose maps so skillfully and beautifully illustrate the text and the route followed by Alexander; and to Candice Gianetti, whose knowledgeable and painstaking editing and copy editing both save us from many a slip, and help us to make the text, the appendices, and our comments accurate, clear, and readable.

Many other people made significant contributions to this volume. Our gratitude for their efforts is expressed in the acknowledgments by James Romm, the chief editor of this book. I would, however, like to express our thanks to Patricia Fogarty for her expert copyediting, and to Christopher Carruth of Cohen Carruth, Inc. for his thorough and excellent index. Finally, my profound thanks go to Edward Kastenmeier, Altie Karper, and Lydia Buechler, our editor, managing editor, and copy chief from Pantheon Books, who stood by us and encouraged us to get on with the work even after we missed our first deadlines.

R.B.S.
July 2010

ACKNOWLEDGMENTS

First and foremost I want to thank Bob Strassler, creator of the Landmark series, for the great boon he has bestowed on all those who read the works of the ancient historians. For many decades, most such readers were denied access to the full richness and complexity of these texts. The Landmark editions have ended their exclusion. They can now take part in explorations formerly open only to scholars, who can make use of commentaries and other specialized materials that rely on a knowledge of Greek. I also want to extend a personal thanks to Bob for opening the doors of the series to a newcomer like myself, despite my initial ignorance in the two crafts that most distinguish the series, mapmaking and book design. Bob's support, guidance and, in the hectic final stages of the book, empathy, have been invaluable to me.

I also want to thank the staff Bob Strassler has assembled to produce the Landmark editions, a team of crack professionals whom I am honored to have worked with. Book designer Kim Llewellyn, copy editor/editor Candy Gianetti, and cartographers Jonathan Wyss and Kelly Sandefer have guided this book forward with unflagging devotion to excellence and with a patience that I sorely tried but somehow never exhausted. Their sharp eyes saved me from countless infelicities and oversights (though I take ownership of any errors that remain). Ingrid MacGillis helped put together the fine collection of artwork that adorns the book. Pamela Mensch, my longtime collaborator, worked tirelessly to produce a translation that is both compelling and faithful to Arrian's Greek, and has achieved a remarkable degree of success.

Many of my colleagues in the Classical Studies community have answered questions or offered encouragement as this book went forward. Gene Borza was an early and invaluable consultant, followed soon afterward by Richard Stoneman, Liz Baynham, Waldemar Heckel, Frank Holt, and Brian Bosworth. I owe each of them sincere thanks for answering the many questions I bombarded them with, and for their excellent contributions to the appendices. Gene, Frank and Richard also generously shared photographs from their private collections, several of which now illustrate this volume. Paul Cartledge, a long-standing friend and supporter of the Landmark series, agreed to take on the task of the introduction despite his many competing commitments, and the volume is much stronger as a result. Others who generously offered their expertise include Michael Flower, John Hale, John Marincola, Duane Roller, Barry Strauss, and Ian Worthington.

My students at Bard College have made helpful comments on the manuscript of the book at various stages, and Lydia Spielberg and Jake Nabel have been top-notch editorial assistants. I owe a further vote of thanks to Bard president Leon Botstein, who encouraged me to undertake this project at a time when I was not sure I could manage it. Jim Ottaway, friend, student, and sponsor of the chair that I occupy, has taken a warm interest that often kept me from losing momentum.

My children, Eve, Abby, and Jonah, and my wonderful wife Tanya, endured much as this book progressed, and I thank them for putting up with it all. At times we all felt like the latest casualties of Alexander's wars, but while I at least had volunteered for combat duty, they were collateral victims. The book is lovingly dedicated to my dad, Alan Romm, in the hopes that the story it tells will provide even half the excitement that he and I shared during Super Bowl XLIV.

James Romm

CHRONOLOGICAL OUTLINE OF EVENTS

by Book/Chapter/Section in Arrian's *Anabasis Alexandrou*

Book 1: The Campaigns in Europe and Western Asia (I)

		Preface	Arrian identifies his chief sources, Ptolemy and Aristoboulos.
Autumn 336	MACEDONIA	1.1.1–3	Philip II is assassinated, Alexander becomes king.
Spring 335	BALKANS	1.1.4–1.2	Alexander puts down revolts of subject peoples.
	DANUBE	1.3–1.4.5	Alexander crosses the river, defeats Getae.
	DANUBE	1.4.6–8	Triballoi offer surrender; Celts send envoys.
	ILLYRIA	1.5–1.6	Rebellious Taulantians and other Illyrians are subdued.
	GREECE	1.7–1.10	Alexander destroys Thebes, receives submission of Greek cities.
Autumn 335	MACEDONIA	1.11.1–2	Alexander presides over athletic games at Aigeai.
Spring 334	HELLESPONT	1.11.3–1.12.1	Alexander leads his army into Asia and visits Troy.
Second Preface		1.12.2–5	Arrian proclaims himself equal to recording Alexander's story.
	GRANICUS RIVER	1.12.6–1.17.2	The Macedonian army defeats Persian forces led by western satraps.
Summer 334	WESTERN ASIA	1.17.3–1.18.2	Alexander takes control of Sardis and Ephesus.
	MILETUS	1.18.3–1.20.1	Alexander takes Miletus by siege and disbands his navy.
	HALICARNASSUS	1.20.2–1.23.6	Halicarnassus is captured, except for its citadel.
Autumn 334	CARIA-LYCIA	1.23.7–1.24.4	Alexander arranges new administrators, sends for new recruits.
Winter 334/3	LYCIA	1.24.5–6	Cities of Lycia surrender to Alexander.

NOTE: Dates in italic type indicate where Arrian's sequence by book/chapter does not follow chronological sequence.

Winter 334/3	PHASELIS	1.25	Alexander son of Aeropos is arrested on conspiracy charges.
	PHASELIS-ASPENDOS	1.26–27.4	Alexander captures coastal cities of Pamphylia.
	PHRYGIA	1.27.5–1.28	Pisidians harass Alexander's army and are subdued.
Spring 333	GORDION	1.29	Army reaches Gordion and is joined by new recruits.

Book 2: The Campaigns in Western Asia (II) and Phoenicia

Spring 333	AEGEAN	2.1.1–3	Memnon conducts Persian naval campaign against the Macedonians.
	AEGEAN	2.1.4–2.5	Persian naval war falters after Memnon's death.
	GORDION	2.3	Alexander undoes a legendary knot.
	GORDION-TARSUS	2.4.1–6	Alexander passes Cilician Gates after subduing Pisidia and Cappadocia.
Summer 333	TARSUS	2.4.7–11	Alexander is seized by a sudden illness.
	TARSUS-SOLOI	2.5.1–8	Alexander defeats Cilicians. Citadel of Halicarnassus falls.
	MALLOS	2.5.9	Alexander settles factional strife.
Autumn 333	MALLOS	2.6.1–2	Alexander learns of Darius' position and sets out to meet him.
	SOCHOI-ISSUS	2.6.3–2.7.1	Darius leaves his prepared battleground, takes up new position.
	ISSUS	2.7.2–2.11	The Macedonians defeat Persian army and seize royal family.
Autumn 333	ISSUS	2.12	Alexander buries his fallen and shows honor to his royal prisoners.
	THAPSACUS	2.13.1–3	Darius and some top officers make their escapes.
	AEGEAN	2.13.4–6	Persian admirals pursue naval war, support King Agis of Sparta.
	ARADOS ISLAND	2.13.7–8	A Phoenician king surrenders to Alexander.
	MARATHOS	2.14	Darius offers a negotiated peace; Alexander rejects the offer.
	DAMASCUS	2.15.1–5	Alexander seizes Persian wealth and deals with captive Greek envoys.
Winter 333/2	PHOENICIA	2.15.6–2.16	Alexander asks to sacrifice to Herakles at Tyre, is rebuffed by Tyrians.
Digression		2.16.1–6	Arrian distinguishes among three different Herakles myths.
Winter 333/2– Summer 332	TYRE	2.17–2.24	Alexander conducts a seven-month siege of Tyre and captures the city with the help of Phoenician ships; many Tyrians are killed after the city falls.
Summer 332	TYRE	2.25.1–3	Darius offers a large grant of territory; Alexander rejects the offer.
Autumn 332	GAZA	2.25.4–2.27.7	Alexander mounts a second determined siege and captures Gaza.

Book 3: The Egyptian Sojourn and the Campaign Against Darius

Winter 332/1	EGYPT	3.1–3.2.2	Alexander takes army into Egypt and founds Alexandria.
	EGYPT	3.2.3–7	Alexander learns of defeats of Persian navy in the Aegean.
	LIBYA	3.3–3.4	Alexander and a small contingent visit oracle of Ammon.
Spring 331	EGYPT	3.5	New administrators take charge of Egypt.
	EGYPT-ASSYRIA	3.6–3.8.2	The army returns to Asia and closes in on the forces led by Darius.
Autumn 331	MEDIA	3.16.1–2	Darius escapes unharmed with a few followers.
	BABYLON	3.16.3–5	Alexander and his troops are warmly welcomed.
Winter 331/30	SUSA	3.16.6–11	Alexander seizes Persian wealth and sends funds and troops to Antipatros.
	OUXIOI TERRITORY	3.17	Alexander subdues a mountain-dwelling tribe.
	PERSIA	3.18.1–10	After victory at the Persian Gates, Alexander enters Persepolis.
Spring 330	PERSEPOLIS	3.18.11–12	Alexander orders the Persian palace complex burned.
	MEDIA	3.19–3.21	Alexander chases Darius' party and finds Darius assassinated.
Summer 330	MEDIA	3.22.1	Alexander decrees a royal burial for Darius' body.
Digression		3.22.2–6	Arrian summarizes the career of the ill-fated Darius.
Summer 330	HYRCANIA	3.23	Alexander defeats the Tapourians, receives surrender of many Persians.
	MARDIAN TERRITORY	3.24.1–3	The Mardians are defeated and surrender.
	HYRCANIA	3.24.4–5	Alexander deals with the Greeks who had sided with Darius.
	ZADRAKARTA	3.25.1–3	News arrives that Bessos has proclaimed himself Persian king.
Autumn 330	AREIA	3.25.3–8	Alexander puts down a revolt by a Persian satrap, Satibarzanes.
	ZARANGIANE	3.26.1–3	Philotas is tried for conspiracy to kill Alexander and executed.
	MEDIA	3.26.4	Parmenion is assassinated on Alexander's orders.
	ZARANGIANE	3.27	The army is purged of suspected conspirators and reorganized.
Winter 330/29	AREIA	3.28.1–3	A second revolt by Satibarzanes is quelled.
Spring 329	BACTRIA-SOGDIANA	3.28.4–29	Alexander's forces pursue Bessos.
	SOGDIANA	3.30.1–5	Bessos, betrayed by his allies, is turned over to Alexander for execution.
	IAXARTES REGION	3.30.6–11	The Macedonians put down an uprising by indigenous tribes.

Book 4: The Campaign in Bactria and Sogdiana

Summer 329	IAXARTES REGION	4.1–4.3.5	Alexandria Eschate is founded; a fierce new uprising is put down.
Autumn 329	MARAKANDA	4.3.6–7	Spitamenes, once an ally, begins guerrilla attacks on the Macedonians.
	IAXARTES REGION	4.4–4.5.1	Alexander crosses the Iaxartes; receives submission of Scythians.
	MARAKANDA	4.5.2–9	Spitamenes destroys a Macedonian relief force, then flees.
Winter 329/8	BACTRA/ZARIASPA	4.7.1–3	Alexander orders the captive Bessos' mutilation before execution.
Digression		4.7.4–5	Arrian disapproves of Alexander's moral deterioration.
Autumn 328	MARAKANDA	4.8–4.9.8	Alexander murders Kleitos, who had taunted him at a banquet.
Winter 328/7	BACTRA/ZARIASPA	4.9.9–4.12.5	Alexander's plan that he be bowed to provokes Kallisthenes' opposition.
Spring 327	BACTRA/ZARIASPA	4.12.6–4.13.7	A plot by royal pages to kill Alexander is exposed.
	BACTRA/ZARIASPA	4.14	The conspirators are executed; Kallisthenes is arrested or perhaps killed.
Spring 328	BACTRA/ZARIASPA	4.15.1–6	Alexander is sought as an ally by the Scythians and by Pharasmanes.
Summer 328	SOGDIANA	4.15.7–4.16.3	The army sweeps the region looking for resisters.
	BACTRIA	4.16.4–4.17.2	Spitamenes makes several attacks on Macedonian positions.
Autumn 328	SOGDIANA	4.17.3–7	Spitamenes is killed by his Scythian allies to forestall an attack by Alexander.
Winter 328/7	NAUTAKA	4.18.1–3	Alexander appoints new satraps for several regions.
Spring 327	SOGDIAN ROCK	4.18.4–4.19.4	Alexander seizes a nearly impregnable fortress held by resisters.
	SOGDIAN ROCK	4.19.5, 4.20.4	Alexander marries Rhoxane, daughter of the chief Oxyartes.
Digression		4.20.1–3	Arrian praises Alexander's chivalrous treatment of women.
Spring 327	PAREITAKENE	4.21	A second rock fortress, held by Khorienes, surrenders to Alexander.
	PAREITAKENE	4.22.1–2	Krateros defeats remaining resistance forces.
Summer 327	INDIAN CAUCASUS	4.22.3–6	Alexander enters the Hindu Kush and is greeted by Taxiles.
	PEUKELAOTIS	4.22.7–8	Part of the army is led through the mountains by Hephaistion and Perdikkas.
Autumn 327	WESTERN INDIA	4.23–4.27	Alexander's army destroys cities of mountain tribes that resist him.
Spring 326	AORNOS ROCK	4.28–30.6	After a massive engineering effort, Alexander captures a lofty stronghold.
	INDUS RIVER	4.30.7–9	The Macedonians cross the river on the bridge of Hephaistion and Perdikkas.

Book 5: The Indian Campaign (I)

Spring 326	NYSA	5.1–2	The army visits a city supposedly founded by Dionysos.
Digression		5.3.1–4	Arrian comments on the tendency to mythicize places in India.
Spring 326	INDUS RIVER	5.3.5–6	Alexander receives gifts from Taxiles, son of the Taxiles he met in the Indian Caucasus.
Digressions		5.4–5.6	Arrian describes the Indus River and the geography of Asia.
Spring 326	INDUS RIVER	5.4.3	Alexander crosses the Indus River.
Digression		5.7–5.8.1	Arrian speculates on how the Indus River was bridged.
Spring 326	TAXILA	5.8.2–3	The army is warmly received by Taxiles, Alexander's ally.
Spring 326	HYDASPES RIVER	5.8.4–5.11.4	Alexander makes feints and sallies to confuse Poros across the river.
	HYDASPES RIVER	5.12–5.18	Select forces cross and defeat Poros and his son in battle.
	HYDASPES RIVER	5.19.1–3	Alexander honors Poros in defeat and makes him a vassal king.
	HYDASPES REGION	5.19.4–6	Alexander founds two new cities and buries his horse, Boukephalos.
	HYDASPES REGION	5.20.1–4	Alexander leads a campaign against the Glauganikai.
	INDIA	5.20.5–6	Abisares, a potentially powerful foe, submits to Alexander.
	INDIA	5.20.7	Troops are sent to put down a revolt in Assakania.
Summer 326	AKESINOS RIVER	5.20.8–10	Many ships are wrecked by a strong current.
	AKESINOS–HYDRAOTES RIVERS	5.21	Alexander pursues a resistance leader also named Poros.
	SANGALA	5.22–5.24	Alexander destroys a resistance stronghold after a bloody siege.
	HYPHASIS RIVER	5.25–5.29.3	The army defies Alexander and refuses to cross; Alexander yields.
	HYDASPES REGION	5.29.4–5	Abisares is appointed satrap.

Book 6: The Indian Campaign (II) and the Return from the East

Autumn 326	HYDASPES–AKESINOS RIVERS	6.1–6.5	Alexander's fleet and army advance toward the Indus River.
Winter 326/5	MALLOI TERRITORY	6.6–6.8.7	The army conducts a bloody campaign against Malloi and Oxydrakai.
	MALLOI TERRITORY	6.8.8–6.11.2	During a siege, Alexander is cut off from help and severely wounded.
Digression		6.11.3–8	Arrian corrects inaccuracies in the historical record.
Winter 326/5	MALLOI TERRITORY	6.12–6.13	The soldiers despair until they see Alexander alive.

Winter 326/5	HYDRAOTES RIVER	6.14.1–3	The Malloi and Oxydrakai offer submission.
Spring 325	INDUS RIVER	6.14.4–6.17.2	Alexander subdues the Brahmans, Mousikanos, and Sambos.
Summer 325	INDUS RIVER	6.17.3–4	Krateros is sent westward with part of the army.
	INDUS DELTA	6.17.5–6.20	Alexander explores the delta and the coast by ship.
Autumn 325	COAST OF INDIA	6.21–6.22.2	Nearkhos prepares his fleet; the Oreitae are subdued.
	GEDROSIA	6.22.3	Alexander prepares to march through a forbidding desert.
Digression		6.22.4–8	The landscape and plant life of Gedrosia.
Autumn 325	GEDROSIA	6.23–6.26	Many troops die during a grueling desert march.
Winter 325/4	CARMANIA	6.27–6.28	Alexander is reunited with Krateros and Nearkhos.
	PASARGADAE	6.29	Alexander deals with a usurper and orders Cyrus' tomb restored.
	PERSEPOLIS	6.30	Alexander executes Orxines, a corrupt local leader.

Book 7: The Return to Babylon

Spring 324	PERSIA	7.1	Alexander sets out to explore the lower Tigris and Euphrates rivers.
Digressions		7.1.2–7.3.6	Arrian ponders Alexander's goals and compares him to famous sages.
Spring 324	SUSA	7.4.1–3	Alexander purges satraps he considers corrupt or incompetent.
	SUSA	7.4.4–8	Alexander and scores of Companions marry Asian women.
	SUSA	7.5	Alexander forgives debtors and awards gold wreaths to officers.
	SUSA	7.6	Tensions grow over Alexander's moves to integrate the army.
	PERSIAN GULF	7.7	Alexander conducts explorations of Tigris and Euphrates mouths.
Summer 324	OPIS	7.8–7.11.7	Alexander faces down a mutiny after reorganizing his army.
	OPIS	7.11.8–9	The end of the mutiny is celebrated with an enormous banquet.
	OPIS	7.12	Krateros is ordered to lead veterans home and to replace Antipatros.
	NESAIAN PLAIN	7.13.1	Alexander views the famous horses of Nesaia.
Digression		7.13.2–6	Arrian discusses the legend of the Amazons.
Autumn 324	ECBATANA	7.14	Hephaistion dies of illness, plunging Alexander into deep grief.
Winter 324/3	COSSAEAN TERRITORY	7.15.1–3	Alexander campaigns against a mountain tribe.
	ASSYRIA	7.15.4–6	Envoys from many peoples approach Alexander.
	ASSYRIA	7.16.1–4	Alexander sends an exploratory mission to Hyrcania.

Key to Maps

Map Configurations

☐ Locator map

☐ Main map

☐ Inset map

Typography

ASIA	Continent or major region
BOEOTIA	Region
Athens	Large city
Cyropolis	Town, village, or other location
Agrianians	People, tribe
Indus R.	Body of water; island; promontory
MT. ORBELOS	Mountain

Cultural Features

• ● Settlements

ɱ Temple

✹ Battle site

═ Road

▢▢▢▢ City walls and fortifications

Natural Features

︿ Mountain
⤳ Mountain range

⌒ River

Marsh

Sea or lake
(approximate extent in Classical Period)

Battle Maps

Macedonian army
Opposing forces

Units

Phalanx and other infantry

Cavalry and mounted units

▮▮▮▮ Chariots

●●● Elephants

Troop movements

·········▷ Pre-battle deployments

– – – – –▷ Past action and initial movements

⟶ Major movements during battle

Water	Land		Elevated terrain

Dates
All dates in this volume and its supporting materials are B.C.E. (Before the Common Era), unless otherwise specified.

BOOK ONE

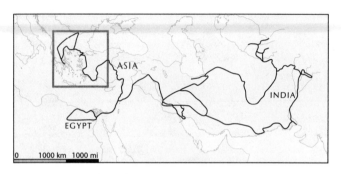

BOOK ONE: THE CAMPAIGNS IN EUROPE AND WESTERN ASIA (I)

Wherever Ptolemy son of Lagos and Aristoboulos son of Aristoboulos concur in their histories of Alexander son of Philip, I record what they say as entirely true; but where their accounts diverge, I have selected the version I consider more plausible and worth relating.[1a] [2] A great deal has been written about Alexander; indeed, there is no figure about whom more writers are more at variance. But, as narrators, Ptolemy and Aristoboulos impressed me as more reliable, in Aristoboulos' case because he served in King Alexander's campaigns, in Ptolemy's not only because of his service under Alexander but also because it would have been more disgraceful for him to speak falsely than for another, given that he, too, was a king.[2a] Furthermore, both men wrote after Alexander had died, when neither coercion nor the prospect of gain would lead them to record anything but what actually occurred. [3] I have also included material written by others when it seemed to me worth relating and not wholly implausible, but only as stories told about Alexander.[3a]

Any readers who are surprised that it would have occurred to me to write this history, after so many others have written theirs, should read the other accounts[3b] and then mine—and then let them say they're surprised.[3c]

PREFACE
Arrian explains the sources he will rely on in composing his history and defends his decision to write yet another history of Alexander.

NOTE: Most locations in the text not identified by a footnote can be found in the Reference Maps section.

Pref.1a For Ptolemy, see the Introduction, §2.3, and Appendix E, Alexander's Inner Circle, §6–7, 11. For Aristoboulos, see the Introduction, §2.4. Arrian's use of both authors as sources is discussed in depth in Appendix A, Arrian's Sources and His Reliability, §10–14.

Pref.2a Ptolemy became ruler of Egypt in the years after Alexander's death and proclaimed himself king in 307. Arrian's decision to trust Ptolemy's writings principally because of his royal position has been mocked by some scholars, who point out that a king whose authority derived from that of Alexander, as Ptolemy's did, had ample incentive to distort the historical record in order to enhance Alexander's stature. A charitable interpretation of Arrian's words might take them to mean that Ptolemy would not have risked a lie, since at the time he published his memoirs there were many veterans of Alexander's campaigns who could gainsay him, and such attacks on his credibility would have compromised his political position.

Pref.3a For more on sources beyond Ptolemy and Aristoboulos, see the Introduction, §2.6–8, and Appendix A, §15–16.

Pref.3b The "other accounts" Arrian refers to here are principally Kleitarkhos, a Greek of the third century who wrote probably several decades after Alexander's death, and the later writers who based their accounts on his (collectively known as the vulgate tradition; see the Introduction, §2.5–7).

Pref.3c Arrian's boastful claim to have written the finest Alexander history is further developed in a second preface at 1.12.2–5. In neither preface does Arrian state his own name—a dramatic break from the conventions of ancient historical writing. For discussion of Arrian's preface and his opinion of his own writing, see Appendix A, §8, 20, 22.

FIGURE PREF.1. Coin minted by Ptolemy in 307 in Egypt displaying his own image. He is portrayed wearing the royal diadem first adopted by Alexander, then worn by several of his generals in the years after his death.

1.1.1–3
Autumn 336
PELOPONNESE
Alexander becomes king and is confirmed as the leader of his father's planned invasion of Asia.

[1] Philip is said to have died during the archonship of Pythodelos[1a] at Athens.[1b] When Alexander, Philip's son, had succeeded to the throne, he visited the Peloponnese.[1c] He was then about twenty years old. [2] On his arrival he assembled all the Greeks who were in the Peloponnese and asked them for the leadership of the Persian campaign, which they had already given to Philip.[2a] All the Greeks granted his request except the Spartans, who replied that it had been their custom never to follow others but to take the lead themselves. [3] Athens,[3a] too, was eager for rebellion, though when Alexander first arrived in the region the awestruck Athenians had ceded him honors even greater than those granted to Philip. Returning to Macedonia,[3b] Alexander prepared for his campaign into Asia.

1.1.4–7
Spring 335
THRACE
Alexander launches a campaign to subdue his Balkan neighbors. His advance into Thrace is checked by a force of Thracians who have occupied Mount Haemus and threaten to loose wagons against any attackers.

[4] In the spring he marched on Thrace against the Triballoi[4a] and Illyrians.[4b] He had learned that they were contemplating revolt, and he also considered it unwise, when embarking on a campaign far from home, to leave neighboring tribes behind without first humbling their spirits. [5] Setting out from Amphipolis,[5a] he invaded the region of Thrace inhabited by the so-called free Thracians,[5b] keeping Philippi and Mount Orbelos[5c] on his left.[5d] Ten days after crossing the River Nestos[5e] he is said to have reached

1.1.1a Ancient historians, who had no universal system for numbering years, routinely used the names of Athenian archons or Roman consuls—officials who served one-year terms—to identify points in historical time.

1.1.1b Philip II, king of Macedonia, was killed by an assassin in the autumn of 336. His remains are almost certainly among those found in the chamber tombs at Aigeai, though there is dispute as to which tomb was his. Most specialists now believe that Tomb I contained Philip and his wife and infant, though some place him in Tomb II. See Appendix Q, The Royal Macedonian Tombs at Aigeai, §5–10, 13.

1.1.1c Peloponnese: Map 1.2.

1.1.2a In 337 the so-called League of Corinth, made up of all the major Greek states except Sparta, had voted to approve Philip's planned Asian campaign and to appoint Philip himself as commander. See Appendix M, Alexander and the Greeks, §2–4.

1.1.3a Athens: Map 1.2.

1.1.3b Macedonia: Map 1.2, inset.

1.1.4a Thrace; Triballoi, location of territory: Map 1.2.

1.1.4b Illyria: Map 1.2, inset.

1.1.5a Amphipolis: Map 1.2, inset.

1.1.5b Free Thracians, location of territory: Map 1.2. Apparently they were "free" in that Philip had not entirely subdued them.

1.1.5c Philippi; Mount Orbelos: Map 1.2, inset. "Mount Orbelos" apparently refers here to the chain shown in the *Barrington Atlas* as the Sapaike (see Bosworth I.54; Bosworth citations throughout this edition refer to his two-volume *A Historical Commentary on Arrian's History of Alexander*—see Bibliography).

1.1.5d There is much dispute over what route Alexander took in this march, partly because Arrian apparently describes a harder and less direct route than that offered by the Strymon valley. Arrian's words have been reinterpreted by Hammond ("Some Passages in Arrian Concerning Alexander," *Classical Quarterly* 30 [1980]: 455–457) to describe a route along the Strymon. The route shown on p. 2, going east along the coast before heading north, is that endorsed by Bosworth (I.52–53).

1.1.5e Nestos River: Map 1.2, inset.

Mount Haemus.[5f] [6] And there, at the narrow path leading up the mountain, he was met by many armed [. . .][6a] and free Thracians standing ready to bar his way; they had occupied the height of Haemus at the very point where the army had to march past. [7] The tribesmen had brought a number of wagons together to form a barricade from which they could defend themselves if they were pressed hard; they also planned to send the wagons down against the ascending Macedonian phalanx[7a] at the steepest part of the mountain, thinking that the more tightly packed the phalanx, the more forcibly the wagons, as they hurtled down, would disperse it.

[8] Alexander considered how he could safely cross the mountain. When he realized that the risk had to be run (as there was no other way past), he relayed his instructions to the hoplites:[8a] when the wagons came rolling down the slope, the men in the wide part of the path, who had enough room to do so, were to break ranks, move to either side, and let the wagons pass down the middle; [9] those stationed where the path was most narrow were to bow down in unison—some were even to fall to the ground—and lock their shields tightly together, so that when the wagons hurtled down, their momentum would, as seemed likely, cause them to leap over the men and continue on without causing harm. The outcome justified Alexander's advice and conjectures. [10] Some of those in the phalanx parted ranks, while elsewhere the wagons, as they rolled over the shields, did little harm; indeed, no one was killed by them.

Finding themselves unhurt by the wagons they had most dreaded, the Macedonians now took courage, raised a shout, and charged the Thracians. [11] Alexander ordered the archers to move from their post on the right wing to the front of the phalanx, where the ground was better, and to shoot at the Thracians wherever they attacked. He himself collected the *agema*,[11a] the shield-bearers,[11b] and the Agrianians[11c] to form his left wing with himself in command. [12] The archers, shooting at the Thracians who sallied forth from the ranks, succeeded in driving them back. The phalanx now joined battle and had no difficulty dislodging the barbarians, who were lightly or

1.1.8–10
THRACE
The wagons roll by harmlessly as the Macedonians either move out of their path or lock shields together. Realizing they are not in danger, the Macedonians prepare to attack.

1.1.11–13
THRACE
The Macedonians rout the Thracians, who flee down the mountain; some perish, but most escape, though without their women, children, and belongings.

1.1.5f   Mount Haemus: Map 1.2.
1.1.6a   A name of a tribe or people has fallen out of the manuscripts.
1.1.7a   Phalanx: the main body of infantry, formed into a rectangular block and moving or fighting in unison; see Appendix D, Alexander's Army and Military Leadership, §2–4.
1.1.8a   In usual parlance, "hoplite" designates a heavy-armed Greek infantryman, fighting with a seven-foot spear and a large shield. But Arrian frequently employs the word (as here) to refer to Macedonian infantry, more properly referred to by the modern term "phalangites" or the ancient term "infantry companions" (*pezetairoi*). See Appendix D, §2, 4.
1.1.11a The term *agema*, here left untranslated, usually denotes a special division of light-armed infantry, assigned to fight in close proximity to the king. The term "honor guard" comes close but does not capture the essentially

combat-centered function of the unit. There was a cavalry *agema* as well.
1.1.11b The shield-bearers (*hypaspists*) were an elite corps of specially equipped infantry (see Appendix D, §3), lighter and more mobile than the heavy infantry who made up the phalanx. A smaller group chosen from this body, and also designated "shield-bearers" in Arrian's text, served as Alexander's personal bodyguard and security force.
1.1.11c As used by Arrian, the term Agrianians usually refers to a light infantry division recruited from a Balkan region northeast of Macedonia (Map 1.2). The long-standing friendship between the Agrianian king and the Macedonian royal house is described further at 1.5.2–4. The recruits this region furnished first to Philip and then to Alexander were evidently of very high caliber and reliability, to judge by the important uses to which they were put. See Appendix D, §6.

poorly armed. The Thracians no longer attempted to engage Alexander, who was advancing from the left, but threw away their weapons and fled as best they could down the mountain. [13] Nearly fifteen hundred of them perished. Few of those who fled were taken alive, on account of their speed and knowledge of the country, though all the women who had accompanied them were captured with their young children and all the property they were carrying.

1.2.1–3
Spring 335
TRIBALLOI TERRITORY
Alexander continues his Balkan campaign with an attack on the Triballoi. Most of these flee to Peuke, an island in the Danube, joining other refugees there.

[1] Alexander sent the plunder back to the cities at the coast, appointing Lysanias and Philotas[1a] to dispose of it. He himself, after crossing the peak, passed over Mount Haemus and marched against the Triballoi, thus reaching the River Lyginus,[1b] which lies a three-day journey from the Danube[1c] as one travels toward Mount Haemus. [2] Syrmos, the Triballoi's king, who had long since learned of Alexander's expedition, sent the Triballoi's wives and children to the Danube, where he told them to cross to Peuke,[2a] one of the river's islands. [3] The Triballoi's Thracian neighbors had fled to this island well in advance of Alexander's approach, and Syrmos himself and his men now joined them. But most of his subjects fled back to the river from which Alexander had himself set out the day before.

1.2.4–7
TRIBALLOI TERRITORY
Alexander lures the Triballoi into battle by sending his more lightly armed troops against them. The Macedonians put the Triballoi to flight, killing many.

[4] When he learned of their move, Alexander turned back, led his men against the Triballoi and came upon them already encamped. Being thus trapped, the Triballoi drew themselves up in battle array at the glen beside the river. Alexander, having himself deepened the phalanx, led his men forward and commanded the archers and slingers to run out ahead and fire their arrows and stones at the barbarians, thinking this might draw them out of the glen and onto open ground. [5] As they came within range of this barrage, the Triballoi ran out to engage the archers, who had no armor, in hand-to-hand combat. When Alexander had thus drawn the barbarians out, he ordered Philotas[5a] to lead the Upper Macedonian cavalry[5b] against the enemy's right wing, where they had advanced farthest after emerging from the glen, and ordered Herakleides and Sopolis to lead the cavalry from Bottiaia and Amphipolis[5c] against their left wing. [6] Having marshaled the remaining cavalry in front of the infantry phalanx, he led both forces against the enemy's center.[6a]

So long as the two sides assailed each other from a distance, the Triballoi held their own; but when the tightly arrayed phalanx attacked them with force, and Alexander's cavalry—thrusting the enemy this way and that, no longer with javelins but with the horses themselves—assailed them from

1.2.1a This Philotas is a different person than the famous son of Parmenion mentioned at 1.2.5. Lysanias is not otherwise known.
1.2.1b Lyginus River: location unknown.
1.2.1c Danube (ancient Istros) River: Map 1.2.
1.2.2a Peuke: exact location unknown. This island in the Danube delta is no longer discernible due to the change of course of the river branches over time.
1.2.5a This Philotas was the eldest son of Parmenion, Alexander's most senior general, and hence, unlike another Philotas mentioned in 1.2.1, occupied a high position among Alexander's inner circle; see Appendix E, §6, 13. He would later fall from grace when implicated in

a conspiracy on Alexander's life (see 3.26).
1.2.5b This regiment is mentioned only here in all of Arrian's narrative; perhaps, as Bosworth suggests (I.58), it was left behind in Europe when Alexander crossed the Hellespont. Upper Macedonia comprised a variety of mountainous regions north and west of the Macedonian heartland.
1.2.5c Botti(ai)a, Amphipolis: Map 1.2, inset.
1.2.6a It is unusual to find Alexander here stationed at the center of the battle line, in front of the infantry phalanx. In almost all his other engagements, he led led an elite unit of horsemen called the Companion cavalry on the right wing.

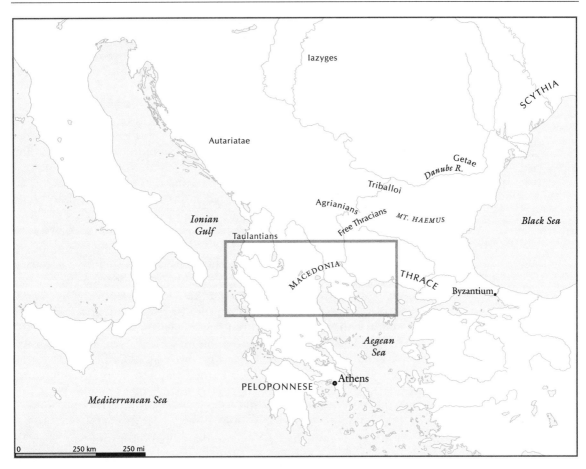

MAP 1.2

every side, the Triballoi were routed and fled through the glen to the river. [7] Three thousand died while fleeing; only a few were taken alive, as the woods beside the river were dense and the gathering darkness robbed the Macedonians' pursuit of its precision. Eleven Macedonian horsemen died, according to Ptolemy, and about forty foot soldiers.

[1] The third day after the battle Alexander reached the Danube.[1a] Europe's largest river, the Danube traverses the most territory, and beyond it dwell the most warlike races, principally the Celtic tribes in whose territory the river's springs emerge, the farthest of whom are the Quadi and the Marcomanni.[1b] [2] It then flows past the Iazyges[2a] in the land of the Sauromatai;[2b] the Getae, who think themselves immortal; the many tribes of the Sauromatai; and then through the Scythians' territory until it flows to its outlets and empties through five mouths into the Black Sea.[2c] [3] There Alexander found his warships, which had arrived from Byzantium[3a] by way of the Black Sea. After filling these ships with archers and hoplites, he sailed for the island to which the Triballoi and Thracians had fled, and tried to force a landing. [4] But the barbarians met his ships wherever they drew near shore. The warships, which were few in number, carried a modest force; the island, in most places, was steep for a landing; and the river's current was swift and hard to deal with, as the island forced it into a narrow channel.

[5] Alexander therefore withdrew his ships and decided to cross the Danube and march against the Getae who dwelt on its farther side.[5a] For he had noticed many of them gathered at the riverbank, nearly four thousand horsemen and more than ten thousand foot soldiers, as though to bar his way should he try to cross. At the same time a longing seized him to pass beyond the Danube.[5b] [6] He himself went aboard ship. Having collected the skins they used for tents, Alexander had them filled with hay. Then he gathered as many as possible of the local vessels made from hollowed-out tree trunks; there were many of these, since the neighboring tribes used them for fishing, for visiting one another up and down the river, and especially for plundering. Using these he ferried across as much of his army as he could. Nearly fifteen hundred horsemen and four thousand foot soldiers made the crossing with Alexander.

1.3.1a   Danube (ancient Istros) River: Map 1.2.
1.3.1b   Quadi and Marcomanni: Germanic tribes of central Europe, unknown to the Greeks and Macedonians of Alexander's time but known to Arrian.
1.3.2a   Iazyges, location of territory: Map 1.2.
1.3.2b   Sauromatai: location of territory unknown (since these are not the same Sauromatai discussed by Herodotus at 4.110–117).
1.3.2c   Getae, location of territory; Scythia; Black (ancient Euxine) Sea: Map 1.2.
1.3.3a   Byzantium: Map 1.2.
1.3.5a   This attack on the Getae (the people known to the Romans as Dacians) did not involve an abandonment of the pursuit of the Triballoi and Thracians, though Arrian leaves obscure the connection between the two maneuvers. By appearing at the Danube in

force, the Getae had demonstrated their support for Syrmos and his Triballoi and their determination to protect his line of retreat. Alexander hoped, by cutting off that line, to surround Syrmos and force him to surrender, without the need of a forced landing on the well-defended island. This was in fact what took place (see 1.4).
1.3.5b   The word *pothos*, translated here as "longing," designates a quality that Arrian, and perhaps one or more of his sources as well, understood to be a defining feature of Alexander's personality; see Appendix C, Alexander the Man (and God?), §7. The crossing of the Danube is the first of several key moments at which Arrian tells us that "a longing seized Alexander" to extend his conquests further or to undertake some bold, difficult endeavor.

FIGURE 1.4. Late-fourth-century iron blade (right) and butt spike (left) of the Macedonian infantry lance, the *sarisa*. These metal pieces were fitted onto two tapered wooden shafts that were joined by a metal socket (center) to form a weapon more than sixteen feet long and weighing fifteen pounds. The *sarisa* was held with both hands at a point about five feet from the butt end.

[1] They crossed at night at a point where a field of tall grain allowed them to come ashore undetected. Toward dawn, Alexander led the men through the field, having ordered the foot soldiers to flatten the grain by holding their *sarisas*[1a] aslant, until they reached untilled ground. As long as the phalanx advanced through the field, the cavalry stayed behind it, [2] but once both forces had passed beyond the rows of grain, Alexander himself led the cavalry to the right wing, ordering Nikanor[2a] to lead the phalanx in rectangular formation. [3] The Getae did not even stay to face his first cavalry charge. For Alexander's daring—his having so easily crossed the largest of rivers in one night without bridging it—confounded their expectations, and they found the phalanx, with its locked shields, utterly daunting and the cavalry's attack ferocious. [4] At first the Getae fled to their city, which lay a few miles from the Danube. But when they saw Alexander rapidly leading the phalanx along the river (a measure he took lest his infantry be surrounded by the Getae who were lying in ambush) and his cavalry out in front, they abandoned their poorly fortified city, taking up on horseback as many of their children and women as the horses could carry. [5] They rushed as far as they could away from the river into the wilderness.

Alexander seized their city and gave all the plunder they had left behind

1.4.1–4

DANUBE RIVER

Alexander advances in secret against the Getae. They are driven off by the surprise appearance of Alexander's army.

1.4.5

DANUBE RIVER

As the Getae flee into the countryside, Alexander seizes their town and offers sacrifice, then returns to his camp.

1.4.1a   The *sarisa* was the infantry spear devised for the Macedonian army by Philip, Alexander's father, at the outset of his reign; see Appendix D, §2. Its exact dimensions are not known, since no examples of the shaft have survived, but it probably exceeded 16 feet in length. In battle it was leveled at the enemy by the first five rows of the phalanx, but it was held aloft at an angle by those farther back, in part to deflect falling javelins, rocks, and arrows. Here it is employed like a scythe to clear dense vegetation that might impede the infantry's march or cause it to lose cohesion.

1.4.2a   Nikanor was one of the sons of Parmenion.

to Meleagros and Philip to convey back to camp, and after razing the town, he offered sacrifices on the bank of the Danube to Zeus the Preserver, to Herakles, and to the Danube itself for letting him cross.[5a] That same day he led all his men safely back to camp.

[6] Envoys now visited Alexander from all the other autonomous tribes settled near the Danube and from Syrmos, the king of the Triballoi.[6a] Envoys also arrived from the Celts who dwelt on the Ionian Gulf.[6b] Men of enormous stature, these Celts had a high opinion of themselves. All the envoys declared they had come desiring Alexander's friendship, [7] and he exchanged pledges with one and all. He asked the Celts what in the human realm they feared the most, expecting that, since his great name had reached the Celts and gone even farther, they would say they feared him above all. [8] But the Celts' reply disappointed him. For as they dwelt far from Alexander and inhabited a place that was hard to reach, and as they saw that Alexander's efforts were directed elsewhere, they said they feared only that the sky might fall on them; and though they admired Alexander, neither fear nor any concern for their advantage had moved them to send these envoys. Alexander declared these men his friends and made an alliance with them before sending them off, though he remarked under his breath, "Big talkers, these Celts!"

[1] Alexander then proceeded toward the Agrianians and Paionians.[1a] There he was reached by messengers, who reported that Kleitos son of Bardylis[1b] had revolted and that Glaukias, the king of the Taulantians,[1c] had joined him. They also reported that the Autariatae[1d] would attack him on his march. Accordingly, Alexander decided to break camp at once. [2] Langaros, the king of the Agrianians,[2a] who had shown himself well disposed to Alexander when Philip was alive and had come to him privately as an ambassador, was now at hand with all the finest and best-equipped shield-bearers he had at his command. [3] When he learned that Alexander was

---

1.4.6–8
Spring 335
DANUBE RIVER
The Danube tribes and the rebel leader Syrmos submit to Alexander. The more distant Celts, however, send a message showing lack of concern over Alexander.

1.5.1–4
AGRIANIAN-PAIONIAN-AUTARIATAE TERRITORY
The European campaign continues. Alexander receives intelligence regarding Illyrian opposition. Langaros, king of the allied Agrianians, offers to support Alexander by attacking the Autariatae himself and is rewarded by Alexander.

1.4.5a Throughout his campaign Alexander was strict in his observance of religious rituals, especially offerings to the gods, and carefully selected the deities to whom he made offerings based on circumstances. Herakles and his father, Zeus, were Alexander's mythic ancestors, and Zeus in this case is doubly appropriate given his role as protector of those in peril. The Danube is here personified as a divine being, as rivers often were.
1.4.6a Triballoi, location of territory: Map 1.2.
1.4.6b Celtic peoples had arrived at the Ionian Gulf (Map 1.2), and in parts of the Balkan and Italian peninsulas, in the fourth century as part of a dramatic expansion from their homeland in central and western Europe.
1.5.1a The Agrianians and Paionians (location of territories: Map 1.2 and inset, respectively) were Balkan peoples dwelling north of Macedonian territory and, since Philip's time, allied to the Macedonian cause.
1.5.1b This Kleitos was king of a tribe of Illyrians (for Illyria, see Map 1.2, inset), an ancient foe of Macedonia. Bardylis, his father (or perhaps uncle), had been killed in battle by Alexander's father, Philip, in 358; Kleitos had subsequently been subdued by Philip about ten years later.
1.5.1c The Taulantians (location of territory: Map 1.2) were another Illyrian people, whose homeland lay near the Greek city of Epidamnos.
1.5.1d The Autariatae (location of territory: Map 1.2), a third Illyrian tribe, as yet unconquered by Macedonia (as shown by Alexander's questions at 1.5.3). All three of the peoples that here unite against Alexander shared the goal of ending the Macedonian hegemony in Europe, which had either destroyed, or threatened to destroy, their autonomy.
1.5.2a Little is known about the Agrianian-Macedonian alliance other than what Arrian reports here, but it was a powerful and enduring bond, to judge by the key role the Agrianian infantry corps would later play in Alexander's army. See Appendix D, §6.

10

asking who and how numerous the Autariatae were, Langaros urged the king to take no account of them, as they were the least warlike of the tribes thereabouts. He said he would himself attack their country, so that they would be forced to attend to their own affairs. At Alexander's urging, Langaros attacked the Autariatae and plundered their country.

[4] Thus the Autariatae had concerns of their own to occupy them, and Langaros was honored greatly by Alexander and received all the gifts that were prized most highly at the Macedonian court. Alexander even agreed to give Langaros his sister Kyna[4a] in marriage when next he came to Pella,[4b] [5] though Langaros died of disease upon returning to his homeland.

Advancing beside the River Erigon, Alexander headed for the city of Pelion, which Kleitos had seized, seeing that it was the strongest place in the region. When Alexander drew near the city, he made camp by the River Eordaikos[5a] and decided to assault the fortress the next day. [6] Kleitos and his party had occupied the densely wooded heights that surrounded the city in order to attack the Macedonians from all sides if they assaulted it. Glaukias, the king of the Taulantians, had not yet arrived.

[7] Alexander led his men against the city, whereupon the enemy, after sacrificing three youths, three maidens, and three black rams, went out to meet the Macedonians in close combat. But after the two sides engaged, the Illyrians abandoned the positions they had occupied, secure though these were, and consequently their sacrificial victims were later found still lying there.

[8] On that day, after forcing the enemy inside the city and making camp near the wall, Alexander decided to seal them off by surrounding the city with ramparts. But on the following day, Glaukias, the king of the Taulantians, arrived with a large army. Thereupon Alexander gave up hope of capturing the city with his present force, since many sturdy fighters had fled inside, and the many others with Glaukias would attack him if he assaulted the wall. [9] He sent Philotas with as many horsemen as he needed for a guard, and all the camp's pack animals, to obtain provisions. When Glaukias learned of Philotas' foraging expedition, he marched out against him and occupied the heights around the plain where Philotas and his men intended to look for food. [10] When it was reported to Alexander that the horsemen and pack animals would be in danger when night fell, he rushed to their rescue, taking the shield-bearers,[10a] the archers, the Agrianians, and nearly four hundred horsemen. He left the rest of the army near the city, fearing that if the entire army withdrew, the enemy forces within the city might emerge and join forces with Glaukias and his men. [11] When Glaukias became aware of Alexander's approach, he left the heights, and the men with Philotas returned safely to camp.

1.5.5–6
ILLYRIA
Alexander advances on the position of Kleitos, the Illyrian king, near Pelion.

1.5.7
ILLYRIA
The Illyrians abandon the heights around Pelion after making sacrifice.

1.5.8–11
ILLYRIA
Alexander's siege operations are interrupted by the arrival of the Taulantian army. Philotas is sent out on a foraging expedition and is surrounded by the Taulantians. Alexander leads a support party that rescues Philotas.

1.5.4a   Kyna (also called Kynna or Kynnane) was Alexander's half-sister, daughter of Philip by an Illyrian woman, Audata. Initially married to her cousin Amyntas, the son of King Perdikkas III, she became a widow after Alexander had Amyntas killed in order

to secure his own claim to the throne.
1.5.4b   Pella: Map 1.2, inset.
1.5.5a   Erigon River; Pelion; Eordaikos River: Map 1.2, inset.
1.5.10a Shield-bearers (*hypaspists*): see Appendix D, §3, 8.

1.5.12
Spring 335
ILLYRIA
Enemies and terrain
both pose obstacles to a
Macedonian retreat.

Yet the forces with Kleitos and Glaukias still appeared to have maneuvered Alexander into a difficult position. [12] For they continued to occupy the heights with many horsemen, javelin men, slingers, and a substantial force of hoplites, while the men confined within the city would come out and press Alexander's troops hard if they departed. And the terrain through which Alexander's army had to pass appeared narrow and wooded, bounded on one side by the river and on the other by a lofty mountain and sheer cliffs, so that the trail would not have accommodated four men-at-arms marching abreast.

1.6.1–4
ILLYRIA
Alexander seeks a way out
of the position he occupies
between two enemy forces.
By having his troops perform
a series of drill maneuvers
followed by a charge, he
succeeds in driving off the
Taulantians.

[1] Alexander then drew up his troops until the phalanx was 120 ranks deep. Stationing 200 horsemen at each wing, he ordered them to keep silent and respond instantly to the word of command. [2] He ordered the hoplites to hold their spears upright at first, but to lower them for an attack when given the signal, and to turn their massed spears now to the right, now to the left. He then marched the phalanx briskly forward, leading it in a zigzag manner, first toward one wing, then toward the other. [3] After thus drawing up several formations and rearranging them at brief intervals, he began from the left wing, arrayed the phalanx in a wedge, and led it against the enemy. The enemy troops had long marveled as they watched the crisp, orderly movements of the men being drilled, and when the attack came they did not await the advancing phalanx but left the first row of hills. [4] Alexander now ordered the Macedonians to raise their war cry and to clang their spears against their shields. The Taulantians, terrified even more by the uproar, hastened back to the city.

1.6.5–6
ILLYRIA
After seizing the high
ground, Alexander begins
to send his troops across
the Eordaikos River.

[5] Noticing that a few of the enemy continued to occupy a hill next to his army's line of march, Alexander ordered his Bodyguards[5a] and the Companions[5b] who attended him to take up their shields, mount their horses, and charge the hill. If when they reached it the occupiers stood their ground, half of his men were to leap down from their horses and engage the horsemen on foot. [6] However, when they saw Alexander's advance, the enemy left the hill and moved to the mountains on either side. Having occupied the hill with his Companions, Alexander sent for the Agrianians and the archers, of whom he had two thousand. He ordered his shield-bearers to cross the river and instructed the Macedonian infantry battalions to follow them. Once across, they were to draw themselves up in order to the left,[6a] so that the phalanx might appear in close formation as soon as they had crossed. Meanwhile, from the hilltop observation post he occupied with the advance guard, Alexander kept a close watch on the enemy's movements.

1.6.5a Apparently the term "Bodyguards" here refers to the coterie of seven officers who attended Alexander's person and not, as elsewhere, to an elite corps of men detailed to fight beside Alexander in battle; see Appendix E, §4.

1.6.5b The term "Companion" is capitalized here and throughout this volume when it refers to the special status, virtually an office, connoted by the Macedonian use of the Greek

word *hetairos*. Alexander kept a formal list of his Companions, the intimates who were invited to dine and drink with him, share his counsels, and fight beside him in the Companion cavalry. See Appendix E, §4.

1.6.6a The meaning of this description seems to be that the infantry units, after crossing the river in a narrow column, deployed into a long line upon reaching the bank, so as to be ready to meet an attack.

[7] When the enemy troops saw Alexander's forces crossing the river, they rushed down the mountains to attack the column's rear as it withdrew. As they drew near, Alexander and the men with him sallied out, and the phalanx raised its war cry as though to move back through the river and attack. The enemy troops, with all of Alexander's forces charging them, gave way and fled, at which point Alexander led the Agrianians and archers on the double to the river. [8] He was the first to get across, and when he saw the enemy attacking his rear guard, he had the siege engines set up on the bank and ordered that they fire every possible kind of missile at farthest range, and also ordered the archers to fire a volley from the middle of the river (for they, too, had started across). The men with Glaukias did not dare to come within range of this barrage, and so the Macedonians crossed the river safely. None of them died in the retreat.

[9] Three days later, when Alexander had learned that the troops with Kleitos and Glaukias had set up camp and had not stationed guards or protected their camp with either a palisade or a ditch, apparently thinking Alexander had departed in fear, and had extended their line beyond what was useful, he recrossed the river, unseen under cover of night, with the shield-bearers, the Agrianians, the archers, and the battalions of Perdikkas and Koinos.[9a] [10] He had left orders for the rest of the army to follow; but when Alexander saw that the time was ripe for an attack, he did not wait for all the units to assemble, but sent the archers and the Agrianians into battle. Arriving unexpected, and attacking a flank of the enemy line where they were likely to engage the enemy at its weakest point with their strongest charge, they killed some men still in their beds and easily captured others who tried to flee. Many perished on the spot, and many others died in the disorderly and panic-stricken retreat. A great many were also taken alive. [11] Alexander's men pursued the Taulantians as far as the mountains. All who managed to escape survived only by throwing away their weapons. Kleitos, who had fled to the city at the start of the engagement, now set it on fire and rejoined Glaukias among the Taulantians.

[1] During this time, a number of Theban exiles, slipping back into Thebes by night with the help of certain persons who sought to stage a revolt,[1a] seized and killed Amyntas and Timolaos, two members of the force occupying the Kadmeia.[1b] Since these men had anticipated no hostilities, they were roaming outside the garrison. [2] Coming forward in the assembly, the exiles incited the Thebans to revolt from Alexander, invoking "free-

1.6.7–8
ILLYRIA
The Taulantians attack the Macedonian rear guard; Alexander repels this attack, then leads the river crossing. A second attack on the rear guard is checked by artillery fire, and the Macedonians reach the opposite bank safely.

1.6.9–11
ILLYRIA
Alexander makes a night raid on the poorly defended camp of the Taulantians and Illyrians. Taken by surprise, many are either captured or killed by the Macedonians, though some escape to the mountains.

1.7.1–3
Summer 335
THEBES
The scene shifts to the Greek city of Thebes. Exiled politicians return here in order to incite an anti-Macedonian revolt; rebels attack two members of the Macedonian garrison force. A rumor of Alexander's death helps the revolt win popular support.

1.6.9a   Koinos was a high officer in Alexander's army, somewhat older than the king (see 5.27.3), and also a son-in-law of Parmenion.

1.7.1a   Thebes, Boeotia: Map 1.9, inset. The exiles mentioned here are almost certainly the anti-Macedonian political leaders whom Philip had forced out of the city after his victory at Chaeronea (Map 1.9, inset). This battle, fought in 338 in the plains near Thebes, resulted in the total rout of a combined Athenian and Theban force seeking

to stop the southward expansion of the Macedonian empire. The treaty Philip imposed on the defeated Greek states afterward bound them to keep pro-Macedonian regimes in power and not allow the reentry of political exiles. See Appendix M, §2, 3.

1.7.1b   This occupying "force" was the Macedonian garrison installed on the Kadmeia, the high ground of Thebes, as part of Philip's post-Chaeronea security measures. The two soldiers ambushed by the Thebans would therefore have been Macedonian guards.

dom" and "autonomy"—noble old words[2a]—and encouraging them to rid themselves of their Macedonian oppressors. The people found the exiles persuasive, especially since they insisted that Alexander had died in the land of the Illyrians. [3] This rumor was indeed making the rounds; it had gained currency because Alexander had been away for a long time and no news had come from him. The result was just what usually happens under such circumstances: in the absence of accurate information, people formed conjectures in keeping with their wishes.

[4] When Alexander learned what was afoot at Thebes, he decided that the developments there could not be neglected.[4a] For he had long been suspicious of Athens, and realized that the Thebans' enterprise would be dangerous if the Spartans, who had long ago become rebels in spirit if not in fact, and some others of the Peloponnesians, and the Aetolians,[4b] whom he did not consider reliable, joined with the Thebans in their revolt. [5] Marching past Eordaia and Elimiotis[5a] and the heights of Stymphaia and Parauaca,[5b] Alexander reached Pelinna[5c] in Thessaly on the seventh day. Setting out from Pelinna, he entered Boeotia[5d] on the sixth day, and the Thebans did not learn that he had passed through the Gates[5e] until he had reached Onchestos[5f] with his entire army. [6] At that point, the men who had fomented the revolt declared that the army from Macedonia was that of Antipatros;[6a] they continued to insist that Alexander was dead, and angrily contradicted those who reported that Alexander himself was leading the army. Some other Alexander had come, they said—namely, Alexander son of Aeropos.[6b]

[7] Starting from Onchestos the next day, Alexander led his army to Thebes and made camp at the grove of Iolaos,[7a] giving the Thebans time, in case they repented their bad decisions, to open negotiations with him. [8] But the Thebans were so far from conceding anything that might lead to an agreement that their horsemen, sallying out from the city with a consider-

---

1.7.4–6
Summer 335
THEBES
Alexander moves swiftly to counter the revolt, fearing its spread. He arrives in Boeotia by rapid marches.

1.7.7–10
THEBES
The Thebans ignore the chance Alexander offers them to come to terms, and instead attack the Macedonian advance guard. Alexander holds off on a full-scale attack, still hoping for a negotiated settlement.

1.7.2a　The sarcastic tone in Arrian's aside reveals his own political perspective; living under the Roman empire as he did, he had good reason to scoff at these long-hollow ideals. But the Thebans of 335 would not have regarded them so cynically. Note that the word "autonomy" in this sentence has been supplied by an editor, since Arrian's aside refers to "words" in the plural, yet the Greek text as we have it contains only one, that is, "freedom."

1.7.4a　Alexander had gotten accurate information about events in Thebes, at a time when the Thebans were utterly deluded about what was happening to Alexander. Throughout his campaigns, Alexander demonstrated a remarkable talent for obtaining better and more current information than his adversaries possessed.

1.7.4b　Athens; Sparta; Peloponnese; Aetolia: Map 1.9, inset.

1.7.5a　Eordaia; Elimiotis (Elim[e]ia): Map 1.9.

1.7.5b　Stymphaia; Parauaea: Map 1.9. Arrian implies that Alexander marched close to these places, but in fact Parauaea was well off to his west. Stymphaia appears as (S)Tymphaia in the *Barrington Atlas* because it is sometimes called Tymphaia.

1.7.5c　Pelinna, Thessaly: Map 1.9.

1.7.5d　Boeotia: Map 1.9, inset.

1.7.5e　The Gates: this probably refers to Thermopylae (Map 1.9, inset), the narrow pass through which an invader could enter central Greece from the north. The Thebans might well have been able to hold this pass against Alexander had they stationed forces there, but the rapidity of the Macedonian advance defied all expectations, as the next two sentences reveal.

1.7.5f　Onchestos: Map 1.9, inset.

1.7.6a　That is, the home guard Alexander had left in Macedonia under the command of Antipatros when he took his expeditionary force into Thrace and Illyria.

1.7.6b　Alexander son of Aeropos is otherwise known as Alexander the Lyncestian. This nobleman held a command in Thrace at the time of the Theban revolt, and so his presence in Onchestos was a realistic possibility. This Alexander would go on to play an ill-fated role in the Asian campaign; see 1.25.

1.7.7a　Iolaos was a mythic hero, a nephew of Herakles, whose cult was prominent at Thebes. The grove in question lay outside the walls of Thebes to the northeast.

14

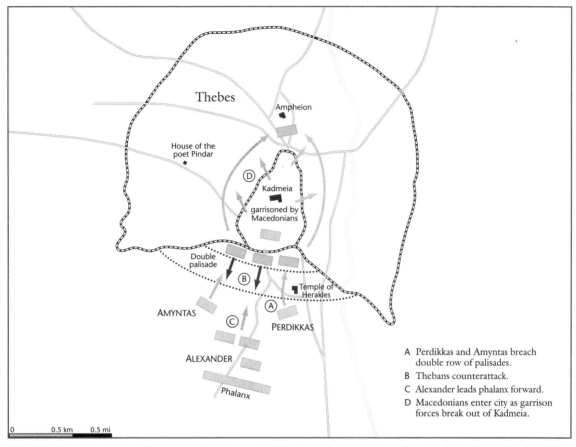

MAP 1.8. THE ASSAULT ON THEBES AS DESCRIBED AT 1.8. According to Arrian, the assault was begun by Perdikkas and Amyntas acting on their own initiative. As their units came under attack, Alexander and the phalanx moved forward to support them and forced an entry into the city.

able number of light-armed troops, fired some shots at the Macedonian advance guards and killed a few of them. [9] Alexander sent out some light-armed troops and archers to check the attack, and his men easily repulsed the Thebans, who were by now approaching his camp. The next day, Alexander marched the entire army around to the gates leading to Eleutherai and Attica.[9a] Even then he did not assault the city walls but made camp not far from the Kadmeia, so that its Macedonian occupiers would have help nearby. [10] For the Thebans had sealed off the Kadmeia with a double palisade and were keeping watch so that no outside aid could reach those who were penned in there, nor could those inside run out and injure them when they were under attack from beyond their walls. Having made

1.7.9a Eleutherai; Attica: Map 1.9, inset. This more southerly position enabled Alexander to cut off communication between Thebes and Athens, a strategically important move because of the risk that the Athenians might (as they were in fact considering) send an army to support the revolt. See Appendix M, §5.

camp near the Kadmeia, Alexander continued to delay, as he still wished to approach the Thebans in friendship rather than risk a confrontation.

[11] At that point, the Thebans who realized what was in their state's best interest were moved to come out to Alexander and seek forgiveness for the commoners who had joined in the revolt.

But the exiles and all who had summoned them, supposing that they would meet with no kindness from Alexander (especially those who were officers of the Boeotian League),[11a] were doing all they could to drum up popular support for the war. But even so, Alexander did not attack the town.[11b]

[1] Ptolemy, however, says that Perdikkas,[1a] who had been put in charge of guarding the Macedonian camp and stood with his own battalion not far from the enemy's palisade, did not wait for Alexander's signal but assaulted the palisade, tore it down, and attacked the Thebans' forward guard.[1b] [2] When Amyntas son of Andromenes saw Perdikkas advancing within the palisade, he followed him, bringing up his own battalion. (Amyntas had been stationed alongside Perdikkas.) Observing these developments, Alexander led up the rest of the army, lest the two engaged units be cut off and find themselves at the Thebans' mercy. [3] He signaled the archers and the Agrianians to run inside the palisade, but kept the *agema*[3a] and the shield-bearers outside. When Perdikkas had forced his way into the second palisade, he was wounded; having fallen there, he was brought back to camp in serious condition, and his life was saved only with difficulty. But the men under his command, falling on the Thebans at the sunken road that runs past the temple of Herakles, hemmed them in with the aid of Alexander's archers. [4] They followed the retreating Thebans as far as the temple, but at that point the Thebans wheeled around with a shout, and the Macedonians were put to flight. Eurybotas, the Cretan captain of the archers,[4a] perished with nearly seventy of his men. The remainder fled to the Macedonians' *agema* and the royal shield-bearers.

[5] At that point Alexander, seeing that his own men were fleeing and that the Thebans who were pursuing them had fallen out of formation, attacked these Thebans with his phalanx in close order and thrust them inside the gates. The Thebans retreated in such terror that when they were

1.7.11a The Boeotian League had been the political instrument by which Thebes had
exerted hegemony over central Greece in
the days before Chaeronea. Officers of that
body evidently bore greater guilt in Alexander's eyes than other political leaders, for
reasons that are not entirely clear.
1.7.11b Arrian's account of the Theban uprising
here begins to diverge considerably from
the narratives of other ancient sources. The
portrait Arrian here constructs of a patient
Alexander, reluctant to attack until circumstances forced him to do so, is contradicted
by Diodorus Siculus, who at 17.9.4–6
depicts Alexander, stung to rage by insults
the Thebans hurled at him from behind
their walls, vowing to utterly destroy the
city that had defied his will.

1.8.1a Perdikkas: see Appendix E, §9, for more on
this important member of Alexander's
inner circle.
1.8.1b Our other sources do not confirm this
unauthorized sally by Perdikkas but instead
portray the Macedonian attack on Thebes
as a deliberate move, ordered by Alexander.
1.8.3a The *agema* was a special division of light-
armed infantry, though there was a cavalry
agema as well. For more, see n. 1.1.11a.
1.8.4a The Cretans were among the few Euro-
peans who trained their youths extensively
in archery. Bowmen recruited from Crete
formed an important auxiliary force in
Alexander's army. He added to the numbers
of this force as his campaign progressed,
after seeing its utility in countering Asian
missile-firing troops.

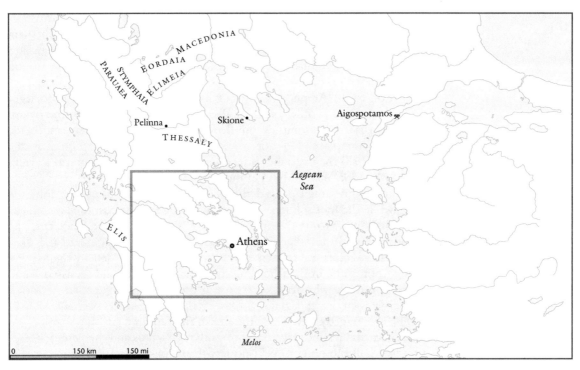

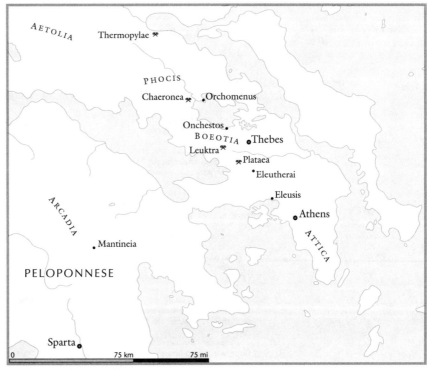

MAP 1.9

driven into the city they did not bar the gates in time, so that all the Macedonians who were following close on their heels rushed along with them inside the walls. (Because the Thebans had posted so many advance guards, their walls were not manned.) [6] Some of the Macedonians, going around the perimeter to the Kadmeia, joined with the garrison there and proceeded on to the Ampheion,[6a] from which point they entered the adjacent sections of the city; others at the walls, which were held now by the troops who had rushed in alongside the fleeing Thebans, scaled them and made for the marketplace. [7] For a short time the Thebans posted at the Ampheion held their ground, but when they were pressed hard on all sides by the Macedonians and by Alexander, who seemed to pop up everywhere, the Theban horsemen dashed through the city and rushed out into the plain, while the foot soldiers tried to save themselves as best they could. [8] After that, it was not the Macedonians[8a] so much as the Phocians, the Plataeans,[8b] and the other Boeotians who, in a rage, slaughtered the Thebans helter-skelter even when they made no move to defend themselves, falling upon some in their houses, upon others who forcibly resisted,[8c] and even upon those who tried to approach the temples as suppliants, sparing neither women nor children.

1.9.1–5
Arrian pauses to compare the suffering of Thebes with other great disasters inflicted by one Greek city on another. He finds that all previous cataclysms pale in comparison to the fate of Thebes.

[1] This tragedy, because of the size of the captured city, the sharpness of the action, and its unexpectedness to both the victims and the perpetrators,[1a] astonished all the other Greeks no less than those who took part in it. [2] For if the reverses that befell the Athenians in Sicily[2a] were as great a calamity in terms of the number of casualties, at least their army was destroyed far from home and included more allied troops than native Athenians, and their city survived and managed to hold out for a long time afterward against the Spartans and their allies, as well as the Great King;[2b] hence it did not leave its victims with a comparable sense of disaster, nor did it evoke the same terror in the other Greeks. [3] Athens' subsequent defeat at Aigospotamoi,[3a] more-

1.8.6a   Ampheion: a temple dedicated to one of Thebes' founding heroes.
1.8.8a   Macedonia: Map 1.9.
1.8.8b   Phocis; Plataea: Map 1.9, inset.
1.8.8c   Arrian's insistence that the Macedonians were not primarily responsible for the slaughter reflects the desire of his source, Ptolemy, to exonerate Alexander from what the Greeks regarded as an atrocity. Diodorus, who, as mentioned in n. 1.7.11b, portrayed Alexander's motives at Thebes in a very different light than Arrian, says that the Macedonians initiated the slaughter of the Thebans, though he also notes that the Boeotian Greeks eagerly followed their lead (17.13.1–6). These neighbors of Thebes had all suffered various forms of violence and oppression during the preceding decades of Theban hegemony, and now took their revenge on the hated regional superpower.
1.9.1a   The idea that the destruction of Thebes came as an unexpected shock even to those

who caused it reinforces Arrian's view that Alexander had been drawn into an all-out attack on Thebes by the unauthorized actions of his subcommanders. Other ancient sources, as already noted, portray the slaughter as an act of policy.
1.9.2a   In 413, an Athenian-led expeditionary force was defeated in Sicily (Map 1.12, locator), and nearly all of more than 40,000 soldiers were either killed or enslaved; hundreds of ships were also lost (see the famous account in Books 6 and 7 of Thucydides).
1.9.2b   The title Great King refers to the King of Persia.
1.9.3a   Aigospotamoi (Aigospotamos): Map 1.9. In 405, Athens lost her entire navy, rebuilt at great expense after the disaster in Sicily, when a Spartan raid captured the ships beached on the shores of the Hellespont. This total defeat led a few months later to the final surrender of Athens to Sparta after almost three decades of on-again, off-again warfare.

over, took place at sea, and though the Athenians were humbled by the pulling down of their Long Walls, the surrender of many ships, and the loss of their empire, their city nevertheless retained its ancient form and before long regained its former power, completely fortified its Long Walls, and again prevailed at sea; it was then their turn to save from the direst dangers the Spartans, who had once terrified them and nearly annihilated their city.[3b] [4] Then again, the Spartan defeats at Leuktra and Mantineia[4a] astonished the Spartans more by the disaster's unexpectedness than by the number of casualties, and the march on Sparta by the Boeotians and Arcadians under Epameinondas frightened the Spartans and their allies more by the surprise of such an unusual sight than by the immediacy of the danger. [5] The conquest of the Plataeans' city, moreover, was no great tragedy, because of both the smallness of the city and [the small number] of those confined in it, the majority having fled to Athens long before.[5a] As for the destruction of Melos and Skione[5b]—these were island dwellings, and their ruin brought more disgrace to those who caused it than any great surprise to the Greek world as a whole.

[6] But in Thebes, the hasty and unpremeditated character of the revolt, and the suddenness of the capture, which came about with little effort on the part of the conquerors,[6a] and the wholesale slaughter of the kind perpetrated by men of the same race taking vengeance for an ancient enmity, and the complete enslavement of the city that was then preeminent among the Greeks for power and renown in warfare—all of these elements were attributed, not unreasonably, to divine wrath. [7] For it was said that the The-

1.9.6–8
Summer 335
THEBES
Onlookers to the calamity
attribute the fall of Thebes
to divine vengeance for
various wrongs the city
has committed.

1.9.3b Arrian here passes quickly through almost forty years of Athenian history. After surrendering to Sparta in 404, Athens was compelled to disband its naval empire and to permit the destruction of part of the Long Walls, a fortified corridor that had given the city secure access to its nearby harbors. Some ten years later, however, these walls were rebuilt and Athens began a second period of naval imperialism, though not nearly on as grand a scale as the first. In 369, two years after the defeat of Sparta by Thebes (see n. 1.9.4b), Athens made common cause with her former enemy to defend it against invasion (Xenophon, *Hellenika* 7.1.1–14). Throughout almost all of this turbulent period, moreover, Athens kept its democratic constitution (what Arrian calls its "ancient form") intact.

1.9.4a Leuktra; Mantineia: Map 1.9, inset. In these two battles, in 371 and 362, Theban troops, commanded by the great general Epameinondas, vanquished those led by the Spartans, whose military skill and prowess had formerly been deemed invincible.

1.9.5a In 427 Plataea was captured by a Spartan-led siege, and its male defenders, slightly more than 200 in number, were executed; the women were enslaved (see Thucydides 3.52–68). The words in brackets in this

sentence have been added to fill a small gap in the Greek text.

1.9.5b At both Skione in 421 and Melos in 415, Athens punished rebellion from, or noncooperation with, its imperial agenda by the execution of all adult males and enslavement of women and children (Thucydides 5.32, 5.116). It is not clear what Arrian means by emphasizing that "these were island dwellings." (Melos alone was a true island, though Skione, isolated at the end of a peninsula otherwise dominated by Athens, had some of the strategic features of one.) Given what he goes on to say about the shamefulness of their destruction, Arrian seems to imply that their vulnerability, in a time of total Athenian naval supremacy, made them nonthreatening; their destruction by Athens could thus only be seen as exemplary punishment rather than a legitimate act of self-defense.

1.9.6a This is another point on which Arrian is at odds with other ancient sources. Diodorus (17.11–12), for example, portrays the battle for Thebes as a close-fought affair in which the Thebans had the upper hand for some time and inflicted substantial casualties on the Macedonians.

bans had paid the full penalty, long after the fact, for their betrayal of the Greeks in the Persian Wars;[7a] and for their occupation of the Plataeans' city during the armistice, and for their complete enslavement of that city, and for their butchery, uncharacteristic of Greeks, of those who had surrendered to the Spartans, and for laying waste the Plataeans' countryside, the very place in which the Greeks, drawn up opposite the Medes,[7b] had repulsed the danger threatening Greece;[7c] and because they had voted to destroy Athens when a motion was proposed among the Spartans' allies concerning the city's enslavement.[7d] [8] Even before the disaster many warning signs were said to have been sent by the gods; these had been ignored at the time, but afterward the memory of them led people to conclude that the event had been prefigured long before.

[9] The allies who had taken part in the action and to whom Alexander entrusted the disposition of affairs in Thebes[9a] decided to garrison the Kadmeia and to raze the city to the ground and distribute its territories (except for consecrated ground) among the allies. All the children, women, and Theban survivors (except for the priests and priestesses, all the guest-friends[9b] of Philip or Alexander, and all who had served as *proxenoi*[9c] of the Macedonians) were enslaved. [10] They say that Alexander saved the house of the poet Pindar and spared his descendants out of reverence for Pindar. In addition to these measures, the allies decided to rebuild and fortify Orchomenus[10a] and Plataea.

1.9.9–10
Summer 335
THEBES
A judicial body formed by Alexander makes final dispositions for the razing of the city and the enslavement of its surviving population. Pindar's house alone is left standing, according to legend, on Alexander's orders.

1.9.7a After the Greek defeat at Thermopylae in 480, Thebes surrendered to the invading Persians and, for the next year, served as their primary base of operations in central Greece.

1.9.7b The Medes were a northern Iranian people who originally ruled the Persians, then came to be ruled by them and assimilated into their power structure. See Appendix G, The Persian Empire and Alexander, §1.

1.9.7c The charges listed here all relate to the events of 431–427, in which Thebes initiated a surprise attack on Plataea (thus violating the Thirty Years' Peace between Athens and Sparta), then, after the town was taken by siege years later, had on the Spartans the execution of all male prisoners and enslavement of females. This extreme (or, in Arrian's view, un-Hellenic) resolution seemed to observers the more unjustified in that Plataea had been the site of the final Greek victory over Persia some fifty years earlier (see Thucydides 3.58).

1.9.7d According to some sources, the Thebans had urged on Sparta either the enslavement or the total destruction of Athens at the conclusion of the Peloponnesian War in 404.

1.9.9a Our sources are unclear as to what sort of judicial body is described here. According to the treaty imposed after the battle of Chaeronea, all decisions concerning members of the Greek League were to be dealt with by the League representatives, who normally met at Corinth. Whether such a distant body could have presided over the fate of Thebes, or whether Alexander instead convened some surrogate body made up of League members then present in Boeotia—of whom the vast majority belonged to the small cities of central Greece that had long been victimized by Theban aggression—is unclear, and our ancient sources give varying accounts. What seems clear is that Alexander did not render the death sentence himself, and that whatever body did so could be counted on to go along with his wishes in the matter.

1.9.9b Guest-friendship (*xenia*), a hallowed institution of ancient Hellas, was a formal relationship, usually formed between eminent citizens of different states, but sometimes between an individual and a whole state. The parties committed themselves to profound mutual obligations, including hospitality, advice, and support.

1.9.9c *Proxenoi* (singular *proxenos*) were citizens and residents of one state who served as friend or representative of a foreign state (much like a modern honorary consul). They provided assistance and attempted to protect the interests of the citizens of their designated city. The office was often hereditary.

1.9.10a Orchomenus, in Boeotia (Map 1.9, inset), and Plataea were two cities that had been traditional enemies of Thebes and victims of its power.

[1] When the Thebans' misfortune was reported to the other Greeks, all the Arcadians[1a] who had started out from home to aid the Thebans[1b] condemned to death those who had encouraged them to do so; the Eleans[1c] received back their exiles, men who were friendly to Alexander. [2] The Aetolians,[2a] having sent representatives of each tribe as their spokesmen, begged Alexander's forgiveness because they, too, had revolted on learning of the Thebans' revolt. The Athenians, who were then celebrating their Great Mysteries,[2b] were thunderstruck when some of the Thebans arrived among them straight from the battle. Abandoning the mysteries, they began transporting their goods from the fields to the city.[2c] [3] The people convened a meeting of the Assembly,[3a] and on Demades'[3b] motion selected ten envoys from among all the Athenians and sent them to Alexander (having chosen men known to be especially friendly to him) to say that the people of Athens were delighted by his safe return from the Illyrians and the Triballoi, even if they had not expressed this sentiment at the time, and by his punishment of the Thebans' revolt.[3c]

[4] Alexander responded in kindly fashion to the embassy, but wrote a letter to the Athenian people demanding the surrender of Demosthenes and Lykourgos, along with Hyperides, Polyeuktos, Khares, Kharidemos, Ephialtes, Diotimos, and Moirokles. [5] He considered these men responsible both for the city's disaster at Chaeronea[5a] and for the later offenses committed at Philip's death against himself and Philip.[5b] He also argued that these men were no less guilty of the Thebans' revolt than the Theban rebels themselves. [6] The Athenians did not give up the men, but sent a second embassy to Alexander, entreating him to let go of his anger against those whose surrender he had demanded. And Alexander relented, perhaps out of reverence for the city, or because he was eager for the expedition to Asia and wanted to leave no cause for resentment behind in Greece. Of those men, however, whose surrender had been demanded but not granted, Alexander ordered Kharidemos alone to go into exile. Kharidemos fled to Asia, to the court of King Darius.[6a]

1.10.1–3
Greek states that supported the revolt quickly reverse policy. Athens sends an embassy to Alexander, seeking to gain his favor.

1.10.4–6
Alexander shows kindness to the Athenians but also demands the surrender of nine of their leading anti-Macedonian politicians. Later, however, he relents in the face of Athenian entreaties and demands the exile of only one of the nine.

1.10.1a Arcadia: Map 1.9, inset.
1.10.1b Arcadian forces apparently went as far as the Isthmus of Corinth during the siege of Thebes, but then waited there to see whether their intervention would be useful. In the end it was not.
1.10.1c Elis: Map 1.9.
1.10.2a Aetolia: Map 1.9, inset.
1.10.2b The Great Mysteries (or Eleusinian Mysteries): an important religious rite celebrated by the Athenians in the autumn.
1.10.2c Withdrawal of the rural population inside the city walls was the standard Athenian response to the threat of attack.
1.10.3a The Assembly was both the legislative and the policy-making body of democratic Athens, in which all citizens could vote on courses of action.
1.10.3b Demades was a leader of the pro-Alexander faction at Athens, and therefore an opponent of Demosthenes, the famous orator who led the anti-collaborationist majority (see n. 1.10.5b).

1.10.3c The sudden reversal of sentiment by the Athenian populace, inclined only a few days earlier to support the Theban revolt, illustrates not only the terror inspired by Alexander's harsh treatment of Thebes but also the existence of a sizable faction within the city that preferred to collaborate with or appease Alexander rather than confront him.
1.10.5a Battle site of Chaeronea: Map 1.9, inset.
1.10.5b Demosthenes, the leading member of the group of proscribed orators, had been the principal advocate of the Athenian militarization that led to the showdown at Chaeronea. He had also celebrated publicly after learning of the assassination of Philip.
1.10.6a According to both Diodorus (17.30.2–6) and Quintus Curtius (3.2.10–19), Kharidemos became a military adviser to the Persian king and was executed in 333 for speaking too frankly about the shortcomings of Persian soldiers.

1.11.1–2
Autumn 335
MACEDONIA
Alexander returns to
Macedonia and presides
over a local athletic contest.
An omen is seen.

1.11.3–5
Spring 334
HELLESPONT
Alexander leaves Antipatros
in charge of his European
empire and crosses into Asia
with his army. On first reaching Asian soil, he sacrifices
to Protesilaos, the mythic
Greek hero who died when
crossing into Asia during
the Trojan War.

1.11.6–8
HELLESPONT
At the point of the crossing,
Alexander performs rituals
and adopts symbols evoking
the legends of the Trojan War.

[1] Having settled these matters, Alexander returned to Macedonia,[1a] where he performed the sacrifice to Olympian Zeus established by Arkhelaos[1b] and celebrated the Olympic Games at Aigeai.[1c] Some say that he also held a contest in honor of the Muses. [2] Word now came that the statue in Pieria[2a] of Orpheus son of Oiagros the Thracian[2b] was sweating continuously. The prophets interpreted this in a variety of ways, but Aristandros,[2c] a Telmessian seer, urged Alexander to take heart, as it had been made clear that the epic and lyric poets and all who concerned themselves with song would have plenty of work composing verses celebrating Alexander and his exploits.

[3] In early spring, Alexander marched to the Hellespont,[3a] having entrusted Macedonian and Greek affairs to Antipatros.[3b] His infantry, including the light-armed troops and archers, numbered not many more than thirty thousand, his cavalry more than five thousand. His route passed alongside Lake Kerkinitis in the direction of Amphipolis and the outlets of the River Strymon.[3c] [4] After crossing the Strymon, he passed Mount Pangaion on his way to Abdera and Maroneia,[4a] Greek coastal settlements. From there he reached the Hebros[4b] and crossed the river easily. [5] Marching through Paetika,[5a] he headed for the River Melas,[5b] crossed it, and arrived in Sestos[5c] twenty days after setting out from home.[5d] On reaching Elaious,[5e] Alexander sacrificed to Protesilaos at that hero's grave, as Protesilaos is thought to have been the first Greek, of those who came with Agamemnon to make war on Troy, to have crossed into Asia. The offering was made in the hope that Alexander's landing might have a more favorable outcome than that of Protesilaos.[5f]

[6] Parmenion[6a] had been assigned to transport the cavalry and most of the infantry from Sestos to Abydos.[6b] These troops crossed in 160 triremes[6c]

1.11.1a Macedonia: Map 1.12.
1.11.1b Arkhelaos was king of Macedonia from about 412 to 399.
1.11.1c Aigeai: Map 1.12. In fact, these games were held at Dion (Map 1.12), another Macedonian city; Arrian has gotten his geography confused. These games are different from the Greek Olympic Games held at Olympia.
1.11.2a Pieria: Map 1.12.
1.11.2b Orpheus, the legendary musician and singer, was by some accounts the son of a Thracian king; by others, of the god Apollo.
1.11.2c Aristandros of Telmessos was the court seer of both Philip and Alexander. He appears often in Arrian's narrative as a prophet who had great influence over Alexander's decisions.
1.11.3a Hellespont: Map 1.12, inset.
1.11.3b Antipatros: this former member of Philip's general staff would remain in command of Alexander's European holdings for the entire course of the Asian campaign. Alexander finally sought to remove him from office for reasons that are not clear (see 7.12). For more on Antipatros, see Appendix E, §15.
1.11.3c Lake Kerkinitis; Amphipolis; Strymon River: Map 1.12.

1.11.4a Mount Pangaion; Abdera; Maroneia: Map 1.12.
1.11.4b Hebros River: Map 1.12.
1.11.5a Paetika: location unknown.
1.11.5b Melas River, possible location: Map 1.12, inset.
1.11.5c Sestos: Map 1.12, inset.
1.11.5d Alexander's route through Thrace (see Book One Route Map) neatly reverses the one followed by Xerxes in his invasion of Greece in 480, thus reinforcing the idea that the Asian campaign was undertaken in retribution for the events of the Persian Wars.
1.11.5e Elaious: Map 1.12, inset.
1.11.5f According to mythic accounts, Protesilaos was shot dead by a Trojan archer at the moment he touched Asian soil.
1.11.6a Parmenion had been sent into Asia in 337 at the head of a Macedonian advance force assigned the task of securing a beachhead. See the Introduction, §7.2–3, and Appendix E, §13, for more on this important figure.
1.11.6b Abydos: Map 1.12, inset.
1.11.6c Trireme: the standard Greek warship in the fifth and fourth centuries, armed with a bronze ram at the front and powered by three banks of rowers. See Appendix D, §13, and Figure D.2.

FIGURE 1.11.
A decaying shield found in Tomb II
at Aigeai, made of wood covered
with gold leaf and ivory bas-relief.
Its central scene depicts Achilles,
Alexander's mythic ancestor, stabbing the Amazon queen Penthesilea.
Too precious to be worn in battle,
this shield bedecked some Macedonian king, perhaps Alexander himself,
on ceremonial occasions.

and many merchant vessels besides. A popular story has it that when crossing
from Elaious to the Achaean harbor,[6d] Alexander himself took the helm of
the admiral's ship, and that when he was halfway across the Hellespont he
sacrificed a bull to Poseidon and the Nereids and poured a libation from a
golden bowl into the sea. [7] It is also said that he was the first to disembark
with his weapons onto Asian soil,[7a] and that he built two altars—one where
he had set out from Europe, the other where he had landed in Asia—in
honor of Zeus Protector of Landings, Athena, and Herakles. Having made
his way up to Troy,[7b] he sacrificed to Trojan Athena, dedicated his armor in
the temple, and took down, in exchange for it, some of the sacred weapons
preserved from the Trojan War. [8] They say that his shield-bearers would
carry these weapons before him into battle. He is also said to have sacrificed
to Priam at the altar of Zeus of the Courtyard, hoping to appease Priam's
wrath against the family of Neoptolemos, to which he himself belonged.[8a]

   [1] When Alexander reached Troy, Menoitios the pilot crowned him
with a golden crown, and then Khares the Athenian,[1a] having arrived

1.12.1
TROY
Alexander visits Troy
and honors his legendary
ancestor Achilles.

1.11.6d Achaean harbor: a landing point near the
ancient city of Troy (Map 1.12, inset).
1.11.7a According to Diodorus (17.17.2), before
coming up onto dry land, Alexander flung
his spear into Asian soil, thus signifying
that he would possess all of Asia by force
of arms. Historians dispute whether
Alexander could have entertained such a
vast goal at this stage of his journey.
1.11.7b In Alexander's day, Troy was no longer
the great city of Homeric times, but a
dusty tourist town.

1.11.8a Priam, aged king of Troy, was ruthlessly
executed by Neoptolemos, Achilles' son,
according to Greek mythic beliefs.
Alexander's mother, Olympias, was
thought to descend from Neoptolemos.
1.12.1a Khares the Athenian was one of the anti-
Macedonian leaders in Athens who,
according to Arrian, had been on Alexander's list of enemies only a few weeks earlier (see 1.10.4). He now apparently
found it expedient to make his peace with
Alexander.

1.12.2–5

SECOND PREFACE

Pausing to make a second introduction to his work, Arrian laments that Alexander lacks a history worthy of his deeds. Arrian parallels the value and nature of his writing with Alexander's vast military accomplishments.

from Sigeion,[1b] and certain others, some of them Greeks, others local residents. [. . .][1c] Some say that Alexander placed a wreath on the tomb of Achilles, and Hephaistion is said to have placed one on Patroklos' tomb.[1d] Legend has it that Alexander accounted Achilles happy for having had Homer to preserve his fame for posterity.

[2] And, indeed, Alexander was right to account Achilles happy on that score especially; for though Alexander was fortunate in other respects, here there was a void, since his exploits were not published to mankind in a worthy manner either in prose or in verse. Nor were his praises sung in lyric poetry as were those of Hieron, Gelon, Theron, and many others who do not bear comparison with him.[2a] Consequently, Alexander's exploits are much less well known than the paltriest of ancient deeds. [3] For the expedition of Cyrus' Ten Thousand against King Artaxerxes, and the sufferings of Klearkhos and the men captured with him, and the march to the coast of those same men under Xenophon's command are much better known, thanks to Xenophon, than Alexander's exploits.[3a] [4] Yet Alexander did not serve under another man's command, nor did he merely defeat those who impeded his march to the coast as he fled from the Great King. One can point to no other man, Greek or barbarian, who performed exploits so numerous and so momentous.[4a]

It was this, I affirm, that spurred me on to write this history, and I have not considered myself unworthy to make Alexander's exploits known to mankind. [5] That much I have discerned about myself, whoever I may be. I need not set down my name, for it is not unknown to men, nor is my country nor my family nor the offices, if any there were, I have held in my own land. But this I do put on record: that these chronicles are my country and my family and my offices, and have been from my youth.[5a] And that is why I do not consider myself unworthy of a foremost place among Greek writers, if indeed Alexander merits a foremost place among warriors.

1.12.1b   Sigeion: Map 1.12, inset.

1.12.1c   There is a small gap in the preserved Greek text here.

1.12.1d   See Appendix E, §8, for more on Hephaistion, Alexander's closest companion and possibly his lover during most of the Asian campaign. The symbolism of this dual offering would have been unmistakable to all onlookers: Alexander, alleged descendant and self-styled avatar of Achilles, and Hephaistion, favored above all followers as highly as Achilles favored Patroklos, each paid obeisance to their heroic models.

1.12.2a   Hieron, Gelon, and Theron were fifth-century Greek tyrants in Sicily who were celebrated for athletic or military victories in the odes of Pindar and others.

1.12.3a   Xenophon's *Anabasis* records the march of a band of Greek mercenaries, hired by Cyrus in 401 to help him usurp the throne, as they made their way, unaided and in dire peril, from Mesopotamia to the Black Sea coast. Xenophon himself, along with Klearkhos,

had helped lead the band of Greeks out of danger. In his career as essayist and historian, Arrian frequently modeled himself on Xenophon (see the Introduction, §1.1) and may even have titled his history of Alexander *Anabasis Alexandrou*, "Alexander's *Anabasis*," so as to evoke parallels with Xenophon's famous text. (The Greek word *anabasis* has no good English equivalent. It means a march or journey inland from a coast, usually as part of a military campaign.)

1.12.4a   Arrian draws a pointed contrast between Xenophon's military achievements and those of Alexander. Xenophon's mercenaries had in fact defeated the armies of the Great King in the battle of Cunaxa, but had also lost their leader there. Their military engagements thereafter had been designed to safeguard a retreat rather than expand a campaign of conquest.

1.12.5a   See the Introduction, §1.1, and Appendix R, Arrian's Life and Works, for the biographical issues raised in this paragraph.

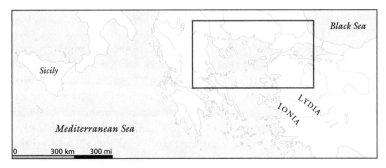

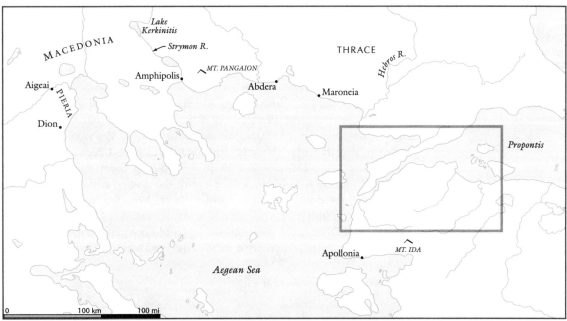

MAP 1.12

1.12.6–7
Spring 334
HELLESPONT
Arrian resumes his narrative.
Alexander continues his
inland march. The city of
Priapus surrenders to his
forward column.

[6] From Troy Alexander went to Arisbe, where his entire army had made camp after crossing the Hellespont, and on the following day proceeded to Perkote.[6a] The next day, after passing Lampsacus,[6b] he encamped near the River Praktios,[6c] which flows from Mount Ida[6d] and empties into the sea between the Hellespont and the Black Sea.[6e] From there he proceeded to Hermoton after passing the city of Kolonai.[6f] [7] His reconnaissance men were sent ahead of the army under the command of Amyntas son of Arrabaios with the squadron of Companions from Apollonia[7a] (whose leader was Socrates son of Sathon) and four squadrons of the Scouts,[7b] as they are called. As Amyntas passed Priapus,[7c] the city was surrendered to him by its inhabitants, and he sent a detachment to receive it with Panegoros son of Lycagoros, one of the Companions.

1.12.8–10
ZELEIA
The Persian satraps in Asia
Minor discuss how best to
meet Alexander's advance.
They reject a scorched-earth
policy.

[8] The Persian commanders were Arsames, Rheomithres, Petenes, and Niphates. With them were Spithridates, the satrap of Lydia and Ionia,[8a] and Arsites, the governor of Hellespontine Phrygia.[8b] These men had made camp near the city of Zeleia[8c] with the barbarian cavalry and the Greek mercenaries.[8d] [9] They held a council when Alexander's crossing of the Hellespont had been reported, and Memnon of Rhodes advised them not to take a chance against the Macedonians, whose infantry, he said, was far superior to their own;[9a] furthermore, he said, the Macedonians had Alexander present, while on their side Darius was absent. He advised them to march ahead, destroy the grazing land by trampling it with the cavalry, and burn the standing harvest, not even sparing the cities themselves; Alexander would not remain in the country, he said, if provisions were scarce. [10] It is reported that Arsites declared at the meeting that he would not permit one house to be burned by the men posted with him. The Persians reportedly sided with

1.12.6a   Arisbe; Hellespont; Perkote: Map 1.12, inset.
1.12.6b   Lampsacus: Map 1.12, inset.
1.12.6c   Praktios River, possible location: Map 1.12, inset. Mount Ida is too far south to possibly be the location of the source of the river. This may be a geographical error on Arrian's part.
1.12.6d   Mount Ida: Map 1.12.
1.12.6e   Black (ancient Euxine) Sea: Map 1.12, locator. The "sea" Arrian here refers to, between the Hellespont and the Black Sea, was called Propontis (Map 1.12 and inset) by other Greek writers and is today called the Sea of Marmara.
1.12.6f   Hermoton; Kolonai: Map 1.12, inset.
1.12.7a   Apollonia: Map 1.12.
1.12.7b   As its name implies, this mounted unit was outfitted for speed and instant readiness, though there is no clear information about what troops were enlisted in it or how they were equipped. They were also known as the *sarisa*-armed cavalry.
1.12.7c   Priapus: Map 1.12, inset.
1.12.8a   Lydia; Ionia: Map 1.12, locator.
1.12.8b   Hellespontine Phrygia: Map 1.12, inset. Arsites was also a satrap, though Arrian

uses a different word here. The satraps, roughly two dozen in number, were appointed by the Persian king to administer the satrapies, or provinces, of the empire, collect taxes, and, especially in this case, organize defense. For the locations of all Persian satrapies mentioned by Arrian, see Ref. Map 1.

1.12.8c   Zeleia: Map 1.12, inset.
1.12.8d   Persian leaders, especially in Asia Minor, had been employing Greek mercenaries as their principal infantry corps for decades. By the treaty imposed by Philip after the battle of Chaeronea, however, Greeks were forbidden to serve the Persian cause. See Appendix G, §9.
1.12.9a   Memnon was well equipped to judge such matters, having led the Persian effort to repulse the Macedonian advance force under Parmenion during the previous two years. Memnon was a talented Greek general who had married Barsine, the daughter of a Persian grandee, and, like many Greeks of his day, had cast his lot with the Persian king rather than with the new Macedonian order in Europe.

FIGURE 1.13.
The Granicus (modern
Biga Çay) as it appears
today is much shallower
than in Alexander's
time, since its waters are
drawn out by pumps for
irrigation. Man-made
floodbanks have also
controlled the river's
spring floods, so that
trees and shrubs have
grown up where the
banks were once bare.

Arsites because they suspected that Memnon was intentionally delaying the
war on account of honor from the King.[10a]

[1] In the meantime, Alexander was advancing to the Granicus River,[1a]
having arrayed the phalanx in two rows,[1b] with the cavalry at the wings; he
had given orders for the baggage train to follow behind. The reconnaissance force under Hegelokhos included the *sarisa*-armed[1c] cavalry and five
hundred light-armed troops. [2] When the army neared the Granicus, the
party from the lookout places galloped up to report that the Persians,
arrayed for battle, had taken up a position beyond the far bank of the river.

1.13.1–2
Spring 334
GRANICUS RIVER
The Macedonian and Persian
armies stand on opposite
banks of the river.

1.12.10a It is unclear whether this means that
Memnon hoped the Persian king would
approve of his delaying the start of the war,
or that he was already receiving honor from
the king and hoped not to lose it by initiat-
ing action that might not succeed. The king
of the Persian empire is meant, as indicated
here and elsewhere in the text by capitaliza-
tion. Arrian, like other Greek writers, often

refers to this monarch simply as "the King."
1.13.1a Granicus River: Map 1.12, inset.
1.13.1b In this formation, the depth of the phalanx
was set at sixteen men, with a space
between the two rows of eight.
1.13.1c *Sarisa*: the infantry spear devised for the
Macedonian army; see n. 1.4.1a. The *sarisa*-
armed cavalry were also known as the
Scouts; see n. 1.12.7b.

Alexander now drew up his entire army in battle order. Parmenion approached him and spoke as follows:[2a]

1.13.3–5
Spring 334
GRANICUS RIVER
Parmenion counsels Alexander to wait and cross the river at dawn, when they may find the Persians unprepared.

[3] "Under the circumstances, sire, I think it would be wise to camp at the bank of the river as we are. For I doubt our enemies, who are far outnumbered by our infantry, would dare to bivouac near us; at dawn we will be able to cross the stream easily and will make it across before they are in formation. [4] I feel it would be unsafe for us to attempt the crossing now, since we will not be able to take the army across in a wide formation. For one can see that the river has many deep spots, and, as you see, the banks themselves are high and steep. [5] So as we climb out in disarray, in a narrow column—the weakest possible formation—the enemy horsemen will charge, having the advantage of a close formation. Thus our first stumble would harm our present standing and might even spoil the outcome of the larger war."

1.13.6–7
GRANICUS RIVER
Rejecting Parmenion's more cautious battle plan, Alexander decides to cross at once.

[6] But Alexander replied, "I know all that, Parmenion. But I would be ashamed, after having easily crossed the Hellespont, if this little stream"—such was the phrase he used to disparage the Granicus—"keeps us from crossing as we are. [7] I would consider it unworthy of the Macedonians' renown and of my quickness to accept risks. And I think the Persians would take courage and think themselves a match for the Macedonians in battle, seeing that up to now their fears have not been confirmed by what they have experienced."

1.14.1–3
GRANICUS RIVER
Alexander orders his troops for battle.

[1] So saying, he sent Parmenion to lead the left wing while he himself led the right. Philotas son of Parmenion had been stationed alongside him on the right wing with the Companion cavalry, the archers, and the Agrianian javelin men. Amyntas son of Arrabaios was stationed next to him with the *sarisa*-armed cavalry, the Paionians, and Socrates' cavalry squadron. [2] Next came the shield-bearers under the command of Nikanor son of Parmenion. Then came the phalanx[2a] of Perdikkas son of Orontes, then that of Koinos son of Polemokrates; that of Krateros son of Alexander; that of Amyntas son of Andromenes; and finally that of Philip son of Amyntas. [3] On the left wing, the Thessalian cavalry, led by Kalas son of Harpalos, was stationed first. Then came the allied cavalry[3a] under the command of Philip son of Menelaos, followed by the Thracians under Agathon. Next came the

---

1.13.2a This first speech of the many that will be encountered in Arrian's text raises the problem of the authenticity of such speeches, discussed in Appendix A, §19. This particular case is doubly problematic, however, because of the conflict among our ancient sources as to how Alexander fought the battle of the Granicus. Parmenion's speech here advises Alexander to rest for the night and attempt a crossing of the river at dawn, and Arrian represents Alexander as rejecting that advice in favor of an immediate crossing. Diodorus (17.19.1–3), however, reports that Alexander did exactly what Parmenion here advises: after bivouacking near the stream, he brought the army

across at dawn, before the Persians could organize themselves to oppose him. There is no possibility of reconciling the two accounts, and no agreement among historians as to which is more credible.

1.14.2a Arrian uses the word "phalanx" here to designate not the entire infantry formation (its usual sense) but the smaller units normally called *taxeis*, or "battalions."

1.14.3a "Allied" in Arrian's usage usually means "Greek." The Greek city-states that had joined the League of Corinth were nominally considered allies of Macedonia, whatever their true sympathies. For more on the allied peoples, see Appendix D, §7.

infantry battalions of Krateros,[3b] Meleagros, and Philip,[3c] which extended to the center of the entire line.

[4] The Persians had nearly twenty thousand horsemen and an only slightly smaller force of foreign mercenary infantry.[4a] The cavalry was drawn out in a long line parallel to the riverbank, and the infantry were posted behind them on the high ground overlooking the river. They could see Alexander himself aiming at their left; the brightness of his weapons and the bustle of the men who attended him were unmistakable. They concentrated their cavalry squadrons at the point on the riverbank that was opposite Alexander.

[5] For a time both armies held their position at the river's edge, shrinking from what lay ahead. There was a great silence on both sides. The Persians were waiting for the Macedonians to enter the river, intending to attack them when they climbed out.

[6] Then Alexander, leaping onto his horse and urging those nearby to follow him and show themselves true men, ordered the Scouts and the Paionians under Amyntas son of Arrabaios to charge into the river with one infantry battalion, following the lead of the squadron of Socrates led by Ptolemy son of Philip.[6a] (That squadron happened to hold the leading role in the entire cavalry on that day.)[6b] [7] Alexander himself, leading the right wing to the sound of war trumpets and the men raising their cry in honor of Enyalios,[7a] entered the stream. As he went he kept stretching out his line diagonal to the direction of the current, so that the Persians might not attack the head of his column as he climbed out of the river.

[1] Where the first troops, those with Amyntas and Socrates, touched the bank, the Persians shot at them from above, some hurling javelins into the river from the bank, others descending to the lower ground at the water's edge. [2] There was a shoving match between the two cavalries— one emerging from the river, the other barring its way—and a dense shower of javelins hurled by the Persians, while the Macedonians assailed the enemy with their spears. But the Macedonians, far outnumbered, suffered in the first assault; they were defending themselves from a low and insecure position in the river, whereas the Persians were assailing them from above. What is more, the strongest contingent of the Persian cavalry had been stationed at this spot, and with them Memnon's sons, and Memnon himself, were

1.14.4
GRANICUS RIVER
The Persians arrange their troops in battle order, placing their cavalry opposite Alexander.

1.14.5
GRANICUS RIVER
The two sides pause before the fighting starts.

1.14.6–7
GRANICUS RIVER
The battle begins. Alexander orders some units to cross the river, then enters the water himself.

1.15.1–3
GRANICUS RIVER
The Macedonians succeed in crossing the Granicus despite Persian opposition. Alexander enters the fray.

1.14.3b Arrian unaccountably puts Krateros' infantry division in two different places, perhaps because he failed to reconcile a dispute between his two major sources (see Bosworth I.118). Some editors delete the first mention of Krateros, which places his position on the right, on the assumption that a scribal error has crept into the text.

1.14.3c Philip is mentioned twice because of his central position. Arrian surveys the battle line first from the right wing to the center, then from the left to the same central point.

1.14.4a These "foreign" mercenaries fighting for

the Persians, like the "allies" fighting for the Macedonians, were Greek.

1.14.6a This Ptolemy is one of several people by that name in Arrian's narrative. He may be the same person as Ptolemy the Bodyguard (1.22.4, 1.22.7) but is certainly different from Ptolemy son of Lagos (Arrian's principal source).

1.14.6b As this sentence informs us, leadership of the cavalry (whatever responsibilities that phrase implies) rotated on a daily basis among the various squadrons.

1.14.7a Enyalios: a Greek war god, roughly identified with Ares.

putting their lives on the line. [3] Thus the first Macedonians to engage the Persians, though they showed themselves brave, were cut to pieces, except for those who wheeled back toward Alexander as he approached. Bringing up the right wing, Alexander now drew near and himself launched an attack on the Persians at the point where the mass of their cavalry had been posted and where the Persian commanders had been stationed.[3a]

A fierce battle was joined around Alexander, [4] and meanwhile battalion after battalion of Macedonians succeeded in crossing the river with no difficulty. Though the battle was fought on horseback, it looked more like an infantry engagement: in a confined space horses contended with horses, men with men, the Macedonians trying to drive the Persians from the bank and force them into the plain, the Persians trying to deny the Macedonians a beachhead and thrust them back to the river. [5] And in this struggle Alexander and his men gained the upper hand, not only because of their strength and experience but because they used cornel-wood spears against the Persians' light javelins.[5a]

[6] At a certain point in the fighting Alexander's spear was shattered. He asked Aretis, a royal groom, for another, but as Aretis' spear had also been shattered—he was fighting valiantly with the remaining half of his broken spear—he showed it to Alexander and urged him to ask someone else. Demaratos the Corinthian, one of the Companions, gave Alexander his spear. [7] Taking it up and catching sight of Mithridates, Darius' son-in-law, riding far out in front and leading a wedge formation of cavalry, Alexander also rode out ahead of the line, struck Mithridates in the face with his spear, and hurled him down. At that moment Rhoisakes rode at Alexander and struck him on the head with a scimitar; [8] Alexander's helmet,[8a] though partially broken, checked the blow. Alexander hurled this man to the ground too, striking with his spear through the man's breastplate and into his chest. Spithridates then raised his scimitar against Alexander from behind, but before he could use it Kleitos son of Dropides[8b] struck him on the shoulder, cutting his arm off with the scimitar still in its grasp. In the meantime, more and more cavalry found themselves able to cross the river, and these joined up with Alexander's forces.

[1] And now the Persians, their faces, and those of their horses, torn by the lances striking them from all sides, were thrust back by the Macedonian cavalry and were injured as well by the light-armed troops who were mingled with them. They gave way first where Alexander was bearing the brunt of the battle. When their center collapsed, both cavalry wings also broke

---

1.15.3a   The strategy described here, in which Alexander directs the main thrust of his attack at the enemy leadership, will be used with devastating effectiveness at Issus (2.11.4) and again at Gaugamela (3.14.2). For more on Alexander's aggressive tactics, see Appendix D, §9–10.

1.15.5a   Arrian blends two points here: the Macedonian *sarisa* (see n. 1.4.1a) was both hard, because made of cornel wood, and several feet longer than the Persian *palton*.

In a cavalry skirmish described by Xenophon (*Hellenika* 3.4.14), the Persian cavalry, armed with superior light spears made of cornel wood, defeats the Greeks, whose spears shatter on impact.

1.15.8a   See Figure 1.15, showing a helmet that could be the one mentioned here; also see Appendix Q, §15.

1.15.8b   This Kleitos, nicknamed Kleitos the Black, was later killed by Alexander (4.8.4–9). For more on Kleitos, see Appendix E, §14.

FIGURE 1.15. A late-fourth-century iron helmet found in Tomb II at Aigeai. The helmet is badly corroded in one spot, leading one scholar, Eugene Borza, to speculate that it might be the one worn by Alexander at the battle of the Granicus and damaged by the sword stroke of Rhoisakes.

and a desperate flight began. [2] Nearly a thousand Persian horsemen died. No serious pursuit was undertaken, as Alexander had turned his attention to the foreign mercenaries who had remained in formation where they were first drawn up—not so much from any firm determination as from terror at the unexpected turn of events. Leading the phalanx against these men, and commanding his horsemen to attack them from all sides, he encircled them and quickly cut them to pieces. No one got away, unless someone was overlooked among the corpses. About two thousand were taken alive.[2a]

[3] Among the Persian commanders, the fallen included Niphates and Petenes; Spithridates, the satrap of Lydia; Mithrobouzanes, the governor of Cappadocia;[3a] Mithridates, Darius' son-in-law; Arboupales, son of Darius and grandson of Artaxerxes; Pharnakes, the brother of Darius' wife; and Omares, the commander of the mercenaries. Arsites escaped from the battle to Phrygia,[3b] and there he died by his own hand, the story goes, because the Persians considered him responsible for their defeat.

[4] On the Macedonian side, some twenty-five of the Companions died in the first attack. Bronze statues of these men stand at Dion.[4a] At Alexan-

1.16.3
GRANICUS RIVER
Arrian lists notable
Persian deaths.

1.16.4–7
GRANICUS RIVER
Alexander comforts his wounded and honors the dead. He sends the surviving Greek mercenaries to Macedonia as slaves. Some of the armor captured in the battle is sent to Athens for a war memorial.

1.16.2a The fate of these prisoners is described at 1.16.6. Alexander's treatment of the Greek mercenaries, as described here by Arrian, is harsh, and it appears even harsher in Plutarch (*Parallel Lives*, "Alexander" 16.13–14), where the mercenaries had first sought to surrender under a negotiated settlement. As at Thebes, Alexander seems to have pressed to their limits the strictures of the League of Corinth, which had forbidden Greek soldiers to serve in foreign armies against other Greeks (see Appendix M, §3). Diodorus (see 17.21) makes no mention of the entire episode.
1.16.3a Cappadocia: Map 1.19, locator.
1.16.3b Phrygia: Map 1.19.
1.16.4a Dion: Map 1.12.

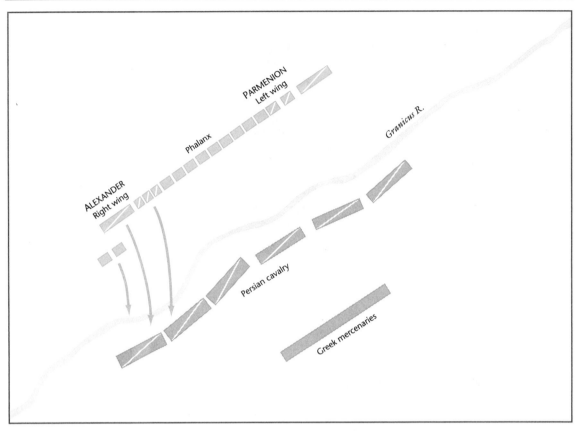

MAP 1.16A. THE FIRST MOVEMENT IN THE BATTLE OF GRANICUS AS DESCRIBED AT 1.14.1–4. The cavalry units of Amyntas and Socrates, stationed to Alexander's left, made the initial move across the river, probably to lure the Persian cavalry down from the heights opposite. The placement of the two infantry units in front of the Macedonian right is speculative, based on the analysis of Bosworth (I.117).

der's command, these statues were sculpted by Lysippos, who was also selected as the only sculptor to fashion a likeness of Alexander.[4b] Among the other horsemen, more than sixty died, while the infantry lost some thirty men. [5] Alexander buried these men the next day with their weapons and other gear, and granted their parents and children exemption from land taxes and all other personal duties or property taxes. He also showed great care for the wounded. He visited them, examined their wounds, inquired how each man came to be wounded, and gave them the opportunity to recount and even embellish their exploits. [6] He honored the Persian commanders with funeral rites and also buried the Greek mercenaries who died fighting on his enemies' behalf. As for the mercenaries he had captured, he

1.16.4b Lysippos was the most prominent Greek sculptor of this period. If it is true that Alexander allowed only Lysippos to sculpt his portrait (as also reported in Plutarch, *Parallel Lives*, "Alexander" 4.1; see also

Appendix L, The *Alexander Romance*, §1), then he was making a remarkably savvy effort to control and manipulate his public image in the Greek world.

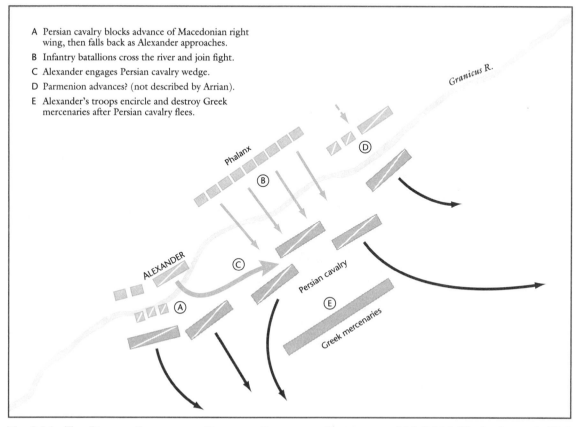

A Persian cavalry blocks advance of Macedonian right wing, then falls back as Alexander approaches.

B Infantry batallions cross the river and join fight.

C Alexander engages Persian cavalry wedge.

D Parmenion advances? (not described by Arrian).

E Alexander's troops encircle and destroy Greek mercenaries after Persian cavalry flees.

MAP 1.16B. THE DECISIVE PHASE OF THE BATTLE OF GRANICUS AS DESCRIBED AT 1.15–1.16.2. The battle was decided by two charges of Alexander's Companion cavalry. The first struck at the left wing of the Persian cavalry, which had come down from the heights above the river to oppose the Macedonian right wing; the second met the advancing horsemen of the Persian center. Alexander became cut off among Persian forces in this second charge and nearly lost his life.

had them bound in shackles and sent to Macedonia to serve as laborers, because though they were Greeks they had disregarded the common resolves of their countrymen and fought against Greece on behalf of the barbarians. [7] He also sent three hundred sets of Persian armor to Athens as a dedicatory offering to Athena on the acropolis,[7a] and even ordered the following words to be inscribed: "Alexander, son of Philip, and the Greeks, except for the Spartans, dedicated these spoils from the barbarians dwelling in Asia."[7b]

1.16.7a This was an extremely deft political move, in that an earlier temple of Athena in Athens, since replaced by the Parthenon, had been destroyed by the Persian invasion of 480. Alexander's offering thus underscored the idea that his Asian campaign was undertaken to avenge the Greek victims of that invasion.

1.16.7b This inscription seeks not only to cast the Asian campaign as a Hellenic crusade against the "barbarians"—despite the fact that Alexander had slain far more Greeks than Persians at the battle of the Granicus—but also to exclude the Spartans, who had declined to join the League of Corinth, from this otherwise Panhellenic cause.

FIGURE 1.16. Greek infantry warriors, known as hoplites, in battle against one another. The carved figures, c. 380, from the Nereid Monument at Xanthos, originally held thrusting spears in their right hands. Greek hoplites were employed by Alexander as support troops and by the Persians as front-line infantry.

1.17.–2
Spring 334
GRANICUS RIVER
Alexander arranges for the administration of Hellespontine Phrygia.

1.17.3–6
Summer 334
SARDIS
Alexander receives the surrender of Sardis and sends an officer to take possession of its citadel. After surveying this lofty site, Alexander lays plans to build a temple of Zeus there; a sudden downpour seems to give divine sanction to those plans.

[1] Alexander appointed Kalas[1a] to serve as satrap of the land Arsites ruled, and ordered the same tribute to be paid as had been paid to Darius. He then commanded all the barbarians who had come down from the mountains and voluntarily submitted to him to return to their homes, [2] and he absolved Zeleia[2a] of guilt, since he realized that the city had joined forces with the barbarians under duress. He sent Parmenion to take possession of Daskyleion,[2b] and this was done, as the guards had abandoned the city.

[3] Alexander now proceeded to Sardis.[3a] When he was about nine miles from the city, Mithrenes, the commandant of the citadel, came to him with the town's leading citizens. These men surrendered the city, as Mithrenes did the citadel and the treasure. [4] Alexander made camp at the River Hermus,[4a] which lies nearly two and a half miles from Sardis, and sent Amyntas son of Andromenes to the city to take possession of the citadel. Thereafter he kept Mithrenes with him in a position of honor, and permit-

1.17.1a Kalas, a Macedonian, here replaces Arsites the Persian as satrap of Hellespontine Phrygia, the Achaemenid province comprising northwest Turkey. In his initial administrative appointment Alexander retained the structure and title of Persian imperial rule, changing only the nationality of the satrap. The system of taxation was also maintained

unchanged, as Arrian goes on to say.
1.17.2a Zeleia: Map 1.12, inset.
1.17.2b Daskyleion, the capital city of the satrapy of Hellespontine Phrygia: Map 1.19.
1.17.3a Sardis (Map 1.19), the capital of the satrapy of Lydia, was the most important imperial center of the Persians in western Anatolia.
1.17.4a Hermus River: Map 1.19.

ted the citizens of Sardis and the other Lydians to keep their ancient customs, and even granted them their freedom.[4b] [5] He ascended to the citadel (the site of the Persian garrison), and the place impressed him as defensible, as it was lofty, steep on all sides, and fenced with a triple wall. He was thinking of building a temple of Olympian Zeus[5a] on the citadel and setting up an altar; [6] and as he was scanning the citadel for a suitable site, a summer storm suddenly broke. Thunder crashed and rain fell from the sky, striking the spot where the Lydian[6a] palace stood; and Alexander supposed the gods were thereby indicating where he should build the temple of Zeus. He issued his commands accordingly.

[7] He left Pausanias, one of the Companions, as governor of the citadel of Sardis; Nikias as assessor and collector of the tribute; and Asandros son of Philotas as ruler of Lydia and the rest of Spithridates' domain, giving him cavalry and as many light-armed troops as seemed sufficient under the circumstances. [8] He sent Kalas and Alexander son of Aeropos to Memnon's territory in command of the Peloponnesians and most of the other allies, except the Argives, who were left behind in Sardis to guard the citadel.

[9] Meanwhile at Ephesus,[9a] when news of the cavalry engagement arrived, the mercenaries manning the garrison fled, taking two of the Ephesians' triremes. They were accompanied by Amyntas son of Antiokhos,[9b] who had fled Macedonia to avoid Alexander. Though he had suffered nothing at Alexander's hands, Amyntas was ill-disposed to the king and thought it would be shameful to be mistreated by him.

[10] Reaching Ephesus on the fourth day, Alexander restored all the exiles who on his account had been banished from the city; dissolving the oligarchy, he established a democracy in its place.[10a] He then ordered that all the tribute that had formerly been paid to the barbarians now be paid to Artemis.[10b] [11] When the common people's fear of the oligarchs had been dispelled, they became eager to kill those who were in favor of calling in Memnon, as well as those who had despoiled the temple of Artemis and those who had thrown down the statue of Philip in the temple and dug up the tomb of Heropythos, the city's liberator, in the marketplace. [12] Syrphax, his son Pelagon, and the sons of Syrphax's brothers were led away from the shrine and stoned to

> **1.17.7–8**
> SARDIS
> Alexander makes administrative arrangements for Lydia.

> **1.17.9**
> EPHESUS
> Persian troops abandon Ephesus after learning about the battle at the Granicus.

> **1.17.10–12**
> EPHESUS
> When he arrives at Ephesus, Alexander establishes a democratic government. This act emboldens the democratic faction to wreak vengeance on the pro-Persian oligarchs, but Alexander quickly puts an end to the violence.

1.17.4b   The meaning of this "freedom" is unclear since, as Arrian reports at 1.17.7–10, the Lydians would continue to pay tribute and would have a Macedonian governor and a garrison installed in Sardis.

1.17.5a   Olympian Zeus: the Zeus who inhabits Mount Olympos, a mountain very close to the borders of Alexander's native Macedonia. Alexander considered Zeus his ancestor, through the line of Zeus' son Herakles. By building a shrine to Olympian Zeus on the acropolis of Sardis, Alexander in effect proclaimed his hegemonic ambitions in Asia.

1.17.6a   Lydia: Map 1.19.
1.17.9a   Ephesus: Map 1.19.

1.17.9b   This is a different Amyntas from the one mentioned at 1.17.3.

1.17.10a The exiles who had been forced out "on [Alexander's] account" were presumably democratic political leaders who, inspired by the successes of the Macedonian advance force under Parmenion, had attempted some years earlier to oust the Persian-installed leadership of Ephesus. Alexander restored them and set up a pro-Macedonian democracy with their collaboration.

1.17.10b Ephesus had a famous temple of Artemis in its territory, partly destroyed by fire in 356. A legend circulating in Hellenistic times made the night of the fire coincide with the night Alexander was born.

death.[12a] But Alexander prevented the Ephesians from seeking out and taking vengeance on others, as he realized that if he granted them permission they would unjustly kill the innocent along with the guilty, either to settle private scores or to seize the property of the victims. Never was Alexander's conduct held in higher esteem than on that occasion, because of what he did in Ephesus.

[1] At this point, envoys from Magnesia and Tralles[1a] approached Alexander and surrendered their cities; he sent Parmenion to receive them, giving him twenty-five hundred mercenary infantry soldiers, about the same number of Macedonians, and nearly two hundred of the Companion cavalry. He sent Alkimkhos son of Agathokles with a comparable force to the Aeolian cities and to all the Ionian[1b] cities still under the barbarians' control. [2] He ordered the oligarchies to be abolished everywhere and democracies established; he permitted each city to have its own laws restored; and he canceled the taxes they had been paying to the barbarians.[2a] Remaining in Ephesus, Alexander performed a sacrifice to Artemis and held a parade with the entire army equipped and arrayed as for battle.

[3] The next day, Alexander started for Miletus[3a] with the rest of the infantry,[3b] the archers, the Agrianians, the Thracian horsemen, the royal company of the Companion cavalry, and three additional companies. He captured the so-called outer city on the first attempt, as the guard had fled. Having made camp there, he decided to besiege the inner city. [4] For Hegesistratos, to whom the garrison of Miletus had been entrusted by the King, had originally sent a letter to Alexander surrendering Miletus; now, however, he had regained confidence, and as the Persian force[4a] was not far off, he intended to save the city for the Persians. But Nikanor, in command of the Greek fleet,[4b] got the jump on the Persians. Having sailed down three days before they touched at Miletus, he anchored 160 ships at the island of Lade,[4c] which lies just offshore. [5] The Persian ships arrived too late, and when their commanders learned that Nikanor had already brought his ships into port at Lade, they lay at anchor near Mount Mycale.[5a] For not only had Alexander occupied Lade in advance by putting his fleet into harbor there; he had also trans-

---

1.17.12a These men were leaders of the pro-Persian oligarchic faction, as the context makes clear. The passions that had been unleashed at Ephesus by Alexander's arrival are revealed by the cruel fate these men suffered. To drag an adversary away from a holy shrine, ordinarily a place of refuge and protection, was a sacrilegious act in the Greek world.

1.18.1a Magnesia; Tralles: Map 1.19. This Magnesia is presumably Magnesia on the Maeander, which is near Tralles, not Magnesia ad Sipylum, which is also in Asia.

1.18.1b Aeolis; Ionia: Map 1.19.

1.18.2a The generous terms Alexander granted to these coastal Greek cities indicate both the political symbolism of granting nominal freedoms to the Greeks, in whose cause the current campaign was purportedly being waged, and the need

to win hearts and minds along the eastern Aegean, where the powerful Persian fleet was expected to arrive at any moment.

1.18.3a Miletus: Map 1.19.

1.18.3b "The rest of the infantry" were those not sent out with Parmenion or Alkimakhos.

1.18.4a This Persian force was the navy, which had been held up by other obligations and by the poor sailing conditions of the spring weather.

1.18.4b The "Greek fleet" was a composite force made up of ships from many cities, all of them bound by terms of the League of Corinth to fight under Alexander's command. The Macedonians had few ships of their own; their national traditions favored land warfare.

1.18.4c Lade: Map 1.19.

1.18.5a Mount Mycale: Map 1.19.

FIGURE 1.18. Architectural model of the harbor area of the ancient city of Miletus.

ported the Thracians and nearly four thousand of the other mercenaries to the island. The barbarians' ships numbered about four hundred.

[6] Nevertheless, Parmenion advised Alexander to fight at sea. Expecting for a variety of reasons that the Greeks would prevail with their fleet, he had been particularly impressed by an omen: an eagle had been seen on the shore near the sterns of Alexander's ships. It was Parmenion's view that if they were victorious, it would be of great advantage to their enterprise as a whole, whereas a defeat would not much matter, since the Persians already had the upper hand at sea. He asserted that he himself was ready to embark with the fleet and run the risk. [7] But Alexander declared that Parmenion was mistaken in his judgment and that his interpretation of the omen was improbable. It would not make sense, he said, with so few ships, to fight at sea against a much larger fleet, and to engage the well-trained navies of the Cyprians and Phoenicians[7a] when their own was untrained. [8] Furthermore, he had no wish to surrender to the barbarians the fate of his experienced and daring Macedonians on an element so uncertain. A naval defeat would considerably harm their early renown in the war, particularly because the Greeks, elated by the news of a naval defeat, would revolt.[8a] [9] Taking these points into account, Alexander argued that this was not the proper time to engage the enemy at sea. Besides, he said, he interpreted the omen differently: the eagle was indeed a favorable omen, but because it was seen

1.18.6–9
MILETUS
Alexander and Parmenion dispute naval strategy. Parmenion wants to engage the larger and better-trained Persian fleet, which Alexander considers too risky. They disagree over interpretation of a bird omen.

1.18.7a Cyprus; Phoenicia: Map 1.19, locator.
1.18.8a Alexander here shows he is under no illu-
sions about the degree of support in mainland Greece for the Macedonians.

on the ground, he rather thought it meant that he would prevail over the Persian fleet from the land.

1.19.1–2
Summer 334
MILETUS
Alexander captures
the inner city.

[1] At that point Glaukippos, a distinguished Milesian who had been sent to Alexander by the people and by the foreign mercenaries to whom the city had mainly been entrusted, declared that the Milesians were willing to grant Alexander and the Persians equal access to their walls and harbors. He expected Alexander to lift the siege on those terms, [2] but Alexander ordered him to return to the city at once and tell the Milesians to prepare to do battle at dawn. Personally directing the placement of siege engines near the wall, Alexander soon broke down part of it and caused many other parts to shake; he then led the army up to launch an attack where the wall had been either thrown down or shaken, while the Persians followed the action from their anchorage at Mycale, mere witnesses to the besieging of their friends and allies.

1.19.3–4
MILETUS
The Macedonian fleet
blocks the harbor. Some
of the defenders reach a
nearby island, but the rest
are trapped in the harbor or
in the city; many are killed.

[3] At that point, the men in Nikanor's fleet, moored at Lade, caught sight of Alexander's attack and made for the harbor of Miletus, rowing along the coast. They anchored their triremes close together at the narrowest point of the harbor's mouth, their prows facing the enemy, and thereby barred the Persian fleet from the harbor and cut the Milesians off from Persian assistance. [4] Then, as the Milesians and the mercenaries were pressed close on all sides by the Macedonians, some of them, flinging themselves into the sea, paddled on their inverted shields to a nameless islet lying offshore from the city, while others, embarking in light vessels and hastening to get ahead of the Macedonians' triremes, were caught at the mouth of the harbor, near the blockading ships. Most, however, perished in the city itself.

1.19.5–6
MILETUS
Alexander spares the Greek
mercenaries provided that
they enlist in his army, and
frees the surviving Milesians.

[5] Now that the city was in his power, Alexander sailed against those who had fled to the island, having ordered his men to carry scaling-ladders on the triremes' prows in order to disembark onto the island's cliffs as though onto a wall. [6] But when he saw that the men on the island were ready to fight for their lives, he was seized with pity for their nobility and steadfastness. He made peace with them on condition that they join his army.[6a] These Greek mercenaries numbered nearly three hundred. As for the Milesians themselves, he released all who had not fallen in the capture of the city and granted them their freedom.[6b]

1.19.7–11
MYCALE-MILETUS-LADE
The Macedonians dislodge
the Persian fleet from its base
at Mycale. When the Persians
fail to spark an engagement
with the Macedonian ships at
Miletus and to take those at
Lade by surprise, they depart
for good.

[7] The Persian ships based at Mycale had been in the habit of sailing out by day against the Greek fleet, hoping to provoke a naval engagement. By night they lay uncomfortably at anchor near Mycale, as they were

1.19.6a This showdown between Alexander and a band of defeated Greek mercenaries came to a very different resolution than the previous one, at the Granicus River (see 1.16.2 and 1.16.6). Evidently both sides in the Miletus engagement had learned something from the earlier encounter: the Greek mercenaries now knew that they would be given no quarter and were therefore prepared to fight to the death, whereas Alexander evidently recognized

that his actions at the Granicus had had the unfortunate effect of alienating a potentially valuable pool of recruits. (Whether he also felt pity for a noble adversary, as Arrian claims, is a matter of interpretation.)

1.19.6b As in the case of the Lydians (see 1.17.4 and n. 1.17.4b), the Milesians received "freedom" in a very limited sense, possibly only exemption from enslavement (see Bosworth I.140).

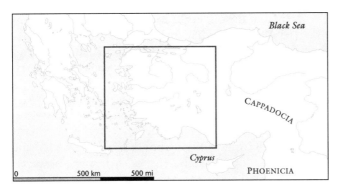

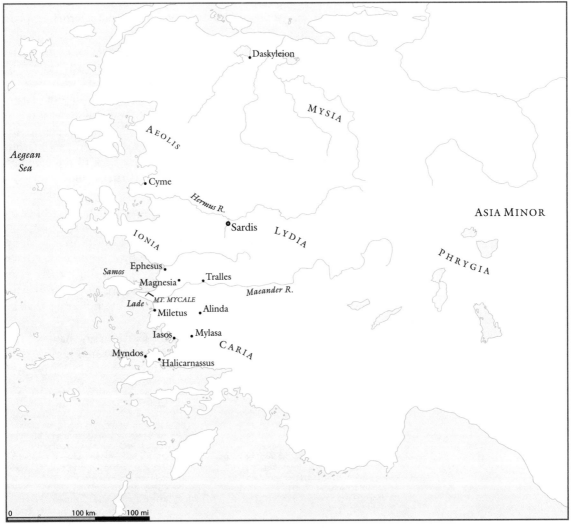

MAP 1.19

obliged to fetch their water from the outlets of the River Maeander,[7a] a considerable distance away. [8] Alexander, while guarding the Milesians' harbor with his ships lest the barbarians force their way through the entrance, sent Philotas to Mycale in command of the cavalry and three units of infantry, with orders to prevent the Persians from disembarking from their ships.[8a] As the barbarians now found themselves virtually besieged on their ships through lack of water and other supplies, they sailed off to Samos.[8b] After obtaining provisions there, they sailed back to Miletus [9] and posted most of their ships in the open sea in front of the harbor, hoping to provoke the Macedonians to engage them in open waters. Five of their ships, however, sailed into the harbor between Lade and the camp, where the Persians hoped to catch Alexander's ships unmanned (they had learned that most of the sailors had dispersed, some to collect firewood, others to gather supplies, and still others to forage for food). [10] But though a number of sailors were absent when the five Persian ships were seen approaching, Alexander manned ten ships with those at hand and straightaway sent them against the five Persian ships with orders to attack prow to prow. When the men in the five Persian ships, to their surprise, saw the Macedonians putting out to sea against them, they turned around while the enemy was still at a great distance and made for the main body of the fleet. [11] In their flight, the Iasians'[11a] ship was captured along with its crew, as it was not swift-sailing, but the other four succeeded in getting safely back to the triremes. Having thus accomplished nothing in Miletus, the Persians sailed away.

[1] Alexander now decided to disband the fleet, as he found himself short of money.[1a] Moreover, he observed that his own fleet was not fit to do battle with that of the Persians, and he was unwilling to endanger any portion of his forces. He also reflected that as he now controlled Asia[1b] with his infantry, he would have no further need of a navy: by capturing the coastal cities he would dissolve the Persian fleet, since it would find no crews to man its ships, nor would it have any place to land along the coast of Asia. The omen of the eagle seemed to support his plan by indicating that he would overpower the ships from the land.[1c]

[2] After settling these matters, he started for Caria,[2a] as he had received word that a large force of barbarians and foreigners[2b] awaited him in Hali-

1.20.1
Summer 334
MILETUS
Alexander disbands his fleet, reckoning that he cannot defeat the Persians at sea.

1.20.2–3
HALICARNASSUS
Alexander marches to Halicarnassus. Both sides prepare for a siege there.

1.19.7a Maeander River: Map 1.19.
1.19.8a That is, after the Persian fleet had left Mycale for its customary daytime sally, Philotas' forces were to seize their base and prevent them from returning to it.
1.19.8b Samos: Map 1.19.
1.19.11a Iasos: Map 1.19.
1.20.1a The cost of maintaining the fleet has been estimated at more than 100 talents per month, probably a greater sum than Alexander was spending to pay his entire phalanx over a comparable period. See Appendix F, Money and Finance in the Campaigns of Alexander.
1.20.1b Asia: Map 1.19. By Asia here, Arrian refers only to Asia Minor (Map 1.19),

not to the whole continent.
1.20.1c The motive Arrian leaves unstated here is fear of disaffection in the Greek fleet (Bosworth I.143). Many historians judge this to be the primary reason for Alexander's surprising decision to send his ships home. Greek sailors in Macedonia's employ had far more autonomy than the Greek mercenary infantry, thanks to their numbers and expertise.
1.20.2a Caria: Map 1.19.
1.20.2b Arrian distinguishes "barbarians" from "foreigners" here, denoting native Persian troops with the first term, Greek and Carian mercenaries with the second.

FIGURE 1.20. The remains of the Myndos gate at Halicarnassus, partially rebuilt in recent times. It was stormed unsuccessfully by Alexander.

carnassus.[2c] After capturing, on the first attempt, all the cities that lay between Miletus and Halicarnassus, he set up his camp slightly more than half a mile from the latter city, seemingly preparing for a lengthy siege. [3] For the nature of the position made it strong, and wherever any weakness had come to light, Memnon had long ago taken precautions. (Memnon himself was at Halicarnassus, having been appointed by Darius as commander of lower Asia[3a] and the whole fleet.) Many foreign mercenaries and Persian troops had also been left behind in the city, and the triremes lay moored in the harbor, so that the sailors, too, were of great assistance to the operations.

[4] On the first day, when Alexander approached the wall at the gates leading to Mylasa,[4a] the city's defenders sallied out and fired off arrows and spears. Alexander's men, mobilizing against these troops, easily repulsed them and forced them to take cover in the city.

[5] Not many days later, Alexander took the shield-bearers, the Companion cavalry, the infantry battalions of Amyntas, Perdikkas, and Meleagros, the archers, and the Agrianians and proceeded around the city to the part facing Myndos,[5a] intending to see whether the wall was more vulnerable there than elsewhere, and also whether it would be possible, with a sudden, surprise raid, to get possession of Myndos. For control of Myndos, he

1.20.4
HALICARNASSUS
The Macedonians win
the initial skirmish.

1.20.5–7
HALICARNASSUS
An attempt by Alexander
to gain control of the nearby
town of Myndos comes to
nothing.

1.20.2c Halicarnassus: Map 1.19.
1.20.3a "Lower Asia" refers to the coast and
islands of Asia Minor. The Greeks often
used terminology based on elevation to
indicate proximity to the sea.
1.20.4a Mylasa: Map 1.19.
1.20.5a Myndos: Map 1.19.

thought, would greatly expedite the siege of Halicarnassus, and in fact the surrender of Myndos had been promised him if he approached unseen under cover of night. [6] According to the terms agreed on, Alexander approached the wall of Myndos near midnight, but no sign of surrender was forthcoming. Since the siege engines and scaling-ladders had not been brought along, as Alexander had set out not to prosecute a siege but to have the city handed over to him by traitors, he brought the Macedonian phalanx up and ordered the men to undermine the wall. The Macedonians brought down one tower; but though the tower fell, this did not force the defenders from the wall. [7] The city's inhabitants defended themselves stoutly, and with the assistance of the many who had already rushed to their aid by sea from Halicarnassus, they made it impossible for Alexander to capture Myndos in so sudden and impromptu a manner. He therefore turned back, having failed to achieve the goal he had set out for, and again applied himself to the siege of Halicarnassus.

1.20.8–10
Summer 334
HALICARNASSUS
Siege operations begin in earnest. Both sides sustain casualties during the Halicarnassians' attempt to burn the Macedonian siege engines.

[8] First he filled up the trench, nearly forty-five feet wide and twenty-two and a half feet deep, that the Halicarnassians had dug in front of their city. This was done in order to make it easier to bring up the siege towers from which Alexander intended to rain missiles on the wall's defenders, and to bring forward the other engines with which he planned to break down the wall. [9] The trench was easily filled, and the siege towers were soon brought forward. A party of Halicarnassians sallied out by night to set fire to the siege towers and all the other engines that had been brought near the wall or stood ready to be wheeled up, but these men were easily driven back into the city by the Macedonian guards and by others who had been awakened by the action itself and hastened to their aid. [10] Nearly 170 of the defenders died, including Neoptolemos son of Arrabaios, the brother of Amyntas, one of the Macedonians who had deserted to Darius. About sixteen of Alexander's men perished, and nearly three hundred were wounded; because they were attacked during the night, they were less able to protect themselves.[10a]

1.21.1–4
HALICARNASSUS
An attack on the wall by two Macedonian hoplites escalates into a full-fledged battle as the Halicarnassians rush to attack them and other Macedonians join them. The city nearly falls.

[1] Not many days later, two hoplites[1a] from Perdikkas' battalion were sharing a tent and drinking together, and each was boasting of his talents and exploits. Warmed by the wine, they were seized by a spirit of rivalry and, on their own initiative, armed themselves and assaulted the citadel wall facing Mylasa, more in order to show off their strength than to provoke a dangerous clash with the enemy. [2] Observing these men from above and noting that there were only two and that they were assaulting the wall without any forethought, some of the citadel's defenders rushed out

---

1.20.10a Though Arrian lists a large number of Macedonians killed and wounded, he still represents the defeat of the Halicarnassian torching party as a fairly easy job for Alexander's men. By contrast Diodorus (17.24.4), who seems to have relied on an account written by one of Halicarnassus' Greek defenders, gives a picture of a far

more closely fought struggle. Diodorus also lists Neoptolemos as a casualty on the Macedonian side, not among the Halicarnassians.

1.21.1a Hoplites: the term is used here, and at several other points in Arrian's narrative, to refer to Macedonian infantrymen rather than Greek. See n. 1.1.8a.

against them. Though the Macedonians were outnumbered and at a disadvantage, as the enemy was attacking and showering missiles on them from above, they nonetheless killed the men who drew near and hurled missiles at those who stood at a distance. [3] At that point others from Perdikkas' forces rushed out to join the fight, as did others from Halicarnassus, and a desperate struggle ensued at the wall. The defenders who had sallied out were driven back inside the gates by the Macedonians, and the city came very close to being captured. [4] For its walls were not being kept under strict guard at the time, and as two towers and the curtain wall between them had fallen to the ground, it would not have been difficult for the army to gain entry through the breach had every man applied himself to the task. The third tower had also been shaken and if undermined might have been brought down with ease. But the Halicarnassians had anticipated this possibility, and in place of the fallen wall had built, from the inside, a crescent-shaped fortification made of brick—an easy task, as there was a multitude of hands.[4a]

[5] The next day, Alexander brought the engines up to the brick wall, and the defenders again sallied out from the citadel to set fire to them. They succeeded in setting ablaze a portion of the wicker screen near the wall,[5a] as well as part of one of the wooden siege towers; the remaining equipment was protected by the men with Philotas and Hellanikos who were responsible for guarding it. But when Alexander himself appeared among those rushing toward them, the defenders dropped the torches with which they had sallied out, and most of them flung away their weapons as well and escaped within the wall. [6] At first, thanks to the nature of their position, which was a commanding one, the defenders retained the upper hand: they could assail the troops fighting in defense of the engines not only from in front but also from the towers that had been left standing on either side of the breach; from these they could fire both from the flanks and practically from behind the men who were assaulting their replacement wall.

[1] Not many days later, when Alexander was again bringing the engines to the inner brick wall, having taken charge of the work himself, the defenders sallied out of the city with all their forces, some at the breached wall where Alexander had stationed himself, others at the Triple Gate, where the Macedonians had never expected to encounter resistance. [2] The defenders threw torches onto the engines and other material that might kindle and fuel a great blaze. But when Alexander and his forces retaliated vigorously, firing enormous stones from the engines in the siege towers and showering the

1.21.5–6
HALICARNASSUS
The defenders again try to torch the siege engines but are driven back to the wall. They harass the besiegers from its heights.

1.22.1–3
HALICARNASSUS
The citizens of Halicarnassus make another attempt to torch the siege weapons, and are again unsuccessful. Many of those attacking Alexander's units cannot easily escape and are slaughtered.

1.21.4a The construction of a lunette wall, to seal off a spot where a breach had begun to open, was a standard strategy employed by the defenders in ancient siege warfare. Arrian's assertion that Halicarnassus almost fell due to a breach in the walls, and that the Macedonians might easily have gained entry at this point—despite the fact that the lunette wall had effectively sealed off this breach—reveals the bias of his sources, who consistently minimize the difficulties Alexander experienced in his military engagements.
1.21.5a The screens were used to shield those operating the siege machinery from the arrows and spears of the defenders.

enemy with missiles,[2a] the defenders were easily routed and fled into the city.[2b] [3] The slaughter there was enormous, more so because the defenders had sallied out in greater numbers and with greater daring. Some of them died fighting at close quarters with the Macedonians, others near the wall that had collapsed, where the passage was too narrow to admit such a throng and the broken portions of the wall could be scaled only with difficulty.

[4] The defenders who sallied out at the Triple Gate were met by Ptolemy, the royal bodyguard,[4a] who was leading the battalions of Adaios and Timandros and some light-armed troops. These forces had no difficulty routing the city's defenders. [5] And it happened that as the Halicarnassians retreated across the narrow bridge over the trench, the bridge broke under the weight of the multitude; many fell into the trench and were trampled by their comrades and died. Many also perished when assailed from above by the Macedonians. [6] But the greatest slaughter occurred near the gates themselves, as they were shut in a moment of panic and before the proper time; the defenders feared that the Macedonians, following close on their heels, might rush in with those who were fleeing. By thus closing the gates they cut off the escape of many of their own side, whom the Macedonians slaughtered at the walls.

[7] The city had come very close to being captured. But Alexander called a halt to the attack, as he still wished to spare Halicarnassus, should the city be surrendered on friendly terms.[7a] Nearly a thousand of the city's defenders had perished, as had some forty of Alexander's men, among them Ptolemy the Bodyguard, Klearkhos the commander of the archers, Adaios the battalion commander, and other notable Macedonians.

[1] The Persian commanders, Orontobates and Memnon, now met and acknowledged that they could not withstand the siege for long, with one portion of the wall already brought down, the other badly shaken, and many of their soldiers either slaughtered in the charges or wounded and past fighting. [2] With this in mind, near the second watch of the night[2a] they set fire to the wooden tower they had erected to counter the Macedonian siege

1.22.4–6
Summer 334
HALICARNASSUS
Those attacking at the Triple Gate meet a similar end when the city's bridge collapses and its gates close during their retreat.

1.22.7
HALICARNASSUS
Alexander halts the Macedonian attack, hoping for a negotiated surrender.

1.23.1–4
HALICARNASSUS
A council is held by Halicarnassus' defending generals, who elect to abandon their position. They torch their own siege equipment as they depart. Alexander has the fire extinguished and occupies the city.

1.22.2a   Apparently this use of catapults to bombard enemy troops during a siege was a new strategy, perhaps devised by Alexander himself (see Bosworth I.148, citing Marsden, *Greek and Roman Artillery*, p. 101). Philip, Alexander's father, had hired numerous Greek engineers to help advance his siege machinery and artillery, and presumably Alexander continued to employ these and other military specialists. See Appendix D, §6.

1.22.2b   Again, Arrian's description of an easy Macedonian victory is very much at odds with other ancient descriptions of the same engagement, notably that of Diodorus. At 17.26.3–17.27.4, Diodorus, seemingly using a source writing from the perspective of the besieged, describes a near victory by the Halicarnassians.

1.22.4a   This is a different Ptolemy from the son of Lagos. He was a member of the corps of shield-bearers responsible for guarding the

king (see n. 1.1.11b). Known only from this passage and 1.22.7, he may be the same person as Ptolemy son of Philip, mentioned at 1.14.6.

1.22.7a   This charitable description of Alexander's motives accords with what Arrian said above regarding the king's hopes for a peaceful settlement with Thebes (see 1.7.7, 1.7.10); and just as in that earlier case, other sources paint a different portrait. Diodorus (17.27.4), for example, has Alexander calling a halt as night was falling, and says nothing about his purported desire for a negotiated resolution.

1.23.2a   The Greeks (and later Romans), who were reliant on the sun to tell time during the day, divided the night into either three or four periods, naming these "watches," based on military parlance. The second watch of the night began approximately two or three hours after midnight.

engines and to the arsenals in which their missiles were stored. They also set fire to the houses near the wall, [3] while other blazes were kindled by the tremendous flames that were borne by the wind from the arsenals and the tower. Some of the defending troops retreated to the citadel offshore, the rest to the fortress known as Salmakis. [4] When a number of deserters from the action reported these developments to Alexander and he himself beheld the great fire, he led the Macedonians out, though it was nearly midnight, and killed the men who were still setting fire to the city, though he decreed that all the Halicarnassians found in their houses were to be spared.

[5] When dawn was breaking and Alexander saw the citadels the Persians and the mercenaries had occupied, he decided not to besiege them, realizing that it would entail no small delay given the nature of their sites and that there was little to be gained now that he had captured the entire city. [6] After burying those who had died during the night, he ordered the men stationed at the engines to convey them to Tralles. After razing Halicarnassus to the ground and leaving behind three thousand mercenary foot soldiers and nearly two hundred horsemen under Ptolemy's[6a] command to garrison the city and the rest of Caria, Alexander set out for Phrygia.[6b]

[7] Alexander appointed Ada to serve as satrap of all of Caria. Ada was the daughter of Hekatomnos and the wife of Hidrieus (who was also her brother, but lived with her as her mate in accordance with Carian custom). When Hidrieus died, he entrusted the government to Ada, it having become customary in Asia ever since the time of Semiramis[7a] for women to rule men. Pixodaros[7b] then expelled Ada and seized power himself. [8] At Pixodaros' death, Orontobates, Pixodaros' son-in-law, was sent by the King to rule the Carians. Ada, meanwhile, had held on to only Alinda,[8a] one of the strongest positions in Caria. She went to meet Alexander when he invaded the region and surrendered Alinda to him and made him her adopted son. Alexander then confirmed her rule over Alinda, and did not decline the title of son, and when he had captured Halicarnassus and prevailed over the rest of Caria, he gave her sovereign power over the entire region.

[1] Some of the Macedonians serving with Alexander had married shortly before the expedition, and he recognized that he should not neglect them. Accordingly, he sent them home from Caria to spend the winter with their wives in Macedonia,[1a] having placed them under the command of

1.23.5–6
HALICARNASSUS
Destroying the surviving portion of Halicarnassus, Alexander leaves two strongholds in enemy hands and moves on to Phrygia.

1.23.7–8
Autumn 334
CARIA
Ada, a dispossessed Carian queen who adopted Alexander as her son, is installed as satrap of Caria.

1.24.1–2
CARIA
Alexander sends recently married troops home for the winter.

1.23.6a   This is clearly not "Ptolemy the Body-guard" (now dead; see 1.22.7) and also not Ptolemy son of Seleukos (who is introduced for the first time at 1.24.1), nor Ptolemy son of Lagos, but a fourth Ptolemy about whom little is known. He appears again only once in Arrian's text, at 2.5.7.
1.23.6b   Tralles; Caria; Phrygia: Map 1.19.
1.23.7a   Semiramis was a legendary queen of ancient Assyria.
1.23.7b   The brother of Hidrieus and Ada, Pixodaros plays a prominent role in one of the most curious episodes of Alexander's younger years, not dealt with by Arrian

but known principally from Plutarch (*Parallel Lives*, "Alexander" 10). Philip, Alexander's father, attempted to form an alliance with Pixodaros by agreeing to the marriage of his son Philip and Pixodaros' daughter. But Alexander, apparently sensing that his half brother Philip was being given preferential treatment, interposed himself and attempted to marry the girl himself. His father was outraged by this move, and a major rift opened between the king and his heir apparent.
1.23.8a   Alinda: Map 1.19.
1.24.1a   Macedonia: Map 1.26.

Ptolemy son of Seleukos,[1b] one of the royal bodyguards, and two of the generals—Koinos son of Polemokrates and Meleagros son of Neoptolemos—as these men, too, had recently married. [2] He directed them to enlist as many horsemen and infantrymen from the country as they could before returning and bringing back their cohort. And for this deed, more than for any other, Alexander was held in esteem by the Macedonians. He also sent Kleandros son of Polemokrates to levy troops in the Peloponnese.[2a]

[3] He sent Parmenion to Sardis, having given him a hipparchy[3a] of the Companions, the Thessalian cavalry, the other allies, and the wagons, with orders to march from Sardis to Phrygia. Alexander himself proceeded to Lycia and Pamphylia,[3b] to win control of the coast and disable the enemy's fleet.[3c] [4] On the first attempt he captured Hyparna,[4a] a strong fortification held by foreign mercenaries, who agreed to depart the fortress under a treaty. Then, having invaded Lycia, he brought Telmessos to terms, and on crossing the River Xanthos accepted the surrender of Pinara, Xanthos (the city), and Patara,[4b] as well as nearly thirty lesser towns.

[5] It was midwinter by the time he had completed these operations, but he went on to invade the land known as Milyas.[5a] The place lies in greater Phrygia but was accounted part of Lycia at the time, by order of the Great King. Envoys from Phaselis[5b] now arrived to establish friendly relations and to crown Alexander with a golden wreath. Most of the cities in lower Lycia sent envoys to make similar overtures. [6] Alexander ordered the inhabitants of Phaselis, of Pisidia,[6a] and of Lycia generally to surrender their cities to the commanders sent to receive them, and they all did so. He himself soon reached Phaselis, whereupon, in addition to these cities, he captured a powerful fort built by Pisidians for the purpose of harassing the region. These barbarians, making the place their base of operations, had been inflicting great harm on the people of Phaselis who were out working the land.

[1] While he was still near Phaselis, it was reported to him that Alexander son of Aeropos was plotting against him.[1a] In addition to serving as a

1.24.3–4
Autumn 334
LYCIA
The Macedonians conduct mopping-up operations in Asia Minor.

1.24.5–6
Winter 334/3
LYCIA
The Lycians surrender to Alexander.

1.25.1–5
PHASELIS
Suspicions arise that Alexander son of Aeropos, brother of two men executed for killing Philip, is conspiring with the Persian king to assassinate Alexander.

1.24.1b This is not the Seleukos who later rose to power in the wars of Alexander's successors, nor the Ptolemy who became king of Egypt. Macedonian noble families chose names of children from a fairly limited pool. Arrian describes this Ptolemy as "one of the royal bodyguards," meaning a member of the corps of shield-bearers responsible for guarding the king (see n. 1.1.11b). A different Ptolemy, encountered at 1.22.4 and 1.22.7, belonged to the seven-man Bodyguard, a different unit from the one mentioned here.

1.24.2a Peloponnese: Map 1.26. According to Arrian (2.20.5), Kleandros returned more than a year later with four thousand Greek mercenaries.

1.24.3a Arrian here uses the term "hipparchy," or cavalry brigade, in a very loose sense. Officially the cavalry was not divided into hipparchies until several years after this; see n. 3.29.7a.

1.24.3b Lycia; Pamphylia: Map 1.26, inset.

1.24.3c Arrian seems to have misunderstood his sources here, as in fact Alexander was operating mostly in the interior at this point, not on the coast.

1.24.4a Hyparna: location unknown.

1.24.4b Telmessos; Xanthos River; Pinara; Xanthos; Patara: Map 1.26, inset. Envoys from Pinara evidently offered surrender to Alexander after he crossed the Xanthos going east, since Pinara itself lies west of that river.

1.24.5a Milyas: Map 1.26, inset.

1.24.5b Phaselis: Map 1.26, inset.

1.24.6a Pisidia: Map 1.26, inset.

1.25.1a Alexander son of Aeropos (also called Alexander the Lyncestian) belonged to a royal house of the province of Lyncestis, a semi-autonomous mountain region that had only recently become firmly subordinated to Macedonian rule. Thus it was natural for Lyncestian royalty to be seen as enemies of the Macedonian crown.

Companion, this Alexander was then in command of the Thessalian[1b] cavalry. He was the brother of Heromenes and Arrabaios, the men who had conspired in the slaying of Philip.[1c] [2] Though he had been accused on that occasion, Alexander had let him off, as the man had been among the first of his friends to come to his side when Philip died, by donning his breastplate and accompanying Alexander to the palace. Later, Alexander had held him in honor at his court and sent him as general to Thrace;[2a] and when Kalas, the cavalry commander of the Thessalians, was sent to take charge of a satrapy, Alexander appointed this man, Alexander son of Aeropos, to head the Thessalian cavalry. The details of the plot were reported in the following way: [3] First Amyntas deserted to Darius[3a] and brought him proposals and letters from Alexander son of Aeropos. Darius then sent Sisines, a trusted Persian at his court, to the coast, ostensibly on a mission to Atizyes the satrap of Phrygia,[3b] but actually to meet with this Alexander and assure him that, if he killed Alexander, Darius would appoint him king of Macedonia and give him a thousand gold talents into the bargain.[3c] [4] But Sisines was caught by Parmenion and divulged his mission, and Parmenion sent him under guard to Alexander, where he repeated his story. Summoning a council of friends, Alexander proposed that they determine what should be done about his namesake. [5] The Companions were of the opinion that Alexander's original decision to entrust the most powerful cavalry company to an untrustworthy man had been unwise, and that Alexander should now get this man out of their midst as soon as possible, before he became more friendly with the Thessalians and incited them to revolt.

[6] Meanwhile, a supernatural event had unnerved the Companions. When Alexander was still besieging Halicarnassus and was taking his midday nap, a swallow, cooing noisily, hovered about his head and perched here and there on his bed, singing in an unusually agitated manner. [7] Since Alexander was exhausted, the swallow was unable to awaken him, but annoyed by the sound, Alexander lightly shooed the swallow away with his hand. But far from fleeing when struck, the bird actually alighted on Alexander's head and did not leave until the king had been completely awakened. [8] Alexander considered the incident significant and communicated it to a seer, Aristandros of Telmessos. Aristandros said it indicated that one of his friends was plotting against him, but that the plot would come to light. For the swallow, he said, is a sociable creature, well disposed to mankind, and more talkative than any other bird.

1.25.6–8
An omen seen earlier at Halicarnassus is now thought to confirm the existence of the suspected plot.

1.25.1b Thessaly: Map 1.26.
1.25.1c Arrian here asserts the idea of a conspiracy behind the assassination of Philip, seemingly without regarding this as a controversial point. But other sources attribute the deed to a lone assassin, Pausanias, and give him purely personal motives. Alexander himself either believed in a conspiracy or pretended to do so because it allowed him to eliminate potential rivals; thus the two other sons of Aeropos mentioned by Arrian, Heromenes and Arribaios, the brothers of the man here accused, had both been executed in the early days of Alexander's reign.
1.25.2a Thrace: Map 1.26.
1.25.3a See 1.17.9.
1.25.3b Phrygia: Map 1.26.
1.25.3c A thousand gold talents was a lavish payment, the gold talent being worth far more than the more usual silver one. For the term "talent" as a monetary unit, see Appendix F, §3.

1.25.9–10
Winter 334/3
After receiving secret orders
sent by Alexander, Parmenion
arrests Alexander son of
Aeropos and puts him
under guard.

1.26.1–2
PHASELIS-PERGE
During the march from
Phaselis to Side, Alexander
is aided by a sudden change
in the winds that enables
him to pass a perilous
stretch of coast.

1.26.3
PERGE
Alexander negotiates with
the Aspendians for the surrender of their city.

1.26.4
SIDE
Arrian digresses on the
origin and language of Side.

1.26.5
SILLYON-ASPENDOS
A Macedonian attack on
Sillyon is broken off when
news arrives that the Aspendians have renounced their
agreement with Alexander.

[9] Putting this together with what he had learned from the Persian, Alexander sent Krateros' brother, Amphoteros son of Alexander,[9a] to Parmenion.[9b] Some Pergaians[9c] accompanied him as guides. Donning native dress lest he be recognized on the journey, Amphoteros reached Parmenion without being detected. [10] He carried no letter from Alexander, as it was not thought appropriate to write explicitly about such a matter. He conveyed his message orally as instructed, whereupon Alexander son of Aeropos was arrested and held under guard.

[1] Setting out from Phaselis, Alexander sent a division of the army through the mountains to Perge, where the Thracians had built a road for him, since the passage would otherwise have been long and difficult. He himself took the coastal route and led his men along the shore. That route presents insuperable difficulties unless the north winds are blowing; when the south winds prevail, it becomes impossible to advance along the shore. [2] On the occasion of Alexander's march, the winds, which had been southerly, changed and blew stiffly from the north—not without divine intervention, as he and his men believed—and made the passage easy and quick.

As Alexander marched onward from Perge, ambassadors from Aspendos[2a] with full powers met him on the road and surrendered their city, but begged him not to install a garrison in it. [3] They got what they asked for with regard to the garrison, but Alexander commanded them to give the army fifty talents toward wages, along with the horses they raised as tribute for the King.[3a] After agreeing to hand over the money and the horses, the ambassadors departed.

[4] Alexander now proceeded to Side.[4a] The Sidetans, who are Cymaeans from Aeolic Cyme,[4b] give the following account of themselves. They say that when the original settlers sent from Cyme touched at Side and disembarked to found a colony, they immediately forgot the Greek language and spoke a barbarian language, though not that of their barbarian neighbors, but a language of their own, a dialect never heard before. And ever since, the Sidetans have spoken a barbarian dialect distinct from that of their neighbors.

[5] Leaving behind a garrison in Side, Alexander advanced to Sillyon,[5a] a formidable place with a garrison of foreign mercenaries and indigenous barbarians. But he was unable to take Sillyon in an initial, spur-of-the-moment assault. When it was reported to him on the march that the Aspendians were refusing to honor their agreements—they would neither hand over the horses to the men who had been sent for them nor pay the money—and that they had packed up supplies from the country and conveyed them into the city, had locked their gates against Alexander's envoys, and were repair-

1.25.9a The Alexander mentioned here, the father of both Amphoteros and Krateros, is a different person from either Alexander son of Aeropos or Alexander the Great.
1.25.9b Parmenion, Alexander's senior general, had been ordered to lead a portion of the army through central Anatolia by a different route (see 1.24.3) and was at this point somewhere in Phrygia.

1.25.9c Perge: Map 1.26, inset.
1.26.2a Aspendos: Map 1.26, inset.
1.26.3a This was a one-time levy rather than a yearly assessment, as is clear from the following chapter.
1.26.4a Side: Map 1.26, inset.
1.26.4b Cyme: Map 1.26.
1.26.5a Sillyon: Map 1.26, inset.

FIGURE 1.26. View of the coastline of Antalya, north of Phaselis. Alexander's route through southern Asia Minor took him along a coast like this, with a narrow track between mountains and sea. He was able to pass, according to Arrian, only because of a sudden shift in wind direction.

ing their walls where these stood in need of reinforcement—hearing all this, Alexander marched the army to Aspendos.

[1] Aspendos has been built, for the most part, on a steep, imposing hill. The River Eurymedon[1a] flows past its citadel. On the level ground surrounding the hill there were a great many dwellings, and these were encircled by a low wall. [2] As soon as the inhabitants learned that Alexander was approaching, they abandoned the wall along with the low-lying houses they thought they could not defend and fled for refuge to the citadel. When Alexander arrived with his forces, he entered the deserted walls and occupied the Aspendians' abandoned houses. [3] When the Aspendians saw that Alexander had arrived in person—something they had not expected—and observed his army surrounding them on all sides, they sent envoys to treat for peace on the terms they had agreed to previously. But Alexander, though he saw that their position was strong and though he was unprepared for a lengthy siege, even so would not make peace on those terms. [4] He ordered the Aspendi-

1.27.1–4
ASPENDOS
Aspendos capitulates at the unexpected arrival of Alexander and is forced to submit to much harsher terms than it had originally agreed to.

1.27.1a   Eurymedon River: Map 1.26, inset.

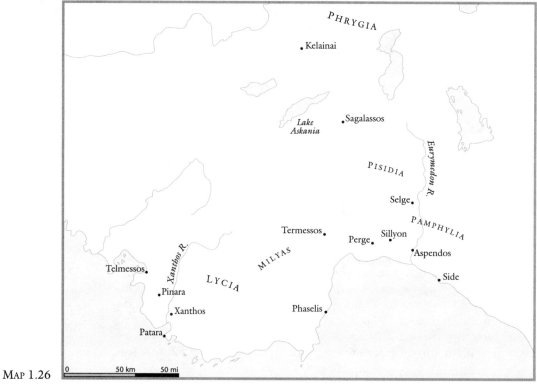

MAP 1.26

ans to hand over their leading citizens as hostages along with the horses they had promised him earlier, to pay a hundred talents instead of fifty, to obey the satrap appointed by Alexander, to pay annual tribute to the Macedonians, and to abide by a judicial decision regarding the territory they had been accused of taking by force from their neighbors.

[5] When the Aspendians had conceded everything, Alexander moved the army to Perge, and from there he started for Phrygia.[5a] His route took him past the city of Termessos,[5b] whose inhabitants are barbarians, Pisidians by race.[5c] They inhabit a lofty position, steep on all sides, and the road that runs past their city is rugged: [6] a mountain extends from their city down to the road, and opposite this mountain stands another, equally steep; these mountains function as gates on the road, and a small force stationed there can make it impossible for an enemy to approach. On the present occasion, the Termessians had sallied out with all their forces and were in possession of both mountains. [7] Observing this, Alexander commanded the Macedonians to make camp there at once, realizing that when the Termessians saw his men bivouacking, they would not stay there with all their forces but would withdraw most of their troops to the city nearby, leaving behind only a guard at the mountains. And it turned out as he had guessed. Most of the Termessians departed and only the guards remained; [8] against these Alexander immediately led the archers, the units of javelin men, and the more lightly armed hoplites. The guards did not stand fast under the volleys of arrows and spears but left their position, and Alexander advanced past the narrows and made camp near the city.

[1] Alexander was now approached by envoys from the Selgians,[1a] who are also barbarian Pisidians. The Selgians inhabit a large city and are formidable warriors. Because they were ancient enemies of the Termessians, they had sent envoys conveying friendly overtures to Alexander, who made a treaty with them and from then on found them trustworthy in every respect. [2] As he had given up hope of capturing Termessos in a short time, Alexander set off for Sagalassos.[2a] It, too, was a large city inhabited by Pisidians, and though all the Pisidians were warlike, the Pisidians of Sagalassos were thought to be the most warlike of all. On that occasion they stood their ground, having occupied a hill in front of their city that was as strong a position as their wall for fighting off an enemy.

[3] Alexander arrayed the Macedonian phalanx in the following order: At the right wing, where he himself was posted, he put the shield-bearers,

1.27.5–8
Winter 334/3
PHRYGIA
Alexander marches from Aspendos to Perge and then into Phrygia. He meets strong resistance by the Pisidians at Termessos but drives them away with artillery fire.

1.28.1–2
TERMESSOS-SAGALASSOS
Alexander allies with Pisidians from Selge, but leaves those of Termessos unsubdued. He marches to Sagalassos, where more Pisidian resistance is encountered.

1.28.3–4
SAGALASSOS
Alexander deploys for a fight.

1.27.5a Arrian does not return to the episode of Sillyon, the fortress Alexander had left untaken when he got the news of Aspendos' revolt. It seems likely that Alexander simply left this position in enemy hands, not wishing to be delayed at this point by a lengthy siege. He did likewise at several other Persian strongholds in Asia Minor (see, for example, the following chapter), counting on his satraps to complete mopping-up operations after the main body of Persian forces had been dealt with.

1.27.5b Termessos: Map 1.26, inset. Arrian calls it Telmessos.
1.27.5c Arrian uses the term "barbarian" in a number of different senses; here it carries a connotation of "primitive" or "uncivilized." The Pisidians still lived by ancient, and often violent, tribal ways, having never accepted Persian domination nor assimilated to Greek cultural norms.
1.28.1a Selge: Map 1.26, inset.
1.28.2a Sagalassos: Map 1.26, inset.

and next to them the infantry companions;[3a] these he extended as far as the left wing, having placed their battalions in an order corresponding to the commanders' daily rotation. [4] He posted Amyntas son of Arrabaios in command of the left wing. Posted in front of the right wing were the archers and the Agrianians, in front of the left wing the Thracian javelin men under the command of Sitalkes. The cavalry were of no use to Alexander on this rugged terrain. Some Termessians who had come to the aid of the Pisidians were drawn up beside them.

[5] Alexander's men, having assaulted the mountain occupied by the Pisidians, were already at the steepest part of the ascent when bands of Pisidians attacked both wings, taking advantage of ground that gave them an easy approach but prevented their foe from advancing. They succeeded in routing the archers, as these had not been well armed and had been the first to approach them. But the Agrianians stood their ground, [6] as the Macedonian phalanx was now approaching and Alexander was visible at its head. When the battle was joined, the barbarians, though unarmed, attacked the hoplites, but, wounded and falling on all sides, they at last gave way. [7] Nearly five hundred of them died, and [. . .][7a] were taken alive. As they were nimble and familiar with the countryside, they retreated with no difficulty, while the Macedonians, burdened with heavy gear and unfamiliar with the paths, were not eager to pursue them. [8] But Alexander followed close on the heels of these fugitives and took the city by storm. Among his own men, Kleandros, the archers' commander,[8a] perished with about twenty others.

Alexander then led his men against the other Pisidians. Some of their strongholds he took by force; the rest were surrendered.

[1] From there Alexander advanced into Phrygia along the shore of the lake named Askania,[1a] where salt crystallizes all by itself; the inhabitants use this salt and have no need for sea salt. He reached Kelainai[1b] on the fifth day. In Kelainai there was a citadel, steep on all sides, that was held by a garrison of a thousand Carians and a hundred Greek mercenaries sent by the satrap of Phrygia. [2] These men negotiated with Alexander and said that if no relief force reached them by the day it had been promised—they specified the date—then they would surrender the place. And Alexander found this plan more to his advantage than besieging a citadel impregnable on all sides. [3] After a ten-day stay he set out for Gordion,[3a] leaving a garrison of fifteen hundred soldiers at Kelainai and appointing Antigonos son of Philip[3b] satrap of Phrygia, making Balakros son of Amyntas commander of the allies in his

1.28.5–8
Winter 334/3
SAGALASSOS
Though their commanding position allows the Pisidians to drive back Alexander's lightly armed troops, they break under the hoplites' assault. The Macedonians capture the city.

1.29.1–4
Spring 333
PHRYGIA
Alexander enters Phrygia and negotiates the surrender of a Persian garrison at Kelainai. He makes administrative arrangements there and marches to Gordion, where Parmenion's forces and the troops from Europe rejoin the main army.

1.28.3a   "Infantry companions" is a term coined by Alexander's predecessors to confer on Macedonian foot soldiers an honorific similar to that traditionally given to the more socially elevated Companion cavalry. It is not clear whether the term referred to a select body of infantry or to the entire phalanx corps, but Arrian uses it here in the latter sense.
1.28.7a   A phrase probably giving the number of prisoners has fallen out of the Greek text.
1.28.8a   This is a different Kleandros from the one

sent to gather recruits in Greece at 1.24.2.
1.29.1a   Lake Askania: Map 1.26, inset.
1.29.1b   Kelainai: Map 1.26, inset.
1.29.3a   Gordion: Map 1.26.
1.29.3b   Antigonos son of Philip is the famous Antigons Monophthalmos ("One-eye") who, together with his son Demetrios, was to play a huge part in the division of the empire after Alexander's death. Due to his posting here in Phrygia, however, he plays no further role in the events of Alexander's Asian campaign.

place. He ordered Parmenion to meet him at Gordion and to bring his troops there with him, and Parmenion and his men duly presented themselves. [4] The newly married Macedonians who had been dispatched to Macedonia reached Gordion with a newly enlisted army led by Ptolemy son of Seleukos, Koinos son of Polemokrates, and Meleagros son of Neoptolemos. This new army included three thousand Macedonian foot soldiers, nearly three hundred and fifty Macedonian horsemen, two hundred Thracian horsemen, and one hundred and fifty Eleans under the command of Alkias of Elis.

[5] Gordion lies on the River Sangarius in Hellespontine Phrygia.[5a] The Sangarius' springs arise in Phrygia, and the river itself, flowing through the lands of the Thracians of Bithynia, empties into the Black Sea.[5b] There Alexander was approached by Athenian ambassadors, who asked him to release the Athenians who had been captured at the Granicus while fighting for the Persians and who were at that time imprisoned in Macedonia with the two thousand captives. [6] When their petition failed, the ambassadors departed. For Alexander did not think it safe, while the war against Persia was still in progress, to let go of the fear he had inspired in those Greeks who had not disdained to fight against Greece on behalf of the barbarians.[6a] But he did reply to the Athenians that when circumstances proved favorable, they should send another embassy to intercede on behalf of the prisoners.

1.29.5–6
GORDION
Alexander declines to free Athenians captured at the Granicus River.

1.29.5a Sangarius River; Hellespontine Phrygia: Map 1.26.
1.29.5b Phrygia; Bithynia; Black (ancient Euxine) Sea: Map 1.26.
1.29.6a The politically skewed phrasing of this sentence characterizes Alexander's army as an extension of "Greece," because its mission had been endorsed and supported by the collective of Greek states making up the League of Corinth. The same body had forbidden Greek mercenary soldiers to fight on the Persian side against their fellow "Greeks." See Appendix M, §3.

BOOK TWO

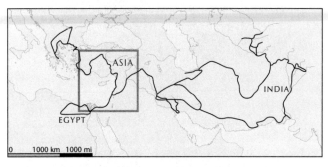

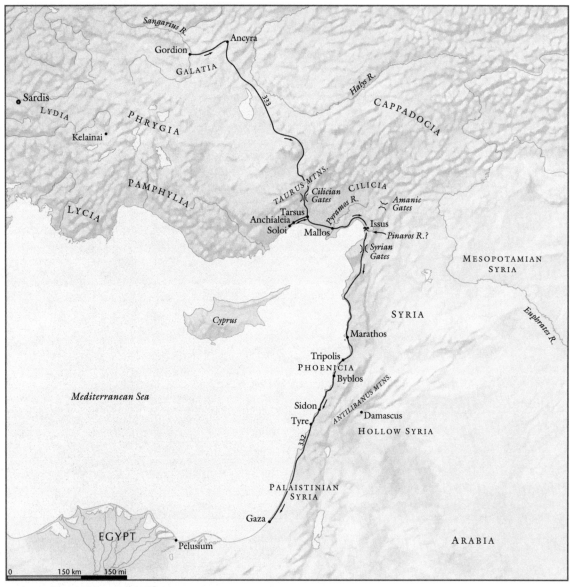

Book Two: The Campaigns in Western Asia (II) and Phoenicia

<big>A</big>fterward Memnon,[1a] who had been appointed by King Darius[1b] as commander of the entire fleet and the entire coast, intending to shift the war to Macedonia and Greece,[1c] seized Chios, which was surrendered by treachery, and from there sailed against Lesbos. Though the Mytilenians[1d] would not come over to him, he got the other cities of Lesbos on his side. [2] Once he had secured their cooperation, he landed at Mytilene and blockaded the city with a double palisade stretching from coast to coast.[2a] After building five fortifications, he easily gained control of the region. While part of his fleet guarded the Mytilenians' harbor, other ships were sent to Sigrion, the headland of Lesbos, where most of the trading vessels from Chios, Geraistos, and Malea[2b] approached the island; this contingent guarded the coast to prevent any assistance from reaching the Mytilenians by sea. [3] At that point Memnon died of disease, and this, more than anything else at that time, damaged the King's cause.[3a]

Autophradates and Memnon's nephew, Pharnabazos son of Artabazos,[3b] to whom Memnon as he died entrusted his power until Darius should make other arrangements, prosecuted the siege vigorously. [4] Barred from their land and blockaded at sea by a large fleet, the Mytilenians negotiated with

2.1.1–3
Spring 333
AEGEAN SEA
Memnon of Rhodes leads a Persian counteroffensive in the Aegean. Siege preparations are laid at Mytilene, but Memnon suddenly dies before his plans can be carried out.

2.1.4–5
MYTILENE
New Persian commanders force Mytilene to submit, then deal harshly with the Mytilenians despite the promised terms of surrender.

NOTE: Most locations in the text not identified by a footnote can be found in the Reference Maps section.

2.1.1a For Memnon's previous role in the Persian effort to resist Alexander's incursion, see 1.12.8–10, 1.20.2–3. See also Appendix G, The Persian Empire and Alexander, §9.

2.1.1b This was Darius III, who had assumed the throne of Persia in 336.

2.1.1c Macedonia; Greece: Map 2.2.

2.1.1d Chios; Lesbos; Mytilene: Map 2.2, inset.

2.1.2a Since Mytilene was built on a promontory projecting into the sea, Memnon hoped to besiege it by using a wall to cut it off from any resupply by land, while his ships blockaded the harbors.

2.1.2b Sigrion Promontory; Geraistos; Malea: Map 2.2, inset.

2.1.3a It is not clear why Memnon should be considered so indispensable to the Persians, since his campaign on Lesbos was immediately

taken up by his successors. It seems likely that Arrian's sources had lionized the Greek general, who had, in their eyes, outstripped the talents of his Persian masters.

2.1.3b Autophradates and Pharnabazos were both high-born Persians. Pharnabazos was one of the many children of Artabazos, a member of the Persian royal family who would eventually join Alexander's regime (see 3.23.7, 3.29.1). Memnon's relationship to Pharnabazos is more complex than Arrian indicates. Memnon had married Barsine, a woman who was both Artabazos' daughter and his own niece (Artabazos having earlier wed Memnon's sister). Thus Pharnabazos, Barsine's brother, was both Memnon's nephew and his brother-in-law. Shortly after the death of Memnon, the widowed Barsine became the mistress of Alexander—a relationship Arrian does not show knowledge of—and bore him a son named Herakles at some point between 327 and 325.

Pharnabazos, and concluded a treaty according to which the mercenaries sent to them by Alexander under the terms of his alliance with them would depart; the Mytilenians would remove the pillars inscribed with their treaty with Alexander, and would become allies of Darius according to the peace made by Antalkidas with King Darius;[4a] and their exiles would return and receive half the property they had possessed at the time of their banishment. [5] These were the terms of the Persians' treaty with the Mytilenians. But once Pharnabazos and Autophradates had entered the city, they established a garrison, appointed Lykomedes of Rhodes as its commander, and installed Diogenes, one of the exiles, as absolute ruler of the city. They also exacted money from the Mytilenians, both by forcibly appropriating it from the rich and by imposing a tax on the state as a whole.

[1] After settling these matters, Pharnabazos sailed for Lycia,[1a] taking with him the foreign mercenaries, while Autophradates proceeded to the other islands. At that point Darius sent Thymondas son of Mentor to receive the mercenaries from Pharnabazos and escort them inland to the King,[1b] and to assign Pharnabazos the powers formerly wielded by Memnon. [2] When Pharnabazos had handed over the mercenaries, he rejoined Autophradates and the fleet. Reunited, Pharnabazos and Autophradates dispatched Datames, a Persian, to the Cyclades with ten ships, while they themselves sailed to Tenedos[2a] with a hundred. Bringing their ships into the so-called northern harbor of Tenedos, they sent representatives to the islanders and ordered them to remove the pillars inscribed with their treaty with Alexander and the Greeks, and to keep peace with Darius, according to the treaty made by Antalkidas with the former Darius.[2b] [3] Though the citizens of Tenedos were better disposed toward Alexander and the Greeks, they surmised that under the circumstances there was no way to survive except by acceding to the Persians' demands, since Hegelokhos, who had been ordered by Alexander to assemble a fleet for a second time,[3a] had not yet acquired a force sufficient for them to expect any immediate help. Thus the cooperation of Tenedos that Pharnabazos and his men secured was more fearful than willing.

[4] Meanwhile, under orders from Antipatros, Proteas son of Andronikos had collected warships from Euboea and the Peloponnese[4a] in order to protect the islands and mainland Greece in case, as had been rumored, the

2.1.4a No doubt Darius II, who reigned during the Peloponnesian War, is meant, though the Peace of Antalkidas (so named for the Spartan who negotiated it) was in fact finalized under his successor Artaxerxes II (in 387). There is further confusion here as to the terms of this treaty: in Arrian's account the Persians seem to regard it as guaranteeing that Aegean islands like Lesbos would support their cause, whereas in fact the treaty gave political autonomy to such places. For more on the Peace of Antalkidas, see Xenophon, *Hellenika* 5.1.25–36.

2.1.1a Lycia: Map 2.2.

2.2.1b Evidently Darius had already begun assembling available land forces in preparation for a major showdown with Alexander, which turned out to be the battle of Issus.

2.2.2a Cyclades; Tenedos: Map 2.2, inset.

2.2.2b Arrian again makes the error he made at 2.1.4 in associating the Peace of Antalkidas with Darius II; see n. 2.1.4a.

2.2.3a The fleet that had initially accompanied Alexander's army had been disbanded after the fall of Miletus (see 1.20.1), one of Alexander's most daring, and ultimately costly, strategic decisions.

2.2.4a Euboea; Peloponnese: Map 2.2, inset.

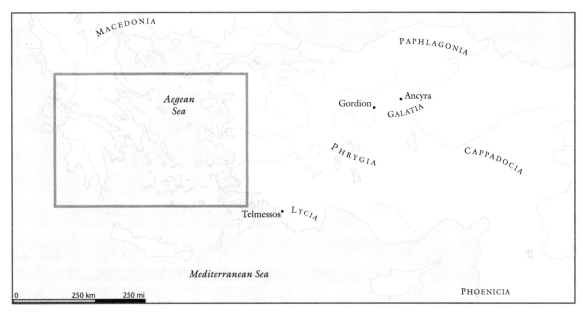

MAP 2.2

barbarians were planning to attack these places by sea.[4b] Informed that Datames was moored near Siphnos with ten ships, Proteas set sail at night with fifteen ships from Chalcis on the Straits of Euripos.[4c] [5] At dawn he put in at the island of Kythnos,[5a] where he bivouacked for the day, both to

2.2.4b Other evidence confirms that various mainland Greek cities expected a Persian attack,
and indeed it is difficult to know why the
Persians did not use their naval superiority
to attack pro-Macedonian cities or stir up
rebellion in divided ones, moves that would

very likely have forced Alexander to return
home from Asia.
2.2.4c Siphnos; Chalcis; Straits of Euripos: Map
2.2, inset.
2.2.5a Kythnos: Map 2.2, inset.

obtain clearer information about the ten ships and because a night attack on the Phoenicians[5b] would be more terrifying. When he had ascertained that Datames was moored with his ships at Siphnos, he sailed there under cover of darkness. Attacking unexpectedly at dawn, he captured eight ships with their crews, but Datames, at the start of the encounter with Proteas' ships, fled with two triremes[5c] and got safely away to the main fleet.

[1] After Alexander had reached Gordion,[1a] a desire seized him to ascend to the citadel, the site of the palace of Gordios and his son Midas, and to see Gordios' wagon and the knot of the wagon's yoke. [2] There was a legend widespread among the local people about that wagon. It said that long ago in Phrygia there was a poor man named Gordios who had a small piece of land that he tilled with two pairs of oxen; with one pair Gordios plowed, with the other he drove his wagon. [3] Once when he was plowing, an eagle alighted on the yoke and remained sitting there until evening when the oxen were unyoked. Astonished at the sight, Gordios went to consult the Telmessian[3a] seers, as the Telmessians were adept at interpreting divine matters; they and their wives and children are endowed from birth with the gift of prophecy. [4] Approaching one of the Telmessian villages, Gordios met a young girl fetching water. He told her about the eagle's behavior, and as she, too, belonged to the race of prophets, she urged him to return to the same place and to sacrifice to Zeus the king. Gordios asked her to accompany him and to prescribe the form of the sacrifice. He performed it as she directed and thereafter married her. A son was born to them, whom they named Midas.

[5] Midas was already a grown man, handsome and noble, when the Phrygians[5a] found themselves afflicted by civil strife. They received an oracle predicting that a wagon would bring them a king who would put an end to their strife. While they were still deliberating about these matters, Midas arrived with his father and mother—in a wagon, no less—and halted at the assembly. [6] Interpreting this as a prophetic sign, the Phrygians decided that Midas was the man the god had said would arrive on a wagon, and appointed him king. Midas then brought their strife to an end and dedicated his father's wagon in the citadel as an offering in thanks to Zeus the king for sending the eagle.[6a] The legend of the wagon also included a prophecy: the man who undid the knot of the wagon's yoke was destined to rule over Asia.

[7] The knot was made from cornel bark, and its end and beginning were nowhere visible. Alexander did not know how to undo the knot, yet he was

2.3.1–6
Spring 333
GORDION
Arrian resumes his account of Alexander, who has spent much of the past winter in Gordion. A local legend there tells how a famous wagon came to be installed on the acropolis long ago. Popular belief among the Gordians holds that whoever undoes the knot of the wagon's yoke will rule all Asia.

2.3.7–8
GORDION
Alexander, sensing a need to live up to his growing reputation, undoes the knot. Violent storms that night seem to confirm the significance of the gesture.

2.2.5b The greater part of the Persian navy was manned by sailors from Phoenicia (Map 2.2).
2.2.5c Trireme: the standard Greek warship in the fifth and fourth centuries, armed with a bronze ram at the front and powered by three banks of rowers. See Figures 2.21 and D.1.
2.3.1a Gordion: Map 2.2. Alexander had earlier (1.29.3–4) arranged to rendezvous in Gordion with the detachments of the army under Parmenion and with the recently married soldiers who had spent the winter of 334–333 at home with their wives.
2.3.3a Telmessos: Map 2.2.
2.3.5a Phrygia: Map 2.2.
2.3.6a The legend of Gordios' wagon must have had special resonance for the Macedonians, since the same Gordios was thought to have lived in their country before migrating to Asia (indeed a region of Macedonia bore the name "the Gardens of Midas" in Alexander's day). The idea that a Phrygian hero had migrated from Europe to Asia, where he established political stability and was made king, established yet another mythic template into which Alexander's campaign could be set.

unwilling to let it remain intact, lest this create public unrest.[7a] Some say that he struck the knot with his sword and cut through it, and then said, "Now it's undone."[7b] Aristoboulos, however, says that after removing the peg from the pole—for a peg had been driven right through the pole and was holding the knot together—he separated the yoke from the pole. [8] How Alexander managed to undo the knot I cannot say with certainty. But he and his entourage undoubtedly left the wagon believing that the prophesied untying of the knot had come to pass; that night thunder and flashes of lightning confirmed the omen. In return Alexander sacrificed the next day to the gods who had revealed these signs and shown him how to undo the knot.

[1] The next day, Alexander set out for Ancyra in Galatia.[1a] An embassy of Paphlagonians[1b] reached him there, surrendered their tribe, and came to terms. They begged him not to invade their country with his army. [2] Alexander told them to follow the orders of Kalas, the satrap[2a] of Phrygia.

Marching to Cappadocia,[2b] Alexander won control of all the country this side of the River Halys,[2c] and a large area beyond it. Appointing Sabiktas[2d] as satrap of Cappadocia, he himself advanced to the Cilician Gates.[2e] [3] When he reached the camp of Cyrus (the Cyrus with whom Xenophon campaigned)[3a] and saw the Gates strongly guarded, he left Parmenion there with the more heavily armed infantry units, while he himself, near the first watch,[3b] took the shield-bearers, archers, and Agrianians[3c] and advanced to

2.4.1–4

ANCYRA–CAPPADOCIA–CILICIAN GATES
On the march from Gordion, Alexander receives the surrender of the Paphlagonians. Gaining control of much territory, he heads for the Cilician Gates. Finding them heavily guarded, light-armed troops led by Alexander frighten away their defenders in a night maneuver, allowing them to enter Cilicia unopposed.

2.3.7a This is an interesting commentary, most likely speculative, on Alexander's private motives. According to Arrian, or one of his sources, Alexander already at this early stage of his campaign saw that he could better control conquered peoples by fostering the idea of the inevitability of his rule.

2.3.7b The comment Alexander makes in this version of the story depends on the multiple implications of the Greek verb *luein*, which can mean both to "untie" a knot in deliberate fashion or to "undo" it more generally. Alexander thus is not cheating, as some commentators have suggested, but proclaiming that the oracle has been fulfilled according to his own interpretation of its wording.

2.4.1a Ancyra in Galatia: Map 2.2.

2.4.1b Paphlagonia: Map 2.2.

2.4.2a The satraps, roughly two dozen in number, were appointed by the Persian King to administer the satrapies, or provinces, of the empire, collect taxes, and organize defense. For the locations of all Persian satrapies mentioned by Arrian, see Ref. Map 1.

2.4.2b Cappadocia: Map 2.2.

2.4.2c Halys River: Map 2.5. That is to say, the western side of the river.

2.4.2d Sabiktas is otherwise unknown; Quintus Curtius gives his name as Abistamenes. In either case he was certainly non-Macedonian and may even have been Persian. Thus he stands as the first in what would become a long line of Asian imperial officers whom Alexander appointed to high positions in his

own regime. Some of these eventually played Alexander false (such as Satibarzanes, see 3.25), while others became his most trusted ministers (like Artabazos, see 3.23, 3.28, 4.17).

2.4.2e Cilician Gates: Map 2.5, Cilicia inset. These "gates"—one of the few passes through the ten-thousand-foot-high Taurus Mountains, between Anatolia and Syria—were so narrow and steep that in spots only four men could pass abreast. Alexander hurried there in hopes of passing through before the Persians could send a force to block the pass; in his haste he left much of Cappadocia unsubdued, and parts of the region remained autonomous or Persian-allied long after.

2.4.3a That is, Cyrus the Younger, who in 401 had traveled this way en route to his engagement with his brother Artaxerxes II (the battle for which he hired the Greek mercenary band eventually led by Xenophon).

2.4.3b The Greeks (and later Romans), who were reliant on the sun to tell time during the day, divided the night into either three or four periods, naming these "watches" based on military parlance. The first watch was the earliest part of the night.

2.4.3c The term "Agrianians," as used by Arrian, usually refers to a light infantry division recruited from a Balkan region known as Agriania, northeast of Macedonia (Map 1.2). See Appendix D, Alexander's Army and Military Leadership, §6.

the Gates by night, intending to attack the guards when they least expected him. [4] His approach did not go undetected, but his daring paid off nonetheless, for when the guards noticed Alexander approaching, they abandoned their posts and fled.[4a]

The next day, near dawn, Alexander passed beyond the Gates with all his forces and proceeded down into Cilicia.[4b] [5] There it was reported to him that Arsames, who had previously intended to preserve Tarsus[5a] for the Persians, having learned of Alexander's passage through the Gates, was planning to abandon the city; and that the Tarsians accordingly feared that Arsames would try to plunder Tarsus before abandoning it. [6] When he heard this, Alexander advanced with all speed to Tarsus with the cavalry and the light-armed troops with the least gear, and consequently Arsames, informed of his swift advance, hastily fled from Tarsus to King Darius without having harmed the city.

[7] Alexander now fell ill from exhaustion,[7a] according to Aristoboulos, though others say that, sweating and overheated and having an intense desire for water, Alexander flung himself into the River Cydnus[7b] for a swim. The Cydnus flows through the center of the city, and as it has its sources in the Taurus Mountains[7c] and flows through open country, its water is cool and clear. [8] Thus Alexander came down with cramps, high fever, and unending insomnia. All of his doctors doubted he would live except Philip of Acarnania, a doctor who kept company with Alexander and who was especially trusted for his medical knowledge and who carried weight in the army for his grasp of affairs in general; this man wanted to treat Alexander with a purgative, and Alexander urged him to do so. [9] It is said that while Philip was preparing the cup, Alexander was given a letter in which Parmenion warned him to be on his guard against Philip; he said he had heard that Philip had been bribed by Darius to poison Alexander. Alexander, it is said, read the letter, and while still holding it, took the cup containing the drug and gave the letter to Philip to read; [10] and while Philip was reading Parmenion's letter, Alexander swallowed the dose. Philip quickly made it clear that the drug was harmless: for he was not disconcerted by the letter, but merely encouraged Alexander and advised him to follow all his other instructions, saying he would recover if he did so. [11] The medicine took effect and Alexander's illness lifted; he showed Philip that he was trusted as a friend, and made it clear to the others in his suite that he firmly refused to suspect his friends and had the strength to face death.

2.4.4a If Arrian's account is correct, then this is the first of several occasions when the Persians abandoned an advantageous position from which they could have done Alexander much harm. However, Quintus Curtius (3.4.4) reports that the Persians never intended to defend the Gates and had left only a tiny reconnaissance force there.
2.4.4b Cilicia: Map 2.5, Cilicia inset.
2.4.5a Tarsus: Map 2.5, Cilicia inset.
2.4.7a There has been speculation that Alexander contracted malaria while in this part of Anatolia, and that this disease, which would have resurfaced from time to time throughout the rest of his life, might have helped bring about his death. For more on the possible role of malaria in Alexander's death, see Appendix O, Alexander's Death: A Medical Analysis, §7–9.
2.4.7b Cydnus River: Map 2.5, Cilicia inset.
2.4.7c Taurus Mountains: Map 2.5, Cilicia inset.

FIGURE 2.4.
The Cilician Gates, the
main pass through the
Taurus Mountains from
central Anatolia to Cilicia,
as seen in a 1909 photo-
graph.

[1] Alexander now sent Parmenion to the other gates, the ones that mark the border between Cilicia and Assyria.[1a] Parmenion had been ordered to seize and guard the passage with the allied infantry, the Greek mercenaries, the Thracians led by Sitalkes, and the Thessalian horsemen. [2] Afterward Alexander himself set out from Tarsus and in one day's march reached the city of Anchiale.[2a]

Legend has it that this city was founded by Sardanapalos the Assyrian.[2b] The city's surrounding wall and its foundations reveal that Anchiale was large when founded and went on to attain great power. [3] The monument of Sardanapalos stood near the city's walls. Upon it stood Sardanapalos himself, his hands brought together as though to clap. An inscription was carved on it in Assyrian characters; [4] the Assyrians said that the epitaph was a line of verse. The sense conveyed by the words was: "Sardanapalos son of Anakyndaraxes built Anchiale and Tarsus in a single day. Eat, drink, and be merry, friend, since all other human things are not worth this"—

2.5.1–2
TARSUS
Parmenion is sent ahead
from Tarsus to secure the
route into Assyria. Alexander
moves to Anchiale.

2.5.3–4
ANCHIALE
A statue of Anchiale's
legendary founder, the
great Sardanapalos, bears
an inscription urging
observers to live only for
sensual pleasures.

2.5.1a Two "gates" (narrow defiles through oth-
erwise impassable terrain) stood between
Cilicia and Assyria—the Syrian Gates
(Syriai Pylai) and the Amanic Gates
(Amanikai Pylai): Map 2.5, Cilicia inset.
Here the action is at the Syrian Gates; for

action at the Amanic Gates, see 2.7.1.
2.5.2a Anchiale (Anchiale[ia]): Map 2.5, Cilicia
inset.
2.5.2b Sardanapalos is the Greek name for Ashur-
banipal, ruler of the Assyrian empire in the
seventh century.

"this" meaning the sound of a hand-clap. The phrase translated as "be merry" was said to be more vulgar in the original.

[5] From Anchiale Alexander reached Soloi,[5a] where he established a garrison and imposed a fine of two hundred silver talents because the city's inhabitants were more favorably disposed to the Persians.[5b] [6] From Soloi, taking three battalions of the Macedonian infantry, all the archers, and the Agrianians, Alexander marched against the Cilicians occupying the mountains. In the course of a mere seven days he expelled some of them by force while bringing others to terms, and returned to Soloi.[6a] [7] There he learned that Ptolemy[7a] and Asandros had defeated the Persian Orontobates, who had been defending the citadel of Halicarnassus along with the cities of Myndos, Caunus, Thera, and Kallipolis; they had also got control of Cos and Triopion.[7b] These generals wrote that Orontobates had been defeated in a great battle; some seven hundred of his infantry and nearly fifty of his cavalry had died, and no fewer than a thousand men had been captured.[7c]

[8] After sacrificing to Asklepios,[8a] Alexander held a parade with his entire army, a torch race, and a competition in athletics as well as music and literature. He then gave his consent for the people of Soloi to be governed by a democracy. After proceeding to Tarsus, he sent the cavalry ahead, having ordered Philotas to lead them across the Aleion Plain to the River Pyramos,[8b] [9] while he himself proceeded to Magarsa with the infantry and the royal squadron, where he sacrificed to Athena of Magarsa. From there he reached Mallos,[9a] where he offered Amphilokhos the sacrifice due to a hero.[9b] On finding the people of Mallos embroiled in civil strife, he brought their strife to an end; he also canceled the taxes they had been paying to King Darius, because the inhabitants were the descendants of Argive colonists, and

2.5.5a Soloi: Map 2.5, Cilicia inset. Soloi was largely a Greek town, and so Alexander took its pro-Persian sympathies very seriously.

2.5.5b Two hundred talents was a crushing fine for such a place, to judge by the fact that Alexander later forgave the quarter of it that the city had not yet paid (see 2.12.2). For the term "talent" as a monetary unit, see Appendix F, Money and Finance in the Campaigns of Alexander, §3.

2.5.6a It is not clear what Alexander sought to accomplish in this weeklong diversion from his main objective, the looming confrontation with Darius. Perhaps he regarded the route through the Cilician Gates as too vulnerable and sought to open up another passage by which men and supplies could reach him from the west.

2.5.7a This is clearly not Ptolemy son of Lagos, Arrian's principal source, but another Ptolemy about whom little is known. He had been put in charge of a cavalry brigade sent to Phrygia at 1.23.6.

2.5.7b Halicarnassus; Myndos; Caunus; Thera; Kallipolis; Cos; Triopion: Map 2.5, Caria inset. The *Barrington Atlas* indicates two

possible sites for Kallipolis, each one situated appropriately to be the Kallipolis that Arrian mentions here.

2.5.7c See 1.23 for the background to these events in coastal Asia Minor. The citadel of Halicarnassus had remained in enemy hands when Alexander set off for Lycia, and other sites in the region had similarly been left to the local Macedonian commanders to deal with on their own.

2.5.8a Asklepios: god of healing and medicine. Alexander was still mindful of the illness he had recovered from recently.

2.5.8b Aleion Plain; Pyramos River: Map 2.5, Cilicia inset.

2.5.9a Magarsa; Mallos: Map 2.5, Cilicia inset.

2.5.9b Amphilokhos was a semidivine being whose cult was centered in Cilicia, so by offering to him "the sacrifice due to a hero," Alexander sought to show himself adaptable to local religious traditions. He would go on to make similar gestures of accommodation at many key points in his campaign, even when dealing with non-Greek traditions, as in Egypt (see 3.1.4 and n. 3.1.4a) and Babylon (see 3.16.4 and n. 3.16.4a).

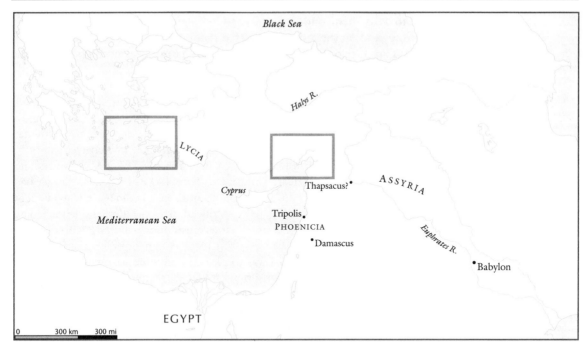

MAP 2.5

Alexander himself claimed to be a descendant of the Argive Heraklids.[9c]

[1] When he was still at Mallos, Alexander received word that Darius had made camp at Sochoi[1a] with all his forces. (Sochoi is in Assyria,[1b] roughly a two-day march from the Syrian Gates.) Alexander reported the news about Darius and his army to the assembled Companions,[1c] and they urged

2.6.1–2
Autumn 333
MALLOS-MYRIANDROS
Alexander receives news that Darius' army is at Sochoi. Advised by his war council, he leads the army in pursuit.

2.5.9c According to a legend well-known to the Greeks long before Alexander, the family that made up the royal Macedonian dynasty was descended from Herakles and had migrated to Macedonia from the Peloponnese. Recent scholarship has questioned whether this legend has any historical basis; see Appendix B, Greek and Macedonian Ethnicity, §3.

2.6.1a Sochoi, approximate location: Map 2.7. Not listed in the *Barrington Atlas*.

2.6.1b Assyria: Map 2.5.

2.6.1c Companions: see Appendix E, Alexander's Inner Circle, §4.

65

2.6.3–7
Autumn 333
SOCHOI
Arrian recounts Persian
movements during the previous few weeks: Darius initially awaits the Macedonians
in a position advantageous
to his superior numbers,
but during the long delays
caused by Alexander's illness
and maneuvers around Soloi,
flattering courtiers persuade
him to shift ground. Ignoring the advice of a Greek
general to remain in position,
Darius, guided (as Arrian
believes) by the hand of a
malevolent fate, moves his
forces to pursue Alexander.

him to lead them out at once. [2] Commending them, he dissolved the meeting, and on the following day led them out against Darius and the Persians. The next day he passed beyond the gates[2a] and encamped near the city of Myriandros;[2b] that night a furious storm arose, a downpour with violent wind, and this detained Alexander in camp.

[3] Darius, meanwhile, was marking time with the army, having selected a plain in Assyria[3a] that was open on all sides, spacious enough to accommodate his army's vast numbers and suitable for cavalry maneuvers.[3b] Amyntas son of Antiokhos, who had deserted from Alexander,[3c] advised Darius not to leave this site, as it furnished an open field for the Persians' numbers and equipment; accordingly, Darius remained there. [4] But when Alexander had lingered for a long time in Tarsus on account of his illness, and had spent considerable time in Soloi, where he sacrificed, held parades, and launched an attack on the mountain Cilicians, Darius' resolution faltered. Moreover, he was eager to adopt whatever viewpoint pleased him most, and, encouraged by associates whose only goal was to please—the same sort who always have consorted and always will consort with kings, to their detriment—he concluded that Alexander was no longer willing to advance [5] and that the news of Darius' own approach was giving him pause. First one man, then another, urged Darius on, declaring that he would trample down the Macedonian army with his cavalry. [6] Amyntas, however, assured the King that Alexander would come to any place once he knew Darius was there, and urged Darius to remain where he was.[6a] But the worse advice won out, since it gave Darius more pleasure at that moment. And perhaps, too, some deity was leading Darius to a position where his cavalry would not be of much use to him, nor his vast numbers of men and javelins and arrows, and where he would not be able to display the brilliance of his army but would cede Alexander and his men an easy victory. [7] For the Persians' power over Asia had now to be usurped by the Macedonians, just as the Medes'[7a] power had been usurped by the Persians and before that the Assyrians' power by the Medes.[7b]

2.6.2a   These are neither the Cilician nor the Amanic Gates mentioned at 2.5.1, but the narrow coastal defile marked by a gate symbol at the mouth of the Pinaros River on Map 2.5, Cilicia inset, and Map 2.7.
2.6.2b   Myriand(r)os: Map 2.5, Cilicia inset.
2.6.3a   This plain is evidently the place named as Sochoi in 2.6.1, a site in Assyria as yet not identified.
2.6.3b   With his great numerical superiority, Darius sought a battle site in a wide, open plain where the full strength of his forces could be deployed. There is much disagreement among historians as to why he eventually abandoned his advantageous position at Sochoi; Arrian's own character-based explanation follows at 2.6.6.
2.6.3c   Amyntas' desertion is also mentioned at 1.17.9.
2.6.6a   Two different narrative patterns, both highly informed by Greek prejudices regarding Persian military prowess, come together in this anecdote. First, Amyntas, the European warrior in exile, here plays the role of the wise

strategist whose advice is ignored by reckless Asian leaders, as happened with Memnon prior to the battle of the Granicus (see 1.12.9–10). Second, Alexander is depicted as an impetuous leader who takes the offensive at every opportunity, in contrast to Darius, who sat waiting at Sochoi to receive Alexander's attack.
2.6.7a   The Medes were a northern Iranian people who originally ruled the Persians, then came to be ruled by them and assimilated into their power structure. See Appendix G, §1.
2.6.7b   Arrian's meditation on the fateful error Darius made in changing ground, which revealed the providential character of the downfall of Achaemenid Persia, creates a grand rhetorical effect, but also distorts the facts: the new position Darius went on to occupy offered him important advantages, even if it did not allow the full exploitation of his numerical superiority. The new position limited Alexander's ability to maneuver and outflank the Persian forces.

[1] After crossing the mountains at the so-called Amanic Gates, Darius advanced toward Issus[1a] and reached the rear of Alexander's army without being observed.[1b] Having gained possession of Issus, he captured the Macedonians who had been left behind as invalids, and had these men tortured and killed.[1c] He advanced, the next day, to the River Pinaros.[1d]

[2] When Alexander heard that Darius had got behind his line of march, he did not credit the report, but embarked some of his Companions in a thirty-oared ship and sent them back to Issus to find out if it was true. Since the coastline there forms a bay, they learned the more easily that the Persians were encamped there, and reported to Alexander that Darius was at hand. [3] Calling together the generals, cavalry commanders, and his allies' officers, Alexander urged them to draw courage from their record of risks successfully run. Their struggle, he pointed out, would be between their own conquering army and men they had already once conquered; and, he said, the god was pursuing a better strategy on their behalf, having given Darius the idea of moving his army from an open space into a narrow one, where the terrain would be wide enough for the deployment of their own phalanx,[3a] but where the Persians would derive no advantage from superior numbers. Nor were these men their match either in physical strength or fighting spirit. [4] For the fight would pit Macedonians against Persians and Medes—men long trained in the hardships of war and accustomed to its perils—against those who had long lived in luxury; and beyond all else, free men against slaves. As for the Greeks who would be fighting other Greeks,[4a] he continued, they would not all be fighting for the same cause, since some would be taking their chances with Darius for a wage, and a meager one at that, while those siding with them would be fighting willingly in defense of Greece. [5] As for their barbarian troops—the Thracians, Paionians, Illyrians, and Agrianians—Alexander noted that the strongest and most warlike

2.7.1
ISSUS
Darius passes Alexander's army unobserved and captures a group of sick and wounded Macedonians left in the rear. He orders these men to be tortured to death.

2.7.2–5
ISSUS
Learning that Darius' army has cut off his lines of communication, Alexander prepares for battle. He addresses his officers and explains his reasons for confidence: the Macedonians have advantages over the Persians in morale, tactics, generalship, and the quality of their allies.

2.7.1a Amanic Gates (Amanikai Pylai); Issus: Map 2.5, Cilicia inset.

2.7.1b Alexander's normally superb reconnaissance failed in this instance to detect Darius' movements. Evidently the Macedonians were so certain that the Persians would advance through the Syrian Gates that they ignored the Amanic Gates, and the high peaks of the Amanus range had kept the two armies out of contact with each other. It is unclear whether Darius intended to surprise Alexander, or indeed whether he even knew Alexander's position at this point. Kallisthenes, who was on the scene at the time, wrote that Darius only learned of Alexander's passing the Cilician Gates after he himself had passed the Amanic Gates (as quoted by Polybius, 12.17.2). For the approach to the battle of Issus, see Map 2.7.

2.7.1c Quintus Curtius (3.8.15) reports a different, and perhaps worse, atrocity here: Darius had the prisoners' hands cut off and their wounds sealed with hot pitch. Then he took them on a tour of the Persian forces and turned them loose to report to Alexander on the enormity of the Persian host.

2.7.1d Pinaros River, possible location: Map 2.5, Cilicia inset. Scholars disagree on the exact location of the ancient Pinaros. There are two principal modern candidates: the Payas and the Deli Çay, some 7 miles apart.

2.7.3a Phalanx: the heavy infantry. The normal depth of a phalanx was eight men, but it could be increased to sixteen or thirty-two upon command.

2.7.4a "Other Greeks" were the many thousands of Greek mercenaries Darius employed as his front-line infantry troops, while Alexander similarly used Greek mercenaries and recruits in his own army. Arrian's assertion that "they would not all be fighting for the same cause" is a distortion on two counts: first, most of Alexander's Greek troops were hired for pay, like those of the Persians; and second, those who served without pay were hardly "fighting willingly in defense of Greece," but, rather, were draftees supplied grudgingly by their home cities in fulfillment of the obligations Philip had placed on them after his victory at Chaeronea.

FIGURE 2.7. Arrowheads (top) used by the army of Alexander's father, Philip (as is clear from the Greek word *Philippou*, meaning "Philip's," on each one), and slingshot bullets (bottom).

2.7.6–7
Autumn 333
ISSUS
Alexander stresses the high stakes of the coming battle, and reminds his men of their past exploits.

tribes in Europe would be drawn up against the laziest and softest tribes of Asia.[5a] And he, Alexander, would be in command, matched against Darius on the other side.

[6] Thus Alexander enumerated the Macedonians' advantages in the coming struggle. He then pointed out that the rewards of running the risk would be great. For it was not Darius' satraps they were now to overpower, nor the cavalry that had been marshaled at the Granicus, nor the twenty thousand foreign mercenaries, but the cream of the Persian and Median forces and of all the Asian tribes who were their subjects.[6a] And, he said, the Great King himself would be present. Accordingly, nothing would be left for them after this struggle but to rule all of Asia and put an end to their many toils. [7] He also reminded them of their brilliant accomplishments for the common good and mentioned any conspicuously daring and noble exploit, naming the man who had performed each deed. He then touched as lightly as possible on the danger he had himself incurred in their battles.

2.7.5a The toughness and vigor of European peoples, as compared with the indolence of Asians, was a standard rhetorical theme in Greek ethnographic thought, endorsed by Alexander's childhood teacher, Aristotle.

2.7.6a A vast exaggeration since, as Alexander knew, Darius had not marshaled the formidable cavalry forces of his eastern provinces for this battle.

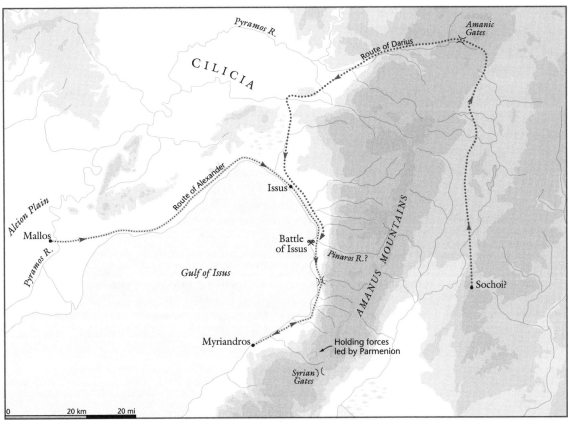

MAP 2.7. THE MOVEMENTS OF THE PERSIAN AND MACEDONIAN ARMIES BEFORE THE BATTLE OF ISSUS. The armies of Darius and Alexander were kept hidden from each other by the Amanus mountain range. Because of this, as Darius' forces came to the coast, they found themselves in the rear of Alexander's army, cutting off its communications, and forcing the Macedonians to fight without a line of retreat.

[8] Alexander is also said to have recalled Xenophon and the Ten Thousand,[8a] whose force, he declared, was not to be compared with his own either in numbers or in any other quality, having had no cavalry, neither Thessalian, Boeotian, Peloponnesian, Macedonian, nor Thracian, nor as many cavalry from other nations as Alexander had in his ranks, nor archers or slingers apart from a few Cretans and Rhodians whom Xenophon had deployed on the spur of the moment when his situation became desperate.[8b]

2.7.8–9
ISSUS
Alexander evokes the example of the Ten Thousand, who defeated a vast Persian army with fewer resources than the Macedonians now possess. Inspired by this speech, the officers surround the king, shaking his hand and asking him to lead them in battle.

2.7.8a   Arrian here refers to the Greek mercenary army hired by Cyrus the Younger in 401, led homeward by Xenophon and others after its employer was killed in battle. Because of the distances covered and the hardships endured, the march of the Ten Thousand was often compared to Alexander's Asian campaign (for example, see 1.12.3–4), and Arrian may have entitled his own treatise *Anabasis Alexandrou* to evoke the parallels with Xenophon's account of that march, the *Anabasis*.

2.7.8b   The army of the Ten Thousand was composed almost entirely of Greek hoplites and was therefore tactically inferior, in Alexander's eyes, to the Macedonian army, with its wide array of infantry, cavalry, and missile-firing units. The emergency Alexander here refers to, in which the Ten Thousand had suddenly deployed slingers and archers, was an attack by Persian missile troops who could not be otherwise countered, described at 3.2–6 of Xenophon's *Anabasis*.

[9] Yet those Ten Thousand had routed the King with all his forces at Babylon itself[9a] and had defeated all the tribes they encountered on their march to the Black Sea.[9b]

He said everything a brave leader would naturally say to hearten brave men on the eve of a dangerous venture, and his troops approached him from all sides, clasped their king by the hand one by one, and with encouraging words urged him to lead them out at once.

[1] But for the time being he ordered his men to have their meal, and sent a few horsemen and archers on to reconnoiter the road to their rear. At nightfall he advanced with the entire army to regain control of the gates.[1a] [2] Near midnight, when he was again in control of the passage, he rested the army for the remainder of the night on the ridges, after carefully posting advance guards. At dawn he descended from the gates by way of the road. While the terrain was narrow, he led the men in column, but as it widened he gradually rolled them out into phalanx formation, bringing one battalion after another from column into line so as to reach the ridge on their right and the sea on their left. [3] His cavalry had until then been posted behind the infantry, but as the army advanced into open country, Alexander set about arraying his forces in battle order: farthest on the right, near the ridge, the infantry *agema*[3a] and the shield-bearers[3b] under the command of Nikanor son of Parmenion; beside these Koinos' battalion, and then that of Perdikkas (these troops extended from the end of the right wing to the center of the hoplites[3c]). [4] Farthest on the left was Amyntas' battalion, then Ptolemy's, and then that of Meleagros. On the left, Krateros had been assigned to lead the infantry; Parmenion held command of the entire left wing, with orders not to lose touch with the coast, lest the barbarians, with their enormous numbers, outflank and surround them.

[5] When Darius received word that Alexander was approaching for battle, he transported roughly thirty thousand horsemen and nearly twenty thousand light-armed troops across the River Pinaros,[5a] in order to draw up the rest of his forces at leisure. [6] First, he posted some thirty thousand Greek mercenaries opposite the Macedonians' phalanx. Then, on either side of these, he posted nearly sixty thousand of the so-called Kardakes, who

---

2.8.1–4
Autumn 333
ISSUS
Alexander rests his army for the night and proceeds at dawn toward Darius' position. Descending from a narrow pass into gradually broadening level ground, Alexander moves his units one by one into battle formation. Parmenion is given command of the left wing and ordered to hug the coast.

2.8.5–8
ISSUS
Darius sets up his cavalry as a screen to conceal his order of battle, then makes his final dispositions. A phalanx of Greek mercenaries is deployed to counter the Macedonian infantry.

2.7.9a Babylon: Map 2.5. Xenophon's mercenary band fought its way easily into the Mesopotamian heartland in 401 and then won the battle of Cunaxa against the reigning monarch, Artaxerxes II, in a bid to put his brother Cyrus on the throne. However, after Cyrus, their leader and employer, was killed in the battle, their victory turned out a hollow one.

2.7.9b Black Sea (ancient Euxine) Sea: Map 2.5. After the battle of Cunaxa (see previous note), the army marched north and west through mostly hostile territory, often attacked by Persian forces and local tribes, losing about a third of their number before reaching the port of Trapezus on the Black Sea coast.

2.8.1a These are the same gates the army passed

through on their way southward, at 2.6.2.

2.8.3a *Agema*: a special division of light-armed infantry, though there was a cavalry *agema* as well.

2.8.3b The shield-bearers (*hypaspists*) were an elite corps of specially equipped infantry (see Appendix D, §3), lighter and more mobile than the heavy infantry who made up the phalanx. A smaller group chosen from this body, and also designated "shield-bearers" in Arrian's text, served as Alexander's personal bodyguard and security force.

2.8.3c Arrian uses "hoplites," uncharacteristically, to refer to Macedonian rather than Greek infantrymen.

2.8.5a Pinaros River, possible location: Map 2.5, Cilicia inset and Map 2.7.

were also hoplites⁶ᵃ (the area where he was arraying his men had room for that many soldiers posted in adjacent units). [7] He also posted nearly twenty thousand men alongside the ridge to his left, opposite Alexander's right; some of these troops found themselves to the rear of Alexander's army, for the ridge where they were posted was deeply recessed at a certain point like a bay of the sea, and past this recess, where the ridge once more bent outward, it left the troops at its base in the rear of Alexander's right wing. [8] The remaining mass of light-armed troops and hoplites, organized by tribes and drawn up too deeply to be of use, was behind the Greek mercenaries and the barbarians arrayed in a phalanx.⁸ᵃ Darius' army was reported to include up to six hundred thousand fighting men.⁸ᵇ

[9] As Alexander advanced and found the terrain widening slightly, he brought the horsemen—the so-called Companion cavalry and the Thessalians—from column into line. He posted these units to his own station at the right wing, and sent the horsemen from the Peloponnese and the other allied cavalry to Parmenion on the left.

[10] When Darius' phalanx had been drawn up in battle array, he recalled by signal the cavalry he had posted in front of the river to ensure the security of his deployment of the army. He posted most of these cavalry opposite Parmenion, on their own right wing near the sea, since the terrain there was better suited to cavalry maneuvers, and placed some of them at the left wing near the ridge. [11] But as it appeared they would be ineffective there for lack of room, he ordered most of them to ride over to the right wing. Darius then took his place at the center of the entire line, the position traditionally held by the Persian kings. (The purpose of this placement has been discussed in the work of Xenophon son of Gryllos.)¹¹ᵃ

[1] At that point Alexander, having noticed that almost the entire Persian cavalry had moved opposite his own left wing, near the sea, where only the Peloponnesians and the other allied cavalry had been posted, quickly sent the Thessalian horsemen to the left, giving them orders not to ride in front of the entire line, lest the enemy notice their change of position, but to pass behind the phalanx without being observed. [2] Alongside the cavalry on the right Alexander posted the Scouts under Protomakhos' command, the Paionians under Ariston, and the archers under Antiokhos.²ᵃ He posted the Agrianians led by Attalos and some of the cavalry and archers at an angle near the mountain at his rear, and as a result his line on the right

2.8.9–11
ISSUS
Advancing into yet wider ground, Alexander deploys his cavalry units on both his wings. Darius withdraws his cavalry screen and posts most of his horsemen to face Parmenion. He then takes his own station at the center of the Persian line.

2.9.1–4
ISSUS
Before the battle begins, Alexander adjusts his dispositions secretly to counter Darius' cavalry strength on the wing nearest the sea and to prevent encirclement on the other wing.

2.8.6a The Kardakes were an elite infantry corps of native Persian troops. There is some dispute as to whether they really were outfitted, as Arrian says here, with hoplite armor.

2.8.8a It was typical of the Persians to fill the space behind their front-line regiments with a mass of poorly trained and poorly equipped infantry, who were not expected to play a major role in the engagement. See Appendix G, §8.

2.8.8b Other sources give totals as low as half of this, but even assuming the lowest figures

are still exaggerated, Darius' army was enormous for its time.

2.8.11a The reference is to Xenophon's *Anabasis*, a work Arrian knew well and frequently emulated (see the Introduction, §1.1–3). At 1.8.22 Xenophon gives two reasons Persian generals take center station: they believe they are safest there, and they can transmit orders down the line faster.

2.9.2a These additional units seem to have been inserted into the battle line as the plain Alexander's forces occupied continued to widen (see Bosworth I.210).

was divided into two wings, one facing Darius and all the Persians beyond the river, the other facing the men posted at the mountain at the Macedonians' rear. [3] Along his left wing Alexander had posted the Cretan archers and the Thracians led by Sitalkes, and next to these contingents, the cavalry of the left wing.[3a] The foreign mercenaries were stationed as a reserve force for the entire army.[3b] Since the phalanx on his right did not seem to be in tight formation, and the Persians seemed likely to outflank them on that side, Alexander ordered two companies of the Companion cavalry (one from Anthemous under Peroidas son of Menestheus, the other the so-called Leugaean company[3c] under Pantordanos son of Kleandros) to pass from the center to the right without being observed. [4] Bringing the archers and some of the Agrianians and Greek mercenaries to the front of his right, he extended his phalanx to outflank the Persians' wing. (Since the Persians posted in the mountains had not come down, but had been easily driven from the foothills and chased to the heights when, at Alexander's order, the Agrianians and a few archers had sallied out against them, Alexander decided he could use the men he had assigned to deal with them to fill up the phalanx; he determined that three hundred horsemen would suffice to keep an eye on the Persians at the heights.)[4a]

[1] When his men had been posted in this order, Alexander led them forward, though regular halts made his approach seem quite leisurely. For Darius was not yet leading the barbarians forward from their original positions; instead he remained at the river's banks, which were steep in many places, and extended a palisade along the stretches that appeared more assailable. This made it clear to Alexander's men that Darius, in his own mind, had already been humbled in spirit.[1a]

[2] Just before the armies met, Alexander rode all along the line, exhorting his troops to be brave and calling out the names and appropriate honors not only of the commanders, but of all the squadron leaders, company commanders, and chiefs of the foreign mercenaries who were distinguished for rank or bravery. A shout went up on all sides to delay no longer, but to

2.10.1
Autumn 333
ISSUS
While Alexander advances, Darius holds his position and fortifies the riverbanks to defend against a Macedonian crossing.

2.10.2
ISSUS
Alexander makes a final exhortation to his troops. Leading the Macedonian right, he mounts a full-speed charge across the river.

2.9.3a   Once again Arrian seems to be describing new postings made necessary as the plain widened and the gap between the central phalanx and the left-wing cavalry had to be filled.

2.9.3b   "Foreign" mercenaries in this case means Greek hoplites. These important infantrymen were kept to the rear of the line because, as Arrian goes on to say, Alexander anticipated he might be outflanked by the Persian forces to his right.

2.9.3c   Cavalry squadrons were normally identified by the region from which they were recruited. The first of the two units named here, "the one from Anthemous" (a district of Macedonia), follows this pattern, but the second, "the so-called Leugaean," is more mysterious; its name does not derive from any known place.

2.9.4a   Arrian's description of this repositioning is rather muddled, but the sequence seems to be: Alexander first sent out a detachment of

Agrianians, archers, and mercenaries to deal with the Persians occupying the foothills; these men succeeded in driving the enemy back where they were no longer an immediate threat; Alexander then used the same three units to extend his phalanx toward the right, outflanking the Persians just where they had initially outflanked him, and sent three hundred cavalry to prevent the Persians on the heights from taking part in the engagement.

2.10.1a   Arrian portrays Alexander's aggressiveness and bravado as the most effective strategy, while implying that Darius' move in fortifying the banks of the Pinaros, so his infantry could more easily defend the river but could not cross it, showed cowardice. In fact, Darius only had to hold his ground to defeat Alexander, since his army had cut off the Macedonian lines of retreat and resupply; the palisade was sensible given the advantages his position offered.

charge the enemy. [3] At first, though Darius' forces were already in sight, Alexander led his men in file at a walking pace, lest the surging of the phalanx in a quicker advance throw it into disarray. But when they were within bowshot, Alexander and those with him, who were stationed on the right, were the first to charge on the double to the river, in order to astonish the Persians with the speed of their approach;[3a] and by coming to blows more swiftly, they hoped to sustain fewer casualties from the Persian archers.

And it turned out as Alexander had surmised. [4] For as soon as the two sides met hand to hand, the Persians posted on their left wing were routed; there Alexander and his men won a spectacular victory. But Darius' Greek mercenaries attacked the Macedonian phalanx where a gap appeared in its right wing; [5] for when Alexander dashed zealously into the river, coming to blows with the Persians posted there and driving them off, the Macedonians at the center did not apply themselves with equal zeal, and when they came to the banks, which were steep at many points, they could not keep their front line in proper order. Spotting the worst breach in the Macedonian phalanx, the Greeks charged right for it. [6] The action there was fierce, as the Greeks tried to drive the Macedonians back to the river and to recover the victory for their own men who were fleeing, while the Macedonians sought not to fall short of Alexander's already conspicuous success, and to preserve the good name of the phalanx, which at the time was spoken of far and wide as invincible. [7] Also, to some extent the Macedonians and Greeks were engaged in an ethnic rivalry.[7a] It was at this spot that Ptolemy son of Seleukos[7b] fell, having proved his bravery, along with nearly 120 other notable Macedonians.

[1] At that point the battalions from the right wing, seeing the Persians opposite them already routed, wheeled about toward Darius' foreign mercenaries, where the Macedonian center was in distress, and drove them back from the river. Having outflanked the breached Persian line, they charged into its side and started cutting down the mercenaries. [2] The Persian horsemen posted opposite the Thessalians did not remain on the opposite bank in the actual engagement, but after boldly fording the stream attacked the Thessalian squadrons.[2a] A desperate cavalry battle ensued, and the Per-

2.10.3–7
ISSUS
Alexander's wing crosses the river and succeeds in punching through the Persian line. But the Macedonian phalanx struggles to make progress through the river, and a gap opens between it and Alexander's units. The Greek infantry fighting for Darius attacks at this weak point and a violent clash ensues, in which Ptolemy son of Seleukos is killed.

2.11.1–2
ISSUS
Alexander's units find their way around to the flank of the Persian center, thus relieving the struggling phalanx, while on the other wing the Persian cavalry mounts a charge. But this effort fails after the horsemen notice Darius' flight and turn to escape the field themselves.

2.10.3a Arrian's picture of Alexander's cavalry charge across the Pinaros is an improbable one, especially if the Pinaros is the modern Payas with its steep embankments. Modern historians have proposed various solutions to this problem. Some believe it was not the Payas but another river with lower banks, either the Deli Çay or the Kuru Çay, on which the battle was fought. One scholar, Nicholas Hammond ("The Battle of the Granicus River," *Journal of Hellenic Studies* 100 [1980]: 73–88), keeps the Payas as the locale but proposes that Alexander and his Companions crossed the river on foot, leading their horses. Still others, following A. M. Devine ("Grand Tactics at the Battle of Issus," *Ancient World* 12 [1984]: 39–59) prefer a sequence in which the Macedonian phalanx units crossed the river first and

cleared a path for the cavalry charge. Maps 2.10 and 2.11 illustrate the course of the battle as Arrian describes it.

2.10.7a Arrian here refers to the difference between the Greek and Macedonian *genos*, a word that can connote racial, national, or ethnic identity. See Appendix B for more discussion of the relationship between Greeks and Macedonians.

2.10.7b Ptolemy son of Seleukos (a different person than Ptolemy son of Lagos, Arrian's principal source) was encountered previously at 1.24.1.

2.11.2a Arrian's description leaps quickly from one side of the battlefield, where Alexander's cavalry had crossed the Pinaros, to the other, where the Persian horse crossed going in the other direction. Arrian leaves unclear the chronological sequence of the two charges, but in our other sources, the Persian charge came first.

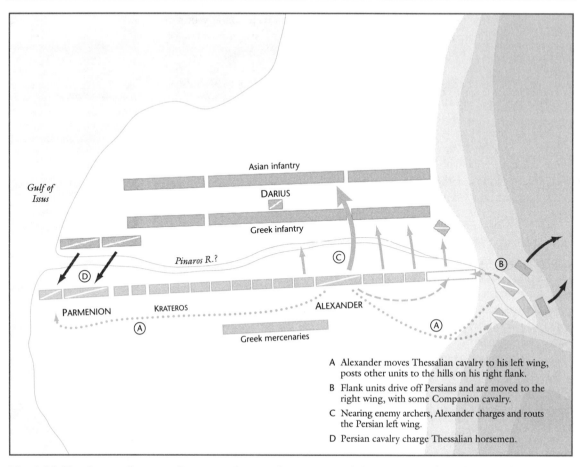

A Alexander moves Thessalian cavalry to his left wing, posts other units to the hills on his right flank.

B Flank units drive off Persians and are moved to the right wing, with some Companion cavalry.

C Nearing enemy archers, Alexander charges and routs the Persian left wing.

D Persian cavalry charge Thessalian horsemen.

MAP 2.10. THE INITIAL PHASE OF BATTLE OF ISSUS AS DESCRIBED AT 2.9–2.11.2. As Alexander moved toward the River Pinaros he thinned out his center to extend his line on both wings. By the time battle was joined his forces outflanked those of Darius despite being fewer in number. The battle commenced with both sides charging across the river, in opposite directions, with their right-wing units.

2.11.3–7
Autumn 333
ISSUS
After seeing his left wing routed, Darius suddenly flees in his chariot, switching to horseback after he reaches rough ground. Alexander pursues him until nightfall, but cannot catch up. He does, however, capture the King's chariot and weapons.

sians did not give way until they noticed that Darius had fled[2b] and that their mercenaries, decimated by the phalanx, were cut off. [3] By now the flight was conspicuous and general. The Persians' horses were suffering in the retreat, carrying their heavily armed riders. As for the horsemen themselves, their enormous numbers were creating panic and disorder: retreating along narrow roads, they trampled one another and thus incurred more injuries from their own side than from their pursuers. Meanwhile, the Thessalians attacked them stoutly, so that just as many horsemen as foot soldiers were slaughtered in the retreat

[4] As for Darius, the moment his left wing was thrown into a panic by

2.11.2b Arrian here anticipates the flight of Darius, an event he narrates in full a few sentences further on.

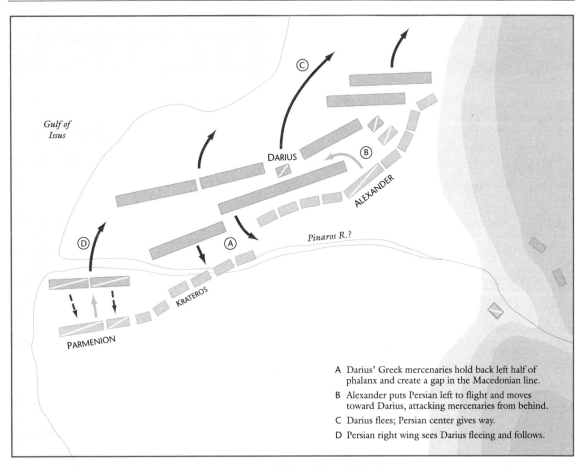

A Darius' Greek mercenaries hold back left half of
   phalanx and create a gap in the Macedonian line.

B Alexander puts Persian left to flight and moves
   toward Darius, attacking mercenaries from behind.

C Darius flees; Persian center gives way.

D Persian right wing sees Darius fleeing and follows.

MAP 2.11. THE BATTLE OF ISSUS AS DESCRIBED AT 2.10.4–2.11.4 With his extended right wing, Alexander was able to get around and behind Darius' front-line infantry once the Persian left had been routed. The approach of Alexander's cavalry caused Darius to flee, according to Arrian, and the Persian right, which had been prevailing up to that point over Parmenion and Krateros, soon followed his retreat.

Alexander and he saw it cut off from the rest of the army, he was among the first to flee, just as he was, on his chariot. [5] As long as he was fleeing on level ground, the chariot conveyed him away in safety; but when he encountered ravines and other difficult terrain, he stripped off his shield and cloak, abandoned the chariot, left his bow behind as well, and fled on horseback. Night fell shortly thereafter and saved him from capture; [6] for Alexander pursued him with all his strength while it was still light, but returned to camp when it grew too dark to see ahead. He seized Darius' chariot, however, and his shield, cloak, and bow. [7] (Alexander's pursuit had been slow to get started, since he had turned back when the phalanx was breached. The pursuit began in earnest once Alexander had seen the foreign mercenaries and the Persian cavalry thrust back from the river.)[7a]

[8] Among the Persian dead were Arsames, Rheomithres, and Atizyes, who had served as cavalry officers at the Granicus. Two Persian nobles, Bubakes and Sauakes, the satrap of Egypt, also perished. Among the rank and file, roughly a hundred thousand men were lost, including more than ten thousand horsemen. Indeed, Ptolemy son of Lagos, who was then with Alexander, reports that when the men who were pursuing Darius reached a ditch, they crossed it by riding over the corpses.[8a] [9] Darius' camp was captured on the first attempt, and Darius' mother, his wife (who was also his sister), and his infant son were taken prisoner. Two daughters[9a] were also captured along with only a few other Persian noblewomen, as the other Persians had recently sent their wives and baggage to Damascus.[9b] [10] Since Darius had also sent away most of his money and all the other trappings of luxury that accompany the Great King even on campaign, no more than three thousand talents were confiscated. But the money in Damascus was soon seized by Parmenion, who had been sent there for that purpose.[10a]

So ended the battle, which was fought in the month of Maimakterion,[10b] during Nikokrates' archonship at Athens.[10c]

[1] The next day, though he had received a sword wound in the thigh,[1a] Alexander visited the wounded, and when the corpses had been gathered, he honored them with splendid funeral rites, the entire army drawn up in its brightest battle array. In his speech Alexander cited everyone who had performed an illustrious exploit in battle, whether he had himself seen the deed performed or had learned of it from general report. He also rewarded the

---

2.11.8–10
Autumn 333
ISSUS
Persian losses include many high officers and a huge number of soldiers. Darius' wife, mother, grown daughters, and infant son are made prisoners, and his treasury of war funds, stored in Damascus, is captured by Parmenion.

2.12.1–2
ISSUS
In the aftermath of the battle, Alexander performs rites for the dead and speaks in honor of the deeds of the living.

2.11.7a   Here, as in a similar situation at the battle of Gaugamela (see 3.15.1 and n. 3.15.1a), Arrian takes pains to show Alexander breaking off pursuit of Darius to aid his own troops. Alexander came under criticism in later years for pursuing personal glory at the expense of his army's safety (see 6.13.4–5), and his tactics at both Issus and Gaugamela, which required his left wing under Parmenion to withstand severe pressure while he himself pressed ahead with the right, may well have been part of that critique. Arrian's careful language in both battle descriptions would, in that case, derive from the portrayal he found in his principal sources, Ptolemy and Aristoboulos. These pro-Alexander writers no doubt stressed Alexander's concern for his own beleaguered forces in an effort to counter charges of recklessness.

2.11.8a   Here as elsewhere, Persian losses are no doubt greatly exaggerated. Macedonian casualty figures are not recorded by Arrian for this battle; other sources give figures ranging from 280 to 1,200 killed.

2.11.9a   Their names were Drypetis and Barsine, according to Arrian's source Aristoboulos and Arrian himself, though our other sources call the latter Stateira. She may have

changed her name from Barsine to Stateira, taking her mother's name to gain greater royal stature, or Aristoboulos may simply have been mistaken. The two princesses were kept in state at Susa during most of Alexander's campaign, along with their grandmother Sisygambis, and were taught Greek by tutors. Finally, in 324, Drypetis and Barsine were married to Hephaistion and Alexander, respectively, in the mass wedding ceremony at Susa (see 7.4.4–5).

2.11.9b   Damascus: Map 2.5.

2.11.10a   For more on Alexander's finances, see Appendix F.

2.11.10b   Because of uncertainties regarding the calendrical system in use at the time, this month may have fallen anywhere from late October to late December of 333.

2.11.10c   Ancient historians, who had no universal system for numbering years, routinely used the names of Athenian archons or Roman consuls—officials who served one-year terms—to identify points in historical time.

2.12.1a   Khares of Mytilene, a Greek writer who was at the battle, reports that Darius himself gave Alexander the thigh wound, though no other historical sources confirm this (F. Jacoby, *Die Fragmente der griechischen Historiker* 125, F 6). For more on Khares, see the Introduction, §2.2.

men with gifts of money, honoring each man according to his deserts. [2] He appointed one of the royal Bodyguards,[2a] Balakros son of Nikanor, as satrap of Cilicia,[2b] and enlisted Menes son of Dionysios to fill his place in the guard. In place of Ptolemy son of Seleukos, who had died in the battle, he appointed Polyperkhon son of Simmias as battalion head. He also forgave the debt of fifty talents still owed him from the fine he had imposed on the citizens of Soloi, and restored their hostages.[2c]

[3] Nor did he neglect Darius' mother, wife, and children. Some writers relate that on the night he gave up the pursuit of Darius, Alexander went to Darius' tent, as it had been reserved for his use. Hearing the sound of women lamenting and other such commotion not far from the tent, [4] he asked who the women were and why their tent had been pitched so near. One of his men said, "Sire, since it was reported to Darius' mother, wife, and children that you have Darius' bow and his royal cloak, and that Darius' shield has been retrieved, they have been wailing for Darius in the belief that he is dead." [5] On hearing this, Alexander sent Leonnatos, one of the Companions, to the women, having instructed him to inform them that Darius was alive, that he had left the weapons and cloak in his chariot when he fled, and that these were all Alexander had. Leonnatos visited the tent, informed the women how matters stood with respect to Darius, and reported that Alexander had given his consent that they be waited upon, honored, and addressed as queens, since the war against Darius had not sprung from enmity but was a lawful struggle for the sovereignty of Asia. [6] So say Ptolemy and Aristoboulos. But it is also reported that on the next day Alexander himself entered the tent, accompanied only by Hephaistion. Darius' mother, in doubt as to which of the two was the king (for they were dressed alike), approached Hephaistion and prostrated herself before him, as he appeared the taller. [7] And when Hephaistion drew back and one of her attendants pointed to Alexander and said that he was Alexander, the queen drew back in shame at her error. But Alexander declared that she had not erred, since Hephaistion, too, was Alexander.[7a]

[8] Though I have recorded these incidents, I do not claim that they are either authentic or entirely implausible.[8a] But if they did take place, I commend Alexander for the compassion he showed the women and for the trust and respect he showed his friend. And if the chroniclers of his career

2.12.3–7
ISSUS
Alexander treats Darius' wife, mother, and daughters deferentially and allows them to retain their royal status. He reportedly gives an ironic reply to Darius' mother when she fails to recognize him and addresses Hephaistion instead.

2.12.8
Arrian finds much to admire in these tales without vouching for their veracity.

2.12.2a Apparently the term "Bodyguards" here refers to the coterie of seven officers who attended Alexander's person and not, as often, to an elite corps of men detailed to fight beside Alexander in battle; see Appendix E, §4.
2.12.2b Cilicia: Map 2.5, Cilicia inset.
2.12.2c Soloi: Map 2.5, Cilicia inset. Alexander had assessed the fine on Soloi at 2.5.5 and had taken hostages as a guarantee of payment, but after his windfall at Issus he could afford to forgive the outstanding portion of the debt.
2.12.7a The point of this quip is somewhat obscure, but it seems to refer to the spiritual unity of close companions. Darius' mother, Sisygambis, went on to become quite fond of Alexander, and reportedly killed herself by refusing food and drink after hearing of his death. The scene depicted here was popular among European painters in the Renaissance and after; Veronese's *The Family of Darius before Alexander* is the best-known example.
2.12.8a As he said he would do in his preface (Preface 1), Arrian here records an episode not found in either of his two main sources, Ptolemy and Aristoboulos, but without vouching for its authenticity.

think it credible that Alexander would have acted and spoken in this way, I commend Alexander on that score as well.[8b]

[1] Darius fled throughout the night with a few members of his suite, but by day was constantly gathering up Persians and foreign mercenaries who had survived the battle. With nearly four thousand in all, he hastened to the city of Thapsacus and the River Euphrates[1a] in order to put that river between himself and Alexander as soon as possible. [2] Amyntas son of Antiokhos, Thymondas son of Mentor, Aristomedes of Pherai, and Bianor the Acarnanian—all of them deserters[2a]—fled at once with roughly eight thousand soldiers under their command, still in their battle order, through the hills to Tripolis in Phoenicia.[2b] [3] There they seized the beached ships on which they had previously crossed from Lesbos.[3a] After launching the number they thought sufficient for their voyage, and torching the rest there in the dockyards to forestall a swift pursuit, they fled to Cyprus and from there to Egypt,[3b] where Amyntas was soon put to death by the inhabitants for meddling in state affairs.[3c]

[4] Meanwhile, Pharnabazos and Autophradates[4a] were marking time off Chios.[4b] After establishing a garrison there, they sent part of the fleet to Cos[4c] and Halicarnassus,[4d] while they themselves, setting sail with a hundred of their best ships, put in at Siphnos.[4e] [5] They were joined there by Agis, the king of the Spartans, who arrived with a single trireme to request that the Persians give him money to fund his war and send as large a naval and infantry force as possible to him in the Peloponnese.[5a]

At that point, news reached them of the battle near Issus. Astonished by what was reported, and fearful that the Chians might revolt when they learned of the defeat, Pharnabazos started for Chios with twelve triremes

---

2.13.1–3
Autumn 333
THAPSACUS
Darius flees to Thapsacus along with some four thousand surviving allies. A number of his mercenaries flee and make for Egypt.

2.13.4–6
AEGEAN SEA–CHIOS
In the Aegean, Persian admirals redeploy and regroup. King Agis of Sparta meets with them to obtain resources for a land war against the Macedonians, but comes away with little.

2.12.8b　Alexander's gracious treatment of the royal Persian women is commended by many ancient sources (some of which Arrian had read; see 4.20) and forms a major theme of the *Alexander Romance* and the medieval legends derived from it (see Appendix L, The *Alexander Romance*). Many of these fanciful accounts stress the sexual restraint Alexander exercised in the presence of his female captives, but it should be noted that some historians believe that Darius' wife bore a child in 331, and that Alexander was the father. In 324 Alexander took a daughter of Darius as his legitimate wife. See 7.4.4 and Appendix K, Alexander's Policy of Perso-Macedonian Fusion, §9.

2.13.1a　Thapsacus, possible location; Euphrates River: Map 2.5.

2.13.2a　The term "deserter" applies much better to Amyntas, a Macedonian who had fled to Darius to escape Alexander's regime (see 1.17.9, 1.25.3, 2.6.3–6), than to the others, who seem to have been Greek mercenary generals serving the Persians as paid employees.

2.13.2b　Tripolis; Phoenicia: Map 2.5.

2.13.3a　Lesbos: Map 2.16, Aegean inset.

2.13.3b　Cyprus; Egypt: Map 2.5.

2.13.3c　According to Quintus Curtius (4.1.29–33),

Amyntas tried to seize control of Egypt while pretending to be acting on Darius' authority; he was killed in an engagement with defending Persian forces.

2.13.4a　Pharnabazos and Autophradates were the leaders of the stalled Persian naval counteroffensive in the Aegean (see 2.1–2).

2.13.4b　Chios: Map 2.16, Aegean inset.

2.13.4c　Cos: Map 2.16, Aegean inset.

2.13.4d　Halicarnassus: Map 2.5, Caria inset.

2.13.4e　Siphnos: Map 2.16, Aegean inset.

2.13.5a　Peloponnese: Map 2.16, Aegean inset. Arrian gives no context to explain this sudden appearance of Agis, the Spartan king who was about to shake up the Macedonian order in Europe. Sparta had stayed outside the League of Corinth when Philip organized it in 338, and had remained deeply resentful of the Macedonians for maintaining the free status of Messene, a province that had long been enslaved by Sparta and forced to supply it with food until its liberation by Thebes in the 360s. Agis had doubtless arranged this meeting with the two main Persian commanders in the Aegean to get help from the other principal enemy of Macedonia and thus prepare for war. On Agis' revolt see Appendix M, Alexander and the Greeks, §9.

and fifteen hundred foreign mercenaries. [6] Having received thirty talents of silver and ten triremes from Autophradates,[6a] Agis dispatched Hippias to take them to his brother Agesilaos at Tainaron,[6b] with instructions that Agesilaos should pay the sailors their full wages and sail immediately to Crete[6c] to settle matters there. Agis himself remained in the islands for the time being, but later joined Autophradates at Halicarnassus.

[7] Alexander appointed Menon son of Kerdimmas as satrap of Hollow Syria[7a] and gave him the allied cavalry to keep watch on the country, while he himself headed for Phoenicia. He was met on the way by Straton, son of Gerostratos the king of the Aradians and of the peoples near Arados.[7b] Gerostratos himself was sailing with Autophradates, as were the other Phoenician and Cyprian kings. [8] Encountering Alexander, Straton crowned him with a golden crown and surrendered to him the island of Arados, Marathos (a large and prosperous city opposite Arados on the mainland), Sigon, and the city of Mariamme,[8a] and all the other places over which he held sway.

[1] While Alexander was still at Marathos, envoys arrived who brought a letter from Darius and who were instructed to appeal personally to Alexander to release Darius' mother, wife, and children. [2] The letter declared that a friendship and an alliance had existed between Philip and Artaxerxes,[2a] but when Arses, Artaxerxes' son, became King, Philip had set about injuring him, though the Persians had done Philip no harm.[2b] And since Darius' accession Alexander had sent no one to his court to confirm their past friendship and alliance, but had crossed with an army into Asia and done the Persians great harm. [3] Accordingly, Darius had journeyed down in person to defend his country and rescue the empire he had inherited. Their battle's outcome had doubtless accorded with the will of some god, and as a king he was now asking a king for his wife, mother, and captured children, and was also ready to form a friendship and an alliance with Alexander. To this end, Darius recommended that Alexander send men back with

2.13.7–8
ARADOS ISLAND
Alexander marches south toward Phoenicia and receives the surrender of the Phoenician king of Arados.

2.14.1–3
MARATHOS
Darius writes to Alexander requesting the return of his captured family. Though he accuses the Macedonians of unwarranted hostility against Persia, he offers to ally himself with Alexander.

2.13.6a Thirty talents and ten triremes was a pittance compared with what Agis might have expected and ultimately needed. Autophradates had been intending to give more aggressive support, but after learning of Darius' defeat at Issus decided to conserve resources for the war in Asia. For more on the value of a talent, see Appendix F, §3.
2.13.6b Tainaron: Map 2.16.
2.13.6c Crete (Creta): Map 2.16, Aegean inset. Control of the island was contested by Spartan and Macedonian forces.
2.13.7a Hollow Syria, Arrian's term for the northern portion of Syria: Map 2.16, Phoenicia inset. Listed as Koile Syria in the *Barrington Atlas*.
2.13.7b Arados Island: Map 2.16, Phoenicia inset. Straton, serving as ruler of the Aradians while his father, Gerostratos, was on campaign in the Aegean, was one of the many Phoenician city-kings in the region Alexan-

der was now entering. Most of them were in charge of naval contingents sailing under Persian command. The surrender of Arados by Straton thus marks the beginning of what was to become a crucial turning point in the Perso-Macedonian war: the defection to Alexander of the Phoenicians serving in the Persian navy.
2.13.8a Marathos; Sigon, possible location; Mariamme: Map 2.16, Phoenicia inset.
2.14.2a Artaxerxes III was king of Persia during the reign of Philip. There is no evidence of an alliance between the two monarchs, and indeed the Persians had chosen to oppose Philip's move against the Greek city of Perinthus in 340 (see 2.14.5 and n. 2.14.5a).
2.14.2b Presumably Darius here refers to an expeditionary force under Parmenion that Philip sent in spring 336 to seize a beachhead in Asia. Arses reigned for only two years, 338–336.

FIGURE 2.14. An iron *kopis*, or cavalry saber, of the type used by the Macedonians, with parts of its decayed wooden scabbard clinging to it. The hilt is in the shape of a bird's head, held together with iron rivets.

Meniskos and Arsimas, the envoys who had come from Persia, so that these men could exchange pledges with him as Alexander's representatives.[3a]

2.14.4–6
Autumn 333
Alexander replies by charging that Persia struck first, and claiming that he has invaded in order to avenge a long series of direct assaults and covert plots against Macedonia and Greece.

[4] Alexander wrote a reply and sent Thersippos along with Darius' envoys, having instructed him to give Darius the letter but not to discuss its contents.[4a] Alexander's letter ran as follows: "Your ancestors came to Macedonia and the rest of Greece and did us great harm, though you had suffered no harm before then.[4b] I, having been made leader of the Greeks and wishing to take revenge on the Persians, made the crossing into Asia, but it was you who began the quarrel. [5] For you went in aid to the Perinthians, who had wronged my father, and Okhos sent a force to Thrace, over which we held sway.[5a] When my father died at the hands of conspirators whom you had organized—as you yourself boasted in letters to one and all—and you killed Arses with Bagoas' help and usurped the throne, violating Persian law and harming Persian interests, and sent the Greeks unfriendly letters about me [6] inciting them to war against me, and sent money to the Spartans and some of the other Greeks (which no other city

2.14.3a   The accounts of Darius' peace offers to Alexander vary significantly among the extant ancient histories, with regard to both what was offered and the timing of the communiqués. Quintus Curtius (4.1.7–10) agrees with Arrian that Darius wrote to Alexander shortly after Issus and proposed a treaty of alliance, but also relates an extravagant offer of ransom for the royal captives that Arrian here omits (though he reports a ransom offer of ten thousand talents in a second letter many months later at 2.25.1–3). Justin (11.12.1–2) supports Curtius' version. Plutarch (*Parallel Lives*, "Alexander" 29.7–8) records a letter from Darius very similar to the one described here by Arrian, but places it at a different point in the war, about a year and a half later. Diodorus Siculus (17.39.1) records that Darius wrote to Alexander after Issus and offered him all the land west of the Halys River (Map 2.5) if he would cease further hostilities; but Alexander suppressed this letter and instead showed a different, forged one to his Companions. It seems

clear that the historical accounts have in this instance become contaminated by a fictional collection of Alexander-Darius correspondence that circulated widely in antiquity, and that the truth about what Darius offered (if anything) and when is very hard to recover.

2.14.4a   Evidently Alexander did not want his envoy to be drawn into any sort of negotiation that might weaken Alexander's uncompromising position. Thersippos is not known outside this episode.

2.14.4b   Alexander refers to the period of Persian domination of Macedonia (Map 2.16, Aegean inset) in the late sixth and early fifth centuries, and the invasions of Greece by Darius and Xerxes in 490 and 480–479.

2.14.5a   Perinthus; Thrace: Map 2.16, Aegean inset. The first of these charges relates to the fact that in 340 Persian assistance helped the city of Perinthus withstand a siege by Philip (see 2.14.2a). As for the alleged invasion of Thrace by "Okhos"—the name Artaxerxes III had held before his ascension to the throne—our other sources offer no enlightenment.

accepted but the Spartans), and sent your agents to destroy my friends and try to destroy the peace that I had arranged for the Greeks[6a]—when you did all this, I marched against you, as you had begun hostilities.

[7] "Now that I have prevailed in battle—over your generals and satraps earlier, and now over you and your own forces—and the gods have given me possession of the country, I am also responsible for all the men who fought on your side, survived the battle, and fled to me, and who remain with me not unwillingly, but have joined my campaign voluntarily. [8] So regard me as master of all of Asia and come into my presence; if you fear you may suffer some harm at my hands, send some of your friends to receive pledges. Approach me and ask for your mother, wife, children, and anything else you like, and receive them; anything you persuade me to give will be yours. [9] And in future, whenever you send word to me, address yourself to me as the king of Asia[9a] and not as an equal, and let me know, as the master of all that was yours, if you have need of anything. Otherwise, I plan to deal with you as a criminal. But if you contest the kingship, hold your ground, fight for it, and do not flee, since I am coming after you wherever you are."

[1] This was the letter Alexander sent to Darius.

When Alexander learned that all the treasure Darius had sent to Damascus[1a] with Kophen son of Artabazos had been captured, and that all the Persians left to guard it had been seized with the rest of the royal belongings, he ordered Parmenion to convey the plunder back to Damascus and guard it there. [2] As for the Greek envoys who had arrived at Darius' court before the battle—the Spartan Euthykles; the Thebans Thessaliskos son of Ismenias, and Dionysodoros, an Olympic victor; and the Athenian Iphikrates son of Iphikrates the general—when Alexander learned these men had been captured, he gave orders for them to be sent to him. [3] When they arrived, Alexander immediately released Thessaliskos and Dionysodoros, though they were Thebans, in part out of a certain compassion for Thebes, and in part because they appeared to have acted pardonably; for when their country had been enslaved by Macedonians, they had looked for any help they could find, for both their homeland and themselves, from Darius and the Persians. [4] Alexander was therefore favorably disposed to both men, though he said he was releasing them for individual reasons: Thessaliskos out of respect for his family (who belonged to the Theban nobility), Dionysodoros on account of his victory at Olympia. As for Iphikrates, while he lived Alexander kept him at court out of friendship for the city of Athens

2.14.7–9
Alexander promises that if Darius submits, his family will be restored to him and he will have anything else he wishes, but if he does not, Alexander will destroy him. He claims the right to be addressed as king of Asia in future communications.

2.15.1–5
DAMASCUS
Alexander takes possession of Persian treasure and deals with captive Greek envoys who have conspired with Persia against Macedonia.

2.14.6a Alexander provides a long list of charges, but most, to the best of our knowledge, are specious. It is true, however, that the Persians sent money to Greece to incite rebellion against Alexander, most notably in the case of the revolt of Thebes in 335; but the Macedonians had already begun their war on the Persian empire by that time.

2.14.9a "King of Asia" appears to be the title

chosen by Alexander to describe his new, and somewhat ambiguous, sovereignty. As a European ruler who had beaten the Persians in an all-out battle, but had not yet taken possession of the Persian capital cities or tokens of royal authority, Alexander was both more and less than a new Great King.

2.15.1a Damascus: Map 2.16, Phoenicia inset.

and in memory of the man's father,[4a] and when he died of disease Alexander sent his bones back to relatives in Athens. [5] Euthykles, on the other hand, was a Spartan, and since Alexander harbored a pronounced hostility toward Sparta at the time, and could find no substantial reason for a pardon based on personal record, he at first put Euthykles under guard, though without shackling him. Later, however, when Alexander had achieved considerable success, he released Euthykles as well.[5a]

[6] Setting out from Marathos, Alexander seized Byblos, which was surrendered to him by negotiation, and Sidon,[6a] where the inhabitants had called him in themselves out of hatred for Persia and Darius. From there he advanced to Tyre,[6b] and was met on the road by Tyrian envoys sent by the populace to declare that the Tyrians had resolved to do whatever Alexander ordered. [7] Alexander commended the city and the envoys (since among them were members of the Tyrian nobility, including Azemilkos' son, the Tyrian king; Azemilkos himself was at sea with the fleet of Autophradates), and ordered them to return and inform the Tyrians that he desired to enter the city and sacrifice to Herakles.[7a]

[1] At Tyre there is a temple of Herakles, the most ancient of those retained in human memory. This was not the Argive Herakles, son of Alkmene; for this Herakles was honored in Tyre many generations before Kadmos[1a] set out from Phoenicia[1b] to take possession of Thebes[1c] and sire a daughter, Semele, who gave birth to Dionysos son of Zeus. [2] Dionysos would have lived two generations after Kadmos, at the time of Labdakos, son of Polydoros and grandson of Kadmos, while the Argive Herakles probably lived about the time of Oedipus son of Laios.[2a] The Egyptians, too, worship a different Herakles—not the Herakles worshiped by the Tyrians or the Greeks, [3] for Herodotus says that the Egyptians consider Herakles one of their twelve gods.[3a] In the same way, the Athenians worship a differ-

2.15.6–7
Winter 333/2
PHOENICIA
Alexander marches through Phoenicia to the important port of Tyre. Meeting envoys from the city en route, he issues a demand to be allowed to sacrifice to a Tyrian god he identifies with his mythic ancestor Herakles.

2.16.1–3
Arrian pauses to differentiate the Herakles of Tyre from the Greek Herakles.

2.15.4a   Iphikrates the elder, the general, led an Athenian military intervention into Macedonia in 368 and helped secure the throne for the Argead royal family, from which Alexander descended.

2.15.5a   The change in attitude probably had less to do with Alexander's success than with Sparta's failure. Most likely Euthykles was released after the defeat of King Agis' revolt, when Sparta was no longer a threat to Macedonian interests.

2.15.6a   Marathos; Byblos; Sidon: Map 2.16, Phoenicia inset.

2.15.6b   Tyre (Tyrus): Map 2.16, Phoenicia inset; Map 2.23. Tyre was an important port city, a naval base that was Persia's best hope for maintaining control of the sea. It was an island in antiquity, though thanks to the mole built by Alexander in the siege described at 2.18–19, it is today a peninsula (see Figure 2.23).

2.15.7a   At Tyre "Herakles" (actually the Phoenician god Melqart) was the focus of a yearly state-sponsored ritual occurring at about the time of Alexander's arrival. Thus Alexander's request to make sacrifice to Tyrian Herakles was, in effect, a challenge to national sovereignty. The Tyrians would have lost autonomy symbolically if they allowed Alexander to dominate this important ritual, and in a more concrete way if he brought a portion of his army into the city with him.

2.16.1a   Kadmos was the mythical founder of Thebes.

2.16.1b   Phoenicia: Map 2.16, Phoenicia inset.

2.16.1c   Thebes: Map 2.16, Aegean inset.

2.16.2a   Laios was the son of Labdakos. This genealogical discussion is designed to show that the Greek Herakles was born much later than the founding of the shrine to Tyrian Herakles, and so the two cannot be the same deity. It is muddled, however, by the introduction of a genealogy of Dionysos. The main argument is that though the Greek Herakles was a contemporary of Oedipus, the great-great-grandson of Kadmos (the founder of Thebes), another Herakles was already worshiped in Tyre before Kadmos' time. Arrian then goes on to assert that the Egyptian Herakles is distinct from both these others.

2.16.3a   See Herodotus, *Histories* 2.43.

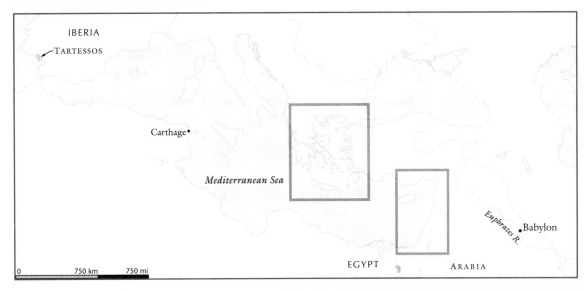

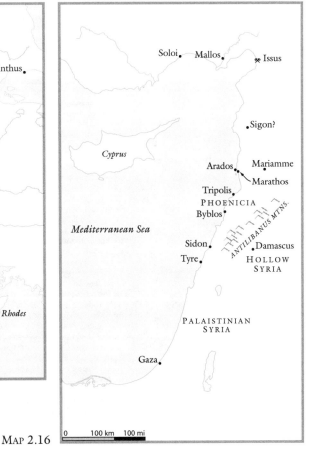

MAP 2.16

ent Dionysos, the son of Zeus and Kore; their mystic hymn the Iakkhos is sung to that Dionysos, not the Theban god.[3b]

2.16.4–6
Arrian advances his theories regarding the Herakles myths, claiming that some should be assigned to the Tyrian Herakles, not the Greek one.

[4] I think that the Herakles honored by the Iberians in Tartessos,[4a] where certain Pillars have also been named after Herakles, is the Tyrian Herakles, since Tartessos is a Phoenician colony, its temple of Herakles is built in the Phoenician style, and the sacrifices are performed in the Phoenician manner.[4b] [5] Eurystheus sent the Argive Herakles to drive off Geryones' cattle and bring them to Mycenae,[5a] but Hekataios the chronicler says that Geryones has no ties to the land of the Iberians, nor was Herakles sent to an island Erytheia beyond the Outer, or Great, Sea. According to Hekataios, Geryones was king of the mainland of Greece near Ambracia and Amphilochia,[5b] and it was from that mainland that Herakles drove off the cattle.[5c] (Nor was this a small undertaking.) [6] I also know that to this day that mainland possesses fertile pastures and nourishes the finest cattle.[6a] And I do not think it improbable that the fame of the mainland cattle, and the name of Geryones, the mainland's king, reached Eurystheus; on the other hand, I think it unlikely that Eurystheus would have known either the name of the king of the Iberians, who live at the farthest reaches of Europe, or whether the cattle grazed in that country are superior, unless some storyteller, introducing Hera into these matters and asserting that she communicated these things to Herakles through Eurystheus,[6b] should wish to cloak the incredible aspects of the story in a myth.[6c]

2.16.3b Arrian bases his comment here on the common Greek confusion between Iakkhos, a minor deity often said to be the son of Zeus and Kore (Persephone), and the god Dionysos; both were celebrated with the ritual salutation "Iakkhe," making them seem identical. By a curious twist of logic, Arrian uses this false identification to prove that there must be two different gods named Dionysos, since the Theban god was known to be the son of Semele, not Kore.

2.16.4a Tartessos; Iberia: Map 2.16.

2.16.4b This temple was in the Phoenician colony of Gadeira (called Gadir by the Phoenicians, Gades by the Romans, today the Spanish city of Cádiz). Gadeira was established inside the Iberian kingdom known to the Greeks as Tartessos (the Tarshish of the Hebrew Bible), but Arrian here confuses the Phoenician colony with the larger province surrounding it. The Pillars of Herakles close to Gadeira are the promontories flanking the body of water today known as the Strait of Gibraltar.

2.16.5a According to Greek myth, the monster Geryones (Geryon) ruled the island of Erytheia somewhere in the Atlantic (here identified by Arrian as "the Outer or Great Sea"). As the tenth of Herakles' twelve labors—undertaken as penance for killing his wife and children (in madness induced by a jealous Hera; see n. 2.16.6b) and directed by Eurystheus, king of Mycenae in the Peloponnese—he had to sail to Erytheia and steal the cattle grazing there.

2.16.5b Ambracia; Amphilochia: Map 2.16, Aegean inset.

2.16.5c Hekataios was an early Greek geographer and genealogist whose works are now mostly lost. Arrian refers to him as an authority for locating Herakles' journey to Erytheia, in quest of the cattle of Geryones, in the Adriatic Sea, not in the Atlantic Ocean, as was commonly supposed; otherwise Arrian would face the difficulty that a Phoenician city that should by logic worship the Phoenician Herakles was also the site of one of the Greek Herakles' most prominent exploits.

2.16.6a Arrian bases his comment here on firsthand knowledge. He had lived in this region as a young man, when he studied with the philosopher Epictetus at Nikopolis (see Appendix R, Arrian's Life and Works, §2).

2.16.6b Hera, wife of Zeus, was thought to have persecuted Herakles throughout his mortal life, angered by the adulterous affair that had begotten him. In Arrian's conception, Hera gave instructions to Eurystheus about the labors Herakles had to perform, including the raid on Geryones' cattle.

2.16.6c Arrian draws on his own knowledge of northwest Greece to back up the point he has already made by way of Hekataios. Since the cattle in this part of the world are exceptionally fine, it makes sense that the adventure of Herakles' theft of the cattle of Geryones was set there and not elsewhere; if Eurystheus, who sent Herakles on the quest, was as Hekataios claimed a native of those parts, then he likely would not have known of any cattle herds as far away as the Atlantic, and any storyteller who ascribes to him such knowledge is dabbling in the supernatural.

[7] It was to this Tyrian Herakles, then, that Alexander said he wished to sacrifice. When the envoys reported this in Tyre, the Tyrians decided to do everything else Alexander commanded, but to receive no Persian or Macedonian in their city, recognizing that this was the most appropriate course of action given their present policy and the safest with regard to the war's outcome, which was still unclear. When the Tyrians' response was reported to Alexander, he angrily sent back the envoys, assembled the Companions, generals, squadron leaders, and cavalry commanders, and spoke as follows:

[1] "Friends and allies, I see it will not be safe for us to march against Egypt[1a] while the Persians control the sea. And for us to leave Tyre behind, its loyalty dubious, to pursue Darius while Egypt and Cyprus[1b] remain in the hands of the Persians would be unsafe for any number of reasons, but particularly when one considers the state of affairs in Greece. [2] For if the Persians regain control of the coast while we proceed with our forces against Babylon[2a] and Darius, they might, by sending out a larger force, shift the war to Greece, where the Spartans are openly at war with us and our control of Athens[2b] is currently founded more on fear than on goodwill. [3] But with Tyre demolished, all of Phoenicia would be in our hands, and the largest and strongest contingent of the Persian navy, namely the Phoenician, would likely come over to us; for the Phoenician oarsmen and marines will not consent to run risks at sea on others' behalf while their cities are under our control. Thereupon Cyprus will either join us willingly or be taken easily in a naval attack. [4] And if we put fleets from Macedonia and Phoenicia into action, and Cyprus joins us as well, our mastery of the sea would be secure, and hence our expedition to Egypt would be easy. And once we have won control of Egypt, we will have no reason to be concerned about Greece or our own home. Secure at home, our renown increased, we will march against Babylon, having cut the Persians off from the sea completely and from all the territory this side of the Euphrates."[4a]

[1] So saying, Alexander had no difficulty persuading his officers to make an attempt on Tyre. And to some extent an omen persuaded him, since on that very night Alexander dreamed that when he was approaching the wall of Tyre, Herakles grasped his right hand and brought him into the city. Aristandros interpreted this to mean that with hard toil Tyre would be captured, since Herakles' feats had also been the fruit of hard toil. For it was obvious that the siege of Tyre would be an enormous task.

[2] The city was an island, fortified on all sides with high walls; in addition, Tyre seemed to have naval superiority at that time, as the Persians still controlled the sea and the Tyrians themselves were in possession of a large fleet. [3] When, despite the difficulties, Alexander won support for his plan, he decided to build a mole extending from the mainland to the city. There is a spot there where the strait forms a shoal; the section near the mainland

2.16.7
TYRE
Winter 333/2
Arrian returns to the history of Alexander's campaign. The Tyrians refuse Alexander entry, insisting on a neutral posture; Alexander angrily summons a war council.

2.17.1–4
TYRE
Alexander addresses his officers and explains the importance of capturing Tyre. Conquest of this vital Persian naval base, he claims, will give the Macedonians control of the seas.

2.18.1
TYRE
In a dream, Alexander sees an apparent omen of victory.

2.18.2–4
TYRE
Tyre's natural advantages and naval superiority do not deter Alexander, who orders a mole built to connect the island city to the mainland.

2.17.1a Egypt: Map 2.16.
2.17.1b Cyprus: Map 2.16, Phoenicia inset.
2.17.2a Babylon (Map 2.16) was the westernmost of four cities the Persian kings used as their
capitals, so Alexander could expect that it would be Darius' primary line of defense.
2.17.2b Sparta; Athens: Map 2.16, Aegean inset.
2.17.4a Euphrates River: Map 2.16.

has shallows and muddy spots, but near the city itself, where the channel is deepest, the water is nearly three fathoms deep.[3a] But there were plenty of stones and an abundance of wood, which Alexander's men laid over the stones. Stakes were easily fixed in the mud, and the mud itself served as a cement to hold the stones in place. [4] The Macedonians showed great eagerness for the task, as did Alexander. He personally directed their every move, offered encouraging words, and lightened the labor by presenting gifts to those whose efforts were outstanding.

As long as they were at work on the section near the mainland, the project went forward with no difficulty, since they were working in shallow water and no one hindered them. [5] But by the time they neared the deeper section and approached the city itself, they were shot at from the high walls and were in serious difficulties, being dressed for work, not combat; and when the Tyrians, who still had control of the sea, sailed out in triremes here and there near the mole, they often made it impossible for the Macedonians to build it up. [6] The Macedonians set two towers at the edge of the mole (which by this time extended far out to sea), and placed siege engines on the towers; these were covered with screens made of skins and hides, to prevent them from being hit by flaming darts shot from the walls, and to shield the men working on them from arrows. And by the same token the Tyrians who were sailing up close to injure the builders would be repulsed with no difficulty, as they could now be shot at from the towers.

[1] But the Tyrians devised the following countermeasure. Filling a cavalry transport ship with dry vine twigs and other kindling, they fixed two masts at the bow and surrounded them with a pen, as large as they could make it, to accommodate the greatest possible quantity of debris and firewood, and on top of that they put pitch, sulfur, and every other substance that stokes up a blaze. [2] Over both masts they stretched a double yardarm, from which they hung basins containing all the flammable material they could find. They also put ballast in the stern to weigh it down and lift the bow. [3] Then, after waiting for a breeze blowing toward the mole, they fastened ropes to the ship and towed it behind their triremes. When they had drawn near the mole and its towers, they threw a torch onto the wood, drew the ship forward as forcefully as they could with the triremes, and drove it onto the edge of the mole. (Once the ship was ablaze, those on board swam away with no difficulty.) [4] At that point the conflagration fell on the towers; and the yardarms, when they broke, poured out all the stuff that had been prepared for fueling the fire. The men from the triremes, holding their position near the mole, shot arrows at the towers so that it would be unsafe to approach them with material to quench the fire. [5] And while the towers were burning, many men rushed out from the city and boarded light vessels, ran their ships ashore here and there at the mole, tore down the palisade that

2.18.5–6
Spring 332
TYRE
The mole goes forward quickly until it comes within range of Tyrian artillery. At that point the Macedonians are forced to construct siege towers from which to supply covering fire.

2.19.1–5
TYRE
The Tyrians counterattack by driving a ship laden with incendiaries onto the mole. This device succeeds in destroying the Macedonian siege towers and a good portion of the mole.

2.18.3a   Arrian speaks in the present tense for the sake of vividness, but by his time the strait described here had become silted up so that Tyre was attached to the mainland, as it is today (see Figure 2.23). Alexander's mole became buried under layers of silt to form the isthmus between Tyre and the mainland.

had been built to shield it, and burned down all the siege engines that the fire from the ship had not reached.

[6] Alexander ordered his men to widen the mole, starting from the shore, so it could accommodate more towers, and instructed the engineers to furnish new siege engines. When these had been prepared, he set out for Sidon,[6a] taking the shield-bearers and the Agrianians, to collect all the triremes that lay ready for him there. For it appeared impossible to conduct the siege while the Tyrians retained the upper hand at sea.

[1] Meanwhile Gerostratos, the king of Arados, and Enylos of Byblos[1a] had learned that their cities were in Alexander's hands.[1b] Leaving Autophradates and his ships,[1c] they went to Alexander with their own fleet and the Sidonians' triremes. Thus Alexander was joined by some eighty Phoenician ships. [2] In the same days there arrived nine triremes from Rhodes,[2a] including their so-called patrol ship, three from Soloi and Mallos,[2b] ten from Lycia,[2c] and a fifty-oared ship from Macedonia[2d] in which Proteas son of Andronikos was captain. [3] Not much later the kings of Cyprus also touched at Sidon with nearly a hundred and twenty ships. For they had heard of Darius' defeat at Issus and were alarmed to learn that all of Phoenicia was now in Alexander's power. Alexander granted all these men an amnesty for past offenses, on the assumption that they had joined the Persian fleet more under duress than by choice.

[4] While his war engines were being built and the ships were being equipped for attack and for service in a naval engagement, Alexander set out for Arabia,[4a] to the Antilibanus range,[4b] taking some of the cavalry squadrons, the shield-bearers, the Agrianians, and the archers.[4c] [5] Capturing a number of places there—occupying some by force, and bringing others to terms—he returned to Sidon ten days later and met up with Kleandros son of Polemokrates, who had arrived from the Peloponnese with nearly four thousand Greek mercenaries.[5a]

[6] When his fleet had been organized, Alexander embarked as many shield-bearers on his decks as seemed to him sufficient for the action, in case the battle's outcome should hinge less on breaking the enemy's line than on fighting at close quarters.[6a] Starting from Sidon, he sailed against

2.19.6
TYRE
Alexander orders construction of a wider mole, and takes steps to procure ships.

2.20.1–3
TYRE
The Phoenicians serving in Persia's navy, learning that their home cities are already in Macedonian hands, begin to desert to Alexander.

2.20.4–5
Summer 332
TYRE-SIDON
While his navy and siege equipment are being readied, Alexander leads a raid into the interior.

2.20.6–8
SIDON-TYRE
Alexander sails from Sidon to Tyre with his newly constituted navy.

2.19.6a Sidon: Map 2.16, Phoenicia inset.
2.20.1a Arados; Byblos: Map 2.16, Phoenicia inset.
2.20.1b The Phoenician Gerostratos had up to this point supported the Persians. Gerostratos' son Straton had earlier surrendered Arados to Alexander in his father's absence (see 2.13.7–8).
2.20.1c That is, leaving the Persian navy, which was at this point trying to secure Persian interests in the Aegean.
2.20.2a Rhodes (Rhodos): Map 2.16, Aegean inset.
2.20.2b Soloi; Mallos: Map 2.16, Phoenicia inset.
2.20.2c Lycia: Map 2.5.
2.20.2d Macedonia: Map 2.16, Aegean inset.
2.20.4a Arabia: Map 2.16.
2.20.4b The Antilibanus mountain range (Map 2.16, Phoenicia inset) forms the eastern side of the valley today known as Bekáa,

in modern Lebanon.
2.20.4c Arrian gives no account of this raid and no explanation of its purpose. Quintus Curtius (4.3.1) says that local tribes had mounted attacks on the Macedonian parties gathering timber for shipbuilding.
2.20.5a Kleandros was sent much earlier to the Peloponnese to hire mercenaries (1.24.2). The outcome of the battle of Issus had no doubt made the job of such recruiters vastly easier, just as it had increased the rate of defections from Darius.
2.20.6a That is, Alexander relied on soldiers who could board enemy ships and overcome their crews, rather than on oarsmen who could give his ships the speed and maneuverability they would need to ram and sink Tyrian vessels.

Tyre, his fleet drawn up in battle array. He himself commanded the right wing (toward the open ocean) in company with the kings of the Cyprians and all the Phoenicians except Pnytagoras,[6b] who with Krateros commanded the left wing of the entire line.[6c]

[7] The Tyrians had previously decided to accept a battle at sea if Alexander brought his ships against them. But now, having unexpectedly caught sight of a vast number of ships—they had not learned before this that Alexander had all the Cyprian and Phoenician vessels— [8] and finding themselves faced with an organized attack—for just before touching at the city, Alexander's fleet had taken up a position, hoping to tempt the Tyrians to fight at sea, and when the Tyrians did not put to sea against them, the fleet had surged forward with a great plashing of oars—the Tyrians decided not to give battle.[8a] Having tightly blocked their harbors' entrances with as many triremes as could fit there, they were standing guard to prevent an enemy fleet coming to anchor in any of these harbors.

[9] When the Tyrians did not put to sea against him, Alexander began naval operations against the city. He decided not to force his way into the harbor facing Sidon, as its mouth was narrow and he saw that many triremes were blocking its entrance, their prows facing seaward. The Phoenicians, however, falling on the three Tyrian triremes moored farthest out, attacked them prow to prow and sank them. The shipwrecked crews had no trouble swimming to the friendly shore. [10] For the time being Alexander's ships anchored along the shore, not far from the newly built mole, where there appeared to be a shelter from the winds.

The next day, Alexander ordered the Cyprians and Andromakhos, the admiral, to blockade the city at the harbor facing Sidon, and the Phoenicians to do the same at the harbor beyond the mole, where his own tent was pitched.[10a]

[1] By that time Alexander had brought many engineers from Cyprus and from all over Phoenicia, and several war engines had been built—some on the mole, others on the horse-transport ships he had brought from Sidon, still others on some of the slower-sailing triremes.[1a] [2] When everything was ready, they brought the engines forward down the newly built mole and from

2.20.6b   Pnytagoras was king of the city of Salamis on Cyprus.

2.20.6c   It is extraordinary how easily Alexander and Krateros, land warriors from childhood seeing their first action at sea, here take command of a naval contingent.

2.20.8a   The broken syntax and breathless pacing of this sentence reproduces the Greek original. Arrian has here tried to capture stylistically the panic of the Tyrians as they see their hopes suddenly dashed.

2.20.10a   The goal of this maneuver was to prevent the Tyrian ships from leaving harbor to interfere with Alexander's naval operations or the construction of his mole.

2.21.1a   Diodorus (17.43.1 and 17.45.1–4) goes into more detail regarding the technological innovations introduced by both sides

during this siege. Alexander's engineers devised catapults large enough to hurl stones capable of smashing the Tyrian walls, apparently the first time artillery weapons had been used against fortifications rather than personnel. The Tyrians for their part made cushions out of hides stuffed with seaweed to absorb the impact of the stones, and further warded them off with some sort of wheel-like device that deflected missile fire as it spun around. Phoenicians were famous in antiquity for their engineering skill, so it is not surprising that Alexander recruited much of the local talent into his army or that both sides in the conflict made rapid advances in military technology over the course of the seven-month siege.

the ships anchored here and there near the wall, and set about putting the wall's strength to the test. [3] The Tyrians, meanwhile, set wooden towers on the battlements facing the mole, from which they meant to fight off the enemy. And whenever the engines came within range, the Tyrians defended themselves by firing their weapons, including flaming arrows that they shot at the enemy ships, so as to terrify the Macedonians seeking to approach the wall. [4] (The Tyrian walls that faced the mole were about 150 feet high and proportionately thick,[4a] and were built of huge stones embedded in cement.)

At the same time, the Macedonian horse-transport ships and the triremes bringing engines to the wall encountered another difficulty: a great many rocks had been cast into the sea, and these prevented the Macedonians from attacking at close range. [5] Alexander decided to pull these rocks from the water, but this job was achieved with difficulty as it had to be done from ships rather than on firm ground; and further trouble was given by the Tyrians, who had covered some of their own ships with armor and regularly sailed past the triremes' anchors and severed their cords, making it hard for the Macedonian ships to remain in place. [6] Alexander armored several thirty-oared ships in the same way and stationed them at an oblique angle in front of the triremes to protect their anchors; even so, divers set about cutting the cords underwater, but the Macedonians foiled the divers by lowering anchors secured with chains instead of cords. [7] From the mole[7a] they now began to fasten nooses to the rocks and pull them from the sea; then, raising them aloft with the engines, they dropped them into the deep water where they would no longer jut out and cause harm. Wherever the approach to the wall had been cleared of obstacles, the ships could now be brought near with no difficulty.

[8] Sorely pressed in every way, the Tyrians decided to launch an attack on the Cyprian ships blockading the harbor facing Sidon.[8a] For many days they hid the mouth of the harbor with stretched-out sails, so that they might not be observed manning their triremes. About midday, when Alexander's sailors had dispersed on necessary errands, and Alexander himself, having left the fleet at the other side of the city, had withdrawn to his tent, [9] the Tyrians, manning three quinquiremes, three quadriremes, and seven triremes[9a]

2.21.4–7
TYRE
Alexander struggles to clear the waters off Tyre so that his ships can bring their weaponry to bear on the walls, while the Tyrians work to prevent him.

2.21.8–9
TYRE
The desperate Tyrians plan a naval sally from their blockaded harbor.

2.21.4a The measurement is regarded by Bosworth (I.247) as a gross exaggeration. It is indeed difficult to imagine that Alexander could have constructed a siege tower high enough to overtop such a wall, but other historians have accepted Arrian's figure without challenge.

2.21.7a It is surprising to find the men on the mole suddenly entering into the task of clearing the rocks, which up to this point has involved only those on the ships. Perhaps from the height of the siege towers they were able to get a better view of the underwater rocks, so as to more accurately lasso them, and better leverage with which to haul them up.

2.21.8a The goal of this move was, presumably, to clear a passageway for a concerted naval attack on the ship-mounted Macedonian siege machines.

2.21.9a The prefixes in the terms "trireme" (*tri-* meaning "three"), "quadrireme" (*quadri-*, "four"), and "quinquireme" (*quinqui-*, "five"), are Latin numbers rather than Greek since our standard ship names come from the Romans. They seem to refer to the number of oarsmen manning each set of oars, though there is dispute about this. In a trireme, rowers sat on three vertically aligned decks, one man to an oar, so that each column of oars totaled three rowers (see Figure D.2). The quadriremes and quinquiremes developed later seem to have used only two oars per column but with larger oars worked by either two or three men each, allowing for more thrust and better efficiency.

FIGURE 2.21. The *Olympias*, a modern reconstruction of a Greek trireme, advancing under oar power with its sails furled. Its ancient forerunners would, however, have left the sails and masts on shore to lighten the vessel for combat.

with their sharpest crews and with those best equipped to fight from the decks and most courageous in naval warfare, rowed out with oars almost motionless, in single file at first and without anyone calling out the oar-strokes.[9b] Then, as they were turning toward the Cyprians and were almost in sight, they raised a great shout, urging one another on, and bore down on the enemy, straining eagerly at their oars.

2.22.1–5
Summer 332
TYRE
Alexander rushes to the relief of the blockading force as the Tyrians set about destroying it. The Tyrians are chased back into their harbor with many ships lost.

[1] On that day it happened that when Alexander withdrew to his tent he did not stay there as usual, but returned after a short time to the ships. [2] The Tyrians, falling unexpectedly upon the moored ships, found some of them quite empty; others, in the uproar of the attack, manned with difficulty by those who happened to be at hand. In the first charge the Tyrians quickly sank the quinquiremes of King Pnytagoras, Androkles the Amathusian, and Pasikrates of Curium;[2a] then they drove all the other ships onto the beach and began smashing them apart.

[3] When Alexander saw the Tyrians' triremes making a breakout, he gave orders for most of his ships, once each was manned, to take up a position at the mouth of the harbor and thereby prevent the other Tyrian ships

2.21.9b Arrian here supplies vivid details of how a sneak attack by ship was carried out. To prevent splashing noises the oars were worked in a very gentle manner, and the *keleustes* who normally provided a beat to the rowers instead kept silent. By keeping in single file the Tyrian ships were pre-

sumably better able to stay behind the screen of sailcloth they had stretched across the harbor entrance.
2.22.2a For Pnytagoras see n. 2.20.6b. He, Androkles, and Pasikrates were all Phoenician dynasts ruling cities in Cyprus.

from sailing out. He himself, taking the quinquiremes he had with him and about five triremes that had got their crews aboard first, sailed around the city to attack the Tyrian ships that had broken out of the harbor. [4] Meanwhile, the Tyrians watching from the walls, catching sight of the enemy attack and seeing Alexander himself on board, shouted to the men on their own ships to turn back; and when their shouts went unheard in the hubbub of those engaged in combat, they tried all kinds of signals to get them to retreat. When the Tyrian ships became aware, too late, of Alexander's attack, they turned back and tried to flee to the harbor. [5] A few managed to escape, but most were assaulted by Alexander's ships; some were disabled, and a quinquireme and a quadrireme were seized right at the harbor's entrance. The crews, however, suffered few casualties; they swam into the harbor with no difficulty when they saw their ships in enemy hands.

[6] Now that the Tyrians could no longer use their ships to improve their chances, the Macedonians brought their siege engines up to the wall. Those that they moved up along the mole proved ineffectual, due to the thickness of the wall, so some of their ships, carrying other such machines, were brought to the side of the city facing Sidon. [7] But when nothing was achieved there either, Alexander moved southward to the wall facing Egypt and tested its strength at every point. And there, after a lengthy battering, the wall crumbled and was even breached in a small part. After bridging the opening with gangways, Alexander made a brief try at an assault, but the Tyrians had no trouble beating back the Macedonians.

[1] Two days later, having waited for a calm, Alexander called his battalion commanders into action and brought the engines mounted on his ships against the city. He first pounded at the wall for a considerable time, and when the breach seemed wide enough, he ordered the ships carrying the siege engines to withdraw; [2] he then brought up two other ships carrying the gangways he intended to throw across the breach in the wall. The shield-bearers took one of the ships (the one in which Admetos[2a] was serving); Koinos' battalion, the so-called *asthetairoi*,[2b] took the other. Alexander himself intended to mount the wall with his shield-bearers wherever he could. [3] To the triremes he gave orders to sail toward both harbors in case they could force an entrance while the Tyrians were occupied in resisting his own party. The ships that had projectiles to be fired from engines and those carrying archers on their decks were ordered to sail around the wall and make landings wherever this could be managed, or to hold their position within range until they had an opportunity to land, so that the Tyrians, assailed from all sides, would not know which way to turn in the terror of the moment.

2.22.6–7
TYRE
The Macedonians now move their siege engines into position and open a breach in a portion of the wall.

2.23.1–3
TYRE
The final assault on Tyre: Alexander prepares to force an entry through the breached wall.

2.23.2a Admetos is not otherwise known.
2.23.2b The term *asthetairoi* has drawn much comment among scholars. It is found only in Arrian's *Anabasis Alexandrou*, in six passages (here and at 4.23.1, 5.22.6, 6.61, 6.21.3, and 7.11.3), all of which clearly refer to some sort of elite infantry status. But just what

troops fell under the heading *asthetairoi*, or what the term means, is unclear. Some editors of Arrian's text believe that in all these passages the word *asthetairoi* arose through scribal error and should be replaced by the more familiar term for phalangites, *pezetairoi*, or "infantry companions."

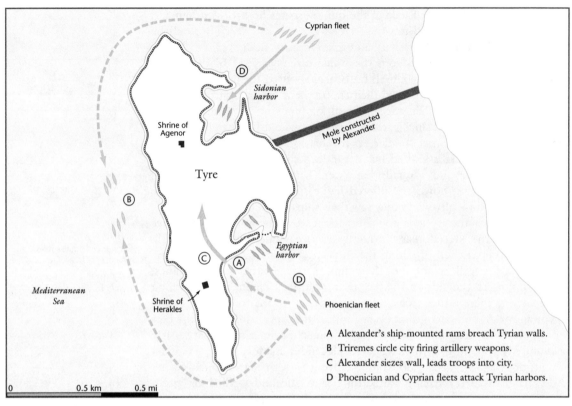

Cyprian fleet

Ⓓ

Sidonian harbor

Shrine of Agenor

Mole constructed by Alexander

Tyre

Ⓑ

Ⓒ   Ⓐ

Egyptian harbor

Mediterranean Sea

Shrine of Herakles

Ⓓ

Phoenician fleet

A Alexander's ship-mounted rams breach Tyrian walls.
B Triremes circle city firing artillery weapons.
C Alexander siezes wall, leads troops into city.
D Phoenician and Cyprian fleets attack Tyrian harbors.

0   0.5 km   0.5 mi

MAP 2.23. THE FINAL ASSAULT ON TYRE AS DESCRIBED AT 2.23–2.24.1. The assault was carried out entirely from Alexander's ships, which by this time had gained mastery of the seas around the city. The mole that had been built at such great cost seems not to have been used at this stage.

2.23.4–6
Summer 332
TYRE
Using gangways, the Macedonians swarm onto the breached wall. A soldier named Admetos is the first to mount the wall, and is instantly killed by a spear. Alexander and his men follow after and capture the wall.

[4] When Alexander's ships approached the city and the gangways were thrown onto the wall from their decks, the shield-bearers used them to climb boldly onto the wall. Admetos proved a brave man on that occasion, and Alexander too went in with them, taking an energetic part in the action and bearing witness to any glorious exploit undertaken in the heat of the action. [5] The wall was captured first at the point where Alexander had stationed himself—the Tyrians were beaten back from it with no difficulty—since for the first time the Macedonians had an approach that was sturdy and not too steep. Admetos mounted the wall first, and as he cheered his men onward, he was struck by a spear and died on the spot. [6] Coming up after him, Alexander and his Companions took the wall.

When some of the towers and their curtain walls were under his control, Alexander proceeded across the battlements to the palace, as the way down into the city appeared easier from there.

FIGURE 2.23. Aerial view of Tyre in 1934. The mole built by Alexander has silted up, forming a land bridge to the mainland.

[1] As for the men on the ships, the Phoenicians, who were moored at the harbor facing Egypt, forced their way in by tearing apart the booms and set about destroying the ships in the harbor, ramming some in the open water and driving others onto the shore. Meanwhile, the Cyprians at the harbor facing Sidon (which did not have a protecting boom) sailed in and immediately captured that part of the town. [2] Most of the Tyrians abandoned the wall when they saw it had been seized. Gathering at a place called the shrine of Agenor,[2a] they went on the attack against the Macedonians, at which point Alexander, advancing against them with his shield-bearers, cut down some who stood and fought there and pursued others who fled.

[3] The slaughter was great, now that those advancing from the harbor were already in control of the town and Koinos' battalion[3a] had entered it as well. The Macedonians advanced, most of them in a rage: they were vexed at the delay caused by the siege, and because the Tyrians had earlier seized

2.24.1–2
TYRE
Alexander's ships get control of both of Tyre's harbors. The Tyrians withdraw from the walls and attempt a last stand at a shrine, but are defeated.

2.24.3–4
TYRE
The Macedonians vent their rage on the Tyrian population, resulting in a tremendous slaughter.

2.24.2a Shrine of Agenor: Map 2.23.
2.24.3a Koinos' battalion consisted of the *asthetairoi*

who had accompanied Alexander in the assault on the breach at 2.23.2.

93

some of their men sailing from Sidon, the Macedonians made them mount the wall so they might be seen from the army's encampment, and cut their throats and flung their bodies into the sea. [4] Nearly eight thousand Tyrians perished;[4a] as for the Macedonians, in the actual assault they lost Admetos, who had proved his bravery as the first man to capture the wall, and twenty shield-bearers. In the course of the entire siege, about four hundred Macedonians died.

[5] Alexander granted an amnesty to all who had fled to the shrine of Herakles,[5a] a group that included a number of Tyrians who held high office, King Azemilkos, and some ambassadors from Carthage who had come to the mother city to pay homage to Herakles according to an ancient custom.[5b] He enslaved all the others: some thirty thousand Tyrians and foreigners were caught and sold.[5c]

[6] Alexander sacrificed to Herakles and in honor of that god held a parade of the armed forces and a naval procession. He also held athletic games and a torch race in the sacred precinct. As for the siege engine with which the wall had been breached, he dedicated this machine in the temple.[6a] He also dedicated the Tyrian ship sacred to Herakles, which he had seized in the naval attack, and affixed an inscription on it, composed by either himself or another, that is not worth recording (which is why I have not taken the trouble to record it).

Thus was Tyre captured, in the month of Hekatombaion, during Niketos' archonship at Athens.[6b]

[1] While Alexander was still engaged in the siege of Tyre, envoys arrived from Darius to report that their King was prepared to give Alexander ten thousand talents for the return of his mother, wife, and children; he also proposed that the entire territory from the Euphrates to the Greek Sea[1a] be Alexander's and that Alexander marry Darius' daughter and become his friend and ally.[1b] [2] When these proposals were announced in an assembly of the Companions, Parmenion reportedly said to Alexander that if he were Alexander he would be content, on those terms, to end the war and run no further risks. Alexander replied that if he were Parmenion, he would do likewise, but since he was

2.24.5
Summer 332
TYRE
Alexander oversees final rituals and settlements at Tyre. Thirty thousand are enslaved.

2.24.6
TYRE
Alexander at last makes the sacrifice to Tyrian Herakles he had requested seven months earlier. He leads celebratory games and rituals in honor of his victory.

2.25.1–3
TYRE
Darius again tries to negotiate a peace with Alexander, offering him half of the Persian empire, a large sum of money, and alliance by marriage. Alexander rejects the offer against the advice of Parmenion.

2.24.4a　Both Diodorus (17.46.4) and Quintus Curtius (4.4.17) give lower figures for the Tyrian dead but also claim that Alexander ordered the crucifixion of a further two thousand military-age males.

2.24.5a　Shrine of Herakles: Map 2.23.

2.24.5b　Carthage (Map 2.16) was founded as a colony of Tyre, and the Carthaginians continued to make ceremonial visits to Tyre at the time of the rites of Melqart. It is also worth noting that the Tyrians, according to Arrian, had expected aid from Carthage in the present siege; perhaps these ambassadors had arrived in connection with that anticipated aid, which never in fact materialized. Alexander, according to Quintus Curtius (4.3.19), declared war on Carthage at the moment of his victory at Tyre.

2.24.5c　Diodorus (17.46.4) gives a much lower

number of enslaved, thirteen thousand.

2.24.6a　Technological triumphs, like spoils of war, were often "dedicated" in temples in the Greek world, that is, set up as both an offering to the god and a showpiece to impress visitors. In the sixth century a Greek engineer named Mandrokles, after building a bridge across the Bosporus that allowed Darius I to invade Europe, dedicated a painting of the bridge in a temple of Hera (Herodotus, *Histories* 4.88).

2.24.6b　The fall of Tyre took place in early August, 332. The month of Hekatombaion in the Attic calendar was roughly July/August.

2.25.1a　By "Greek Sea" Arrian means the Aegean Sea (Map 2.16, Aegean inset). Euphrates River: Map 2.16.

2.25.1b　See n. 2.14.3a regarding the variant versions of Darius' letters in the different sources.

Alexander, he would answer Darius as he did in fact answer him. [3] For he said he had no need of Darius' money nor of any part of the country instead of the whole, since the money and the entire country were his. And he would marry Darius' daughter if he wished to; he would marry her even if Darius failed to offer her.[3a] He urged Darius to come to him in person if he wished to be treated generously. When Darius heard this, he gave up hope of coming to terms with Alexander, and again set about preparing for war.

[4] Alexander now decided to launch his expedition to Egypt.[4a] All of so-called Palaistinian Syria had already come over to him except a eunuch named Batis[4b] who held power in the city of Gaza.[4c] Batis had brought in Arab mercenaries and over a long period of time had stored up enough food for a long siege. Confident that the place would never be taken by force, he decided not to let Alexander enter the city.

[1] Gaza lies nearly two and a half miles from the sea. One ascends to it across deep sands, and the sea by the city is formed wholly of shoal water. Gaza was a large city, built on a high mound and surrounded by a strong wall. It was the last city one passed on the way from Phoenicia[1a] to Egypt before entering the desert.

[2] When Alexander first approached the city, he made camp where the wall appeared particularly vulnerable, and ordered that siege engines be put together.[2a] The engineers, however, argued that owing to the height of the mound it would be impracticable to attempt to capture the city by force. [3] But in Alexander's view, the harder the conquest, the more it should be attempted; the exploit would greatly astound his enemies by its unexpectedness, whereas a failure to capture the city, if reported to the Greeks and to Darius, would disgrace him. It was decided to heap up a mound around the city so that, from atop this mound, the siege engines could be brought against the walls on a level plane. The mound was mainly raised at the southern wall, where the city appeared more vulnerable.

[4] When the Macedonians judged that the mound had been raised to the proper height, they set the engines upon it and brought them forward to the walls of Gaza. And at that point, as Alexander was sacrificing—he had been garlanded, and was about to slaughter the first victim, according to custom[4a]—a bird of prey flew over the altar and dropped onto his head a stone it had been carrying in its claws. Alexander asked the seer Aristandros what the omen meant, and he replied, "Sire, you will capture the city, but today you must take care to protect yourself."

2.25.4
Autumn 332
GAZA
Alexander sets a course for Egypt; Gaza, an important city on the way, prepares to resist.

2.26.1
GAZA
Gaza's formidable defenses include its location atop a high mound.

2.26.2–3
GAZA
Alexander camps outside Gaza's walls and begins siege operations, despite the misgivings of his engineers. He orders the army to build a mound adjoining the one that protects Gaza, bringing the siege engines level with the city walls.

2.26.4
GAZA
As Alexander prepares to attack the walls, a bird drops a stone on his head. Aristandros interprets this event as an omen that the king may be wounded in the coming battle.

2.25.3a Alexander did in fact marry Darius' eldest daughter in 324. See Appendix K, §9.
2.25.4a Egypt: Map 2.16.
2.25.4b Batis was probably a Persian installed in Gaza as puppet ruler or garrison commander. His name is given as Betis or Babemesis by other sources. For his fate, see n. 2.27.7a.
2.25.4c Palaistinian Syria; Gaza: Map 2.16, Phoenicia inset.
2.26.1a Phoenicia: Map 2.16, Phoenicia inset.

2.26.2a Either the siege engines from Tyre had not yet arrived (see 2.27.3 and n. 2.27.3a) or, more likely, they had been broken down into sections for easier transport and were now reassembled.
2.26.4a Alexander was scrupulous in his religious observances throughout his reign. Here, before undertaking a major assault, he conducts a sacrifice to seek the favor of the gods, wearing a garland on his head as was customary in such rituals.

FIGURE 2.27. Drawing of a torsion-driven artillery weapon of the kind used by Alexander. The bow at the front was drawn back by the winch at the rear, twisting taut a set of ropes or hairs. The bow was then yanked forward by the sudden untwisting of the ropes when the winch was released.

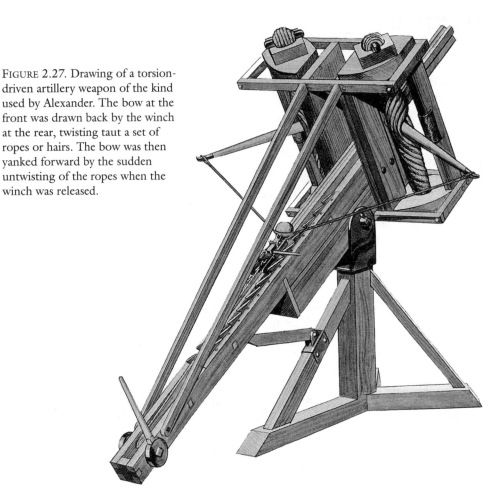

2.27.1–2
Autumn 332
GAZA
Alexander ignores the omen and is wounded by a catapult shot in the shoulder.

[1] When Alexander heard this, he held himself back for a time near the siege engines and out of range of enemy fire. But when the Arabs charged out from the city, set fire to the engines, used the heights to bombard the Macedonians who defended themselves below, and sought to thrust them from the raised mound, Alexander either intentionally disobeyed the seer or, distracted in the heat of battle, failed to recall the prophecy. Taking the shield-bearers with him, he rushed to aid the Macedonians where they were pressed hardest. [2] He kept them from being forced from the mound into shameful flight, but was himself hit by a shot from a catapult; it passed through his shield and breastplate and struck his shoulder. When he realized that Aristandros had been right about the wound, he was delighted, since he thought that in light of Aristandros' prophecy he would also capture the city.

[3] Alexander's wound proved difficult to treat. But meanwhile, the siege engines with which Alexander had captured Tyre had been sent for, and they now arrived by sea. Alexander ordered a mound to be raised up around the city on all sides, nearly 400 yards wide and 250 feet tall.[3a] [4] When his engines had been built and brought up to the mound and used to batter the wall down over a good distance, and when underground passages had been dug here and there and the soil carried away without the enemy noticing, the wall fell in ruins in many places, subsiding over the space that had been hollowed out. With their artillery[4a] the Macedonians were controlling a large area and driving the defenders from their towers. The inhabitants withstood three assaults, though many of their men were dead or wounded. [5] On the fourth, however, Alexander advanced the Macedonian phalanx from all sides. At one point he threw down the undermined wall, while at another he broke apart a long stretch that had already been pounded by his engines, so that the assault with ladders, where the wall had fallen in ruins, was easily managed.

[6] The ladders were placed against the wall, whereupon all the Macedonians who claimed some measure of courage competed to be the first to take the wall; the first man to do so was Neoptolemos, one of the Companions and a member of the Aiakid clan.[6a] Battalion after battalion now climbed up with their officers. [7] As soon as a number of the Macedonians had entered the fortress, they broke open the various gates as they reached them and let in the entire army. The people of Gaza, though their city was now occupied, nevertheless joined battle, and all who resisted there perished, each man where he had been posted.[7a] Alexander enslaved their women and children. After peopling the city with neighboring tribesmen, he used Gaza as a stronghold for conducting the war.

2.27.3–5
GAZA
The siege engines used at Tyre arrive and, from atop the new mound, are put to work against the walls of Gaza. After numerous attempts the Macedonians succeed in forcing a large breach.

2.27.6–7
GAZA
The Macedonians take the wall and open the gates to the rest of the army, killing all those who continue to fight. Later, Alexander orders the women and children enslaved and resettles Gaza with supporters of his cause.

2.27.3a This command seems to repeat what Alexander had already ordered and his engineers had accomplished at 2.26.3–4. It seems likely that Arrian has recorded a duplicate account of the same action, perhaps because he was working from two main sources, the histories of Ptolemy and Aristoboulos. Alternatively, one might suppose that Alexander here orders a complete circuit mound, whereas before he had concentrated on Gaza's southern sector.
2.27.4a For more on artillery, see Appendix D, §6.
2.27.6a The Aiakids were the ruling family in Molossia, a region west of Macedonia that was closely allied to the Macedonian

royal house after the marriage of Philip to Olympias, Alexander's mother, a Molossian princess. They claimed descent from the mythic hero Neoptolemos, son of Achilles, and that claim enabled Alexander to believe (or claim) that he had the blood of Achilles in his veins.
2.27.7a Quintus Curtius (4.6.26–30) gives the figure of ten thousand killed in the assault on Gaza, and also reports that Alexander took a cruel revenge on Batis, dragging him still alive behind a chariot. There is no consensus about the veracity of this report, which is not confirmed by other sources.

BOOK THREE

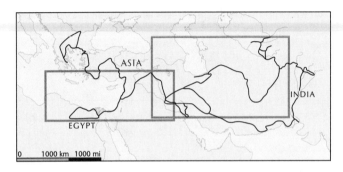

BOOK THREE: THE EGYPTIAN SOJOURN
AND THE CAMPAIGN AGAINST DARIUS

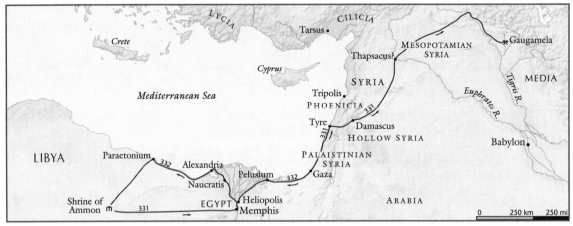

From Gaza to Egypt, and from Egypt to Gaugamela (3.1–3.15)

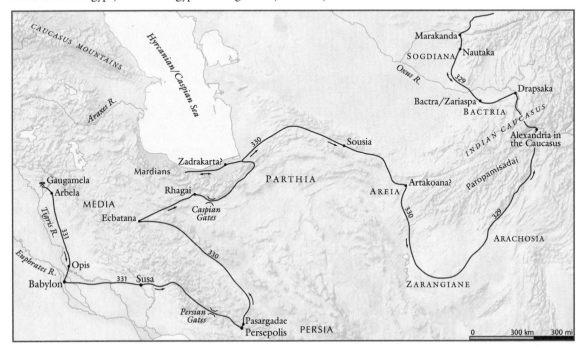

From Gaugamela to Sogdiana (3.16–3.30)

$\mathbb{A}$lexander now started for Egypt,[1a] and after a six-day march from Gaza reached Egyptian Pelusium.[1b] His navy had accompanied him, sailing along the coast, when he left Phoenicia[1c] for Egypt, and it was already moored at Pelusium when he arrived. [2] Mazakes the Persian, who had been appointed satrap[2a] of Egypt by Darius, had been informed about the battle at Issus and Darius' disgraceful flight and the fact that Phoenicia, Syria,[2b] and the greater part of Arabia[2c] were in Alexander's power; having no Persian forces available, Mazakes received Alexander amicably in the cities and the country. [3] Alexander established a garrison at Pelusium, and after commanding his officers to sail up the river as far as Memphis, he himself proceeded to Heliopolis, keeping the Nile[3a] on his right. After taking control of all the places along his route, which were all surrendered by their inhabitants, he marched across the desert and arrived in Heliopolis.

[4] From there he crossed the Nile and journeyed to Memphis, where he sacrificed to the gods and in particular to Apis,[4a] and held a competition in athletics and the arts. The most distinguished experts in these fields came from Greece to compete. From Memphis he sailed downriver toward the sea, taking the shield-bearers[4b] aboard ship as well as the archers, the Agrianians,[4c] and the royal squadron of the Companion cavalry.[4d] [5] On reach-

3.1.1–3
Winter 332/1
GAZA–NILE DELTA–HELIOPOLIS
Alexander turns westward and heads for Egypt. He arrives at Pelusium and meets no resistance from the satrap. Towns on his way to Heliopolis surrender to him.

3.1.4–5
MEMPHIS–NILE DELTA
After observing rites designed to cement his solidarity with the Egyptians, Alexander sails down the Nile to its delta. Thinking the mouth of the Nile to be a favorable location for a city, Alexander founds the first Alexandria there.

NOTE: Most locations in the text not identified by a footnote can be found in the Reference Maps section.

3.1.1a Egypt: Map 3.2, BX.
3.1.1b Gaza; Pelusium: Map 3.2, BY
3.1.1c Phoenicia: Map 3.2, AY.
3.1.2a The satraps, roughly two dozen in number, were appointed by the Persian king to administer the satrapies, or provinces, of the empire, collect taxes, and organize defense. For the locations of all Persian satrapies mentioned by Arrian, see Ref. Map 1.
3.1.2b Issus; Syria: Map 3.2, AY.
3.1.2c Arabia: Map 3.2, BY.
3.1.3a Memphis; Heliopolis; Nile River: Map 3.2, BY.
3.1.4a The cult of Apis, a deity who took the form of an unblemished bull, was indigenous to Egypt, and had been famously disrespected

by Egypt's Persian masters (see Herodotus, *Histories* 3.27–29). By pointedly including Apis in his rites of worship, Alexander was demonstrating to the Egyptians that his occupation of their country would be milder and more tolerant than that of the Persians.
3.1.4b The shield-bearers (*hypaspists*) were an elite corps of specially equipped infantry; see Appendix D, Alexander's Army and Military Leadership, §3.
3.1.4c Agrianians: as used by Arrian, usually refers to a light infantry division recruited from a Balkan region northeast of Macedonia (Map 3.2); see Appendix D, §6.
3.1.4d The Companion cavalry was an elite unit of horsemen typically led by the king himself as his principal striking arm. The subgroup of this unit known as the royal squadron was assigned to fight alongside the king in battle.

ing Canopus he sailed around Lake Mareotis and disembarked at the site of present-day Alexandria,[5a] the city named after him. The site struck him as very beautiful for a new settlement, and he imagined that a city founded there would prosper. A sudden passion for the project seized him, and he himself marked out where the marketplace was to be built and decided how many temples were to be erected and to which gods they were to be dedicated—the Greek gods as well as Egyptian Isis[5b]—and where the wall was to be built around the city. With these plans in mind he offered sacrifices, and the omens proved favorable.[5c]

[1] The following story is also told, and I, for one, find it credible. Alexander is said to have wanted to leave the builders with an outline of the proposed wall, but had nothing with which to mark the surface of the ground. It occurred to one of the builders to gather the barley meal the soldiers carried in their mess kits, and to lay it down along the ground where the king indicated. In this way the city's circuit wall was outlined. [2] The seers pondered this incident, particularly Aristandros of Telmessos, many of whose other predictions are said to have come true. They then predicted that the city would be prosperous in every way, especially with respect to the fruits of the earth.[1a]

[3] At that point Hegelokhos landed in Egypt and reported to Alexander that the Tenedians, having revolted from the Persians, had come over to their side (for the Tenedians had in fact taken the Persian side against their will) and that the people of Chios[3a] had invited his forces into the city in spite of the men occupying it, whom Autophradates and Pharnabazos[3b] had put in power. [4] Pharnabazos had been captured, as had Aristonikos the tyrant of Methymna,[4a] who had sailed into the harbor of Chios with five light ships belonging to pirates, not realizing that the harbor was in the power of Hegelokhos' forces; Aristonikos had been deceived by the men in control of the harbor's booms, who led him to believe that the fleet anchored there belonged to Pharnabazos. [5] Hegelokhos went on to say that all the pirates had been killed there by his men. However, he brought Aristonikos to Alexander, along with Apollonides the Chian, Phesinos, Megareus, and all the others who had taken part in the Chians' revolt and seized control of the island's government. [6] He had captured Mytilene from Khares, brought the other cities of Lesbos to terms, and sent Amphoteros with sixty ships to Cos[6a] at the

3.2.1–2
Winter 332/1
NILE DELTA
Seers predict that the city will flourish because the circuit of its walls is traced with lines of grain.

3.2.3–7
EGYPT
Hegelokhos, leader of the pro-Macedonian naval forces in the Aegean, arrives to report the total suppression of the Persian-backed insurrection there.

3.1.5a Canopus; Lake Mareotis; Alexandria (site of): Map 3.2, BX.
3.1.5b Egyptian Isis: another example of Alexander's policy of religious inclusiveness, like his sacrifice to Apis in Memphis.
3.1.5c Among our ancient sources, only Arrian and Plutarch (*Parallel Lives*, "Alexander" 26) date the founding of Alexandria to a point just prior to Alexander's visit to the Ammonion, the oracle or shrine of Ammon at what is now called the Siwa oasis. The other writers place it after Alexander's return from the shrine of Ammon. There is as yet no consensus among historians as to

which version is more credible.
3.2.1a In Plutarch (*Parallel Lives*, "Alexander" 26.8–10) and Quintus Curtius (4.8.6), the omen consists not just of the spreading of barley but also of the arrival of a flock of birds that devour it, giving more point to the interpretation.
3.2.3a Tenedos; Chios: Map 3.2, AX.
3.2.3b Autophradates and Pharnabazos were the Persian admirals who had inherited leadership of the Aegean counteroffensive after the death of Memnon (see 2.1.3).
3.2.4a Methymna: Map 3.2, AX.
3.2.6a Mytilene; Lesbos; Cos: Map 3.2, AX.

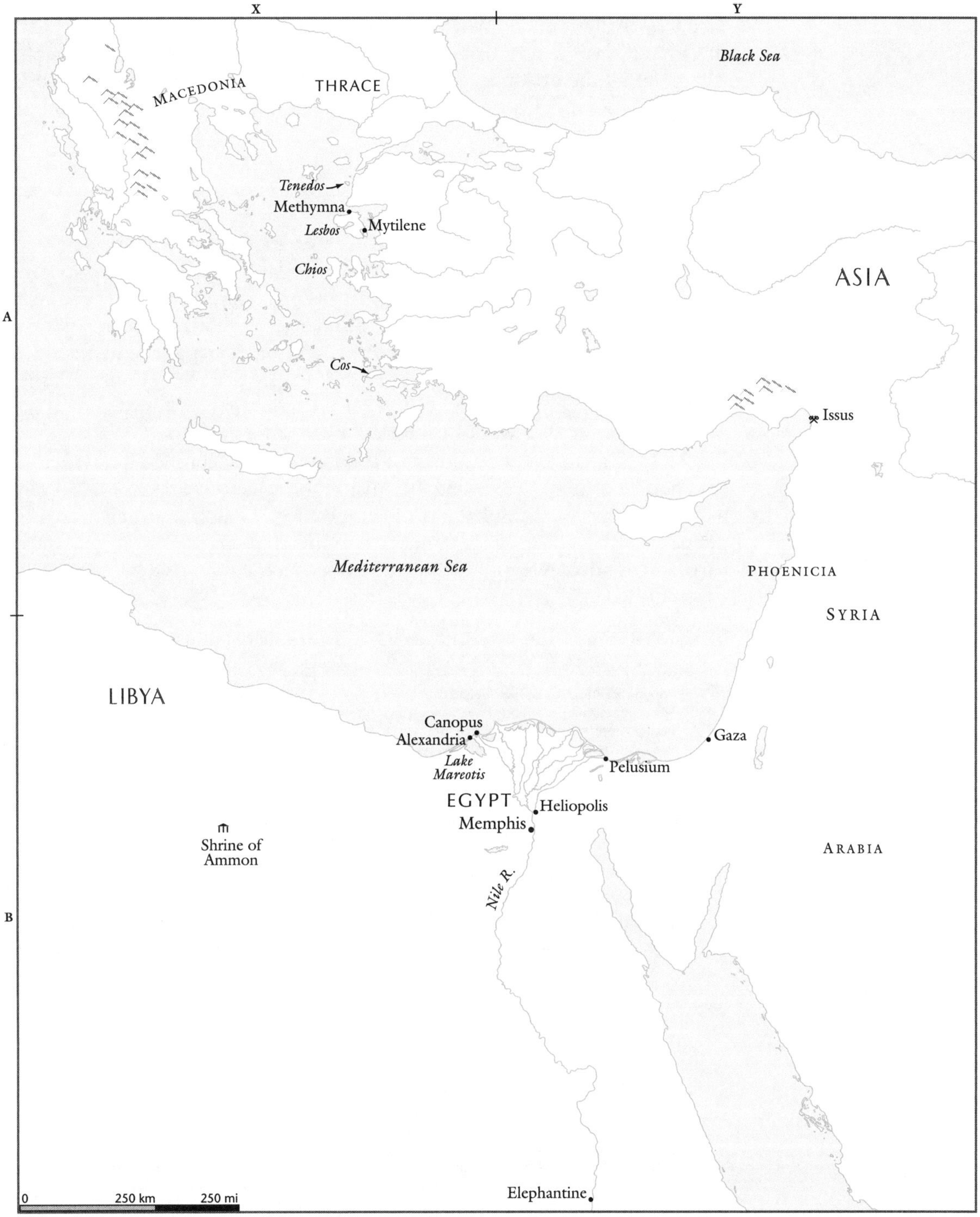

X | Y

Black Sea

MACEDONIA   THRACE

Tenedos
Methymna
Lesbos   Mytilene

Chios

ASIA

A

Cos

Issus

Mediterranean Sea

PHOENICIA

SYRIA

LIBYA

Canopus
Alexandria
Lake Mareotis   Gaza

Pelusium

EGYPT   Heliopolis
Memphis

ARABIA

Shrine of Ammon

Nile R.

B

0   250 km   250 mi

Elephantine

MAP 3.2

islanders' invitation; and when he had landed on Cos himself he found that the island was already in Amphoteros' hands. [7] Hegelokhos brought Alexander all the prisoners except Pharnabazos, who had eluded his guards on Cos.[7a] Alexander sent the tyrants back to their respective cities to be dealt with as the citizens wished, but sent Apollonides and the Chians under strict guard to Elephantine[7b] in Egypt.

[1] A sudden desire now seized Alexander to visit and consult Ammon[1a] in Libya,[1b] both because the oracle of Ammon was said to be truthful and because Perseus and Herakles had consulted it: the former when he was sent against the Gorgon by Polydektes, the latter when he was seeking Antaios in Libya and Bousiris in Egypt.[1c] [2] Alexander was engaged in a rivalry with Perseus and Herakles, as both heroes were his kinsmen.[2a] Moreover, he sought to trace his own birth to Ammon,[2b] just as the myths trace the births of Perseus and Herakles to Zeus. In any case, he set out with this in mind and imagined that he would obtain more precise knowledge of his own affairs, or at least would say he had obtained it.

[3] Taking the coastal route to Paraetonium,[3a] he traveled a distance of two hundred miles, according to Aristoboulos, across a land not wholly without water, but uninhabited. From Paraetonium he headed into the interior, to the oracle of Ammon. The route is deserted and for the most part sandy and waterless. [4] But Alexander met with considerable rainfall,

3.3.1–2
Winter 332/1
LIBYA
Arrian gives Alexander's reasons for wanting to visit the famous oracle of the god Ammon. Alexander sets off on a long march through the Libyan desert.

3.3.3–6
PARAETONIUM
Alexander reportedly receives divine aid on his march to the oracle.

3.2.7a This is the last we see of the Persian admiral Pharnabazos, though we know from other sources that he survived through the end of Alexander's reign. At some point this talented, esteemed Persian leader must have stopped fighting on Darius' behalf.

3.2.7b Those tyrants sent home to their native cities were promptly executed, as Alexander could have anticipated. The decision to keep the deposed Chian rulers under guard at Elephantine (Map 3.2, BY) posed a problem, in that Alexander's decree to the Chians, known from a recovered inscription, specified that all Persian agents captured on the island had to be tried by the Greek delegates assembled in Corinth. It is not clear why, or whether, Alexander made exception to his policy here.

3.3.1a The Egyptian god Ammon (or Ammun, or Amon-Re) had been absorbed into the Greek religious system, as had most Egyptian deities, by means of assimilation to a more familiar Hellenic figure, in this case Zeus. Hence he is often referred to by both ancient and modern writers as Zeus Ammon, and was depicted by the Greeks as a young male figure with ram's horns curling from his head. The shrine of Ammon (Map 3.5, BX) at modern Siwa, a Sahara Desert oasis in the northwest of Egypt, had been known to the Greek world for centuries as an important source of oracular prophecy, and many Greeks are known to have visited it in the fifth and fourth centuries. A cult of Ammon was established at Athens in the fourth century.

3.3.1b Libya: Map 3.2, BX. For the ancient Greeks, Libya was all of Africa (which to them meant

primarily North Africa) except for Egypt.

3.3.1c In Greek mythology, Perseus and Herakles were both sons of the god Zeus famous for fulfilling perilous quests. Perseus was ordered by Polydektes, a suitor of his mother, Danaë, to slay the Gorgon Medusa, while Herakles (among other labors) defeated the Libyan giant Antaios, a wrestler whose strength was invincible so long as he remained in contact with the ground. Neither hero is known from sources other than Arrian to have consulted the oracle at Ammon.

3.3.2a Alexander's family traced its descent from Herakles through Temenos, grandson of Herakles, a legendary ruler of Argos. His connection to Perseus is more obscure, and this offhand mention by Arrian is in fact the earliest record we have of it.

3.3.2b In this sentence, Arrian clearly states that even before visiting the shrine of Ammon, Alexander had conceived the idea that he was the son (not merely a lineal descendant) of the god Ammon. This is surprising information and, if reliable, holds important implications for the question of Alexander's self-conception; see Appendix C, Alexander the Man (and God?), §16. If Alexander was crowned pharaoh upon his entry into Memphis, this may have suggested to him the idea of divine parentage, since in the conception of the Egyptians, the reigning pharaoh was a son of Ammon. However, the crowning is reported only in the *Alexander Romance*, the least reliable of all the ancient sources, and there is no certainty among historians that it did indeed take place.

3.3.3a Paraetonium: Map 3.5, BX.

FIGURE 3.3. A typical coin issued
by Alexander's mints. The image
on the left is often misidentified as
his portrait. In fact it is Herakles,
his mythic ancestor, wearing the
helmet made from the impenetra-
ble skin of the Nemean lion. The
reverse shows Zeus seated on a
throne, holding an eagle and a
scepter, with the legend "Alexandrou" (Alexander's).

and this was attributed to the gods. The gods were also felt to be at work in
the following incident: Whenever the south wind blows in that country, it
buries the route in sand; the markings of the route disappear and it is
impossible to find one's way, just as in an ocean of sand. No mountain, tree,
or unshifting hill rises up by which wayfarers may judge their course, as
sailors do by the stars. Accordingly, Alexander's army went astray, and his
guides were in doubt. [5] Ptolemy says that two snakes, uttering sounds,
advanced in front of the army, and that Alexander ordered his officers to
follow them and to put their trust in the gods; the snakes led the way to the
oracle and back again. [6] But Aristoboulos says, and most other accounts
agree with him, that two ravens flew ahead of the army and became Alexander's guides. And I can confidently declare that divinity aided him in some
way, since such a view accords with what one might reasonably expect;[6a] but
the exact truth of the story has been lost in the welter of conflicting
accounts.

[1] The site of the shrine of Ammon[1a] is surrounded by a sandy and
waterless desert, yet this small area at the center, five miles wide at most, is
full of cultivated trees—olives and palms—and is the only place thereabouts
where dew forms. [2] The place has a spring unlike any other on earth: at
midday its water is cold to the taste and still more to the touch, as cold as
water can be; yet as the sun declines toward evening, the water grows
warmer, and from evening until midnight grows warmer still, reaching its
warmest at midnight. Past midnight it gradually cools, and by early morning is cold, though it is coldest at midday.[2a] This cycle is repeated every day.
[3] Also, salt deposits form there naturally and can be harvested by digging;
these are sometimes brought to Egypt by the priests of Ammon. For when-

3.4.1–4

SHRINE OF AMMON
Arrian describes the unusual
spring and salts of the oasis
where the temple is located.

3.3.6a   Arrian's reasoning here seems to be that,
         because the route to the shrine of Ammon
         was so difficult to find that Alexander could
         not have gotten there without the help of
         the gods.
3.4.1a   Shrine of Ammon (Ammun): Map 3.5, BX.
3.4.2a   A similar spring at the shrine of Ammon

is described by Herodotus (*Histories*
4.181.3–4) and labeled by him "the Spring
of the Sun." Modern visitors to the spring
have not found variations in temperature,
but the water does emit gases that might
give the impression of steam (Bosworth
II.273).

ever these priests journey to Egypt, they place the salt in baskets woven from palm leaves, and present it as a gift to the king of Egypt or to someone else. [4] The grains of this salt are large (some of them larger than three fingers' breadth) and as clear as crystal. Purer than sea salt, it is used in sacrifices by the Egyptians and by all who are scrupulous in their religious observances.

[5] Alexander marveled at the place and posed his questions to the god Ammon. When he had heard what his heart desired (as he said),[5a] he led the army back to Egypt, returning by the same road, according to Aristoboulos, though Ptolemy says they took another, a road that led straight to Memphis.

[1] Several embassies from Greece reached Alexander in Memphis,[1a] and he sent no envoy away without granting his requests. A force sent by Antipatros also arrived.[1b] It included some four hundred Greek mercenaries under the command of Menoitas son of Hegesandros and nearly five hundred horsemen from Thrace[1c] under Asklepiodoros son of Eunikos. [2] Alexander sacrificed to Zeus the King[2a] and held a parade of his armed forces and a competition in athletics and the arts. He then set Egypt's administrative affairs in order. He appointed two Egyptians, Doloaspis and Petisis, as governors of Egypt, and divided the territory of Egypt between them. But as Petisis declined the office, Doloaspis took over the entire realm. [3] As garrison commanders, Alexander appointed two Companions: Pantaleon of Pydna, in Memphis, and in Pelusium,[3a] Polemon son of Megakles of Pella. He appointed Lykidas of Aeolis to lead the mercenaries, and as their secretary he named Eugnostos son of Xenophantes, one of the Companions. As the Companions' overseers he named Aiskhylos and Ephippos son of Khalkides. [4] He granted rule over nearby Libya[4a] to Apollonios son of Kharinos, and that over Arabia near Heroonpolis[4b] to Kleomenes of Naucratis. Alexander ordered Kleomenes to allow the governors to rule

Sidebar

3.4.5
Winter 332/1
SHRINE OF AMMON
Alexander consults the oracle. After hearing "what his heart desired," he leads the army back to Egypt.

3.5.1–6
MEMPHIS
Alexander receives reinforcements and makes administrative arrangements for Egypt's governance.

Footnotes

3.4.5a Arrian pointedly gives no information about what Alexander asked or what answers he received. This reticence indicates to some historians that the entire interview between Alexander and the priests of the oracular shrine was conducted in private, without witnesses, and that all reports found in other sources about its content are fabrications. Nonetheless, those reports do exist and must be taken into account in any assessment of this episode. Plutarch (*Parallel Lives*, "Alexander" 27) quotes "most writers" for the report that Alexander asked whether his father's murderers had all been punished; the high priest urged him to correct his speech, since his father was not a mortal. Alexander then asked whether *Philip*'s murderers had been punished, along with another question: whether he himself was destined for world rule. The priest gave him assurance that he would indeed rule the globe and that Philip's assassins had been punished. (Diodorus Siculus [17.51.2–3] and Quintus Curtius [4.7.27–28] record very much the

same questions and answers as the ones Plutarch attributes to "most writers," but vary their order.) Plutarch then goes on to record a variant tradition, accepted by many scholars as genuine, according to which Alexander kept secret the details of his meeting with the priest of Ammon, but wrote to his mother, Olympias, that he would confide its substance to her, alone and in person, upon his return to Macedonia. On Alexander's relationship to Ammon, see Appendix C, §16.

3.5.1a Memphis: Map 3.5, BY.

3.5.1b This was one of many contingents of reinforcements sent to Alexander by Antipatros, head of the Macedonian home guard.

3.5.1c Thrace: Map 3.5, AX.

3.5.2a It is likely that the god in question was Ammon, from whose oracle Alexander had just returned. Ammon was commonly identified with Zeus by the Greeks.

3.5.3a Pelusium: Map 3.5, BY.

3.5.4a Libya: Map 3.5, BX.

3.5.4b Arabia; Heroonpolis: Map 3.5, BY.

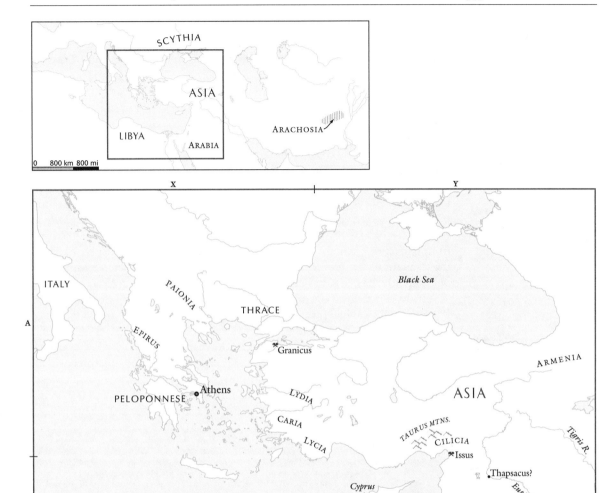

MAP 3.5

their own districts according to age-old custom, but to collect taxes from them himself; the governors were ordered to remit their taxes to Kleomenes.[4c] [5] He appointed Peukestas son of Makartatos and Balakros son of Amyntas as generals of the forces being left behind in Egypt; Polemon son of Theramenes was appointed as admiral of the fleet. In Arrhybas'[5a] place, Alexander appointed Leonnatos son of Onasos as Bodyguard,[5b] since Arrhybas had died of disease. [6] Antiokhos, the archers' commander, had also died, and in his place Alexander appointed Ombrion, a Cretan. He appointed Kalanos as commander of the allied infantry Balakros had led, since Balakros was being left behind in Egypt.

[7] It is said that Alexander, marveling at how strongly defended Egypt was by its natural position, distributed rule over the country among several persons, since he did not think it safe to entrust sovereignty of the whole land to a single man.[7a] And it seems to me that the Romans have learned from Alexander how to keep watch over Egypt, as they send no one from their senate to be governor; instead, Egypt's governor is selected from the body of citizens classed as knights.[7b]

[1] At the beginning of spring Alexander proceeded from Memphis to Phoenicia. The Nile[1a] was bridged for him at Memphis, as were all its canals. When he reached Tyre,[1b] his fleet[1c] had already arrived. Alexander again sacrificed to Herakles and held a competition in athletics and the arts. [2] The *Paralos*[2a] then arrived from Athens,[2b] bringing two ambassadors, Diophantos and Achilles; every man on board was also part of the embassy. These men obtained all the goals for which they had been sent out; Alexander even released all the Athenians captured at the Granicus.[2c] [3] When he

---

3.5.7
EGYPT
Alexander's overall principle was to divide power in Egypt so as to prevent it from rebelling against his rule.

3.6.1–3
Spring 331
PHOENICIA
Alexander returns to Asia to confront Darius once again. He also takes measures to deal with insurrection brewing in the Peloponnese.

3.5.4c Kleomenes was given financial but not political control over Egypt, in part to prevent his having too much power and autonomy. Alexander was well aware that Egypt had broken away several times from Persian imperial control, and that its natural defenses made it hard to reconquer; a rebellious governor there could give him considerable difficulty. Kleomenes did not in fact rebel, but his financial regime was infamous for extortion and abuse (see 7.23.6).

3.5.5a Apart from what Arrian tells us here, nothing else is known of this Arrhybas.

3.5.5b This is the same Leonnatos referred to by Arrian at 6.28.4 as "son of Anteas"; it is unclear which was his true patronymic. He was encountered earlier, at 2.12.5, where he served as Alexander's emissary to the Persian women captured at Issus. Apparently the term "Bodyguard" here refers to the coterie of seven officers who attended Alexander's person and not, as often, to an elite corps of men detailed to fight beside Alexander in battle; see Appendix E, Alexander's Inner Circle, §4.

3.5.7a That is, Alexander feared that a single subordinate, left in charge of such an easily defended place, would break away from his empire and found a separate kingdom. This fear was later borne out when, after Alexander's death, his general Ptolemy seized Egypt

and held it successfully through the strife-torn decades that followed, thus founding the Ptolemaic dynasty that endured until the coming of Julius Caesar in the mid first century (see the Epilogue, §8, 17).

3.5.7b Arrian here inserts a rare observation based on his own experience of imperial administration under the Romans. Rome, too, had apparently striven not to put an ambitious or powerful leader in charge of such a tempting prize as Egypt. With the Greek word *hippeas* ("knights") Arrian translates the Latin *equites*, a Roman aristocratic order ranking below the patricians or senatorial class. Because senators were barred by law from certain kinds of mercantile activities, tax farming—one of the principal obligations of the governor of Egypt—usually fell to the *equites*.

3.6.1a Memphis; Phoenicia; Nile River: Map 3.5, BY.
3.6.1b Tyre (Tyrus): Map 3.5, BY.
3.6.1c The ships under the command of Hegelokhos (see 3.2.3–7), which had completed their mission in the Aegean.
3.6.2a The *Paralos* was a sacred ship used by Athens for state diplomatic missions.
3.6.2b Athens: Map 3.5, AX.
3.6.2c Two years earlier Alexander had refused a similar request (see 1.29.5–6). Evidently he felt himself to be in a stronger position now, from which he could afford clemency.

FIGURE 3.5. A late-fourth-century Egyptian carving from the so-called Barque Shrine, in the Temple of Ammon at Luxor, shows Alexander as pharaoh receiving the ankh (a symbol of eternal life) from the god Horus. A hieroglyphic inscription indicates that the shrine was rebuilt on Alexander's orders, though no other written account of such a project exists.

received word of an uprising against him in the Peloponnese,[3a] he sent Amphoteros to aid the Peloponnesians who had been dependable in the war with Persia and who were not following the Spartans. The Phoenicians and Cyprians[3b] were ordered to send a hundred ships to the Peloponnese in addition to those Alexander was sending under Amphoteros' command.

[4] Alexander himself was now starting inland for Thapsacus and the River Euphrates,[4a] having appointed Koiranos of Beroia to collect taxes in Phoenicia, and Philoxenos to collect them in Asia west of the Taurus.[4b] In their place, as guard of the funds he had with him, Alexander appointed Harpalos son of Makhatas,[4c] who had just returned from exile.

3.6.4–8

PHOENICIA

Alexander makes administrative appointments and staff changes in Asia. Harpalos becomes royal treasurer after briefly deserting Alexander, then being restored to favor.

3.6.3a   Peloponnese: Map 3.5, AX. Apparently the revolt led by King Agis of Sparta is meant here, but there is some question as to whether it had begun by this point.
3.6.3b   Cyprus: Map 3.5, BY.
3.6.4a   Thapsacus, possible location; Euphrates

River: Map 3.5, BY.
3.6.4b   Taurus Mountains: Map 3.5, AY. By "Asia west of the Taurus," Arrian designates the Anatolian peninsula.
3.6.4c   Harpalos was one of Alexander's oldest friends; see Appendix E, §16.

109

[5] Harpalos had first gone into exile during Philip's reign[5a] because of his loyalty to Alexander. Ptolemy son of Lagos had been exiled for the same reason, as had Nearkhos son of Androtimos, Eriguios son of Larikhos, and Laomedon, Eriguios' brother. For Alexander and Philip had viewed each other with suspicion after the latter had married Eurydike and dishonored Olympias, Alexander's mother.[5b] [6] At Philip's death, everyone who had gone into exile on Alexander's account returned. Alexander appointed Ptolemy as Bodyguard, Harpalos as treasurer (since his body was unfit for warfare),[6a] Eriguios as cavalry commander of the allies, his brother Laomedon (who was bilingual) as commander of the barbarians taken in war, and Nearkhos as satrap of Lycia[6b] and the neighboring territory as far as the Taurus range.[6c] [7] Shortly before the battle of Issus,[7a] Harpalos was persuaded by Tauriskos, a despicable man, to desert with him.[7b] After making his way to Alexander of Epirus in Italy,[7c] Tauriskos died there, whereupon Harpalos fled to the Megarid.[7d] But Alexander persuaded him to return, after giving assurances that he would not suffer for his desertion. And no harm came to Harpalos on his return; in fact, he was again appointed treasurer.[7e]

Alexander sent Menandros, one of the Companions, to Lydia[7f] as satrap. [8] Klearkhos was ordered to take charge of the mercenaries Menandros had been commanding. In Arimmas' place as satrap of Syria,[8a] Alexander appointed Asklepiodoros son of Eunikos, since Arimmas was thought to have been slack in the preparations he had been ordered to make for the army's inland march.[8b]

3.6.5a Arrian here turns the clock back to 337 to recount the first departure of Harpalos from Alexander's side, a true "exile" imposed by Alexander's father. Harpalos departed from Alexander again in 331, as will be described at 3.6.7, this time in a voluntary flight (though Arrian uses the same Greek word to describe both episodes). It is this second "exile" from which he has just returned.

3.6.5b See Plutarch, *Parallel Lives*, "Alexander" 9–10, for more details. Of the five men Arrian says were exiled for Alexander's sake, all except Laomedon are mentioned by Plutarch; they were suspected of having urged Alexander to propose a marital liaison with a powerful Carian clan, in defiance of his father's wishes.

3.6.6a Harpalos suffered from a physical disability of a kind not specified by our sources.

3.6.6b Lycia: Map 3.5, AX.

3.6.6c It is interesting to note that, in this first major set of administrative appointments, Alexander relied heavily on friends from boyhood who had shown him great loyalty.

3.6.7a Issus: Map 3.5, AY.

3.6.7b Nothing is known of either Tauriskos or the circumstances of Harpalos' desertion, aside from what Arrian says here.

3.6.7c Epirus; Italy: Map 3.5, AX. Alexander of Epirus was Alexander the Great's maternal uncle and king of Epirus, the realm neigh-

boring Macedonia to the west; at the time he was leading a military venture into southern Italy. Evidently, in the period before the battle of Issus, Tauriskos and Harpalos regarded Alexander of Epirus' prospects more favorably than those of their own monarch.

3.6.7d The Megarid is the region surrounding Megara (Map 2.16, Aegean inset).

3.6.7e Arrian's digression on Harpalos' flight and restoration is only the first chapter of a tangled tale. At 3.19.7, Arrian relates that, in the summer of 330, Harpalos was put in charge of guarding the treasure Alexander seized from the Persians at Persepolis. Then in 324, Harpalos betrayed Alexander a second time and fled to Greece with money intended to raise an anti-Macedonian revolt; the episode has been lost from Arrian's narrative due to the gap in the text after 7.12. After the Athenians refused to take him in, Harpalos went to Crete, where one of his own officers assassinated him. See Appendix M, Alexander and the Greeks, §10.

3.6.7f Lydia: Map 3.5, AX.

3.6.8a Syria: Map 3.5, BY.

3.6.8b This replacement marks the first of Alexander's many "upgrades" of his administrative staff. Arrian does not specify the manner of Arimmas' removal, but in later cases, satraps suspected of perfidy or incompetence were routinely executed.

[1] Alexander reached Thapsacus in the month of Hekatombaion,[1a] during Aristophanes' archonship[1b] at Athens, and found the river spanned by two bridges. For Darius had entrusted the guardianship of the river to Mazaios,[1c] who had been guarding it with roughly three thousand horsemen and . . . foot-soldiers,[1d] two thousand of whom were Greek mercenaries. [2] The Macedonians had not connected the bridge to the opposite bank, as they feared that Mazaios' men might attack the bridge where it ended. But as soon as Mazaios heard that Alexander was approaching, he fled with the entire army. And once Mazaios had fled, the bridges were thrown across to the opposite bank, and Alexander crossed them with his army. [3] He then advanced inland, keeping the Euphrates and the mountains of Armenia[3a] on his left, through the country known as Mesopotamia.[3b] When he set out from the Euphrates, he did not take the road that led directly to Babylon,[3c] since everything was more practicable for the army on the other road: it was easier to obtain green fodder for the horses and provisions for the men, and the heat was not so intense. [4] Men from Darius' army who had spread out along the route to reconnoiter were captured, and these men reported that Darius had taken up a position at the Tigris[4a] and was determined to bar Alexander's way should he try to cross; they also said that the army with Darius was much larger than the force that had fought in Cilicia.[4b]

[5] On hearing this, Alexander hastened to the Tigris. When he arrived, he found neither Darius nor the guard Darius had left behind. He crossed the river—a difficult task only because the current was swift, not because anyone barred his way.

[6] Alexander now gave the army a rest. When an almost total eclipse of the moon occurred,[6a] Alexander sacrificed to the Moon, the Sun, and the Earth, the deities said to be responsible for this phenomenon. Aristandros thought the eclipse was a favorable omen for the Macedonians and Alexander, and that the battle would take place that month. He said that the sacrifices foreshadowed a victory for Alexander. [7] Starting from the Tigris, Alexander marched across Assyria,[7a] keeping the Gordyenian[7b] Mountains on his left, the Tigris on his right.

[1] On the fourth day after Alexander had crossed the river, his Scouts reported that enemy horsemen could be seen in the plain, though their numbers could not be estimated. Arraying the army, Alexander advanced as for battle, whereupon other Scouts,[1a] who had made a more exact observa-

3.7.1–4
Summer 331
THAPSACUS
Alexander crosses the Euphrates unopposed and advances into Mesopotamia.

3.7.5
TIGRIS RIVER
Alexander crosses the Tigris without opposition.

3.7.6–7
Autumn 331
ASSYRIA
Given omens thought to be favorable, Alexander leads the army forward.

3.8.1–2
ASSYRIA
Having crossed the river, the Macedonians encounter an advance guard of Persian cavalry and capture a few riders.

3.7.1a   The month of Hekatombaion in the Attic calendar was roughly July/August.
3.7.1b   Archonship: ancient historians, who had no universal system for numbering years, routinely used the names of Athenian archons or Roman consuls—officials who served one-year terms—to identify points in historical time.
3.7.1c   Mazaios was a satrap who had headed various provinces and had become one of Darius' most trusted officials.
3.7.1d   The number of infantry has become lost in the transmission of Arrian's text.
3.7.3a   Armenia: Map 3.5, AX.

3.7.3b   Mesopotamia: Map 3.10, AX.
3.7.3c   Babylon: Map 3.10, BY.
3.7.4a   Tigris River: Map 3.10, BY.
3.7.4b   Cilicia: Map 3.5, AY. That is, at the battle of Issus.
3.7.6a   The eclipse is dated to September 20, 331.
3.7.7a   Assyria: Map 3.10, BX.
3.7.7b   Gordyenian Mountains: precise location unknown. Gordyene: Map 3.10, AX.
3.8.1a   The mounted Scouts, sometimes called the *sarisa*-bearing cavalry, were Alexander's principal reconnaissance unit. Probably they only carried *sarisas* in battle.

tion, rode up to report that there seemed to be no more than a thousand horsemen.[1b] Taking the royal squadron, one squadron of Companion cavalry, and those of the Scouts who were Paionians,[1c] Alexander went forward on the double, having ordered the rest of the army to follow at a marching pace. When the Persian horsemen saw the swift approach of Alexander's troops, they fled as fast as they could. Alexander, in pursuit, pressed them hard; [2] most of them escaped, though Alexander's men killed those whose horses became exhausted as they fled, and took others alive along with their horses. From these men the Macedonians learned that Darius was not far off, with a large force.

[3] Indeed, the Indians[3a] who dwelt near the Bactrians had rushed to Darius' aid, along with the Bactrians themselves and the Sogdians;[3b] these contingents were all under the command of Bessos, the satrap of Bactria.[3c] The Sacae, a Scythian tribe related to the Scythians who dwell in Asia, were also accompanying them, not as Bessos' subjects but in fulfillment of the terms of their alliance with Darius. Their commander was Mauakes, and they were mounted bowmen. [4] Barsaentes, the satrap of the Arachosians, was leading the Arachosians and the so-called mountain Indians.[4a] Satibarzanes, the satrap of Areia, was leading the Areians. Phratarphernes was leading the Parthians, Hyrcanians, and Tapourians, all of whom fought on horseback. Atropates led the Medes[4b] with whom the Kadousioi, Albanoi, and Sakasenai had been posted. [5] Orontobates, Ariobarzanes, and Orxines were leading the Red Sea tribes.[5a] The Ouxioi and Susians were commanded by Oxathres son of Abulites. Boupares was leading the Babylonians. The displaced Carians,[5b] together with the Sittacenians, had been posted with the Babylonians. Orontes and Mithraustes led the Armenians, Ariakes the Cappadocians. [6] Mazaios was leading the contingent from Hollow Syria and all the Mesopotamians.

3.8.3–6
Autumn 331
GAUGAMELA
Arrian describes Darius' army: a force of forty thousand cavalry and a million infantry, made up of units drawn from all across Asia.

3.8.1b It is unclear whether Darius meant to oppose the crossing of the Tigris but failed to get significant forces there in time, or whether his scouts were lying at 3.7.4 when they claimed such forces were already in place. In either case, it seems that the Persians lost an important strategic opportunity, since they could have mounted an effective defense at the Tigris.

3.8.1c This is Arrian's only reference to the Paionian Scouts (Paionia: Map 3.5, AX), obviously a different group than the Scouts proper (who were probably native Macedonians). Elsewhere he distinguishes "the Paionians" and "the Scouts" as two separate units, though they often fight in close proximity (see 3.12.3).

3.8.3a Arrian uses the term Indians to refer to a wide array of peoples living east of the Indian Caucasus/Paropamisos (Map 3.10, locator; modern Hindu Kush). Here he specifies the westernmost segment of that group, also described at 3.8.6 as "the Indians dwelling west of the Indus." For the locations and tribal territories mentioned in 3.8.3–6, see Map 3.10 and its directory.

3.8.3b The term Sogdians has been adopted in this text for the inhabitants of Sogdiana, in keeping with common modern usage. The more

correct term would be Sogdianians.

3.8.3c As satrap of Bactria, Bessos commanded one of the most effective cavalry units in the Persian battle line. He would go on to play a large role in the events following the battle of Gaugamela.

3.8.4a The mountains by which this race of Indians is known are presumably the Indian Caucasus/Paropamisos. They are thus yet another nation living on the western edge of India, like those discussed in n. 3.8.3a.

3.8.4b The Medes were a northern Iranian people who originally ruled the Persians, then came to be ruled by them and assimilated into their power structure.

3.8.5a "Red Sea tribes" refers to those located on or near what ancient writers called the Red Sea (not the modern Red Sea but the Persian Gulf), which in this case is the entire coast south of Arabia and Persia.

3.8.5b These are most likely descendants of the Carians (Caria: Map 3.5, AX) who, along with the Ionian Greeks, revolted from the Persians in 499 and were defeated several years later. It was not uncommon for the Persians to punish rebellious peoples by deporting them into the interior of their empire.

Darius' entire army was said to include nearly forty thousand cavalry, a million infantry, two hundred scythe-bearing chariots,[6a] and a modest number of elephants (the Indians dwelling west of the Indus had about fifteen).[6b]

[7] With this force Darius had encamped at Gaugamela, near the River Boumelos,[7a] roughly seventy-five miles from the city of Arbela,[7b] on completely level ground. The Persians had long since leveled the uneven ground thereabouts, making it fit for chariot-driving and for use by the cavalry. For some were trying to convince Darius that he had fallen short in the battle at Issus[7c] owing to the narrowness of the battlefield, and Darius was easily convinced.

[1] When the captured Persian spies reported this to Alexander, he remained where he was for four days. He gave the army a rest after its march and fortified the camp with a ditch and a palisade, as he had decided to leave behind the baggage train and all the soldiers unfit for battle, and to proceed to the battlefield with troops carrying only their arms. [2] Taking his forces at night, he set out near the second watch,[2a] intending to join battle with the barbarians at daybreak. When Darius received word that Alexander was drawing near, he marshaled his army for battle, and Alexander led his own men forward, likewise drawn up in battle array. The armies were about seven miles apart and not yet within sight of each other, since the terrain that separated them was hilly.

[3] When Alexander was about four miles away and his army was descending these hills, he caught sight of the barbarians and halted the phalanx. Again calling together the Companions, generals, and squadron leaders, and the commanders of the allies and the foreign mercenaries, he asked them whether he should immediately advance the phalanx from its present position, as the majority urged, or follow Parmenion's advice [4] and make camp where they were, reconnoiter the entire area to find out if there was anything suspicious or difficult, or any concealed ditches or stakes fixed in the ground, and inspect the enemy's arrangements more carefully. Parmenion's view prevailed, and they made camp where they were, in the order in which they were going to advance into battle.

[5] Taking the light-armed troops and the Companion cavalry, Alexander rode all around, inspecting the entire ground where his action would be fought. After returning to camp and again convening the same officers, he said that there was no need for him to inspire them for battle, as they had long been inspired by their own bravery and their excellent record. [6] He expected each of them to urge his own men on, each captain to encourage

---

3.8.7
GAUGAMELA
Darius takes up a position at Gaugamela, where the Persians have prepared the ground for cavalry maneuvers.

3.9.1–2
GAUGAMELA
Darius and Alexander make preparations for battle as Alexander's army approaches the Persian position.

3.9.3–4
GAUGAMELA
At a distance of four miles from the enemy, Alexander, on Parmenion's advice, makes camp to conduct further reconnaissance.

3.9.5–8
GAUGAMELA
Alexander addresses his officers, impressing upon them the need to keep good order and follow the chain of command.

3.8.6a Darius had assembled quite a large contingent of these by-now antiquated war machines, which were designed to charge lines of infantry and slash them with the blades mounted on their wheels.

3.8.6b Numerical estimates of military strength are controversial in any ancient history, and this one is no exception. Two points, however, seem to be widely agreed upon: the "million" Persian infantry, whatever their actual number, did not contribute much strength to Darius' army, since only a

few elite corps were capable of holding their own against the Macedonian phalanx; and the Persian cavalry, though perhaps less numerous than Arrian reports, nevertheless far outnumbered the seven thousand horsemen of the Macedonians.

3.8.7a Gaugamela; Boumelos River, possible location: Map 3.10, AX.
3.8.7b Arbela: Map 3.10, BX.
3.8.7c Issus: Map 3.10, AX.
3.9.2a The second watch began approximately two or three hours after midnight.

his company, each squadron leader his own squadron, each battalion commander his battalion, and each infantry commander the phalanx that had been entrusted to him, since in this battle they were fighting not for Hollow Syria, as previously, or for Phoenicia,[6a] or even for Egypt;[6b] on this occasion, the sovereignty of all of Asia would be decided. [7] Accordingly, there was no need to make long speeches heartening men who were naturally disposed to fight nobly. Instead, they should urge each man to look to his own orderly conduct at the moment of danger, and to keep a strict silence when there was need to advance in silence, and to send up a glorious shout when it was fitting to shout, and to raise their most terrifying war cry by shouting "Alalai!" when the time was right for doing so. [8] The officers themselves should obey instructions swiftly, and swiftly pass them on to their units, and everyone should bear in mind that the entire outcome depended on each man's conduct: negligence on anyone's part endangered them all, while every man's diligent effort contributed to their common success.[8a]

3.10.1–4
Autumn 331
GAUGAMELA
Alexander rejects Parmenion's advice that the Macedonians should mount a night assault on the Persian position. Arrian comments on the wisdom of this decision.

[1] When Alexander had encouraged the men with these words and others, not many, in the same vein, and when his officers had in turn urged him to rely on them, he ordered the army to dine and rest. Parmenion, they say, went to him in his tent and advised him to attack the Persians at night, since the enemy would be surprised and confused by the attack and more terrified if it came at night. [2] But Alexander replied, because others were listening,[2a] that it would be disgraceful to steal the victory; instead, he said, Alexander must win openly and without trickery. His high-flown rhetoric seemed less an expression of arrogance than of self-confidence in the face of danger, and I think he was calculating accurately in this regard: [3] at night, whether or not men have been sufficiently prepared for battle, it often happens that many things turn out contrary to calculation and the stronger are foiled while victory goes to the weaker, against the expectations of both. Though Alexander took many chances in his battles, he recognized that the night posed dangers. Furthermore, if Darius were again defeated but the attack came secretly and at night, he would not be forced to concede that he and the men he led were inferior; [4] whereas if Alexander's men should meet with an unexpected reverse, they would find themselves in a country friendly to their enemies, who were moreover familiar with the region, while they themselves, lacking such familiarity, were surrounded by enemies, many of whom were prisoners of war who might join in attacking them at night even if the Macedonians' victory were not decisive, let alone if they were defeated. I commend Alexander for these calculations, no less than for his public display of heroics.

3.9.6a Hollow Syria; Phoenicia: Map 3.10, BX.
3.9.6b Egypt: Map 3.10, locator.
3.9.8a Here, as in other passages, Arrian's portrait of Alexander's leadership stresses the king's attention to organization, efficiency, and chain of command. The authenticity of the speech is of course

uncertain; see Appendix A, Arrian's Sources and Reliability, §19.

3.10.2a This remark is one of several that shows Arrian or his source to be rather cynically attuned to Alexander's need to present himself to his followers in heroic poses; see 2.3.7 and 3.3.2 for other instances.

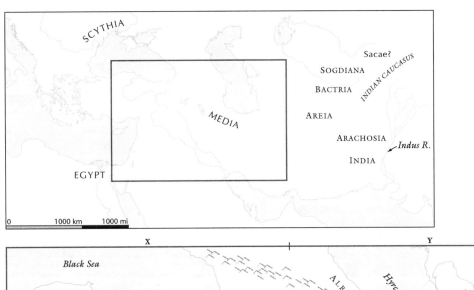

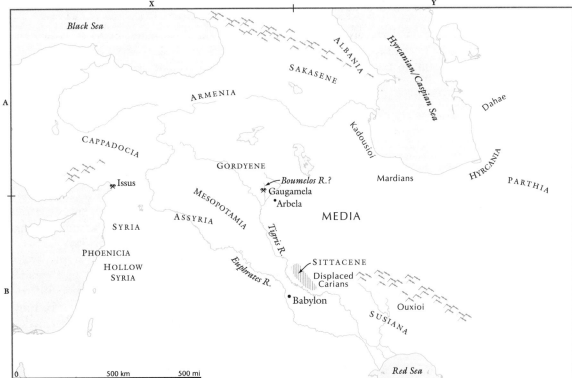

MAP 3.10. POINTS OF ORIGIN OF DARIUS' FORCES AS DESCRIBED AT 3.11.3–7

Albanoi, AY	Dahae, AY	Medes, AY	Sittacenians, BY
Arachosians, locator	Displaced Carians, BX	Mesopotamians, AX	Sogdians, locator
Areians (Ar[e]ia), locator	Hollow Syrians (Koile Syria), BX	Ouxioi, BY	Susians (Susiana), BY
Armenians, AX	Hyrcanians, AY	Parthians, AY	Tapourians (Tapouroi), AY
Babylonians, BY	Indians, locator	Red Sea tribes, BY	
Bactrians, locator	Kadousioi, AY	Sacae, possible location, locator	
Cappadocians, AX	Mardians (Mardoi), AY	Sakesenai, AY	

115

3.11.1–2
Autumn 331
GAUGAMELA
The Persians spend the night
standing at arms, thereby
losing morale.

3.11.3–7
GAUGAMELA
Arrian reviews the Persian
order of battle, drawing on
a source who claimed to
have had access to the written battle plans. Darius
places himself at the center
of the line behind elephants,
chariots, and crack infantry
regiments, with cavalry and
scythe-bearing chariots on
either wing.

3.11.8–10
GAUGAMELA
Arrian next reviews the
Macedonian order of battle.
Alexander's Companion
cavalry occupies the right
wing, with allied cavalry on
the left under Parmenion.
The phalanx and other
infantry units hold the
center.

[1] That night Darius and his army remained arrayed for battle in their original order, since their camp had not been securely fortified and they feared that the enemy might attack them at night. [2] If anything ruined their prospects at this juncture, it was that they had been standing idle for a long time under arms, and that the fear that is bound to arise on the eve of great dangers did not spread through their ranks only at the last moment, but had been troubling them for a long time and had come to dominate their spirits.

[3] The army was marshaled in the following order.[3a] (According to Aristoboulos, Darius' battle order had been committed to writing and was later confiscated.) The left wing was held by the Bactrian cavalry, the Dahae, and the Arachosians; the Persians were posted next (their cavalry and infantry mixed together) and next to them the Susians, and next to the Susians the Kadousioi. [4] This was the order of the left wing up to the middle of the entire phalanx. On the right, the contingents from Hollow Syria and Mesopotamia had been posted first, followed by the Medes; next came the Parthians and Sacae, then the Tapourians and Hyrcanians, and finally the Albanoi and Sakesenai. These were the contingents on the right up to the middle of the entire phalanx. [5] The center was held by King Darius, the King's kinsmen, the Persian Apple Bearers,[5a] the Indians, the so-called displaced Carians, and the Mardian archers. The Ouxioi, Babylonians, Red Sea tribes, and Sittacenians had been posted behind them in deep formation.[5b] [6] In front of the left wing, facing Alexander's right, stood the Scythian cavalry, nearly a thousand Bactrians, and a hundred scythe-bearing chariots. The elephants were posted in front of the royal squadron, along with fifty chariots. [7] The Armenian and Cappadocian[7a] cavalry had been posted in front of the right wing with fifty scythe-bearing chariots. The Greek mercenaries had been stationed on either side of Darius and the Persians, opposite the Macedonian phalanx, on the assumption that these were the only contingents that could effectively counter it.

[8] Alexander's army was marshaled as follows. The Companion cavalry held the right wing. The royal squadron under Kleitos son of Dropides had been posted in front of the Companion cavalry, and next to Kleitos' squadron stood the squadrons of Glaukias, Ariston, Sopolis son of Hermodoros, Herakleides son of Antiokhos, Demetrios son of Althaemenes, Meleagros, and Hegelokhos son of Hippostratos, in that order. The entire Companion cavalry was led by Philotas son of Parmenion. [9] In the Macedonian phalanx, the *agema*[9a] of the shield-bearers was posted right beside the cavalry; beside them stood the rest of the shield-bearers under

3.11.3a See Appendix D, Map D.1, for an illustration of the order of battle described here and in 3.12.1–5.
3.11.5a The Persian Apple Bearers were an elite corps of royal bodyguards whose spears were fitted with golden ornaments shaped like apples at the butt end.
3.11.5b As was standard for the Persians, a throng of

untrained infantry was massed at the rear, where they were not expected to engage the enemy.
3.11.7a For the points of origin of Darius' commanders and forces at 3.11.3–7, see Map 3.10.
3.11.9a *Agema*: a special division of light-armed infantry, though there was a cavalry *agema* as well.

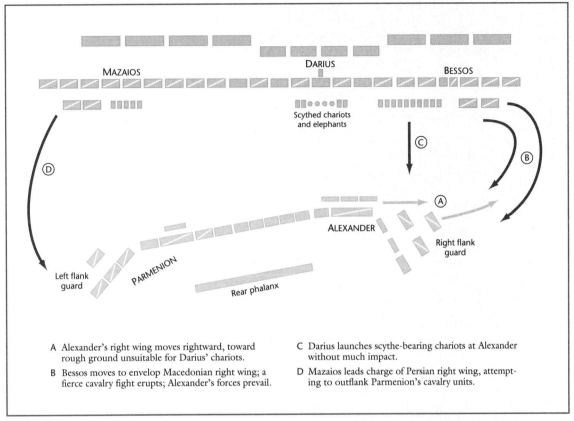

A Alexander's right wing moves rightward, toward rough ground unsuitable for Darius' chariots.

B Bessos moves to envelop Macedonian right wing; a fierce cavalry fight erupts; Alexander's forces prevail.

C Darius launches scythe-bearing chariots at Alexander without much impact.

D Mazaios leads charge of Persian right wing, attempting to outflank Parmenion's cavalry units.

MAP 3.11. OPENING PHASE OF THE BATTLE OF GAUGAMELA AS DESCRIBED AT 3.13.1–3.14.4. Knowing that Darius, with superior numbers, would be able to outflank him, Alexander posted a second, rearward-facing phalanx behind his front line and put slanting flank guards on either wing. As he moved forward toward Darius he shifted his whole army to the right, as though to outflank Darius on that side, and held his left wing back at an oblique angle. He hoped to win the battle with his right wing, where the expert horsemen of the Companion cavalry were posted, before his left had engaged the Persian right, for with his shorter line he could not hope to prevail on both wings simultaneously. Darius, however, eventually ordered his right, under Mazaios, to charge Alexander's left wing.

Parmenion's son Nikanor. Beside the shield-bearers stood the battalions of Perdikkas son of Orontes, Meleagros son of Neoptolemos, Polyperkhon son of Simmias, and Amyntas son of Philip.[9b] Amyntas' battalion was led by Simmias, since Amyntas had been sent to Macedonia[9c] to levy troops. [10] The battalion of Krateros son of Alexander held the left wing of the phalanx, and Krateros himself had command of the infantry on the left. Stationed next to the infantry were the allied cavalry under Eriguios son of Larikhos; beside them, at the left wing, stood the Thessalian[10a] horsemen under Philip son of Menelaos. Parmenion son of Philotas commanded the

3.11.9b An error; Amyntas was actually the son of Andromenes.

3.11.9c Macedonia: Map 3.19a.
3.11.10a Thessaly: Map 3.19a.

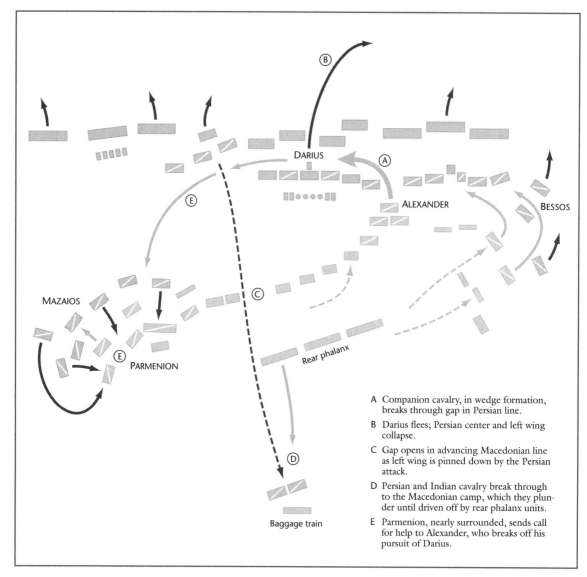

A Companion cavalry, in wedge formation, breaks through gap in Persian line.

B Darius flees; Persian center and left wing collapse.

C Gap opens in advancing Macedonian line as left wing is pinned down by the Persian attack.

D Persian and Indian cavalry break through to the Macedonian camp, which they plunder until driven off by rear phalanx units.

E Parmenion, nearly surrounded, sends call for help to Alexander, who breaks off his pursuit of Darius.

MAP 3.12. THE CRITICAL POINT OF THE BATTLE OF GAUGAMELA AS DESCRIBED AT 3.14–3.15.1. Alexander's rightward move forced the Persians to stretch their line, creating a hole between rapidly shifting units. He formed his Companion cavalry into a wedge and drove it straight into that hole, making for Darius' position at center. Darius recognized the danger and fled the battle in his chariot, pursued by Alexander. Much of the Persian center and left followed Darius in flight. On the other side of the field, Mazaios was making good headway against the Macedonian left under Parmenion, and some Indian and Persian cavalry exploited a gap in Macedonian lines to plunder the baggage train at the rear. Parmenion's position was deteriorating rapidly until, in Arrian's account (contradicted by other sources), the old general sent a distress message to Alexander and summoned him back from the pursuit of Darius. Alexander made his way back to Parmenion through waves of retreating enemy cavalry and helped drive off Mazaios' forces.

entire left wing, and around him stood the Pharsalian[10b] horsemen, the strongest and largest contingent of the Thessalian cavalry.

[1] Such was the order in which Alexander had marshaled his front line. But he also posted a second line, so that the phalanx could become double-fronted. The officers of this reserve force had been instructed to wheel about and meet the barbarians' attack if they saw their comrades surrounded by the Persian army. [2] But if it should become necessary either to extend or to close the line, half the Agrianians, under Attalos, had been posted next to the royal squadron on the right wing, but at an angle to it,[2a] with the Macedonian archers under Brison, and beside the archers the so-called old mercenaries under Kleandros. [3] In front of the Agrianians and the archers stood the mounted Scouts and the Paionians,[3a] led by Aretes and Ariston. Posted in front of all these contingents was the mercenary cavalry under Menidas. Half the Agrianians and archers had been posted with Balakros' javelin men in front of the royal squadron and the other Companions; these contingents had been stationed opposite the scythe-bearing chariots. [4] Menidas and his men had been instructed to charge the enemy in the flank as they were turning if the latter rode around their wing. Such were the arrangements at Alexander's right wing. The contingents that had been posted at an angle on the left included the Thracians[4a] under Sitalkes, and beside them the allied cavalry under Koiranos and the Odrysian cavalry[4b] under Agathon son of Tyrimmas. [5] Posted in front of all these contingents was the foreign mercenary cavalry under Andromakhos son of Hieron.[5a] The Thracian infantry had been posted as a guard for the baggage train. Alexander's entire army included nearly seven thousand cavalry and about forty thousand infantry.[5b]

[1] As the armies were now drawing near each other, Darius could be seen, along with his troops: the Persian Apple Bearers, the Indians, the Albanoi, the displaced Carians, and the Mardian archers, all of whom were posted opposite Alexander and the royal squadron. But Alexander began heading more to his right, and the Persians shifted in response to this move, now far outflanking his army with their left wing. [2] The Scythian cavalry,

3.12.1–5
Autumn 331
GAUGAMELA
Alexander stations a second phalanx line behind the main one in case of encirclement, and forms two flanking forces to connect the two lines.

3.13.1–4
Autumn 331
GAUGAMELA
Battle is joined on the Macedonian right wing, where Alexander strives to counter an attempt by the Persians to outflank him.

3.11.10b Pharsalus: Map 3.19a.
3.12.2a It is unclear just what sort of formation Arrian describes here, but generally the phrase "at an angle" is taken to mean a right angle or something close to it, so that the Macedonian front and rear phalanxes were connected by the two flanking forces to form, in essence, a rectangle.
3.12.3a Paionia: Map 3.19a.
3.12.4a Thrace: Map 3.19a.
3.12.4b Odrysian cavalry: the cavalry from Odrysian Thrace (Map 3.19a).
3.12.5a Two different units of "mercenary cavalry" are listed by Arrian, one at the front of the right-wing flanking force, under Menidas, the other under Andromakhos at the front of the opposite flank. Evidently both units received the orders Arrian records only in

the first instance: to lead the charge against any Persian forces that got past the ends of the Macedonian line, taking them in the flank as they rounded the corners. These precautions show that Alexander, aware of his great numerical disadvantage, expected to be outflanked by Darius.
3.12.5b The numbers Arrian gives puts Alexander at almost a six-to-one disadvantage in cavalry and twenty-five–to–one in infantry, with no weapons at all to counter Darius' scythed chariots and elephants. Though the numbers are doubtless exaggerated, it is not unthinkable that Alexander's forces, with training, experience, and tactics far superior to those of any other military, might have been a match for an enemy several times their size.

FIGURE 3.12.
Two images from the central scene of the huge Alexander Mosaic (approximately 19 feet by 10 feet), found on the floor of a house in the buried city of Pompeii, depicting the battle of either Issus or Gaugamela. Both were resolved as shown here, with Darius fleeing in his chariot (opposite) before Alexander's cavalry charge. The template was probably copied from a Greek painting done within a few decades of the battle, perhaps based on eyewitness accounts.

riding parallel to Alexander's line, were already making contact with the troops posted in front of it, but Alexander continued to move to the right and was about to leave the ground the Persians had leveled. Fearing that if the Macedonians advanced to the unleveled ground the Persians' chariots would be of no use, Darius commanded the men posted in front of his left wing to ride around the Macedonians' right, where Alexander was leading, so that they would not extend their wing any farther.[2a] [3] When this happened, Alexander commanded Menidas' mercenary cavalry to charge them. Sallying out to meet this force, the Scythian horsemen and the Bactrians posted with them routed Menidas' cavalry, as the barbarians far outnumbered them. Alexander then ordered Ariston's Paionians[3a] and the mercenaries to attack the Scythians, and the barbarians gave way. [4] But the rest of the Bactrians, having drawn near the Paionians and the mercenaries, rallied their own fleeing troops and made the cavalry engagement a close contest. Alexander's men were falling in greater numbers. They were pressed hard on account of the barbarians' superior numbers and because

3.13.2a The characterization of Darius' generalship here is consistent with the picture Arrian draws at Issus and elsewhere. Uncertain of his own prowess and that of his forces, the Persian king seeks instead to press his topographic advantages, in this case overextending his left wing in an effort to preserve them. We are perhaps meant to infer that Alexander, aware of this psychological weakness in his adversary, had foreseen this

response when he ordered his line to move rightward.

3.13.3a The text reads "Aretes' Paionians," but Aretes has been mentioned as head of the Scouts, not the Paionians at 3.12. Either Arrian has slipped here (as is assumed) or something has fallen out of the text between "Aretes" and "Paionians," so that we should understand that Alexander ordered two different waves of cavalry to attack.

the Scythians and their horses had been better equipped for defense.[4a] But even so, the Macedonians[4b] withstood their attacks; assaulting one squadron after another, they were driving them out of formation.

[5] By that time the barbarians had sent their scythe-bearing chariots out against Alexander himself, intending to throw his phalanx into disarray. Here especially they were cheated of their hopes. For just as the chariots were approaching, the Agrianians and Balakros' javelin men (both contingents were posted in front of the Companion cavalry) hurled their javelins; seizing the chariots' reins, they pulled down the drivers, then stood around the horses and stabbed at them. [6] Some of the chariots also passed right through the Macedonian lines; for they separated ranks, as they had been instructed to do, at the points where the chariots charged. This was the chief reason the chariots themselves and those against whom they were driven escaped unharmed. These chariots, too, were seized by the grooms of Alexander's army and the royal shield-bearers.[6a]

[1] Now that Darius was leading his army against the entire phalanx, Alexander ordered Aretes to attack the cavalry trying to surround their right wing. [2] For a time Alexander himself led his men in column, but when the cavalry, charging the Persians who were trying to surround the

3.13.5–6
Autumn 331
GAUGAMELA
Darius' scythe-bearing chariots fail to inflict great damage on the Macedonian infantry.

3.14.1–3
GAUGAMELA
Seeing a break in the Persian left wing, Alexander charges through it and makes straight for Darius, putting him to flight.

3.13.4a Both riders and horses were outfitted with chain mail, a measure possibly devised for this battle to counter the known strength of the Macedonian cavalry.
3.13.4b That is, those fighting on Alexander's side,

though in this case not ethnically Macedonian.
3.13.6a It is unclear why these "royal shield-bearers" are placed in the rear of the Macedonian lines, since the shield-bearers as a whole were posted in the front (see 3.11.9).

121

FIGURE 3.13. A relief from the ruins of the Persian palace at Persepolis, depicting a royal infantry guard corps of the kind Darius mustered around himself at Gaugamela.

Macedonians' right wing, first breached the barbarian phalanx, Alexander wheeled about opposite the gap, arrayed the Companion cavalry and the nearby portion of the phalanx in a wedge formation, and led them at full speed and with a war cry toward Darius himself. [3] For a brief period the fighting was hand to hand, but when Alexander and his horsemen pressed the enemy hard, shoving the Persians and striking their faces with spears, and the Macedonian phalanx, tightly arrayed and bristling with pikes, was already upon them, Darius, who had long been in a state of dread, now saw terrors all around him; he wheeled about—the first to do so[3a]—and fled. The Persians who were trying to surround the Macedonian wing also took fright when Aretes and his men attacked them in force.

[4] Here the Persians' flight was desperate, and the Macedonians in pursuit were slaughtering their enemies as they fled. But elsewhere, Simmias and his battalion were unable to join Alexander in the pursuit; having halted the phalanx, they fought where they were, as the Macedonians' left was reported to be in trouble. [5] There they had broken formation, and some Indians and Persian cavalry now burst through the gap and made for the Macedonian baggage train. A desperate action ensued here.

3.14.4–6
Autumn 331
GAUGAMELA
On the Macedonian left, a gap in the line allows the Persians to break through and plunder the baggage train before troops from the reserve phalanx arrive and put them to flight.

3.14.3a Our other sources for the battle portray Darius' flight as a desperate expedient, adopted only after all hope was lost. In general Arrian gives Darius much less stature as a soldier and a king than do the other Alexander historians.

For the Persians boldly attacked many unarmed men who had not expected anyone to cut through the double phalanx, and the barbarian prisoners of war joined the Persians at the crucial moment in attacking the Macedonians. [6] But the commanders of the reserves for the Macedonians' first phalanx soon learned what was happening; facing about as they had been instructed to do, they assaulted the Persians' rear and killed many who were crowded around the baggage train, though some turned tail and escaped.[6a] Meanwhile, the Persians at the right wing, not yet aware that Darius had fled, rode around Alexander's left and assaulted Parmenion's troops.

[1] At that point, when for the first time the Macedonians found themselves attacked on both sides, Parmenion quickly sent a messenger to Alexander to report that their men were in trouble and needed help. When this was reported to Alexander, he turned back from further pursuit.[1a] Wheeling about with the Companion cavalry, he hastened toward the barbarians' right. First he attacked the fleeing enemy cavalry,[1b] the Parthians, some Indians, and even some Persians, the largest and strongest contingents. [2] This was the most fiercely fought cavalry engagement of the entire battle. For the barbarians, posted many rows deep (as they had been arrayed in squadrons), encountered Alexander's troops face to face and resorted neither to javelin throwing nor to countermarching of horses, which are common in cavalry actions. Instead, each man strove on his own to force a breakout, as this was their only hope of rescue. They eagerly struck and were struck without mercy, as they were no longer contending for another's victory but each for his own survival. Some sixty of Alexander's Companions fell in that action, and Hephaistion[2a] himself was wounded, as were Koinos and Menidas. Yet here, too, Alexander prevailed. [3] All the Persians who managed to break through Alexander's forces fled for their lives.

Alexander himself now approached to engage the enemy's right wing. At that point the Thessalian horsemen, who had fought gloriously, did not prove inferior to Alexander in the action. But the barbarians' right wing was already fleeing when Alexander encountered them.[3a] He therefore turned back to pursue Darius, and pursued him as long as there was light. [4] Parmenion and his men followed, pursuing the enemy forces in their sector.

3.15.1–2
GAUGAMELA
Parmenion, surrounded by Persian cavalry outflanking the Macedonian left, urgently requests assistance from Alexander. The king therefore gives up pursuit of Darius and returns to the fray, meeting stern resistance from fleeing Persian units.

3.15.3–4
Autumn 331
GAUGAMELA
Alexander arrives at Parmenion's position to find the Persians already in flight and so turns back toward the pursuit of Darius. Parmenion siezes the enemy's supply caravan.

3.14.6a Our other sources portray this episode at the baggage train as a large, deliberate, and effective assault, not a mere plundering raid. Arrian's account also raises the question of how Indian and Persian units evaded Alexander's rear phalanx as they headed for the baggage train, and some have doubted it on these grounds.

3.15.1a See n. 2.11.7a. Our other sources give different versions of this episode, in which Alexander did not receive Parmenion's message (Diodorus 17.60.7–8) or received it but returned to find Parmenion already victorious (Plutarch, *Parallel Lives* "Alexander" 33.9–11). There seems to have been debate in the aftermath of the battle as to whether Parmenion was to blame for Darius' escape or whether

Alexander had pressed ahead too fast without regard for his own left wing.

3.15.1b That is, as he crossed from one wing to the other, moving behind enemy lines, Alexander first encountered, coming toward him, the central Persian units fleeing in the path of Darius. Meanwhile, other Persian units farther to the right (facing Parmenion) were as yet unaware of Darius' flight and were still attacking.

3.15.2a For more on Hephaistion, Alexander's most intimate friend and confidant, see Appendix E, §8.

3.15.3a This is a rare instance in Arrian's narrative where hard-pressed Macedonian forces are able to turn the tide of battle without the personal intervention of Alexander.

FIGURE 3.14. The infantry phalanx of the Macedonians was divided into small units of 256 men each, like the one shown here. The *sarisas* of the first five rows were held level; soldiers farther back could carry their *sarisas* vertically or rest them on the shoulders of the men ahead of them.

But when Alexander had crossed the River Lykos,[4a] he made camp to give his men and horses a brief rest. Parmenion, meanwhile, captured the barbarians' camp, baggage train, elephants, and camels.[4b]

3.15.5
Autumn 331
ARBELA
Alexander captures Darius' possessions, though not Darius himself, at Arbela.

[5] Having rested his horsemen until midnight, Alexander hastened toward Arbela,[5a] intending to capture Darius there with all his treasure and all the royal accouterments. He reached Arbela the next day, having covered more than seventy miles since the battle. Alexander did not find Darius at Arbela, since Darius, having taken no rest, was still fleeing. But his treasure and all his furniture were seized. His chariot and shield were captured for the second time; his bow and arrows were also taken.

3.15.6
Arrian reports an astonishing number of Persian dead and wounded, but light Macedonian losses.

[6] Nearly a hundred of Alexander's men perished, and more than a thousand horses died from wounds and the stress of the pursuit. Almost half of these horses belonged to the Companion cavalry. There were said to be nearly three hundred thousand barbarian corpses, but far more men were captured than killed,[6a] and the elephants were captured, as were all the chariots that had not been shattered in the battle.

3.15.7
The victory fulfills Aristandros' prophecy.

[7] So ended the battle, which took place in the month of Pyanepsion,[7a]

3.15.4a   Lykos River, possible location: Map 3.19b, AY.

3.15.4b   It is odd to find the elephants reappearing only now, at the end of the battle account, and in the camp at the rear rather than in the front lines (where Arrian had placed them at 3.11.6). Indeed, our sources give little clue as to why these beasts, so important a factor in Alexander's Indian campaign, seem to play no role in this battle at all.

3.15.5a   Arbela: Map 3.19b, AY.

3.15.6a   These wildly exaggerated casualty figures would give the Macedonian army an unheard of three-thousand–to–one kill ratio over the Persians. Whatever propagandist first generated these numbers had little regard for credibility.

3.15.7a   This is a calendrical error. The battle actually occurred in the Athenian month of Boedromion (roughly September/October in the Attic calendar), not the month of Pyanepsion (October/November).

FIGURE 3.15. This astronomical tablet found at Babylon records events from the weeks prior to and following the battle of Gaugamela, and contains one entry that fixes the date of the battle at October 1 by the Julian calendar. The entries on the reverse side describe Alexander's proclamations to Babylon and entry into the city. The anonymous scribe who recorded these events refers to Darius as "king of the world" in the entries leading up to the battle, then gives the same title to Alexander in the entries that follow it.

during Aristophanes' archonship at Athens. And Aristandros' prophecy, that the battle would take place in the same month as the lunar eclipse and would be a victory, was fulfilled.

[1] Immediately after the battle, Darius hastened past the Armenian mountains[1a] toward Media. As the Bactrian[1b] cavalry had been posted with him in the battle, they joined him in the flight.[1c] The Persians who accompanied him included the King's kinsmen and a few of the so-called Apple Bearers. [2] He was also joined by some two thousand foreign mercenaries under the command of Patron the Phocian and Glaukos the Aetolian. He had chosen to flee to Media on the supposition that after the battle Alexander would advance toward Susa and Babylon.[2a] For the road to Babylon was inhabited from beginning to end and was not impassable for pack animals; furthermore, Babylon and Susa were clearly the prizes of the war. The road to Media, on the other hand, would make hard travel for a large army.

[3] Darius was not mistaken. Setting out from Arbela, Alexander advanced directly toward Babylon, and when he was not far from the city, leading his forces in battle array, all the Babylonians came out to meet him with their priests and rulers, each group of citizens bearing gifts and surrendering the city, the citadel, and their treasure. [4] On entering

3.16.1–2
MEDIA
Accompanied by several elite corps, Darius heads northeast to Media, assuming Alexander will go southeast.

3.16.3–5
BABYLON
Rather than pursue Darius, Alexander enters Babylon and is greeted warmly. He appoints administrators and orders the rebuilding of destroyed temples.

3.16.1a Armenian mountains: precise location unknown. Armenia: Map 3.19b, AX.
3.16.1b Media; Bactria: Map 3.19b, locator.
3.16.1c The survival, more or less intact, of the

Bactrian cavalry under Bessos was to pose grave implications for Alexander in the years to come.
3.16.2a Susa; Babylon: Map 3.19b, BY.

Babylon, Alexander ordered the Babylonians to rebuild all the temples Xerxes had destroyed, including the temple of Bel, a god the Babylonians especially esteem.[4a] He appointed Mazaios as satrap of Babylon, Apollodoros of Amphipolis as commander of the soldiers left behind with Mazaios, and Asklepiodoros son of Philon as collector of the taxes.[4b] [5] He also sent Mithrenes to Armenia as satrap, since this man had surrendered the citadel at Sardis.[5a] In Babylon Alexander also met with the Chaldaeans[5b] and did everything they advised with regard to the Babylonian temples. He even sacrificed to Bel in the manner they prescribed.

[6] Alexander started for Susa and was met on the road by the son of Susa's satrap and a courier from Philoxenos (Alexander had dispatched Philoxenos to Susa right after the battle). The letter from Philoxenos related that the Susians had surrendered their city and that all the treasure was being kept safe for Alexander. [7] Twenty days after leaving Babylon, Alcxander reached Susa. On entering the city, he received the treasure—nearly fifty thousand talents of silver[7a]—and the rest of the royal property. Many other objects were captured there, including everything Xerxes had brought back with him from Greece, in particular bronze statues of Harmodios and Aristogeiton.[7b] [8] These Alexander sent back to Athens,[8a] and today they stand in the Athenian Kerameikos at the point where we ascend to the acropolis, just opposite the Metroon and not far from the altar of the Eudanemoi.[8b] (Anyone who has been initiated into the mysteries

3.16.6–8
Winter 331/30
SUSA
Alexander seizes the imperial capital Susa, with its enormous treasury, and repatriates art treasures found there to Greece.

3.16.4a The magnificent step pyramid of the god Bel (also sometimes called Marduk) was probably not destroyed by Xerxes, though he had, according to Herodotus, despoiled the place of its cult statue. In any case, Xerxes and the Persians in general, were regarded by the Babylonians as religious oppressors, so Alexander's decree ordering the rebuilding of the temples (and his own participation in their rites; see 3.16.5) was, if nothing else, an effort to win support among the Babylonians. Alexander resumed his plan to rebuild the temple of Bel when he returned to Babylon in 323; see 7.17.2–3.

3.16.4b As he had done in Egypt, Alexander retained the local, Persian-appointed (indeed, in this case, native Persian) political leadership already in place, but transferred all military and fiscal responsibilities to hand-picked Greek and Macedonian officers. It is a remarkable testament to Alexander's pragmatism that he could entrust the satrapy of Babylonia to Mazaios, who just a few days earlier had fought as Darius' senior general and led the fierce attack on Parmenion.

3.16.5a Sardis: Map 3.19a.

3.16.5b Chaldaea was a region of southern Mesopotamia, part of the old Babylonian empire. Because its inhabitants were known for mastery of astrology, science, and religious lore, the term "Chaldaean" came to signify to the Greeks a Babylo-

nian astrologer, and in particular a priest serving the cult of Bel-Marduk.

3.16.7a Fifty thousand talents was a phenomenal sum. For more on the talent as a monetary unit, see Appendix F, Money and Finance in the Campaigns of Alexander, §3.

3.16.7b Harmodios and Aristogeiton were democratic heroes who had helped break the hold of the Peisistratid tyranny that dominated Athens throughout most of the sixth century.

3.16.8a The return of these statues to Athens carried enormous symbolic weight. First, it underscored the idea that Alexander's campaign was being waged on behalf of the Greeks who had suffered in the Persian invasion of 480, in particular the Athenians. Second, the return of the statues of Harmodios and Aristogeiton highlighted the liberal political values Alexander claimed to represent, in contrast to the alleged tyranny of the Persians.

3.16.8b The name Kerameikos originally referred to the state cemetery outside Athens' northwest walls, but came to refer, as it does here, to the whole northwestern quadrant of the city. It includes the agora, or market square, the location of the Metroon, the building where the important government body called the Boule met. Arrian's mention here of the altar of the Eudanemoi gives us our only clue as to the location of this shrine.

of the two goddesses at Eleusis is familiar with the altar of the Eudanemoi, which stands on its pavement.)[8c]

[9] Alexander then sacrificed in the traditional manner and held a torch race and an athletic competition. After appointing Abulites the Persian as satrap of Susiana; Mazaros, one of the Companions, as commander of the fortress at Susa; and Arkhelaos son of Theodoros as general, he proceeded against the Persians.[9a] He sent Menes down to the coast as governor of Syria, Phoenicia, and Cilicia,[9b] [10] having given him nearly three thousand talents of silver to carry to the coast; from this money he was instructed to send Antipatros as much as he needed for the war with the Spartans.[10a] Amyntas son of Andromenes also reached Susa with the troops he had brought from Macedonia.[10b] [11] Distributing these men, Alexander assigned the horsemen to the Companion cavalry and added the foot soldiers to the other units, assigning them by tribes. He established two companies in each cavalry squadron, though there had never been cavalry companies previously, and named as their captains those among the Companions who had distinguished themselves for bravery.

[1] Starting from Susa and crossing the River Pasitigris, Alexander invaded the land of the Ouxioi.[1a] The Ouxioi who inhabited the plains obeyed the satrap of Persia and gave themselves up to Alexander on that occasion. But the so-called mountain Ouxioi, who were not subjects of Persia, sent messengers to notify Alexander that they would not let him and his army make use of the passage to Persia unless they received the same fee the Persian king used to pay them for his passage. [2] Alexander sent word back by these messengers, telling the Ouxioi to meet him at the pass—which they controlled, and thus thought they owned the route to Persia—where he, too, would pay them their fee.

Taking the royal bodyguards,[2a] the shield-bearers, and nearly eight thousand other troops, he traveled at night along a back road, the Susians acting as his guides. [3] Having traversed a rough and scarcely passable road in one day, he fell upon the Ouxioi villages, took considerable plunder, and

3.16.9–11
SUSA
Alexander makes further administrative appointments, incorporates new recruits, and reorganizes the army.

3.17.1–2
Winter 331/30
OUXIOI TERRITORY
Alexander mounts an attack on the mountain-dwelling Ouxioi, a defiant tribe as yet unconquered even by the Persians.

3.17.3–6
OUXIOI TERRITORY
Finding the pass they have always commanded in Alexander's hands, the Ouxioi retreat to the mountains, but the Macedonians hold these as well. Many are killed, and the rest must pay tribute to Alexander.

3.16.8c Much is obscure about this sentence. We do not know much about the Eudanemoi (apparently an Athenian clan responsible for tending the cult of certain wind gods), nor about the "pavement" of their altar that Arrian refers to so vaguely. It does seem possible to conclude from this reference, however, that Arrian himself was an initiate into the cult of the "two goddesses," Demeter and Persephone, at Eleusis, near Athens.
3.16.9a That is, against the other major cities in the Persian heartland (besides Babylon) rather than against Darius.
3.16.9b Syria; Phoenicia; Cilicia: Map 3.19b, BX.
3.16.10a By now Alexander had received news of the revolt of King Agis, though it is unclear just when he received it (see 3.6.3 and n. 3.6.3a). There is even more uncertainty about the timing of the suppression of the revolt and the transmission of this

news to Alexander. It is possible that Antipatros had already crushed the rebellion before Alexander's victory at Gaugamela, though the king could not have known of this until some weeks later; at best he would have had to wait until spring for news from Greece to reach him.
3.16.10b Arrian has not made previous mention of this recruiting mission, but other sources tell us that Amyntas was dispatched to Macedonia from Gaza about a year earlier. His contingent of recruits was reportedly huge: more than thirteen thousand infantry and almost fifteen hundred cavalry, according to Quintus Curtius (5.1.40–41).
3.17.1a Pasitigris River, possible location; Ouxioi: Map 3.19b, BY.
3.17.2a The royal bodyguards here are the same thousand-man *agema*, or "royal squadron," mentioned elsewhere. See Appendix D, §3.

killed many inhabitants still in their beds. The rest fled to the mountains. Alexander now hastened to the pass, where the Ouxioi expected to meet him with all their forces and receive their fee. [4] He sent Krateros ahead to seize the heights, where he thought the Ouxioi would retreat if they were pressed hard. Rushing onward, he got to the passage first. Arraying his men for battle, he led them from the higher ground against the barbarians. [5] Astounded by Alexander's speed, and put at a disadvantage by the very terrain they had particularly relied on, the Ouxioi fled without even coming to blows. Some of them died in flight at the hands of Alexander's men, and many died on the road, which was steep. But most of them, fleeing up the mountains, ran into Krateros' men and were destroyed by them. [6] These were the gifts of honor the Ouxioi received from Alexander, and when they asked him for possession of their own land, they obtained it with difficulty, and had to pay him an annual tribute. Ptolemy says that Darius' mother entreated Alexander to give the Ouxioi their country to dwell in.[6a] They were required to pay an annual tribute of a hundred horses, five hundred yoke animals, and thirty thousand head of cattle. For the Ouxioi had no money or arable land; on the contrary, most of them were herdsmen.

[1] Alexander now sent the baggage train, the Thessalian horsemen, the allies, the foreign mercenaries, and all his army's other heavy-armed troops with Parmenion, who was to lead them against Persepolis[1a] by way of the wagon road leading into the Persians' homeland. [2] Alexander himself took the Macedonian infantry, the Companion cavalry, the mounted Scouts, the Agrianians, and the archers and hastened along the route through the mountains. When he reached the Persian Gates,[2a] he came upon Ariobarzanes, the satrap of Persepolis, with some forty thousand foot soldiers and seven hundred horsemen. Ariobarzanes had walled off the Gates and made camp near the wall in order to bar Alexander's way. For the time being Alexander made camp where he was; on the following day he arrayed his troops and led them in an assault on the wall. But since the place appeared hard to capture owing to the rough terrain, and since his men, assailed from higher ground and hit by catapult fire, were sustaining many casualties, he withdrew for the moment to the camp. [4] But some of his

3.18.1–6
Winter 331/30
PERSIAN GATES
Leading half the army through mountainous terrain, Alexander encounters a blockade of a strategic pass, the Persian Gates. Alexander plans to approach by an unwatched path and make a surprise attack on the blockade, aided by a reserve force that will be summoned by a signal.

3.17.6a As Bosworth has noted (I.323), it is hard to see why Darius' mother would intercede with Alexander on behalf of a rugged hill tribe that had for decades demanded transit fees from the Persians. This improbability gives support to the alternate accounts found in Diodorus (17.67) and Quintus Curtius (5.3.14–15): the intercession came on behalf of a member of the royal family, Madates, satrap of Ouxioi territory, who had mounted a stern and effective resistance to Alexander in the mountain passes leading into Persia. Arrian makes no mention of Madates or the troubles Alexander had in dealing with him, instead relating the above tale of an easy triumph over disorganized tribesmen. It is possible that his source, in this case Ptolemy, omitted the Madates episode because it closely resembled the campaign Arrian describes here but showed Alexander having far more difficulty with local opposition. Arrian may have transferred the anecdote of the queen mother's intervention from one campaign to the other.

3.18.1a Persepolis: Map 3.19b, BY. The translation here relies on Bosworth's suggestion (I.329) that Arrian here and elsewhere in this chapter uses the name Persai to denote the city of Persepolis rather than, as it can also mean, the Persian people.

3.18.2a Persian Gates: Map 3.19b, BY.

prisoners told him of another path that would lead him around to the Gates. Since this path was said to be rugged and narrow, he left Krateros in camp with his own battalion and that of Meleagros, a few archers, and nearly five hundred horsemen, [5] with orders to assault the wall as soon as he knew that Alexander had made his way around and was approaching the Persians' camp (he would easily know this, since Alexander's trumpets would sound a signal). Alexander set out at night and, after covering about twelve miles, went on ahead with the shield-bearers, Perdikkas' battalion, the nimblest of the archers, the Agrianians, the royal squadron of the Companion cavalry,[5a] and one additional cavalry tetrarchy;[5b] with the prisoners showing the way, they advanced by an indirect route toward the Gates. [6] Meanwhile Alexander ordered Amyntas, Philotas, and Koinos to lead the rest of the army[6a] to the plain and to bridge the river that had to be crossed in order to advance on Persepolis.[6b] He himself took a difficult and rugged road and led his men along it, mostly on the double.

Falling on the first barbarian guard before daylight, he destroyed it and most of the second guard as well; [7] most of the third guard fled, and such was their fear that they did not flee to Ariobarzanes' camp but dropped everything and ran to the mountains. Consequently, Alexander's attack, near dawn, took the enemy by surprise. And just as he was assaulting the ditch, the trumpets sounded the signal, and Krateros led his men against the fortification.[7a] [8] Their enemies, attacked from all sides, fled without even attempting to fight; but as they were hemmed in on all sides, both where Alexander was pressing them hard and where Krateros' men were running to the scene, most of them were forced to turn back and flee to the walls. But these were already occupied by the Macedonians; [9] for Alexander, having foreseen what would happen, had left Ptolemy[9a] there with nearly three thousand foot soldiers, and accordingly most of the barbarians were cut to pieces by the Macedonians in hand-to-hand combat,

3.18.7–9

PERSIAN GATES

Alexander's approach goes undetected, and the coordinated attack succeeds. The Persians are slaughtered as they try to flee, though their leader, Ariobarzarnes, escapes.

3.18.5a The cavalry *ilē*, or "squadron," was a unit of up to 250 horsemen. One such *ilē* was dubbed "royal" and had the special assignment of accompanying the king in battle.

3.18.5b This is the only mention in our sources of a cavalry tetrarchy. Its name indicates that it was made up of four subdivisions, but how large these were, or how they were composed, is unclear.

3.18.6a The rest of the army: that is, the soldiers he had taken with him from camp but who were not in the group leading the assault. There were now three detachments of troops under Alexander's command—those in camp with Krateros awaiting the signal to attack, those detailed to bridge the Persian Araxes River, and those proceeding along the narrow path with Alexander—as well as the heavy-armed troops following Parmenion down the wagon road. The purpose of sending the bridge-building crew on

ahead was to ensure swift passage to Persepolis to the east once the blockade was smashed, and thus to prevent the removal of its treasures.

3.18.6b The river meant is the Araxes in Persia (possible location, Map 3.19b, BY), not the river by the same name in Central Asia.

3.18.7a The narrow path followed by Alexander must have been indirect indeed, since it took him most of the night to reach the Persian position, whereas Krateros, traveling a straight route, appears to have gotten there in a very short time.

3.18.9a It is unclear whether this means Ptolemy son of Lagos, one of Arrian's principal sources, or another of the Ptolemys accompanying Alexander, perhaps Ptolemy son of Philip (see 1.14.6). None of the other Alexander historians mention a Ptolemy in their accounts of this episode.

FIGURE 3.18A. The ruins of the palace complex at Persepolis. Some of the ruins still bear traces of the fire that, according to Arrian, was started on Alexander's orders.

while others, in a flight that became desperate, flung themselves from the cliffs and perished. Ariobarzanes himself fled to the mountains with a few horsemen.

[10] Alexander now hastened with his men to the river, found the bridge already in place, and crossed easily with the army. He then hurried on to Persepolis and arrived before the guards had time to plunder the treasure; he also seized the treasure in the coffers of Cyrus the First in Pasargadae.[10a] [11] He appointed Phrasaortes son of Rheomithras as satrap of Persepolis.

He also set the Persian palace on fire against the advice of Parmenion, who argued that it was ignoble to destroy what was now his own property, and that the peoples of Asia would not pay heed to him in the same way if

3.18.10–12
Winter–Spring 330
PERSEPOLIS
Alexander's speedy advance allows him to capture the treasuries of Persepolis and Pasargadae before they can be removed. In the spring, Alexander orders the burning of the royal palace, against the advice of Parmenion, in order to pay the Persians back for offenses against the Greeks.

3.18.10a The hoard of treasure at nearby Pasargadae (Map 3.19b, BY), reported by other sources to be 6,000 talents, was large by Greek standards but minuscule in comparison with what Alexander had already seized at Susa and Persepolis: 50,000 talents of silver (according to Arrian) in the former case, and as much as 120,000 (according to the vulgate sources; Arrian gives no figure) in the latter. The Persians had used the palaces of these three cities to stockpile the wealth accrued in two centuries of imperial taxation; by Herodotus' reckoning (*Histories* 3.95.2) they were already taking in more than 14,000 talents per year in the early fifth century. Indeed, the unlocking of this wealth of precious metals by Alexander was to have profound economic impact. See Appendix F, §4, 6.

FIGURE 3.18B. The remains of the palace of Darius I at Persepolis. Darius had sent the invasion forces that attacked Athens in 490, one of the acts of aggression that Alexander, in Arrian's account, decided to avenge.

they assumed he had no intention of governing Asia but would merely conquer and move on. [12] But Alexander declared that he wanted to pay back the Persians, who, when they invaded Greece, had razed Athens and burned the temples, and to exact retribution for all the other wrongs they had committed against the Greeks. It seems to me, however, that in doing this Alexander was not acting sensibly, nor do I think there could be any punishment for Persians of a bygone era.[12a]

3.18.12a The burning of the Persepolis palace, which left the vast complex the charred ruin that can still be seen in southern Iran today, is one of the most controversial and contested aspects of Alexander's campaign. Appendix H, Alexander at Persepolis, discusses the burning of the palace and its ramifications. Arrian's version is contradicted by the vulgate sources, which characterize the arson as an unplanned act of vandalism, conceived and committed during a night of revelry. According to these accounts, a Greek courtesan named Thaïs suggested the idea as an act of revenge that would please the Greeks, and a drunken Alexander tossed the first torch.

Most historians deem Arrian's version more credible. A further problem arises from the report in Diodorus (17.70.2–6) that Alexander allowed his troops to pillage Persepolis on first entering the city, and that this sack was carried out with wanton cruelty and destructiveness; Arrian's account bears no trace of such an episode. The general picture drawn by the vulgate sources is thus of a conqueror who, following his total victory over Darius, turned into a reckless despoiler, whereas Arrian maintains an image of Alexander as a temperate and rational leader, even while expressing disapproval of this particular policy choice.

3.19.1–4

Spring 330

MEDIA-ECBATANA

After his sojourn in Persepolis, Alexander resumes the pursuit of Darius. On his arrival in Media he learns of the Persian king's military weakness.

[1] Alexander now headed for Media, as he kept hearing reports that Darius was there. Darius had decided that if Alexander remained at Susa and Babylon, he would himself remain in Media, in case there was any sedition among Alexander's forces; but if Alexander should march against him, he would go farther into the interior, to the Parthians and into Hyrcania[1a] as far as Bactra,[1b] laying waste the entire countryside and making Alexander's route impassable. [2] He sent the women, his remaining furniture, and the covered carriages to the place known as the Caspian Gates; he himself remained in Ecbatana[2a] with the forces he had chosen from those at hand. On hearing of this, Alexander advanced toward Media. Attacking the Paraetacae[2b] in their country, he subjugated them and appointed Oxathres son of Aboulites the satrap of Susa, as their satrap. [3] When it was reported to him en route that Darius had decided to meet him in battle and again try the chances of war, and that he had been joined by his Scythian[3a] and Kadousian[3b] allies, Alexander gave orders for the pack animals and their keepers, along with the other gear, to follow behind, while he led the rest of the army forward, armed for battle. In twelve days he reached Media. [4] There he learned that Darius lacked sufficient forces to do battle, that his Kadousian and Scythian allies had not come, and that Darius was intending to flee. Alexander now increased his pace. When he was roughly a three-day journey from Ecbatana, he was met by Bisthanes son of Okhos[4a] (Okhos had been king of the Persians before Darius); [5] Bisthanes reported that Darius had fled four days earlier with the treasure from Media, about seven thousand talents, and an army of nearly three thousand cavalry and six thousand infantry.

3.19.5–8

Summer 330

ECBATANA

On the way to Ecbatana, Alexander learns that Darius has fled the city. In Ecbatana, Alexander decommissions his Greek allied troops with generous pay, and allows them to re-enroll on a volunteer basis. He orders Parmenion to transfer the treasury to Harpalos and then march with an army into Hyrcania.

On his arrival in Ecbatana, Alexander sent the Thessalian cavalry and the other allies[5a] back to the coast, having paid them their full wages and given them an additional two thousand talents out of his own funds. [6] Any man who wished to continue to serve with him as a mercenary was ordered to set down his name, and it turned out that a considerable number did so. Alexander appointed Epokillos son of Polyides to lead the departing troops to the coast, taking other horsemen to guard them, since the Thessalians

3.19.1a The following locations can be found on Map 3.19b: Media, locator; Susa, BY; Babylon, BY; Parthia, AY; Hyrcania, AY.

3.19.1b Bactra and Zariaspa (Map 3.19b, locator) are two different names for the capital city of Bactria.

3.19.2a Caspian Gates; Ecbatana: Map 3.19b, BY.

3.19.2b Paraetacae (Paraetacene): Map 3.19b, BY. These are a different people than the Pareitakai mentioned at 4.22.1.

3.19.3a Scythia: Map 3.19b, locator.

3.19.3b Kadousioi, location of territory: Map 3.19b, AY.

3.19.4a Okhos was Artaxerxes III's name before his ascension to the throne; see n. 2.14.2a.

3.19.5a These were the units supplied by the Greek city-states, Sparta excepted, under the terms accepted by the League of Corinth (see Appendix M, §3). By dismissing them from service, Alexander

was tacitly acknowledging that the stated goals of the invasion as it was first approved by the League—the punishment of Persia and the liberation of its Hellenic subjects—had been achieved. He also no doubt had reckoned that, with Darius unable to field another army for a major confrontation, the services of such conscripts—who, apart from the Thessalian cavalry, had never been asked to do much for the war effort anyway—were no longer needed; and that with Greece itself now pacified after the defeat of King Agis, news of which had certainly reached Alexander by this point, these troops no longer served much purpose as hostages either. The vulgate sources differ from Arrian in placing the release of the Greek troops after the death of Darius (see n. 3.23.1a).

FIGURE 3.19. Two 1934 photos of the entrance to the Caspian Gates. The inset box on the aerial photo (above) shows the entry to the pass, the same point depicted in the close-up below.

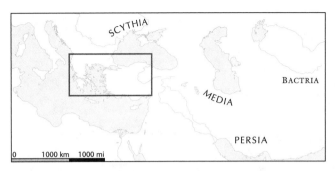

MAP 3.19A

had sold their horses there. Alexander also ordered Menes to see to it, when they reached the coast, that these men were conveyed in triremes[6a] to Euboea.[6b] [7] He also assigned Parmenion the job of depositing the Persian treasure in the citadel at Ecbatana and handing it over to Harpalos; for he left Harpalos in charge of the treasure and posted some six thousand Macedonians, both cavalry and a few light-armed troops, to guard it. Parmenion himself was then to take the mercenaries, the Thracians, and all the other horsemen except the Companion cavalry and march past Kadousian country into Hyrcania.[7a] [8] Kleitos, the commander of the royal squadron, was instructed, when he reached Ecbatana from Susa, where he had been left ill,

3.19.6a Trireme: the standard Greek warship in the fifth and fourth centuries, armed with a bronze ram at the front and powered by three banks of rowers.
3.19.6b Euboea: Map 3.19a.

3.19.7a This mission, evidently an effort to clear out resistance in the north and cut off a possible escape route for Darius, was never carried out, for unexplained reasons. Parmenion would remain in Ecbatana.

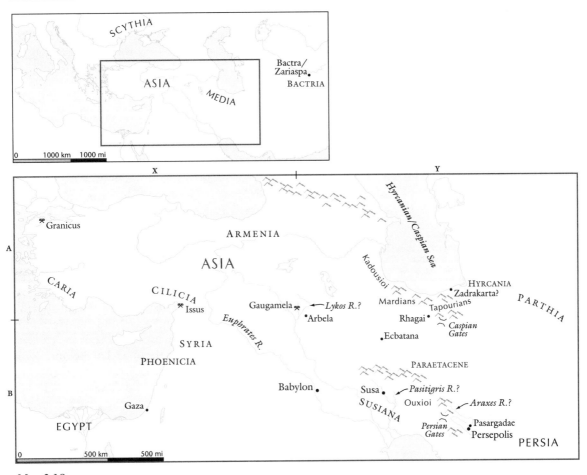

MAP 3.19B

to take command of the Macedonians Alexander was now leaving behind to guard the treasure and to proceed on the road to Parthia,[8a] where Alexander himself was also about to go.

[1] Taking the Companion cavalry, the Scouts, the mercenary cavalry under Eriguios' command, the Macedonian phalanx (except for the men assigned to guard the treasure), the archers, and the Agrianians, Alexander went after Darius. Owing to the urgent pace of the march, many of his soldiers were left behind exhausted, and the horses were dying; [2] undeterred, he hastened onward and reached Rhagai[2a] on the eleventh day. For anyone traveling at Alexander's pace the place lies a day's journey from the

3.20.1–4
Summer 330
RHAGAI
With a composite force designed for mobility, Alexander sets out at top speed in pursuit of Darius, pausing to rest only when he learns his foe is out of reach.

3.20.2a Rhaga(i): Map 3.19b, AY.

Caspian Gates,[2b] but before Alexander could get there, Darius had already passed the Gates. Many of those who fled with Darius deserted him in the course of the flight and withdrew, each man to his own country, and no small number gave themselves up to Alexander. [3] Having given up hope of overtaking Darius by a close pursuit, Alexander remained in Rhagai for five days and allowed his army to rest.[3a] He appointed Oxydates, a Persian, as satrap of Media. (Oxydates had been arrested by Darius and confined at Susa,[3b] a circumstance that encouraged Alexander to trust him.) Alexander himself then proceeded to Parthia. [4] On the first day, he made camp near the Caspian Gates; on the second, he passed beyond them and advanced to the edge of inhabited territory. In order to obtain provisions there, as he had heard that the country ahead was a wasteland, he sent Koinos on a foraging expedition with some horsemen and a few foot soldiers.

3.21.1–5
Summer 330
MEDIA
Alexander resumes his high-speed pursuit when he learns that Darius has been overthrown in a coup led by Bessos and is a prisoner of those fleeing with him.

[1] At that point Bagistanes, a distinguished Babylonian, reached Alexander from Darius' camp with Antibelos, one of Mazaios' sons. These men reported that Darius had been arrested by Nabarzanes, the commander of the cavalry that had fled with him; by Bessos, the satrap of Bactria; and by Barsaentes, the satrap of the Arachosians and Zarangians. [2] On hearing this, Alexander advanced even faster, accompanied only by the Companions, the mounted Scouts, and the strongest and nimblest foot soldiers. He did not even wait for Koinos' party to return from their foraging expedition, but put Krateros in charge of the men left behind, with orders to follow but not to make forced marches. [3] The men with Alexander carried only their weapons and two days' rations. Having marched throughout the night until noon the next day, he gave the army a brief rest and again marched all night long. At daybreak he reached the camp from which Bagistanes had started, [4] but encountered none of the enemy. As for Darius, Alexander learned that he had been arrested and was being transported in a covered carriage, and that Bessos held power in Darius' place and had been named commander by the Bactrian horsemen and all the other barbarians who had fled with Darius, with the exception of Artabazos and his sons and the Greek mercenaries. These men had remained loyal to Darius but had been unable to prevent what was happening; they had left the main road and were on their way to the mountains by themselves, taking no part in the acts of Bessos and his followers.[4a] [5] The men who had seized Darius, Alexander learned, had decided that if they heard that Alexander was pursuing them, they would surrender Darius to him and get something out of it for themselves; but if they learned that he had turned back, they would assemble as large an army as they could and preserve their power in common. Finally, Alexander learned that Bessos,

3.20.2b　Caspian Gates: Map 3.19b, BY. Bosworth (I.339) measures the distance from Rhaga(i) to the Caspian Gates at 51 miles.
3.20.3a　The implication seems to be that the deserters gave information as to Darius' whereabouts and so caused Alexander to rethink his pursuit strategy.
3.20.3b　Susa: Map 3.19b, BY.
3.21.4a　Artabazos' decision to flee into the hills and avoid the guilt of Darius' murder was a politic one, for he was later appointed satrap by Alexander and entrusted with several important commands (see 3.23.7 and n. 3.23.7a).

because of his close relationship with Darius and because the deed was done in his satrapy, was for the moment in command.

[6] It was plain to Alexander, when he heard this report, that he must pursue these men with all possible vigor. His own men and horses were already exhausted by the constant strain, but he nevertheless pressed on. After traveling a great distance, marching through the night until noon the next day, he reached a village where those leading Darius had made camp the day before. [7] On hearing that the barbarians had decided to travel at night, he asked the inhabitants if they knew of any shortcut leading to the fugitives. They said they did know of one, but the road was deserted as it lacked water. Alexander ordered them to lead him to that road. As he realized that the foot soldiers would not follow him at his rapid pace, he dismounted some five hundred horsemen, selected the fittest officers of the infantry and the other units, and ordered them to mount the horses carrying their regular infantry weapons.[7a] [8] He ordered Nikanor, the commander of the shield-bearers, and Attalos, who led the Agrianians, to take the men who were being left behind and lead them along the road Bessos' party had taken, equipping them as lightly as possible; he ordered the rest of the infantry to follow in regular formation. [9] Alexander himself, starting in the afternoon, led his men on the double. At dawn, after traveling nearly forty-five miles overnight, he caught up with the barbarians marching in disorder and unarmed. A few of them tried to defend themselves, but the majority, as soon as they caught sight of Alexander himself, fled without even coming to blows. Those who turned and resisted also fled after a few had fallen. [10] For a time Bessos and his confederates took Darius with them in a covered carriage, but when Alexander drew near, Satibarzanes and Barsaentes wounded Darius, left him there, and fled with six hundred horsemen. Darius died from his wounds shortly thereafter, before Alexander had seen him.[10a]

[1] Alexander sent Darius' body back to Persepolis[1a] and ordered that he be buried, like all his royal predecessors, in the royal tombs. He appointed Amminapes the Parthian as satrap of Parthia and Hyrcania.[1b] Amminapes had been among those who, along with Mazakes, surrendered Egypt[1c] to Alexander. One of the Companions, Tlepolemos son of Pythophanes, was conjointly assigned to help oversee Parthian and Hyrcanian affairs.

[2] This was the end of Darius, who died in the month of Hekatombaion during Aristophon's archonship at Athens. In military matters,

Right margin notes:

3.21.6–10
MEDIA
Taking only a highly mobile force with him, Alexander races down a desert road to head off Bessos' party. He catches up with them at dawn the next day and puts most to flight. Two of Bessos' party stab Darius and leave him to die before Alexander can reach him, while they and Bessos use the diversion to make their escape.

3.22.1
Alexander accords Darius a royal burial.

3.22.2–6
Arrian summarizes the reign of Darius: a continuous string of disasters beginning from the moment he ascended the throne.

3.21.7a By this move Alexander sought to gain the best combination of mobility and combat strength. The many lightning-quick command decisions Alexander made during this pursuit put his logistical genius into high relief: by the final stage of the chase he had shed slower-moving units at several points along hundreds of miles of unfamiliar and often inhospitable country, delegating leadership for each group and arranging how each was to

rendezvous with the advance force.
3.21.10a The more fanciful versions of the Alexander legend, including that found in the *Alexander Romance* and often depicted in manuscript illustrations, portray Darius dying in Alexander's arms and proclaiming him heir to the throne with his last breath.
3.22.1a Persepolis: Map 3.19b, BY.
3.22.1b Hyrcania: Map 3.19b, AY.
3.22.1c Egypt: Map 3.19b, BX.

the man could scarcely have been more cowardly or misguided;[2a] but in other areas he did nothing amiss, or rather he lacked the opportunity, since as soon as he ascended the throne he found himself at war with the Macedonians and Greeks. Thus even if he had wanted to persecute his subjects, he would have found it impossible to do so, since the danger he faced was graver than theirs. [3] Throughout his life he was afflicted by one disaster after another, nor was there any respite after his accession. His misfortunes began with the satraps' cavalry disaster at the Granicus.[3a] Then, right away, Ionia and Aeolis were in enemy hands, along with both Phrygias, Lydia, and all the Carians except for the Halicarnassians.[3b] [4] Soon Halicarnassus was also captured, and shortly afterward the entire coast as far as Cilicia.[4a] Then came his defeat at Issus,[4b] where he saw his mother, wife, and children taken prisoner. Then Phoenicia[4c] and all of Egypt were lost. He then disgraced himself at Arbela,[4d] where he was among the first to flee, thereby losing the largest army of the entire barbarian race. [5] A fugitive from his own empire, a wanderer finally betrayed to the utmost by his own party, he became at one and the same time a king and a prisoner carried off in dishonor. Finally he was destroyed by a conspiracy of his closest associates. Such was Darius' fate while he lived, [6] but when he died he met with a royal burial, his children were raised and educated by Alexander as if Darius were still on the throne, and Alexander became his son-in-law.[6a] Darius was about fifty years old when he died.

[1] Collecting the troops that had been left behind in the pursuit, Alexander advanced into Hyrcania,[1a] which lies to the left of the road leading to Bactra.[1b] The country is bounded on one side by lofty, densely wooded mountains. Its plain extends to that region's branch of the Great Sea.[1c] Alexander was advancing to Hyrcania because he had learned that Darius'

3.23.1–2
Summer 330
HYRCANIA
Alexander moves into Hyrcania to pursue forces loyal to Darius and to subdue the Tapourians.

3.22.2a It must be stressed here that Arrian's picture of Darius is persistently more negative than that drawn by our other sources, especially in the matter of military prowess. There is good evidence elsewhere that Darius showed personal bravery at both Issus and Gaugamela, and notwithstanding his loss of those two battles, his generalship was at least competent. Arrian also ignores Darius' success in reconquering rebellious Egypt in 335.

3.22.3a Granicus (battle site on the Granicus River): Map 3.19b, AX.

3.22.3b Ionia; Aeolis; Phrygia; Hellespontine Phrygia; Lydia; Halicarnassus: Map 3.19a. Caria: Map 3.19b, AX.

3.22.4a Cilicia: Map 3.19b, AX.

3.22.4b Issus: Map 3.19b, AX.

3.22.4c Phoenicia: Map 3.19b, BX.

3.22.4d In mentioning Arbela (Map 3.19b, AY), Arrian is referring to the battle of Gaugamela. For Arrian's commentary on the use of Arbela as the name of the battle, see 6.11.5–6.

3.22.6a Darius' eldest daughter, known both as Barsine and as Stateira, was wed by

Alexander in 324 (see 7.4.4). As for the education of Darius' children, Diodorus (17.67.1) reports that Alexander had them tutored in Greek—hardly the curriculum Darius would have prescribed.

3.23.1a This is the point at which Diodorus and Quintus Curtius place the decommissioning of the Greek allied troops, which according to Arrian took place several weeks earlier. Both these sources also report that Alexander had to persuade his remaining troops to go forward into Hyrcania, since they felt that the death of Darius had put an end point to the war.

3.23.1b Bactra/Zariaspa: Map 3.19b, locator.

3.23.1c The "Great Sea" usually means Ocean, which the Greeks thought surrounded Europe, Asia, and Africa on all sides. Arrian seems to accept a theory, prevalent in his day, that the Hyrcanian/Caspian Sea (Map 3.19b, AY) was an inlet of Ocean. Alexander reportedly sent an expedition to the Hyrcanian Sea, just before his death, to determine whether this was so. See Appendix N, Alexander's Geographic Notions, §2, and Ref. Map 8b.

mercenaries had fled to the Tapourian Mountains; he also intended to subdue the Tapourians[1d] themselves. [2] Dividing the army into three parts, he himself advanced along the shortest and roughest road with the largest and nimblest division. He dispatched Krateros against the Tapourians with his own and Amyntas' battalions, some archers, and a few horsemen. Eriguios was ordered to take command of the mercenaries and the rest of the cavalry and lead them along the main road, which was longer, together with the wagons, the baggage train, and all the other camp followers.

[3] After passing over the first mountains, Alexander made camp. Taking the shield-bearers, the nimblest of the Macedonian phalanx, and some archers, he traveled a difficult, nearly impassable road, leaving guards behind at the points that looked dangerous lest the barbarians who held the mountains attack the troops following at a distance. [4] After traversing the narrows with the archers, he camped in the plain near a small river. There he was approached by Darius' officer Nabarzanes, Phrataphernes the satrap of Hyrcania and Parthia,[4a] and the most distinguished Persians of Darius' suite, who gave themselves up.[4b] [5] After a four-day stay he picked up the men who had been left behind on the road. Most had come through safely, except the rear guard of Agrianians, who had been attacked by the barbarian mountain-dwellers; but the barbarians had been worsted in the skirmish and had withdrawn.

[6] Setting out from there, Alexander advanced to Zadrakarta,[6a] a city in Hyrcania. At that point he was joined by Krateros and his men, who had not encountered Darius' mercenaries but had gained possession of the entire region through which they had just traveled, partly by use of force and partly through the surrender of the inhabitants. Eriguios also arrived with the baggage train and wagons. [7] Shortly thereafter, Artabazos[7a] reached Alexander with three of his sons, Kophen, Ariobarzanes,[7b] and Arsames. They were accompanied by envoys from Darius' mercenaries and by Autophradates, the Tapourians' satrap. Alexander confirmed Autophradates in the satrapy and kept Artabazos and his sons with him in positions

3.23.3–5
TAPOURIAN MOUNTAINS
While taking his column through the mountains, Alexander is approached by several high-ranking Persian fugitives wishing to surrender.

3.23.6–9
ZADRAKARTA
Important Persian officers surrender to Alexander and are given positions of honor in his regime, but the Greek mercenaries who fought with Darius are rebuffed in their attempt to negotiate a surrender.

3.23.1d Tapourians (Tapouroi), location of territory: Map 3.19b, AY. The Tapourian Mountains correspond to the modern-day Elburz Range.

3.23.4a Evidently Phrataphernes had replaced Amminapes, who had been appointed satrap of Hyrcania and Parthia just before this (see 3.22.1) but must have been removed for some unknown reason.

3.23.4b These men had fled with Darius and had connived at his overthrow, but had not participated in his murder and so could expect some clemency from Alexander. Quintus Curtius (6.4.8–13) quotes a letter from Nabarzanes to Alexander in which the Persian tries to justify his role in the coup, claiming in essence that he had no choice and asking for a guarantee of amnesty. Phrataphernes would go on to become Alexander's most reliable Persian adherent, and his sons would be

appointed to high-ranking positions in the army (see 7.6.4).

3.23.6a Zadrakarta, possible location: Map 3.19b, AY. The *Barrington Atlas* shows two possible locations for this city; the one indicated on Map 3.19b has been deemed the more likely by Bosworth (I.351).

3.23.7a Artabazos was a distinguished Persian nobleman, one of whose sons (not accompanying him here) was Pharnabazos, the admiral who had led the Persian forces in the Aegean after Memnon's death. It is also worth noting that, as father of a woman with whom Alexander had a sexual liaison several years earlier, Artabazos was the grandfather of Alexander's only known child to this point, a son named Herakles.

3.23.7b This is evidently a different Ariobarzanes than the satrap of Persepolis mentioned at 3.18.2.

of honor, as they were Persians of the first rank and had kept faith with Darius. [8] But he refused to come to any agreement with the Greek envoys who begged him to negotiate terms for the surrender of all the mercenaries, since he regarded their having joined forces with the barbarians against Greece, in violation of Greek decrees,[8a] as a grave offense. He urged all of them to come to him and give themselves up, placing themselves in his hands to be treated as he pleased, or else find refuge wherever they could. [9] The envoys declared that they and all the other mercenaries would turn themselves over to Alexander, and urged him to send an officer along with them to escort their forces to him in safety. The mercenaries were said to number nearly fifteen hundred men. Alexander sent them Andronikos son of Agerros and Artabazos.[9a]

[1] Alexander now advanced against the Mardians[1a] with the shield-bearers, the archers, the Agrianians, the battalions of Koinos and Amyntas, half the Companion cavalry, and the mounted javelin men, for by this time their unit had been formed.[1b] [2] As he passed through most of this territory he killed many Mardians as they fled, including some who ventured to resist, and took many alive. It had been a long time since anyone had invaded the country of the Mardians to make war on them, both on account of the rough terrain and because the tribe was poor and warlike. As they had no fear that Alexander would attack them, especially since he had already advanced beyond them, they were the more caught off guard. [3] Many of them fled to the mountains, which in their country are lofty and steep, thinking Alexander would not come after them. But when he reached them even there, they sent envoys and surrendered themselves and their country. Alexander released them, but appointed Autophradates as their satrap (he was also the Tapourians' satrap).

[4] Returning to the camp from which he had set out for the Mardians' country, Alexander found that the Greek mercenaries had arrived along with the envoys who had been sent to King Darius: the Spartans Kallistratidas, Pausippos, Monimos, and Onomas, and Dropides the Athenian.[4a] Arresting them, Alexander held them under guard, though he released the envoys from Sinope,[4b] since Sinope was not a member of the League of the Greeks;[4c] and as the Sinopeans were Persian subjects, Alexander did not

---

3.24.1–3
Summer 330
MARDIAN TERRITORY
Alexander proceeds against the Mardians and obtains their surrender.

3.24.4–5
HYRCANIA
Alexander deals with the Greek mercenaries who fought against him in the service of Persia, and with envoys from the Greek cities.

3.23.8a Under Philip, Alexander's father, the League of Corinth had forbidden Greek mercenaries to serve the Persian crown. See Appendix M, §3.

3.23.9a The fact that a Persian could be dispatched to take charge of a contingent of Greek prisoners is indicative of the way racial and national allegiances were rapidly giving way at Alexander's court to a kind of hierarchy of reliability. Alexander seems to have regarded Artabazos, who had remained loyal to the Persian cause, as worthy of honor and trust, whereas the Greeks who had sold their services to a foreign nation were held in contempt.

3.24.1a Mardians (Mardoi), location of territory: Map 3.19b, AY.

3.24.1b Alexander appears to have adapted to the new type of opponent he was encountering, small bands fighting from mountain redoubts and in rough terrain, by creating a force of more lightly armed cavalry capable of quick movement.

3.24.4a These envoys must have been sent prior to or during King Agis' rebellion, to enlist Persian aid, hence the predominance of Spartans among them.

3.24.4b Sinope: Map 3.19a.

3.24.4c The League of Corinth; see Appendix M, §3.

think it unreasonable of them to send an embassy to their own king. [5] He
also released the Greeks who had been serving the Persians as mercenaries
before the peace and alliance had been concluded with the Macedonians,[5a]
as well as Herakleides, the Chalcedonians' envoy.[5b] He ordered the other
mercenaries[5c] to serve in his army for the same pay as before, and posted as
their commander Andronikos, a man who had been in charge of them
previously and had evidently taken great pains to save his men.

[1] After settling these matters, Alexander proceeded to Zadrakarta, the
largest Hyrcanian city and the site of the Hyrcanian palace. After a fifteen-
day visit, during which he performed his customary sacrifices and held an
athletic competition, Alexander proceeded to Parthia.[1a] From there he
advanced to the Areian frontier and reached Sousia,[1b] an Areian city, where
he was joined by Satibarzanes, the Areian satrap. [2] Confirming Satibarzanes in his satrapy, Alexander sent Anaxippos, one of the Companions,
along with him, having given him some forty mounted javelin men so that
he could establish guards at regular intervals to ensure that no Areians
would be injured by the army on its march.[2a] [3] At that point, Alexander
received a visit from a party of Persians, who reported that Bessos was wearing the tall tiara[3a] and the royal attire, was calling himself Artaxerxes instead
of Bessos,[3b] and was claiming to be the king of Asia. Bessos' followers
included some Persians who had fled to Bactra[3c] and many of the Bactrians
themselves. He was also expecting a force of Scythian auxiliaries.

[4] Now that all his forces had joined him, Alexander set out for Bactra.
He was joined en route by Philip son of Menelaos, who had arrived from
Media[4a] with the mercenary cavalry under his own command, the Thessalian volunteers who had remained with the army, and Andromakhos'
foreign troops. Nikanor son of Parmenion, the shield-bearers' commander,
had already died of disease. [5] On his way to Bactra Alexander received

3.25.1–3
ZADRAKARTA
Moving eastward through
Parthia and Areia, Alexander
gets word that Bessos has
proclaimed himself Darius'
successor and is assembling
an army in Bactria.

3.25.4–6
Autumn 330
ZADRAKARTA–ROAD TO
BACTRA–ARTAKOANA
Alexander starts out for
Bactra but learns en route
that Satibarzanes has
mounted a rebellion in Areia.
He heads back at top speed
to suppress the revolt.

3.24.5a The reference is to the treaty Philip
imposed after his victory at Chaeronea (by
which Greek mercenaries were forbidden
to serve the Persian crown). Those Greek
mercenaries who had already entered
Persian employ before the treaty were
considered exempt from its terms.
3.24.5b Nothing is known of this Herakleides. It is
possible that he came not from Chalcedon
(in the Greek, Kalkhedon) but from
Carthage (Karkhedon), since Karkhedonion
is the reading of the manuscripts. Most
modern editions, including this one, have
preferred the change to Kalkhedonion
because the name of the envoy appears to
be Greek, not Punic.
3.24.5c Those who had joined the Persian cause
after the treaty forbade them to do so, and
who were therefore subject to punishment
had they not done as Alexander asked.
3.25.1a Parthia: Map 3.28. Arrian is silent here
about a sensational episode reported by
the vulgate sources (Diodorus 17.77,
Quintus Curtius 6.5.24–32, Justin 12.3),
in which Thalestris, queen of an Amazon

tribe dwelling to the north, approached
Alexander in Zadrakarta in hopes of
conceiving a child by him; Alexander
stayed with her for thirteen days of sexual
congress, and then both monarchs went
on their way. Plutarch (*Parallel Lives*,
"Alexander" 46) discusses the legend but
rejects it as a fiction, on the grounds that
Alexander does not mention the
encounter in a letter from this period in
which he discusses an alliance by marriage
offered by a Scythian king.
3.25.1b Ar(e)ia; Sousia: Map 3.28, Sogdiana inset.
3.25.2a It is noteworthy both that Alexander
feared his men would pillage the countryside on his way through Areia and that he
took steps to prevent this.
3.25.3a Only the Persian king was permitted to
wear a tall, peaked version of the felt hat,
variously called the tiara or *kitaris*,
commonly worn by Persian aristocracy.
3.25.3b Persian monarchs often assumed a regnal
name upon ascending the throne.
3.25.3c Bactra/Zariaspa: Map 3.28, Sogdiana inset.
3.25.4a Media: Map 3.28.

word that Satibarzanes, the Areian satrap, had killed Anaxippos and his mounted javelin men and was arming the Areians and mustering them in the city of Artakoana,[5a] the site of the Areian palace. Satibarzanes had decided, when he learned that Alexander was advancing, to proceed with his forces to Bessos and join him in attacking the Macedonians wherever he encountered them. [6] When all this was reported to Alexander, he stopped his march to Bactra. Taking the Companion cavalry, the mounted javelin men, the archers, the Agrianians, and the battalions of Amyntas and Koinos, and leaving the rest of his forces there under Krateros' command, he hastened against Satibarzanes and the Areians and reached Artakoana after covering nearly seventy-five miles in two days.

[7] When Satibarzanes realized that Alexander was nearby, he was so astonished by the speed of Alexander's approach that he fled with a few Areian horsemen. He was abandoned by most of his soldiers during his flight when they, too, learned that Alexander was approaching. Alexander, meanwhile, went here and there in swift pursuit of all those who he learned had taken part in the revolt and had in the course of it abandoned their villages. After killing some of the insurgents and enslaving others, he appointed Arsakes, a Persian, as satrap of the Areians. [8] Rejoined by the troops left behind under Krateros, Alexander advanced to Zarangiane[8a] and reached its capital. Barsaentes, who was then in control of the country and had been among those who had attacked Darius in his flight, escaped to the Indians west of the Indus[8b] when he learned that Alexander was approaching. But the Indians arrested Barsaentes and sent him to Alexander, who put him to death for having betrayed Darius.[8c]

[1] It was in Zarangiane that Alexander learned of the plot of Philotas, Parmenion's son.[1a] Ptolemy and Aristoboulos both say that it had been reported to him earlier, in Egypt, but had not seemed credible to him given his long-standing friendship with Philotas, the honor he had bestowed on Philotas' father, Parmenion, and the faith he had in Philotas himself. [2] Ptolemy

3.25.5a Artakoana (Artacavan), possible location: Map 3.28, Sogdiana inset.
3.25.8a Zarangiane (Drangiane): Map 3.28.
3.25.8b Indus River: Map 3.28.
3.25.8c Arrian fails to note that the arrest of Barsaentes came much later, after Alexander had brought his army into India.
3.26.1a Arrian here speaks of "the plot of Philotas" as though the man's guilt were established, but the historical record is more ambiguous. The events referred to obliquely by Arrian at 3.26.2, but recounted in detail by other sources, are as follows: Philotas was on guard duty outside Alexander's tent when he was approached by a certain Kebalinos with information about a plot to assassinate the king. The plot was said to have been organized by Dimnos, a lower-ranking Companion. For the next two days Philotas failed to inform Alexander of what he had heard, and Kebalinos finally reported the plot to one of the royal pages instead, who passed on the information to Alexander. Philotas was thus

guilty of a dereliction of duty, but there is no evidence that he was involved in Dimnos' plot. Dimnos died before he could give information. His lover and co-conspirator Nikomakhos named several other members of the plot, but Philotas was not among them. In assessing this episode, it is important to bear in mind that Philotas, son of Alexander's senior general Parmenion, was widely disliked and occasionally mistrusted by the other high-ranking officers in Alexander's army. Parmenion's high stature and growing estrangement from Alexander made Philotas a potential threat. The other Companions seem to have seized on Philotas' lapse as a pretext to destroy him, and Alexander was easily persuaded to give his assent. However, it should also be noted that Philotas' failure to report the plot to Alexander was quite possibly intentional. Had the plot succeeded, Philotas' position, and that of his father, Parmenion, would have been greatly strengthened. See the Introduction, §7.1–3, and Appendix E, §6.

relates that Philotas was tried before the Macedonians, that Alexander accused him aggressively, and that Philotas defended himself, and that the informers who testified brought clear proof against Philotas and his associates. Laying particular stress on Philotas' admission that he had been aware of a plot being hatched against Alexander, the Macedonians convicted him of having said nothing to the king, though he visited his tent twice a day. [3] The Macedonians executed Philotas and his fellow conspirators with a volley of javelins. As for Parmenion, Alexander moved against him by sending Polydamas, one of the Companions, with a letter to Kleandros, Sitalkes, and Menidas, the commanders in Media; these men had been posted with the army under Parmenion's command, [4] and these were the men at whose hands Parmenion died. Perhaps Alexander could not believe that Parmenion had taken no part in his own son's plot, or perhaps, even had he not taken part, there was a danger in Parmenion remaining alive once his son had been executed, given the high rank he held with Alexander himself and his popularity with the army—not only with the Macedonians, but also with the mercenaries, whom he had often led, both in the normal course of duty and beyond it, at Alexander's command.

[1] They also say that Amyntas son of Andromenes was brought to trial at the same time, as were his brothers Polemon, Attalos, and Simmias, on the grounds that they, too, had taken part in the plot against Alexander out of loyalty to Philotas and fellowship with him. [2] And most people were more inclined to believe in the plot because Polemon, one of Amyntas' brothers, had fled to the enemy when Philotas was arrested. But Amyntas, who awaited trial with his brothers and defended himself forcefully, was acquitted, and as soon as he was released he demanded in the assembly to be allowed to go to his brother and bring him back to Alexander. [3] The Macedonians consented. Departing that very day, Amyntas brought Polemon back, and in doing so made it much more evident than before that he was innocent. But shortly thereafter, while besieging a village, he was hit by an arrow and died of the wound, and thus his acquittal afforded him no greater benefit than that of dying with his reputation intact.

[4] Alexander now appointed two hipparchs[4a] for the Companions, Hephaistion son of Amyntor and Kleitos son of Dropides, and divided the Companions' battalion in two, as he would not have wanted one man, not even his dearest friend, to have charge of so many horsemen,[4b] especially as the men of that battalion were the bravest and most renowned in the entire cavalry. He then visited the tribe known in ancient times as the Ariaspians[4c] but later named the Euergetai, or "Helpers," because they had

3.27.1–3
ZARANGIANE
Four other officers, all brothers, are implicated in the conspiracy. One, Amyntas, stands trial and is acquitted, then goes off to fetch back his brother Polemon, who had fled before being arrested.

3.27.4–5
ZARANGIANE
After splitting the command of the Companion cavalry in two, Alexander moves into the territory of the Ariaspians, whom he rewards with generous treatment. Demetrios, a member of the royal Bodyguard, is arrested for having conspired with Philotas.

3.27.4a "Hipparch" means "cavalry commander." It is used here by Arrian loosely, since there was already a team of other officers who had the title hipparch by this time (see n. 3.29.7a).
3.27.4b Arrian's forthright explanation for this reorganization of command under two hipparchs or cavalry commanders seems to be the correct one. In the aftermath of the

Dimnos conspiracy, Alexander realized the danger in allowing any of his officers to have too much power. Hephaistion, his oldest and most trusted friend, thus assumed a position of leadership not merited by his experience or military talents. See Appendix E, §8.
3.27.4c The Ariaspians (Ari[m]aspai), location of territory: Map 3.28.

joined with Cyrus son of Cambyses in his campaign against the Scythians. [5] When Alexander had honored these men both for their ancestors' devotion to Cyrus and because he observed that they were not governed as the other barbarians in the region were but laid claim to as great a share of justice as the most powerful of the Greeks, he left them free, and added to their domain as much of the neighboring territory as they requested (which was very little). Then, after sacrificing to Apollo, he arrested Demetrios, one of his Bodyguards, as he suspected the man of having taken part in Philotas' plot. In Demetrios' place Alexander appointed Ptolemy son of Lagos.[5a]

[1] After settling these matters, Alexander advanced against Bactra and Bessos, bringing the Zarangians and Gedrosians[1a] to terms in the course of his march. He also brought the Arachosians to terms, appointed Menon as their satrap, and even made contact with the Indians[1b] on Arachosia's eastern borders. Alexander reached all these tribes through deep snow. Provisions were scarce, and his troops suffered greatly. [2] Informed that the Areians[2a] had again revolted—Satibarzanes[2b] having invaded their country with the two thousand horsemen he had received from Bessos—Alexander sent Artabazos the Persian and two of the Companions, Eriguios and Karanos, to their country. He also ordered Phratapherness, the Parthian satrap, to join them in attacking the Areians. [3] The troops with Eriguios and Karanos fought a fierce battle with Satibarzanes, and the barbarians did not give way until Satibarzanes, engaging in hand-to-hand combat with Eriguios, was struck in the face with Eriguios' spear and died. At that point the barbarians gave way and fled pell-mell.

[4] Alexander, meanwhile, was advancing to the Caucasus Mountains,[4a] where he founded a city and named it Alexandria.[4b] After sacrificing there to all the gods to whom he customarily sacrificed, he passed over the Caucasus, having appointed Proexes, a Persian, as satrap of the region, and having left behind Neiloxenos son of Satyros, one of the Companions, as overseer in charge of a company.

[5] The Caucasus range, according to Aristoboulos, is as lofty as any in Asia, though it is mostly bare, at least on its western side. It extends over so great a distance that the Taurus range, which forms the boundary of Cilicia and Pamphylia,[5a] is said to be a spur of the Caucasus, as are other large ranges that have been distinguished from it by a variety of different names according to the custom in each region. [6] In the Caucasus crossed by Alexander, nothing grows but the pistachio tree and the

---

3.28.1–3
Winter 330/29
ZARANGIANE–ARACHOSIA
Alexander pursues Bessos deep into Central Asia, sending officers back to Areia to put down another revolt there.

3.28.4
Spring 329
INDIAN CAUCASUS
Alexander crosses the Indian Caucasus into Bactria in pursuit of Bessos.

3.28.5–7
Arrian describes the Indian Caucasus and its vegetation.

3.27.5a   Ptolemy son of Lagos here becomes a top officer, though he had held no commands on the campaign thus far (except perhaps at 3.18.7). Alexander seems to have promoted long-standing friends to positions nearest him, in the wake of the Philotas affair (see Appendix E, §7).
3.28.1a   Gedrosia: Map 3.28.
3.28.1b   Arachosia; India: Map 3.28.
3.28.2a   Ar(e)ia: Map 3.28, Sogdiana inset.
3.28.2b   Satibarzanes was the former satrap of Areia and leader of the first rebellion

there, some months earlier.
3.28.4a   Caucasus Mountains: Map 3.28. There were several mountain ranges known to the Greeks as "the Caucasus." In this case the Indian Caucasus/Paropamisos range (modern Hindu Kush) is meant. See Appendix N, §8, and Ref. Maps 8a and 8b.
3.28.4b   Alexandria in the Caucasus: Map 3.28, Sogdiana inset.
3.28.5a   Taurus Mountains; Cilicia; Pamphylia: Map 3.28, Pamphylia inset.

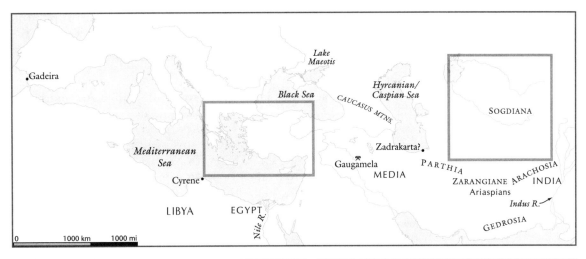

MAP 3.28

silphium plant,[6a] according to Aristoboulos. The range was nevertheless inhabited by many tribes, and many flocks and herds also grazed there, since herd animals delight in silphium; if they see silphium even from a great distance, they run to it, graze on its flower, and dig up and devour its root. [7] That is why, in Cyrene,[7a] the inhabitants drive their flocks as far as possible from the places where their silphium grows. They even build fences around the silphium, so that if herds do draw near they cannot get to it, since the plant is highly prized by the Cyrenaeans.

3.28.6a The slopes of the Indian Caucasus mountains do indeed flourish with asafetida (a medicinal plant), which seems to be the plant referred to as silphium here.

3.28.7a Cyrene (Map 3.28) was a Greek city in Libya (North Africa) famous for silphium and wealthy from its trade.

145

3.28.8–10
Spring 329
NAUTAKA
Bessos retreats across the
Oxus before Alexander's
relentless advance, having
failed to stop the Macedonians by denying them
provisions.

[8] Meanwhile, with the help of the Persians who had participated in Darius' arrest, nearly seven thousand of the Bactrians themselves, and the Dahae who dwell on that side of the River Tanais,[8a] Bessos was laying waste the land along the base of the Caucasus with the intent of discouraging Alexander's advance by making the country between him and Alexander barren and incapable of yielding needed provisions. [9] But Alexander kept on coming; though the deep snow and lack of needed supplies posed difficulties, he advanced nonetheless.[9a] When Bessos received word that Alexander was not far off, he crossed the River Oxus and burned the vessels on which he had crossed; he then withdrew to Nautaka in Sogdian[9b] territory. [10] He was accompanied by the troops with Spitamenes and Oxyartes, the horsemen from Sogdiana, and the Dahae from the Tanais. As for the Bactrian cavalry, when they learned that Bessos had decided to flee, they dispersed to their various homes.

3.29.1–4
BACTRIA
Alexander penetrates into
Bactria and sends his troops
across the Oxus River on
hide floats.

[1] After reaching Drapsaka and giving the army a rest, Alexander led his troops to Aornos and Bactra, the largest cities in Bactria.[1a] He captured them on the first attempt and left a garrison in the citadel of Aornos under the command of Arkhelaos son of Androkles, one of the Companions. Alexander appointed Artabazos the Persian as satrap of the other Bactrians after they joined his side rather readily. [2] Alexander led the army to the River Oxus, which originates in the Caucasus and is the largest river Alexander and his army reached in Asia, except for the rivers of India, for those are the largest of all. The Oxus empties into the Great Sea in Hyrcania.[2a] [3] When Alexander attempted to cross the river, he found the task impossible at every point, for the river was roughly three-quarters of a mile wide and its depth was not proportionate to its width, but much deeper; it was sandy-bottomed and swift-flowing, so that piles fixed in its bed could not be seated securely in the sand and were easily dislodged by the current alone. [4] A further difficulty was that wood was scarce, and it seemed there would be a long delay if they had to fetch from a distance enough wood to bridge the stream. So, collecting the hides with which the soldiers roofed their tents, Alexander ordered that these be filled with the driest possible chaff, tied up, and carefully stitched together so as not to let water in.

3.28.8a The river here called the Tanais (Map 3.28, Sogdiana inset; the modern Syr Darya) was more widely known in the ancient world as the Iaxartes. For the problem of its nomenclature, see 3.30.7–9 and n. 3.30.7a, and Appendix N, §4–6.

3.28.9a It is likely that Alexander crossed the Indian Caucasus (modern Hindu Kush) by what is now known as the Khawak Pass, a more difficult crossing than the nearby Shibar Pass. In that case Bessos would probably have concentrated his scorched-earth efforts in the wrong area, anticipating that Alexander would follow the easier route.

3.28.9b Oxus River; Nautaka; Sogdiana: Map 3.28, Sogdiana inset.

3.29.1a Drapsaka; Aornos; Bactra/Zariaspa; Bactria (Baktrianoi): Map 3.28, Sogdiana inset. The Aornos mentioned here is different from the famous citadel Aornos Rock captured later, at 4.28.

3.29.2a That is, into the Hyrcanian/Caspian Sea (Map 3.28), which Arrian regarded as a gulf of Ocean (hence "Great Sea"). The Amu Darya (ancient Oxus) River today empties into the Aral Sea, but it may in fact have fed the Hyrcanian in antiquity. In any case Greco-Roman geographers did not recognize the Aral as a separate body of water from the Hyrcanian. For more on geographical knowledge and assumptions in Alexander's time, see Appendix N and Ref. Maps 8a and 8b.

FIGURE 3.28.
Stuffed animal skins were used as floats on the Amu Darya (known to ancient Greeks as the Oxus) in the early twentieth century (top), much as Alexander and his troops used them. They were also employed for crossing rivers long before Alexander, as seen in this detail from a relief that once decorated the seventh-century palace of Sennacherib in Assyria (bottom).

When filled and stitched together, these hides were numerous enough to transport the army across in five days.

[5] Before crossing the river, Alexander selected the oldest Macedonians, who were now past fighting, and sent them home with the Thessalian[5a] volunteers who had remained with him. He also dispatched Stasanor, one of the Companions, to Areia, having ordered him to arrest Arsakes the Areian satrap, who he thought had been slack in performing his duties,[5b] and to assume the satrapy of Areia in his place.

[6] After crossing the Oxus, Alexander led the army at a rapid pace to the place where he had learned Bessos and his forces were gathered. At that point, messengers reached him from Spitamenes and Dataphernes and reported that if those two men were sent even a modest force under the command of an officer, they would seize Bessos and hand him over to Alexander; they were even now holding him under house arrest. [7] When Alexander heard this, he rested the army and led it onward at a more relaxed pace than before, but dispatched Ptolemy son of Lagos with three hipparchies[7a] of Companion cavalry, all the mounted javelin men, the infantry battalion of Philotas, one brigade of shield-bearers, all the Agrianians, and half the archers, with orders to march at a rapid pace to Spitamenes and Dataphernes. Ptolemy advanced as ordered and, after covering a ten-day march in four days, reached the place where the barbarians with Spitamenes had camped the day before.

[1] Ptolemy then learned that Spitamenes' and Dataphernes' resolve with regard to Bessos' surrender was not firm. Leaving the infantry behind with orders to follow in battle array, he himself, advancing with the cavalry, reached a village where Bessos and a few soldiers were. [2] Spitamenes and his men had already departed, as they were ashamed to be the ones to surrender Bessos. Posting the cavalry in a circle around the village (a wall fitted with gates had been built around it), Ptolemy sent a message to the barbarians in the village, informing them that they could depart unharmed once they had surrendered Bessos. Ptolemy and his men were admitted into the village; [3] after seizing Bessos, Ptolemy withdrew. Sending a messenger, he asked Alexander how he should conduct Bessos into Alexander's presence. Alexander ordered him to bring Bessos naked, bound in a dog

3.29.5
Spring 329
OXUS RIVER
Aging veterans are sent home to Macedonia. The satrap of Areia is replaced.

3.29.6–7
OXUS RIVER
Messengers from Spitamenes inform Alexander that Bessos is being held prisoner in Sogdiana and will be surrendered.

3.30.1–3
SOGDIANA
Spitamenes leaves Bessos prisoner in a village but departs with his men. The inhabitants give up Bessos to Ptolemy, who brings him before Alexander naked and bound.

3.29.5a Macedonia; Thessaly: Map 3.28, Pamphylia inset.
3.29.5b The translation here follows Bosworth (I.375), who supposes that Arsakes had failed to do enough, in Alexander's eyes, to resist Satibarzanes' invasion. Others render the passage as "seemed guilty of treason" or the like.
3.29.7a This is Arrian's first use of the term "hipparchy" in its correct sense, to designate a squadron of Companion cavalry led by a commander, or hipparch. He gives no insight as to how or why these units were formed, evidently in 330 or 329. Their creation is unrelated to the

splitting of the Companions into two general commands at 3.27.4; it is clear from the passage above that there were at this stage more than three hipparchies, perhaps six, and only two general commanders. The hipparchy scheme is loosely analogous to the division of the infantry phalanx into battalions, each serving under its own leader, able to function as an independent unit or to combine with any number of others. The number of hipparchies varied, from perhaps as many as ten to as few as four (see 7.6.4).

collar, and stand him on the right of the road along which he and the army were going to march; Ptolemy carried out these orders.

[4] When Alexander caught sight of Bessos, he halted his chariot and asked him why he had abducted Darius, his king, his kinsman, and his bene-factor, led him away in chains, and then murdered him. Bessos replied that he had not acted alone but in concert with the men in Darius' suite, so that they might obtain a guarantee of safety from Alexander. [5] At these words Alexander ordered Bessos to be whipped and the herald to recite all the offenses Alexander had reproached him with in his question. Abused in this manner, Bessos was sent back to Bactra to be put to death.[5a] That is what Ptolemy has written about Bessos. Aristoboulos, on the other hand, has written that it was Spitamenes, Dataphernes, and their followers who brought Bessos to Ptolemy and surrendered him to Alexander naked and bound in a dog collar.

[6] After supplementing his cavalry with the local horses, since many of his horses had died in the crossing of the Caucasus and on the march to and from the Oxus, Alexander led his men toward Marakanda,[6a] the royal seat of Sogdiana. [7] From there he proceeded to the River Tanais. This Tanais, which according to Aristoboulos has been given a different name, Orxantes,[7a] by the local barbarians, has its source in the Caucasus; it, too, empties into the Hyrcanian Sea.[7b] [8] The Tanais that the historian Herodotus says is the eighth of the Scythian rivers—he says it rises from a large lake and flows into an even larger one called Lake Maeotis[8a]—would be a different Tanais. There are some who consider this Tanais the boundary between Asia and Europe; [9] according to them, starting from the corner of the Black Sea, Lake Maeotis and this River Tanais, which empties into it, form the bound-ary between Asia and Europe, just as the sea between Gadeira and the Libyan nomads separates Libya from Europe. According to these writers, Libya is divided from the rest of Asia by the River Nile.[9a]

[10] In this region, some Macedonians who were dispersed on a forag-ing expedition were massacred by the barbarians. The perpetrators, who numbered up to thirty thousand, fled to a very rugged mountain that was steep on all sides. Taking the most mobile of his troops, Alexander advanced

3.30.4–5
SOGDIANA
After being ordered to account for his crimes against Darius and being whipped, Bessos is sent to his former capital for execution.

3.30.6–9
TANAIS/IAXARTES RIVER
Alexander marches to the river called variously the Tanais, the Orxantes, and the Iaxartes. Arrian pauses to distinguish this Tanais from the Scythian river of the same name, a river discussed by Herodotus and adopted by many as the boundary between Europe and Asia.

3.30.10–11
TANAIS/IAXARTES RIVER
After they kill some Macedonians out foraging, local barbarians retreat to a mountain, which the Macedonians assault and manage to take, though many are wounded, includ-ing Alexander. More than twenty-two thousand barbarians die there.

3.30.5a   Bessos was in fact only tortured at Bactra, then sent to Ecbatana for execution (see 4.7.3).
3.30.6a   Marakanda: Map 3.28, Sogdiana inset.
3.30.7a   Orxantes or something like it was the local name Aristoboulos recorded for the river (the modern Syr Darya) he thought of as an extension of the Tanais (the modern Don), a river far to the west. Later Greek writers called it the Iaxartes, and this became its standard name. Whether Arrian knew the river by the name Iaxartes is unclear; at 7.16.3 his manuscripts have the name Oxyrtes, but this seems to be a textual corruption, and most modern editions replace it with Iaxartes. In other places, Arrian follows Aristoboulos in

calling this river Tanais, even though he knew that the theory that connected the two rivers was in error. To reflect the complexity he tried to capture with his nomenclature, the double name Tanais/Iaxartes (Map 3.28, Sogdiana inset) is used in the notes and maps of this edition. See Appendix N, §4–6, for more discussion and Ref. Map 8a.
3.30.7b   Hyrcanian/Caspian Sea: Map 3.28. Neither the real Tanais nor the Iaxartes empties into this body of water. Knowl-edge of this region's geography was sketchy in Arrian's time.
3.30.8a   Lake Maeotis: Map 3.28.
3.30.9a   Black (ancient Euxine) Sea; Gadeira; Libya (North Africa); Nile River: Map 3.28.

against them. [11] The Macedonians then launched several assaults on the mountain. At first they were assailed by the barbarians and driven off; among the many who were wounded, Alexander himself was hit by an arrow that passed through his leg and fractured his fibula. But even so, he captured the place. Some of the barbarians were massacred there by the Macedonians, but many also died by hurling themselves from the cliffs. Out of thirty thousand, no more than eight thousand escaped alive.[11a]

3.30.11a Arrian makes no mention of an incident reported by Quintus Curtius shortly after the arrest of Bessos. According to Curtius (7.5.28–35), in Bactria Alexander came upon a colony of the Branchidai, a Greek religious order that in 480 had betrayed a wealthy temple in Miletus to the Persian invaders. When the Persians were defeated, the Branchidai fled into the interior of Asia to escape reprisals. Alexander, after consulting with the Milesians in his army, ordered the massacre of the colony and the total destruction of the site. The story is confirmed only by one other source, the geographer Strabo (11.11.4), and there is dispute as to whether it should be believed.

BOOK FOUR

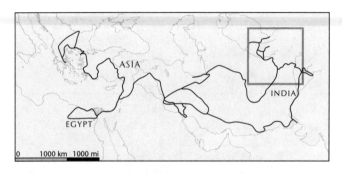

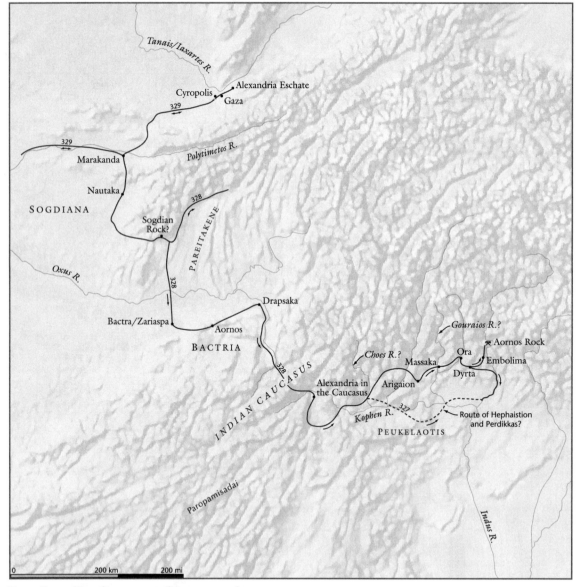

BOOK FOUR: THE CAMPAIGN IN BACTRIA AND SOGDIANA

Not many days later, envoys reached Alexander from the Scythians known as the Abii,[1a] the same tribe whom Homer praised in his poetry, saying they are supremely just.[1b] The Abii dwell in Asia and retain their independence, mainly as a result of their poverty and upright ways. Envoys also arrived from the European Scythians, the largest tribe in Europe.[1c] [2] Alexander sent some of the Companions[2a] back with these men, ostensibly as a deputation to make a pact of friendship, though the escort's larger purpose was to spy out the nature of the Scythians' land, the size of their population, their customs, and the equipment they carried into battle.

[3] Alexander intended to found a city near the River Tanais and to name the city after himself. For the place seemed suitable for a city that would rise to greatness; it would also prove advantageous should an invasion of Scythia ever take place, and would serve as a defensive outpost for the country against raids by the barbarians who dwelt beyond the river. [4] He imagined that the city would become important by virtue of the number of those who would settle there and the brilliance of its name.[4a]

At that point, the barbarians who dwelt by the river seized and killed the

4.1.1–2
Summer 329
NORTHERN SOGDIANA
Alexander receives envoys from the Scythians dwelling on either side of the river Arrian calls Tanais.

4.1.3–5
TANAIS/IAXARTES RIVER
Alexander orders the founding of another Alexandria as an outpost on the river. The local tribes rise in revolt against Macedonian rule and are joined by the Sogdians and some Bactrians.

NOTE: Most locations in the text not identified by a footnote can be found in the Reference Maps section.

4.1.1a The Abii (location of territory: Map 4.8, inset) Homer wrote about were a mythic people, but the name became attached, probably first by Alexander himself, to a real tribe dwelling in northern Sogdiana.

4.1.1b Homer talks of "the mare-milking, milk-drinking Abii, most just of men" in *Iliad* 13.4–6.

4.1.1c Scythia: Map 4.8. Arrian here subscribes to the general belief he cites in the previous chapter (see 3.28.8 and n. 3.28.8a, 3.30.7–8 and n. 3.30.7a) that the river he calls the Tanais, but was more widely known to Greek writers as the Iaxartes (Map 4.8, inset; modern Syr Darya), forms the boundary between Asia and Europe, which he thinks stretches far to the east.

Though Arrian himself knew that this eastern Tanais was a separate river from the Scythian one (Map 4.8; modern Don), he nonetheless treats it as a continental boundary, the role many Greeks had earlier assigned to the Scythian Tanais. Thus "European" and "Asian" Scythians would inhabit the same longitudes but dwell on opposite banks of the river; see Appendix N, Alexander's Geographic Notions, §4–6.

4.1.2a Alexander kept a formal list of his Companions, the intimates who were invited to dine and drink with him, offer their counsel, and fight beside him in the Companion cavalry. See Appendix E, Alexander's Inner Circle, §4.

4.1.4a The city Alexander would found here would become known as Alexandria Eschate ("Farthest Alexandria"); see Map 4.8, inset.

Macedonian soldiers garrisoned in their cities.[4b] They also took steps to strengthen the cities' fortifications. [5] Most of the Sogdians, incited by the party that had arrested Bessos,[5a] joined in the revolt, and as a result some of the Bactrians also took part in it. It may be that they truly feared Alexander; on the other hand, they may have given as a pretext for their revolt the fact that he had summoned the governors of the country to Zariaspa,[5b] the largest city, to a meeting, and that meeting seemingly portended nothing good for them.

[1] When this had been reported to Alexander, he ordered the infantry companies to make ladders—each company was instructed to make a certain number—while he himself, setting out from the camp, advanced against the first city, Gaza;[1a] the barbarians of the region were reported to have fled for refuge to seven cities. [2] Alexander sent Krateros to the city known as Cyropolis,[2a] the largest of the seven and the place where the greatest number of barbarians had gathered. Krateros had been instructed to camp near the city, surround it with a trench and a palisade, and assemble as many siege engines as he needed, so that the city's inhabitants, their attention diverted by Krateros and his men, would be unable to aid the other cities. [3] Alexander himself proceeded against Gaza and upon arrival gave the signal to assault the wall, an earthen structure of no great height, and to place the ladders against it on all sides. As the infantry attacked, his slingers, archers, and javelin men hurled their missiles[3a] at the wall's defenders and fired projectiles from siege engines. The rain of missiles soon cleared the wall of defenders. The ladders were put in place at once, and the Macedonians climbed up onto the wall. [4] Obeying Alexander's instructions, they killed all the men there and made off with the women, children, and other plunder. Alexander then led his men straight to the second city, captured it in the same manner on the same day, and dealt with the captives in the same way. He then led his men to the third city and captured it the next day on the first attempt.

[5] While he was engaged in these exploits with the infantry, he sent the cavalry to the two nearby cities with orders to keep close watch on those within the walls, lest they learn of the capture of their neighbors' cities and

4.2.1–4
Autumn 329
TANAIS/IAXARTES RIVER
Alexander orders Krateros to mount siege operations against the largest of seven rebel strongholds, Cyropolis, while he himself captures Gaza and two other forts and metes out a harsh punishment.

4.2.5–6
TANAIS/IAXARTES RIVER
Two other rebel strongholds are put under close guard by the Macedonian cavalry, and their inhabitants are slaughtered as they attempt to flee.

4.1.4b These "barbarians," the tribes of northern Sogdiana (Map 4.8, inset), here begin a major uprising against Macedonian rule. Their anger seems to have been touched off by the founding of the city on the Iaxartes, Alexandria Eschate, which signaled to them that the Macedonians intended a permanent occupation, not just a plundering raid. (The term Sogdians has been adopted in this text for the inhabitants of Sogdiana, in keeping with common modern usage. The more correct term would be Sogdianians.)
4.1.5a This party was led by Spitamenes, who was about to become a determined leader of the anti-Alexander insurgency. Why he had

collaborated with the Macedonians in the arrest of Bessos but then turned against them is unclear.
4.1.5b Zariaspa and Bactra (Map 4.8, inset) are two different names for the capital city of Bactria.
4.2.1a This Gaza (Map 4.8, inset) should be distinguished from the Phoenician port of the same name, captured by Alexander at 2.26–27.
4.2.2a Cyropolis: Map 4.8, inset.
4.2.3a "Missile" is used in this volume to translate the Greek word *belos*, encompassing all hurled or fired projectiles (stones, arrows, javelins, and the lead bullets or stones used by slingers).

of Alexander's imminent approach and contrive to flee; for in that case they would be difficult to catch. It turned out as he had guessed, and the cavalry was dispatched in the nick of time. [6] For when the barbarians who occupied the two cities not yet captured saw smoke rising from the city nearest them as it burned, and when some of the disaster's survivors arrived to report in person their city's fall, they fled in a crowd with all speed. But their path was barred by Alexander's cavalry, drawn up in close array, and most of them were cut down.

[1] After thus capturing the five cities in two days and enslaving those seized there, Alexander advanced against the largest city, Cyropolis. This city had been fortified with a higher wall than the others, as it had been built by Cyrus; and as most of the region's barbarians, including the fiercest warriors, had fled there for refuge, it was not so easy for the Macedonians to capture it on the first attempt. Alexander brought engines to the wall, intending to shake it apart and to launch attacks wherever it had been breached. [2] But then he noticed that the outlets of a river that flowed through the town only in winter were dry at that time and thus created a gap in the walls large enough to afford his soldiers access to the city. So he took the bodyguards, the shield-bearers, the archers, and the Agrianians,[2a] and while the barbarians were occupied with his siege engines, he slipped unnoticed into the city by way of the outlets, taking with him only a few men at first; [3] then, breaking open the gates nearest that point from inside, he easily admitted the rest of his men.[3a] Though the barbarians realized that their city was already occupied, they made a stand nonetheless against Alexander and his troops, and attacked with vigor. Alexander himself received a powerful blow from a stone on his head and neck;[3b] Krateros was shot with an arrow, and many other officers were also wounded. But even so, the Macedonians drove the barbarians from the marketplace. [4] At that point, the men who had been attacking the wall captured it, as it had by then been deserted by its defenders. In the first seizure of the city, roughly eight thousand enemy fighters perished; the rest, out of an original fifteen thousand who had taken refuge there, fled to the citadel. Putting a ring of camps around them, Alexander kept them under guard for one day, whereupon the barbarians, who had no water, gave themselves up.

[5] Alexander seized the seventh city on the first attempt. Ptolemy says that the inhabitants surrendered themselves. Aristoboulos, however, says that this city too was captured by force, and that Alexander killed all who were caught in it. Ptolemy, on the other hand, says that Alexander divided

4.3.1–4
CYROPOLIS
Alexander joins Krateros at Cyropolis and leads an assault on the city, gaining entrance through the water-courses perforating the walls. More than eight thousand defenders are killed when the city falls.

4.3.5
TANAIS/IAXARTES RIVER
Arrian gives differing accounts of the fate of the seventh rebel fortress.

4.3.2a The shield-bearers (*hypaspists*) were an elite corps of specially equipped infantry; see Appendix D, Alexander's Army and Military Leadership, §3. The term Agrianians, as used by Arrian, usually refers to a light infantry division recruited from a Balkan region northeast of Macedonia (Map 1.2); see Appendix D, §6.

4.3.3a It is ironic that Alexander takes Cyropolis, the city of Cyrus, by sneaking through dry water conduits, since Cyrus himself had reportedly captured Babylon by just the same device (see Herodotus, *Histories* 1.191).

4.3.3b Plutarch (*Parallel Lives*, "Alexander" 45.5, *Moralia* 341b) reports that this injury was grave enough to cause partial loss of vision.

the captives among various units of the army, with orders that they be bound and guarded until he left the region, so that no one responsible for the revolt might be left to his own devices.[5a]

[6] At that point, an army of Asian Scythians reached the banks of the River Tanais.[6a] Most of them had heard that some of the barbarians on the farther side of the river had revolted from Alexander, and they intended, in the event that any significant revolt was in progress, to join in attacking the Macedonians. It was also reported that Spitamenes and his men were besieging the forces left in Marakanda[6b] garrisoning the citadel. [7] Thereupon, Alexander sent Andromakhos, Menedemos, and Karanos against Spitamenes and his men, with nearly sixty cavalry Companions, eight hundred mercenaries under Karanos' command, and nearly fifteen hundred mercenary infantry. Pharnoukes the interpreter, a Lycian by birth, was posted to lead these forces,[7a] as he was conversant with the language of the barbarians in the region and seemed in general to be adept at dealing with them.

[1] Alexander then spent twenty days fortifying the city he intended to found, and peopling it with Greek mercenaries, those of the neighboring barbarians who wished to join the settlement, and Macedonians who were unfit for fighting.[1a] After performing his customary sacrifices to the gods, he held a competition in horsemanship and athletics. When he observed that the Scythians were not retreating from the riverbank [2] but were shooting arrows from it into the river (which was not broad at that point) and brazenly insulting Alexander in a manner typical of barbarians—saying that he would not dare to attack the Scythians or that he would learn the difference between Scythians and the natives of Asia—Alexander was provoked. He decided to cross over and attack them, and was preparing the hides for the crossing.[2a] [3] But when he sacrificed, the omens were not favorable for a crossing. Alexander found this hard to bear, but controlled himself and stayed put. When the Scythians did not desist, he again sacrificed for the crossing, and again Aristandros the seer declared that the signs

---

4.3.5a According to Bosworth (II.21), the implication here is that the captives who had supported the rebellion would be sold into slavery after Alexander's departure and thus neutralized. We later learn of extensive recruitment from this region of auxiliary forces for the Macedonian army.

4.3.6a Either these "Asian" Scythians had fled to the northern (European) bank of the river or else Arrian meant to say "European Scythians," for as the next sentence makes clear, they were assembling north of the river (that is, in "Europe").

4.3.6b Marakanda: Map 4.8, inset.

4.3.7a It would be unusual for a foreigner and a nonmilitary man like Pharnoukes to have command of these forces, and in the end it turned out to be a grave error, at least in Aristoboulos' version of events (see 4.6.1). There may be an effort here to lay blame at

the feet of a non-Macedonian for the debacle about to unfold.

4.4.1a The settlers described here are no doubt typical of the groups Alexander called on to people his new "cities" throughout Central Asia. The Greeks left behind in these garrison towns attempted to flee back to Europe on two occasions, once when they believed Alexander had been killed in India and again shortly after Alexander's death (see the Epilogue, §6), indicating that their participation in the settlement project was not voluntary.

4.4.2a As before at the Oxus (3.29) and long ago at the Danube (ancient Istros) River (1.3.6), Alexander planned to make his troops' hide tent covers into floats for crossing the river. A more elaborate version of the scheme would be used again at the Hydaspes River in India (5.12.3).

showed Alexander to be in danger. Alexander replied that it was better, after subjugating almost all of Asia, to brave the worst danger than to be a laughingstock in the eyes of the Scythians, as Darius, Xerxes' father, had been years ago.[3a] But Aristandros refused to interpret the divine signs otherwise merely because Alexander wished to hear a different interpretation.

[4] When the hides had been prepared for Alexander's crossing and his troops stood in armed array at the river, the siege engines, on signal, began firing at the Scythians who were riding along the bank. A number of Scythians were wounded, and one man, struck by a shot that passed straight through his ox-hide shield and breastplate, fell from his horse. Astonished by their enemy's ability to shoot from a distance and by the loss of one of their brave men, the Scythians retreated a little from the bank. [5] Seeing them thus thrown into disorder by his barrages, Alexander signaled by trumpet blast to cross the river, and led the way himself; the rest of the army followed him. He got the archers and slingers onto the shore first, and ordered them to sling their stones and shoot their arrows at the Scythians, to prevent them from getting near the infantry phalanx as it emerged from the river, before the entire cavalry had crossed.

[6] When his men were assembled on the bank, Alexander began by sending one regiment of mercenaries and four squadrons of *sarisa*-armed[6a] cavalrymen against the Scythians. The Scythians withstood the charge of these units and began riding around them in a ring while firing arrows; many against few, they easily evaded attack. Alexander then mixed the archers, the Agrianians, and the rest of Balakros' light-armed troops in with the cavalry and led them against the Scythians.[6b] [7] When they had come close, he commanded three regiments of Companions and all the mounted javelin men to charge the enemy, while he himself, hastening forward with the remaining cavalry, attacked with his squadrons in column. Thus the Scythians could no longer wheel their entire cavalry around in circles as before, for Alexander's cavalry was now harassing them, and at the same time the light-armed troops mixed in with the horsemen were preventing them from wheeling about safely.

Then the Scythians bolted openly. [8] Up to a thousand of them fell, as did Satrakes, one of their commanders, and nearly 150 were captured. But the pursuit was rapid, and difficult due to the extreme heat, and the entire army was afflicted by thirst; and Alexander himself, as he drove onward, drank whatever sort of water there was in that country. [9] Since the water was bad, a severe flux attacked his stomach, and for that reason the pursuit of the Scythians was not carried through to the end. Had Alexander not fallen ill, I imagine that they all would have perished in their flight. Having

4.4.4–5
TANAIS/IAXARTES RIVER
The attack proceeds despite the ill omens. A volley of catapult fire drives the Scythians back and enables the Macedonians to cross the river.

4.4.6–7
TANAIS/IAXARTES RIVER
Though initially put on the defensive by the Scythian mounted archers, Alexander changes his dispositions and gains the upper hand.

4.4.8–9
TANAIS/IAXARTES RIVER
Alexander puts the Scythians to flight, but is forced to abandon pursuit after contracting diarrhea from drinking fetid water.

4.4.3a The story of Darius' invasion of Scythia in the late sixth century, which resulted in a humiliating Persian retreat, is related by Herodotus in Book 4 of the *Histories*.

4.4.6a The *sarisa* was the infantry spear devised for the Macedonian army by Philip, Alexander's father, at the outset of his

reign; see Appendix D, §2.

4.4.6b The purpose of this intermingling seems to be that the light infantry could direct sling and arrow fire at the enemy while themselves staying behind the protective screen of the cavalry.

fallen into grave danger, Alexander was conveyed back to the camp, and thus Aristandros' prophecy was fulfilled.

[1] Shortly thereafter, Alexander was approached by envoys sent by the Scythian king to explain what had occurred. They said that the action had not been sanctioned by the Scythian community, but was the work of bandits out for plunder; the king himself, on the other hand, was ready to obey Alexander's orders. Alexander made a gracious reply; though he considered it ignoble, if he distrusted the king, not to proceed against him, it was inconvenient for him to do so at that time.

[2] At Marakanda, when Spitamenes and his men assaulted the citadel, the Macedonians on guard there sallied out against them. After killing some of the enemy and driving away the rest, they returned to the citadel with no losses. [3] Spitamenes, on receiving word that the men Alexander had sent to Marakanda were approaching, abandoned the siege of the citadel and retired to the inaccessible regions of Sogdiana.[3a] Pharnoukes and his fellow commanders, in their eagerness to drive him out entirely, pursued him as he withdrew to the frontier of Sogdiana and, without taking account of what they were doing, entered the territory of the Nomad Scythians.[3b] [4] Spitamenes, meanwhile, had enlisted nearly six hundred Scythian horsemen and was encouraged by his alliance with the Scythians to stand and fight the approaching Macedonians. But when he had arrayed his men on level ground near the Scythian desert, he chose neither to await the attack of the enemy forces nor to attack them himself, but rode in a circle around their infantry phalanx while firing arrows. [5] When Pharnoukes' forces attacked them, Spitamenes easily escaped, since his horses were swifter and, for the moment, fresher, whereas Andromakhos'[5a] horses, in need of fodder after their long march, were in distress. Whether the Macedonians stood their ground or retreated, the Scythians assaulted them with zeal.

[6] Since many Macedonians were now being wounded by arrows, and some were even falling, their commanders arrayed the soldiers in a square[6a] and withdrew to a glen near the River Polytimetos,[6b] where the barbarians could no longer shoot at them easily and their own infantry might be more effective. [7] Karanos, the cavalry commander, without having consulted Andromakhos, attempted to cross the river to position his cavalry safely on the opposite bank. The foot soldiers followed him,

4.5.1
Autumn 329
TANAIS/IAXARTES RIVER
The Scythian king offers apparent submission, which Alexander, though mistrustful, accepts for reasons of expediency.

4.5.2–5
MARAKANDA
Arrian returns to the account (begun at 4.3.6–7) of the Macedonian troops besieged by Spitamenes. The Macedonians force Spitamenes to retreat, and reinforcements under Pharnoukes drive him deeper into Sogdiana. There Spitamenes receives assistance from his Scythian allies and attacks, to devastating effect.

4.5.6–9
POLYTIMETOS RIVER
Under a barrage of arrows, the Macedonians fall back to the Polytimetos River, and one cavalry commander makes a spontaneous decision to cross it. The infantry follows him into the river in disorder. Seeing the disarray of the Macedonians, the Scythians press their advantage and destroy the entire relief force.

4.5.3a Sogdiana: Map 4.8, inset. The translation here is based on a suggestion made by Bosworth (II.33) that *ta abata* ("inaccessible regions") should be read in place of the manuscript text, *ta basileia* ("the palace"). Other editors read *ta boreia*, "the northern parts," or assume that *ta basileia* is correct and some other Sogdian palace is meant (besides the one in Marakanda).

4.5.3b Nomad Scythians: location unknown. At 7.16.4, in Arrian's only other reference to this mysterious tribe, they are located on the northeast shore of the Caspian Sea, but

here they seem to dwell much farther east. Arrian may have confused the Caspian and Aral seas, as many Greek writers did.

4.5.5a Andromakhos is the name given at 4.3.7 to one of the cavalry commanders of the relief force, and so it has been restored here in place of the manuscript reading "Aristomakhos."

4.5.6a Arraying soldiers in a square was a defensive move designed to minimize losses during a retreat.

4.5.6b Polytimetos River: Map 4.8, inset.

though no orders had been given, and since the riverbanks were steep, they entered the water in a panicked, disorderly throng. [8] Aware of the Macedonians' error, the barbarians, as they were already mounted, rushed from all sides to the stream. Some pursued the Macedonians who had already crossed and were retreating; others, taking a position in front of those who were crossing, confined them in the river [9] while their comrades rained arrows on them from the flanks; still others attacked those who were entering the river. The result was that the Macedonians, at a loss and under attack from all sides, fled for refuge to a small island, one of several in the river. Encircling them, the Scythians and the horsemen with Spitamenes shot all of them down. A few they captured alive, but all of those they killed.

[1] But Aristoboulos says that the greater part of the army was slaughtered by an ambush. The Scythians, concealed in a wooded preserve, attacked the Macedonians by surprise after battle had been joined. In Aristoboulos' account, the ambush occurred at the moment Pharnoukes was resigning from command and giving it to those who had been sent with him, declaring that he was inexperienced in military affairs and had been sent by Alexander to negotiate with the barbarians rather than to take charge in battles, whereas they were Macedonians and Companions of the king. [2] But Andromakhos, Karanos, and Menedemos declined to accept command, in part so as not to appear to be making changes on their own authority contrary to Alexander's orders, and in part being unwilling, at so difficult a moment, to take any part in the fight except as private soldiers, lest in the event of a calamity they be thought to have managed the entire affair incompetently. It was in this confusion and breakdown of discipline that the barbarians attacked and cut them all to pieces so that no more than forty horsemen and about three hundred foot soldiers got safely away.

[3] When these events were reported to Alexander, he was grieved by his soldiers' misfortune and resolved to march in haste against Spitamenes and the barbarians who accompanied him. Taking half the Companion cavalry, all the shield-bearers, the archers, the Agrianians, and the nimblest of the phalanx, he proceeded to Marakanda,[3a] as he had been informed that Spitamenes had returned to that city and was again besieging the men in the citadel. [4] Covering more than 180 miles in three days,[4a] Alexander approached the city at dawn on the fourth day. When his approach was reported, Spitamenes and his men did not hold their ground, but left the city and fled. [5] Alexander pursued them closely. When he reached the site of the recent battle, he buried the soldiers as circumstances permitted and pursued the fugitives as far as the desert. At that point, turning back, he plundered the country and killed the barbarians who had fled for refuge to

4.6.1–2
POLYTIMETOS RIVER
An alternative version of the episode given by Aristoboulos has the Scythians attacking from ambush at a moment of confusion in the Macedonian chain of command.

4.6.3–5
MARAKANDA
Alexander hastens to Marakanda and destroys some of the strongholds reportedly supporting the rebellion, but Spitamenes and his men escape unharmed.

4.6.3a Marakanda: Map 4.8, inset.
4.6.4a An astounding rate of speed, the highest of any given in Arrian's narrative. It is almost

certainly greatly exaggerated (see Bosworth II.35).

their strongholds, since they, too, were reported to have joined in attacking the Macedonians. He traversed the entire territory watered by the River Polytimetos.

[6] The Polytimetos disappears at the edge of a desert. Though its volume is substantial, the river vanishes in the sand. Many other rivers, even those of great strength that flow throughout the year, vanish there in the same way: the Epardus, which flows through the Mardians' country; the Areios, which takes its name from the land of Areia; and the Etymandros, which flows through the land of the Euergetai.[6a] [7] All these rivers are so large that none is inferior in size to the Peneios, the Thessalian river that flows through vale of Tempe and empties into the sea. The Polytimetos is much larger than the Peneios.

[1] After carrying out these operations, Alexander reached Zariaspa,[1a] where he remained until the worst of winter had passed. Phratapherenes, the satrap[1b] of Parthia,[1c] now came to him, along with Stasanor, who had been sent to Areia to arrest Arsakes.[1d] They were escorting Arsakes, bound in chains, along with Brazanes, whom Bessos had appointed as satrap of Parthia, and some others who had revolted with Bessos. [2] At the same time, Epokillos, Melamnidas, and Ptolemy, the commander of the Thracians,[2a] returned there from the coast, having escorted the allies to the sea along with the treasure sent with Menes.[2b] Asandros also arrived at that time, as did Nearkhos,[2c] leading an army of Greek mercenaries.[2d] [. . .], the satrap of Syria,[2e] and Asklepiodoros, the governor, also arrived from the coast with their forces.

[3] Calling an assembly of those who were present, Alexander had Bessos brought before them. After accusing him of having betrayed Darius, he commanded that Bessos' nose and the tips of his ears be cut off[3a] and

4.6.6–7
POLYTIMETOS RIVER
Arrian notes that the river, like some other streams, has its waters entirely absorbed by dry desert soil.

4.7.1–2
Winter 329/8
BACTRA/ZARIASPA
Alexander takes up winter quarters, and new recruits join him.

4.7.3
BACTRA/ZARIASPA
In a public assembly, Alexander denounces Bessos and orders that he be mutilated and then executed.

4.6.6a We know the locations of the Mardians (Mardoi) and of Ar(e)ia and the Euergetai or Ariaspians (Ariaspai/Ari[m]aspai), all on Map 4.22, but the rivers named here cannot be located.
4.7.1a Bactra/Zariaspa: Map 4.8, inset.
4.7.1b The satraps, roughly two dozen in number, were appointed by the Persian king to administer the satrapies, or provinces, of the empire, collect taxes, and organize defense. For the locations of all Persian satrapies mentioned by Arrian, see Ref. Map 1.
4.7.1c Parthia: Map 4.8.
4.7.1d Arrian reports, at 4.18.1, that Phratapherenes and Stasanor rendezvoused with Alexander a year later. It is possible that confusion in Arrian's sources led him to erroneously report their meeting twice.
4.7.2a This Ptolemy who commanded Thracians is a different person than any of the various Ptolemies encountered thus far (see 1.14.6, 1.22.4, 1.23.6, 1.24.1, 2.11.8). He is unknown outside this passage.
4.7.2b For the dispatch of these men, see 3.16.9–11, 3.19.6.
4.7.2c Nearkhos of Crete, a friend of Alexander's

since boyhood, was to become one of the campaign's more important officers. He had been summoned to Bactria from his original post as satrap of Lycia and Pamphylia (see 3.6.6). See Appendix E, §11.
4.7.2d According to Quintus Curtius (17.83.9), mercenaries also arrived at this time from Antipatros, who no longer needed them in Europe after the defeat of Agis' revolt. The total number of Greek troops now joining Alexander is given by Curtius as more than twenty thousand, an immense infusion of manpower that would allow Alexander to continue garrisoning the eastern provinces.
4.7.2e Syria: Map 4.8. The satrap of Syria's name here is given as Bessos in the manuscripts, but this is generally assumed to be a scribal error.
4.7.3a Disfigurement of the face was a typical Persian form of punishment. In Herodotus' *Histories* (3.154), Zopyrus, a Persian noble, cuts off his own nose and ears in order to pretend that he is a victim of the King's wrath.

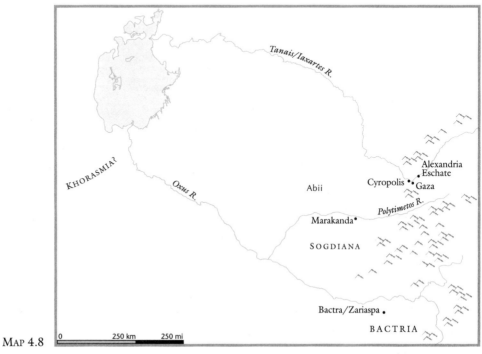

MAP 4.8

that he be taken to Ecbatana to be put to death in the assembly of the Medes[3b] and Persians.[3c]

[4] For my part, I do not approve of the excessive punishment inflicted on Bessos. I consider the mutilation of the extremities to be a barbarian custom, and I admit that Alexander was led on gradually to emulate the luxuriousness of the Medes and Persians and the differences of status the barbarian kings maintained between themselves and their subjects.[4a] I by no means commend the fact that Alexander, though a descendant of Herakles, substituted the apparel of the Medes for traditional Macedonian dress, or that he was not ashamed to exchange the *kitaris*[4b] of the conquered Persians for the headgear that he, their conqueror, had long worn.[4c] [5] I can commend none of this, but I surmise that one need look no further than Alexander's great successes for proof that neither physical strength nor illustrious birth nor uninterrupted success in war even greater than Alexander's—even if a man should circumnavigate Libya[5a] and Asia and conquer them, as Alexander meant to do,[5b] or add Europe, as the third part of his empire, to Asia and Libya—none of these things, I surmise, can gain a man happiness unless that man, whose achievements are seemingly so great, should at the same time possess the power to govern his passions.

[1] Here it will not be out of place for me to relate the tragedy of Kleitos son of Dropides and the dismay it caused Alexander, though these events occurred a little later.[1a] Among the Macedonians there was a day held sacred to Dionysos, and on that day, every year, Alexander performed a sacrifice in the god's honor. [2] But that year, they say, Alexander neglected Dionysos and sacrificed to the Dioskouroi, it having for some reason occurred to him to sacrifice to them. The drinking went on far into the night (for by now Alexander's drinking had taken on a more barbarian

---

4.7.4–5

Arrian, beginning a long discussion of Alexander's excesses and failures of self-restraint, expresses disapproval of Alexander's treatment of Bessos and reflects on his adoption of Persian court dress.

4.8.1–3

Autumn 328

MARAKANDA

Arrian looks ahead nearly a year, to the time when Alexander murders his friend and officer Kleitos during a drunken argument.

4.7.3b The Medes were a northern Iranian people who originally ruled the Persians, then came to be ruled by them and assimilated into their power structure.

4.7.3c Arrian does not describe the execution of Bessos, and our other sources give varying versions of it, all of them gruesome: Quintus Curtius (7.5.40) has him mutilated, crucified, and finally shot with arrows. Plutarch (*Parallel Lives*, "Alexander" 43.6) has him dismembered by the force of two bent trees springing apart. Diodorus Siculus (17.83.9) reports a less fantastical sort of dismemberment, followed by the scattering of the body parts.

4.7.4a The implicit contrast here is with the Macedonian version of monarchic rule, in which the king was not nearly so far elevated. See Appendix K, Alexander's Policy of Perso-Macedonian Fusion, §2.

4.7.4b The *kitaris* was a kind of Persian headdress, also called a tiara, that was worn folded down by most Persians but high and upright, with an encircling diadem, by the reigning king.

4.7.4c Arrian somewhat exaggerates the degree of Alexander's change of regalia. The king did

not "substitute" Eastern dress for Macedonian, according to our other sources, but combined the two, and he never adopted the upright *kitaris*, which served as the Persian crown, but wore the more discreet diadem, a purple-striped ribbon encircling the head. See Appendix K, §4.

4.7.5a Libya (North Africa): Map 4.22.

4.7.5b See 7.1 for a further discussion of Alexander's supposed plan for world conquest. At the time of his death, in 323, Alexander was certainly preparing for a campaign to subdue the Arabian peninsula, and there were further indications that an attack on Carthage (part of Africa or "Libya") was also in his near-term plans, but probably not a circumnavigation of Africa (see Appendix N, §9).

4.8.1a Starting here and continuing through 4.14, Arrian uses a thematic rather than chronologic arrangement (dates are shown in italics), grouping together events from autumn 328 through spring 327 that, in his view, show Alexander's loss of self-restraint. If the text followed a strict chronology, the murder of Kleitos would come after 4.17.3, during the last phase of the campaign to subdue Sogdiana and capture Spitamenes.

character),[2a] and on that occasion there was some talk about the Dioskouroi, and how their paternity, stolen from Tyndareus, had been traced to
Zeus.[2b] [3] And some of the company, the sort of men who are forever
corrupting and ruining the state affairs of kings, sought to flatter Alexander
and maintained that Kastor and Polydeukes did not deserve to be compared
with Alexander and his exploits. In their drunken talk they even touched on
Herakles, regarding whom they said that jealousy proved an obstacle for
living men and prevented their being properly honored by their friends.

[4] Kleitos, it had long been clear, was oppressed by Alexander's adoption of a more barbarian way of life and by his flatterers' remarks. On this
occasion, since he too was affected by the wine, he said he would not allow
them to show disrespect for religion or seek to bestow a "graceless grace"
on Alexander by belittling the exploits of the ancient heroes. [5] He
remarked that the present company were making Alexander's exploits
greater and more wondrous than they really were, and that in any case
Alexander had not achieved his conquests all by himself; they were in large
part the work of the Macedonians. Alexander was vexed at Kleitos' words.
Nor do I myself commend what he said, for I think it sufficient, when such
drinking is under way, for a man to keep his views to himself, and not give
offense by flattering, as others do.[5a] [6] But when some of the company
also touched on Philip's achievements, asserting—unjustly—that he had not
accomplished anything great or marvelous, hoping with this as well to curry
favor with Alexander, Kleitos could no longer contain himself. Claiming
that Philip's deeds ranked highest, he belittled Alexander and his deeds—
Kleitos was by now quite drunk—and said a great deal more, casting in
Alexander's teeth that he had saved his life during the cavalry action against
the Persians at the Granicus.[6a] [7] And finally, extending his right hand
haughtily, he said, "This was the hand, Alexander, that saved you then."

Alexander could no longer bear Kleitos' drunken insolence. He leaped
up in a fury and was restrained by his fellow banqueters. Kleitos would not
stop taunting him. [8] Alexander shouted for his shield-bearers;[8a] when no

4.8.4–7
Autumn 328
MARAKANDA
Kleitos' dislike of Alexander's newly adopted ways,
and of the excessive praise
heaped on the king by flatterers, leads him to insult
and belittle Alexander at a
court drinking party.

4.8.7–8
Autumn 328
MARAKANDA
Alexander responds violently
and is restrained by his
companions. As Kleitos
continues his insults, Alexander breaks free, grabs a
nearby weapon, and strikes
the man dead.

4.8.2a Drinking habits, like the wearing of sumptuous clothes, were considered by the Hellen-
ized world a marker of the boundary
between Greek and barbarian. The Macedonians were actually considered intemperate
drinkers by the Greeks, but in Arrian's
account their native habits are made to seem
moderate and civilized by contrast with
Asiatic self-indulgence. Once again his
discussion here is at variance with his final
eulogy (7.29.4), where he claims that
Alexander stayed up late at drinking parties
only for the company of his friends, not for
the wine.

4.8.2b The Dioskouroi, the twins Kastor and Polydeukes (called Castor and Pollux by the
Romans), born to the mortal Leda, were
sometimes identified as sons of her husband,
King Tyndareus of Sparta, and at other
times as sons of Zeus. In some accounts one
twin sprang from Zeus and the other from

Tyndareus. Their mixture of divine and
mortal parentage, seen also in the mythology surrounding Herakles, made them
especially relevant as models for Alexander,
who was reputed by some (perhaps at his
own urging) to have sprung from both
Philip and Ammon.

4.8.5a Arrian here seems to speak out of personal
experience as a high official in the Roman
administration who was often in the
company of emperors. His remark about
avoiding flattery fits such a context better
than the episode he is narrating, which
involved insult rather than flattery.

4.8.6a See 1.15.8 for Arrian's account of this episode.

4.8.8a A special detachment of the shield-bearers
served as part of Alexander's personal bodyguard. By calling for them here, Alexander
signaled that he suspected Kleitos'
remarks—and perhaps also the attempt to
restrain him—to be traitorous acts.

one obeyed, he said that this was exactly what had happened to Darius when he was arrested by Bessos and his followers and led away, a king in name only. Alexander's Companions were no longer able to restrain him. He leaped up; some say that it was a spear he snatched from one of his bodyguards and used to strike Kleitos, killing him, [9] while others say he used a *sarisa* snatched from one of the guards.

Aristoboulos does not say how the drinking bout got started but maintains that Kleitos had only himself to blame. For when Alexander, infuriated, leaped up as though he would destroy him, Kleitos was hauled away by Ptolemy son of Lagos, who was among Alexander's Bodyguard,[9a] and taken through the doors and over the wall and ditch of the citadel where this was happening. But, unable to restrain himself, Kleitos came back a second time and crossed paths with Alexander, who was calling out "Kleitos!" and said, "Here's Kleitos! Here I am, Alexander!" And at that moment, struck by the pike, Kleitos died.

[1] For my part, I utterly deplore the insolence Kleitos displayed toward his king, and I pity Alexander for his misfortune: he showed himself mastered on that occasion by two vices, namely anger and drunkenness, neither of which should get the better of a sensible man. [2] But I commend Alexander's conduct in the aftermath, for he recognized immediately that he had committed a savage act. There are some who report that he leaned the *sarisa* against the wall, intending to fall on it, on the grounds that now that he had killed his friend while drunk it was dishonorable for him to live. [3] But most historians offer a different account and say that Alexander took to his bed and lay prostrate in grief, calling out Kleitos' name and that of Kleitos' sister Lanike, who had nursed him,[3a] saying that he had after all made her a fine return for her nursing now that he was grown; [4] for she had seen two of her own sons die fighting for him, and now he had himself killed her brother with his own hand. Again and again he called himself the murderer of his own friends, and went without food and drink for three days and completely neglected all other care of his person.

[5] In light of these events, some of the prophets "sang the wrath" of Dionysos,[5a] because Alexander had neglected to sacrifice to that god. Persuaded with some difficulty by his Companions, Alexander took food and gave some slight attention to his person. He also made an offering to Dionysos, since he was not unwilling to have the calamity attributed to a god's wrath rather than his own baseness. [6] I commend Alexander highly for neither arrogantly dismissing an evil act nor proving baser still by

4.8.9
Autumn 328
MARAKANDA
In Aristoboulos' version of the episode, Kleitos does more to provoke Alexander and brings retribution on himself.

4.9.1–4
Autumn 328
MARAKANDA
Arrian gives his own opinion on the murder of Kleitos and reports two versions of Alexander's deep remorse afterward.

4.9.5–6
Autumn 328
MARAKANDA
Alexander ends three days of remorse-stricken fasting and isolation. He endorses the idea that the god Dionysos had taken a hand in the disaster.

4.8.9a It is noteworthy that this account of the events leading up to Kleitos' murder, in which Ptolemy is singled out for his efforts to prevent the disaster, derives not from Ptolemy's own memoirs but from those of Aristoboulos. Ptolemy had been promoted to the seven-man Bodyguard in the wake of the Philotas conspiracy about

two years before this (see 3.27.5).

4.9.3a Several sources attest that Kleitos' sister Lanike, who was some thirty years Alexander's senior, had indeed been his wet-nurse.

4.9.5a Arrian's wording here recalls the opening of the *Iliad*, where Homer urges the muse to "sing the wrath" of Achilles.

becoming a defender or advocate of his offensive conduct. Instead, he conceded that, being human after all, he had erred.

[7] There are some who say that Anaxarkhos the sophist was summoned to console Alexander. Finding the king moaning on his bed, Anaxarkhos laughed and said that Alexander had not appreciated that this was why the ancient sages made Justice sit beside Zeus—namely, to show that anything ordained by Zeus was done with justice. It therefore followed that the acts of a great king should be considered just, first by the king himself and then by the rest of mankind. [8] Anaxarkhos' words gave Alexander comfort on that occasion, though in my view he did Alexander an injury greater than the misfortune then afflicting him if he held it to be the view of a wise man that the king's duty is not, after all, to act justly after diligent reflection, but that anything done by a king, in whatever manner, is to be considered just.

[9] For it is reported that Alexander wanted his subjects to make a ritual bow when greeting him,[9a] the underlying idea being that he was more the son of Ammon than of Philip, and was now[9b] showing his admiration for Persian and Median ways by changing his apparel and adopting new arrangements for the way others attended on him. And as his court included many flatterers, notably the sophist Anaxarkhos and Agis of Argos, an epic poet, there was no lack of men willing to grant him that token of submission.

[1] It is said that Kallisthenes of Olynthos,[1a] a man who had attended Aristotle's lectures, a somewhat rough-hewn fellow, disapproved of this. Here I agree with Kallisthenes, though I find his other views unreasonable, if what has been written is true and he actually declared that Alexander and his exploits depended on him and the history he was writing; [2] and that he had appeared on the scene not to acquire renown from Alexander, but to convey Alexander's renown to mankind; and that Alexander's association with divinity depended not on the tales Olympias made up about his birth, but on what he, Kallisthenes, would write and publish about him. [3] Some have also related that Philotas once asked Kallisthenes whom he thought the people of Athens held in highest regard, and Kallisthenes replied, Harmodios and Aristogeiton, since they had killed one of the two

4.9.7–8
Autumn 328
MARAKANDA
Anaxarkhos, a court philosopher, reportedly tries to justify the murder under a doctrine of divine right of kings.

4.9.9
Winter 328/7
BACTRA/ZARIASPA
Continuing to glance forward in time, Arrian relates how Alexander attempts to introduce the Persian ritual of *proskynesis*.

4.10.1–4
Winter 328/7
BACTRA/ZARIASPA
Kallisthenes, Alexander's court historian, opposes the introduction of the ritual.

4.9.9a   The ritual of *proskynesis* had been a hallmark of Persian court ceremony for generations and, in the eyes of many Greeks, a symbol of barbarian political culture. It might take varying forms, ranging from a slight bow of the head, accompanied by a finger-kissing gesture, to a very deep bow or even self-prostration, depending on the difference in rank between the person making the gesture and the one receiving it. The Persian king demanded *proskynesis* of visitors to his court, even forcing them on pain of death, according to Herodotus (*Histories* 7.136). But the Greeks ordinarily paid such reverence only to their gods, and so Alexander's plan to institute the ritual might well be interpreted, as it was

by Kallisthenes at 4.11.2–5, as a desire to be worshiped. For more on Alexander's possible aspirations to divinity, see Appendix C, Alexander the Man (and God?), §16–17, and Appendix K, §7.

4.9.9b   The time frame is left vague, but we know from other sources that the events of the next few chapters took place at Bactra early in 327, several months after Kleitos' murder.

4.10.1a   Kallisthenes of Olynthos was a grandnephew of Aristotle and a distinguished Greek intellectual. Alexander had taken him along on his campaign as a kind of official historian/propagandist. Only a few sentences of his historical account survive in quotations by later authors.

tyrants and brought down a tyranny.[3a] [4] Philotas then asked whether it was possible for a man who had slain a tyrant to obtain asylum in any Greek city he wished, and Kallisthenes replied that if no other Greeks offered him asylum the Athenians would, since on behalf of Herakles' children they had even gone to war with Eurystheus, the tyrant of Greece at the time.[4a]

[5] With regard to Kallisthenes' opposition to Alexander on the question of the ritual bow, the following story is widely accepted. It had been agreed between Alexander and the sophists and the most illustrious Persians and Medes[5a] in his court to introduce this topic at a drinking party. [6] Anaxarkhos opened the discussion by saying that Alexander would more justly be considered a god than Dionysos or Herakles, not only in view of his many extraordinary exploits, but also because Dionysos was a Theban and therefore unrelated to the Macedonians, and Herakles was an Argive who likewise had no ties to Macedonia, except that he was related to Alexander; for Alexander was a Heraklid;[6a] [7] it would be more just for the Macedonians to pay divine honors to a king who was one of their own. And, in any case, there could be no doubt that once Alexander had departed the human sphere they would honor him as a god. Would it not be more just to honor him while he lived than after his death, when the honor would be of no benefit to him?

[1] When these and similar remarks were made by Anaxarkhos, all who were part of the plan applauded his speech and were indeed ready to begin making the ritual bow. But most of the Macedonians were angered by his speech, though they kept silent. [2] Kallisthenes now interrupted and said,[2a] "Anaxarkhos, I declare that Alexander is worthy of any honor that is due a human being. But human honors have been distinguished by mankind from those accorded to the gods, in a great many ways: the building of temples and the setting up of statues and precincts have been given to the gods, sacrifices and libations are performed for them, and hymns are composed in their honor, whereas eulogies are composed for human beings. But nowhere is the distinction more plainly marked than in this very practice of

4.10.5–7
Winter 328/7
BACTRA/ZARIASPA
The scene is set for Kallisthenes to take his stand when a faction of Alexander's supporters, coached in advance by the king, brings up during a banquet the idea of paying Alexander the honor of *proskynesis.*

4.11.1–5
Winter 328/7
BACTRA/ZARIASPA
Kallisthenes, addressing Anaxarkhos before the assembled banqueters, delivers a forceful speech in opposition to the proposed ritual, asserting that it blurs the distinction between humans and gods.

4.10.3a Kallisthenes' praise of the "tyrant slayers" Harmodios and Aristogeiton, who had conspired to assassinate one of two ruling sons of Peisistratos, founder of the tyranny that dominated sixth-century Athens, carries somewhat dark overtones, given that Kallisthenes himself was soon to be accused of taking part in a conspiracy against Alexander. Quite possibly the anecdote was promulgated by pro-Alexander factions seeking to cast suspicion on Kallisthenes' reputation.

4.10.4a The reference is to a mythical war fought by Athens to end the persecution of the sons of Herakles by Eurystheus.

4.10.5a Persia; Media: Map 4.8. For Persians and Medes, see n. 4.7.3b.

4.10.6a According to a legend well known to the

Greeks long before Alexander, the family that made up the royal Macedonian dynasty was descended from Herakles and had migrated to Macedonia from the Peloponnese. See Appendix B, Greek and Macedonian Ethnicity, §3.

4.11.2a There is no consensus as to how closely the speech that follows reflects Kallisthenes' actual words. It contains much that could have been easily invented, but nothing that obviously has been. Significantly, it is the second-longest speech of Arrian's text (exceeded only by Alexander's speech at the Hyphasis River, 5.25.3–5.26) and falls almost exactly at the center of that text. Clearly Arrian wanted to give full play to the themes developed here (see Appendix A, Arrian's Sources and Reliability, §19).

FIGURE 4.10. Reliefs from the palaces of Xerxes (above) and Darius (right) at Persepolis (late sixth to early fifth century) attest to the worshipful attitude with which courtiers attended the Persian kings. Alexander's attempt to introduce the ritual bow of *proskynesis* at his court would have imported this Asian conception of semidivine kingship into a European court that was unfamiliar with it.

bowing. [3] For human beings greet one another with a kiss, but divinity, I suppose because it is seated on high and must not be touched, is honored with a bow, and choruses are established for the gods, and hymns are sung to them. And this is not at all surprising, since even the gods themselves receive a variety of different honors; and still other honors—by Zeus!—distinct from those paid to the gods are paid to heroes. [4] Thus it would be unreasonable to confound all these things, exalting human beings by offering them excessive honors, or degrading the gods unduly (if that is conceivable) by according them the honors paid to mortals. Alexander would surely not tolerate it if some private citizen thrust himself into royal honors by means of an unjust election or vote! [5] The gods would have even more right to be vexed with human beings who usurp divine honors or let others make them usurpers.

"By any standard, Alexander both is and is thought to be the bravest of brave men, the most kingly of kings, the commander most worthy to command. [6] And you, of all people, Anaxarkhos, should have been the one to advance this argument and to cut off the opposing one, since you attend Alexander in order to instruct and educate him. It was indeed wrong of you to open this discussion. Instead you ought to recall that you are not attending or advising a Cambyses or a Xerxes,[6a] but Philip's son, a member of the house of Herakles and Aiakos, whose ancestors came to Macedonia from Argos[6b] and have continued to rule the Macedonians not by force but by law. [7] Even Herakles himself did not receive divine honors from the Greeks during his lifetime, nor even after his death, until permission was given by the god at Delphi to honor him as a god.

"Perhaps, one must think like a barbarian because our discussion takes place in a barbarian land. Even so I think it fit to remind you, Alexander, of Greece, for the sake of which you made this entire expedition—to annex Asia to Greece. [8] And consider this: will you, on your return there, also compel the Greeks, the freest of men, to bow before you, or will you keep your distance from the Greeks but impose this dishonor on the Macedonians? Or will you make some final distinction when it comes to honors, and be honored by the Greeks and Macedonians in the human and Greek manner, while receiving barbarian honors only from the barbarians? [9] But if it is said about Cyrus son of Cambyses that he was the first man to have his subjects bow down to him, and that after him this indignity became an institution among the Persians and Medes, one should bear in mind that the Scythians, men who were poor but independent, taught that very Cyrus a lesson—a lesson other Scythians later taught Darius, and the Athenians and Spartans taught Xerxes, and Klearkhos and Xenophon and their Ten

4.11.6–7
Winter 328/7
BACTRA/ZARIASPA
Kallisthenes reminds the company that they follow a European, not an Asian, monarch.

4.11.8–9
Winter 328/7
BACTRA/ZARIASPA
Kallisthenes expands on the contrast between European and Asian court rituals. He ends by recalling a string of European military victories over Asians, implying that in freedom lies strength.

4.11.6a   Cambyses and Xerxes were two early Persian kings (late sixth and early fifth centuries, respectively), known for wielding power arrogantly or even—in Cambyses' case—abusively.
4.11.6b   A mythic account of the origins of the Macedonian royal family traced both Alexander and Philip to a divine ancestor, Herakles, and to a Greek city, Argos. See Herodotus, *Histories* 8.137–139, for one version of the myth. Alexander's mother, Olympias, a Molossian, was thought to have descended from Aiakos, a mythic ancestor of Achilles.

Thousand taught Artaxerxes, and Alexander—without having his people bow down before him—taught this Darius."[9a]

[1] In making these and similar remarks Kallisthenes greatly vexed Alexander, though what he said pleased the Macedonians. Realizing this, Alexander sent word[1a] to the Macedonians telling them to think no more of the bowing ritual. [2] But in the silence that followed these words, the most distinguished Persians stood up and one by one performed their bows. When Leonnatos, one of the Companions, judged that one of the Persians had made his bow in a clumsy manner, he mocked the man for his abject appearance.[2a] Alexander lost his temper with Leonnatos on that occasion, though they were later reconciled.

The following story has also been recorded. [3] Alexander was passing around a golden drinking cup, and gave it first to those with whom he shared an agreement about the bowing ritual. The first man to drain the cup stood up, made his bow, and was kissed by Alexander;[3a] then each man did the same in his turn. [4] When the cup came to Kallisthenes, he drained it and approached Alexander to kiss him, though he had not made his bow. As Alexander happened to be talking to Hephaistion at the time, he did not notice whether Kallisthenes had made his bow. [5] But when Kallisthenes approached to kiss Alexander, Demetrios son of Pythonax, one of the Companions, mentioned that Kallisthenes was approaching without having made a bow. And Alexander did not allow Kallisthenes to kiss him, whereupon the latter said, "I'll go away one kiss poorer."

[6] For my part, I commend none of these actions, which reveal Alexander's arrogance at the time and the rudeness of Kallisthenes. I consider it sufficient, however, for a man to conduct himself decorously, and to enlarge his king's deeds as far as he is able, once he has seen fit to attend a monarch. [7] Accordingly, I find it understandable that Alexander conceived a hatred of Kallisthenes, given the latter's ill-timed outspokenness and reckless arrogance. I imagine that this was why those who denounced Kallis-

4.12.1–2
Winter 328/7
BACTRA/ZARIASPA
Kallisthenes' speech finds approval among the Macedonians, and Alexander backs off the attempt to introduce the new ritual.

4.12.3–5
Winter 328/7
BACTRA/ZARIASPA
Another anecdote about Kallisthenes shows him refusing to practice *proskynesis* and thereby losing Alexander's favor.

4.12.6–7
BACTRA/ZARIASPA
Arrian expresses disapproval of the behavior of both Kallisthenes and Alexander in this episode, and sees in it the origins of Alexander's willingness to believe charges leveled at Kallisthenes in the Pages' Conspiracy.

4.11.9a Kallisthenes ends his speech with a list, going back more than two centuries, of conflicts in which the Persians had been beaten. In each case, Kallisthenes implies, the greater degree of individual freedom enjoyed by Persia's foes had given them the strength to defeat the mighty empire. He refers first to Cyrus' alleged invasion of the Massagetai (described by Herodotus in his *Histories* 1.201–216, but not confirmed by modern historians); then to the failed incursion across the Danube (ancient Istros) by Darius I (517); then to the battles of Salamis and Plataea (480–479), in which Greek forces defeated the invasion led by Xerxes; the battle of Cunaxa (401), where a Greek mercenary army led by the Spartan general Klearkhos defeated the army of Artaxerxes, in the expedition immortalized by Xenophon in the *Anabasis*. He concludes by invoking the recent show-

downs at Issus and Gaugamela.
4.12.1a Evidently Alexander was not present in the same room as the banqueters and so communicated with them by messenger. It is unclear how this implied arrangement coheres with the bowing scene that follows, in which Alexander and his Persian subjects appear to be together.
4.12.2a Quintus Curtius (8.5.22–8.6.1) tells a story of similar import but involving Polyperkhon, not Leonnatos. According to Plutarch (*Parallel Lives*, "Alexander" 74.2–3), Kassandros, the son of Antipatros, reacted with similar ridicule when he first beheld a Persian doing *proskynesis* before Alexander (see n. 7.27.1b).
4.12.3a This ritual, in which the king bestows favor on his nobles by way of a kiss, appears to have been adapted by Alexander from Persian custom. There is no evidence that it was traditional in the Macedonian court.

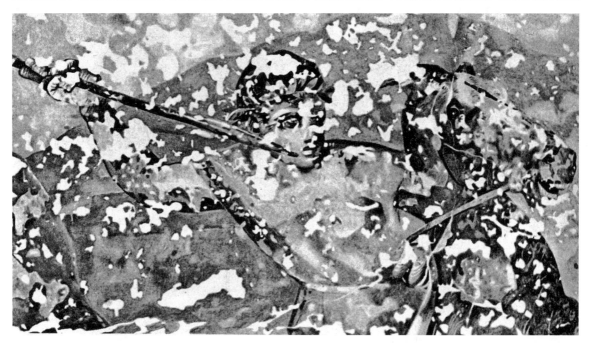

FIGURE 4.13. A youthful hunter prepares to spear a lion in this image from a painted frieze atop Tomb II in the Aigeai royal burial complex, revealing the importance of hunting in the life of the Macedonian elite. The figure was identified as Alexander the Great by its excavator, Manolis Andronikos, but later scholars have questioned that theory.

4.13.1–2
Spring 327
BACTRA/ZARIASPA
Arrian again turns the clock forward to describe how the Pages' Conspiracy, in which Kallisthenes became implicated, arose out of a rash punishment Alexander allegedly inflicted on Hermolaos, one of his adolescent pages.

thenes were readily believed—both those who claimed he had taken part in the conspiracy against Alexander by his pages, and those who maintained that he himself had instigated the conspiracy. The plot came about in the following way.

[1] Since Philip's day it had been the custom for all the sons of Macedonian officers, when they reached adolescence, to be enlisted into the king's service. In addition to serving the king's personal needs, the pages were entrusted with the task of watching over him when he slept. Whenever he went riding, they would take the horses from the grooms, lead them up, and help the king mount in the Persian manner, and they shared with him the rivalry of the hunt. [2] One of their number was Hermolaos son of Sopolis, who was thought to have an interest in philosophy and for that reason was a follower of Kallisthenes. There is a story that in the course of a hunt, when a wild boar was charging Alexander, Hermolaos struck the boar before Alexander could. The wounded beast fell, and Alexander, having missed his chance, lost his temper with Hermolaos and in his anger ordered that Hermolaos be whipped in the presence of the other pages; he also took away Hermolaos' horse.

[3] Grieved at the insult, Hermolaos told Sostratos son of Amyntas, his comrade and lover, that his life would not be worth living unless he took vengeance on Alexander for the insult. Sostratos, since he was in love with Hermolaos, was easily persuaded to join him. [4] These two succeeded in enlisting the participation of Antipatros, son of Asklepiodoros who had been the satrap of Syria; Epimenes son of Arsaios; Antikles son of Theokritos; and Philotas[4a] son of Karsis the Thracian. Antipatros' turn came for night watch duty, and the conspirators agreed to kill Alexander that night by attacking him while he slept. [5] But it turned out, according to some writers, that, entirely of his own accord, Alexander stayed up drinking until it was day. But Aristoboulos tells the following story. A Syrian woman, who was possessed by divine spirits, used to follow Alexander about. At first she elicited nothing but ridicule from Alexander and the members of his suite. But when everything she said in her inspired state had come true, she was no longer ignored by Alexander but was allowed access to him night and day, and often kept watch over him while he slept. [6] On this occasion, when Alexander left the drinking party, the woman, who was in her possessed state, met him and begged him to return and drink for the rest of the night. And since Alexander regarded this as an omen, he returned and drank, and thus the Pages' Conspiracy failed.[6a]

[7] The next day, Epimenes son of Arsaios, one of the conspirators, spoke of the affair to his lover, Kharikles son of Menandros. Kharikles then spoke of it to Eurylokhos, Epimenes' brother, whereupon Eurylokhos went to Alexander's tent and communicated the entire affair to Alexander's Bodyguard Ptolemy son of Lagos.[7a] Ptolemy informed Alexander, who ordered the arrest of those named by Eurylokhos. Stretched on the rack, the pages confessed their plot and named some others as fellow conspirators.

[1] According to Aristoboulos, the pages claimed that Kallisthenes had induced them to make the attempt, and Ptolemy concurs with his account. Most writers, however, view the matter differently and say that because Kallisthenes had already incurred Alexander's hatred and Hermolaos was especially friendly to Kallisthenes, Alexander had no difficulty believing the worst about Kallisthenes. [2] A number of writers have also recorded that when Hermolaos was summoned before the Macedonians, he admitted that he had conspired, saying that it was no longer possible for a free man to bear Alexander's insolence, and recounting all that had happened: Philotas'

4.13.3–6
Spring 327
BACTRA/ZARIASPA
Hermolaos gains the sympathy of other pages, and they plan to kill Alexander in his sleep. Two accounts differ as to why Alexander chose to stay up drinking that night, thus robbing the conspirators of their chance.

4.13.7
Spring 327
BACTRA/ZARIASPA
The plot is revealed and the conspirators are arrested and put to torture.

4.14.1–2
Spring 327
BACTRA/ZARIASPA
Arrian notes the differing accounts of how Kallisthenes became implicated, then summarizes the justification Hermolaos reportedly gave for the planned murder.

4.13.4a This is a different Philotas than the son of Parmenion executed in an earlier conspiracy episode (3.26).

4.13.6a Here, as elsewhere (see 7.29.4), we see evidence that Aristoboulos' memoir was at pains to minimize Alexander's drinking. In Aristoboulos' version Alexander does not voluntarily stay late at the drinking party, but is bidden to do so by the

prophetess. See Appendix A, §12.

4.13.7a This is one of many places where Arrian's source Ptolemy son of Lagos has highlighted his own services to Alexander by diminishing that of others. According to Quintus Curtius (8.6.22), Leonnatos was on duty with Ptolemy when this report arrived.

wrongful end and the still more unlawful end of Parmenion and of the others who were put to death at the time; the drunken slaying of Kleitos; the Median apparel; the plan (not yet discarded)[2a] to require the bowing ritual at court; and Alexander's drinking and sleeping habits.[2b] Unable to bear these things any longer, he had wanted to free himself and the other Macedonians.

[3] Hermolaos and his fellow prisoners were stoned to death by those present at the hearing. Aristoboulos says that Kallisthenes, bound in shackles, was carried here and there with the army train and subsequently died of disease. Ptolemy, on the other hand, relates that he was tortured on the rack and then hanged.[3a] Thus, even wholly trustworthy writers who kept company with Alexander at the time do not agree in their writings about events that were public and known to them personally. [4] Though many different versions of these events have been reported, let what I have set down suffice. Though these incidents occurred a little later, I have set them down alongside the story of Alexander and Kleitos in the belief that, for the purposes of my narrative, it is more appropriate to include them here.

[1] A second embassy from the European Scythians reached Alexander, accompanied by the envoys he had himself sent to the Scythians. (The Scythian king who was on the throne when Alexander had dispatched these men had just died, and his brother was now reigning.) [2] The purpose of the Scythians' embassy was to declare that the Scythians were willing to follow all of Alexander's orders. From their king the envoys brought all the gifts that are prized most highly in Scythia. The king also wished to give Alexander his daughter in marriage, as a firm pledge of his friendship and alliance;[2a] [3] but if Alexander considered it beneath him to marry the Scythian princess, the king was willing to give the daughters of the Scythian satraps and of all the other Scythian chieftains to Alexander's most trusted followers. The king also declared that he would come in person, if he were so commanded, to hear all of Alexander's commands from Alexander himself. [4] At that point Alexander also received a visit

Margin notes

4.14.3–4
Spring 327
BACTRA/ZARIASPA
Hermolaos is stoned to death with his coconspirators. Accounts differ as to whether Kallisthenes too was executed on the spot or died later of disease while in prison.

4.15.1–4
Spring 328
BACTRA/ZARIASPA
Arrian ends the digression (starting at 4.8) that took his narrative forward in time and returns to the events of early 328. At this time, the European Scythians send an embassy to Alexander, offering a marriage alliance. The king of the Khorasmians also visits Alexander and proposes a joint expedition against his neighbors.

Footnotes

4.14.2a   This contradicts what Arrian said above in his own account of the *proskynesis* affair, that Alexander abandoned the idea of introducing the ritual almost at the same moment it was raised.

4.14.2b   This is the first hint in Arrian's narrative that Alexander's drinking may have begun getting out of hand, a charge refuted by one of his sources, Aristoboulos (see Aelian, *Varia Historia* 3.23). The "sleeping habits" referred to here are connected to overconsumption of alcohol. According to one piece of ancient testimony, apparently a fragment of a log of Alexander's campaign, by 324 the king was regularly sleeping whole days following late-night drinking bouts; see Appendix C, §11.

4.14.3a   There are no good grounds for choosing between these two versions of Kallisthenes' fate. Some historians don't believe Alexander would summarily execute a prominent Greek writer and relative of Aristotle, while

others have no trouble with that idea. Plutarch (*Parallel Lives*, "Alexander" 55.9), who endorses Aristoboulos' version, claims that the point of hauling Kallisthenes about in chains was to have him tried by his Greek countrymen at some later date.

4.15.2a   This marriage offer is perhaps connected to a story, reported by the vulgate sources, that an Amazon queen named Thalestris visited Alexander in Hyrcania and slept with him for nearly two weeks in an effort to get pregnant by him (see n. 3.25.1a). The authenticity of the story was already disputed in antiquity (see Plutarch, *Parallel Lives* "Alexander" 46). Since the Scythian tribes of this region were known for allowing their women to ride and hunt (Herodotus, *Histories* 4.117, for example), it is easy to imagine that a Scythian princess could be transformed by legend into an Amazon queen.

from Pharasmanes, the Khorasmian[4a] king, who arrived with fifteen hundred horsemen. Pharasmanes declared that his country shared a border with the Colchian race and the Amazons; he promised to act as a guide and to provision the army if Alexander wished to attack the Colchians and Amazons and subdue the local tribes all the way to the Black Sea.[4b]

[5] Alexander replied graciously to the Scythian envoys and in a manner that served his present interest, but said he had no need for a Scythian marriage. After complimenting Pharasmanes and forming a friendship and an alliance with him, Alexander declared that the timing was not opportune for a march to the Black Sea. On commending Pharasmanes to Artabazos the Persian, whom he had appointed to manage the affairs of Bactria,[5a] and to all the other satraps whose territories bordered on his, he sent Pharasmanes back to his own settlements. [6] He said that for the time being he was occupied with India,[6a] because once he had subdued the Indians he would control all of Asia. But with Asia in his power he would return to Greece and would advance from there to the Black Sea by way of the Hellespont[6b] and the Propontis[6c] with all his land and naval forces.[6d] He said he expected Pharasmanes to defer until then all the promises he was making at present.

[7] Alexander went a second time to the River Oxus[7a] and decided to advance into Sogdiana,[7b] since it was reported that many of the Sogdians had fled for refuge to their strongholds and were refusing to obey the satrap Alexander had appointed. When he had made camp at the River Oxus, a spring of water emerged not far from his tent, and near it a spring of oil.[7c] [8] When the marvel was reported to Ptolemy son of Lagos, the Bodyguard, he informed Alexander, who performed all the sacrifices the seers prescribed in response to the omen. Aristandros said that the spring of oil was a sign of future hardships, but that it also foreshadowed victory after the hardships.[8a]

4.15.5–6
BACTRA/ZARIASPA
Alexander declines both offers and sets his sights on the conquest of India.

4.15.7–8
OXUS RIVER
At the Oxus River, Alexander encounters a natural wonder that is taken as an omen.

4.15.4a Khorasmia, possible location of territory: Map 4.8, inset.
4.15.4b Colchis: Map 4.8. The "Colchian race" referred to here are the legendary people from whom Jason was said to have stolen the Golden Fleece. The Amazons too were well known in Greek mythology as a tribe of warrior women who had once been defeated by the Greeks at the very threshold of Attica. Pharasmanes probably exploited the romance surrounding these names to entice the Macedonians, the new superpower, into attacking the nomadic tribes bordering his territory and therefore enlarging his own sphere of influence. He could not possibly have expected them to go as far west as the land of the Colchians, however, nor can his Hyrcanian realm be said to share a border with that land. Either he deliberately telescoped the distance to the Black (ancient Euxine) Sea, thinking this stratagem would make Alexander more likely to take on the campaign, or else his European listeners, who had only vague ideas of regional geography, misunderstood him.
4.15.5a Bactria: Map 4.8, inset.
4.15.6a India: Map 4.8. This is Arrian's first reference to the invasion of India, which will occupy much of the remainder of his narrative.
4.15.6b Hellespont: Map 1.12, inset.
4.15.6c Propontis: Map 1.12 and inset.
4.15.6d Shortly before his death Alexander planned to send an exploratory party into this region, principally to determine whether the Hyrcanian/Caspian was an inland sea or a gulf of Ocean (see 7.16.1–2), so he did indeed have plans to stage further campaigns here or to develop the region economically.
4.15.7a Oxus River: Map 4.8 and inset.
4.15.7b Sogdiana: Map 4.8, inset.
4.15.7c The word Arrian uses for this substance usually denotes olive oil. The Greeks had no name as yet for petroleum.
4.15.8a Aristandros disappears from Arrian's narrative after this last, unremarkable prophecy. It is likely that he died shortly after this point.

4.16.1–3
Summer 328
MARAKANDA
Alexander crosses into Sogdiana to deal with opposition there. He splits his army into five columns and makes a wide sweep through the province; then Hephaistion is commissioned to resettle the population. The hunt for Spitamenes continues.

[1] Leaving Polyperkhon, Attalos, Gorgias, and Meleagros behind in Bactria with orders to guard the country lest the local barbarians make trouble, and to destroy those who were still in revolt, Alexander crossed with part of the army into Sogdiana. [2] Dividing his force into five parts, he assigned one division to Hephaistion, and another to Ptolemy son of Lagos, the Bodyguard. He named Perdikkas to lead the third, and Koinos and Artabazos to lead the fourth. Taking command of the fifth division himself, Alexander advanced toward Marakanda.[2a] [3] Each of the other commanders launched attacks wherever good opportunities arose, forcibly removing some who had fled to their strongholds, and bringing others to terms. When all of Alexander's forces had traversed the greater part of Sogdiana and reached Marakanda, he dispatched Hephaistion to resettle the population in the cities of Sogdiana.[3a] Koinos and Artabazos were sent to Scythia,[3b] as Spitamenes was reported to have fled there for refuge. With his remaining forces, Alexander advanced against the places in Sogdiana still under the rebels' control and demolished them with no difficulty.

4.16.4–5
BACTRIA
Spitamenes, backed by new Massagetan allies, raids a Bactrian fort and kills the Macedonians guarding it, then moves to threaten the forces at Bactra/Zariaspa.

[4] While Alexander was thus occupied, Spitamenes and some of the Sogdian fugitives, who had fled to the country of the Scythians known as the Massagetai,[4a] assembled six hundred Massagetan horsemen and proceeded to one of the forts in Bactria. [5] Attacking the garrison head (who was not expecting an enemy) and the guards on duty, they slaughtered the soldiers and seized the commander as a prisoner. Taking courage from their capture of the fort, they approached Zariaspa[5a] a few days later. Though they had decided not to attack the city, they surrounded it and carried away considerable plunder.

4.16.6–7
BACTRIA
The small Macedonian force left in Bactra/Zariaspa sallies out and strikes a blow against the Massagetai, but is ambushed by Spitamenes on its way back to the town.

[6] A few cavalry Companions had been left behind ill in Zariaspa. With them were Peithon son of Sosikles, who had been assigned to the royal retinue in Zariaspa, and Aristonikos, the kithara-player. Having recovered their strength after being ill, these men had resumed bearing arms and mounting their horses. On learning of the Scythians' raid, they assembled nearly eighty mercenary horsemen who had been left behind as a garrison for Zariaspa, along with some of the royal pages, and sallied out against the Massagetai. [7] In the first assault, they fell on the unsuspecting Scythians, seized all their plunder, and killed several of the men who were carrying it away. But returning in disorder for want of a commander, they were caught in an ambush by Spitamenes and the Scythians and lost seven Companions and sixty mercenary horsemen. Aristonikos died there, having proved himself a braver man than any mere musician. Peithon was wounded and taken alive by the Scythians.

4.16.2a   Marakanda: Map 4.8, inset.
4.16.3a   This settlement program probably involved moving nomadic and agrarian tribes to the newly founded, Greek-style cities, where they could be watched by Macedonian garrisons, and where, it was hoped, they would adopt a settled, urban way of life that would make them more easily incorporated into the empire.
4.16.3b   Scythia: Map 4.8.
4.16.4a   Massagetai: Map 4.22, inset, AX.
4.16.5a   Bactra/Zariaspa: Map 4.22, inset, BX.

FIGURE 4.16. The ruined walls of medieval Balkh, in what is now Afghanistan, are thought to stand on the site of ancient Bactra/Zariaspa.

[1] When this was reported to Krateros,[1a] he quickly marched against the Massagetai, who made haste to flee toward the desert when they learned that he was almost upon them. Following close on their heels, Krateros caught up with them not far from the desert, where more than a thousand other Massagetan horsemen had joined them. [2] The Macedonians and

4.17.1–2
BACTRIA
Krateros learns of the fighting at Bactra/Zariaspa and hastens there. He catches up to the Massagetai as they flee into the desert and defeats them.

4.17.1a Arrian does not tell us where Krateros
        was at this point or what his orders were.
        It is likely he was stationed in Bactria

with the other commanders mentioned
at 4.16.1.

175

Scythians fought a pitched battle, and the Macedonians were victorious. A hundred and fifty Scythian horsemen perished; the rest had no difficulty reaching safety by slipping into the desert, where it was impossible for the Macedonians to pursue them farther.[2a]

[3] Meanwhile, Alexander granted the request of Artabazos,[3a] who was now elderly, to be relieved as satrap of Bactria, and named Amyntas son of Nikolaos his successor. He left Koinos there with his own battalion and that of Meleagros and nearly four hundred of the cavalry Companions, all the mounted javelin men, some Bactrians and Sogdians, and all the others posted with Amyntas, with orders to obey Koinos and to pass the winter in Sogdiana, both to guard the country and to lie in wait for Spitamenes; they were to ambush and arrest him anywhere he might wander during the winter. [4] When Spitamenes and his men saw that every place was controlled by Macedonian garrisons and that escape had become impossible, they ventured to attack Koinos and his army, in the hope that they might be more evenly matched with their enemy with that quarter of their enemy's array. On reaching Gabai,[4a] a strong position on the frontier between the Sogdians' land and that of the Massagetan Scythians, they easily persuaded nearly three thousand Scythian horsemen to join them in an attack on Sogdiana. [5] (These Scythians live in dire poverty, and as they have no cities or settled communities and hence do not fear for treasured possessions, they are easily persuaded to engage in one war after another.)[5a] On learning that these horsemen were approaching with Spitamenes, Koinos and his comrades went out to meet them with the army. [6] Their battle was a fierce one, and the Macedonians were victorious. More than eight hundred barbarian horsemen fell, while Koinos' force lost twenty-five horsemen and twelve foot soldiers.

Spitamenes was now deserted by the Sogdians who had remained with him, and by most of the Bactrians. These men approached Koinos and surrendered to him. [7] Since the Massagetan Scythians had fared poorly, they plundered the baggage trains of their Bactrian and Sogdian comrades-in-arms and fled to the desert with Spitamenes. When word reached them that Alexander was on the march and heading to the desert, they cut off Spitamenes' head and sent it to Alexander, hoping by this action to keep him away from their territory.[7a]

4.17.3
Autumn 328
SOGDIANA
Koinos is left in charge of forces detailed to spend the winter guarding Sogdiana and watching for Spitamenes.

4.17.4–6
SOGDIANA
Spitamenes gathers a large band of Scythian guerrillas and attacks Koinos' forces, but suffers a decisive defeat. In its wake, his allies begin to desert him.

4.17.7
SOGDIANA
The Massagetai, fearing that Alexander will march against them to capture Spitamenes, cut off the head of the rebel chief.

4.17.2a   There is no mention of the fate of Peithon, who was presumably killed by his Scythian captors.

4.17.3a   Artabazos was a former adherent of Darius who had come over to Alexander after the King's murder (see 3.21.4, 3.23.7). He was also father of Barsine, mother of Alexander's son Herakles.

4.17.4a   Gabai: location unknown. The *Barrington Atlas* (Maps 3 [F3], 92 [G4]) shows a possible site for a city named Gabai, but this cannot be the site of the city mentioned here by Arrian. It is hardly located on a frontier between Sogdiana and the territory of the Massagetai, which would be far

to the northeast on the Tanais/Iaxartes River.

4.17.5a   Behind this comment lies an implicit endorsement of Alexander's city-founding and resettlement policies in central Asia. Nomadic and rootless tribes were assumed by the Macedonians, and by the Greco-Roman world generally, to be naturally inclined toward brigandage and violence. The cure for their perceived lawlessness was assumed to lie in urbanization, which would give them a stake in maintaining a settled political order.

4.17.7a   In Quintus Curtius' version (8.3.1–16), Spitamenes is beheaded by his wife.

[1] At that point Koinos returned to Alexander at Nautaka,[1a] as did Krateros, Phrataphernes, the satrap of Parthia, and Stasanor, the satrap of Areia, after carrying out all of Alexander's orders. [2] Giving his army a rest near Nautaka, as it was the dead of winter, Alexander dispatched Phrataphernes to the Mardians and Tapourians[2a] to bring back the satrap Autophradates, who had often been sent for by Alexander, but had not obeyed the summons. [3] Alexander sent Stasanor to the Zarangians[3a] as satrap, and Atropates to the Medes to assume the satrapy of Media,[3b] as Oxydates appeared to be remiss in his duty. He sent Stamenes to Babylon, as he had been informed that Mazaios, the Babylonian governor, had died. He sent Sopolis, Epokillos, and Menidas to bring him the army from Macedonia.[3c]

[4] At the first appearance of spring[4a] Alexander advanced to the rock in Sogdiana,[4b] as he had been informed that many of the Sogdians had fled there for refuge. The wife and daughters of Oxyartes the Bactrian[4c] were said to have fled to the rock as well, Oxyartes having conveyed them there for safekeeping on the assumption that the place was impregnable. For Oxyartes had also revolted from Alexander.

Alexander supposed that once the rock had been taken, the Sogdians who wished to revolt would have nowhere else to turn. [5] But when he had marched to the rock, he found that the approach was steep on all sides and that the barbarians had gathered in the provisions necessary for a long siege. A heavy snow made the ascent more difficult for the Macedonians and at the same time brought the barbarians an abundant supply of water. But even so, Alexander decided to attack the place. [6] For an arrogant remark made by the barbarians had fired his thirst for glory and his wrath. When they had been summoned to discuss terms, and he had offered them the opportunity to withdraw in safety to their homes if they surrendered the place to him, they had laughed and in their native language had urged Alexander to seek soldiers with wings to capture the mountain for him, since no other men were of concern to them. [7] Thereupon Alexander

---

4.18.1–3
Winter 328/7
NAUTAKA
While resting his troops in winter quarters, Alexander makes administrative changes in the Asian satrapies.

4.18.4
Spring 327
SOGDIANA
Oxyartes, a Sogdian tribal leader, prepares to resist Alexander from a rock thought to be impregnable.

4.18.5–7
SOGDIAN ROCK
Alexander marches to the rock and examines Oxyartes' strong position. But stung by a verbal challenge from the Sogdians that only men with wings could threaten them, he decides to assault the rock, offering rich rewards to the troops if they succeed.

4.18.1a Nautaka: Map 4.22, inset, AX.
4.18.2a Mardians (Mardoi); Tapourians (Tapouroi), location of territories: Map 4.22.
4.18.3a Zarangiane (Drangiane): Map 4.22.
4.18.3b Media: Map 4.22.
4.18.3c Arrian is vague about this contingent of reinforcements, but his wording could imply that Alexander here set in motion the extraction of the Macedonian home guard, until now under Antipatros' command, for use in his continuing Asian campaign (see Bosworth II.123–124). If that is indeed what is meant here, then Alexander would be seeking to commit the whole of Macedonia's military-age male population to the Asian campaign, a policy for which he has been harshly criticized by some historians; but unfortunately there can be no certainty. In any case, it appears that "the army from Macedonia" was never brought into Asia, for whatever reason.

4.18.4a The time marker used by Arrian here may be an effort to cover up a disastrous error committed by Alexander. According to Quintus Curtius (8.4.1–17), the army left camp too early in the year and was soon beset by a bad winter storm; it had to be rescued with an emergency shipment of provisions after more than 2,000 men were lost. Arrian apparently alludes to this otherwise omitted event at 4.21.10, where he also indicates that the army was on the march in winter, not early spring.
4.18.4b Sogdian Rock, possible location: Map 4.22, AX. Its exact location is unknown. Arrian's reference to it here indicates it was a well-known fortress; other sources call it the rock of Ariamazes or the rock of the Oxus.
4.18.4c Oxyartes the Bactrian was formerly one of Bessos' followers (see 3.28.10).

announced a reward of twelve talents for the first man to scale the mountain; the rewards for the second and third man were announced in turn, and finally a reward of three hundred darics[7a] was promised to the last man to reach the top. The Macedonians, who were already eager, were spurred on still more by the proclamation.

4.19.1–4
Spring 327
SOGDIAN ROCK
Three hundred Macedonian climbers ascend the rock face at night. Some thirty fall to their deaths, but the rest succeed in seizing the rock's heights. Alexander announces to the Sogdians that their challenge has been met, and they quickly surrender.

[1] When everyone who had acquired rock-climbing expertise in Alexander's sieges had assembled—they numbered nearly three hundred—and had prepared small iron pegs (the ones used to secure their tents) to be fixed in the snow wherever it looked frozen solid and where any bare ground showed through, and had bound the pegs to strong linen cords, they went out at night to the sheerest face of the rock, where the fewest guards had been posted. [2] They fixed some of the pegs in the ground where it was visible, others in the snow where it was least likely to break up, and pulled themselves up at various parts of the rock. Some thirty men perished in the ascent, and their bodies were not recovered for burial, since they had fallen here and there in the snow. [3] The rest, having ascended near dawn and reached the mountain's peak, waved signal flags toward the Macedonians' camp as Alexander had instructed them to do. Alexander sent a herald and ordered him to shout to the barbarians' advance guard to delay no longer, but to give themselves up, as Alexander had indeed found the men with wings, and the heights of the mountain were in their hands. And as he spoke, the herald pointed to the soldiers atop the crest. [4] The barbarians were astounded by the unexpectedness of the sight. Imagining that even more of Alexander's men, armed to the teeth, were in possession of the heights, they gave themselves up, so terrified were they at the sight of those few Macedonians. Many of the barbarians' wives and children were taken prisoner, including Oxyartes' wife and daughters.

4.19.5–6
SOGDIAN ROCK
Alexander conceives a passionate desire for Rhoxane, the beautiful daughter of Oxyartes, now his captive. He elects to marry her rather than treat her as a concubine.

[5] Oxyartes had a virgin daughter of marriageable age. Her name was Rhoxane, and the men who served with Alexander said she was the most beautiful woman they had seen in Asia except for Darius' wife. It is said that when Alexander saw her he fell in love with her, and having been thus smitten by passion, he declined to rape her like a captive, but considered it not beneath his dignity to marry her.[5a] [6] And I find more to commend than blame in this action of Alexander's. Somehow in the case of Darius' wife, who was said to be the most beautiful woman in Asia, either Alexander felt no desire, or he restrained himself, though he was a young man at the very peak of his success, when men are apt to run wild. But Alexander respected

4.18.7a For the talent, see Appendix F, Money and Finance in the Campaigns of Alexander, §3, 5. The daric was a Persian unit of currency, introduced by Darius I.

4.19.5a Alexander's first marriage, and the only one that resulted in an heir to the throne, has spawned much romantic lore and legend, all of which is ignored by Arrian here. The marriage was in fact almost certainly a political act, designed to secure a powerful ally in a volatile and unstable region, rather than a love match (see Appendix I, Alexander in Central Asia, §7). Very little is known of Rhoxane, despite the fact that she was notionally queen mother of Macedonia for more than fifteen years before being executed in 309 or 308 (see the Epilogue, §4, 11).

and spared her, showing great self-control and a perfectly appropriate desire to be well thought of.[6a]

[1] There is also a story that shortly after the battle between Darius and Alexander at Issus, the eunuch who had been bodyguard to Darius' wife got away from his captors and made his way to Darius. When Darius saw him, he asked first whether his daughters, wife, and mother were alive.[1a] [2] When he heard that they were alive and that they were addressed as royalty and were waited on as deferentially as at Darius' court, Darius asked whether his wife had remained faithful to him. On learning that she had, he asked whether Alexander ever forced himself on her, whereupon the eunuch, swearing an oath, said, "Sire, your wife is just as you left her, and Alexander is the best and most self-restrained of men." [3] On hearing this, Darius raised his hands to the sky and uttered this prayer: "O Zeus the King, to whom has been entrusted the management of the affairs of mortal kings, I pray you to preserve my rule over the Persians and Medes, as you granted it to me. But if in your sight I am no longer king of Asia, give my power to no one but Alexander."[3a] Thus temperate actions are not overlooked, even by one's enemies.

[4] When Oxyartes learned that his children were captured and that Alexander was taking an interest in his daughter Rhoxane, he took courage and came before Alexander, who treated him honorably, as one would expect in such happy circumstances.

[1] When he had settled affairs in Sogdiana and the rock was in his possession, Alexander proceeded to Pareitakene,[1a] as a large group of barbarians were said to be in possession of another rock, a stronghold in Pareitakene known as the Rock of Khorienes.[1b] Khorienes himself had fled to it with several other chieftains. [2] The rock, from foot to summit, measured roughly two and a half miles,[2a] and its circumference measured nearly seven and a half miles. The rock itself was steep on all sides. There was only one ascent, and this was narrow and not easily scaled, a path forced onto the steep terrain; it made for difficult climbing even in single file and with no one barring the way. The rock was also surrounded by a deep ravine,[2b] so that anyone who intended to bring an army up to attack it

4.20.1–3
Arrian relates an anecdote concerning Darius' gratitude for Alexander's respectful treatment of the captive Persian queen.

4.20.4
SOGDIAN ROCK
Alexander is reconciled with Oxyartes.

4.21.1–2
PAREITAKENE
A second group of resisters, led by Khorienes, takes refuge on a second rock plateau, a tall outcropping surrounded at its base by a deep ravine.

4.19.6a See 2.12.3–7, where Arrian reports other chivalrous behaviors of Alexander toward Darius' wife but ignores the question of rape or a sexual relationship. Later literature, such as the *Alexander Romance*, made much of Alexander's abstinence, but Plutarch (*Parallel Lives*, "Alexander" 30.1) reports that Darius' wife died in childbirth, and some have speculated that the child was Alexander's.

4.20.1a For the capture of Darius' wife, mother, and daughters after the battle of Issus, see 2.12.3–7.

4.20.3a The idea that Darius had wanted Alexander to become his heir, undoubtedly a fiction, was elaborated in the *Alexander Romance*, some of which have Darius handing his power to Alexander at the moment of his death. For more on this work and its influence, see Appendix L, The *Alexander Romance*.

4.21.1a Pareitakene: Map 4.22, inset, AX.

4.21.1b Quintus Curtius (8.2.19–33) writes of a "Rock of Sisimithres" that Alexander attacked in late 328, and this is taken by some historians to be the same episode as the one Arrian describes here, but under a different name and moved several months earlier in time. But Bosworth (II.135), relying on the *Metz Epitome*, which mentions both, believes that Khorienes and Sisimithres are two different leaders on two different rocks.

4.21.2a The distance here is that of the trail one would travel from base to top.

4.21.2b Arrian's description of a ravine encircling a steep rock seems implausible. Quintus Curtius (8.2.19–33) more convincingly speaks of a ravine leading away from the rock, filled with rushing water running down from it. What Arrian describes here may have been a ditch dug by the defenders.

would have to fill in the ravine well in advance, in order to lead an assault from level ground.

[3] But even so, Alexander applied himself to the task. His daring and success had advanced to such a point that he thought no place should be beyond his reach or ability to conquer. Felling the silver firs (there were many enormous fir trees all around the mountain), he had ladders made, so that there would be a way down into the ravine for the army; there was no other way to descend into it. [4] By day Alexander himself supervised the work, keeping half the army engaged on it; by night his Bodyguards—Perdikkas, Leonnatos, and Ptolemy—took turns supervising the rest of the army, which had been divided into three parts and assigned to the night shift. By day they could complete no more than thirty feet, and by night slightly less, though the entire army was engaged in the work—so difficult was the site and the task undertaken there. [5] Descending into the ravine, they drove in stakes where it was narrowest, spacing them so as to make them strong and able to bear the materials laid upon them. On the stakes they laid wicker work woven into the shape of a bridge, and binding these woven pieces together, they poured earth onto them from above, so that the army could approach the rock from level ground.[5a]

[6] At first the barbarians viewed the undertaking with contempt, thinking it utterly impossible. But by the time arrows were reaching the rock,[6a] and they found themselves unable, from above, to hinder the Macedonians—who had built protective screens beneath which they could work without risk of injury—Khorienes, utterly panicked by what was happening, sent a herald to Alexander requesting that Oxyartes be sent up to him. [7] Alexander sent Oxyartes, who arrived and persuaded Khorienes to turn himself and the place over to Alexander. For, he said, when it came to force, there was no place Alexander and his army could not conquer; but if Khorienes put his trust in Alexander's honesty and friendship [. . .].[7a] He spoke highly of the king's honesty and fairness, offering his own case, along with other examples, to bolster his claim. [8] Persuaded by these arguments, Khorienes himself visited Alexander with some of his kinsmen and friends. Replying humanely to his visitor and giving him a pledge of friendship, Alexander kept Khorienes at his side, but told him to send some of his party to the rock to urge its occupiers to surrender the place. [9] The position was then surrendered by those who had taken refuge there, whereupon Alexander himself, taking nearly five hundred shield-bearers, ascended to

4.21.5a Arrian's account does not give a clear picture of this engineering operation. In particular, it is uncertain from his language whether the stakes were fixed vertically in the bottom of the chasm or horizontally along its sides. Bosworth (II.137) asserts the former, on the assumption that the work is taking place in the ravine described by Curtius (see n. 4.21.2b), which was filled with rushing water. In any case, the point of the opera-

tion seems clear enough: to speed up the landfill process by creating a support-work partway up the ravine, allowing the space beneath to be left void.

4.21.6a That is, after the landfill had risen high enough to allow the Macedonians to get within bowshot range of the rock's summit.

4.21.7a The end of this sentence appears to have fallen out of the manuscripts.

get a look at the rock. And far from treating Khorienes unfairly, Alexander entrusted the place to him and made him governor of all the tribes over whom he had formerly held sway.

[10] It happened that Alexander's army had suffered hardships as a result of the winter weather, as it snowed heavily during the siege,[10a] and his men were also distressed by a shortage of supplies. But Khorienes said he would give the army provisions for two months, and he distributed grain and wine from the stores on the rock, and salted meat, tent by tent. When giving these supplies, he claimed he would not be using up even a tenth of what had been prepared for the siege. From then on Khorienes was even more esteemed by Alexander, on the grounds that he had surrendered the rock by choice rather than by necessity.

[1] Having achieved his aims, Alexander himself proceeded to Bactra,[1a] but sent Krateros with six hundred cavalry Companions, Krateros' own infantry battalion, and the battalions of Polyperkhon, Attalos, and Alketas, against Katanes and Austanes,[1b] the last remaining rebels in Pareitakene. [2] In the fierce battle fought against these men, Krateros and his forces were victorious. Katanes died fighting there, and Austanes was arrested and conducted to Alexander. Of the barbarians with Katanes and Austanes, a hundred and twenty horsemen and fifteen hundred foot soldiers perished. Their mission accomplished, Krateros and his men also proceeded to Bactra. (It was in Bactra that Alexander had his painful experience connected with Kallisthenes and the pages.)[2a]

[3] When spring ended, Alexander advanced with the army to India,[3a] leaving Amyntas in Bactra with thirty-five hundred horsemen and ten thousand foot soldiers. [4] Crossing the Caucasus[4a] in ten days, he reached Alexandria,[4b] the city he had founded in the land of the Paropamisadai[4c] on his first expedition to Bactra. Alexander dismissed the governor he had originally appointed to rule the city, as the man appeared to be managing its affairs ineptly. [5] After adding new settlers to Alexandria drawn from various neighboring peoples and the soldiers who were unfit for fighting, Alexander ordered Nikanor, one of the Companions, to put the city's affairs in order. He appointed Tyriespis as satrap of the country of the Paropamisadai and the territory that extended to the River Kophen.[5a]

4.21.10
PAREITAKENE
Khorienes cements the new alliance by reprovisioning Alexander's army.

4.22.1–2
BACTRA/ZARIASPA
Krateros is dispatched to mop up further resistance in Pareitakene.

4.22.3–5
Summer 327
ALEXANDRIA IN THE CAUCASUS
Alexander crosses the Caucasus a second time, on his way into India. Reaching Alexandria in the Caucasus, he makes new administrative appointments.

4.21.10a Arrian's chronology is inconsistent here, since he reported earlier that Alexander had marched to the Sogdian Rock "at the first appearance of spring." The contradiction can probably be explained by Arrian's attempt to excuse Alexander for a premature departure from winter quarters (see n. 4.18.4a).
4.22.1a Bactra/Zariaspa: Map 4.22, inset, BX.
4.22.1b Katanes and Austanes appear to be two other regional resistance leaders, not otherwise mentioned by Arrian.
4.22.2a Arrian refers to the plot to kill Alexander, which he has already described at 4.14.3.

4.22.3a India: Map 4.22. Arrian gives no motivation or rationale for Alexander's invasion of India, but for some modern analysis see Appendix J, The Indian Campaign, §1.
4.22.4a The Indian Caucasus/Paropamisos (modern Hindu Kush): Map 4.2, inset, BX.
4.22.4b Alexandria in the Caucasus: Map 4.22, inset, BY. Alexander's founding of this city was described at 3.28.4.
4.22.4c Paropamisadai (Arrian spells it Parapamisadai): Map 4.22, inset, BX.
4.22.5a Kophen River: Map 4.22, inset, BY.

FIGURE 4.22. The Khyber Pass, leading into India by way of Peukelaotis. According to some theories, this was the route taken by Hephaistion and a large body of the Macedonian army.

4.22.6
Summer 327
KOPHEN RIVER
The leaders of India west of the Indus, including Taxiles, submit to Alexander, promising him their war elephants.

[6] On reaching Nicaea[6a] and sacrificing to Athena, he advanced to the Kophen, having sent a herald ahead to order Taxiles and the tribes west of the River Indus to present themselves at their first opportunity. Taxiles and the other leaders, arriving with the gifts most prized by the Indians, duly presented themselves and promised to give Alexander all the elephants at their disposal, nearly twenty-five in number.[6b]

4.22.6a Nicaea: location unknown.
4.22.6b Diodorus (17.86.3–4) and Quintus Curtius (8.12.5) tell us more about this embassy to Alexander. The man here called Taxiles was the aging ruler of the important Indian city of Taxila (Map 4.22, inset, BY). His son, whom Diodorus calls Mophis and Curtius calls Omphis, had earlier persuaded Taxiles to make an alliance with the Macedonians and invite them to Taxila, in hopes of using Alexander's power to support his own regional ambitions. His gift of

elephants was a demonstration of trust and friendship, since trained elephants were a powerful weapon of war in ancient India (see Appendix D, §16). Shortly after meeting with Alexander, Taxiles died, and his son Omphis/Mophis took the regnal name Taxiles formerly used by his father. Arrian did not distinguish between the father and son, and introduces the younger Taxiles at 5.3.5 as though he were the same person as the Taxiles who greets Alexander here.

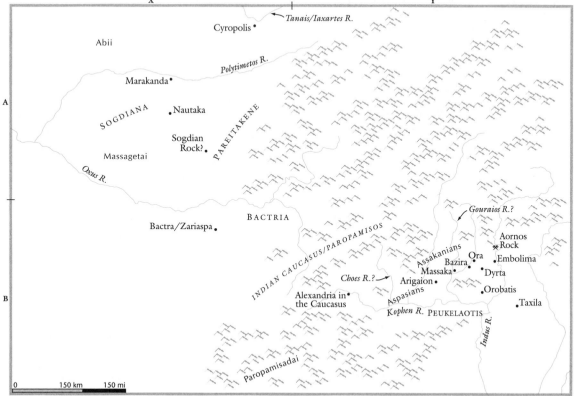

MAP 4.22

4.22.7–8
Summer 327
PEUKELAOTIS
Alexander sends Hephaistion and Perdikkas ahead to the Indus with a large force, ordering them to subdue the region and prepare to cross the river. Hephaistion captures Peukelaotis' principal city, held by a recalcitrant leader, after a lengthy siege.

4.23.1–3
Autumn 327
WESTERN INDIA
Entering the westernmost regions of India, Alexander hastens to head off the reported exodus of potential resisters. In his first battle he pens up a group of hostile inhabitants but is wounded, as are two of his officers.

[7] Dividing the army, Alexander sent Hephaistion and Perdikkas to Peukelaotis, which lay on their route to the Indus,[7a] with the battalions of Gorgias, Kleitos,[7b] and Meleagros, half the Companion cavalry, and all the mercenary horsemen, with orders to subdue, by force or diplomacy, the tribes they encountered on their march and, on reaching the Indus, to prepare all necessary equipment for crossing the river. Taxiles and the other governors were dispatched with these troops and carried out all of Alexander's orders when they reached the Indus. [8] But Astis, the governor of Peukelaotis, stirred up trouble, and thereby brought about his own demise and the downfall of the city in which he had taken refuge.[8a] For Hephaistion and his men captured the city after besieging it for thirty days; Astis himself was put to death, and Sangaios was put in charge of the city. (Having deserted Astis earlier, Sangaios had gone over to Taxiles, and had thereby won Alexander's trust.)

[1] Leading the shield-bearers, all the cavalry Companions who had not been posted with Hephaistion, the battalions of the so-called *asthetairoi*,[1a] the archers, the Agrianians, and the mounted javelin men, Alexander advanced to the country of the Aspasians,[1b] Gouraians,[1c] and Assakanians.[1d] [2] After traveling a rough and mountainous road beside the river known as the Choes[2a] and managing a difficult crossing, Alexander ordered the mass of infantry to follow him at a walking pace; taking all the horsemen, and mounting nearly eight hundred Macedonian foot soldiers on horseback with their infantry shields,[2b] he led these forward in haste, as he had received word that the local barbarians had fled for refuge to the nearby mountains and to the towns that offered strong defensive positions. [3] Attacking the first city in his path the moment he arrived there, he routed the men posted outside it, and forced them to take refuge inside the walls, though he himself was wounded by an arrow that pierced his breastplate and entered his shoulder. The wound gave him no trouble, as his breastplate kept the arrow from passing right through the shoulder. Ptolemy son of Lagos was also wounded, as was Leonnatos.

4.22.7a Peukelaotis; Indus River: Map 4.22, inset, BY. There is uncertainty about the routes through the mountains followed by both Alexander's contingent and that led by Hephaistion and Perdikkas. Alexander probably went by way of the Shibar and Salang passes; the Khyber Pass is a possible route for the other commanders (see Figure 4.22).
4.22.7b This Kleitos is obviously a different person than the Kleitos murdered by Alexander the previous year. Alexander's men distinguished the two men named Kleitos by referring to the one killed by Alexander as "the Black" and the other as "the White."
4.22.8a This unnamed city cannot be identified with certainty.
4.23.1a There is little information available about

what this corps consisted of.
4.23.1b Aspasians (Aspasioi), location of territory: Map 4.22, inset, BY.
4.23.1c Gouraians: precise location of territory unknown. Gouraios River, possible location: Map 4.22, inset, BY. The Gouraios is usually identified with the modern Panjkora River.
4.23.1d Assakanians (Assakanoi), location of territory: Map 4.22, inset, BY.
4.23.2a Choes River, possible location: Map 4.22, inset, BY.
4.23.2b This tactic was designed to permit the swift transport of infantrymen but still allow them use of their heavy weaponry when they arrived at the scene of a confrontation.

[4] Alexander then made camp near the city where the wall appeared most vulnerable. A double wall had been built around the city; at dawn the next day, the Macedonians easily forced their way through the first wall, which had not been properly constructed, while at the second wall the barbarians held out briefly. But when the scaling ladders had been placed against this wall and the defenders were being wounded by shots from all sides, they did not stand their ground, but poured through the gates, heading to the mountains. [5] Some of them perished in the flight, and the Macedonians, enraged that Alexander had been wounded by these people, slew everyone they captured, though most of the defenders escaped to the mountains, which were not far off.[5a]

After razing the city to the ground, Alexander led his men to another city, Andaka.[5b] The city surrendered after negotiating terms, and when Alexander had taken possession, he left Krateros there with the other infantry officers to destroy all the other cities that refused to come over willingly, and to settle the country's affairs as advantageously as circumstances permitted.

[1] Alexander himself, leading the shield-bearers, the archers, the Agrianians, the battalions of Koinos and Attalos, the cavalry *agema*[1a] and up to four hipparchies[1b] of the other Companions, and half the mounted bowmen to the river [...][1c] a city where the Aspasians' governor was. After covering considerable ground, he reached the city on the second day. [2] When the barbarians learned that Alexander was approaching, they set fire to the city and fled to the mountains. Alexander's troops followed the fugitives closely as far as the mountains. There was a great massacre of the barbarians until they found safety by reaching the rugged country well ahead of their pursuers.

[3] When Ptolemy, accompanied by some shield-bearers, caught sight of the leader of the local Indians near a hill, he pursued the man on horseback, though he was very much outnumbered. But as his horse had difficulty running up the hill, Ptolemy left the animal behind, handing it to one of his shield-bearers, and pursued the Indian on foot. [4] When the Indian saw Ptolemy drawing near, he and his shield-bearers turned around to face him. Striking at close quarters with his long spear, the Indian pierced Ptolemy's breastplate at the chest, but the breastplate blocked the blow. Striking with

4.23.4–5
WESTERN INDIA
A siege operation forces the inhabitants of an unnamed city to flee, and the pursuing Macedonians kill all they capture in revenge for Alexander's wound. Alexander razes this city and receives the surrender of the next, Andaka.

4.24.1–2
WESTERN INDIA
Alexander moves on to another city, whose inhabitants set fire to their dwellings and try to flee at his approach. The Macedonians slaughter many as they flee.

4.24.3–5
WESTERN INDIA
During the pursuit, Ptolemy engages in single combat with the Indian leader and kills him. A battle breaks out over possession of the corpse; the Macedonians prevail, but with difficulty.

4.23.5a This first engagement in the India campaign sets the pattern for much of the grim action that would follow in the next two years. The local rulers of India, unlike the tribal chiefs of Central Asia, had never been fully incorporated into the Persian empire and were not accustomed to foreign domination. With the exception of Taxiles, their resistance was more determined, and their acquiescence more short-lived, than those Alexander had dealt with elsewhere, and the military tactics of the Macedonians became more severe and unsparing (see Appendix J, §12).

4.23.5b Andaka: location unknown.
4.24.1a The term *agema* has been used earlier by Arrian to refer to an elite infantry squadron. Here it designates cavalry. In both cases the units involved were assigned to fight in close proximity to the king.
4.24.1b Alexander evidently began dividing the Companion cavalry into hipparchies, or squadrons, in 330 or 329 (see 3.29.7 and n. 3.29.7a). The number of hipparchies varied, from perhaps as many as ten to as few as four (see 7.6.4).
4.24.1c Some words are missing from the transmitted text here.

his own weapon, Ptolemy drove straight through the Indian's thigh, felled the man, and stripped him of his gear. [5] The Indians who attended this man, when they saw their commander lying there, held their ground no longer. But when other Indians from the mountains saw the leader's corpse being taken up by their enemies, they were appalled. Running down from the heights, they engaged in a fierce battle near the hill for possession of the body. But by then Alexander was at the hill with his infantrymen, who had dismounted from their horses. These men attacked the Indians and managed, with difficulty, to drive them to the mountains; thus they kept possession of the corpse.

4.24.6–7
ARIGAION
At Arigaion, Alexander finds another town burned and deserted by its inhabitants. He appoints Krateros to resettle the site with friendly locals and invalided veterans.

[6] On crossing the mountains, Alexander descended to a city called Arigaion.[6a] He found that the city had been burned down by its inhabitants and that the people had fled. Krateros and his troops joined him there, having performed all the tasks assigned them by the king. [7] As Arigaion seemed to Alexander to have been settled on an opportune site, he ordered Krateros to fortify it and people it with volunteers from the neighboring tribes and any of his own men who were unfit for fighting. He himself advanced to the region where most of the local barbarians had reportedly fled for refuge. On reaching a mountain range, he made camp at its foot.

4.24.8–10
Winter 327/6
WESTERN INDIA
Observing reports of an immense host of enemy forces, Alexander divides his army into segments.

[8] At that point, Ptolemy son of Lagos, who had been dispatched by Alexander on a foraging expedition and had advanced with a few men to reconnoiter, reported to Alexander that he had seen more fires in the barbarians' camp than in Alexander's. [9] Alexander was incredulous as to the number of fires, but since he understood that there was a cohort of barbarians in that area, he left a part of the army there, in the camp they had already set up near the mountain, and took with him what seemed a sufficient force in light of Ptolemy's report. As soon as they saw the enemy's fires nearby, Alexander divided the army into three parts. [10] He put Leonnatos the Bodyguard in charge of one division, assigning him the battalions of Attalos and Balakros; the second division, which included a third of the royal shield-bearers, the units of Philip and Philotas, two regiments of archers, the Agrianians, and half the cavalry, was assigned to Ptolemy son of Lagos; and Alexander himself led the third division, positioned where there appeared to be the largest concentration of barbarians.

4.25.1–4
WESTERN INDIA
The battle between Alexander's tripartite forces and the huge throng of Indians results in a Macedonian victory, with more than forty thousand prisoners taken.

[1] When the Indians, looking down from high ground, noticed the Macedonians approaching, they took courage from their superiority in numbers; and in their contempt for the Macedonians, who appeared to be few, they came down to the plain. Here a pitched battle was fought, but Alexander defeated these men without much trouble. [2] Ptolemy's men were drawn up on uneven ground, while the barbarians were in possession of a hill and were formed into deep columns, so Ptolemy led his companies to what seemed to be the hill's most vulnerable point. He did not surround the hill completely, but left a space for the barbarians in case they wished to

4.24.6a Arigaion: Map 4.22, inset, BY.

flee. [3] The battle against these men was also a fierce one, owing to the difficulty of the terrain and because these Indians were not like the other barbarians of that region, but were by far the most warlike. Nevertheless they too were driven from the mountain by the Macedonians. And Leonnatos' men in the third segment of the army were equally successful, as they also defeated their opponents. [4] Ptolemy says that the total number of prisoners taken exceeded forty thousand, that more than two hundred and thirty thousand oxen were seized,[4a] and that Alexander selected the finest among them—the ones plainly superior in beauty and size—and wished to send them to Macedonia to work the land.

[5] Thereafter Alexander led his men to the territory of the Assakanians;[5a] for word had reached him that the Assakanians, in possession of nearly two thousand horsemen, more than thirty thousand foot soldiers, and thirty elephants, were preparing to fight. Krateros, who had by then fortified the city whose settlement he had been left behind to organize, brought Alexander the more heavily armed contingents of the army along with the war engines, in case a siege became necessary. [6] Alexander himself, leading the Companion cavalry, the mounted javelin men, the battalion of Koinos and Polyperkhon, the thousand Agrianians, and the archers, advanced against the Assakanians through Gouraian territory. [7] He managed a difficult crossing of the Gouraios[7a] (from which the region takes its name), since the river was deep and its current swift, and round rocks in the water made the footing slippery. But when the barbarians noticed Alexander approaching, they did not dare to join forces against him, but disbanded, each to their several cities, which they intended to defend and preserve.

[1] Alexander led his men first against Massaka,[1a] the largest city in the region. When he was nearing its walls, the barbarians, taking courage from the nearly seven thousand mercenaries from farther east in India who had joined them, charged out against the Macedonians when they saw them setting up camp. [2] Alexander, having observed that the battle would be fought near the city, wanted to draw the inhabitants farther from their walls, so that if a rout took place—and he knew that there would be a rout[2a]—it would be harder for them, when they fled, to reach their city in safety. So when he saw the barbarians, he ordered the Macedonians to wheel about and retreat to a particular hill, roughly a mile from the place where he had decided to camp. [3] The enemy now took heart, imagining

4.25.5–7
ASSAKANIAN TERRITORY
Resistance forces sent by the Assakanians scatter as Alexander approaches.

4.26.1–4
MASSAKA
The Macedonians attack Massaka. When the inhabitants make a sortie outside their walls, Alexander surprises them with a feigned retreat followed by a charge, and drives them back in. Alexander receives a minor arrow wound in the ankle.

4.25.4a   The number of both prisoners and cattle are gross exaggerations, claims Bosworth (II.126), basing his reasoning on the modern population and grazing capacity of this region. It is noteworthy that Arrian attributes this information to Ptolemy, who, as leader of the victorious troops, had obvious motives for amplifying the scale of what was achieved.
4.25.5a   Assakanians (Assakanoi), location of territory: Map 4.22, inset, BY.
4.25.7a   Gouraios River, possible location: Map

4.22, inset, BY. The Gouraios is usually identified with the modern Panjkora River.
4.26.1a   Massaka: Map 4.22, inset, BY.
4.26.2a   This is an interesting insight regarding Alexander's self-confidence, even when he faced huge numbers of hostile Indian warriors. The superior armaments, training, and tactics of his army had already demonstrated that any obstacles in India could be overcome, with the possible exception of large elephant brigades.

that the Macedonians were already giving way, and swept toward them at full speed, all out of formation. When their arrows were nearly reaching his men, Alexander gave the signal, and the phalanx wheeled about and charged the enemy. [4] The mounted javelin men, the Agrianians, and the archers ran out first and joined battle with the barbarians; Alexander himself was leading the phalanx. The Indians were astonished by the unexpected turn of events, and as soon as they found themselves fighting at close quarters, they gave way and fled to the city. Nearly two hundred of them perished;[4a] the rest were forced inside their walls. Alexander advanced the phalanx toward the city and received a minor arrow wound in the ankle.

[5] The next day, having brought the siege engines forward, he easily battered down a section of the wall, though the Indians mounted a brave defense against the Macedonians who were trying to force their way through the breach. Alexander therefore recalled the army for that day. The next day, the Macedonians' assault was stronger, and a wooden tower was brought forward, from which the archers shot arrows, while engines fired missiles. Though the Macedonians succeeded in pushing the Indians back a good distance, they could not yet force their way into the city. [6] On the third day, having again advanced the phalanx and thrown a bridge from an engine across the breach in the wall, Alexander led up the shield-bearers, the very unit that had demolished Tyre for him in the same way.[6a] With many men eagerly pushing forward, the overburdened bridge collapsed and the Macedonians fell with it. [7] When the barbarians saw what was happening, they raised a shout and assailed the Macedonians from their walls with rocks and arrows and anything else they happened to be holding or could lay their hands on at the moment. Running out through the gates, which were just small openings in their curtain walls, they assaulted the confused Macedonians at close quarters.

[1] Alexander sent Alketas with his battalion to take up the wounded and to recall to the camp all who were still fighting. On the fourth day, another gangplank was brought up to the wall in the same manner by another engine. [2] As for the Indians, while the leader in those parts survived, they fought fiercely. But when he was hit by a shot from a catapult and perished, they sent representatives to negotiate with Alexander, as some of their men had fallen in the prolonged siege and most were wounded and unfit for fighting. [3] And Alexander was glad to spare brave men. He made peace with the Indian mercenaries on condition that they be posted with the rest of his army and serve under him; they emerged with their weapons and set up their own camp on a hill opposite the camp of the Macedonians. It was their intention to flee to their own settlements under cover of night, as they were unwilling to bear arms against other Indians. [4] When

4.26.5–7
Winter 327/6
MASSAKA
During the siege of Massaka, a breach in the walls is opened but stoutly defended. When the Macedonians try to climb over the wall from a siege tower, their gangway collapses and many troops end up at the mercy of the Massakans.

4.27.1–4
MASSAKA
The siege continues, but after the Massakans' leader is shot dead, the city opens negotiations. Alexander allows the Indian mercenaries safe conduct out of the city and attempts to hire them into his own army, but orders their massacre after learning of their plan to run away. Massaka is then taken by storm.

4.26.4a The relatively light Indian losses here can be attributed to the fact that the Macedonians did not have their cavalry in play (Alexander himself was fighting on foot).

Much higher casualty rates resulted when the Macedonians pursued fleeing infantry with their cavalry.
4.26.6a See 2.20.6, 2.23.2.

Alexander was informed of this, during the night he posted his entire army around the hill and cut to pieces the Indians who were thus encircled;[4a] then he took the city by storm, since it had been deserted by its defenders, and seized Assakanos' mother and daughter.[4b]

[5] In the entire siege, twenty-five of Alexander's men died. Alexander then sent Koinos to Bazira,[5a] supposing that its inhabitants, when they learned of the capture of Massaka, would surrender. He also sent Attalos, Alketas, and Demetrios, the cavalry commander, to Ora,[5b] another city, with orders to surround it with a wall until he could get there himself. [6] At a certain point, Ora's inhabitants sallied out against Alketas and his men, whereupon the Macedonians, routing them easily, drove them back into their city. Koinos met with no success in Bazira, as its inhabitants, trusting to the strength of their position, which rose to a great height and was well fortified on all sides, showed no sign of surrender.

[7] Informed of this, Alexander started for Bazira, but when he learned that some of the neighboring barbarians were planning to slip unnoticed into Ora, having been sent by Abisares[7a] for that purpose, he went to Ora first. He ordered Koinos to fortify a strong site near the city of Bazira and to man it with an adequate garrison, so that the city's inhabitants could not safely make use of the countryside, and then to bring the rest of the army and join up with him. [8] When the inhabitants of Bazira saw Koinos departing with most of the army, they disdained the Macedonians and imagined that they would be no match for themselves in battle. They rushed out into the plain, and a fierce battle was fought. Nearly five hundred of the barbarians fell there, and more than seventy were taken alive. The rest, having fled into the city, were now barred more firmly from the countryside by the men posted at the fort. [9] Meanwhile, Alexander's siege of Ora did not prove difficult: immediately attacking the walls, he got control of the city on the first attempt and seized the elephants that had been left there.

4.27.5–6
BAZIRA-ORA
Alexander sends detachments to deal with two other centers of resistance, Bazira and Ora.

4.27.7–9
BAZIRA-ORA
Bazira is left under the guard of a small holding force, which tempts the inhabitants to make a sally, but their attack fails. Meanwhile, Alexander moves against Ora and quickly takes the city by siege.

4.27.4a The massacre of the Indian mercenaries is reported differently by Diodorus (17.84.1–3) and Plutarch (*Parallel Lives*, "Alexander" 59), in ways that suggest Alexander was guilty not just of extreme harshness, as even Arrian's account suggests, but of treacherous double-dealing. In Diodorus' version, Alexander seems to reframe the terms of the safe conduct under which the mercenaries had left the city to mean that they could be attacked as soon as they had passed beyond its walls. Whatever the true circumstances of the massacre were, it seems clear that Alexander seized an opportunity to annihilate a potential source of future resistance.

4.27.4b The mother here referred to, named Kleophis according to Quintus Curtius (8.10.22), was left in charge of the

Assakanians after the death of her husband, the local dynast Assakanos. Arrian does not say how or when Assakanos died, though some have assumed he was the unnamed Indian leader killed by Ptolemy at 4.24.3–5. Since Assakanos (according to Quintus Curtius) was dead before the siege of Massaka began, he cannot be "the leader" killed by artillery fire at 4.27.2.

4.27.5a Bazira: Map 4.22, inset, BY.
4.27.5b Ora: Map 4.22, inset, BY.
4.27.7a Abisares was an Indian regional ruler who initially decided to side with the enemies of Alexander. He was deemed one of two principal opposition leaders (Poros was the other). However, in the end Abisares decided to make an accommodation with the invaders.

[1] When the inhabitants of Bazira learned of this, they felt that their predicament was hopeless. They left the city near midnight.[1a] The other barbarians did the same: leaving their cities, they all fled to the so-called Aornos Rock.[1b] The rock is an enormous landmark in the region. According to legend, not even Herakles, son of Zeus, had been able to capture it. [2] I cannot say positively whether the Theban, Tyrian, or Egyptian Herakles actually reached India; I rather think he did not, but when men want to exaggerate their difficulties, they say that not even Herakles could have overcome them. I believe that it was just so in the case of this rock: Herakles' name became associated with it as a boast.

[3] They say that the rock's circumference measures nearly twenty-five miles and that its height at its lowest measures a mile and a quarter. There is but one way up, and it is handmade and rugged. At the peak there is a plentiful, spring-fed supply of pure water, a wood, and fertile land—enough for a thousand men to cultivate.

[4] When Alexander heard the place described, a longing seized him to capture this mountain too, not least on account of the Herakles legend. He made Ora and Massaka watch posts for the region and completely fortified Bazira as a city. [5] Hephaistion and Perdikkas, after fortifying another city, Orobatis,[5a] left a garrison there and proceeded to the River Indus.[5b] On their arrival, they set about bridging the river according to Alexander's orders. [6] Alexander appointed Nikanor, one of the Companions, as satrap of the territory west of the Indus. Alexander himself first headed for the river, and after bringing to terms Peukelaotis,[6a] a city lying at no great distance from the river, he established a Macedonian garrison there and named Philip as commander; he also secured a number of other small cities that had been founded near the Indus. He was accompanied by Kophaios and Assagetes, the governors of the region.[6b] [7] After reaching Embolima,[7a] a city near the Aornos Rock, he stationed Krateros there with a division of the army, having ordered him to supply the city with as much food as possible and everything else needed for a long stay, so that the Macedonians, making the city their base of operations, might wear out the rock's occupiers with a long siege if they could not capture them in the initial assault.

[8] Taking the archers, the Agrianians, Koinos' battalion, and a hand-picked group of the nimblest and best-armed men from the rest of the phalanx, along with some two hundred of the cavalry Companions and nearly a hundred mounted bowmen, Alexander headed toward the rock. On that day he made camp at a site he considered suitable; the next day, advancing a little farther toward the rock, he again made camp.

4.28.1a The manuscripts of Arrian's work have a mysteriously vague phrase at the end of this sentence, "and fled to the rock." If the text is sound, it seems that some rock other than Aornos, first mentioned in the next sentence, is meant. But most editors delete the phrase as a scribal error.
4.28.1b Aornos Rock: Map 4.22, inset, BY.
4.28.5a Orobatis: Map 4.22, inset, BY.
4.28.5b Indus River: Map 4.22, inset, BY.
4.28.6a Peukelaotis: location unknown. This is evidently a different Peukelaotis from the one subdued by Hephaistion at 4.22.7–8.
4.28.6b These two collaborators are not otherwise known.
4.28.7a Embolima: Map 4.22, inset, BY.

FIGURE 4.28. The slopes of Pir Sar, the site known to Alexander as Aornos Rock, are cut through by deep ravines. The Macedonians had to fill in one such ravine in order to get within artillery range of the Indian stronghold. After that, their catapults and torsion bows were able to scatter the rock's defenders, clearing a path for the final assault.

[1] At that point some of the neighboring tribesmen came to Alexander, surrendered, and promised to guide him to the most vulnerable part of the rock, a position from which he could easily capture the place. With these men as guides, Alexander sent Ptolemy son of Lagos, the Bodyguard, in command of the Agrianians and the light-armed troops, including some picked shield-bearers, with orders that when he had captured the place, he should secure possession with a strong holding force and send a signal that it was in his hands. [2] Following a rugged and barely passable road, Ptolemy took possession of the place without attracting the barbarians' notice. When he had fortified it all around with a palisade and a ditch, he held up a torch from a hilltop where it would be seen by Alexander. The flame was seen at once, and on the following day Alexander led the army forward, but because the barbarians were resisting his advance and the terrain was rough, he was unable to make headway. [3] When the barbarians realized that Alexander's advance had

4.29.1–3
AORNOS ROCK
With the help of informants, Alexander sends Ptolemy to seize a strategic position near the rock. Ptolemy gets possession of the place and fortifies it, but Alexander is prevented from bringing in the main force, and the Indians nearly dislodge Ptolemy from the position.

191

bogged down, they turned and attacked Ptolemy and his men. A fierce battle was fought between the barbarians and the Macedonians, the Indians striving to tear down the palisade, Ptolemy to protect his position. The barbarians, getting the worst of it in the exchange of fire, withdrew at nightfall.

[4] Alexander selected one of the Indian deserters who was especially trustworthy and knowledgeable about the region, and sent him with a letter to Ptolemy, directing him to attack the barbarians from the heights when Alexander attacked the rock, and not to be content merely to hold his position. Assailed from both sides, the Indians would be in doubt about which way to turn. [5] Alexander himself, starting from the camp as soon as it was day, led the army along the route by which Ptolemy had ascended unseen, having calculated that if, by forcing his way through, he joined up with Ptolemy's detachment, his task would pose no further difficulty. And so it turned out. [6] Until midday the battle was fierce, the Macedonians forcing their way up the ascent, the barbarians shooting at them as they advanced. But when the Macedonians did not give way, and one company after another climbed up and relieved those who had preceded them, they managed to get the ascent under their control near evening and joined up with Ptolemy's detachment. Thereafter, the entire army, reunited, advanced against the rock itself. But it was still impossible for them to attack,[6a] and they suspended their efforts for that day.

[7] At dawn Alexander ordered each soldier to cut a hundred stakes. When these had been cut, he began heaping up a large mound,[7a] starting from the crest of the hill where they were encamped and extending to the rock. For it seemed to him that from the mound their arrows could reach the rock's defenders, as could the shots fired from catapults. Every man took part in the work of raising the mound, and Alexander himself stood by as supervisor, giving praise when the work was performed with zeal, chastising when it failed to progress swiftly.

[1] On the first day, the army raised the mound about two hundred yards. The next day the slingers, hurling stones at the Indians from the rising mound, together with the shots fired from the engines, repulsed the Indians who were sallying out against the Macedonians at work on the mound. The mound-building went on without interruption for three days; on the fourth, a few of the Macedonians, forcing their way, gained possession of a small rise on the same level as the rock. Losing no time, Alexander extended the mound, as he wished to join it to the hill that the few Macedonians were now holding for him.

Margin notes

4.29.4–6

AORNOS ROCK

Alexander gets a message to Ptolemy instructing him to attack the next day, while Alexander's forces advance and try to make contact with him. This strategy unites the two armies at the spot seized by Ptolemy, but further advance is blocked.

4.29.7

AORNOS ROCK

To prepare a surface on which he could advance his siege engines and his army, Alexander sets the men to work filling in a chasm that separates him from the rock.

4.30.1

AORNOS ROCK

As work on the mound progresses, the Macedonians bring their artillery weapons to bear and gain ground.

Footnotes

4.29.6a Arrian omits a crucial topographical detail that explains Alexander's halt here: as is implied in what follows, a deep ravine stood between his position and the rock itself. This feature of the landscape had also gone unmentioned (in Arrian's account, at least) by Alexander's Indian guides, who had promised that ascent of the rock would be easy from Ptolemy's position. Perhaps they did not reckon with Alexander's need to bring heavy siege engines to bear on the rock to soften its defenses.

4.29.7a Arrian implies that the stakes were used as a framework to hold the earth and the fill being heaped into the ravine.

[2] The Indians were astounded at the indescribable daring of the Macedonians who had forced their way to the hill. Observing that the mound was now attached to the hill, they ceased further resistance and, sending heralds to Alexander, they said they were willing to give up the rock if he would make peace with them. But they were actually planning to spend the day prolonging the negotiations and to disperse that night, each tribe to its own settlement. [3] When Alexander got wind of this, he gave the barbarians time to retreat and removed the guards that surrounded the place on all sides.[3a] He waited until they had started their withdrawal and then took some seven hundred of the bodyguards and shield-bearers to the abandoned part of the rock. Alexander himself was the first to scale it, and the Macedonians, drawing one another up at various points, came up after him. [4] At a signal they turned on the retreating barbarians, killing many of them as they fled; the rest, in a panic to get away, hurled themselves off the cliffs and perished.

[5] The rock Herakles had failed to capture was now in Alexander's hands, and he sacrificed on it and established a garrison there, placing Sisikottos in charge. (Sisikottos had long ago deserted from the Indians to Bessos in Bactra, and when Alexander had taken possession of Bactria, Sisikottos had joined forces with him and shown himself especially trustworthy.)

Starting from the rock, Alexander invaded the land of the Assakanians,[5a] as he had received word that Assakanos' brother, with his elephants and a great many of his barbarian neighbors, had fled to the mountains there. Alexander arrived at the city of Dyrta[5b] but not before the inhabitants had left, nor did he find them in the surrounding countryside. The next day he sent out Nearkhos[5c] and Antiokhos, the commander of the shield-bearers; [6] he gave Nearkhos the command of the Agrianians and the light-armed troops, Antiokhos the command of his own and two additional regiments. The two men were sent to explore the country and to capture any barbarians they could find for questioning about the region. Among other matters, Alexander was especially concerned to learn about the elephants.[6a]

[7] As for Alexander, he now led his men to the Indus, and his army, as it advanced, leveled a road, since the terrain thereabouts was otherwise impassable. In the course of their march they arrested a few barbarians, from whom they learned that the Indians of the region had fled to Abisares[7a] and had left their elephants grazing there near the Indus. Alexander commanded these men to lead him to the elephants. [8] Many of the Indians hunt elephants, and Alexander had eagerly added a number of these

4.30.2–4
AORNOS ROCK
The Indians on the rock, distressed at Alexander's progress, sue for peace, secretly intending to escape by night. Alexander takes possession of "invincible" Aornos Rock and massacres many of the escaping Indians.

4.30.5–6
AORNOS ROCK–
ASSAKANIAN TERRITORY
Alexander puts Sisikottos in charge at Aornos Rock and returns to the territory of the Assakanians, where he has heard there is further resistance, led by a local ruler.

4.30.7–8
Spring 326
INDUS RIVER
Alexander, advancing to the Indus, learns that the inhabitants of the region have already fled, leaving their elephants behind. Alexander captures some of these for use by his army.

4.30.3a   The duplicitous entrapment of the Indians on Aornos Rock is reminiscent of the treacherous way Alexander dealt with the mercenaries at Massaka at 4.27.3–4.
4.30.5a   Assakanians (Assakanoi), location of territory: Map 4.22, inset, BY. Alexander has already attacked the Assakanians at 4.25.5, but this new target seems to be a more easterly sector of their territory, ruled by a separate dynast (the brother of

Assakanos). The intervening action, the siege of Aornos, had taken the Macedonians farther north.
4.30.5b   Dyrta: Map 4.22, inset, BY.
4.30.5c   For Nearkhos, who was shortly to become invaluable to Alexander, see 4.7.2 and n. 4.7.2c, and Appendix E, §11.
4.30.6a   That is, to learn how many war elephants his potential enemies could draw on.
4.30.7a   For the Indian ruler Abisares, see 4.27.7 and n. 4.27.7a.

hunters to his retinue. These men now accompanied him in the hunt. Two of the animals perished after flinging themselves from a cliff while being chased; the rest, when they were captured, let themselves be mounted and were marshaled with the army.

4.30.9
Spring 326
INDUS RIVER
Alexander has a fleet of
ships constructed for use
on the Indus.

[9] When Alexander happened upon a wood suitable for felling near the river, he had it cut down for him by the army, and ships were built, which conveyed the army down the Indus to the bridge Hephaistion and Perdikkas had built for him long before.

BOOK FIVE

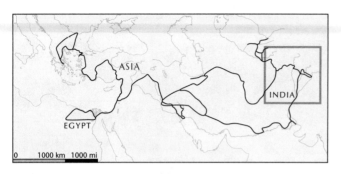

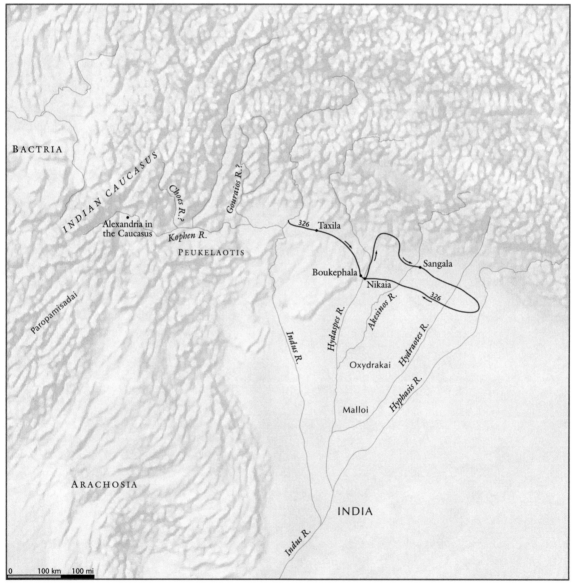

BOOK FIVE: THE INDIAN CAMPAIGN (I)

In the country Alexander invaded between the River Kophen and the Indus,[1a] a city known as Nysa[1b] was said to have been settled. The city was said to have been founded by Dionysos after he had subdued the Indians—whoever that Dionysos may have been, and whenever and from wherever he made war on the Indians.[1c] [2] For I am unable to determine whether or not the Theban Dionysos,[2a] starting from Thebes or the Lydian Tmolos, led an army into India and attacked many warlike tribes unknown to the Greeks of that period, but subdued none of them by force except the Indians. Of course, one must not examine ancient tales about the divine too minutely. For stories that strike a listener as incredible because they violate our sense of what is probable begin to seem credible when an element of the divine is added.[2b]

[3] When Alexander attacked Nysa, the Nysaians sent him their leading citizen, a man named Akouphis, and with him thirty envoys of the highest renown, to entreat Alexander to leave the city in the god's keeping. [4] When the envoys entered Alexander's tent, they found him seated, covered with dust from the journey, wearing his armor and helmet and holding his spear. Astonished at the sight, they fell to the ground and kept silent for a long time. But Alexander raised them up and urged them to take courage,

5.1.1–2
Spring 326
NYSA
Alexander arrives at the city of Nysa in western India. Arrian questions the legends according to which Dionysos had founded Nysa.

5.1.3–6
NYSA
Alexander's attack on Nysa prompts the city's leader, Akouphis, to plead that the city should remain free on account of its connection to Dionysos. He cites the presence of ivy near the town as proof of that connection.

NOTE: Most locations in the text not identified by a footnote can be found in the Reference Maps section.

5.1.1a Kophen and Indus rivers: Map 5.5, inset.
5.1.1b Nysa: location unknown. The mythic origins of this fabled city in western India are recounted at 5.1.5–6.
5.1.1c According to Greek legends, the god Dionysos, before arriving in the Hellenic world, traveled through Asia, spreading the refinements of civilized life among the peoples there. The additional idea that he "made war on the Indians," as Arrian says here, seems to postdate Alexander's invasion of that land, and can thus be seen as an attempt to supply mythic archetypes for Alexander after the fact. Whereas Herakles had served as Alexander's most prominent

model/rival in the first half of his campaign, Dionysos comes increasingly to take on that role as Alexander moves into the East.
5.1.2a Arrian here appears to leave open the possibility that there was more than one god named Dionysos, just as he had earlier (2.16.1–6) allowed for two deities sharing the name Herakles. If the conquest of India cannot be fit into the legends of the "Theban" Dionysos, then perhaps, Arrian suggests, it was another god of the same name who carried it out.
5.1.2b The train of thought here is that since a mythic element is often added by storytellers to enhance the plausibility of otherwise incredible stories, a historian cannot apply the normal tools of investigation to such tales.

whereupon Akouphis began and spoke as follows: [5] "Sire, the Nysaians entreat you, out of respect for Dionysos, to leave them free and independent. For when Dionysos had subdued the Indians and was returning to the Greek Sea,[5a] he founded this city, peopling it with soldiers unfit for fighting who were also his revelers, as a memorial for later generations of his wandering and his conquest—just as you founded an Alexandria near the Caucasus[5b] and another in Egypt.[5c] By now you have founded many more, and will found others in the course of time, thus showing the world exploits more numerous than those of our founder.[5d] [6] Dionysos named the city after Nysa, his nurse, and named the country Nysaia. And the mountain that lies near the city he named Meros, as legend has it that Dionysos grew in Zeus' thigh.[6a] Since then, we have inhabited Nysa as a free city and have governed ourselves in an independent and orderly manner. Let this be your proof that Dionysos founded Nysa: ivy, which grows nowhere else in India, grows in our country."[6b]

[1] It gratified Alexander to hear all these details, and he was ready to believe the stories told about the wandering of Dionysos; he also wanted Nysa to be a creation of Dionysos, since he had himself now reached the point Dionysos had reached and would go even farther. He also thought that the Macedonians, given the chance to rival Dionysos' exploits, would not decline to join him in further toils.[1a] [2] He granted the inhabitants of Nysa their freedom and independence. When he inquired about their laws and learned that their government was run by a select group of nobles,[2a] he expressed his approval and required them to send him some three hundred of their horsemen, and to pick out and send the hundred highest-ranking of the men who led their government (these numbered three hundred altogether). Akouphis, whom Alexander appointed as governor of the region around Nysaia, was to select the hundred. [3] On hearing this, Akouphis is said to have smiled, and when Alexander asked him why he was laughing, Akouphis replied: "How, sire, should a single city, deprived of a hundred good men, still be governed well? If you care for the Nysaians, take the three hundred horsemen—take more if you wish—but in place of the

5.2.1–4
Spring 326
NYSA
Alexander sees an opportunity for self-aggrandizement in the legends of Nysa's founding and grants the city its autonomy. He also accedes to Akouphis' request and abandons his demand for high-ranking hostages.

5.1.5a The Greek Sea is the Aegean Sea.
5.1.5b Alexandria in the Caucasus: Map 5.5, inset. Several mountain ranges were known to the Greeks as "the Caucasus." In Arrian the Indian Caucasus (also known as the Paropamisos; modern Hindu Kush) is meant. See Appendix N, Alexander's Geographic Notions, §8, and Ref. Map 8.
5.1.5c Alexandria, Egypt: Map 5.5, BX.
5.1.5d See n. 5.1.1c.
5.1.6a Mount Meros: Map 5.5, inset. The Greek word for "thigh" is *meros*. According to Greek myth, Zeus destroyed Dionysos' mother, Semele, by appearing to her in the form of a thunderbolt, and then saved the embryonic Dionysos by sewing him up inside his thigh.
5.1.6b The ivy plant was considered sacred to Dionysos, and ivy fronds were worn by his

celebrants. Partly because of this connection, and also because of its actual geographic diffusion, ivy was thought to be a European plant that could have found its way into Asia only with the help of a god.
5.2.1a Arrian's language here hints at the dissatisfaction brewing among Alexander's troops. Our other sources are more explicit about the war-weariness of the army at this stage and its lack of motivation for the Indian campaign. In Arrian the discontent of the troops appears to emerge more abruptly, in the mutiny at the Hyphasis River (5.25).
5.2.2a Literally, "by the *aristoi*," an untranslatable Greek term that combines notions of wealth, social standing, moral virtue, and political power. In the rest of this chapter various translations have been employed in an effort to capture some of the nuances of this word.

hundred you ordered to be chosen from the nobility, take twice the number of inferior men, so that when you return, you may find the city in the same good order." [4] Since what he said seemed reasonable, Akouphis won over Alexander, who ordered him to send the horsemen but no longer to ask for the hundred chosen men, nor even to request others in their place. But Akouphis was obliged to send him his own son and his daughter's son.[4a]

[5] A sudden desire seized Alexander to visit the place where certain memorials of Dionysos, as the Nysaians boasted, were to be seen. He went to Mount Meros with the Companion cavalry and the infantry *agema*[5a] and saw that the mountain abounded in ivy and laurel and had groves of all kinds; it was thickly shaded and had all manner of wild beasts to hunt. [6] The Macedonians, glad to see the ivy (which they had not seen for a long time, as there was none elsewhere in India, not even where there were vines), eagerly fashioned wreaths from it, donned them at once, and sang Dionysos' praises, calling on the god by his various names. Alexander sacrificed there to Dionysos and feasted with his Companions.[6a] [7] Some have also reported (if anyone can find this credible) that many of the prominent Macedonians in Alexander's inner circle, having crowned themselves with ivy and invoked the god, were possessed by Dionysos, honored the god with cries of "Evoi!" and flew into a Bacchic frenzy.[7a]

[1] One is free to believe or disbelieve those tales, however one wishes to take them. For my part, I do not wholly agree with Eratosthenes of Cyrene,[1a] who says that everything the Macedonians attributed to the gods was an exaggeration designed to win Alexander's favor. [2] For example, he says that when the Macedonians saw a cave in the land of the Paropamisadai[2a] and heard some local legend (or invented one themselves), they spread a report that this was in fact the cave in which Prometheus had been imprisoned, and that the eagle had visited it to feast on his entrails, and that Herakles, on his arrival, had killed the eagle and freed Prometheus from his bonds.[2b] [3] In his account, the Macedonians transferred the Caucasus

5.2.5–7
MOUNT MEROS
Alexander visits the mountain said to contain landmarks of Dionysos' visit. There some of his officers supposedly don ivy wreaths and lose themselves in the ecstatic rites of the god.

5.3.1–4
Arrian discusses the critique of such legends offered by Eratosthenes, who claimed that stories in which Alexander rivals the gods were exaggerated or invented for propaganda purposes. The historian neither agrees nor disagrees.

5.2.4a Presumably Akouphis' son and grandson were to be hostages to ensure the continuing loyalty of the city.

5.2.5a The Companion cavalry was an elite unit of horsemen typically led by the king himself as his principal striking arm. The *agema* was a special division of light-armed infantry, though there was a cavalry *agema* as well.

5.2.6a The Companions were the intimates who were invited to dine and drink with Alexander, share his counsels, and fight beside him in the Companion cavalry. See Appendix E, Alexander's Inner Circle, §4.

5.2.7a The Bacchic revel is reported by Quintus Curtius (8.10.16–18) and Justin (12.7.8). Justin, summarizing the work of his Roman forerunner Pompeius Trogus (see the Introduction, §2.6), characterizes it as a spontaneous frenzy gripping the troops, much to the displeasure of Alexander. The ecstatic rites of Dionysos, as seen in Euripi-

des' *Bacchae*, for example, were considered inappropriate for men of affairs, such as soldiers, statesmen, and rulers.

5.3.1a Eratosthenes: a famous Greek scholar and geographer of the third century who rejected many mythic beliefs about distant parts of the world.

5.3.2a Paropamisadai, location of territory: Map 5.5, inset. Arrian spells it Parapamisadai.

5.3.2b The events surrounding Prometheus' binding and release were dramatized in a famous trilogy by Aeschylus, of which *Prometheus Bound* survives. Because this play, and the myth generally, situated the place of Prometheus' punishment at the ends of the earth, it was very much to Alexander's credit to appear to have reached this locale (see Appendix N, §8). For another comment by Arrian about the Macedonians' names for the places in this region as they relate to Alexander's achievements, see 5.5.3.

range[3a] from the Black Sea to the eastern regions of the earth, and the land of the Paropamisadai to India, calling Mount Paropamisos[3b] the Caucasus for the sake of Alexander's reputation, so that he would actually have crossed the Caucasus. [4] And in India, when they saw oxen branded with a club, they took this as a sign that Herakles had reached India.[4a] Eratosthenes is equally skeptical about the wandering of Dionysos. In my own view, the authenticity of these stories should remain an open question.

[5] When Alexander arrived at the Indus,[5a] he found the bridge Hephaistion had built for him,[5b] several small vessels, and two thirty-oared ships. In addition, nearly two hundred talents[5c] of silver had arrived as a gift from Taxiles[5d] the Indian, along with three thousand oxen for sacrificing, more than ten thousand head of cattle, and some thirty elephants. [6] Seven hundred Indian horsemen had also arrived from Taxiles as an auxiliary force. Taxiles also gave Alexander control of Taxila, the largest city between the Indus and the Hydaspes.[6a] Alexander then sacrificed to all the gods to whom he customarily sacrificed and held a competition in athletics and horsemanship at the river. The omens proved favorable for a crossing.

[1] The Indus is the largest river in Asia and Europe besides the Ganges, another Indian river. Its springs are on this side of Mount Paropamisos (or Caucasus), and the river empties into the Great Sea[1a] south of India. The Indus is double-mouthed, and both its outlets form shallow shoals, as do the five outlets of the Danube.[1b] It forms a delta similar to the delta in Egypt; the Indus' delta is known, in the Indian language, as Patala. As these facts about the Indus are not in dispute, let me record them here. [2] Other Indian rivers—the Hydaspes, Akesinos, Hydraotes, and Hyphasis[2a]—are much larger than the rest of the rivers in Asia. But they are smaller—much smaller, in fact—than the Indus, while the Indus is itself smaller than the Ganges. Ktesias[2b] actually reports—if one can regard Ktesias as a reliable

Margin notes

5.3.5–6
Spring 326
INDUS RIVER
Supplied with money, cavalry, and food by Taxiles, Alexander takes his army to the Indus, already bridged for him by Hephaistion, and prepares to cross.

5.4.1–2
INDUS RIVER
Arrian describes the Indus River, which he calls the second-largest river in Asia and Europe.

Footnotes

5.3.3a Caucasus Mountains: Map 5.5, AX. Eratosthenes' analysis is consistent with his scorn for geographic mythmaking generally. He accused Homer, for instance, of taking episodes from Mediterranean waters and moving them into Ocean in the *Odyssey*. In the argument Arrian repeats here, he claims that a mountain range bordering the Black (ancient Euxine) Sea (Map 5.5, AX) has similarly been moved into India.

5.3.3b Indian Caucasus/Paropamisos: Map 5.5, inset. For another comment by Arrian about how the Macedonians' names for places in this region magnified Alexander's achievements, see 5.5.3.

5.3.4a India: Map 5.5, BY, and inset. The club-branding Paropamisadai tribe is discussed again by Arrian in his *Indika* (5.12), where they are given the name Sibai. He says there that if the club brand was indeed a reminiscence of Herakles, it must be of the Tyrian or Egyptian, not the Greek, Herakles.

5.3.5a Indus River: Map 5.5, inset.

5.3.5b Perdikkas and Hephaistion were sent to build this bridge at 4.22.7.

5.3.5c For the talent as a monetary unit, see Appendix F, Money and Finance in the Campaigns of Alexander, §3.

5.3.5d Arrian does not distinguish this Taxiles, called Omphis or Mophis before his accession, from his father, also called Taxiles, encountered at 4.22.6–8 (see n. 4.22.6b). According to Quintus Curtius (8.12.4–18) and Diodorus (17.86.4), Omphis/Mophis had recently taken power in Taxila after his father's death; probably he assumed the name Taxiles as a mark of his new stature.

5.3.6a Taxila; Hydaspes River: Map 5.5, inset.

5.4.1a The Greeks thought the Great Sea, which they also called the Outer Sea and Ocean, surrounded Europe, Asia, and Africa on all sides. For more on Alexander's geographic notions, see Appendix N, §2.

5.4.1b Danube (ancient Istros) River: Map 5.5, AX.

5.4.2a Akesinos (Arrian's spelling is Akesines), Hydraotes, and Hyphasis rivers: Map 5.5, inset.

5.4.2b Ktesias, a Greek doctor living at the Persian court in the late fifth century, wrote a largely fantastical account of India called the *Indika*, the same title later used by Arrian.

source—that the Indus' banks are five miles apart where the river is narrowest, twelve and a half miles apart where it is broadest. For the most part its breadth falls somewhere between these extremes.[2c]

[3] At dawn Alexander and his army crossed the Indus into India.[3a] I have not, in this history, recorded the Indians' customs, nor whether the country produces any extraordinary animals, nor the quantity or kind of fish or whales to be found in the Indus, Hydaspes, Ganges, or other Indian rivers; nor have I mentioned the ants that mine their gold, nor the guardian griffins, nor all the other tales that have been written—more for pleasure than for describing what actually exists, on the assumption that all the bizarre tales invented about the Indians will not be disproved by anyone.[3b] [4] But Alexander and those who shared his campaigns did disprove most of them—except for some that they themselves invented. They proved that none of the Indians had gold (none of the tribes, at any rate, that Alexander reached with his army, and he reached a great many); that they had no taste for luxurious living; that they were large in stature, in fact the tallest men in Asia, most of them eight feet tall or nearly so;[4a] that they were blacker than all the other races except the Ethiopians; and that they were by far the noblest warriors among the inhabitants of Asia at that time. [5] As for the ancient Persians, who under Cyrus son of Cambyses wrested rule over Asia from the Medes[5a] and either conquered other peoples or brought them over willingly,[5b] I cannot, with any accuracy, compare them with the Indians. In fact, the Persians of that period were poor; they inhabited a rugged country, and their customs especially resembled those of the Spartan training. As for the defeat the Persians suffered in Scythia,[5c] I cannot even conjecture whether it came about through the difficulties of the terrain or some other error on Cyrus' part, or whether the Persians were inferior militarily to the Scythians of that region.[5d]

[1] I shall, however, write a separate account of India that will include all that is most reliable in the narratives of those who took part in Alexander's campaigns, including that of Nearkhos, who sailed the Great Sea along the

5.4.3–5
INDUS RIVER–INDIA
Alexander crosses the Indus. His entry into India proper prompts Arrian to declare that he will not indulge in legend-mongering in his account of India. Among the truths about that land revealed by Alexander are the strength and valor of its inhabitants, reminiscent of the Persians in the time of Cyrus I.

5.5.1
Arrian promises to treat Indian matters more fully in a future work. For now he will present only the essentials of its geography.

5.4.2c Arrian's exaggerated claim for the breadth of the Indus is part of the general pattern of huge Indian rivers he found in his sources; see also 5.20.8–10, 6.4.2, 6.14.5, 6.18.5. Ptolemy in particular exaggerated river widths to make Alexander's feats of crossing them more glorious.

5.4.3a Here, and again at 5.6.3, Arrian uses the term India to refer to the lands east of the Indus. Elsewhere in the text he uses it more informally to refer to lands east of the Indian Caucasus/Paropamisos (modern Hindu Kush). The latter is the more standard ancient usage.

5.4.3b The Greek literary tradition concerning India included many bizarre accounts of grotesque animal and plant life. Herodotus (*Histories* 3.102) first popularized the tale of ants that mine gold in the Indian mountains.

5.4.4a This is a patent exaggeration, as Arrian

himself makes clear at 5.19.1, where he describes eight-foot-tall Poros as having exceptional height.

5.4.5a The Medes were a northern Iranian people who originally ruled the Persians, then came to be ruled by them and assimilated into their power structure.

5.4.5b Cyrus the Great founded the Persian empire in the mid-sixth century. He and his followers were legendary for their toughness and bravery. See Appendix G, The Persian Empire and Alexander, §1.

5.4.5c Scythia: Map 5.5, AX.

5.4.5d The words Arrian earlier quoted from Kallisthenes (see 4.11.9) attribute Cyrus' defeat to the ruggedness and political autonomy of the Scythians. The Persian invasion of Scythian lands under Cyrus is described by Herodotus in the *Histories* 1.201–214.

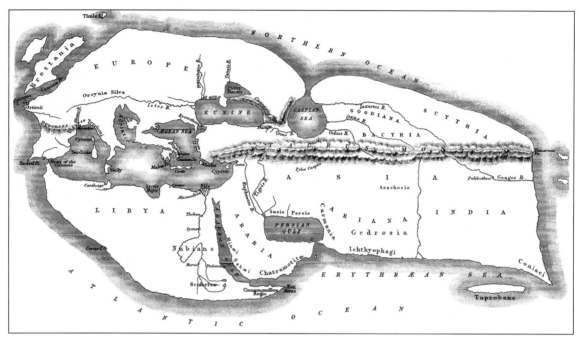

FIGURE 5.5. World map described at the beginning of the second century B.C.E. by Eratosthenes and other Greek geographers, and adopted in large part by Arrian (drawn by a nineteenth-century cartographer based on the writings of these authors). Europe is divided from Asia along an east–west axis by an assumed line of the mountains Arrian calls the Taurus and the Indian Caucasus or Paropamisos.

coast of India, and of Megasthenes and Eratosthenes, both reputable men.[1a] I will also discuss the customs of India and will describe any unusual animals bred there, along with Nearkhos' voyage along the coast of the Outer Sea.[1b] [2] Let me restrict myself, in the present work, to matters sufficient for a discussion of Alexander's achievements.

The Taurus range, starting from Mycale, the mountain directly opposite the island of Samos, is the boundary of Asia.[2a] Forming a boundary to the land of the Pamphylians and Cilicians, it extends into Armenia, and from

5.5.2–5
Asia can be divided by an east–west line that follows its two great mountain chains, the Taurus and Paropamisos. This line forms a watershed between north- and south-flowing rivers.

5.5.1a Arrian refers here to his short work the *Indika*, an account of the sea voyage ordered by Alexander that began at the Indus mouth and ended at Babylon. Nearkhos commanded the fleet and wrote the narrative of his experience that served as Arrian's major source. Megasthenes went to India some two decades after Alexander's death (according to the usual dating; but Bosworth places his visit much earlier) and spent much time at the court of Chandragupta, the first of the Maurya rulers; he compiled his observations of India into a treatise also titled *Indika*. Eratosthenes, as has been noted, was a scholar of the third century who discussed India at length in his geographical writings.

5.5.1b The term Outer Sea, like Great Sea, presup-

poses that the Indian Ocean was ultimately connected to the Atlantic and thus formed part of the stream of Ocean thought to surround the known world (see Ref. Map 8b).

5.5.2a The geographic scheme Arrian discusses at 5.5.2–5.6.3 follows Hellenistic geographers like Eratosthenes, who divided the known world along an east–west axis consisting of the Taurus and Caucasus chains (see Figure 5.5). It is unclear why Arrian refers to this axis as a "boundary of Asia," since it is clear from what follows (see 5.6.1) that "Asia" extends both to the north and south of it. Perhaps here he has superimposed his own conceptual scheme in which Europe extends eastward all across the northern half of the world (see 4.1.1 and n. 4.1.1c).

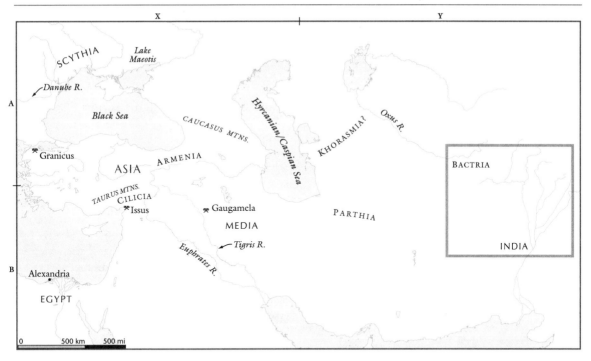

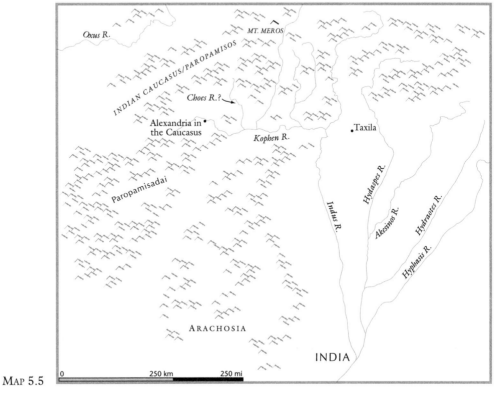

MAP 5.5

there to Media, skirting the land of the Parthians and Khorasmians,[2b] [3] and in Bactria[3a] joins the Paropamisos range,[3b] which in fact the Macedonians who served with Alexander called the Caucasus, reportedly with an eye to exalting Alexander's accomplishments, so that it could be said that Alexander had actually passed beyond the Caucasus, victorious in arms.[3c] But perhaps the Indian Caucasus is continuous with the Scythian Caucasus, just as the Taurus range is continuous with the Indian Caucasus. That is why I myself have formerly referred to the Indian range as the Caucasus and will continue to do so in the future. [4] The Caucasus extends as far as the Great Sea in the east, on the Indian coast.[4a] Thus all the noteworthy rivers of Asia arise from the Taurus and the Caucasus. Some flow to the north; of these, some empty into Lake Maeotis, some into the so-called Hyrcanian Sea,[4b] which is itself an inlet of the Great Sea.[4c] [5] Others flow southward— the Euphrates, the Tigris,[5a] the Indus, the Hydaspes, Akesinos, Hydraotes, and Hyphasis,[5b] and all the rivers that lie between these and the Ganges; these rivers empty into the sea or pour into marshes and disappear, as the Euphrates disappears.

[1] Anyone who thinks of Asia as divided, from west to east, by the Taurus range and the Caucasus is aware that Asia's two largest divisions arise from the Taurus itself, one extending to the south and southwest, the other to the north and northeast. [2] Asia's southern division is in turn divided into four land masses,[2a] and Eratosthenes and Megasthenes consider the land of India the largest of the four. (Megasthenes had dealings with Sibyrtius, the satrap[2b] of Arachosia, and often says he visited Sandrakottos,[2c] the Indian king.) The smallest of the four, bounded by the Euphrates, lies toward the Aegean Sea. The two land masses bounded by the Euphrates and the Indus, even taken together, do not deserve to be compared with India. [3] Eastern India is bounded on the south by the Great Sea; the Caucasus forms its northern boundary as far as the juncture with the Taurus range. The Indus, as it flows to the Great Sea, forms India's western and northwestern boundary.

5.6.1–3
India forms the largest of the regions into which the southern half of Asia can be subdivided, using its major rivers and mountain chains as boundaries. India is defined by the Caucasus to the north, the Indus to the west, and the Great Sea to the east and south.

5.5.2b The following locations can be found on Map 5.5: Cilicia, BX; Armenia, AX; Media, BX; Parthia AY; Khorasmia, possible location, AY.

5.5.3a Bactria: Map 5.5.

5.5.3b Indian Caucasus/Paropamisos: Map 5.5, inset.

5.5.3c For another report by Arrian of the Macedonians' geographical misconceptions, see 5.3.2 and n. 5.3.2b.

5.5.4a Arrian, like most Greek geographers, assumes that India was the easternmost land of Asia and was bounded by the waters of Ocean, here referred to as the Great Sea, to the east. See Appendix N, §1, 3.

5.5.4b Lake Maeotis; Hyrcanian/Caspian Sea: Map 5.5, AX.

5.5.4c Arrian, like most in his time, thought that the Hyrcanian/Caspian was a gulf of the surrounding Ocean (or Great Sea) rather than a landlocked sea. Alexander was in fact preparing to investigate this theory at the time of his death (see 7.16.2 and Appendix N, §2).

5.5.5a Euphrates and Tigris rivers: Map 5.5, BX.

5.5.5b Indus, Hydaspes, Akesinos, Hydraotes, and Hyphasis rivers: Map 5.5, inset.

5.6.2a Eratosthenes had first created these divisions, which he called *sphragides*, as a way of dealing with the enormous size of the southern half of Asia.

5.6.2b The satraps, roughly two dozen in number, were appointed by the Persian king to administer the satrapies, or provinces, of the empire, collect taxes, and organize defense. For the locations of all Persian satrapies mentioned by Arrian, see Ref. Map 1.

5.6.2c King Sandrakottos is better known to us as Chandragupta, founder of the Mauryan empire.

Most of India[3a] is a plain, and this plain, it is surmised, was formed by deposits from the rivers. [4] For in other lands as well, plains that lie near the sea have been formed by the nearby rivers; and places have from ancient times been named after rivers. For example, there is a plain named after the Hermus, which emerges in Asia from the mountain of Mother Dindymene[4a] and empties into the sea beside Smyrna, an Aeolic city. Other instances include the plain of the Cayster (a Lydian plain named after a Lydian river), the plain of the Caicus in Mysia, and in Caria the plain of the Maeander, which extends as far as Miletus, an Ionian city.

[5] As for Egypt, the historians Herodotus and Hekataios (though it's possible the works on Egypt were written by someone other than Hekataios) both call it "the gift of the river;"[5a] moreover, Herodotus has demonstrated with clear proofs that that is so, since the country itself is actually named after the river. (Homer sufficiently proves that the river the Egyptians and peoples outside Egypt now call the Nile was in ancient times called Aegyptus when he says that Menelaos stationed his ships at the outlet of the River Aegyptus.)[5b] [6] Accordingly, if one river in each country—and these rivers are not large—can, while pouring forth to the sea, build up a large area of land, carrying down mud and silt from the regions near their sources, there is no valid reason to doubt, with respect to the land of India, that it is mostly a plain and that the plain has been formed by deposits from its rivers. [7] As for the Hermus, Cayster, Caicus, Maeander, and all the rivers of Asia that empty into this Inner Sea,[7a] they do not deserve, even taken all together, to be compared with one of the Indian rivers for volume of water—not to mention the Ganges, India's largest river, with which not even the Egyptian Nile, nor the Danube, which flows through Europe, deserves to be compared. [8] But all those rivers combined do not even equal the Indus, which emerges, already immense, from its sources, and after receiving the water of fifteen rivers, all of them larger than the rivers of Asia, and imposing its name upon them,[8a] empties into the sea. For the present this is all I need say about India. Let the rest be reserved for my treatise on that country.[8b]

[1] As to the method by which Alexander built the bridge at the Indus, neither Aristoboulos nor Ptolemy, whom I principally follow, discusses it. Nor can I guess with any accuracy whether the stream was bridged with

5.6.4–8
Most of India is an alluvial plain. It is quite possible that such a large landmass was formed by the deposition of rivers, if one compares the size of Indian rivers with other, smaller streams that have also laid down tracts of land.

5.7.1–5
INDUS RIVER
Arrian cannot say how the Indus was bridged by Alexander, but supposing it might have been by the pontoon method favored by the Romans, he provides a description of that method.

5.6.3a   See n. 5.4.3a.
5.6.4a   The "mountain of Mother Dindymene" (a Phrygian goddess also known as Kybele) is Mount Dindymos.
5.6.5a   Meaning that the land was created from alluvial silt. Herodotus goes to great lengths to support this theory at *Histories* 2.10–15. The phrase "gift of the river" is used by Herodotus at 2.5, quite possibly quoted from the *Periegesis* of Hekataios of Miletos. This Greek geographical treatise, now lost, dealt with Egypt as part of its second book; later ancient scholars were uncertain about the authorship of this book, prompting Arrian's cautious comment in the parenthesis.

5.6.5b   Arrian here refers to Homer's *Odyssey* 6.281, where the river of Egypt is itself called Aegyptus. The name Aegyptus comes from Egyptian words meaning "house of the spirit of Ptah," originally used to refer to the city of Memphis at the apex of the Nile Delta.
5.6.7a   By the term Inner Sea, Arrian signifies the Mediterranean Sea (Map 5.5, BX). For Arrian's conception of the Inner Sea, see Ref. Map 8a.
5.6.8a   A colorful way of expressing the idea that the name Indus prevails over that of its tributary rivers.
5.6.8b   The treatise referred to is the *Indika*, where Arrian does indeed discuss Indian geography and ethnography in the first sixteen chapters.

FIGURE 5.7A. This 1890 photograph shows a pontoon bridge built of boats across the upper Indus, probably similar in construction to the Indus bridge Hephaistion and Perdikkas built in 327 on Alexander's orders.

ships, as the Hellespont was bridged by Xerxes and the Bosporos and the Danube by Darius,[1a] or whether a bridge was built straight across it. I rather think it was bridged with ships, since the depth of the water would not have accommodated a fixed bridge, nor could so extraordinary a work have been completed in so short a time. [2] And if in fact the stream was bridged with ships, I cannot even conjecture whether these were lashed together with cords and moored in line, as Herodotus says the Hellespont was bridged, or whether Alexander employed the method the Romans used when they built their bridges at the Danube and the Celtic Rhine, and on all the occasions when they were forced to bridge both the Euphrates and the Tigris.[2a]

[3] But the quickest method I know of is the Roman method of bridging with ships, which I will now describe, since it is worthy of notice. At a

5.7.1a The pontoon bridges built by the Persians over the Bosporos, the Danube (ancient Istros) River, and the Hellespont in the late sixth and early fifth centuries were considered marvels of engineering; see Herodotus, *Histories* 4.88–89, 7.36.

5.7.2a The Danube (ancient Istros) and Tigris rivers were both bridged by the Romans as part of Trajan's wars, and Arrian may have been an eyewitness to one or both events, since he may have fought in Trajan's Parthian campaign as a young man (see Appendix R, Arrian's Life and Works, §3). The bridging of the Danube is vividly depicted on Trajan's Column in Rome (see Figure 5.7b). The Euphrates and the Rhine were both bridged more than once by the Romans in wars that preceded Arrian's time.

FIGURE 5.7B. The Roman bridging of the Danube in 102 C.E. is shown on the bottom level of the column of Trajan in Rome. The Danube is personified as a god at left. Arrian may have witnessed the construction of this vast bridge and, if so, he drew on his recollections when discussing Alexander's bridging of the Indus.

signal, the ships are sent downstream, not with their bows forward, but as if they are backing water. The current, as one might guess, carries them downstream, but a light rowing vessel holds them back until it can guide them to their assigned positions. Then pyramid-shaped wicker containers, filled with unhewn stones, are let down from the prow of each ship, in order to hold the ship in place against the current. [4] As soon as one ship is secured in place, another, just far enough away to support what will be laid over the gap, is brought to anchor, prow against the current. Timbers extending from both boats are quickly laid down level and flush, and planks are placed over them crosswise to bind them together. The same process is repeated from one ship to the next until the stream has been bridged. [5] On each end of the bridge, gangways are laid down and fixed in place to provide a safer approach for horses and yoke animals. The gangways also fasten the bridge to the banks. Before very long the whole task is completed, and with much uproar, though while the work is in progress there is no sense of disorder: the cheers of encouragement, when- ever they occur on each ship, and the reprimands for shirking do not prevent the instructions from being heard or slow the work's progress.

5.8.1
INDUS RIVER
Arrian reiterates that he does not know how the Indus was bridged.

5.8.2–3
Spring 326
TAXILA
Alexander takes the army across the Indus River and marches to Taxila, where he is warmly received.

5.8.4–5
HYDASPES RIVER (WEST BANK)
Learning that Poros intends to oppose his crossing of the Hydaspes River, Alexander has his Indus fleet taken apart and reassembled on the Hydaspes. He marches to the river at the head of a combined Indo-Macedonian army.

5.9.1–3
HYDASPES RIVER (WEST BANK)
The Macedonians take up position on the bank of the Hydaspes, opposite Poros' position. Alexander orders maneuvers designed to confuse Poros about his plans and to keep the Indians constantly on their guard.

[1] These methods have been employed by the Romans since ancient times, but I cannot say how the Indus was bridged by Alexander, since the matter has not been discussed even by the men who served with him. I suppose he used a method very like that of the Romans, but if he actually used some other, so be it.

[2] When he had crossed the Indus, Alexander again sacrificed according to custom. Setting out from the river, he reached Taxila, a large and prosperous city—the largest between the Indus and the Hydaspes.[2a] The local Indians and Taxiles, the city's governor, received him in a friendly manner, and Alexander added to their domain as much of the neighboring territory as they requested. [3] Envoys now reached him from Abisares,[3a] the king of the mountain Indians, in company with Abisares' brother and other highly distinguished men, including representatives bearing gifts from the local chieftain Doxareus. Alexander again sacrificed in Taxila according to custom and held a competition in athletics and horsemanship. Having appointed Philip son of Makhatas[3b] as satrap of the Indians of that region, he left a garrison in Taxila with those of his soldiers who through illness were unfit for fighting. He then advanced toward the River Hydaspes.

[4] For he had received word that Poros,[4a] who was now at the far bank of the Hydaspes with his entire army, was determined either to prevent Alexander from crossing or to attack him if he tried to cross. When Alexander learned this, he sent Koinos son of Polemokrates back to the Indus with orders to dismantle all the vessels at the crossing there and to convey them to the Hydaspes. [5] The vessels were dismantled and brought to him—the shorter vessels were cut in two, the thirty-oared vessels in three—and the sections were conveyed on carts as far as the bank of the Hydaspes. There the vessels were rebuilt, and the assembled fleet was again in full view, now at the Hydaspes. Then, taking the force with which he had reached Taxila and five thousand of the Indians Taxiles and the local governors had brought him, Alexander advanced to the Hydaspes.

[1] Alexander made camp at the bank of the Hydaspes, and Poros was observed on the opposite bank with his entire army and his troop of elephants. Poros, remaining in position across from where he saw Alexander bivouacked, guarded the crossing himself and posted guard units at all the other points where the river was easier to ford, appointing commanders for each, since he intended to prevent the Macedonians from crossing.

5.8.2a Taxila; Indus and Hydaspes rivers: Map 5.5, inset.
5.8.3a Abisares (mentioned at 4.27.7) was an Indian regional ruler who initially decided to side with the enemies of Alexander. He was deemed one of two principal opposition leaders (Poros was the other). However, in the end Abisares decided to make an accommodation with the invaders; see 5.20.5–6, 5.29.4–5.
5.8.3b This Philip was last encountered as a leader

of an infantry unit (4.24.10). He remained satrap of India only briefly; Arrian reports at 6.27.2 that he was killed by his own troops.
5.8.4a Poros, Alexander's last great antagonist, known to Indian history as Paurava, was ruler of the realm between the Akesinos and Hydaspes rivers. It was with the objective of countering Poros' power, primarily, that Taxiles had invited Alexander into the region and supported his army so generously.

FIGURE 5.8. The ruins of a Greek-style settlement found on the site of ancient Taxila. These remains date from the century after Alexander's, when Greek military adventurers once again used Taxila as their base.

[2] Observing this, Alexander decided to move his forces frequently in order to keep Poros in doubt. He divided the army into many parts, some of which he himself led up and down the countryside plundering enemy territory[2a] or looking for points where the river appeared more fordable, while also appointing various commanders to other divisions and sending them off again and again in different directions. [3] Meanwhile, grain was being conveyed to Alexander's camp from all quarters on the west side of the Hydaspes, so it was clear to Poros that Alexander meant to remain on the bank until winter, when the water level would drop and he could cross at many points. Alexander's vessels, sailing up and down the river, and the stuffing of the hides with hay,[3a] and the riverbank teeming here with cavalry, there with infantry—all this allowed Poros no rest, nor could he even select a single position suitable for defense and concentrate his forces there.

5.9.2a   Apparently some of the rulers west of the
         Hydaspes had still refused to submit to
         Alexander's sovereignty.
5.9.3a   As at the Danube (1.3.6), the Oxus (3.29),

and the Tanais/Iaxartes (4.4.2), Alexander
here has his troops' hide tent covers made
into floats for crossing the Hydaspes (see
5.12.3).

[4] For the time being, all the Indian rivers, swollen and turbid, were flowing swiftly, since it was the season of the year when the sun is turning after the summer solstice, when it rains constantly in India and the snows of the Caucasus, where the springs of most of the rivers lie, melt and greatly increase the volume of the rivers.[4a] But in winter the rivers diminish and become small and clear, and it is possible to ford them at various points, except for the Indus, the Ganges, and perhaps some others. The Hydaspes, at any rate, becomes fordable.

[1] Accordingly, Alexander publicly declared that he would await that season if he were prevented from crossing immediately. But he continued to watch for an opening nonetheless, in the hope that he might somehow steal across swiftly without being detected. He realized that he would be unable to cross where Poros himself had made camp by the bank of the Hydaspes, for in addition to Poros' large number of elephants, a vast army, drawn up and armed to the teeth, would attack his men as they emerged from the river. [2] Also, he imagined that his horses would refuse to set foot on the opposite bank, since the elephants would immediately charge and the sight and sound of the beasts would terrify them; even before that point, he realized, his horses would not remain on the hide floats ferrying them across but would panic and leap into the water when they caught sight of the elephants on the other side.[2a] [3] So Alexander planned to steal across in the following manner. He made a nightly practice of leading a large cavalry force here and there along the bank and of having the men raise shouts, war cries, and every kind of uproar made by troops when they prepare to make a crossing. Poros, on the other side, would then march with his elephants to the point opposite the hubbub. Thus Alexander got Poros into the habit of making flank marches. [4] But when this had been going on for a long time, and nothing occurred beyond the shouting and the war cries, Poros gave up responding to the sallies of Alexander's cavalrymen; judging that there was no cause for alarm, he remained in camp, though he saw to it that scouts were posted everywhere along the bank. And once Alexander had made Poros complacent about the nightly sorties, he contrived the following plan.

[1] A promontory jutted out from the bank of the Hydaspes where the river bent at a sharp angle. The promontory itself was thickly wooded, and across from it, in the river, lay an island that was wooded and trackless, being uninhabited. After spotting the island opposite the promontory,

5.9.4a Arrian here describes the monsoon season, which indeed begins around the time of the summer solstice. But the text as it stands gives the mistaken impression that the time of Alexander's engagement with Poros was during the monsoon season, rather than, as Arrian himself else-where states (see 5.19.3 and n. 5.19.3b), and as other sources confirm, in spring. One solution to this inconsistency is to take the above sentence, describing the cresting of the Indian rivers, as referring to the general pattern of the monsoons, and not as a description of conditions at the time of Alexander's operations. It is possible that some text has been lost from the manuscripts (as Bosworth believes, II.272) that would have made this context clearer.
5.10.2a Cavalry horses were known to be unwilling to advance against unfamiliar creatures such as elephants and camels.

FIGURE 5.11. A coin minted by Ptolemy in Egypt (left) after Alexander's death depicts the conqueror wearing a helmet made from an elephant's scalp, in place of the more familiar lion skin worn by Herakles on Alexander's own standard coinage (see Figure 3.3). The exemplar of the elephant-scalp helmet may be the so-called Mir Zakah coin (center and right), named for the Afghan village where it was found in 1992. It depicts Alexander on one side and a striding elephant on the other. If genuine, it may have been issued by Alexander himself, but specialists are divided about its authenticity.

Alexander decided that, since both places were wooded enough to conceal the attempt at crossing, he would try to get the army across at that point. [2] The promontory and the island were both nearly twenty miles from the main camp. Alexander had stationed guards all along the bank at intervals that made it possible for them to see one another and to hear orders easily, no matter where they were issued. For many nights, shouts were raised on all sides and fires were kept burning.

[3] When Alexander had decided to attempt the passage, preparations for crossing went forward openly throughout the camp. Krateros was left behind in camp with his own hipparchy,[3a] the Arachosian cavalry and horsemen from the Paropamisadai, the battalions of Alketos and Polyperkhon from the Macedonian phalanx,[3b] and the governors of the local Indian tribes and their five thousand men. [4] Krateros had been ordered not to cross the stream until Poros had left camp to attack Alexander's forces, or until he learned that Poros had fled and Alexander's men had won a victory. "If Poros takes part of his army to attack me, and the rest of his men are left in camp with the elephants, stay where you are. If, on the other hand, Poros leads all his elephants against me and leaves part of his army in camp, make haste to cross. For only the elephants prevent you from disembarking the horses; the rest of Poros' force will not dismay them."

5.11.3–4
Spring 326
HYDASPES RIVER (WEST BANK)
With orders that Arrian quotes in direct speech, Alexander tells Krateros to hold position with a large force and act as a decoy to prevent Poros from moving.

5.11.3a Alexander evidently began dividing the Companion cavalry into hipparchies, or squadrons, in 330 or 329; see 3.29.7 and n. 3.29.7a. The number of hipparchies varied, from perhaps as many as ten to as few as four; see 7.6.4.

5.11.3b Phalanx: the heavy infantry. Normal depth was eight men, but it could be increased to sixteen or thirty-two upon command.

5.12.1–4
Spring 326
HYDASPES RIVER (WEST BANK)
Stationing other units on the west bank with orders to cross the river in stages, Alexander proceeds with the main attack force to his chosen crossing point, where ships and hide rafts have been prepared. A thunderstorm helps to drown out the army's noises as they launch these vessels, and the wooded island serves as a screen to conceal their crossing.

[1] Such were Krateros' instructions. Between the island and the main camp where he had been left behind, Meleagros, Attalos, and Gorgias had been posted with the mercenary horsemen and foot soldiers. These men were also instructed to cross in sections, dividing up their forces, once they saw the Indians engaged in battle.

[2] Alexander selected the *agema* of the Companions,[2a] the hipparchies[2b] of Hephaistion, Perdikkas, and Demetrios, the cavalry of the Bactrians and Sogdians, the Scythian horsemen, the mounted bowmen of the Dahae, and, from the phalanx, the shield-bearers,[2c] the battalions of Kleitos and Koinos, the archers, and the Agrianians,[2d] and led these men forward unseen, keeping a good distance from the bank lest he be spotted taking them to the island and the promontory he had chosen for the crossing. [3] There the hide floats that had been brought to the place much earlier were being filled with hay and carefully stitched together under cover of night. A heavy rain fell that night and helped to conceal Alexander's preparations and his attempt to cross, since the thunder and rain drowned out the clash of weapons and the uproar caused by the relay of orders. [4] Most of the ships, including the thirty-oared ships that had been cut in pieces, had been conveyed to that spot, reassembled where they could not be seen, and concealed in the woods. Near dawn, the wind and rain had subsided, and when his cavalry had embarked on the hide floats, and all the foot soldiers the ships could accommodate had boarded, they crossed by way of the island, lest they be observed by Poros' spies before they had sailed past the island and were a short distance from the bank.

5.13.1–3
HYDASPES RIVER (WEST BANK)
Alexander leads his forces across and disembarks them, only to discover they have reached not the opposite bank of the river but a second midstream island. The troops are forced to wade through deep water in order to reach their destination, after Poros' scouts have already spotted them and gone to inform their leader.

[1] Alexander embarked on a thirty-oared ship and crossed the stream with three of his Bodyguards[1a]—Ptolemy, Perdikkas, and Lysimakhos—and Seleukos (a Companion who later became king)[1b] and half the shield-bearers. Other thirty-oared ships carried the rest of the shield-bearers. As soon as they sailed by the island, it became clear that they were making an assault on the riverbank, and the Indian scouts, spotting their onslaught, rode to Poros as fast as their horses could carry them. [2] Having disembarked first and taken with him the troops from the other thirty-oared ships, Alexander marshaled the horsemen as they disembarked (they had

5.12.2a　This *agema* was an elite cavalry unit, as distinct from the infantry *agema* mentioned at 5.2.5.
5.12.2b　On hipparchies, see n. 5.11.3a.
5.12.2c　The shield-bearers (*hypaspists*) were an elite corps of specially equipped infantry (see Appendix D, Alexander's Army and Military Leadership, §3), lighter and more mobile than the heavy infantry who made up the phalanx.
5.12.2d　The term Agrianians, as used by Arrian, usually refers to a light-infantry division recruited from a Balkan region known as Agriania, northeast of Macedonia; see Appendix D, §6.
5.13.1a　Apparently the term "Bodyguards" here refers to the coterie of seven officers who

attended Alexander's person and not, as often, to an elite corps of men detailed to fight beside Alexander in battle; see Appendix E, §4.
5.13.1b　The qualification attached to Seleukos' name is odd, because both Lysimakhos and Ptolemy also had themselves crowned at about the same time as Seleukos. Arrian calls attention to the first appearance in his narrative of Seleukos, who was later to play such an important role in the struggle to succeed Alexander (see the Epilogue §10, 14), but Lysimakhos is also mentioned here for the first time without similar fanfare.

been ordered to disembark first) and led them forward in battle order. But in his ignorance of the area, he had unknowingly landed not on firm ground but on an island; it was a second large island, and its size had concealed the fact that it was an island, separated from the other bank by a narrow channel of the river. [3] Meanwhile, the pouring rain, which continued through much of the night, had swelled the stream, with the result that Alexander's cavalry at first did not find a ford, and it was feared that in order to cross they would need to mount another effort equal to the first. But then a ford was discovered, and Alexander led his men across it, though with difficulty: for where the water was deepest, it was over the chests of the foot soldiers, while the horses barely kept their heads above water.[3a]

[4] When he had also crossed that expanse of water, he led the cavalry *agema* and the strongest men selected from the other hipparchies to the right wing. He posted the mounted bowmen in front of the entire cavalry. As for the infantry, he posted the royal shield-bearers, under Seleukos' command, next to the cavalry. Beside the shield-bearers he posted the royal *agema*, and beside the *agema* the rest of the shield-bearers in an order corresponding to the rotation of commands for that day. At both ends of the phalanx he posted the archers, the Agrianians, and the javelin men.

[1] Having thus arrayed his army, he commanded the infantry, a force numbering almost six thousand, to follow in formation at a marching pace. He himself, since he sensed that he had the upper hand in cavalry, took only the horsemen, who numbered nearly five thousand, and led them forward on the double. He ordered Tauron, the archers' commander, to bring his men up with the cavalry and to deploy them rapidly as well. [2] He had decided that if Poros' men attacked him with their full strength, he would either overcome them easily by attacking with his cavalry or hold them off until the infantry joined the action. But if, in their astonishment at the extraordinary daring of the crossing, the Indians should flee, he would follow closely on their heels, for the greater the slaughter in the retreat, the lighter his task would be thereafter.

[3] Aristoboulos says that Poros' son arrived with nearly sixty chariots before Alexander made his last crossing from the small island, and that he would have been able to prevent Alexander's crossing, which was difficult even with no one preventing it, if the Indians had leaped down from their chariots and attacked Alexander's men as they landed. Instead, Poros' son drove past with his chariots and thereby enabled Alexander to cross safely. Alexander sent the mounted bowmen out against these men, and they were driven off easily after sustaining casualties. [4] Others say that a battle also took place at the landing site between the Indians who had arrived with

5.13.4
HYDASPES RIVER (EAST BANK)
Having gotten his men across to Poros' side of the river, Alexander arrays them for battle.

5.14.1–2
HYDASPES RIVER (EAST BANK)
Alexander hurries forward with five thousand cavalry and some archers, planning to make a quick assault while the infantry moves up more slowly.

5.14.3–6
Spring 326
HYDASPES RIVER (EAST BANK)
Poros' son, leading a chariot force, arrives first at Alexander's landing point, though there is dispute over the size of this force and why it failed to stop Alexander from crossing the river. In Arrian's opinion, it was a large force but arrived too late to prevent the crossing.

5.13.3a Arrian here speaks as though the men were wading in the river, but earlier he described the hides and boats that had been prepared to carry them across. Arrian's sources seem to have exaggerated the difficulties Alexander overcame in his last great battle. Bosworth (II.282) also points out that the amount of time that would be required for a crossing of the type described here would far surpass the time Arrian allots for it. There must have been more than one ford available, so that the army encountered deep water for only short stretches.

Poros' son and Alexander at the head of his cavalry. According to that account, Poros' son arrived with a larger force, and Alexander himself was wounded by him, and Alexander's favorite horse, Boukephalos, was also wounded by Poros' son and killed. But Ptolemy son of Lagos says otherwise; [5] for he too says that Poros' son was sent out, but not with a mere sixty chariots, and I agree with his account. For it is not likely that Poros, when he heard from his scouts that Alexander himself, or at least some portion of his army, had crossed the Hydaspes, would have sent his son out with only sixty chariots. [6] If these were sent out for spying, they would be too numerous and too unwieldy for a fast retreat; whereas if they were sent to prevent enemy troops from landing and to attack those who had already emerged from the river, they would have been wholly inadequate. Instead, according to Ptolemy, by the time Poros' son arrived with two thousand horsemen and a hundred and twenty chariots, Alexander had already completed his crossing from the island.

[1] Ptolemy also says that Alexander began by sending the mounted bowmen against them, while he himself advanced with the cavalry, as he thought that Poros was approaching with his entire force and that this advance unit of horsemen was the spearhead of Poros' army. [2] But when Alexander had gained an accurate sense of the Indians' numbers, he made a lightning attack with his own cavalry. The Indians fled when they caught sight of Alexander himself and his mass of horsemen, who were attacking not in line but squadron by squadron.[2a] Up to four hundred Indian horsemen fell, as did Poros' son. The chariots were captured along with their horses; they had proved heavy in the retreat and were of no use in the action itself on account of the mud.

[3] When the horsemen who were able to save themselves by flight had reported to Poros that Alexander himself had crossed the river in force and that his son was dead, Poros nevertheless could not make up his mind what to do, since the men who had been left behind with Krateros in the main camp opposite were clearly attempting to cross the river.[3a] [4] In the end Poros chose to advance against Alexander and to fight it out, with his entire army, against the most powerful body of Macedonians and the king himself; but he left a few of the elephants with a modest force at the camp to scare Krateros' cavalry away from the bank. Taking his entire cavalry force of up to four thousand horsemen, all his three hundred chariots, two hundred elephants, and the effective units of his infantry—nearly thirty thousand men[4a]—Poros advanced against Alexander. [5] When he came upon an area

5.15.1–2
Spring 326
HYDASPES RIVER (EAST BANK)
After learning the size of the Indian force engaging him, Alexander launches a cavalry charge and puts the Indians to flight. Their heavy chariots bog down in the muddy ground.

5.15.3–7
HYDASPES RIVER (EAST BANK)
Poros commits the majority of his army to meeting Alexander's forces and makes his battle dispositions. He posts elephants in his front line as a moving bulwark, with infantry divisions between and behind them and with cavalry at the wings.

5.15.2a The phrase translated "squadron by squadron" (Greek *kat'ilas*) is not well understood. It seems in this case that Alexander kept his cavalry arranged in a column rather than spreading them out in a line.

5.15.3a If Arrian's account is correct, Krateros moved into the river prematurely, for Alexander ordered him to wait until Poros had marched off with his elephants (see

5.11.4). But Krateros was not one to jump the gun or disobey orders, so Arrian may have misunderstood his sources here.

5.15.4a The number of Poros' forces at this battle is a subject of dispute. Bosworth (II.292), reasoning on the basis of the length of the Indian line, believes that Arrian's source, Ptolemy, has greatly exaggerated the strength of Poros' army to increase the glory of Alexander's victory.

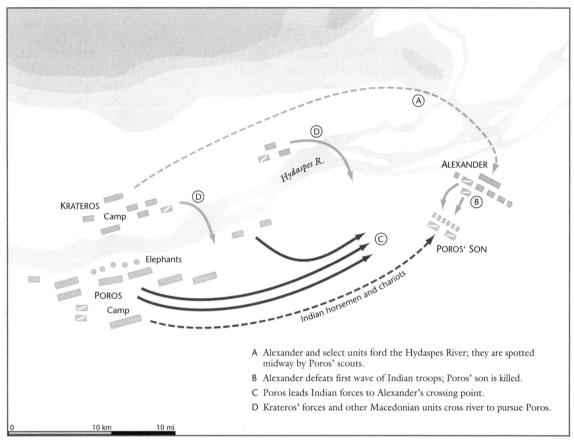

A Alexander and select units ford the Hydaspes River; they are spotted midway by Poros' scouts.

B Alexander defeats first wave of Indian troops; Poros' son is killed.

C Poros leads Indian forces to Alexander's crossing point.

D Krateros' forces and other Macedonian units cross river to pursue Poros.

MAP 5.15. THE FIRST PHASE OF THE BATTLE OF THE HYDASPES AS DESCRIBED AT 5.12.2–5.18.1. Alexander is shown crossing the Indus at a point some 20 miles from his base camp, and forming up his battle line in time to meet the first wave of Indian attackers, led by Poros' son.

where no mud was visible, a sandy, level plain with firm footing for the charges and maneuvers of his cavalry, he arrayed his forces, starting with a line of elephants, each animal placed less than a hundred feet from the next, so that the line would be equal in length to that of the opposing infantry phalanx and might terrify the horsemen surrounding Alexander. [6] In any event, Poros did not expect that his adversaries would dare to thrust themselves into the spaces between the elephants, not with their cavalry, given the horses' fear, still less with the foot soldiers whose forward progress would be barred by the onslaught of heavily armed Indians and who would be trampled underfoot when the elephants wheeled on them. [7] Next, Poros posted the foot soldiers not on the same line as the elephants, but in a second line close enough behind them that their companies could be posted in the intervals between the beasts. He also stationed infantry at the wings even beyond the elephants; beyond the infantry at each wing he posted his

FIGURE 5.16. The so-called elephant medallion was apparently cast in very small numbers after the battle of the Hydaspes. It seems to show Alexander standing and holding a thunderbolt in the guise of Zeus on one side, mounted and pursuing a fleeing elephant on the other. The elephant is ridden by two Indian foes, one of whom is often identified as Poros.

5.16.1–3
Spring 326
HYDASPES RIVER (EAST BANK)
Alexander, leading the cavalry, is rejoined by the infantry. He allows them to rest from the river crossing and then prepares his attack. Leading his own cavalry force on a rightward flanking maneuver, he details Koinos to lead other horsemen in the opposite direction, with instructions to pursue any Indian cavalrymen that ride out to meet Alexander.

cavalry, and in front of the cavalry, likewise at each wing, the chariots.

[1] Such was Poros' battle array. As soon as Alexander saw the Indians drawn up in order, he halted his own cavalry so as to await the infantry who were still approaching. But when the phalanx, hastening up on the double, had joined him, he did not immediately array the troops for battle and lead them forward, lest he deliver up exhausted and panting men to the unwearied barbarians. Instead he had his cavalry ride back and forth in circles in front of his infantrymen, giving them an interval in which to catch their breath. [2] When he saw the Indians' battle order, he decided not to lead his men forward against their center, since the elephants stood on the front lines and the phalanx had densely filled in the intervals between them; he feared the combination of forces that Poros, after calculating carefully, had posted there. Instead, since his cavalry was superior to that of Poros, he took most of it and rode past the enemy's left wing, intending to launch his attack there. [3] He sent Koinos[3a] against the right with his own cavalry division and that of Demetrios, having ordered him to keep close behind the barbarians once they had glimpsed Alexander's approach and ridden out to counter it.[3b] He assigned the command of the infantry phalanx to Seleukos, Antigenes,[3c] and Tauron and ordered them not to join the action until they saw that the Indians' infantry and horsemen were thrown into disorder by his cavalry.

5.16.3a Koinos inexplicably appears here as a cavalry commander, whereas elsewhere (at 4.16.2, for example) Arrian describes him as leading an infantry unit.
5.16.3b The words here translated "against the right" could just as easily mean "toward the right." On the first interpretation, Alexander told Koinos to move leftward and get in position to attack the Indian right wing from behind, as it moved against Alexander

(see Map 5.16). But the other reading is also possible; Koinos in that case would have moved rightward. Both versions of the maneuver seem equally possible and equally problematic, so the passage remains ambiguous.
5.16.3c This is Arrian's first mention of Antigenes, later commander of the elite Silver Shields infantry unit and a major figure in events after Alexander's death. See the Epilogue, §8.

[4] When he was within range of enemy fire, Alexander sent the mounted bowmen, who numbered nearly a thousand, against the Indians' left wing, so as to confuse the Indians stationed there with a barrage of arrows and incursions of horses. Alexander swiftly overtook the barbarians' left with the Companion cavalry, taking pains to attack them in the flank while they were still in disarray and before their cavalry could be drawn up in line.

[1] Meanwhile, the Indians had brought their horsemen together from all sides and were riding parallel to Alexander and drawing out their line to match his progress.[1a] Koinos and his men, following Alexander's instructions, appeared behind them. Once the Indians saw this, they were forced to deploy their cavalry in two directions, the largest and strongest part facing Alexander, the other facing Koinos and his men. [2] This tactic upset the Indians' formation and their presence of mind. Alexander, seeing his opportunity at the moment their cavalry changed direction, attacked the men nearest him, and as a result the Indians did not even await his charge but were driven back to their line of elephants as though to a friendly wall. [3] At that point the commanders of the elephants led the beasts against the cavalry, and the Macedonian phalanx advanced to meet the elephants, hurling javelins at the men mounted upon them,[3a] and shooting at the beasts themselves from all sides. The action was like none of their previous battles; for the beasts sallied out against the battalions of foot soldiers and ravaged them wherever they turned, despite their keeping in close formation, while the Indian horsemen, seeing their infantry joining the fight, turned back and charged the Macedonian cavalry.

[4] But when Alexander's men regained the upper hand—for they far surpassed the Indians in strength and experience[4a]—the Indians were again forced back to the elephants. At that point, Alexander's entire cavalry united in one troop, not in response to an order, but in consequence of the engagement itself; and wherever it assaulted the Indian ranks, these suffered heavy losses. [5] As the elephants were now confined in a narrow space, their friends were injured by them no less than the enemy, trampled underfoot when the beasts wheeled and shoved. As the Indian horsemen were also confined in a narrow space near the elephants, they suffered a heavy slaughter. Meanwhile, most of the elephants' mahouts had been struck down by javelins, and the elephants themselves, some of them wounded, others overcome by their toils and bereft of their masters, no longer remained in formation. [6] Driven senseless by their misery, they attacked friends and foes alike,

5.16.4

HYDASPES RIVER (EAST BANK)
The attack begins. The Macedonian mounted archers render the Indian left wing vulnerable to an assault by Alexander.

5.17.1–3

HYDASPES RIVER (EAST BANK)
The Indian cavalry pursues Alexander and is caught between his contingent and that of Koinos. They retreat behind the protective screen of the elephants. The infantries of both sides join the fray, and the Indians succeed in using their elephants to harass the Macedonian phalanx.

5.17.4–6

HYDASPES RIVER (EAST BANK)
Alexander's veterans, relying on their years of experience in battle, turn the tide. The elephants in the Indian line cause great confusion, harming both Alexander's army and the Indians in their panic and distress.

5.17.1a   Following Bosworth (II.299) and others, we should imagine that this movement of the Indian cavalry, and the corresponding pursuit by Koinos' regiment, took place in the rear of the Indian lines rather than in front, as some have supposed.

5.17.3a   Though facing a major elephant force for the first time, the Macedonians seem to have already understood that a trained war elephant could be rendered ineffective if its trainer-rider was killed.

5.17.4a   This seems to be the crucial point: though Arrian's sources have done their best to emphasize the risks Alexander ran in the battle with Poros, the high degree of training and discipline his troops had attained meant that victory was assured even against an army equipped with elephants. There is also a suggestion in Arrian's language here that the Macedonians enjoyed numerical superiority.

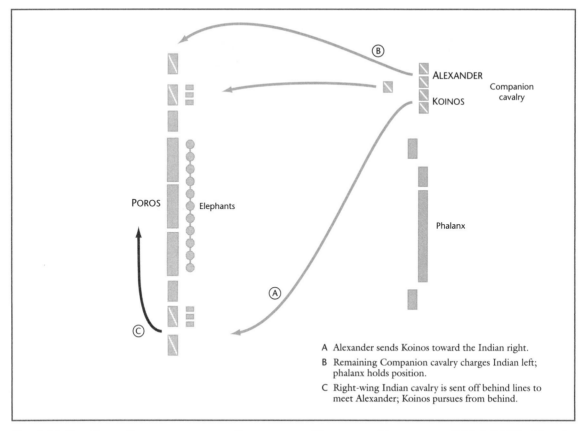

A Alexander sends Koinos toward the Indian right.

B Remaining Companion cavalry charges Indian left; phalanx holds position.

C Right-wing Indian cavalry is sent off behind lines to meet Alexander; Koinos pursues from behind.

MAP 5.16. THE MAJOR ENGAGEMENT OF THE BATTLE OF THE HYDASPES AS DESCRIBED AT 5.16.3–5.17.1. After the arrival of Poros' forces at Alexander's crossing point. Alexander's key move was to send cavalry led by Koinos "toward the (Macedonian) right" or "against the (Indian) right"—Arrian's language is unfortunately ambiguous. The map is based on the latter interpretation. In this reading, Alexander anticipated that the Indians would draw cavalry from their right wing to meet his attack on the left, and planned for Koinos to take these relief forces in the rear. It is unclear how Koinos avoided detection as he moved into position.

and thrust themselves in all directions, trampling and killing. The Macedonians, who were attacking the beasts in an open field and at their own discretion, were able to give ground when charged, then follow behind and hurl javelins when the beasts turned their backs; it was the Indians, who were at close quarters with the elephants, who incurred the most harm from them.

5.17.7
Spring 326
HYDASPES RIVER (EAST BANK)
Alexander orders his phalanx to advance in tight formation. The Indian army, routed, flees the field.

[7] When the beasts were worn out, and their charges were no longer vigorous—when they merely trumpeted and retired, like ships backing water—Alexander completely surrounded their entire unit with his cavalry and gave the signal for the foot soldiers to lock their shields, draw themselves into the tightest possible formation, and advance the phalanx. And thus all but a few of the Indian horsemen were cut to pieces in the action.

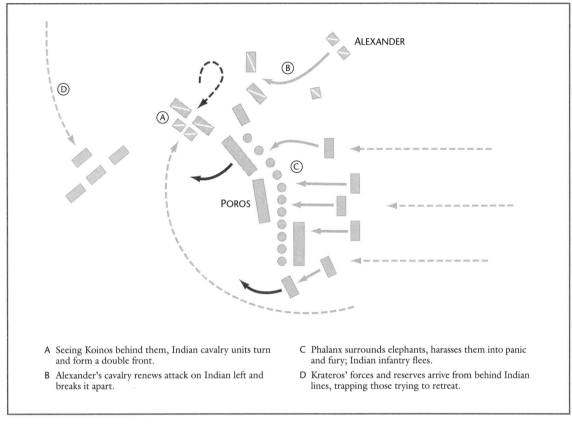

A Seeing Koinos behind them, Indian cavalry units turn
   and form a double front.
B Alexander's cavalry renews attack on Indian left and
   breaks it apart.

C Phalanx surrounds elephants, harasses them into panic
   and fury; Indian infantry flees.
D Krateros' forces and reserves arrive from behind Indian
   lines, trapping those trying to retreat.

MAP 5.17. THE FINAL PHASE OF THE BATTLE OF THE HYDASPES AS DESCRIBED AT 5.17.2–5.18.1. In Arrian's
description, the battle became a rout after Koinos' surprise move startled and disordered the Indian cavalry.
Alexander's renewed attacks smashed the Indian left wing, and the Macedonian phalanx, kept out of the fight
until now, brought its weapons to bear against the elephants arrayed in the center. The Indians soon lost control
of these beasts and fled in panic, only to be boxed in by Krateros' reserve forces, which by then were arriving at
the battlefield.

Their foot soldiers were already being cut down, as the Macedonians were
attacking them from every side. At that point, where a gap appeared in
Alexander's cavalry, all the Indians turned and fled.

[1] At the same time, Krateros and all the other officers of Alexander's
army who had been left at the bank of the Hydaspes began to cross the
river when they saw Alexander prevailing decisively. These men caused no
less of a slaughter in the Indians' retreat, having arrived fresh for the
pursuit as replacements for Alexander's exhausted men. [2] Almost twenty
thousand Indian foot soldiers and some three thousand horsemen were
killed. All their chariots were destroyed. Two of Poros' sons died, as did
Spitakes, the chief of the local Indians, the officers in charge of the

5.18.1–3

HYDASPES RIVER (EAST BANK)
Krateros and the men
stationed across the Hydaspes
now ford the river to aid in
the slaughter of the Indians.
Losses on the Indian side are
huge; only a few hundred
Macedonians are killed.

elephants and chariots, and all the cavalry commanders and generals of Poros' army. [. . .]²ᵃ Also captured were the elephants that did not perish there. [3] On Alexander's side, about eighty of the eight thousand foot soldiers who had taken part in the initial assault were killed. As for the cavalry, ten of the mounted bowmen, whose task it had been to begin the battle, were killed, along with about twenty Companions and some two hundred other horsemen.

[4] Poros had performed great exploits in the battle, not only as a general but as a noble soldier. And when he saw the slaughter of his horsemen, and some of his elephants fallen, while others, bereft of their masters, were wandering about pitiably, and when most of his infantry had perished, he did not emulate Darius, the Great King, who retreated, the first of his men to flee.⁴ᵃ [5] Instead, Poros stood his ground as long as any portion of the Indian force held firm, until at last, wounded in the right shoulder—the only part of him that was exposed as he ranged over the battlefield, since his breastplate, remarkable for its strength and joint work, as was plain to those who saw it later, protected the rest of his body from missiles—then and only then did he turn his elephant about and retreat.⁵ᵃ

[6] Alexander, having seen that Poros was a great man who had acquitted himself nobly in the battle, was eager to save him. First he sent Taxiles the Indian to him, and Taxiles, having ridden up to what seemed to him a safe distance from Poros' elephant, bade him halt the beast, since escape was now out of the question, and listen to Alexander's proposals. [7] When Poros caught sight of Taxiles, his old enemy, he wheeled about and made ready to hurl his javelin at him, and indeed might have killed him if Taxiles had not seen what was coming and ridden away from Poros. Even then Alexander did not grow angry with Poros, but sent others to him in turn, and in particular Meroes, an Indian, because he learned that the man was an old friend. [8] Poros heard what Meroes had to say, and then was suddenly overcome by thirst. He halted his elephant and dismounted, and when he had quenched his thirst and recovered himself, he urged Meroes to conduct him to Alexander at once.

[1] Meroes complied. When Alexander learned that Poros was approaching, he met him in front of the line with a few of the Companions. Halting his horse, he marveled at Poros' height (which appeared to exceed eight feet),¹ᵃ his beauty, and the fact that his spirit was plainly unbowed: he approached Alexander as one brave man would approach

5.18.2a A sentence or two, completing the casualty lists and giving the number of prisoners captured, has fallen out of the manuscripts here.

5.18.4a Darius, the Persian emperor, was the first to flee after realizing his ultimate defeat in the battle at Issus (2.11.4–7) and again at Gaugamela (3.14.3).

5.18.5a A medallion struck by Alexander in very small numbers, perhaps as a gift to his senior officers in the Indian campaign, depicts a fleeing elephant pursued by a

spear-wielding cavalryman (see Figure 5.16). One of the two figures riding the elephant is generally thought to be Poros, and the cavalryman is thought to be Alexander, even though, according to accounts of the battle of the Hydaspes, the two did not encounter each other until after the fighting had ceased.

5.19.1a Arrian tends to exaggerate the height of Indians (see n. 5.4.4a), but by the accounts of all ancient sources, Poros was indeed exceptionally tall.

another, having contended honorably against another king on behalf of his kingdom. [2] Alexander spoke first and urged Poros to say what he hoped would befall him. Poros is said to have replied, "Treat me like a king, Alexander." Pleased with the response, Alexander said, "That will be done, Poros, on my own account. But on your account, say what would be to your liking." Poros replied that everything was contained in that wish. [3] And Alexander, even more pleased with this response, granted Poros sovereignty over the very Indians he had been ruling and added another territory even more extensive than his former domain.[3a] Thus he had treated a brave man like a king, and thereafter enjoyed the man's unswerving loyalty. So ended the battle against Poros and the Indians beyond the Hydaspes, which took place in the month of Mounykhion,[3b] during Hegemon's archonship[3c] at Athens.

[4] At the battlefield and at the site from which he set out to cross the Hydaspes, Alexander founded two cities. He named one of them Nikaia, in honor of his victory over the Indians,[4a] the other Boukephala,[4b] in memory of his horse Boukephalos, who died there. [5] The horse had not been wounded but had succumbed to the heat and old age (he was about thirty years old)[5a] after years of sharing Alexander's toils and dangers. Enormous in stature and noble in spirit, Boukephalos had been mounted only by Alexander, since the horse had refused to carry any other riders. He had been branded with the mark of an ox head, which some say was the source of his name;[5b] others say that though the rest of his body was black, his head was marked with a white shape that resembled an ox head. [6] Boukephalos went missing once in Ouxioi[6a] country, whereupon Alexander issued a general proclamation stating that he would kill every one of the Ouxioi unless they brought back his horse. The horse was brought back as soon as the proclamation was issued, so great was Alexander's regard for Boukephalos and so great the barbarians' fear of Alexander. May this serve as my brief tribute to Boukephalos for Alexander's sake.

[1] When those who had died in the battle had been honored by Alexander with the appropriate ceremony, he performed for the gods the customary rites that honor victories, and held a competition in athletics and horseman-

5.19.4–6
NIKAIA-BOUKEPHALA
Alexander founds two cities: Nikaia, in honor of his victory, and Boukephala, in honor of his horse who died.

5.20.1–4
INDIA
After holding a victory celebration and games, Alexander marches against a tribe neighboring the realm of Poros and puts their territory under Poros' control.

5.19.3a It is surprising to find Alexander so willing to trust a man who had until this moment been a determined foe, but his judgment of Poros' character was borne out by later events. Poros remained a faithful vassal of the Macedonians throughout the rest of his life. He was assassinated for unknown reasons by a Macedonian garrison commander in 318.

5.19.3b The month of Mounykhion in the Attic calendar corresponds to late April/early May by our calendar. This passage raises the likelihood that the text of 5.9.4, which in its received condition dates the battle of the Hydaspes after the summer solstice, is somehow corrupt.

5.19.3c Ancient historians, who had no universal system for numbering years, routinely

used the names of Athenian archons or Roman consuls—officials who served one-year terms—to identify points in historical time.

5.19.4a Nikaia: Map 5.25, inset. The name is derived from the Greek word *nike*, meaning "victory."

5.19.4b Boukephala: Map 5.25, inset.

5.19.5a Boukephalos' age seems exaggerated but is within the realm of possibility. The information that Boukephalos was not wounded but died of exhaustion also contradicts our other sources, which claim that the horse died from wounds incurred in the battle (a tradition referred to by Arrian himself at 5.14.4).

5.19.5b *Boukephalos* in Greek means "ox head."

5.19.6a Ouxioi, location of territory: Map 5.25.

ship at the bank of the Hydaspes,[1a] where he had first crossed with the army. [2] He left Krateros behind with a portion of the army to build and fortify the cities he was founding there, while he himself advanced against the Indians whose land bordered on Poros' empire.[2a] Their tribe was known as the Glauganikai,[2b] according to Aristoboulos, though Ptolemy calls them the Glausai; the name, whichever it was, does not concern me. [3] Alexander marched toward their country with half the Companion cavalry, picked men from each of the infantry battalions, all the mounted bowmen, the Agrianians, and the archers. Everyone came to terms with him. [4] He seized some thirty-seven cities, the smallest of which had no fewer than five thousand inhabitants, while many had more than ten thousand. He also took many villages no less populous than the cities, and gave the country to Poros to govern. After reconciling Poros and Taxiles, he sent Taxiles back to his own settlements.

[5] At this time envoys arrived from Abisares,[5a] offering the surrender of Abisares himself and his entire domain to Alexander. Though before the battle Abisares had intended to side with Poros, he now sent his own brother to Alexander with the other envoys, bringing money and forty elephants as a gift for Alexander. [6] Envoys had also arrived from the autonomous Indians[6a] and from another Indian chieftain whose name was also Poros. Alexander ordered Abisares to come to him in person immediately, and threatened that if he failed to do so, he would soon see Alexander and his army in a place where the sight would not please him.[6b]

[7] Meanwhile, Phrataphernes, the satrap of Parthia and Hyrcania,[7a] had come to Alexander with the Thracian troops who had been stationed with him. Messengers also arrived from Sisikottos, the satrap of Assakania,[7b] to report that the Assakanians had killed their governor and revolted from Alexander. Alexander sent Philip and Tyriespis with an army to meet the rebels, having instructed them to settle matters in and around Assakania and restore order.

[8] Alexander proceeded to the River Akesinos.[8a] The Akesinos is the only Indian river whose size Ptolemy son of Lagos has recorded. He says that where Alexander crossed it with his army on boats and hides the Akesinos' current is swift; that the water becomes rough and turbid as it rushes over large, sharp rocks; and that the channel is two miles wide. [9] The passage was easy for those who crossed on the hides, but of the men who crossed in

5.20.5–6
INDIA
Alexander negotiates the surrender of Abisares, a former ally of Poros' in the anti-Macedonian resistance.

5.20.7
INDIA
News arrives of a revolt in Assakania; Alexander sends forces to subdue it.

5.20.8–10
Summer 326
AKESINOS RIVER
Alexander proceeds to the river and crosses it in spite of a dangerous current. Many ships are wrecked and their crews drowned.

5.20.1a Hydaspes River: Map 5.25, inset.
5.20.2a It was not mere desire for conquest that led Alexander to march against this neighboring tribe, but an additional motive, unmentioned by Arrian but clear from other sources: he needed the timber found in these regions for the construction of the fleet that, as Alexander had already resolved, would be used to explore the Indus River.
5.20.2b Glauganikai/Glausai, location of territory: Map 5.25, inset. The Glauganikai

dwelt in the wooded highlands between the Hydaspes and Akesinos rivers.
5.20.5a On Abisares, see n. 5.8.3a.
5.20.6a That is, Indians not subject to the rule of one or another local dynasty.
5.20.6b One of few threats on which Alexander did not make good; see 5.29.4–5.
5.20.7a Parthia; Hyrcania: Map 5.25.
5.20.7b Assakanians (Assakanoi), location of territory: Map 5.25, inset.
5.20.8a Akesinos River: Map 5.25, inset. Arrian spells its name Akesines.

boats, a great many drowned when their boats were wrecked on the rocks and dashed to pieces. [10] Judging from this account, one could reasonably surmise that those who have written about the size of the Indus[10a] are not far from the truth when they report that the Indus is five miles wide on the average, but that at its narrowest (and hence deepest) it contracts to a width of nearly two miles.[10b] (At many points that is the width of the Indus.) And I conjecture that Alexander chose to cross the Akesinos where the stream was widest so that he might have a lazier current to deal with.

[1] After crossing the river, Alexander left Koinos and his battalion at the bank with orders to oversee the crossing of the remaining troops, who would be transporting food and other provisions from the Indian territory already subject to Alexander. [2] He sent Poros back to his own settlements with orders to rejoin him after selecting the best Indian warriors and to bring with him any elephants he had at his disposal.[2a] Alexander now intended to pursue, with the most mobile of his troops, the second Poros, the bad one,[2b] as it had been reported to him that the man had abandoned his country and fled. [3] This Poros, while Alexander and the other Poros had been at odds, had sent envoys to Alexander, surrendering himself and his territory, more out of hatred for the other Poros than out of friendship for Alexander. But when he learned that that Poros had been set free and was governing another large territory in addition to his own, he took fright, not at Alexander, but at Poros his namesake, and fled from his own kingdom, taking with him all the fighting men he could persuade to join him in his flight.[3a]

[4] Advancing against this man, Alexander reached the Hydraotes,[4a] another river that joins the Indus. (The Hydraotes is as wide as the Akesinos, but its current is slower.) On his way to the Hydraotes, Alexander had left guards at all the most strategic points, so that the men with Krateros and Koinos might traverse most of the country in safety when foraging.

[5] Alexander now gave Hephaistion a portion of the army—two phalanxes of infantry, his own and Demetrios' regiments of horsemen, and half the archers—and dispatched him to the land of the rebellious Poros with orders to hand it over to the other Poros. Also, if Hephaistion encoun-

5.21.1–3
AKESINOS RIVER
Leaving Koinos to safeguard his supply route, Alexander gathers forces for the pursuit of a fugitive rebel leader, also named Poros. This second Poros had tried to ally with Alexander earlier but after the battle of the Hydaspes had feared the increasing power of his rival, Poros, under Alexander's dominion.

5.21.4
HYDRAOTES RIVER
The pursuit of Poros takes Alexander across another river, the Hydraotes.

5.21.5–6
HYDRAOTES RIVER
Hephaistion is detailed to secure the allegiance of the kingdom abandoned by the fugitive and any other tribes encountered along the Hydraotes.

5.20.10a Indus River: Map 5.25 and inset.
5.20.10b Arrian here reasons that if the Akesinos is as wide and strong as Ptolemy claims, then the Indus, to which it is but one of many tributaries, must really be as vast a river as is claimed. See 5.4.2 and n. 5.4.2c or Arrian's tendency to exaggerate Indian river widths.
5.21.2a It is a mark of Alexander's versatility as a general that here, only a few weeks after his first experience of the broad-scale use of war elephants, he was prepared to adopt them himself as an offensive weapon. As things turned out he never had the chance to use them in combat, but his generals relied heavily on them in the years after his death (see the Epilogue, §14).
5.21.2b It is not Arrian but his sources who call this Poros "bad." Alexander's soldiers distinguished the two men named Poros—one of whom had gone over to Alexander, while the other revolted—as "good Poros" and "bad Poros."
5.21.3a This second Poros fled to the kingdom of the Gandaridae (Diodorus 17.91.1), identified by Bosworth (II.325) as the people of the Ganges valley. If that is correct, then Poros' flight would mark the first known point at which the Nanda kingdom on the Ganges became involved in the events triggered by Alexander.
5.21.4a Hydraotes River: Map 5.25, inset.

tered any tribes of autonomous Indians dwelling near the banks of the Hydraotes, he was to secure their allegiance and entrust them to Poros. [6] Alexander himself crossed the Hydraotes with none of the difficulty he had experienced when crossing the Akesinos. As he advanced beyond its bank, it turned out that most of the inhabitants made terms with him, including some who had earlier borne arms against him. Some others fled, and these he captured and subdued by force.

[1] At that point Alexander received word that a number of other autonomous Indians, including the tribe known as the Kathaioi,[1a] were preparing for battle in case he approached their country, and were summoning all the tribes whose territory bordered theirs, and who were likewise autonomous, to assist them. [2] Moreover, they intended to use a well-fortified city, Sangala,[2a] as their base of operations. The Kathaioi were considered experienced and highly courageous warriors, as were two other Indian tribes, the Oxydrakai and the Malloi.[2b] When, a short time previously, Poros and Abisares and their forces had made war on these tribes and had roused many other autonomous Indians against them, the attackers ultimately retired without having accomplished anything worthy of their preparations. [3] When this was reported to Alexander, he hastily advanced against the Kathaioi. After a day's march from the Hydraotes, he approached a city called Pimprama.[3a] The Indians who inhabited it were known as the Adrestae.[3b] [4] They came to terms with Alexander.

After allowing his army to rest the next day, Alexander proceeded on the third day to Sangala, where the Kathaioi and their neighbors had assembled in front of the city and arrayed themselves for battle. They had occupied a hill that was steep in some places but not in others. Having placed wagons in a circle around the hill, they had used them to create a triple palisade and were encamped within it. [5] When he had taken note of the barbarians' numbers and the nature of their position, Alexander arrayed his troops in the order that seemed to best suit the circumstances. He instantly sent out the mounted bowmen against the defenders with orders to ride by and shoot at them from a distance, so that the Indians would not sally out before the Macedonians had formed up in position, but would suffer injuries within their stronghold even before the battle began. [6] At the right wing he posted the cavalry *agema* and Kleitos' regiment; next to them he posted the shield-bearers, and beside the shield-bearers the Agrianians. At the left he posted Perdikkas with his own regiment and the battalions of the *asthetairoi*.[6a] Having divided the archers, he posted half of them at each wing. [7] As he was marshaling his forces, he was joined by the infantry and the cavalry who made up the rear guard; he divided the cavalry and posted half of it at each wing, and distributed the newly arrived infantry into the

5.22.1a Kathaioi, location of territory: Map 5.25, inset. This volume does not follow the *Barrington Atlas* in equating the Kathaioi with the Xathrians (Xathroi).
5.22.2a Sangala: Map 5.25, inset.
5.22.2b Oxydrakai; Malloi, location of territo-

ries: Map 5.25, inset.
5.22.3a Pimprama: location unknown.
5.22.3b Adrestae, location of territory: Map 5.25, inset.
5.22.6a Little is known about the makeup of the elite unit called *asthetairoi*. See n. 2.23.2b.

phalanx to make it more solid. Taking the horsemen who had been posted on the right, he led them against the wagons at the Indians' left, for the place seemed more accessible on that side, and the wagons had not been crowded together so densely.

[1] When the Indians did not sally out from their wagons against the approaching cavalry but climbed onto them and shot at the Macedonians from a distance, Alexander realized that this was not a job for the cavalry. Leaping down from his horse, he led the infantry phalanx forward on foot. [2] The Macedonians had no difficulty forcing the Indians from the first circle of wagons; but at the second circle the Indians, drawn up in battle order, easily fought the Macedonians off, as they stood in closer formation in the smaller circle and the Macedonians were not approaching from an open space as before, but were pulling the first wagons out of the way and charging, in no kind of order, through the gaps between them as the opportunity arose. Yet even from the second circle the Indians were thrust back by the phalanx. [3] The Indians of the third circle held their ground no longer, but fled as fast as they could and locked themselves inside the city walls.[3a]

That day Alexander made camp with the infantry around the city, as far as the phalanx could surround it. He could not completely encircle the city with his army, as the wall extended for a considerable distance. [4] But in the space his troops could not fill, at a short distance from the wall, there was a lake, and Alexander posted cavalry around it; for the water was not deep, and he guessed that the Indians, grown fearful after their recent defeat, would abandon the city at night. [5] And it turned out he had guessed correctly. Near the second watch,[5a] most of the Indians poured out of the city, only to encounter the advance guards of the Macedonian cavalry. The first group of Indians was cut to pieces by the horsemen, and those who followed, seeing that the lake was surrounded by guards, drew back into the city.

[6] Alexander now built a double palisade wherever the lake did not bound the city, and strengthened the guard stationed around the lake. He was planning to bring siege engines forward to throw down the wall; but deserters from the city informed him that, on that very night, the Indians intended to make their escape from the city by crossing the lake, where there was a gap in the palisade. [7] Alexander therefore posted Ptolemy son of Lagos at that spot, giving him three units of shield-bearers, all the Agrianians, and one unit of archers. Pointing to the place where he guessed the barbarians were most likely to force their way, he said:[7a] "As soon as you see

5.23.1–2
SANGALA
After fierce fighting on the hilltop, the Macedonians dislodge the Indians from their entrenched position and force them to take refuge inside Sangala.

5.23.3–5
SANGALA
Alexander puts a circuit of troops around Sangala, including cavalry positioned to guard the most likely exit point. At night the Indian troops, attempting a breakout, are driven back by these horsemen and again penned up in the city.

5.23.6–7
SANGALA
A stronger perimeter guard is put in place, with Ptolemy assuming a key command, after Alexander learns that the Indians will once again attempt a night sortie.

5.23.3a That is, the Indians abandoned the rings of wagons they had set up outside Sangala and took refuge within the city itself.

5.23.5a The Greeks (and later Romans), who were reliant on the sun to tell time during the day, divided the night into either three or four periods, naming these "watches" based on military parlance. The second watch of the night was approximately two or three hours after midnight.

5.23.7a The sudden introduction of direct address reminds us that Ptolemy son of Lagos, who is here receiving his first important combat command, was one of Arrian's two principal sources for the *Anabasis Alexandrou*. He must have recounted this episode in particularly close detail, both because he would have remembered it more clearly than others and because it highlighted his own high position among Alexander's officers.

them pressing forward there, bar their way with your army and order the trumpeter to sound the alarm. As for you others, my officers: when the signal is given, advance to the fray with the forces you each command, wherever the trumpet summons you. As for me, I shall not stand aloof from the action."

5.24.1–3
Summer 326
SANGALA
Ptolemy orders the construction of a barricade to frustrate the escape attempt and readies his men. As soon as the Indians are seen escaping, he leads an attack that kills many and drives the rest back into Sangala.

[1] Such were Alexander's instructions, and Ptolemy, collecting as many as he could of the wagons left behind in the initial flight, placed them across the fugitives' intended path, so that their difficulties might seem greater in the dark; and he gave orders that the stakes meant for the palisade, cut but not yet fixed in the ground, be gathered in piles here and there between the lake and the wall. His soldiers performed these tasks under cover of darkness. [2] It was already nearing the fourth watch[2a] when the barbarians, just as Alexander's informants had foretold, opened the gates nearest the lake and ran toward the water. But they did not elude the guards or their appointed commander, Ptolemy. His trumpeters sounded the alarm, and in an instant Ptolemy himself, with his forces armed and arrayed for battle, advanced against the barbarians, [3] who were blocked by the wagons and the palisade that had been thrown up between the wall and the lake. When the trumpet sounded and Ptolemy's men attacked them, killing them one after another as they emerged from between the wagons, they went back into the city. Nearly five hundred of them died in the retreat.

5.24.4–5
SANGALA
After siege equipment arrives, the Macedonians seize Sangala and inflict enormous casualties on those inside.

[4] At that point Poros arrived with the rest of the elephants and nearly five thousand Indians, and the siege engines that had been built for Alexander were now brought up to the wall. But before any part of the wall had been battered down the Macedonians undermined it (since it was built merely of brick), placed gangways all around it,[4a] and took the city by storm. [5] Some seventeen thousand Indians died in the capture, and more than seventy thousand were taken prisoner; three hundred chariots and five hundred horses were seized. In Alexander's army, a few short of a hundred died in the entire siege. The number of wounded, more than twelve hundred, was out of proportion to the number of dead. Among the wounded were several officers, including Lysimakhos the Bodyguard.

5.24.6–7
SANGALA
Eumenes is sent to secure the cooperation of neighboring towns in exchange for a security guarantee, but the occupants flee before he arrives. Five hundred invalids left behind meet their deaths.

[6] After burying the dead according to his custom, Alexander gave his clerk Eumenes[6a] nearly three hundred horsemen and sent him to the two cities that had revolted at the same time as Sangala. Eumenes was ordered to inform their inhabitants that Sangala had been captured and that they would suffer no harsh treatment from Alexander if they remained where

---

5.24.2a See n. 5.23.5a. The fourth watch was just before dawn.

5.24.4a These gangways were portable wooden walkways placed so as to allow the invading troops to easily climb over the rubble of the collapsed wall.

5.24.6a This is the first appearance in the text of a figure who went on to play an important role in the years following Alexan-

der's death. Eumenes was a Greek scribe, first recruited by Alexander's father, Philip, to be in charge of royal correspondence and archives. Alexander had up to now employed him in a similar capacity but from this point onward began to entrust him with military assignments. See Appendix E, §12, and the Epilogue, §8, 10.

they were and received him amicably, just as none of the other autonomous Indians who had surrendered willingly had been treated harshly. [7] But as these Indians had grown fearful (for they had already received word that Alexander had taken Sangala by storm), they abandoned their cities and fled; and when their flight had been reported to him, Alexander made haste to pursue them. Most of them got a head start and succeeded in escaping, as the pursuit was long delayed. But all who, owing to weakness, were left behind in the retreat, nearly five hundred men, were caught by the army and died.[7a]

[8] When he had decided against pursuing the fugitives farther, Alexander returned to Sangala, razed the city to the ground, and added the country to the domain of the Indians who had from ancient times been autonomous but had now come over to him willingly. He sent Poros and his forces to establish garrisons in the cities that had come over to him, while he himself advanced with the army to the River Hyphasis[8a] so that he might also subdue the Indians who dwelt beyond it. For he saw no end to the war as long as any enemy remained.

[1] The country beyond the Hyphasis was said to be prosperous and its inhabitants able farmers and brave fighters whose domestic affairs were conducted in an orderly manner: the common people were ruled by the nobles, who governed equitably. These Indians also had many more elephants than any other of their countrymen, and what is more, elephants of surpassing size and courage.[1a] [2] These reports stirred Alexander's desire to go farther. But the Macedonians had by now grown quite weary of their king's plans, seeing him charging from labor to labor, danger to danger. Various meetings were held in the camp; in some (the meetings of the most moderate), the men merely lamented their lot; in others, they positively refused to follow, even with Alexander leading them. When Alexander learned of this, he summoned his battalion officers, before the soldiers' agitation and faintheartedness could increase, and spoke as follows:

[3] "I have noticed, Macedonians and allies, that you no longer follow me into dangers with the same zeal, and I have therefore called you together so that I may either persuade you to follow me onward or be persuaded by you to turn back. If you find fault with any of your previous

---

5.24.8

HYPHASIS RIVER
After Alexander razes Sangala, he advances to the Hyphasis River, intending to take his army across.

5.25.1–2

HYPHASIS RIVER
The Macedonian army begins to chafe at Alexander's plans to continue the campaign eastward. Alexander calls his officers together and addresses them.

5.25.3–6
Summer 326
HYPHASIS RIVER
Alexander begins his speech by cataloguing the past conquests and successes of the army, in order to demonstrate that they have nothing to fear from any enemy.

5.24.7a   Arrian does not say that they were killed by the army, though we should probably assume this. Perhaps he is seeking to soften the grim realities of what Bosworth has called "one of the more repulsive acts of the campaign" (II.336). The sequence of events after Sangala reveals much about the tragedies that result from encounters between two nations that neither trust nor understand each other. Alexander probably would have granted security guarantees in exchange for compliance, but the panicked local population felt they must get away from him at all costs; and he, already pressured by numerous rebellions, with his lines dangerously

extended, treated their flight as an act of resistance rather than self-preservation.

5.24.8a   Hyphasis River: Map 5.25, inset.

5.25.1a   These reports refer to the kingdom of Magadha, governed by the Nanda dynasty. Alexander was perhaps aware that the dynasty, though superficially powerful, was mistrusted by its subjects and could be easily overcome by an invader, as Chandragupta, founder of the Mauryan empire, subsequently demonstrated when he conquered the Nandas a few years hence. Plutarch (*Parallel Lives*, "Alexander" 62.9) represents Chandragupta, whom he calls Sandrakottos, as disparaging Alexander for having failed to attack the Nandas.

exertions or with me as your leader, there is no point in my saying anything more. [4] But if, through those exertions, we now control Ionia,[4a] the Hellespont, both Phrygias,[4b] Cappadocia, Paphlagonia, Lydia, Caria, Lycia, Pamphylia, Phoenicia, Egypt, the Greek region of Libya,[4c] part of Arabia, Hollow Syria and Mesopotamian Syria, [5] and Babylon; the Susians, Persians, and Medes and the nations they ruled, as well as those they did not rule, those beyond the Caspian Gates, beyond the Caucasus, the Tanais and the lands beyond the Tanais—Bactria, Hyrcania, and the Hyrcanian Sea; if we drove the Scythians all the way to the desert; and if, in addition, the River Indus flows through our realm, as well as the Hydaspes, Akesinos, and Hydraotes, why do you shrink from adding the Hyphasis and the tribes beyond it to our empire—the empire of the Macedonians? [6] Are you afraid that other barbarians may withstand your attack? But these either come over to our side willingly or, if they attempt to flee, are captured; and those who flee leave us a deserted land, to be handed over to our allies and those who have joined us of their own accord.

[1] "What limit should a man of noble nature put to his labors? I, for one, do not think there is any, so long as those labors lead to noble accomplishments. But if anyone longs to hear when our wars will come to an end, let him know that we are not far from the Ganges and the Eastern Sea,[1a] with which, I promise you, the Hyrcanian Sea will turn out to be joined. For the Great Sea girdles the entire earth.[1b] [2] I will show the Macedonians and their allies that the waters of the Indian[2a] and Persian[2b] gulfs flow together, as the Hyrcanian Sea flows into the Indian Gulf. From the Persian Gulf our fleet will sail around Libya as far as the Pillars of Herakles;[2c] and

---

5.26.1–2
Summer 326
HYPHASIS RIVER
By asserting the connectedness of the seas and the scope of their advances so far, Alexander argues that a universal empire, bordering Ocean in all directions, is within the army's grasp.

5.25.4a For the locations mentioned in 5.25.4–5, unless otherwise noted, see Map 5.25 and its directory.

5.25.4b "Both Phrygias" refers to Phrygia (Map 5.25) and Hellespontine Phrygia (Ref. Map 4).

5.25.4c The Greek region of Libya is called Cyrene.

5.26.1a The reference is to the Pacific Ocean, or perhaps the Bay of Bengal; see Appendix N, §9.

5.26.1b The idea that the Hyrcanian/Caspian Sea was a gulf of the great external Ocean (or Great Sea, as it is called here) had long been accepted by Greek geographers, though it was challenged by Herodotus. Alexander himself felt sufficient doubt over this doctrine that, after his return to Babylon in 324, he planned to send an expedition to explore the Hyrcanian's perimeter (see 7.16.1–3; his death forestalled the plan). In this speech, however, he insists on the interconnectedness of the Hyrcanian Sea and the other waters bounding Asia, as a way of convincing his men that their conquests do indeed have a natural terminus: if they go forward to the Eastern Sea, which Alexander claimed was close at hand, they would have subdued the entire landmass of Asia as defined by the circuit of waters surrounding it (see Appendix N, §3 and Ref. Map 8b).

5.26.2a Indian Gulf: Map 5.25, BY. This name for what we call the Arabian Sea is used only on this occasion. At 5.6.3 Arrian calls the same body of water "the Great Sea" (see Appendix N, §3).

5.26.2b Persian Gulf: Map 5.25, BX.

5.26.2c The Pillars of Herakles are two promontories that sit on either side of what today we call the Strait of Gibraltar. The idea that Alexander contemplated an African campaign, directed principally against Carthage, comes from the tradition of the "Last Plans," discussed in more detail by Arrian at 7.1.1–4. Here that idea is conjoined with another geographic theory: the circumnavigability of Africa. It is a theory disputed by Greek geographers but very congenial to the goal of this speech—that is, the construction of a global empire defined by terminal water boundaries. Whether Alexander would in fact have proposed to his weary and war-worn soldiers the conquest of yet another continent after Asia is very much to be doubted (see Appendix N, §9). The improbability of such an argument supports the view of Bosworth (II.344–345) that this speech reads like a rhetorical set-piece composed by the author rather than words actually spoken by Alexander (see Appendix A, Arrian's Sources and Reliability, §19).

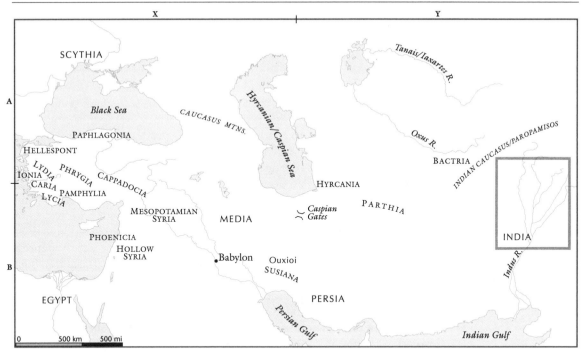

MAP 5.25. ALEXANDER'S EMPIRE AT ITS GREATEST
EXTENT AS DESCRIBED AT 5.25.

All locations appear on the main map unless inset specified.

5.26.3–4
HYPHASIS RIVER
Any enemies left unsubdued
will raise rebellion and force
the army to undertake new
dangers.

5.26.5–6
Summer 326
HYPHASIS RIVER
The example of Herakles
should teach the Macedo-
nians about the rewards of
their labors. Great empires
demand great efforts.

5.26.7–8
HYPHASIS RIVER
Alexander reminds his men
that he fights alongside them
on equal terms, and freely
shares the booty of war with
them. Those who leave now
will forfeit vast riches.

5.27.1–3
HYPHASIS RIVER
After a long silence, Koinos
replies to Alexander, saying
he speaks for the rank and
file who are not present. He
asserts his right to speak
freely given his age, rank,
and record of distinguished
service.

from those Pillars, all of Libya lying inside them becomes ours, and all of Asia, and our empire's boundaries become those that god has set for the earth itself.

[3] "But if we turn back now, many warlike races will be left unconquered between the Hyphasis and the Eastern Sea, and many others northward to the Caspian Sea, and the Scythian tribes not far beyond them. What must be feared is that if we turn back, the tribes we do not now hold securely may be stirred to rebel by those not yet under our control. [4] And then many of our toils will be profitless, or else we shall have to again undertake fresh toils and dangers.

"Only stand fast, Macedonians and allies! For those who labor and face dangers achieve noble deeds, and it is sweet to live bravely and die leaving behind an immortal fame. [5] Or are you unaware that our ancestor,[5a] not content to remain in Tiryns or Argos, or even in the Peloponnese or Thebes, attained such glory that from a man he became, or was thought to become, a god? Even the labors of Dionysos, a more delicate god than Herakles, were not few in number. But we have passed even beyond Nysa,[5b] and the Aornos Rock, which Herakles could not capture, belongs to us. [6] You must add what still remains of Asia to what you have already acquired—a tiny portion to a great tract. After all, what great or noble thing would we ourselves have accomplished, had we sat in Macedonia and thought it sufficient merely to safeguard our own country, by repelling our Thracian neighbors or the Illyrians or Triballoi[6a] or those Greeks who were not our allies—and nothing more?

[7] "Certainly, if I had led you into toils and dangers without incurring these myself, I would understand it if you lost heart before I did, since you would have borne the toils alone and reaped their rewards for others. But as it is, we have shared the toils, and have shared just as much in the dangers, and the prizes are there for us all. [8] The country is yours, and you govern it as satraps. As for treasure, the larger share is already coming to you; and when we have completed the conquest of Asia, then, by Zeus, when I have not merely fulfilled but exceeded your hopes of wealth, I will send home those who wish to return to their own country or will lead them back myself, and make those who remain here the envy of those who depart."

[1] When Alexander had said these and similar words, there was a long silence, as those present did not dare to contradict the king but were unwilling to yield. Meanwhile, Alexander repeatedly urged anyone to speak who wished to, if there was anyone who held an opposing view. Even so, the silence persisted. Then, after a long time, Koinos son of Polemokrates took courage and spoke thus:

"Since you yourself, sire, do not wish to compel the Macedonians to follow you but declare that you will lead them onward only after persuading them, and that, should they persuade you instead, you will not resort to

---

5.26.5a "Our ancestor" means Herakles.
5.26.5b Nysa: location unknown. For more on Nysa, see 5.1.1–5.2.4.

5.26.6a The following appear on Map 1.2: Thrace; Illyrians (Illyrikoi), location of territory, inset; Triballoi, location of territory.

force: I will speak not on behalf of ourselves here present; we have been honored above the rest, and most of us have already received the rewards of our labors, and because of our preeminence, we are eager to satisfy you in everything. Instead I will speak for the mass of the army. [3] But even while speaking on their behalf I will say not what will please them, but what I think most advantageous for you in the present circumstance and what will bring the most security in the future. My age gives me the right to state what I think best without concealment, as does the honor you have accorded me in the eyes of my comrades and the unhesitating boldness I have shown in toils and dangers thus far.

[4] "It is the very greatness of the success achieved by you as leader and by those who set out with you that makes it expedient, in my view, to set some limit to our toils and dangers. For you surely see how many Macedonians and Greeks set out with you and how many of us are left. [5] You sent the Thessalians home from Bactria, perceiving that they were no longer eager for our toils,[5a] and you were right to do so. Of the other Greeks, those who have been settled in the cities you founded do not remain there entirely of their own will;[5b] and both the Macedonian forces and those who have shared our toils and dangers have lost some of their comrades in battle, while others, wounded from past fighting, are strewn across Asia. [6] But most have died of disease, and the few who are left no longer have the bodily vigor they once had, while their spirits have sunk even further. In all of them there is a longing for parents (in those, at any rate, whose parents are still living), a longing for wives and children, and a longing for their homeland,[6a] for which they may be pardoned, since thanks to the honor you have afforded them they will return great men instead of lowly, wealthy instead of poor.

[7] "Do not lead them onward now against their will! For you may find that unwilling combatants will not prove equally formidable in the field. But return, if you wish, to your own country, and when you have seen your mother and settled the Greeks' affairs and brought these many great victories to your father's house, then start afresh with a new expedition, if you like, against those same Indian races who dwell in the east, or to the Black Sea, if you prefer, or against Carthage[7a] and the Libyan tribes who dwell beyond the Carthaginians. [8] These things are for you, as our commander, to decide. Other Macedonians and other Greeks will follow you, young men instead of old, unwearied instead of exhausted, who from inexperience will have no immediate fear of war and will harbor eager hopes for the future.[8a] And they will follow you the more eagerly when they see your

5.27.4–6
HYPHASIS RIVER
Koinos reminds Alexander of how many troops have been killed, wounded, or left behind in Asian settlements, and how weary and homesick the others have become.

5.27.7–9
HYPHASIS RIVER
Koinos exhorts Alexander to return to his home base and refresh the army with new recruits. He warns the king not to count on continued success, for the army would be lost if he were to meet with misfortune.

5.27.5a Alexander had sent some of the older Macedonians and the Thessalian volunteers home; see 3.29.5.
5.27.5b Certainly this was true of the Greeks settled in Bactria and Sogdiana, who were about to revolt and head home after hearing false reports of Alexander's death (see the Epilogue, §6).
5.27.6a This appeal to home and family is more rhetoric than reality. By this time the troops who had been in Asia for almost a

decade had become habituated to army life, and most of them had taken Asian wives, with whom they had had children, during the campaign. In the years after Alexander's death few of these long-term veterans showed much desire to return to Europe.
5.27.7a Carthage: Map 7.2, BX.
5.27.8a Koinos' rhetoric here is every bit as artificial and ill-fitting as Alexander's above. Both king and officer knew well that the army's long experience of battle was its greatest asset.

FIGURE 5.27. Detail of a painted frieze from a Macedonian tomb, discovered in 1994 at Aghios Athanasios, near Thessalonica. This frieze gives us one of our clearest images of how Alexander's troops were dressed and equipped. As depicted here, they wear the standard military cloak, known as a *chlamys*, and either the brimmed *kausia* hat or an elaborately plumed helmet. Though armed, they maintain relaxed poses; they are standing beside a banquet (not shown). The date of the painting has yet to be determined, but it may be nearly contemporary with Alexander.

5.28.1–5
HYPHASIS RIVER
Seeing his officers cheer Koinos' speech, Alexander threatens to go on anyway and to leave the unwilling behind. But after withdrawing to his tent for three days and sensing no change of heart within his army, Alexander claims to find the omens unfavorable for further advances and proclaims an end to the march.

former comrades-in-arms returned to their settlements, wealthy now instead of poor, famous instead of obscure.

"Finally, sire, nothing is so honorable as self-restraint in the midst of good fortune. For while you are in command of such an army we have nothing to fear from our enemies, but it is not in men's power to anticipate and thereby guard against what comes from god."

[1] By the time Koinos had finished speaking, his hearers were in an uproar. Many even shed tears, making it plainer still that they had no heart for further dangers and would be glad to turn back. Vexed at Koinos' frankness and at the timidity of his other officers, Alexander broke up the assembly. [2] The next day, he called the same men together and angrily declared that he himself would go on, but would force no Macedonian to accompany him, and that he would have men who followed their king willingly. Those who wished to return home were free to depart, he said, and to tell their families that they had returned after deserting their king among his enemies. [3] So saying, he went back to his tent and did not allow any of the Companions to enter, on that day or for the next two days, as he was waiting to see whether some change of heart, such as often occurs in a mass

of soldiers, would move the Macedonians and allies and make them readier
to obey. [4] A great silence now fell on the camp. Yet the men, though
clearly grieved by Alexander's anger, were not swayed by it. According to
Ptolemy, Alexander continued to perform sacrifices for the crossing, but the
omens were not favorable. [5] Then, as everything seemed to favor retreat,
he assembled his senior Companions and those closest to him and
announced to the army that he had decided to turn back.

[1] The soldiers sent up a shout of the kind a motley crowd would send
up in its joy, and most of the men shed tears. Some even approached the
royal tent and called down many blessings on Alexander because he had
consented to be conquered by them alone. Alexander then divided the
army into units and ordered the men to build twelve altars, equal in height
to the largest siege towers and even wider than such towers, as offerings in
thanks to the gods who had brought him so far as a conqueror and as
memorials of his labors.[1a] [2] When the altars had been built, he performed

5.29.1–2
Summer 326
HYPHASIS RIVER–
AKESINOS RIVER
The army rejoices at news
of the turn, and Alexander
sets them to work building
twelve giant altars to mark
his farthest progress. The
"good" Poros is left as vassal
ruler of the easternmost
territories.

5.29.1a The location of these altars, if they indeed
existed, has never been found. Other
sources report that Alexander also ordered
the building of enormous stables and

bunk-houses, so that any invaders coming
from the east would think the empire was
inhabited by giants.

5.29.3

AKESINOS RIVER

Alexander finds that a city he had ordered built by Hephaistion is now complete and ready for settlement.

5.29.4–5

NIKAIA-BOUKEPHALA

Alexander receives gifts from Arsakes and Abisares, and confirms Abisares as vassal ruler of his own former territory. He recrosses the Hydaspes River and makes repairs to his two foundations there.

sacrifices on them in the customary manner and held a competition in athletics and horsemanship. He gave the territory as far as the Hyphasis to Poros to govern, and he himself turned back toward the Hydraotes; after crossing that river, he proceeded to the Akesinos.[2a] [3] There he found that the city he had ordered Hephaistion to fortify[3a] was completely built. Peopling it with all the neighboring tribesmen who volunteered to settle there and the mercenaries who were unfit for battle, he made ready for his voyage to the Great Sea.[3b]

[4] At that point, Arsakes, the governor of the country bordering that of Abisares, visited Alexander along with Abisares' brother and other relatives, bringing gifts of the kind the Indians especially prize and some thirty elephants from Abisares (illness prevented Abisares from coming himself).[4a] In the course of their visit, the envoys arrived whom Alexander had sent to Abisares. [5] As Alexander had no difficulty crediting their report, he appointed Abisares as satrap of his own country and assigned Arsakes to Abisares' realm. Having fixed the taxes they were to pay,[5a] he again sacrificed at the Akesinos. Recrossing the river, he reached the Hydaspes, where he set the army to work repairing the damage caused by rains in the cities of Nikaia and Boukephala[5b] and put all the country's other affairs in order.

5.29.2a   Hyphasis, Hydraotes, Akesinos rivers: Map 5.25, inset.

5.29.3a   Arrian has made no record earlier of Alexander ordering Hephaistion to build this city, nor do our other sources mention it.

5.29.3b   The "voyage to the Great Sea" means the voyage down the Indus to its mouth, where the river enters waters that Alexander thought of as part of the world-encircling Ocean or Great Sea (see Appendix N, §2). Arrian leaves unstated the motives for the journey: to further subdue conquered India, to explore new

waterways and routes of navigation, and to give his rebellious army a surrogate labor in place of the stymied advance to the east.

5.29.4a   Abisares had been summoned some weeks before this to appear in person before Alexander as a demonstration of goodwill (see 5.20.6).

5.29.5a   This is one of the few times Arrian refers explicitly to tribute assessments on the Indians. Alexander probably made many of these.

5.29.5b   Hydaspes River; Nikaia; Boukephala: Map 5.25, inset.

BOOK SIX

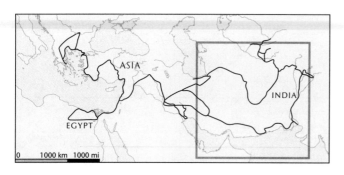

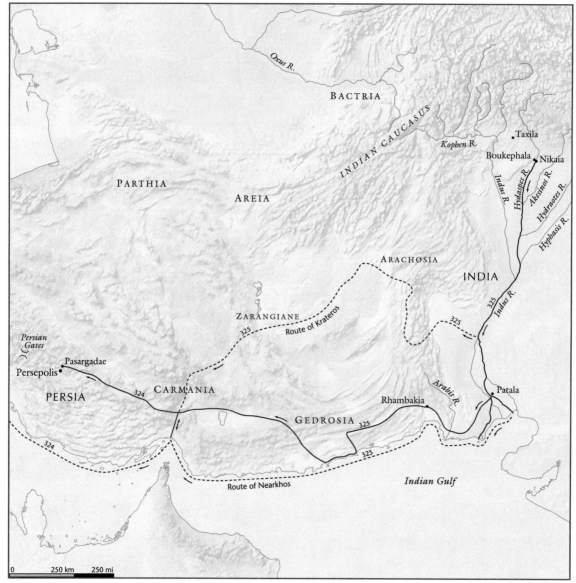

BOOK SIX: THE INDIAN CAMPAIGN (II) AND THE RETURN FROM THE EAST

Now that many thirty-oared ships and ships with one and a half banks of oars had been prepared for Alexander at the banks of the Hydaspes,[1a] along with many horse transports and all the other vessels used for conveying an army by river, Alexander decided to sail down the Hydaspes to the Great Sea.[1b] [2] As he had previously seen crocodiles in the Indus (the only river in which they are found except the Nile) and beans growing near the banks of the Akesinos[2a] of the kind the land of Egypt produces, and as he had heard that the Akesinos empties into the Indus, Alexander imagined he had discovered the sources of the Nile:[2b] [3] he supposed that the Nile, arising from somewhere in India,[3a] flowed through a vast desert where it lost the name Indus; that thereafter, when it began to flow through inhabited territory, it was called either the Nile, by the local Ethiopians[3b] and Egyptians, or Aegyptus, the name it was given by Homer, who named it after the country through which it flowed; and that it then emptied into the Inner Sea.[3c] [4] When writing to Olympias about

6.1.1–6
Autumn 326
NIKAIA-BOUKEPHALA
Alexander prepares to sail down the Hydaspes and the Indus to the Indian Ocean, using his newly constructed fleet. He assumes a connection between the Indus and the Nile on the basis of their shared flora and fauna, but later realizes his error.

NOTE: Most locations in the text not identified by a footnote can be found in the Reference Maps section.

6.1.1a Hydaspes River: Map 6.11, inset.

6.1.1b Arrian does not often use a separate name for the body of water into which the Indus River flows (what we call the Arabian Sea, an arm of the Indian Ocean), but at 5.25.2 he has Alexander refer to it as the Indian Gulf (see Map 6.11).

6.1.2a Indus and Akesinos (Arrian's spelling is Akesines) rivers: Map 6.11, inset.

6.1.2b Egypt; Nile River: Map 6.11.

6.1.3a India: Map 6.11 and inset.

6.1.3b Ethiopia: Map 6.11.

6.1.3c By the term Inner Sea, Arrian signifies the Mediterranean Sea (Map 6.11). The idea of a connection between the Indus and Nile rivers may seem to modern readers inherently untenable, but it should be recalled that the Greek geographers had no clear sense of where, or whether, Africa and Asia were divided (see Appen-

dix N, Alexander's Geographic Notions, §7, and Ref. Map 8a), and had long been at an impasse in their search for the source of the Nile. Moreover, Alexander, as seen at 5.26, had a strong interest in understanding how the waterways of his new empire were connected so that its many parts would be more accessible to travel and military expeditions. His imagination must have been stirred by the possibility that he had simultaneously solved one of science's most perplexing riddles—the source of the Nile—and stumbled upon a quick and easy route homeward from farthest India to the Mediterranean. Indeed, his journey down the Indus (described in this book), and his decision to take his army westward along a coastal rather than an inland route, can be largely explained by his desire to find a new maritime link between India and the imperial heartland, once the promise of a Nile–Indus connection had vanished.

India,[4a] Alexander mentioned, among other things, that he thought he had found the source of the Nile, basing conjectures about momentous matters on slim and trivial evidence. [5] But when he inquired about the Indus in greater detail, he learned from the inhabitants that the Hydaspes unites with the Akesinos, the Akesinos with the Indus, whereupon the two earlier rivers give up their name; that the Indus, being double-mouthed, then empties into the Great Sea; and that it has no connection at all with Egypt. At that point, Alexander struck out what he had written about the Nile in the letter to his mother. [6] Since he intended to sail down the rivers to the Great Sea, he ordered the preparation of ships for that purpose. The ships were manned by the Phoenicians, Cyprians, Carians,[6a] and Egyptians who were accompanying the army.[6b]

[1] Here Koinos, who was among the most trusted of Alexander's Companions,[1a] died of disease.[1b] To the degree circumstances permitted, Alexander gave him a splendid funeral.

After assembling the Companions and all the Indian envoys who had approached him, Alexander appointed Poros king of all the Indian territory captured thus far:[1c] all seven tribes and their cities, which numbered more than two thousand.

[2] He divided the army as follows. Under his own command he embarked all the shield-bearers,[2a] the archers, the Agrianians,[2b] and the cavalry *agema*.[2c] Krateros led a division of the infantry and cavalry along the right bank of the Hydaspes; Hephaistion advanced on the other bank in command of the largest and strongest division of the army and the elephants, which now numbered nearly two hundred. These forces had been ordered to advance as swiftly as they could to the capital ruled by Sopeithes.[2d] [3] Philip, the satrap[3a] of the territory that extended beyond the Indus toward

6.1.4a Throughout his campaign (see also 7.12.5–7), Alexander evidently kept up a warm and active correspondence with his mother, Olympias, who had by this time returned to her native Molossia. Two letters purporting to contain Alexander's descriptions of India, one addressed to Olympias and the other to Aristotle, have been preserved in some versions of the *Alexander Romance*, but their contents are fantastic and they are almost certainly not authentic.

6.1.6a Phoenicia; Cyprus; Caria; Map 6.11.

6.1.6b Arrian's language here seems to imply that Alexander had brought naval crews with him into India, perhaps anticipating that he would eventually reach Ocean by marching eastward.

6.2.1a The Companions were the intimates who were invited to dine and drink with Alexander, share his counsels, and fight beside him in the Companion cavalry. See Appendix E, Alexander's Inner Circle, §4.

6.2.1b The death of Koinos, coming so soon after his prominent role in the mutiny at the Hyphasis River (5.27–5.28), has aroused suspicions of foul play (see, for example, Bosworth II.355), but these remain mere speculation.

6.2.1c "Indian territory" here must mean lands east of the Indus. Those to the west were under the control of the satrap named Philip, as related at 6.2.3.

6.2.2a The shield-bearers (*hypaspists*) were an elite corps of specially equipped infantry; see Appendix D, Alexander's Army and Military Leadership, §3.

6.2.2b The term Agrianians, as used by Arrian, usually refers to a light infantry division recruited from a Balkan region known as Agriania, northeast of Macedonia.

6.2.2c The term *agema* has been used earlier by Arrian to refer to an elite infantry squadron; here it designates cavalry. In both cases the units involved were assigned to fight in close proximity to the king.

6.2.2d Sopeithes is mentioned only here by Arrian. He was presumably a local ruler who had promised to receive Alexander's army amicably.

6.2.3a The satraps, roughly two dozen in number, were appointed by the Persian king to administer the satrapies, or provinces, of the empire, collect taxes, and organize defense. For the locations of all Persian satrapies mentioned by Arrian, see Ref. Map 1.

Bactria,[3b] had been ordered to follow with his own troops after an interval of three days. Alexander sent the Nysaian horsemen back to Nysa.[3c] Nearkhos led the entire fleet on Alexander's behalf; the pilot of Alexander's own ship was Onesikritos, who falsely claimed, in the history he wrote about Alexander, that he was the ship's captain, though he was actually the pilot.[3d] [4] According to Ptolemy, whom I principally follow, the fleet included nearly eighty thirty-oared ships; the total number of vessels, including the horse transports, the light vessels, and all the other river vessels (both those that had long been in service on the rivers and those newly built) fell a few short of two thousand.[4a]

[1] When all his preparations were complete, the army boarded the ships at dawn, and Alexander sacrificed to the gods according to his custom and to the River Hydaspes as prescribed by the seers. After boarding his ship, he stood at the bow and poured a libation from a golden cup into the river, invoking both the Akesinos and the Hydaspes, as he had learned that the Akesinos, the largest of all the other rivers, joined the Hydaspes at a point not far away; he also invoked the Indus, into which the Akesinos empties with the Hydaspes. [2] After pouring a libation to Herakles,[2a] his ancestor, and to Ammon[2b] and all the other gods to whom he customarily sacrificed, he gave orders for the trumpet to sound the signal for setting sail. When the signal was given, the fleet set sail in proper order. For instructions had been issued with regard to the distances that were to be maintained between the horse transports, the warships, and the vessels transporting naval gear, so they would not sail downstream in random order and collide with one another. Even the swift-sailing vessels were not permitted to sail ahead out of formation.

[3] The din caused by the rowing resembled nothing heard before, arising as it did from so many ships advancing under oar at the same time. A roar of voices also arose from the signalmen calling out "stroke, pause" and from the rowers whenever they plunged together through the swells and sent up a shout. The riverbanks, which in many places were higher than the ships, confined the shout in a narrow space where its volume greatly increased, and reflected it back and forth between them, while empty glades here and there on either side of the river re-echoed the sound and helped to swell it. [4] Meanwhile the horses, visible on the horse transports, astonished the barbarian onlookers, since horses had never before been seen on ships in India. (There was no memory of Dionysos' campaign against the Indians'[4a] having included a fleet.) Therefore, the Indians who were present

6.3.1–2
NIKAIA-BOUKEPHALA
With sacrifices to the gods and flourishes of trumpets, the fleet sets off down the Hydaspes.

6.3.3–5
HYDASPES RIVER
The noise raised by the huge fleet, echoing through the steep riverbanks and deserted glades, astonishes the Indian onlookers, as does the spectacle, unknown in their lands, of horses being carried on ships.

6.2.3b   Bactria: Map 6.11.
6.2.3c   Nysa: location unknown. For the Nysaian horsemen, see 5.2.2–4.
6.2.3d   Nearkhos and Onesikritos, Greek seamen who played important parts in Alexander's fleet, seem to have had a very contentious relationship (see 7.20.9–10). Both later wrote accounts of the expedition highlighting their own roles. On Nearkhos, see Appendix E, §11.
6.2.4a   This figure doubles what is claimed by other sources and is also hard to reconcile with the report Arrian himself gives in his *Indika*

(19.7) that there were eight hundred ships in Nearkhos' Indian Ocean fleet.
6.3.2a   The dynasty to which Alexander belonged traced its descent to the god Herakles and thus ultimately to Zeus.
6.3.2b   Ammon was commonly identified with Zeus by the Greeks. On Alexander's relationship to Ammon, see Appendix C, Alexander the Man (and God?), §16.
6.3.4a   See 5.1.1–2 and n. 5.1.1c for the idea that Dionysos had conquered India before Alexander.

when the fleet got under way ran alongside it for a great distance. [5] And other Indians allied with Alexander, when the roar of the oarsmen and the noise of the rowing reached their ears, ran down to the bank and followed alongside the fleet, chanting in their barbarian manner. (The Indians have been extraordinarily devoted to song and dance ever since the days of Dionysos and those who celebrated his mysteries in India.)

6.4.1–3
Winter 326/5
HYDASPES RIVER
Alexander's fleet moves down the Hydaspes, making contact with the land army at prearranged points. A new campaign looms as Alexander learns that two powerful nations to the south, the Malloi and the Oxydrakai, are preparing to resist his advance.

[1] Voyaging in this way, Alexander landed, on the third day, at the point where Hephaistion and Krateros had been ordered to make camp on opposite banks of the river. He waited there for two days, and when Philip reached him with the rest of the army,[1a] Alexander sent him ahead with his forces to the River Akesinos[1b] with orders to advance along the river's bank. He again sent off the forces with Krateros and Hephaistion after instructing them about their route. [2] He himself sailed down the Hydaspes,[2a] whose width on the downstream voyage was never narrower than two and a half miles. Anchoring at the banks wherever he chanced to put in, he would make terms with the local Indians if they surrendered to him; any who ventured to resist he subdued by force. [3] He then hastened to the land of the Malloi and the Oxydrakai,[3a] as he had learned that they were the most populous and warlike of the Indian tribes in the region, and he had received word that they had sent away their wives and children to the strongest of their cities and intended to meet him in battle. He quickened his pace in order to catch them off guard and in disarray when their preparations were not yet complete.

6.4.4–5
HYDASPES AND AKESINOS
RIVERS
At the juncture of the Hydaspes and the Akesinos, rough, noisy rapids cause the crews to become confused and stop rowing.

[4] Setting out again, on the fifth day he reached the juncture of the Hydaspes and the Akesinos. From the juncture of these two rivers one quite narrow river[4a] emerges, and because it is so narrow, its current is swift, and incredible whirlpools arise where the stream eddies back on itself; the water billows and forms enormous swells, so that even from a distance one can hear the roar of the rapids. [5] Alexander had been told of this by the natives and had in turn informed the army. But all the same, when his men drew near the juncture, the sound of the river was so loud that the sailors stopped rowing, not by order but because the signalmen were struck dumb with amazement and the sailors themselves were perturbed by the sound.

6.5.1–3
AKESINOS RIVER
The violent currents play havoc with the fleet, spinning the lighter boats around in circles and causing grave damage to the heavier ones.

[1] When they were not far from the juncture, the helmsmen ordered the crews to row as hard as possible to get past the narrows, so that the ships would not plunge into the eddies and be capsized but would overcome the force of the backwash with their rowing. [2] All the merchant-ships that were spun around by the current suffered no harm from the spinning, though it terrified the sailors; the vessels were set straight and kept on course by the current itself. The warships, however, did not leave the

6.4.1a Philip had been requested to bring troops from the region west of the Indus and follow in Alexander's rear (6.2.3). Evidently Alexander was anticipating a hard fight down the Indus, for which greater numbers would be required.
6.4.1b Akesinos River, Map 6.11, inset.
6.4.2a Hydaspes River: Map 6.11, inset.
6.4.3a Malloi; Oxydrakai, location of territories:

Map 6.11, inset. Since the Greeks and Macedonians were vague as to the distinctions between the Oxydrakai and the Malloi, and since the rivers of the Indus valley have changed course over the centuries, it is difficult to locate these groups on a map.
6.4.4a The single river that emerges from the junction of the Hydaspes and Akesinos retains the name Akesinos; see 6.14.5.

whirlpool unscathed, as they did not ride as high over the turbid waves and the vessels with two banks of oars were unable to keep their lower oars above water. [3] When these boats came broadside to the eddies, the oars that were caught in the water and not raised up in time were broken off. Thus many of the ships were in distress, and two of them fell foul of each other, so that the ships themselves were destroyed and many of those on board drowned.

When the river widened, the current was no longer so difficult and the eddies did not whirl the ships around with the same force. [4] Bringing the fleet to anchor near the right bank where there was a shelter from the current, a landing place, and a promontory that jutted out into the river, a spot useful for collecting wrecked ships and any survivors clinging to them, as Alexander now did. After having the damaged ships repaired, he ordered Nearkhos to sail downstream as far as the Malloi's frontier, while he himself conducted a raid on the territory of the barbarians who were not submitting to him, and thus prevented them from aiding the Malloi. He then rejoined the fleet.

[5] Now Hephaistion, Krateros, Philip, and their forces were once again with Alexander. Transporting the elephants across the Hydaspes[5a] along with Polyperkhon's battalion, the mounted bowmen, and Philip and his army, Alexander appointed Krateros to lead them; he sent Nearkhos with the fleet, ordering him to keep three days ahead of the army. [6] Dividing the rest of the army into three parts, he ordered Hephaistion to keep five days ahead of him, so that if men fleeing his own troops hastened forward, they would come upon Hephaistion's men and be captured; similarly, giving Ptolemy son of Lagos a division of the army, Alexander ordered him to follow behind at a three-day interval so that any who turned back to avoid Alexander would encounter Ptolemy and his troops. [7] Those sent ahead to the juncture of the Akesinos and the Hydraotes[7a] were ordered to wait there until Alexander had arrived and the forces with Krateros and Ptolemy had joined him.

[1] Taking the shield-bearers, the archers, the Agrianians, Peithon's[1a] battalion of the so-called *asthetairoi*,[1b] all the mounted bowmen, and half the Companion cavalry, Alexander marched across a waterless region against the Malloi, one of the autonomous Indian tribes. [2] On the first day, he encamped near a meager water source roughly twelve miles from the River Akesinos. After giving the army a little time to dine and rest, he gave orders for every pail or pitcher anyone owned to be filled with water. Marching for the remainder of the day and throughout the night and covering about fifty miles,[2a] at daybreak he reached a city where many of the

6.5.4
AKESINOS RIVER
At a calmer spot, Alexander collects his damaged ships and has them repaired. He leads a raid on a nearby tribe suspected of aiding the resistance and sends Nearkhos on ahead.

6.5.5–7
AKESINOS RIVER
The land army is divided into three divisions so as to mop up as many escaping members of the resistance as possible. The three parts are ordered to rejoin forces at the juncture of the Akesinos and the Hydraotes.

6.6.1–3
MALLOI TERRITORY
Leading some of his fittest and most mobile units, Alexander makes a rapid night march through a desert in order to take the Malloi by surprise. He arrives at dawn outside their city and slaughters many who have not had time to arm or take cover; the rest are besieged within the walls.

6.5.5a Arrian's text here does not make sense, since the army had already left the Hydaspes behind and were journeying down the Akesinos. It is possible that in compiling his sources he has gotten this passage out of its proper order and that it belongs with the events of 6.4.1; or he may have written "Hydaspes" instead of "Akesinos."
6.5.7a Hydraotes River: Map 6.11, inset.
6.6.1a This is Arrian's first mention of Peithon son of Agenor, who would go on to play a large

role in the Indian campaign. He should be distinguished from Peithon son of Krateuas (first mentioned at 6.28.4), who became a principal rival for power after Alexander's death; see the Epilogue, §6.
6.6.1b *Asthetairoi*: very little is known about the composition of this elite unit.
6.6.2a Either the distance has been exaggerated here or the time lapse reduced. Fifty miles was a possible march for Alexander's army in two days and a night, not one.

Malloi had taken refuge. [3] Never imagining that Alexander would approach them across the desert, most of them were outside the city and unarmed; and it became obvious why Alexander had taken that route—namely, because the road that was hard for him to travel was the road his enemies never believed he would take.[3a] He fell on these men unexpectedly, and as they were unarmed and offered no resistance, he killed many of them;[3b] when the rest took refuge inside the city, he posted horsemen around the wall in a circle. (Since his infantry phalanx[3c] had not yet caught up with him, he used the cavalry in place of a palisade.)

[4] As soon as the infantry arrived, he sent Perdikkas, along with his own and Kleitos' hipparchies[4a] and the Agrianians, to another Mallian city where many of the local Indians had taken refuge, with orders to keep watch over the inhabitants but not to engage in an action until he arrived; he was not to let anyone escape from that city and carry word to the other barbarians that Alexander was approaching. He himself now assaulted the walls;[4b] [5] but the barbarians abandoned these, in the belief that they could no longer defend them after so many had died in the first assault or been sidelined by their wounds. Instead they fled to the citadel, and for a time they defended themselves from the higher ground, a position hard to assail. But when the Macedonians attacked them stoutly from all sides, and Alexander himself appeared now here, now there in the thick of the fight, this citadel was taken by storm, and all who had fled there for refuge, nearly two thousand, were killed.

[6] As for Perdikkas, when he reached the city to which he had been sent, he found it deserted. On learning that its inhabitants had fled only recently, he marched on the double in their track. The light-armed troops accompanied him as fast as they could. When he caught up with the fugitives, he killed everyone except those who escaped into the marshes.

[1] After giving his men time to dine and rest, Alexander marched onward at the first watch. Covering a great distance overnight, he reached the Hydraotes at daybreak. There he learned that many of the Malloi had already crossed the river. Coming upon others who were even then making their way across, he slaughtered many of them, [2] and lost no time crossing at the

Margin notes

6.6.4–5
Winter 326/5
MALLOI TERRITORY
Perdikkas is sent to guard a nearby Malloi city to prevent word of Alexander's approach from spreading. Meanwhile, Alexander assaults the undefended walls; they are captured, and the Malloi within are killed en masse as they flee.

6.6.6
MALLOI TERRITORY
Perdikkas arrives too late to prevent the neighboring Malloi from fleeing, but he kills many of the refugees.

6.7.1–3
HYDRAOTES RIVER
Alexander attacks another body of Malloi troops at the Hydraotes, and sends Peithon to capture those who escape his onslaught.

Footnotes

6.6.3a Alexander's most potent and reliable weapon was the psychological damage he inflicted by showing up where his enemies least expected him; see Appendix D, §15.

6.6.3b This is one of many episodes in the Indian campaign that have been characterized by Alexander's critics as terrorism. The wanton slaughter of unarmed and fleeing Malloi, most of them noncombatants, does seem to have been part of a strategy of deliberate and calculated cruelty.

6.6.3c Phalanx: the heavy infantry. Normal phalanx depth was eight men, but it could be increased to sixteen or thirty-two upon command.

6.6.4a Alexander began dividing the Companion cavalry into hipparchies well before this, to prevent any single commander from having too much power (see 3.29.7 and

n. 3.29.7a). Apparently the number of such subdivisions multiplied over time. Arrian speaks of three hipparchies, comprising only a portion of the Companion cavalry, and in the passage above there appear to be at least that many if not more. The total number may have gone as high as ten.

6.6.4b That is, the walls of the refugee stronghold, the same city Alexander had attacked the previous day. Arrian specifies that "Alexander himself" led the assault, the first of many indications that by this time the Macedonian troops, weary and impatient to leave India, were not advancing willingly, even when ordered forward by the king. Alexander threw himself into the vanguard so as to embarrass any troops who were hanging back. See also 6.7.4–6, 6.9.3.

same spot and pursuing the Malloi who had gotten a head start on him. He killed many of them and took others prisoner, but the majority escaped to a well-fortified position. When his infantry caught up to him, Alexander sent Peithon and his battalion after the fugitives with two hipparchies of cavalry; [3] this detachment captured the place at the first attempt and enslaved any of the Malloi who had not perished in the initial assault and had escaped to it. Their mission accomplished, Peithon and his men returned to the camp.

[4] Alexander himself led his forces against a city of the Brahmans,[4a] having learned that some of the Malloi had fled there as well. Approaching the city, he led the phalanx in close formation up to the wall on all sides. When the inhabitants saw their walls undermined and were themselves driven back by arrows and stones, they too abandoned their walls, took refuge in their citadel, and ventured to defend themselves. When a few of the Macedonians rushed in on them, the inhabitants, wheeling about in a mass, drove some of the attackers out and killed about twenty-five who were retiring. [5] Alexander then ordered his men to place scaling ladders all around the citadel and to undermine its wall. And when an undermined tower fell and a breach in the curtain wall made the citadel more vulnerable, Alexander, climbing up first, was seen in possession of the wall. [6] The other Macedonians, catching sight of him, were ashamed, and ascended the wall at various points. By then the citadel was in their hands. As for the Indians, some of them set fire to their houses, were caught in them, and perished, but most of them died fighting. Nearly five thousand died in all, and few were taken alive owing to the courage of those who fought.

[1] After remaining there for one day, Alexander advanced the next day against the other Malloi. He found their cities abandoned and learned that the inhabitants had fled to the desert. [2] He then gave the army a day's rest and on the following day sent Peithon and Demetrios, the cavalry commander, back to the river with the forces under their command, along with as many light-armed troops as their task required. [3] He ordered them to march along the river's bank; and if they found Malloi who had escaped into the many wooded areas near the bank, they were to kill any who did not surrender voluntarily. The troops with Peithon and Demetrios did indeed find many in the woods and killed them.

[4] Alexander himself marched to the largest city of the Malloi, as he had learned that many Malloi from other cities had sought refuge there. But even that city had been abandoned by the Indians when they learned that Alexander was approaching. Having crossed the Hydraotes and stationed themselves

6.7.4–6
MALLOI TERRITORY
Alexander attacks a city inhabited by Brahman holy men. The walls are again undefended and the inhabitants flee to high ground. When Alexander personally leads an ascent of the wall, the city is taken and many Indians are killed.

6.8.1–3
MALLOI TERRITORY
Peithon and Demetrios are sent out to kill anyone who does not surrender.

6.8.4–5
HYDRAOTES RIVER
Attacking a Malloi city said to have become the base of an enemy army, Alexander again finds it deserted and sets off in pursuit of the forces that left it.

6.7.4a   Arrian's conception of these Brahmans is rather fuzzy. In the current passage he seems to think of them as a tribe; at 6.16.5 he comes closer to the truth by calling them "the wise men [*sophistai*] of India," though he also uses the same term at 7.1.5 to describe the students and ascetics whom Alexander encountered at Taxila. In fact the Vedic religious order known as Brahmans or Brahmins included two subgroups, one that believed in renunciation of temporal life and material goods, and another that took an active part in politics and even warfare. In his *Indika* Arrian thought more carefully about such distinctions (see 11–12), but in the *Anabasis* he blurred them. At 7.2.2 he speaks of "the Indian sages who go naked," perhaps in an effort to distinguish the ascetic Brahmans from the politically active group he here calls by that name. See Appendix J, The Indian Campaign, §10–11.

6.8.6–7
Winter 326/5
HYDRAOTES RIVER
Fifty thousand enemy troops
await him at the Hydraotes.
They repel a cavalry attack,
but when the infantry arrives,
they flee to a neighboring
stronghold.

6.8.8
MALLOI TERRITORY
Alexander puts a cordon
around this new enemy
position and rests his army
for the night.

6.9.1–3
MALLOI TERRITORY
Alexander's division bursts
through the outer walls and
forces the Malloi into their
citadel. As his men put
ladders into position for an
assault on this stronghold,
Alexander, impatient with
their slow efforts, grabs a
ladder and ascends it himself,
followed by Peukestas and
Leonnatos; a fourth man,
Abreas, ascends another
ladder nearby.

along its banks (as these were high), they were waiting to bar Alexander's way. [5] Informed of this, Alexander took all the cavalry he had with him and proceeded to the place on the Hydraotes where the Malloi had reportedly taken up position, leaving orders for the infantry to follow him.

When he reached the river and saw the enemy troops drawn up on the opposite side, he immediately advanced into the water, accompanied only by the cavalry. [6] The Indians, seeing Alexander in the middle of the river, made a hasty retreat from the bank, though they maintained formation as they did so, and Alexander pursued them with his cavalry alone. Once the Indians, who numbered roughly fifty thousand, noticed that only horsemen were pursuing them, they wheeled about and fought fiercely. Alexander saw that their phalanx was drawn up in close formation; and because his own infantry had not yet arrived, he sent his cavalry in a circle around the Indians and made charges here and there, but avoided coming to close quarters. [7] Now the Agrianians arrived, along with the elite units of light-armed troops he normally kept with him and the archers; the infantry phalanx was also seen approaching at no great distance. With all these terrors bearing down on them, the Indians turned and fled headlong to the strongest city in the region, [8] and Alexander, in close pursuit, killed many.

Those who got away from that engagement locked themselves inside the city, and as soon as Alexander reached it he surrounded it with horsemen. When his infantry joined him, he made camp that day around the wall, since only a few hours of daylight remained and his army was exhausted, the foot soldiers by their long march, the horsemen by the constant pursuit of those who were fleeing and, even more, by the fording of the river.

[1] The next day, after dividing the army in two, Alexander led one division up to assault the wall; Perdikkas brought up the other. By then the Indians were no longer willing to meet the Macedonians' attack, but left the city walls and fled together to the citadel. Alexander and his men broke apart a gate and entered the city far in advance of the others. [2] Perdikkas' division came up behind them and scaled the walls with difficulty; only a few of his men carried ladders, for when they saw the walls deserted by the defenders, they imagined that the city had been taken. But when the citadel was seen to be still in enemy hands, with many stationed before it to fight off their attack, some of the Macedonians set about undermining the wall, while others, placing ladders wherever they could, tried to fight their way through to the high ground. [3] Suspecting that the Macedonians bringing the ladders were shirking, Alexander snatched a ladder from one of them, placed it against the wall, and ascended it himself, hunched under his shield. Peukestas climbed up after him, carrying the sacred shield that Alexander had taken from the temple of Athena in Troy and kept with him, the shield that was carried before him in battle.[3a] After Peukestas, Leonnatos the Bodyguard[3b] ascended

6.9.3a   The sacred weapons taken from the temple
of Athena are described at 1.11.7–8.
6.9.3b   Leonnatos was one of the seven Bodyguards, whose duties included protecting

the king's person in combat—a job Alexander here makes extremely difficult; see
Appendix E, §4.

by the same ladder, while Abreas, one of the men who received double pay,[3c] ascended by another.

[4] The king was now near the wall's rampart. Propping his shield on it, he thrust some of the Indians back into the city, while slaying others with his sword and thus clearing that part of the wall. The shield-bearers, grown fearful on the king's behalf, hastily forced their way up the same ladder and broke it—so that those ascending fell down and made it impossible for others to climb up. [5] Standing on the wall, Alexander found himself fired at from the towers that stood nearby on all sides (since none of the Indians dared to come near him) and also by men in the citadel who were hurling their javelins from close range, as there happened to be a mound of earth very near the wall at that point. As it was clear to all that this was Alexander, both by the brightness of his arms and by his extraordinary daring, he decided that if he remained where he was, he would be risking his life without performing any noteworthy exploit, whereas if he leaped down inside the wall, he might strike fear into the Indians; and even if this tactic failed, since he had to risk his life in any case, he would die nobly, having performed exploits that merit study by future generations. With these thoughts in mind, he leaped down from the wall into the citadel. [6] Planting himself firmly against the wall, he killed a number of men in hand-to-hand combat, including the Indians' leader, whom he struck with his sword in the midst of a furious attack. As they came on he hit them with stones, now this man, now that one, while anyone who came closer he dispatched with his sword. The barbarians were no longer willing to come near him, but surrounded him on all sides and fired at him with any weapon they happened to have or could grab at the moment.

[1] At that point Peukestas and Abreas, the man who received double pay, and after them Leonnatos, the only men who reached the top of the wall before the ladders broke,[1a] also leaped down to defend the king. Abreas now fell, struck in the face by an arrow, and Alexander himself was also struck, the arrow piercing his breastplate and entering his upper body above the breast; according to Ptolemy, air came hissing out from the wound, along with spurts of blood.[1b] [2] While his blood remained warm, Alexander defended himself, though he was in a bad way; but when a huge rush of blood gushed from the wound along with a hiss of air, he was overcome with vertigo and faintness and collapsed, slumping over his shield. Peukestas, who stood over him when he fell and protected him with the

6.9.4–6
MALLOI TERRITORY
When Alexander's troops try to mount one of the ladders, it breaks, making further ascent impossible. Alexander finds himself alone atop the wall and a target for many enemy archers and spearmen. Reasoning that he might use his perilous situation as a way to win glory, he leaps down inside the walls, fighting off swarms of attackers with sword and stones.

6.10.1–2
MALLOI TERRITORY
Three Macedonians who went with Alexander strive to help him, but Abreas is hit by an arrow. Then Alexander takes an arrow in the lung and, bleeding heavily, loses consciousness. Peukestas and Leonnatos are wounded as they try to protect him.

6.9.3c Arrian's mention of double pay is one of the few references in any of our sources to the pay scale of Macedonian troops. At 7.23.3–4 he describes the rank and pay of Macedonians and Persians in Alexander's new mixed-race army. See also n. 7.23.3b and Appendix F, Money and Finance in the Campaigns of Alexander, §4.

6.10.1a In the previous chapter Arrian recounts the breaking of one ladder. Diodorus (17.98)

specifies that two ladders broke, but different ladders from the one climbed by Alexander, again leaving one ladder available for use by support troops. In neither case are the particulars of the episode very clear.

6.10.1b The hissing air is an unmistakable sign of a punctured lung. See Appendix O, Alexander's Death: A Medical Analysis, §9.

6.10.3–4
Winter 326/5
MALLOI TERRITORY
The Macedonian troops
outside the walls, unable to
see what is taking place in
the citadel, make desperate
efforts to get in to help their
king. A few scale the wall
and rush to aid Alexander.
Finally they succeed in breaking open a gate and entering
en masse.

6.11.1–2
MALLOI TERRITORY
The Macedonians slaughter
the entire population of the
city while tending to Alexander's wound. Various sources
give differing accounts of
who treated him, an example
of the ways historical events
are falsely reported and
recorded.

6.11.3–8
Arrian pauses in his narrative
to set the historical record
straight on various matters:
the site where Alexander was
wounded, the personnel who
aided him when he was
trapped in the rebel town,
and the place where the battle
of Gaugamela was fought.

sacred shield from Troy, and Leonnatos on the other side were both hit as well, and Alexander was almost gone from loss of blood.

[3] By this time the Macedonians' assault was faltering. Those who saw Alexander assailed on the wall and leaping into the citadel were roused by devotion and fear that the king might suffer harm in taking senseless risks. Since their ladders were broken, they improvised various means of scaling the wall, some of them fixing pegs in the earthen rampart and creeping up with difficulty by hanging onto these, others climbing up on one another's shoulders. [4] The first man to scale the wall threw himself down into the city where he saw the king lying, then another and another, with everyone raising a wail and a war cry. A desperate battle was already being fought around Alexander, his men taking turns protecting him with a shield, when some of the Macedonians, having broken the bar with which the gate in the curtain wall was secured, entered the city a few at a time. The rest, leaning their shoulders against the gate where it was ajar and thrusting it inward, threw open the citadel.

[1] At that point some began killing the Indians—slaying them all, including women and children—and others carried the king away on his shield. He was doing poorly, and it was not yet known if he would live. Some have written that Kritodemos, a doctor from Cos,[1a] of the family of the Asklepiads,[1b] made an incision and drew the arrow from the wound. Others have written that no doctor was present in the emergency and so Perdikkas the Bodyguard lanced the wound with his sword at Alexander's urging and extracted the arrow.[1c] [2] The extraction of the arrow was accompanied by a heavy loss of blood, causing Alexander to faint again, and the fainting slowed his blood loss. A great many other versions of this episode have been recorded, and Rumor, having taken up the story and passed it on, preserves even to our day what it heard from those who contrived these lies originally. And it will never cease passing falsehoods on to others, unless it is deterred by this history.

[3] In the first place, it is universally claimed that this calamity befell Alexander among the Oxydrakai, whereas it occurred among the Malloi,[3a] an autonomous Indian tribe. It was a Malloi city, and those who struck Alexander were Malloi who had indeed decided to join forces with the Oxydrakai and fight alongside them. But Alexander, marching against them across the desert region, had reached them before the Oxydrakai could get help to them or they could help the Oxydrakai. [4] It is also universally

6.11.1a Cos (Map 6.11), an island in the eastern Aegean, was famous for the skill of the doctors who trained there.

6.11.1b The Asklepiads were a Greek guild of physicians, partly religious and partly scientific in orientation, who claimed descent from Asklepios, the god of healing and medicine.

6.11.1c Quintus Curtius (9.5.25–29) concurs with the first version, but gives the doctor's name as Critobulus. No other extant

source besides Arrian names Perdikkas as the man who performed the emergency surgery. Plutarch gives a detailed narrative of the scene in which the arrow was extracted from Alexander's chest (*Moralia* 343d and following) that is unfortunately truncated, apparently by the loss of the end of the text, before the identity of the surgeon is revealed.

6.11.3a Oxydrakai; Malloi, location of territories: Map 6.11, inset.

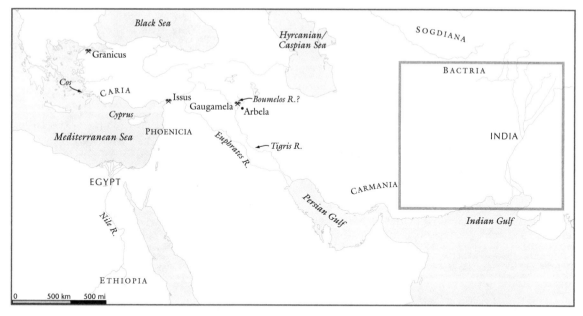

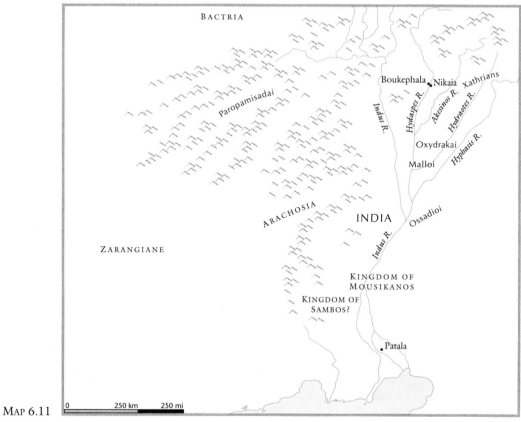

MAP 6.11

247

FIGURE 6.12. This iron cuirass decorated with gold, and once lined with leather, was found in Tomb II of the royal burial complex at Aigeai. Alexander may have worn one much like this when he was struck by an Indian arrow, which had been shot with sufficient force to penetrate his armor.

claimed that the final battle with Darius, in which he fled and did not halt his flight until he was arrested by Bessos' party and died as Alexander was approaching, took place at Arbela, just as the one before it took place at Issus, and the first cavalry battle took place at the Granicus.[4a] [5] But though the cavalry battle did take place at the Granicus and the second battle at Issus, Arbela is far from the place where Darius and Alexander fought their final battle (the largest figure reported for the distance is seventy-five miles; the smallest, sixty-three miles). But Ptolemy and Aristoboulos say that the battle took place at Gaugamela, near the River Boumelos.[5a] [6] Gaugamela was not a city, but a large village; the place was not notable, nor was its name pleasing to the ear. Accordingly, I presume that Arbela, being a city, carried off the glory of the great battle. But if we must accept that a battle fought so far from Arbela actually took place there, then we should also say that the naval battle at Salamis took place at the Isthmus of Corinth, and that the battle at Euboean Artemision took place near Aegina or Sounion.[6a] [7] With regard to the question of who held their shields over Alexander in his peril, everyone agrees that Peukestas was there, but there is still no consensus about Leonnatos or even about Abreas, the man who received double pay. Some say that Alexander, struck on his helmet by a club, grew dizzy and fell, but rose up again only to be struck by an arrow that pierced his breastplate and entered his chest. Ptolemy, however, says that the wound in the chest was the only one Alexander

6.11.4a Arbela; Issus; Granicus River: Map 6.11.
6.11.5a Gaugamela; Boumelos River, possible
          location: Map 6.11.
6.11.6a Arrian cites two famous battles of the
          Persian Wars, both of which were fought at

places much less prominent than the more familiar landmarks nearby, as a way to make his point about the Arbela/Gaugamela confusion.

received. [8] But in my opinion, the most serious lapse on the part of Alexander's historians is this: some writers have reported that Ptolemy son of Lagos climbed up the ladder with Alexander, along with Peukestas, and held the shield over him as he lay there, and that this was why Ptolemy came to be nicknamed Savior.[8a] Ptolemy himself, however, has written that he was not even present at that action, but was leading other troops to fight other battles against other barbarians.

Let the above digression remain on record, so that those in the future may not be careless in their narration of exploits and calamities so momentous.

[1] While Alexander remained there to be treated for his wound, the first report to reach the camp from which he had set out against the Malloi was that he had died of it. At first, as the news passed from one to another, the entire army raised a wail. But when they had ceased wailing, the troops grew disheartened and perplexed as to who would command the army, [2] since a great many officers were held in equal esteem by both Alexander himself and the Macedonians; they had no idea how they would get home safe, surrounded as they were by so many warlike tribes, some of whom had not yet become allies and would be likely to fight fiercely for their freedom, while others would revolt once their fear of Alexander was dispelled. As for the rivers the Macedonians would encounter on their homeward journey, the troops imagined they would be unfordable in that season. Everything seemed insurmountable and impossible if they had lost Alexander. [3] When word came that Alexander was alive, they scarcely believed it, as they doubted he was likely to live. And when a letter arrived from him saying he would soon come down to the camp, most of them in their terror did not think it genuine, but guessed that it had been forged by his Bodyguards and generals.

[1] With this in mind, and with an eye to preventing unrest in the army, Alexander had himself conveyed to the banks of the River Hydraotes[1a] as soon as he was strong enough. He traveled down the river by ship (for the camp lay at the juncture of the Hydraotes and the Akesinos,[1b] where Hephaistion waited with the army and Nearkhos was holding the fleet), and when the ship carrying him drew near the camp, Alexander gave orders for his cloth screen to be removed from the stern so that he might be clearly seen by one and all. [2] The men were still in doubt, thinking it was really Alexander's corpse being conveyed, until the ship touched at the bank and Alexander held up his hand to the multitude. The soldiers sent up a shout, some of them lifting their hands to the sky, others toward Alexander himself; many even wept in spite of themselves at the unhoped-for boon. Some of his shield-bearers brought out a litter to carry him from the ship, but he ordered them to bring him his horse instead. [3] When he was seen

6.12.1–3
Winter 326/5
MALLOI TERRITORY
The army believes that Alexander is dead and becomes disheartened at the prospect of fighting its way home without him.

6.13.1–3
HYDRAOTES RIVER
Alexander reassures his troops by appearing before them and demonstrating his vigor. They are overcome with joy and relief.

6.11.8a Quintus Curtius (9.5.21) places Ptolemy at the scene of Alexander's wounding. Ptolemy's epithet Soter ("savior") was in fact awarded to him by the Rhodians in 304, after he lifted the siege imposed on their city by Demetrios. See the Epilogue, §14.
6.13.1a Hydraotes River: Map 6.11, inset.
6.13.1b Akesinos River: Map 6.11, inset.

once again on horseback, the entire army roared with cheers, and the banks and all the nearby woods echoed with the sound. Nearing his tent he dismounted so as to be seen walking as well. The soldiers approached him from all sides, some touching his hands, others his knees, still others his clothes; some sought only to set eyes on him from close at hand, offer their good wishes, and depart. Some were flinging garlands, others all the many kinds of flowers that India brings forth at that season.

6.13.4–5
Close associates remonstrate with Alexander for being too reckless; Arrian believes he was powerless to stop himself. One anonymous soldier approves Alexander's daring and thereby becomes a favorite of the king.

[4] Nearkhos relates that some of Alexander's friends were severe with him, reproaching him because he put himself in danger out in front of the army; they said this was not the part of a general but of a soldier. I have the impression that Alexander was annoyed by their remarks because he recognized that these were true and that he had deserved his friends' criticism. But Alexander was mastered by passion for battle and lust for glory just as others are mastered by other pleasures, and he lacked the self-control to keep clear of danger. [5] Nearkhos relates that a certain elderly Boeotian (he does not mention the man's name) learned that Alexander was vexed by his friends' reproaches and stern looks. The man approached him and in the Boeotian dialect said, "Alexander, these deeds are the work of men." He also added a line of iambic verse, something to the effect that whoever seeks to achieve something is obliged to suffer.[5a] The man found immediate favor with Alexander and thereafter became his close friend.

6.14.1–3
Winter 326/5
HYDRAOTES RIVER
The Malloi and Oxydrakai surrender to Alexander on fixed terms, explaining their earlier resistance as the result of their long history of fiercely guarded independence.

[1] After this, envoys from the remaining Malloi reached Alexander and surrendered their tribe. The Oxydrakai also sent along their cities' commanders, the heads of their provinces, and 150 of their most distinguished citizens, who had been authorized to make terms with Alexander and were bringing him India's most valuable gifts; these men, too, surrendered their tribe. [2] They said they should be pardoned for having failed to send him an embassy long ago; even more so than other tribes, they longed to keep their freedom and autonomy, which they had enjoyed from the time Dionysos came to India until Alexander's day. But if it seemed best to Alexander—as legend had it that he, too, was descended from a god—they would accept as satrap whomever he appointed and pay whatever tribute he thought fit to impose. They were also ready to provide however many hostages Alexander requested. [3] He asked for a thousand of the tribe's strongest men, whom he would either keep as hostages or press into military service until the wars against the rest of the Indians came to an end. Choosing from among their strongest and most important men, they sent him this thousand; they also sent five hundred chariots and their drivers, though Alexander had not requested them. Alexander appointed Philip[3a] as satrap of these tribesmen and of the Malloi survivors.[3b] He released their hostages[3c] but kept the chariots.

6.13.5a   This is almost certainly a line from a lost tragedy, but the exact play or context is unknown.
6.14.3a   This Philip was previously encountered at 4.24.10 and 5.8.3.
6.14.3b   Malloi, location of territory: Map 6.11, inset. Arrian's casual mention of "Malloi

survivors" is telling; the Macedonian campaign in this region had taken many tens of thousands of lives.
6.14.3c   It is unclear why Alexander first demanded these hostages, then returned them. Perhaps he was merely testing the willingness of the local peoples to comply.

[4] Alexander settled these matters and saw to it, in the delay caused by his wound, that many new vessels were built; he then put seventeen hundred of the Companion cavalry aboard the ships, the same number of light-armed troops as before, and some ten thousand soldiers, and sailed a short way down the Hydraotes. After the Hydraotes joined the Akesinos, he sailed down the Akesinos (since past the juncture the name Akesinos wins out over the other) until he reached its juncture with the Indus.[4a] [5] For these four immense and navigable rivers join their waters in the River Indus, though they do not keep their own names: the Hydaspes empties into the Akesinos, at which point the stream is called the Akesinos; the Akesinos in turn empties into the Hydraotes, though it is still called the Akesinos thereafter; even after receiving the water of the Hyphasis[5a] it keeps its name until it empties into the Indus; but on joining the Indus, the Akesinos yields its name. Thereafter I can well believe that the Indus, until it divides at the delta, is twelve miles wide or perhaps even wider;[5b] along that stretch it is more like a lake than a river.

[1] Alexander waited at the juncture of the Akesinos and the Indus until Perdikkas arrived with his forces, having subdued the Abastanes, an autonomous tribe, along the way. Then new thirty-oared ships reached Alexander, as did merchant vessels that had been built for him in the land of the Xathrians.[1a] Another autonomous Indian tribe, the Sogdoi,[1b] now joined his side. Envoys also approached him from the Ossadians,[1c] also an autonomous Indian tribe, to surrender their people. [2] Alexander fixed the juncture of the Akesinos and the Indus as the boundary of Philip's satrapy and left with him all the Thracians and as many battalions as seemed sufficient to monitor the region. He ordered Philip to build docks at the juncture of the rivers and to found a city there in the expectation that it would be great and renowned.[2a]

[3] It was then that Oxyartes the Bactrian, the father of Rhoxane, Alexander's wife, paid a visit. Alexander appointed him as satrap of the Paropamisadai,[3a] having dismissed Tyriespis, the former satrap, after receiving word that Tyriespis was not conducting affairs in an orderly manner.

[4] Then, having transported Krateros with the greater part of his army and the elephants across to the Indus' left bank—the route along that side seemed easier for a heavily burdened army, and because the neighboring tribes were not invariably friendly—Alexander sailed downstream to the capital of the Sogdoi. There he fortified another city and built other docks, and his damaged vessels were repaired. He appointed

6.14.4–5
Spring 325
HYDRAOTES, AKESINOS, AND
INDUS RIVERS
Alexander resumes his downstream voyage with an augmented fleet. He sails down the Hydraotes to the Akesinos and then to the Indus. Arrian pauses to explain the river system of the Indus valley.

6.15.1–2
AKESINOS AND INDUS RIVERS
More tribes surrender to Alexander. Philip is left in charge of the garrison of the region, with orders to build a new city at the juncture of the Akesinos and the Indus.

6.15.3
INDUS RIVER
Alexander makes Oxyartes satrap of the region.

6.15.4–7
INDUS RIVER
The voyage down the Indus continues. Krateros leads the land army, while Alexander proceeds by ship to the realm of Mousikanos, a local ruler of uncertain loyalty. Mousikanos submits to Alexander after the Macedonians take him by surprise, and Alexander confirms him in his rule over the territory.

6.14.4a Indus River: Map 6.11, inset.
6.14.5a Hydaspes and Hyphasis rivers: Map 6.11, inset.
6.14.5b For another example of Arrian's tendency to exaggerate the width of Indian rivers, see 5.4.2 and n. 5.4.2c.
6.15.1a Xathrians (Xathroi), location of territory: Map 6.11, inset. This volume does not follow the *Barrington Atlas* in equating the Xathrians with the Kathaioi.
6.15.1b Sogdoi: the name of this little-known tribe has been inserted into the text in some editions, based on Alexander's visit to their

capital at 6.15.4; the location of their territory is unknown. Note that the Sogdoi of the Indus valley are a different people from the Sogdians dwelling north of Bactria.
6.15.1c Ossadians (Ossadioi), location of territory: Map 6.11, inset.
6.15.2a If Philip founded this city as ordered, its name has not survived. The *Barrington Atlas* does not show any city at the juncture of the Indus and the Akesinos.
6.15.3a Paropamisadai, location of territory: Map 6.11, inset.

Peithon[4a] as satrap of the territory extending from the juncture of the Indus and the Akesinos to the sea, including the entire Indian seaboard. [5] He again sent Krateros on with the army,[5a] while he himself sailed down to the Kingdom of Mousikanos,[5b] which was reported to be the most prosperous in India.[5c] Mousikanos had not yet met him to surrender himself and his country, nor sent envoys to conclude an alliance, nor even sent gifts suitable for a great king nor requested anything of Alexander. [6] Alexander's voyage down the river was conducted with such speed that he reached the borders of Mousikanos' country before the king was aware that Alexander had set out against him. Taken quite by surprise, Mousikanos quickly presented himself to Alexander, bringing India's most valuable gifts and all his elephants; surrendering himself and his tribe, he acknowledged that he had done wrong, which was actually the surest way, where Alexander was concerned, for anyone to obtain what he wanted. [7] And accordingly Alexander responded to these overtures by pardoning Mousikanos. Alexander then stopped to admire the city and the country, and granted sovereign power to Mousikanos. Krateros was assigned to fortify the citadel. This was done while Alexander was still present, and a garrison was established, since Alexander considered the position suitable for controlling and keeping watch over the neighboring tribes.

[1] From there Alexander took the archers, the Agrianians, and the cavalry that was sailing with him and advanced against a certain Oxikanos,[1a] the chieftain of that region, as the man had neither come to him personally nor sent along envoys to offer the surrender of himself and his country. [2] Attacking as soon as he arrived, Alexander stormed and captured two of the largest cities in Oxikanos' domain; in the second of these, Oxikanos himself was also captured. Alexander gave the plunder to the army, but kept the elephants himself. The other cities in the region surrendered when Alexander approached, with none venturing to resist, so greatly had all the Indians by now, in their own minds, been reduced to servitude, thanks to Alexander and his good fortune.

[3] He then led the army against Sambos, the self-appointed satrap of the mountain Indians. Sambos had reportedly fled when he learned that Mousikanos, his long-standing enemy, had been released by Alexander and was ruling his own country. [4] As Alexander drew near Sindimana, the capital of Sambos' country,[4a] the gates were thrown open to him and Sambos' relatives went out to meet Alexander with their elephants and a tally of their riches. They explained that Sambos had fled not out of hostility to him, but from fear of Mousikanos' release. [5] Alexander then

6.16.1–2
Spring 325
INDUS VALLEY
Alexander moves against another noncompliant local chief, Oxikanos, and takes the man prisoner in a lightning attack.

6.16.3–5
SINDIMANA
Sambos, another local ruler, is reported to have fled his city in fear of his old enemy Mousikanos. Alexander takes over his territory and suppresses a revolt led by Brahman holy men.

6.15.4a   The text reads "Oxyartes and Peithon," but the first name seems to have been introduced in error, perhaps by the copyist rather than Arrian himself. Oxyartes was given a different satrapal post at 6.15.3.

6.15.5a   The text adds "through the land of the Arachosians and Zarangians," but Krateros in fact is sent to these regions at 6.17.3, and the phrase in question seems to have been taken in error from that later passage.

6.15.5b   Kingdom of Mousikanos: Map 6.11, inset.
6.15.5c   India: Map 6.11 and inset.
6.16.1a   Little is known of this chieftain or his location. Diodorus (17.102.5) and Quintus Curtius (9.8.11–13) call him Portikanos; Curtius adds that he ruled a people called the Praesti.
6.16.4a   Kingdom of Sambos, possible location: Map 6.11, inset.

captured another city that had revolted, and killed as many of the Brahmans, who are the wise men among the Indians, as had taken part in the revolt.[5a] (I will discuss the Brahmans' wisdom, if wisdom it is, in my account of India.)[5b]

[1] Then word was received that Mousikanos had revolted. Sending the satrap Peithon son of Agenor against him with an adequate force, Alexander advanced against the cities Mousikanos controlled. He razed some of them to the ground after enslaving their inhabitants; in others he established garrisons and built citadels. After attending to these matters, he returned to the camp and the fleet. [2] Thereafter Mousikanos was arrested and brought to him by Peithon, and Alexander ordered that he be hanged in his own country along with the Brahmans who were responsible for the revolt. Alexander was also approached by the ruler of the land of Patala,[2a] which as I said is the delta formed by the River Indus (and is even larger than the Egyptian delta). The man surrendered himself, his property, and his entire country to Alexander, [3] who sent him back to his own realm to make all necessary preparations for receiving the army.

Alexander then dispatched Krateros to lead the battalions of Attalos, Meleagros, and Antigenes, some of the archers, all the Companions, and other Macedonians who were being sent home as unfit for combat, to Carmania by way of Arachosia and Zarangiane,[3a] and entrusted him with the elephants.[3b] [4] The other land forces, those Alexander had not taken by ship to the coast, were put under the command of Hephaistion, while Peithon was conveyed across the river on Alexander's orders with the mounted javelin men and the Agrianians, to the bank opposite Hephaistion and his army; Alexander ordered him to find settlers for the cities already fortified there and, if any revolt broke out among the local Indians, to restore order and then join him in Patala.

6.17.1–2
INDUS VALLEY
Mousikanos revolts and is captured and executed. His cities are either destroyed or put under garrison occupation, and more Brahman rebels are killed. Another local ruler surrenders, giving Alexander apparent control of the Indus delta.

6.17.3–4
Summer 325
INDUS VALLEY
The army is split into segments. Krateros is to lead many of the heavier units west to Carmania. Peithon and Hephaistion lead land forces on either side of the Indus.

6.16.5a The brutal suppression of this Brahman-led revolt and an earlier massacre of Brahmans at 6.7.4–6 were particularly ugly episodes, since the Brahmans were admired for their wisdom and devotion to religious principles. Plutarch presents a fanciful dialogue between Alexander and the Brahman leaders of "Sabbas'" revolt (as Plutarch calls it), in which the Brahmans outwit Alexander and are pardoned by him (*Parallel Lives*, "Alexander" 64). According to the account of Kleitarkhos used by both Diodorus (17.102.6) and Quintus Curtius (9.8.15), Alexander killed more than 80,000 Indians in the campaign to end Sambos' revolt, but this figure is no doubt exaggerated. See Appendix J, §10–11.

6.16.5b Arrian's *Indika* does not contain an account of the Brahmans that fulfills this promise, though it does contain a brief discussion of Indian sages (11.1–8). Possibly Arrian refers here to a different treatise than the *Indika*, one that he never wrote or that has been lost. Arrian also provides

a brief commentary on the wisdom of the Indian sages at 7.1.5–7.2.4.

6.17.2a Arrian first uses the name Patala at 5.4.1. Here and at 6.17.5 and 6.18.5, he refers to the entire delta of the Indus; elsewhere (6.18.2, 6.20, 6.21.3) he uses the same name for the city at the apex of the delta. Patala: Map 6.11, inset.

6.17.3a The following locations can be found on Map 6.11: Carmania; Arachosia, inset; Zarangiane (Drangiane), inset.

6.17.3b This is one of many points at which Alexander separated himself from Krateros by putting the older general in charge of a column other than his own. It is probably significant in this context that Krateros was seen as the most reactionary member of Alexander's senior staff, ideologically opposed to the king's policies of racial and cultural fusion. Alexander trusted and relied on Krateros but seems not to have liked him much; he never made Krateros a member of his Bodyguard, as he did his other top commanders. See Appendix E, §10.

[5] On the third day of his voyage, Alexander received word that the governor of Patala[5a] had decamped and fled, and that he had taken most of the city's inhabitants with him and left his country deserted. Alexander now sailed against him in even greater haste. When he reached Patala, he found the city and the country deserted by its inhabitants and laborers. [6] He sent the most mobile of his troops to pursue the fugitives; and when some of these were arrested, he sent them ahead to urge the rest to return and not be afraid, as the city was theirs to inhabit as before and the land theirs to work. Many of the city's inhabitants returned.

[1] After ordering Hephaistion to build a citadel in Patala, Alexander sent men to the desert nearby to dig wells and make the country habitable. These men were attacked without warning by some of the neighboring barbarians, who slaughtered a number of them, though when the barbarians lost several of their own men, they fled to the desert. The men who had been sent out accomplished their appointed tasks when Alexander, having learned of the barbarians' attack, sent out an additional force to share their labor.

[2] Near Patala the Indus splits into two large branches, both of which retain the name Indus all the way to the sea. At the juncture Alexander built an anchorage and docks. While this work was advancing, he decided to sail down the right-hand branch of the river to the sea. [3] Giving Leonnatos nearly a thousand horsemen and some eight thousand hoplites[3a] and light-armed troops, Alexander sent him to the island of Patala[3b] with orders to march the army alongside the fleet. Then, taking his swiftest ships, including all those with one and a half banks of oars, all the thirty-oared ships, and some light vessels, Alexander sailed down the right-hand branch of the river; [4] but, as he lacked a guide (since the Indians of the region had fled),[4a] he had a very hard voyage. A storm arose the day after he set sail, and the wind blowing contrary to the current made huge troughs in the river and shook the ships so violently that most were in distress and some of the thirty-oared were completely wrecked. The latter ran aground before being broken to pieces in the water. [5] New ships were built to replace them. Having sent the most mobile of his light-armed troops to the country beyond the bank, Alexander seized some Indians, and these men subsequently served as guides for the voyage. When they reached the place where the river widened (at its broadest it was twenty-five miles wide), a heavy gale from the Outer Sea[5a] fell upon them, and their oars could scarcely be raised in the billows; but the ships sought refuge in a canal to which the guides steered them.

6.17.5a   It is unclear whether this "governor" (*hyparchos*) of Patala is the same man as the "ruler" (*arkhon*) who had offered his submission at 6.17.2. If so, the man's change of allegiance came even more quickly than that of Mousikanos; see 6.15.5–6 and 6.17.1.

6.18.3a   Hoplite: a heavily armed Greek citizen foot soldier, who fought in a phalanx.

6.18.3b   Arrian here calls an island what is more commonly referred to as a delta. The land on which Patala was built was surrounded by water on all sides, with branches of the Indus to the east and west and the sea to the south.

6.18.4a   A telling admission of the costs Alexander had incurred with his forceful tactics.

6.18.5a   The Outer Sea is another name for the Great Sea; see n. 6.1.1b.

[1] When they had anchored there, the Great Sea's ebb tide occurred, which left their ships on dry land. As Alexander's men had not known about the tide in advance, it gave them a great shock at the time, and an even greater shock later on when the water rose and the ships floated.[1a] [2] All the ships that were in the mud when the tide flooded in were raised up unharmed, and, having suffered no damage, resumed sailing; but the ships that were left on drier land and in precarious positions were broken in pieces, either by falling against one another when the tide rushed in or by being dashed to the ground. [3] Alexander repaired these ships as best he could and sent men downstream in two light vessels to inspect the island the natives had told him to anchor at on his seaward voyage; they said it was called Cilluta.[3a] When Alexander received word that there were anchorages at the island and that it was large and had water, he sent a force to occupy it, while he himself advanced beyond it with his best ships to have a look at the river's outlet into the sea and find out whether it would give them an easy route into open water.

[4] Advancing twenty-five miles past the island, they found another island, this one in the open sea.[4a] Returning to the island in the river and anchoring near its tip, Alexander sacrificed to all the gods to whom he said Ammon had instructed him to sacrifice. The next day, he sailed down to the other island (the one in the sea); on landing there he sacrificed again, performing different sacrifices to different gods and in a different manner, claiming that he performed them in accordance with an oracle from Ammon. [5] Having passed beyond the Indus' outlets, he sailed into the ocean, purportedly to see if any land rose up nearby, though it seems to me he mainly wanted to have sailed the Great Sea beyond India.[5a] There he sacrificed bulls to Poseidon and cast them into the sea,[5b] and, after pouring a libation and casting the golden cup and mixing bowls into the sea as an offering of thanks, he prayed to Poseidon to protect the navy he planned to send with Nearkhos to the Persian Gulf and the mouths of the Euphrates and the Tigris.[5c]

6.19.1–3
CILLUTA
The fleet gets a surprise when the oceanic tides of the delta first strand, then float the ships. A reconnaissance mission goes downstream to explore a midriver island described by the guides, and finds it suitable as a naval station.

6.19.4–5
INDIAN OCEAN
Alexander sails out past the Indus' mouth and finds another island. He returns there the next day and makes sacrifice. He then sails into the open ocean and sacrifices again, beseeching Poseidon to safeguard Nearkhos' voyage back to the Persian Gulf.

6.19.1a   Since tidal changes are small in the Mediterranean and Aegean, the European sailors had no experience of this phenomenon.

6.19.3a   Cilluta: location unknown. Arrian later called Cilluta the "island in the river" to distinguish it from the "island in the ocean" (see 6.19.4).

6.19.4a   This island cannot be easily correlated with any modern site, but it has been linked to a small rock outcropping called "the Boat" by local inhabitants (Wood, Michael, *In the Footsteps of Alexander the Great: A Journey from Greece to Asia*, Berkeley: University of California Press, 1997, p. 207).

6.19.5a   Since this "Great Sea" was assumed to be part of Ocean, the primeval and mysterious entity girding the known world, Alexander must have deemed his entry into it a glorious and almost supernatural feat (see Appendix N, §2). There is a rhetorical exercise by the elder Seneca (*Suasoria* 1), a Roman orator, that depicts Alexander's counselors urging him not to attempt to enter Ocean, for fear of the monsters he would find there.

6.19.5b   At 1.11.6, at the start of the Asian campaign, Alexander had similarly sacrificed a bull to mark the crossing of the Hellespont. The repetition of the gesture here seems designed to provide a sense of closure to the campaign and a symmetry between East and West.

6.19.5c   Persian Gulf; Euphrates and Tigris rivers: Map 6.11.

6.20.1–5
Summer 325
PATALA
Alexander explores the
second of the two Indus
branches and finds it to be an
easier route to the sea than
the first. He begins preparing the way for Nearkhos'
sea voyage by ordering wells
dug along the coast, building
docks and shipyards, and
laying in supplies.

6.21.1–3
Autumn 325
COAST OF INDIA
While the fleet awaits the
end of the monsoon winds,
Alexander leads a segment
of the army westward along
the coast to dig wells and
to launch an attack on the
Oreitae, a tribe that had
not yet made gestures of
submission.

[1] On his return to Patala he found that the citadel had been built and that Peithon had arrived with his army, having completed all the tasks he had been sent to perform. Hephaistion was assigned to fortify the anchorage and build the docks, since Alexander intended to leave a large fleet of ships near Patala, where the River Indus divided.[1a] [2] Alexander now sailed back down to the Great Sea by way of the other branch of the Indus,[2a] to learn which of the river's outlets was more navigable. (Roughly two hundred and twenty-five miles separate the outlets of the Indus.) [3] On the downstream voyage he reached a spot where the river emptied into a large lake. Here the river, and perhaps other streams in that region as well, empties into the lake, making it enormous and very much like a bay of the sea.[3a] And in fact deep-sea fish, larger than the species found in our sea,[3b] could already be seen in it. Anchoring at a place on the lake to which the guides had directed him, Alexander left most of the troops and all the light vessels there with Leonnatos. [4] Passing beyond the Indus' outlet with the thirty-oared ships and the ships with one and a half banks of oars, he advanced into the open sea, having discovered that the outlet of the Indus he had just used was the more navigable of the two. Securing his ships on the beach, he advanced with some of the horsemen on a three-day march along the shore, reconnoitering the country past which the fleet would sail and ordering wells to be dug so that the sailors could get water.[4a] [5] Returning to his ships, he sailed up to Patala and ordered a part of the army to perform the same tasks at the coast and then to return to Patala. When he had sailed back down to the lake, he built another anchorage and another set of docks; leaving a garrison there, he brought in a four-month supply of grain for the army and busied himself with all the other preparations for the voyage along the coast.

[1] It was then a difficult time of the year for sailing, since the annual winds were blowing, which at that season arise, not from the north as in our region, but from the Great Sea to the south.[1a] [2] But from the beginning of winter (that is, from the setting of the Pleiades) to the winter solstice, the weather was reported to be suitable for sailing. For throughout that time, because the land is soaked with heavy rains, there are mild breezes for a

6.20.1a The improvements ordered at Patala (Map 6.27, BY) show that Alexander was planning to make this an important naval station, facilitating shipping and communications with the center of the empire. The land route into India, across the Indian Caucasus/Paropamisos (modern Hindu Kush), was arduous in summer and impossible in winter, so a sea route had to be developed if India was to be integrated with the other Asian territories. This goal does much to explain the otherwise irrational march through Gedrosia (6.22–6.26).
6.20.2a Indus River: Map 6.27, BY. This is the western branch of the Indus River.
6.20.3a This "lake" was in fact a bay or inlet of some kind; Quintus Curtius confirms that it contained salt water (9.10.1). Its precise

location has not been determined.
6.20.3b "Our sea" is the Mediterranean Sea: Map 6.11.
6.20.4a Nearkhos' ships, like most ancient sailing vessels, were not designed to carry large quantities of supplies; they were expected to put to shore each night to resupply themselves. Digging wells was thus the principal mission of Alexander's land army during this march. Without them the fleet had no way to keep itself watered.
6.21.1a The monsoon winds in this region of South Asia in fact blow more nearly from the southwest than from the south. They prevail from June to September. Alexander, having readied the fleet for its voyage by late August, must have learned from indigenous peoples about the imminent change in wind patterns.

coasting voyage under either oars or sails. [3] Nearkhos, who had been put in command of the fleet, awaited the sailing season, while Alexander, setting out from Patala, advanced with the entire army as far as the River Arabis.[3a] From there, taking half the shield-bearers, half the archers, the battalions of the so-called *asthetairoi*, the *agema* of the Companion cavalry, a squadron from each cavalry regiment, and all the mounted bowmen, he turned left and proceeded to the coast, to dig wells so that the fleet would have plenty of water throughout their voyage along the coast, and to launch a surprise attack on the Oreitae,[3b] a local Indian tribe that had long been autonomous, as they had made no friendly overture to him and the army. Hephaistion was appointed to lead the forces that had been left behind. [4] The Arabitai,[4a] another autonomous tribe, who dwelt near the River Arabis, decided that they were not equal to fighting Alexander but were also unwilling to submit; they fled into the desert when they learned he was approaching.

After crossing the Arabis, a narrow river containing little water, and traversing by night a long stretch of desert, Alexander arrived at dawn near the inhabited region. He ordered the infantry to follow him in marching order. Taking the horsemen with him, having himself divided them into squadrons to spread them out over as much ground as possible, he advanced into Oreitan territory. [5] All the Oreitae who ventured to resist were cut to pieces by Alexander's horsemen, and many were captured alive. Alexander then made camp near a small water source, and when Hephaistion and his forces joined him, he proceeded onward. On his arrival at Rhambakia,[5a] the largest Oreitan village, he admired the site and imagined that a city settled there would become large and prosperous. Hephaistion was left behind to attend to it.

[1] Again taking half the shield-bearers and the Agrianians, the cavalry *agema*, and the mounted bowmen, Alexander proceeded to the borders between the land of the Oreitae and Gedrosia.[1a] He had received a report of a narrow passage there, and that the Oreitae, drawn up with the Gedrosians, were stationed in front of it to bar his way. [2] They had indeed been stationed there; but when Alexander's approach was reported, most of them fled from the passage and abandoned their post, while the commanders of the Oreitae approached Alexander and surrendered themselves and their tribe. He ordered these men to summon the Oreitae in their numbers and send them to their various settlements, on the understanding that they would suffer no harm. He appointed Apollophanes as satrap of these tribes; [3] Leonnatos the Bodyguard, in command of all the Agrianians, some of the archers and horsemen, and other foot soldiers and Greek mercenary horsemen, was left behind among the Oroi[3a] to assist him. Apollophanes

6.21.4–5

COAST OF INDIA
Another tribe in the region, the Arabitai, flee into the desert at the army's approach. Taken by surprise, the Oreitae are massacred and taken prisoner. A city is planned on the site of one of their villages.

6.22.1–3

GEDROSIA
A force of Oreitae and Gedrosians, intending to stop Alexander's progress, loses heart at his approach. Alexander appoints a satrap for this region and leaves behind a garrison before proceeding to Gedrosia.

6.21.3a Arabis River: Map 6.27, BY.
6.21.3b Oreitae/Oroi, location of territory: Map 6.27, BY. Arrian seems to use "Oroi" as an alternate name for the Oreitai, though some editors understand him to be denoting a place, "Ora." The Greek spellings would be the same in every instance

where this name occurs.
6.21.4a Arabitai, location of territory: Map 6.27, BY.
6.21.5a Rhambakia: Map 6.27, BY.
6.22.1a Gedrosia: Map 6.27, BY.
6.22.3a Another name for the Oreitae; see n. 6.21.3b.

was ordered to wait there until the fleet sailed past, and then to people the city and to arrange matters so that the region's inhabitants might pay more heed to him as satrap. Hephaistion having arrived with the troops left in the rear, Alexander himself took most of the army and advanced to Gedrosia across a land that was for the most part uninhabited.

[4] Aristoboulos reports[4a] that myrrh trees taller than those found elsewhere have grown abundantly in that desert, and that the Phoenicians[4b] who accompanied the army in pursuit of trading opportunities would collect the gum of the myrrh, of which there was an enormous quantity, since it came from huge trunks and had never before been collected. They would carry it away by loading it onto their pack animals. [5] The fragrant root of spikenard[5a] is also said to abound in that desert; it too was gathered by the Phoenicians. So much of it was trampled underfoot by the army that a sweet fragrance arising from the trampled spikenard pervaded the country. [6] According to Aristoboulos, there are other trees in this desert, including one whose leaf resembles a laurel's; this species grows where the waves of the sea wash over the land: the trees are left on dry land by the ebb tide, but when the water returns, they appear to be growing in the sea. And even where these trees have taken root in hollow places from which the tide does not recede and where their roots are perpetually under water, the tree is not harmed by the sea.[6a] [7] Some of the trees thereabouts are forty-five feet tall and were in bloom at that season. Their flowers particularly resemble the white violet, though their fragrance is much sweeter. The earth there also brings forth a thistle stalk[7a] whose thorn is so strong that when it becomes entangled in the clothes of a horseman riding by, it pulls the horseman down from his horse instead of separating from its stalk; [8] hares too, it is said, have their fur caught in the thorns as they dart by and are snared in this way, just as birds are snared with birdlime or fish with hooks. The thorn is easily cut with a knife, and the stalk of the cut thorn emits abundant juice—more than figs produce in spring, and sharper-tasting.

[1] From there Alexander advanced through Gedrosia along a difficult road, where there were no supplies and even water was often not to be found; the men were forced to do much of their traveling at night and to venture farther from the sea, though Alexander was eager to stay near the coast, both to see what harbors there were and to make all possible preparations for the fleet as it passed by—digging wells or making arrangements for a market or an anchorage. [2] But as the entire coast of Gedrosia was uninhabited,[2a] Alexander sent Thoas son of Mandrodoros down to the sea with

6.22.4a Aristoboulos was one of Alexander's principal sources. For more on Aristoboulos, see the Introduction, §2.4, and Appendix A, Arrian's Sources and Reliability, §10, 12.
6.22.4b Phoenicia: Map 6.27, locator.
6.22.5a The herb Arrian here calls *nardos* (spikenard) may actually be lemongrass. Its precise identity is not known.
6.22.6a The tree described is the mangrove.

6.22.7a The plant described here appears to be the *Acacia catechu*, or cutch tree. It has thorns two to three inches thick that are said to be strong enough to puncture truck tires.
6.23.2a The lack of inhabitants meant, for Alexander, a lack of information about surrounding territory, a similar problem to that he had encountered in his Indus delta explorations (see 6.18.4).

FIGURE 6.23. View of Gedrosia, along the route followed by Alexander and his troops. The landscape is marked by barren sands and rugged, rocky hills.

a few horsemen to see whether any anchorage was to be found, or any source of water near the sea, or any other source of supplies. [3] On his return Thoas reported that he had found some fishermen dwelling in cramped huts at the shore; that the huts had been built of cockle shells fitted together, and roofed with fish spines; and that the little water these men used was obtained with difficulty by scraping away the shingle, and even then it was not always fresh.

[4] When Alexander reached a part of Gedrosia where there was an abundance of grain, he loaded what he had found onto the baggage trains and, having marked the shipments with his seal ring, gave orders for them to be conveyed to the coast.[4a] But while Alexander was heading to the way station closest to the sea, the soldiers and the guards, paying little heed to his seal, consumed the grain themselves and shared it with those who were suffering most from hunger, [5] for they were so overpowered by their misery that they took more account of the death that was in sight and already upon them than of any danger from the king that was unseen and still to come. And Alexander, recognizing the need that drove them, pardoned their transgressions. He sent Kretheus of Kallatis to convey provisions—everything he had been able to collect by scouring the countryside—to the troops sailing

6.23.4–6
GEDROSIA
Hunger drives Alexander's men to break into food supplies meant for Nearkhos, but the king overlooks this defiance of his orders. Urgent steps are taken to secure food for both the army and the fleet.

6.23.4a   That is, to be deposited for Nearkhos and
            the fleet. The impress of the seal ring was
            intended to ward off pilferage.

259

with the fleet, [6] and the inhabitants of the inland areas were ordered to convey cattle, dates, and as much grain as they could grind to a market where the soldiers could buy it. Telephos, one of the Companions, was sent to another location with a modest supply of ground grain.

6.24.1–3
Autumn 325
GEDROSIA
Arrian says most writers speculate that Alexander chose to march through Gedrosia in order to outdo the former great conquerors Semiramis and Cyrus, whose armies were destroyed in that desert. Only Nearkhos asserts that Alexander was ignorant of the perils he would encounter, and that his main motive was resupply of the fleet.

[1] Alexander proceeded to Gedrosia and reached its royal seat, a place named Poura,[1a] a full sixty days after starting from the land of the Oroi.[1b] Most of the chroniclers of Alexander's career say that all the hardships his troops suffered in Asia, even taken together, do not deserve to be compared with the hardships of that march. [2] They say that Alexander was not ignorant of the journey's difficulty (only Nearkhos maintains that he was); on the contrary, he had heard that no previous army had ever got safely across that region except Semiramis in her retreat from India, and, as the local people reported, she survived with only twenty of her soldiers, while Cyrus son of Cambyses survived with only seven.[2a] [3] For Cyrus, too, was said to have arrived there with the intention of invading India, though before he could do so he lost most of his army on account of the desolation and difficulty of that route. When these incidents were reported to Alexander, the chroniclers say, he was roused to rival Cyrus and Semiramis. It was for that reason and also to be able to provision the fleet from near at hand that Alexander chose that route, according to Nearkhos.

6.24.4–6
GEDROSIA
Arrian summarizes the reports of the chroniclers on the difficulties of the march, which forged through forbidding territory with constant shortages of water.

[4] The burning heat and lack of water destroyed a great part of the army and particularly the pack animals. The deep and scorching sand killed off the beasts, and many of them succumbed to thirst, since they encountered high hills of deep, loose sand that did not support their weight but engulfed them as if they were stepping in mud or in untrampled snow. [5] Moreover, in the climbs and descents, the horses and mules were even more afflicted by the unevenness of their path and its instability. The army was especially oppressed by the long marches, forced on them by the fact that water was scarce and found only at irregular intervals. [6] Whenever they could cover the necessary distance at night and reach water in the morning, they had some relief from hardship; but when their journey was prolonged and they were still marching when daylight caught up with them, they suffered in the heat and were afflicted with a never-ending thirst.

6.25.1–3
GEDROSIA
More details of the gruesome march: Pack animals are killed and eaten by the army, while Alexander pretends not to notice. Those too afflicted to keep up are left stranded in the desert for lack of carts to convey them.

[1] The destruction of the pack animals was widespread and was the deliberate work of the army. Whenever their provisions ran out, the men would band together and slaughter most of their horses and mules, eat their flesh, and then report that the animals had died of thirst or exhaustion. And there was no one to establish the truth of what had occurred, both because of the labor involved and the fact that everyone was committing the same crimes. [2] Alexander was not unaware of what was happening but saw that

6.24.1a Poura: location unknown.
6.24.1b Oreitai/Oroi, location of territory: Map 6.27, BY.
6.24.2a Semiramis, a legendary queen of Assyria, was supposed to have conquered India many centuries before this time (see Diodorus 2.16–19), but historical evidence

about either her or her march through Gedrosia is lacking. Cyrus the Great founded the Achaemenid Persian empire in the sixth century and was famous for his conquests of Babylonia and Lydia, but this is our only reference to the idea of his invading India.

feigned ignorance was a better remedy for the situation than conscious acquiescence. It was also no longer easy to transport the troops who were weakened by disease or who were exhausted and had been left by the roadsides. For not only had pack animals become scarce, but the men had themselves broken up the wagons, both because these could not be dragged through the deep sand and because at the outset of the march the wagons had forced them to take not the shortest routes but those with the best surfaces. [3] So the sick were left behind, along with those who were exhausted or could not bear the heat or lack of water. And there was no one to transport them or to stay and take care of them; as the march was conducted in great haste, the needs of individuals had to be neglected out of concern for the army as a whole. Some men were also overcome by sleep while on the march, since the men generally marched at night. Later, when they arose, those who were still able to do so followed in the army's tracks, and those few were saved, but most perished in the sand like men who fall overboard at sea.

[4] The army met with another misfortune that especially oppressed the men, the horses, and the pack animals. Rain is brought to Gedrosia, as to India, by the monsoons, and it falls not on the plains but in their mountains, where clouds are borne by the wind and pour out rain without passing over the mountains' crests. [5] At one point the army had made camp near a streambed that contained a scanty supply of water; it was for the sake of this water that the site had been chosen. Near the second watch[5a] of the night, the stream, unseen by the army, filled up with rainwater. It overflowed with such force that it killed most of the women and children accompanying the army, and the king's own gear, along with all the pack animals that were still surviving, was washed away and never seen again. The men themselves barely got safely away with their weapons, and not even with all of them.

[6] Many even died from drinking too much water, when in their exhaustion and thirst they came upon a plentiful supply. For this reason Alexander generally let the army bivouac not near water but at a distance of some two or three miles, so that the men and animals might not perish by falling in throngs on the water supply; he was also concerned to prevent the men who were least able to control themselves from walking into the springs or streams and fouling the water for the rest of the army.

[1] At this point a noble deed of Alexander's, perhaps his noblest, should not, it seems to me, be forgotten, whether it was performed in that region or even earlier among the Paropamisadai (as some have reported).[1a] The army was marching across the sands in the already scorching heat, as it had to cover the distance to a source of water that lay ahead. Alexander himself, though badly afflicted with thirst, was nevertheless leading the way,

6.25.4–5
GEDROSIA
Rainfall in the mountains causes a stream to flood, and the army's camp is largely destroyed.

6.25.6
GEDROSIA
A further danger lay in the excessive drinking of water when supplies suddenly permitted.

6.26.1–3
GEDROSIA
Arrian relates an anecdote in which Alexander refused a drink of water despite parching thirst, since there was not enough for others to drink, too.

6.25.5a The Greeks (and later Romans), who were reliant on the sun to tell time during the day, divided the night into either three or four periods, naming these "watches" based on military parlance. The second watch of the night was approximately two or three hours after midnight.

6.26.1a Quintus Curtius situates a similar episode in the deserts of Sogdiana (7.5.10–12), while Plutarch places it in Bactria during the pursuit of Bessos (*Parallel Lives*, "Alexander" 42.7–10).

on foot, so that the other soldiers might bear their toils more lightly, as they generally do when hardship is shared equally. [2] Then some of the light-armed troops who had split off from the army to search for water found a shallow gully in which there was a small, scanty spring. After taking pains to collect the water, they went in haste to Alexander as though bearing some great treasure; when they drew near him, they poured the water into a helmet and took it to the king. [3] Alexander is said to have received it and praised the men who had brought it, but then to have taken it and poured it out in the sight of all. And the army was so encouraged by this gesture that one would have guessed that everyone had drunk the water that Alexander had poured out. For this deed, a testament to his endurance and his leadership, I especially commend Alexander.

[4] The following incident also befell the army in that region. The guides of the march at last declared that they no longer recalled the route, all landmarks in the sand having been blown away by the wind. For there was nothing, in the masses of sand heaped up equally on all sides, by which to discern the route, no familiar tree or hill that was stable and unshifting. Nor had they learned to rely on the stars at night or the sun by day to guide their journey, the way the Phoenicians navigate by the Little Bear and other peoples by the Great Bear.[4a] [5] At that point Alexander, realizing that he should lead the army to the left, took some horsemen with him and went on ahead. When these men's horses were exhausted by the heat, he left most of them behind, rode on with five, and found the sea; and upon ordering the gravel scraped away on the beach he found sweet, clear water. The entire army joined him there, and for seven days they marched beside the sea, fetching water from the shore. Then, since the guides now recognized the route, he led the army into the interior.

[1] When he reached the capital of Gedrosia, Alexander rested the army. He stripped Apollophanes of his satrapy,[1a] as he realized that the man had not carried out his orders, and appointed Thoas as satrap of the region. When Thoas died of disease, Sibyrtius succeeded to the satrapy; he had recently been posted as satrap of Carmania, but was now appointed to govern the Arachosians and Gedrosians,[1b] while Tlepolemos son of Pythophanes took his place in Carmania. [2] The king was already on his way to Carmania when word reached him that Philip, the satrap of India, had been killed, the victim of a plot hatched by the mercenaries, and that Philip's Macedonian body-

6.26.4–5
Autumn 325
GEDROSIA
After the army becomes lost, Alexander miraculously finds his way to the shore and uncovers a supply of fresh water.

6.27.1–2
Winter 325/4
GEDROSIA-CARMANIA
Once the army emerges from the desert, Alexander replaces a satrap he considers lax in his duties. Word arrives of the murder of Philip, satrap of India, by men under his command.

6.26.4a The last star in the tail of the constellation Little Bear (our Little Dipper) is the North Star (Polaris), a valuable aid to navigation because it holds an almost constant position close to the northern celestial pole. The Great Bear (Big Dipper), which circles around Polaris during the night, can also be used as a way to find true north; it is brighter and easier to see, but less reliable. The Phoenicians, the ancient world's most renowned navigators, were thought by the Greeks to have discovered the utility of the Little Bear and to have relied on this

constellation, while other peoples preferred the more visible Great Bear.

6.27.1a According to Arrian's *Indika* (23.5), Apollophanes was already dead by this time, killed in a battle fought between Nearkhos' ship-borne forces and the Oreitae. Either Arrian has written the wrong name here or Alexander had not yet received word of Apollophanes' death when he issued the orders regarding his removal from office.

6.27.1b The following locations can be found on Map 6.27: Carmania, BX; Arachosia, BY; Gedrosia, BY.

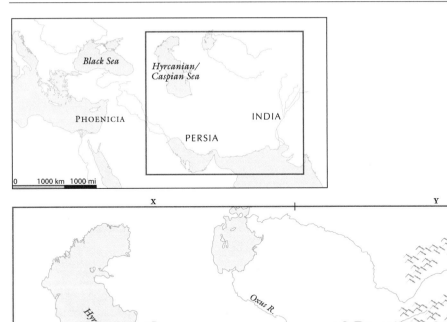

Black Sea

PHOENICIA

Hyrcanian/
Caspian Sea

INDIA

PERSIA

0   1000 km 1000 mi

X

Y

A

Oxus R.

Hyrcanian/Caspian Sea

INDIAN CAUCASUS/PAROPAMISOS

HYRCANIA

PARTHIA

AREIA

Indus R.

MEDIA

ARACHOSIA

INDIA

SUSIANA

Tigris R.

Susa

ZARANGIANE

Indus R.

Euphrates R.

Pasargadae

Persepolis

Arabis R.

Patala

B

PERSIA

CARMANIA

GEDROSIA   Rhambakia

Persian Gulf

Oreitae/Oroi
Arabitai

Ichthyophagoi

Indian Gulf

0   500 km   500 mi

MAP 6.27

guards had killed his murderers, some of whom were caught in the act, the rest seized afterward. When Alexander learned of this, he sent letters to Eudamos[2a] and Taxiles in India, ordering them to tend to affairs in the country previously governed by Philip until such time as he sent out a new satrap.[2b]

[3] When Alexander had reached Carmania, Krateros arrived with the rest of the army and the elephants;[3a] he also brought along Ordanes, who had been arrested for raising revolt and causing trouble. Stasanor, the satrap of the Areians and Zarangians, also arrived, as did Pharismanes son of Phrataphernes, the satrap of the Parthians and Hyrcanians.[3b] Alexander was also joined by Kleandros, Sitalkes, and Herakon,[3c] the generals who had been left behind with Parmenion in charge of the army in Media[3d] and were now bringing with them the greater part of that army. [4] Many of Kleandros' and Sitalkes' men had been accused by the native peoples and by the army itself of having despoiled shrines, disturbed ancient tombs, and injured their subjects by rash and reckless behavior. When this was reported, Alexander had the offenders put to death so that all the remaining satraps, governors, and chieftains might hesitate to offend in like manner lest they suffer the same fate. [5] And this, more than anything, maintained order among the tribes, whether they had been taken in war or had joined Alexander willingly, despite how numerous they were and how different from one another: under Alexander's sovereignty, the rulers were not allowed to injure the peoples they ruled. On that occasion, Herakon was acquitted of the charges; but shortly thereafter, accused by the Susians of having despoiled the shrine in Susa,[5a] he paid the price. [6] Stasanor and Phrataphernes and their forces arrived, bringing Alexander an enormous number of pack animals and many camels; they had guessed, when they learned that he was marching to Gedrosia, that the army would suffer the fate that it had in fact suffered. These men and the camels and pack animals had arrived in the nick of time. Alexander distributed all the animals to the officers man by man, and proportionately to the squadrons, companies, and regiments.

[1] Certain writers have also related the following story (an untrustworthy one, in my opinion): Yoking two covered wagons together, Alexander reclined with his Companions and was entertained by flute players as he led his men through Carmania. The troops accompanied him, bedecked with garlands and making merry, and food and all sorts of luxuries were collected by the Carmanians and set before them along their route. These arrange-

Margin notes

6.27.3–6
Winter 325/4
CARMANIA
At Carmania, Alexander's forces are reunited with those whom Krateros had led across the Indian Caucasus/Paropamisos and joined by units once under the command of Parmenion in Media. Some of these men, accused of abuses by the Medians, are executed on Alexander's orders as an example to other administrators.

6.28.1–4
CARMANIA
Arrian retells a story he does not himself believe, that Alexander indulged in banqueting and revelry as he was borne along through Carmania. The true account, Arrian believes, is that Alexander conducted sacrifices and games in Carmania to celebrate his return from India. Peukestas is here elevated to the rank of Bodyguard.

Footnotes

6.27.2a This is Arrian's only mention of Eudamos, captain of a contingent of Thracian mercenaries left behind in India as a garrison force. He was later to become the murderer of Poros under mysterious circumstances (Diodorus 19.14.8).

6.27.2b Alexander died before appointing Philip's successor. Poros and Taxiles continued to govern India as vassal kings, with Eudamos exercising power as a kind of surrogate satrap.

6.27.3a Krateros had been detailed to lead many of the heavier units westward by an

inland route (see 6.17.3).

6.27.3b The following locations can be found on Map 6.27: Ar(e)ia, AY; Zarangiane (Drangiane), BY; Parthia, AX; Hyrcania, AX.

6.27.3c Kleandros, Sitalkes, and Herakon were among the subcommanders of Parmenion whom Alexander had recruited to kill their senior officer in the wake of the execution of Philotas; see 3.26.3, where Kleandros and Sitalkes are mentioned (along with another assassin, Menidas).

6.27.3d Media: Map 6.27, BX.

6.27.5a Susa: Map 6.27, BX.

FIGURE 6.28. The Gedrosian coast, along the route taken by Nearkhos' fleet.

ments were said to have been organized by Alexander in imitation of the revelry of Dionysos, [2] who reportedly traversed the greater part of Asia after subjugating the Indians and was given the name Triumph, for which reason the processions held in honor of military victories are also called triumphs.[2a] But neither Ptolemy nor Aristoboulos has recorded these details, nor has anyone else one might regard as a competent authority.[2b] For my part, it is enough to have set them down with the proviso that I do not consider them credible. [3] But this I do report, following Aristoboulos: Alexander sacrificed in Carmania[3a] in gratitude for his victory over the Indians and the army's escape from Gedrosia,[3b] and organized a competition in athletics and music. He also enrolled Peukestas in the Bodyguards. Alexander had already decided to appoint Peukestas as satrap of Persia,[3c] but wanted him first to enjoy this honor and pledge of good faith on account of his exploit among the Malloi.[3d] [4] Up to that time Alexander had had seven Bodyguards: Leonnatos son of Anteas, Hephaistion son of Amyntor, Lysimakhos son of Agathocles, and Aristonous son of Peisaios, all of them from Pella; Perdikkas son of Orontes, from Orestis; Ptolemy son of Lagos, and Peithon son of Krateuas, both from Eordaia. He now added an eighth Bodyguard: Peukestas, the man who had covered Alexander with a shield.

[5] Meanwhile Nearkhos, after passing the territory of the Oroi,[5a] the Gedrosians, and the Fish-eaters[5b] on his voyage, landed at the inhabited part of the Carmanian coast. Traveling up from the coast with a small party, Nearkhos briefed Alexander about his voyage along the coast through the Outer Sea.[5c] [6] Alexander then sent Nearkhos back to the coast to sail onward to Susian territory and the outlets of the River Tigris.[6a] In a sepa-

6.28.5–6
Winter 325/4
CARMANIA
Nearkhos and his fleet, safely arrived in Carmania, rendezvous with Alexander and relate the events of their voyage. Alexander sends them on to the mouth of the Tigris.

6.28.2a The Greek word is *thriambos*, which was later borrowed by the Romans and latinized as *triumphus*. In Greek usage it designated only a procession of revelers celebrating Dionysos. The public procession commemorating a military victory referred to by Arrian was exclusively a Roman custom.

6.28.2b The story of the revels in Carmania can be found in Diodorus (17.106.1), Quintus Curtius (9.10.24–29), and Plutarch (*Parallel Lives*, "Alexander" 67). The elaborate description in Plutarch is certainly a wild exaggeration, though perhaps there was some sort of celebratory banquet that gave rise to the story. The tale of the revel at Nysa follows a similar pattern, in which Alexander and his men lose all self-control in the grip of a Bacchic frenzy, and is similarly suspect as a piece of anti-Alexander propaganda (see 5.2.7 and n. 5.2.7a).

6.28.3a Carmania: Map 6.27, BX.

6.28.3b Gedrosia: Map 6.27, BY.

6.28.3c Persia: Map 6.27, BX. The term Persia here and at 6.28.7 and 6.29.1, 2 designates the central satrapy of the Persian empire, sometimes called Persis (including by Arrian and the *Barrington Atlas*). This edition has opted for the more familiar name.

6.28.3d Peukestas had been one of the three

Macedonians who scaled the walls of the Mallian town (Malloi territory, Map 6.11, inset) along with Alexander and helped protect the king from enemy fire (see 6.10.1–2).

6.28.5a Oreitae/Oroi, location of territory: Map 6.27, BY.

6.28.5b The so-called Fish-eaters (Ichthyophagoi; Map 6.27, BY) were a people who dwelt along the mountainous coast of Gedrosia (see Figure 6.28).

6.28.5c Arrian here makes only a cursory and toneless reference to the ordeal endured by Nearkhos, recounted at length in his *Indika*. Departing India in haste after attacks by indigenous peoples, Nearkhos was delayed by contrary winds and lost contact with the land army that was supposed to help provision the fleet. The rest of the three-month journey was plagued by shortages of food and water. Nearkhos mounted attacks on primitive peoples of the region on several occasions, but they had few supplies. When Nearkhos at last found signs that the land army was nearby and reconnected with it, Alexander had trouble recognizing his malnourished and weather-worn senior admiral.

6.28.6a Susiana; Tigris River: Map 6.27, BX.

rate account I will describe, following Nearkhos himself, the voyage from the Indus[6b] to the Persian Sea[6c] and the outlet of the Tigris;[6d] thus another Greek account about Alexander remains to be written, later perhaps, if my own desire and the will of the gods so move me.

[7] Alexander ordered Hephaistion to lead the largest division of the army, the baggage train, and the elephants along the coastal route from Carmania to Persia, since his march would take place in wintertime, when the part of Persia near the coast always received ample sunshine and produced abundant supplies.

[1] Alexander himself, with the most mobile of his foot soldiers, the Companion cavalry, and a division of archers, proceeded to Pasargadae[1a] in Persia. He dispatched Stasanor to his own realm.[1b] [2] When he reached the Persian border, Alexander found that Phrasaortes was no longer serving as satrap, having died of disease while Alexander was still in India; instead, though Alexander had not appointed him, Orxines[2a] was managing Persian affairs, as he did not deem it beneath him, in the absence of another governor, to maintain order in Persia for Alexander. [3] Atropates, the Median[3a] satrap, also reached Pasargadae, escorting Baryaxes—a Mede who had been arrested for wearing his *kitaris* upright[3b] and declaring himself king of the Persians and Medes—along with the men who had taken part in his revolt and rebellion. Alexander had these men put to death.

The desecration of the tomb of Cyrus son of Cambyses,[3c] [4] which was found ruined and ransacked, distressed Alexander, as Aristoboulos reports. Cyrus' tomb was in the royal park in Pasargadae. A grove of many kinds of trees had been planted around it. The grove was irrigated, and deep grass had grown in the meadow. [5] The tomb itself was rectangular in shape and had a base built of squared stone; this base supported a roofed stone chamber fitted with a door so narrow that a man of moderate height had difficulty passing through it.[5a] In the chamber lay a golden sarcophagus in which Cyrus' body had been buried, and beside the sarcophagus stood a couch, its feet made of beaten gold; a Babylonian tapestry served as a carpet, and thick purple robes as coverlets. [6] A military cloak and various tunics of Babylonian workmanship had been placed on the couch. Aristo-

6.28.7
CARMANIA
Hephaistion is dispatched with an army to march along the coast in tandem with the fleet.

6.29.1–3
PASARGADAE
Alexander, with a flying column, moves on to Pasargadae, the old Persian capital. A pretender to the Persian throne is executed there, along with his supporters.

6.29.4–8
PASARGADAE
Alexander grieves at the destruction and spoliation of the tomb of Cyrus, a sumptuous monument dedicated to the greatness of the Persian royal line.

6.28.6b   Indus River: Map 6.27, AY and BY.
6.28.6c   Persian Sea (Persian Gulf): Map 6.27, BX.
6.28.6d   The Greeks of Alexanders' expedition thought that the Euphrates did not have an outlet to the sea but, rather, ended in marshes (see 5.5.5).
6.29.1a   Pasargadae: Map 6.27, BX.
6.29.1b   That is, Alexander's satrapies Are(i)a and Zarangiane (Drangiane). For the locations of all Persian satrapies mentioned by Arrian, see Ref. Map 1.
6.29.2a   Orxines was a Persian nobleman who had fought against Alexander at Gaugamela (see 3.8.5). His self-appointment to the vacant Persian satrapy was to lead to his downfall (see 6.30.1–2).
6.29.3a   The Medes were a northern Iranian

people who originally ruled the Persians, then came to be ruled by them and assimilated into their power structure.
6.29.3b   The *kitaris* was a kind of Persian headdress, also called a tiara, which was worn folded down by most Persians but high and upright, with an encircling diadem, by the reigning king.
6.29.3c   Cyrus (c. 600–529) was the great conqueror who founded the Achaemenid Persian dynasty more than two centuries before the time of Alexander.
6.29.5a   Arrian's description fits the structure at the site of ancient Pasargadae, in modern Iran, known today as the tomb of Cyrus (see Figure 6.29), but there is no definitive evidence that the two are in fact identical.

boulos reports that there were Median trousers, garments dyed in blue, some of them dark, others of various hues, collars of linked metal, scimitars, and earrings of precious stones set in gold. A table stood there, and between the table and the couch lay the sarcophagus containing Cyrus' body. [7] Within the enclosure, near the ascent leading to the tomb, there was a small chamber built for the Magi[7a] who had guarded the tomb even in the days of Cambyses son of Cyrus. The office of guardian passed from father to son, and the king used to provide these guardians with a fixed daily allowance that included a sheep, wheat flour, and wine, and a horse each month to sacrifice to Cyrus.[7b] [8] The tomb had an inscription in Persian characters that read, "You there! I am Cyrus son of Cambyses, who founded the Persian empire and reigned as king of Asia. Do not begrudge me my monument."[8a]

6.29.9–11
Winter 325/4
PASARGADAE
Alexander directs Aristoboulos to supervise the reconstruction of the tomb. His attempts to find the robbers come to naught.

[9] Alexander had made up his mind to visit the tomb of Cyrus should he conquer the Persians,[9a] and he now found that everything in it had been carried away except the sarcophagus and the couch. The tomb's despoilers had even mutilated Cyrus' body by removing the lid from the sarcophagus and tossing out the corpse. They had tried to make the sarcophagus more compact and easy to carry, in some places cutting pieces off, in others crushing it; but when their efforts did not succeed, they departed, leaving the sarcophagus in place. [10] Aristoboulos reports that he himself was ordered by Alexander to restore Cyrus' tomb to its original condition; to deposit in the sarcophagus as much of Cyrus' body as had been preserved and to replace the lid; to repair everything that had been damaged; to spread the couch with garlands; to reproduce, item by item, everything that had been placed in the tomb; to re-create its ancient arrangement; to obliterate traces of the little door, partly by laying stones against it and partly by plastering it with clay; and to stamp the clay with the royal seal. [11] Alexander then arrested the Magi who had guarded the tomb and had them tortured in order to learn who had desecrated it; but under torture they denounced none of their own people or anyone else, nor were they

---

6.29.7a The Magi were a powerful priestly caste who attended the Persian king under the Achaemenid empire, interpreted dreams and signs, and presided over various state rituals. According to Herodotus (*Histories* 1.132), a magus was required to be present at all religious sacrifices, as a kind of intermediary between the worshiper and the gods. Arrian gives our only evidence for the role of the Magi in tending the tombs of the Persian kings, but this fits with their other known duties.

6.29.7b Persian state records found at Persepolis confirm the fact that yearly allowances of food and wine were given to the guardians of royal tombs. However, the allotment of horses for sacrifice to the tomb's occupant would be unique, if Arrian's information is accurate. The Persians are known to have sacrificed horses to

a god the Greeks identified as the Sun (Xenophon, *Cyropaedia* 8.3.12; Herodotus, *Histories* 7.113). During his lifetime, Cyrus apparently kept a herd of sacred white horses (see Herodotus, *Histories* 1.189).

6.29.8a There is no trace of this inscription on the walls of the structure assumed to be Cyrus' tomb, and no other feature of the structure clearly connects it with Cyrus. Legend has it that the inscription was effaced at the time of the Arab conquest of Persia, in the seventh century C.E., by local inhabitants who wished to save the pre-Islamic monument from destruction.

6.29.9a Arrian seems to frame this as an intention Alexander had before he started his Asian campaign, but the manuscripts may have become corrupt here and the Greek text has been revised by some editors.

FIGURE 6.29. The tomb usually identified as that of Cyrus the Great, at Pasargadae.

otherwise proved to have been accomplices in the deed, and therefore Alexander released them.[11a]

[1] Alexander then proceeded to the Persian palaces that he had previously burned down, as I mentioned when I expressed my disapproval of the act.[1a] (Alexander himself disapproved of it on his return.)[1b] The Persians now told many tales about Orxines, who had been governing the Persians

6.30.1–3
PERSEPOLIS
Alexander revisits the burned palace complex at Persepolis. Orxines, who had been acting as satrap over the Persians, is hanged for his greed and cruelty, and Peukestas is appointed in his place.

6.29.11a The desecration of Cyrus' tomb remains a mystery to this day. According to Plutarch (*Parallel Lives*, "Alexander" 69.3–4), a Macedonian named Poulamakhos plundered the tomb, motivated presumably by greed, and was executed for his crime by Alexander. Arrian does not mention Poulamakhos or any other perpetrator, but strongly implies at 6.30.2 that Orxines, the interim satrap, had some part in the crime. It is also possible that the Magi, who were hardly reconciled to being ruled by an invader, despoiled the tomb as a way to make the new Macedonian administrators look incompetent and arouse local opposition.

6.30.1a This burning of the palaces at Persepolis was described at 3.18.11–12. Persepolis: Map 6.27, BX.
6.30.1b This is Arrian's only mention of the idea that Alexander regretted the burning of the Persepolis palaces. Quintus Curtius (5.7.11), who with the other vulgate sources claims that Alexander burned the Persepolis palaces on a drunken whim, depicts him as regretting the act immediately afterward.

since Phrasaortes' death; [2] it was proved that Orxines had despoiled shrines and royal tombs and had unjustly executed many Persians. Alexander had the man hanged, and made Peukestas the Bodyguard satrap over the Persians,[2a] a man he considered thoroughly trustworthy; his courageous action in the city of the Malloi, where he had braved danger and helped to save Alexander, especially commended him.[2b] Beyond that, Peukestas was not ill disposed to the barbarian way of life, as he made clear from the moment he was appointed; [3] he was the only Macedonian who adopted Median apparel, learned the Persian language, and adopted the Persian manner in everything. Alexander praised him for this, as did the Persians, who were pleased with him for honoring their own ways in preference to those of his ancestors.

6.30.2a   By "Persians" Arrian here refers to the
          inhabitants of the satrapy of Persia (see
          Ref. Map 1).
6.30.2b   Peukestas was given an honorary promo-

tion to the rank of Bodyguard (at 6.28.4)
for protecting Alexander with the sacred
shield at the Mallian town (see 6.10.2,
6.11.7–8).

BOOK SEVEN

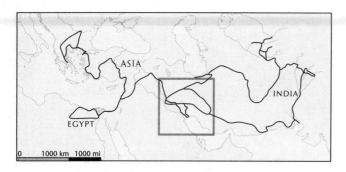

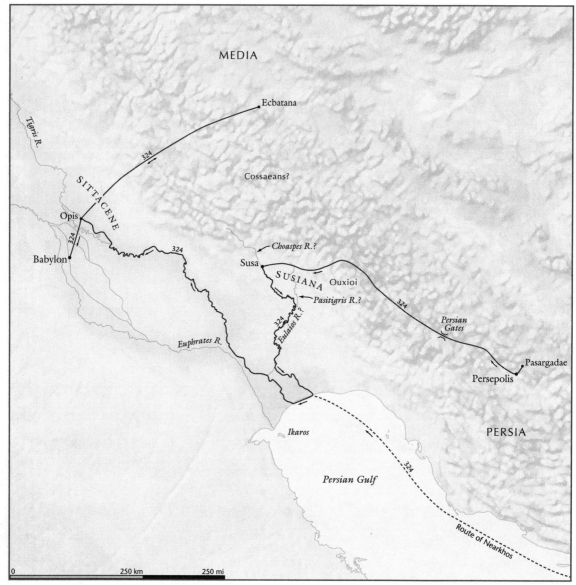

Book Seven: The Return to Babylon

W hen Alexander reached Pasargadae and Persepolis, a sudden longing seized him to sail down the Euphrates and Tigris to the Persian Sea[1a] and to see the place where the rivers met the ocean, as he had done at the Indus,[1b] and to explore that stretch of coastline. [2] And there are some who say that Alexander was planning to circumnavigate most of Arabia,[2a] Ethiopia,[2b] Libya, and the nomads who dwell beyond Mount Atlas, and thus sail to Gadeira and sail on into our sea;[2c] then, after subjugating Libya and Carthage,[2d] he would indeed have earned the right to call himself king of all of Asia.[2e] [3] (Since the kings of the Persians[3a] and Medes[3b] had ruled not even a small fraction of Asia, they had not been justified in calling themselves Great Kings.)[3c] Thereafter, according to some sources, he planned to sail into the Black Sea to Scythia and Lake Maeotis; others say he meant to sail to Sicily and the headland of Iapygia,[3d] since, as they claim, he was already unsettled by the Romans'

7.1.1–4
Spring 324
PASARGADAE-PERSEPOLIS
Alexander sets out to explore the Persian Gulf, prompting Arrian to speculate on how far into the unknown the king's restless spirit would have carried him, had he lived longer.

NOTE: Most locations in the text not identified by a footnote can be found in the Reference Maps section.

7.1.1a Pasargadae; Persepolis; Euphrates River; Tigris River; Persian Sea (Persian Gulf): Map 7.2, Persian Gulf inset.

7.1.1b Indus River: Map 7.2, India inset.

7.1.2a Arabia (Map 7.2, Persian Gulf inset) was indeed Alexander's next objective; see 7.19.6–7.20.2.

7.1.2b Ethiopia: Map 7.16.

7.1.2c By "our sea," Arrian signifies the Mediterranean (Map 7.2, BX).

7.1.2d The following locations can be found on Map 7.2: Libya (North Africa), BX; Atlas Mountains, BX; Gadeira, AX; Carthage, BX. A document known as the *Hypomnemata*, or Last Plans, of Alexander, found among the king's papers at the time of his death according to Diodorus Siculus (18.4.2–6), called for a campaign that would spread Macedonian territory to the Strait of Gibraltar and the construction of a road all along the North African coast, mentioning Carthage as an objective. These plans also called for construction of an enormous fleet, perhaps with the ultimate goal of challenging

Carthage for control of the western Mediterranean, along with other projects (see the Epilogue, §5). Some scholars doubt the authenticity of all or part of these Last Plans.

7.1.2e The idea that Alexander contemplated a circumnavigation of Libya (North Africa), attributed here to Arrian's sources, was asserted by Arrian at 4.7.5, and by Alexander himself in his speech at the Hyphasis (5.26.2). But that speech shows signs of having been composed by Arrian (see Appendix A, Arrian's Sources and Reliability, §19) and it is doubtful Alexander actually contemplated undertaking the voyage described here. See Appendix N, Alexander's Geographic Notions, §9.

7.1.3a Persia: Map 7.2, Persian Gulf inset.

7.1.3b The Medes (Media: Map 7.2, BY) were a northern Iranian people who originally ruled the Persians, then came to be ruled by them and assimilated into their power structure.

7.1.3c This claim is hyperbolic even if Arrian is here considering Africa to be part of Asia, as Greek writers sometimes did (see Herodotus, *Histories* 4.41, for example).

7.1.3d The following locations can be found on Map 7.2: Black (ancient Euxine) Sea, AX; Scythia, AX; Lake Maeotis, AY; Sicily, BX; Iapygia, AX.

growing renown.³ᵉ [4] For my part, I cannot ascertain with any accuracy what plans Alexander was pondering,⁴ᵃ nor is it my concern to guess, though I do not hesitate to assert that he would have planned nothing trivial or insignificant, nor would he have ceased striving no matter what he had already acquired, even if he had added Europe to Asia or the British Isles⁴ᵇ to Europe. Instead, he would have sought beyond the known for something unknown, vying with himself in the absence of any other rival.

[5] It is with this in mind that I commend the Indian sages,⁵ᵃ some of whom Alexander reportedly encountered in the open air in a meadow where they were accustomed to pass their time in discussion. It is said that at the sight of Alexander and his army they merely stomped on the ground with their feet. When Alexander inquired, through interpreters, what the gesture meant, they replied, [6] "King Alexander, each man can have only so much land as this on which we are standing. You are human like the rest of us, except that in your restlessness and arrogance you travel so far from home, making trouble for yourself and others. Well, you will soon be dead and will have as much land as will suffice to bury your corpse."

[1] At the time, Alexander praised the speakers and their remarks, though he acted otherwise and did the opposite of what he praised. Similarly, he is said to have admired Diogenes of Sinope.¹ᵃ Coming upon Diogenes lying in the sun at the Isthmus,¹ᵇ Alexander halted with his shield-bearers¹ᶜ and infantry companions¹ᵈ and asked the man if he needed anything. Diogenes replied that he needed nothing, other than for Alexander and his men to stand aside and stop blocking his sunlight.¹ᵉ [2] So Alexander was not wholly removed from a better way of thinking, but he was, to a great degree, overpowered by ambition.²ᵃ When he arrived in Taxila²ᵇ and saw the Indian sages

7.1.5–6
Looking back to events in India two years earlier, Arrian contrasts the insatiability of Alexander's drives with the attitude of the Indian sages, who once reminded Alexander that death would rob him of all he had striven for in life.

7.2.1–4
Though Alexander did not follow their teachings, Arrian believes he admired men like Diogenes, the Greek philosopher, and Dandamis, the Indian holy man, who desired nothing more than the basic necessities of life. Alexander failed to attract Dandamis into his entourage but did succeed with Kalanos, one of Dandamis' students.

7.1.3e   The Roman republic was at this time engaged in regional wars with the other peoples of central Italy, but had already distinguished itself as a power to be reckoned with. There is no evidence that Alexander knew anything of Italian affairs, however; his eye was usually turned toward the East, not the West.

7.1.4a   Arrian shows no knowledge of the Last Plans document cited by Diodorus (see n. 7.1.2c).

7.1.4b   The following locations can be found on Map 7.2: Europe, AX; Asia, BX; Britain, AX.

7.1.5a   Evidently the religious ascetics of Taxila; see n. 6.7.4a. On the themes of the anecdotes in this chapter, see Appendix L, The *Alexander Romance*, §5.

7.2.1a   Diogenes of Sinope (Sinope: Map 7.2, AX) is the famous founder of the Cynic school of philosophy, which, in part, taught men to live in such a way as to satisfy only their most basic needs and to regard everything else as superfluous.

7.2.1b   The Isthmus of Corinth, the neck of land connecting central Greece to the Peloponnese. Alexander journeyed to the Peloponnese in 336, at the very start of his reign (see 1.1.1), when Diogenes was living at Corinth.

7.2.1c   Shield-bearers: an elite corps of specially equipped infantry lighter and more mobile

than the heavy infantry who made up the phalanx.

7.2.1d   The infantry companions (*pezetairoi* in Greek) were the members of the phalanx, sometimes also called hoplites by Arrian and phalangites by modern historians (see Appendix D, Alexander's Army and Military Leadership, §2–4.

7.2.1e   This legendary quip of Diogenes' is related on several occasions by Plutarch (*Parallel Lives*, "Alexander" 14.1–5; *Moralia* 331f–332a, 605d, 782a–d).

7.2.2a   Arrian's train of thought in this whole opening segment of Book 7 is obscure. He appears to be trying to have it both ways: he admires Alexander's unquenchable ambition on the one hand, but also suggests that the path of the Indian sages was appealing to Alexander and would have been a "better way of thinking." Many late Greek texts roughly contemporary with Arrian's were exploring the contrast between eastern quietism and western imperialism; see Appendix L, §5.

7.2.2b   For the visit to Taxila (Map 7.2, India inset), the Indian city most friendly to the Macedonians, see 5.8.2–3. Taxila at this time was the seat of several religious schools, drawing students from all over the Indus valley.

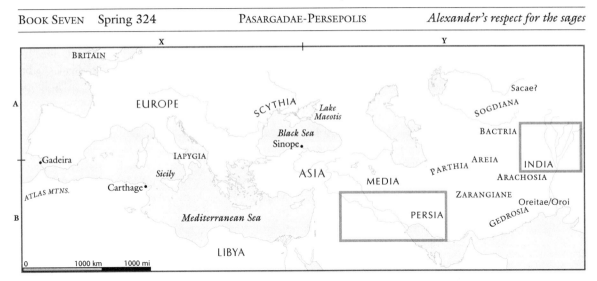

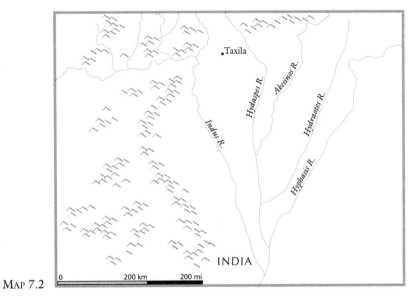

MAP 7.2

who go naked, he was seized by a desire to have one of them join him, since he admired their endurance. The oldest sage, whose name was Dandamis[2c] (the others were his disciples), said that he would neither join Alexander himself nor allow the others to do so. [3] He is said to have replied that if Alexander was really a son of Zeus, then so was he; that he needed nothing from Alexander but was content with his lot;[3a] and that, from what he could see, Alexander's men were wandering at length over land and sea for no good reason, nor was there any limit to their many wanderings. In any event, he desired nothing Alexander had the power to bestow, nor was he afraid to be deprived of anything under Alexander's control. [4] While he lived, the land of India, bearing its fruit in season, was all he needed, and when he died, he would depart from his body as from an unseemly companion. The result was that Alexander did not after all try to coerce him, recognizing that the man was free. But Kalanos, one of the local sages, was persuaded to join Alexander's suite—the same Kalanos who, according to Megasthenes' account,[4a] the sages themselves said was utterly lacking in self-control. They reproached him because he abandoned the happiness to be gained with them and served a master other than god.

[1] I have mentioned these incidents because in any history of Alexander it is essential to speak of Kalanos. It is said that Kalanos' health deteriorated in Persia,[1a] though he had never been ill previously. But he refused to live the life of an invalid and told Alexander that he was content to die as he was, before reaching an extreme of suffering that would force him to change his way of life. [2] For a long time Alexander tried to argue with him; but when he saw that Kalanos would not yield, and would make an end in some other way if his wishes were not honored, he ordered a pyre to be built according to Kalanos' instructions and ordered his Bodyguard[2a] Ptolemy son of Lagos to take charge of it. Some say that Kalanos was preceded by an escort of horses and men, some wearing armor, others carrying all manner of incense for the pyre; others say that the men carried gold and silver cups and royal robes. [3] A horse was prepared for Kalanos himself, since his illness made it impossible for him to walk; but when he could not ride either, he was conveyed on a litter, crowned with garlands in the Indian fashion and chanting Indian songs, which the Indians say were hymns in praise of their gods.

7.3.1–6

PERSIA

Arrian describes in detail the self-immolation of Kalanos, the Indian sage who had accompanied Alexander into Persia, as an example of the kind of self-mastery and determination that also characterized Alexander himself.

7.2.2c The lost memoirs of a Greek in Alexander's service, Onesikritos (see 7.5.6), told of the Macedonians' fascination with the religious devotees at Taxila and of several contacts between the two peoples, including the embassy sent by Alexander to Dandamis referred to here (see Strabo 15.1.63–65, where the sage's name is given as Mandanis). In later literature the same character, under the name Didymus, became the central figure in a number of texts (see Appendix L, §5).

7.2.3a Dandamis' retorts here make better sense if we understand that, according to Onesikritos (see Strabo 15.1.68), messengers were sent to summon Dandamis to "Alexander the son of Zeus," promising him gifts if he complied but threatening punishment for refusal. Arrian has transmit-

ted the responses but omitted the demands that preceded them.

7.2.4a Megasthenes was a Greek diplomat who spent time in India in the years following Alexander's death. He wrote some of his observations of Indian society in a treatise called *Indika*, now lost. According to Strabo (15.1.68), Megasthenes heard reproaches of Kalanos' intemperance among the sages at Taxila.

7.3.1a Persia: Map 7.2, locator. The term Persia here designates the central satrapy of the Persian empire, sometimes called Persis (by Arrian and the *Barrington Atlas*, among others). This edition has opted for the more familiar name.

7.3.2a The Bodyguard was a coterie of seven officers who attended Alexander's person.

FIGURE 7.3. These examples of the art of Gandhara, the ancient region today comprising nothwest India, north Pakistan, and eastern Afghanistan, attest to the cultural interactions that began with Alexander's invasion and continued long afterward. Greek sculptural styles were absorbed and adapted by Bactrian and Indian artists, producing a Hellenic-type banqueting scene (top) and a Buddha wearing a typically Greek himation (right). Even Homeric myth made its way into the region, to judge by what seems to be a version of the Trojan horse story (bottom) carved by a Gandharan artist.

[4] It is said that the horse that had been provided for his use was of the royal Nesaian breed,[4a] and that before he mounted the pyre he presented it to Lysimakhos,[4b] one of those who studied with him. As for the cups and rugs Alexander had ordered to be thrown on the pyre in Kalanos' honor, Kalanos distributed them among his followers. [5] Then, mounting the pyre, he lay down in a decorous manner in sight of the entire army. Alexander did not think it decent to witness such a spectacle, the man having been his friend, but the rest were amazed to see that Kalanos remained motionless in the fire. [6] When the fire was kindled by those to whom the duty had been given, Nearkhos[6a] says that trumpets blared, by Alexander's order, and the troops shouted "Alalai!" as they used to do when marching into battle, and the elephants joined in with their high-pitched war cry in honor of Kalanos.[6b] Competent writers have recorded these details about Kalanos the Indian, which are not utterly without value for mankind, or at least for anyone who cares to comprehend how powerful and unconquerable is the human will to accomplish whatever it desires.

[1] Then[1a] Alexander sent Atropates to his satrapy.[1b] On reaching Susa,[1c] he arrested Aboulites and his son Oxathres and had them put to death for abusing their power.[1d] [2] Many offenses had indeed been committed by those in control of the territories conquered by Alexander—offenses against temples, tombs, and the inhabitants themselves; for the king's expedition to India had been prolonged, and people doubted he would return home safe from all those tribes and elephants. They imagined he would perish beyond the Indus, Hydaspes, Akesinos, and Hyphasis;[2a] [3] and the disasters that befell him in Gedrosia[3a] further encouraged the nearby satraps to reject the idea of his return.[3b] What is more, it cannot be denied that at that period

7.3.4a Herodotus (*Histories* 7.40.2) writes that there is a large plain in Media called the Nesaian Plain from which it is presumed these renowned horses came, but its location is not known.
7.3.4b Lysimakhos, a member of Alexander's Bodyguards (see 5.13.1), was destined to play a long and central role in the struggle for control of Alexander's empire, as Arrian hints at 7.18.5 (see n. 7.18.5a).
7.3.6a Nearkhos was not present himself at this point, having been sent on by sea (see 6.28.6). Perhaps he recorded what he had heard about the incident from others.
7.3.6b Different versions of this spectacular suicide have been recorded by Diodorus (17.107.1–6), Strabo (15.1.68), and other sources.
7.4.1a After his loosely organized meditations on Alexander's goals and the Indian sages, Arrian here resumes his narrative from the point he had reached at the end of Book 6.
7.4.1b Atropates' satrapy (province) was Media. For the locations of all Persian satrapies mentioned by Arrian, see Ref. Map 1.
7.4.1c Susa: Map 7.2, Persian Gulf inset.
7.4.1d Abulites and Oxathres were the satraps of Susiana and Pareitakene, respectively. Plutarch (*Parallel Lives*, "Alexander" 68) reports that Alexander executed Oxathres himself, by

running him through with a *sarisa*, a long spear used by the infantry.
7.4.2a Indus, Hydaspes, Akesinos (Arrian's spelling is Akesines), and Hyphasis rivers: Map 7.2, India inset.
7.4.3a Gedrosia: Map 7.2, BY.
7.4.3b These satraps were not the only ones who seem to have counted on Alexander's not returning from India. A renegade Macedonian, Harpalos, an old friend of Alexander's who had been put in charge of the royal treasury in Babylon, had run riot during Alexander's Indian campaign, spending vast sums on his own pleasures and those of his imported Greek courtesans. Alarmed by Alexander's approach, Harpalos left Babylon and headed to Greece with a contingent of troops and huge amounts of embezzled money, hoping to arouse the resentful Athenians to revolt against Macedonian rule. He failed to persuade the Athenians to break away from Alexander and was ultimately killed by one of his hired soldiers. The episode is not dealt with in our text of Arrian, partly due to a page that was lost from the manuscript (see 7.12.7 and n. 7.12.7a). See Appendix E, Alexander's Inner Circle, §16, and Appendix M, Alexander and the Greeks, §10.

Alexander is said to have become quicker to accept accusations as wholly trustworthy and to impose severe punishments on those who were convicted even of minor offenses, on the assumption that in the same state of mind they might commit serious ones.

[4] Alexander also held weddings at Susa for himself and his Companions. He himself married Darius' eldest daughter, Barsine,[4a] and, according to Aristoboulos, another wife as well: Parysatis, the youngest of Okhos' daughters (he was already married to Rhoxane, the daughter of Oxyartes the Bactrian).[4b] [5] To Hephaistion he gave another daughter of Darius, Drypetis, his own wife's sister, since he wanted Hephaistion's children and his own to be cousins.[5a] To Krateros he gave Amastrine, the daughter of Oxyartes, Darius' brother. To Perdikkas he gave the daughter of Atropates the Median satrap. [6] To Ptolemy his Bodyguard and to Eumenes his royal secretary he gave the daughters of Artabazos, Artacama and Artonis.[6a] To Nearkhos he gave the daughter of Barsine[6b] and Mentor, to Seleukos the daughter of Spitamenes the Bactrian.[6c] In like manner he gave the other Companions the Persians' and Medes' most distinguished daughters, about eighty in number.

The weddings were held in the Persian manner. [7] Chairs were placed in order for the bridegrooms, and after the toasts were drunk, the brides arrived and each sat down beside her bridegroom. The grooms took their brides by the hand and kissed them. The king did so first, and after him the others, all at the same time, followed his example. Alexander's conduct on that occasion was felt to be particularly generous and amiable. [8] On receiving their wives, each man led his own away. All the brides received dowries from Alexander, and he commanded all other Macedonians who had married Asian wives to

7.4.4–6
SUSA
To cement bonds of kinship between his own leadership and the Persian nobility, Alexander arranges marriages between his Companions and the daughters of leading Persian families. He himself takes two wives, the daughters of the two most recent Persian kings.

7.4.7–8
SUSA
Arrian describes the mass wedding, held according to Persian custom. Alexander generously dowers all Asian women marrying Macedonians.

7.4.4a   Barsine is usually known by the name she is given in the other sources, Stateira (see n. 2.11.9a). She is not to be confused with another Barsine with whom Alexander had had a sexual liaison several years earlier, resulting in an illegitimate son named Herakles (see n. 7.4.6b).

7.4.4b   Macedonian kings were traditionally polygamous. By marrying women from both of the principal lines of the Persian royal family—Stateira/Barsine was the daughter of Darius III and Parysatis the daughter of Artaxerxes III (here called Okhos), two kings from collateral branches of the Achaemenid house—Alexander evidently intended to secure his claim on the Persian throne and to fuse the bloodlines of the Persian and Macedonian dynasties. See Appendix K, Alexander's Policy of Perso-Macedonian Fusion, §9.

7.4.5a   Both Hephaistion's bride Drypetis and Alexander's wife Stateira/Barsine were reportedly murdered by Rhoxane, with the collaboration of Perdikkas, after the deaths of their husbands (Plutarch, *Parallel Lives*, "Alexander" 77). However, there has been speculation that Plutarch erred and that it was really Stateira and Parysatis, Alexander's two Persian wives, who were killed.

7.4.6a   For Artabazos, see 3.23.7 and n. 3.23.7a. Since he was the grandfather of Alexander's

son Herakles, the selection of his daughters as brides for Ptolemy and Eumenes seems to have been intended to forge a blood tie between their children and Alexander's, as Arrian says explicitly in the case of Hephaistion. The same is true of Nearkhos, who also married into Artabazos' family. It is interesting to see how high these three subcommanders had risen in Alexander's esteem during the Indian campaign; none of them had figured prominently in the king's entourage until then.

7.4.6b   This Barsine, a different woman than the Barsine mentioned at 7.4.4, was a daughter of Artabazos with whom Alexander had fathered a child several years before this. Mentor, her first husband, was the brother of Memnon, a prominent Greek general who had fought on Darius' side against Alexander (see 1.12.9–10, 2.1.1).

7.4.6c   The name of Spitamenes' daughter was Apame, according to Plutarch. This last union mentioned by Arrian is the only one we know of to have lasted; the other generals apparently repudiated their Persian brides after Alexander's death. Some scholars believe that by the phrase "Spitamenes the Bactrian" Arrian designates a different person from the Spitamenes encountered in Books 3 and 4, though this volume assumes they are the same.

have their names registered. There turned out to be more than ten thousand, and these men, too, received wedding gifts from Alexander.

[1] He also thought it an opportune moment to pay off all his soldiers' debts, and he ordered each man to register how much he owed, with the idea that they would receive the money. At first only a few registered their names, as the soldiers feared that this was a test, a way for Alexander to discover which of his men were not getting by on their pay and which were living extravagantly.[1a] [2] When it was reported that few of the men were registering and that those who held promissory notes were hoping to conceal the fact, Alexander reproached the men for their distrust. He declared that the king should speak nothing but the truth to his subjects, and that none of them should ever imagine he would do otherwise. [3] He had tables set up in the camp with money on them, and instructed his clerks to pay the debt of any man who presented a promissory note, but not to take down his name. The soldiers now believed that Alexander was speaking the truth, and were more thankful that their names had not been made known than that their debts had been cleared. This gift to the army is said to have amounted to twenty thousand talents.[3a]

[4] Alexander also bestowed a number of other gifts in recognition either of rank or of conspicuous courage in the heat of battle. He awarded golden crowns to those who had distinguished themselves for valor, presenting the first to Peukestas for having covered him with a shield, [5] the next to Leonnatos for having done the same[5a] and in recognition of the risks he had run in India[5b] and the victory won among the Oroi.[5c] (With the force that had been left with him, Leonnatos had taken a stand against the Oreitan rebels and their neighbors and overpowered them in battle, and was thought to have put the affairs of the Oroi in good order.) [6] Alexander also gave a crown to Nearkhos, who had now arrived at Susa,[6a] for his voyage from India through the Great Sea.[6b] Onesikritos,[6c] the pilot of the royal ship, was also awarded a crown, as were Hephaistion and all the other Bodyguards.

[1] Alexander also received visits from the satraps of his newly founded

7.5.1–3
Spring 324
SUSA
Alexander offers to pay the debts of all his soldiers, but the men are mistrustful and reluctant to reveal their debts. Alexander then offers them the chance to clear their debts anonymously.

7.5.4–6
SUSA
Golden wreaths are given to the heroes of the Indian campaign.

7.6.1–5
SUSA
Alexander receives a force of thirty thousand Persian youths, trained on his orders to fight in the Macedonian manner. This move upsets the native Macedonians, already wary of Alexander's other concessions to Persian custom: his wearing of Median dress, his adoption of the Persian marital rite, and his incorporation of Persian forces into the elite cavalry units of the army.

7.5.1a An interesting glimpse into the deteriorating relations between the rank-and-file soldiers and the army leadership, Alexander in particular. Arrian pays little attention to this important development, since it reflects poorly on Alexander.

7.5.3a For the talent as a monetary unit, see Appendix F, Money and Finance in the Campaigns of Alexander, §3.

7.5.5a Peukestas and Leonnatos both protected Alexander when he was wounded in the Mallian town, as described at 6.10.1–2. Only Peukestas is there said to have held a shield over Alexander, but evidently both men did so.

7.5.5b India: Map 7.2 and India inset.

7.5.5c Oroi/Oreitae, location of territory: Map 7.2, BY. Oroi and Oreitae (see "Oreitan" in previous sentence) are apparently two different names for one tribe, as explained in n. 6.21.3b. In the *Indika* (23.5) Arrian supplies more information about Leonnatos' bravery among the Oroi.

He fought a major battle there in an effort to protect Nearkhos' camp, killing some six thousand attackers while sustaining only small losses.

7.5.6a Susa: Map 7.2, Persian Gulf inset. Nearkhos arrived before the mass wedding ceremony recounted at 7.4.7–8, since he was one of the bridegrooms there (see 7.4.6).

7.5.6b See n. 6.28.5d, which summarizes Nearkhos' ordeal in making a coastal voyage westward from India on the Great Sea, or Ocean, as the Greeks called what is today known as the Indian Ocean. The full narrative of the reconnection of the fleet and the army is given by Arrian in the *Indika* (33).

7.5.6c Onesikritos was mentioned at 6.2.3. He was a Greek who, like Nearkhos, possessed naval expertise that the Macedonians largely lacked. Onesikritos and Nearkhos shared command during the westward voyage of the Indian Ocean fleet, and each later wrote a memoir emphasizing his own role at the expense of the other.

cities[1a] and the other territory taken in war. They brought with them about thirty thousand adolescent boys, all the same age, whom Alexander called his Epigonoi.[1b] They had been issued Macedonian arms and were trained for war in the Macedonian manner. [2] Their arrival is said to have vexed the Macedonians, who felt that Alexander was doing his utmost to lessen his future dependence on his countrymen. The Macedonians were indeed highly distressed by Alexander's Median apparel; and the fact that the weddings had been performed in the Persian manner displeased most of them, even those who had themselves taken part as bridegrooms, notwithstanding that they had been greatly honored that the king had treated them as equals. [3] They were also vexed at Peukestas, the satrap of the Persians, who had taken to wearing Persian apparel and speaking Persian to please Alexander.[3a] It grieved them as well that Bactrian, Sogdian, Arachosian, Zarangian, Areian, and Parthian[3b] cavalrymen, along with Persian[3c] cavalrymen (the so-called Euakai), were being distributed into the Companion cavalry, provided that they were preeminent in rank, appearance, or some other quality.[3d] [4] Furthermore, a fifth hipparchy[4a] had been created: it was not entirely barbarian, but when the whole cavalry was increased in size, barbarians were enrolled in it, and the *agema*[4b] now included Kophen son of Artabazos; Hydarnes and Artiboles, sons of Mazaios; Sisines and Phradasmenes, sons of Phratapherdes, the satrap of the Parthians and of Hyrcania;[4c] [5] Itanes, son of Oxyartes and brother of Rhoxane, Alexan-

7.6.1a   It is not clear what "satraps of . . . cities" refers to. Perhaps Arrian has used the term "satrap" loosely here to refer to some lesser official rather than the province administrators appointed by the Persian king.

7.6.1b   The Greek name Epigonoi (literally, "offspring") signifies a younger contingent trained or educated to take the place of their elders. Alexander had ordered the recruitment of the Epigonoi some two years before this, according to Diodorus (17.108), though Arrian first mentions them here. Diodorus claims they were recruited to serve as leverage against the unruly and mutinous Macedonian troops. See Appendix K, §8.

7.6.3a   See 6.30.2–3, where Peukestas' receptivity to Persian language and customs is first noted. The fact that no other Macedonian administrators had bothered to learn Persian is remarkable, and telling. By contrast, Alexander had Greek taught to the Epigonoi, according to Plutarch (*Parallel Lives*, "Alexander" 47.6), and to the Persian royal family, according to Diodorus (17.67.1).

7.6.3b   The following locations can be found on Map 7.2: Bactria, AY; Sogdiana, AY; Arachosia, BY; Zarangiane (Drangiane), BY; Ar(e)ia, AY; Parthia, AY.

7.6.3c   Persia: Map 7.2, and Persian Gulf inset.

7.6.3d   The appointment of Asian horsemen to the elite Companion cavalry was a radical move on Alexander's part (see Appendix K, §10). Unfortunately Arrian gives us our only account of it, and does not indicate when it occurred. Scholars' opinions vary widely, from

330 to 324. The issue of the integration of Asian cavalries into the Companions is raised again by the Macedonian troops at 7.8.2.

7.6.4a   Arrian implies that the number of hipparchies, or cavalry squadrons, had diminished from eight or more in 327 (see 4.24.1 and n. 4.24.1b) to four, with a fifth added to accommodate new Asian recruits. Brunt suggests that losses in the Gedrosia march had diminished the numbers of Companions (P. A. Brunt, trans., *Arrian: Anabasis of Alexander*, Books 1–4 [Cambridge: Harvard University Press, 1976], lxxiii).

7.6.4b   *Agema*: usually a special division of light-armed infantry, though here the term refers to a cavalry unit, first mentioned at 4.24.1. Since the *agema* was an elite unit, made up of those most favored by the king, the inclusion of Asian nobles in it especially galled the more conservative among the Macedonians.

7.6.4c   All the Asian recruits mentioned in this list are the sons of powerful Persian nobles who had once opposed Alexander but then became his adherents and were given high administrative posts: Artabazos was satrap of Bactria (4.15.5), Mazaios of Babylon (3.16.4), and Phratapherdes of Parthia and Hyrcania (3.23.4). Alexander was aware of the danger that such men could turn against him, as another Persian satrap, Satibarzanes, had done (see 3.25.1–2 and 3.28.2–3). One motive for keeping their sons in his service, then, was to have hostages ensuring the loyalty of the fathers. See Appendix K, §10.

der's wife; and the brothers Aigobares and Mithrobaios.[5a] Hystaspes the Bactrian had been appointed as their commander, and they had been issued Macedonian spears instead of barbarian javelins. All these developments troubled the Macedonians, who felt that Alexander now was going entirely over to the barbarian side in his attitudes and regarded Macedonian customs and the Macedonians themselves with disrespect.

[1] Alexander ordered Hephaistion to lead most of the infantry to the Persian Gulf,[1a] while he himself, now that the fleet had sailed up to Susian territory,[1b] embarked on the ships with the shield-bearers, the *agema*, and a few cavalry Companions and sailed down the River Eulaios[1c] toward the sea. [2] When he was near the river's outlet, he left most of the ships behind, including those that had been damaged. Taking only his swiftest ships, he went by sea from the Eulaios to the outlets of the Tigris.[2a] The other ships were sent down the Eulaios to the canal that connects that river to the Tigris, and entered the Tigris by way of that canal.

[3] Of the two rivers, the Euphrates and the Tigris, that enclose Assyria[3a] (this is why the country has been called Mesopotamia,[3b] or "land between the rivers," by the inhabitants), the Tigris, flowing through much lower ground than the Euphrates, receives the water of many canals that connect it to that river as well as the water of several other rivers, and consequently increases in volume before it empties into the Persian Gulf. It is an enormous stream, fordable nowhere until its outlet, as none of its water is expended on the land. [4] For the land in the Tigris' vicinity lies higher than the water, and the river empties neither into the canals nor into any other river, but receives their streams and nowhere furnishes water to irrigate the land. [5] The Euphrates' water level, on the other hand, is higher. The level of the river is everywhere even with its banks, and many canals have been cut from it, some of which flow year-round and supply water to the inhabitants on either bank. Other canals are created to irrigate the land whenever water is scarce, since the country receives little rainfall. The Euphrates eventually trickles away into shallows and marshes and flows no farther.[5a]

[6] After sailing the length of the shoreline separating the Eulaios and the Tigris, Alexander sailed up the Tigris to the site where Hephaistion had made camp with all his forces. From there Alexander sailed to Opis,[6a] a city settled on the Tigris. [7] On the upstream voyage, he destroyed the river's weirs and made the channel completely level. These weirs had been built by

7.6.5a   Itanes, Alexander's brother-in-law, is mentioned only here. His father Oxyartes was at this point satrap in the Paropamisos (see 6.15.3). Aigobares and Mithrobaios must have been important Persian nobles, but they are otherwise unknown to us.
7.7.1a   Persian Gulf: Map 7.2, Persian Gulf inset.
7.7.1b   Susiana: Map 7.9, BY.
7.7.1c   Evidently Eulaios is another name for the waterway formed by the upper Choaspes River and the lower Pasitigris, which at this time were joined by a canal. Eulaios (Eulaeus), Pasitigris, and Choaspes rivers

and canal, possible locations: Map 7.2, Persian Gulf inset.
7.7.2a   Tigris River: Map 7.2, Persian Gulf inset.
7.7.3a   Euphrates River; Assyria: Map 7.2, Persian Gulf inset.
7.7.3b   Mesopotamia: Map 7.9, BX.
7.7.5a   Contradicted by 7.19.3, where Nearkhos sails up the Euphrates from the sea. It may be that the river, which was drained by canals in spring (see 7.21.2–5), reached the sea at some times of the year but not others.
7.7.6a   Opis: Map 7.9, BX.

the Persians to prevent anyone's sailing up from the sea to their country and getting the better of them with a naval force—a measure devised because the Persians were not a naval people, and the succession of weirs made it impracticable to sail upstream on the Tigris. Alexander said that such devices were the work of men who were not the sort to prevail in arms,[7a] whereas he had no need of such a precaution; indeed he demonstrated that it was not even effective, since he easily cut through the structures the Persians had erected with such zeal.

[1] On reaching Opis, Alexander assembled the Macedonians and announced that he was discharging from the army all who through age or disability were unfit to serve. He was sending them home, and he would reward them richly enough to arouse the envy of the Macedonians at home and excite their desire to share the same dangers and toils.[1a] [2] Alexander undoubtedly assumed his words would please the Macedonians. But since they felt they had already been slighted by Alexander and were considered useless in war, they were vexed yet again, and not unreasonably, by his words. Throughout the whole army the men had been exasperated on many other occasions. By now they had often been pained by Alexander's Persian apparel, as it conveyed the same message, and by his supplying the Epigonoi with Macedonian equipment, and his inclusion of foreign cavalrymen in the ranks of the Companions. [3] Accordingly, they could not bear to sit silent but began telling him to send them all home and to wage war by himself along with his "father," referring mockingly to Ammon.[3a]

Alexander was quicker to anger at that period, and in consequence of being attended in barbarian fashion was no longer as kind to the Macedonians as in the past. As soon as he heard the men's protests he leaped down from the platform with his officers, ordered them to arrest the principal agitators, and pointed out to the shield-bearers the men they should arrest, thirteen in number. He commanded that they be led away for execution.[3b] Thunderstruck, the rest fell silent, whereupon Alexander again mounted the platform and spoke as follows:

7.8.1–2
OPIS
At Opis, Alexander tries to decommission aging or unfit Macedonian veterans, but the Macedonians take this as yet another sign that they are being replaced by foreign troops, and refuse to go along.

7.8.3
OPIS
Alexander wades into the rebellious throng and orders the immediate arrest and execution of thirteen of its leaders. Arrian admits that the king's character had been adversely affected by the obsequies showered on him by his Asian subjects.

7.7.7a Alexander characteristically regarded defensive military tactics as ignoble or cowardly. His destruction of the Tigris weirs was no doubt partly in preparation for a combined sea and land expedition against the Arabs, already planned for the following year (see 7.19.6).

7.8.1a The manuscripts of Arrian's text have a single Greek word (*menousin*) in this sentence indicating that Alexander rewarded those who stayed with him rather than those who were sent home. However, this word is deleted by many modern editors, including the editor of this volume. Alexander's goal was to advertise his success and spur new enlistments, which could best be achieved by rewarding those returning to Macedonia. The word in question may have been inserted by a scribe who misunderstood the king's strategy. It is worth noting, however, that at 5.26.8, facing

down the mutineers at the Hyphasis River, Alexander promises to make those who *remain* with him the envy of those who depart, which argues in favor of the manuscript reading.

7.8.3a The Macedonians' mockery of their king here is one of the most significant pieces of evidence found in Arrian to indicate that Alexander himself had fostered the idea of his divine parentage; see Appendix C, Alexander the Man (and God?), §16. In retelling the episode of Alexander's visit to the oracle of Ammon, Arrian studiously avoids comment on this point (see 3.4.5 and n. 3.4.5a).

7.8.3b Alexander's summary imposition of the death sentence stands in marked contrast to the Philotas affair (3.26.1–3) and the conspiracy of the pages (4.13–14), where he conducted elaborate, albeit rigged, judicial procedures.

7.9.1–5

Summer 324

OPIS

Alexander begins his speech to his men by reminding them of how far they progressed under his father's leadership—from backward shepherds to rulers of the Greek world and the Balkans.

[1] "I will speak not to quell your longing for home, Macedonians, for you may go wherever you wish as far as I am concerned, but so you may realize, as you depart, who we are, you and I, that you should act toward me in this way. [2] I will begin, as is appropriate, with Philip, my father, who took you up when you were helpless wanderers, most of you dressed in skins, pasturing a few flocks in the mountains and fighting ineptly to protect them from your neighbors, the Illyrians,[1a] Triballoi,[1b] and Thracians.[1c] He gave you cloaks to wear instead of skins, led you down from the mountains to the plains, and made you able to hold your own in battle against your barbarian neighbors, so your safety depended not on your mountain strongholds but on your own courage. He made you city dwellers, and by means of laws and good customs gave you an orderly way of life. [3] He made you masters of the very barbarians who had plundered you earlier of men and property—you who had been their slaves and subjects—and added the greater part of Thrace to Macedonia.[3a] Having captured the most advantageous places along the coast, he opened up the country to trade, made it safe for you to work the mines, [4] and made you masters of the Thessalians,[4a] who in times past had frightened you half to death. By humbling the Phocians,[4b] he made your route into Greece broad and open instead of narrow and difficult.[4c] As for the Athenians and Thebans[4d] who were always lying in wait for us, he brought them so low, at a time when I myself was sharing his toils,[4e] that instead of our paying tribute to the Athenians[4f] and obeying the Thebans, it was their turn to look to us for their security. [5] On his arrival in the Peloponnese[5a] Philip again put state affairs in order. Appointed as leader with full powers over the rest of the Greeks in the expedition against the Persians,[5b] he conferred as much renown on the Macedonian people as on himself.

7.9.6–8

OPIS

Under his own leadership, Alexander reminds his men, Macedonians have attained global empire and untold wealth.

[6] "Such are the benefits conferred on you by my father. But though substantial when judged by themselves, they appear small when compared with the benefits I have conferred. Having inherited from my father a few gold and silver cups, with not even sixty talents in the treasury and with debts incurred by Philip amounting to nearly five hundred talents, I myself borrowed an additional eight hundred[6a] and set out from the land from

7.9.1a Illyria: Map 7.9, inset.
7.9.1b Triballoi: Map 7.9, AX.
7.9.1c Thrace: Map 7.9, inset.
7.9.3a Macedonia: Map 7.9, inset. Philip campaigned in various parts of Thrace in the 350s, in the early phase of his expansion.
7.9.4a Thessaly: Map 7.9, inset.
7.9.4b Phocis: Map 7.9, inset.
7.9.4c The Phocians controlled a route into central Greece that circumvented the pass of Thermopylae, historically a choke point where invasions from the north could be stopped or slowed.
7.9.4d Athens; Thebes: Map 7.9, inset.
7.9.4e The reference is to the battle of Chaeronea in 338, in which Alexander had helped Philip defeat the combined armies of Thebes and Athens (see Appendix M, §2).

7.9.4f At least one Macedonian city appears on lists kept by the Athenians of the tributary states in their empire.
7.9.5a Peloponnese: Map 7.9, inset. Philip followed up his victory over the Athenians and Thebans with a sally into the Peloponnese in 338.
7.9.5b In its first meeting, in 337, the League of Corinth affirmed the right of Philip to lead the conglomerate Greek and Macedonian forces against Persia. For more on the League of Corinth, see Appendix M, §3.
7.9.6a This is the only place where we hear of such a huge debt, though Plutarch confirms that Alexander had to borrow at the start of his expedition (*Parallel Lives*, "Alexander" 15; *Moralia* 327d and 342d). All of Philip's revenue from his Thracian mines was used in creating and maintaining his army.

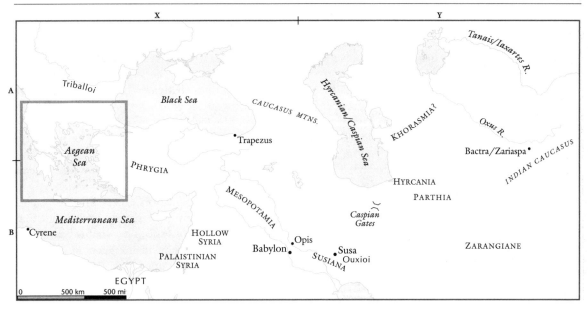

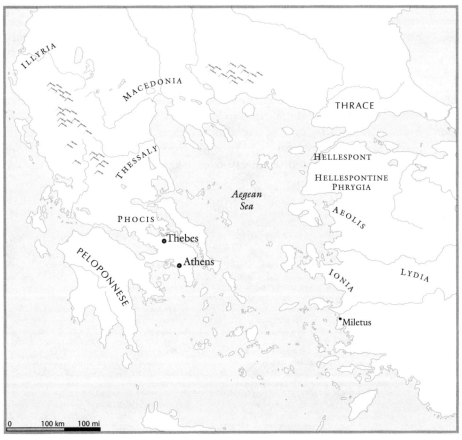

MAP 7.9

which you were barely able to get a living. Heading straight for the Hellespont,[6b] I opened a passage for you, though the Persians then held sway at sea. [7] Overpowering the Persian satraps with my cavalry, I added all of Ionia to your domain and all of Aeolis, both Phrygias, and Lydia, and took Miletus[7a] by siege. As for all the other countries that came over to me willingly: upon their surrender, I gave them to you for your own profit. [8] The treasures from Egypt[8a] and Cyrene,[8b] all of which I acquired without a battle, go to you; Hollow Syria, Palaistinian Syria, and Mesopotamia are your property; Babylon, Bactra, and Susa[8c] are yours; and the wealth of the Lydians, the treasures of the Persians, the riches of India,[8d] and the surrounding Ocean are yours. You are the satraps, you the generals, you the commanders.[8e]

[9] "As for me, what is left to me after these labors except this purple and this diadem?[9a] I have acquired nothing in my own name, nor can anyone point to treasures of my own, but only your possessions or what is being kept safe on your behalf. For there would be no point in my keeping anything, since I eat the same food as you do and take the same sleep. Though, for that matter, I doubt that my food is as dainty as the fare some of you eat, and I know I keep awake and stand watch for you, so that you may sleep soundly.[9b]

[1] "But perhaps you feel that it was you who were toiling and suffering hardships, while I acquired these treasures as your leader without toil and hardship. But who among you imagines that he has toiled more on my behalf than I have on his? Come on, then—let any of you strip and show his wounds, and I will show mine. [2] For in my own case, there is no part of my body, at least not in front, that has been left unwounded, and there is no weapon, held or hurled, whose marks I do not carry. On the contrary, I have been wounded by the sword when fighting hand to hand, pierced by arrows, struck by shots from catapults, and hit time and again by rocks and clubs.[2a] For your sake, for the sake of your renown and your wealth, I led you, a conquering army, through every land and sea, every river, every mountain, and every plain.

7.9.9
Summer 324
OPIS
Alexander insists that he has made all his efforts not in pursuit of personal gain, but for the sake of his people.

7.10.1–4
OPIS
Alexander reminds his men of the wounds he has received in battle and other ways in which he has shared their lot, as well as his generosity in honoring them in life and in death.

7.9.6b Hellespont: Map 7.9, inset.
7.9.7a The following locations can be found on Map 7.9, inset: Ionia; Aeolis; Hellespontine Phrygia; Lydia; Miletus. Phrygia: Map 7.9, BX.
7.9.8a Egypt: Map 7.9, BX.
7.9.8b Cyrene: Map 7.9, BX. This autonomous Greek city had not yet fallen under Macedonian control by this time, but perhaps had agreed to pay some sort of indemnity.
7.9.8c The following locations can be found on Map 7.9: Hollow Syria (Koile Syria), BX; Palaistinian Syria, BX; Mesopotamia, BX; Babylon, BX; Bactra/Zariaspa, AY; Susa, BY.
7.9.8d India: Map 7.2 and India inset.
7.9.8e Alexander's rhetoric here resembles what he used against the Hyphasis mutiny (see 5.26.8), where he also claimed that the army had received all the power and wealth of the empire. However, as Koinos replied, this claim applied only to the high-ranking officers in the army, not to the rank and file.
7.9.9a Alexander refers to the two most visible

symbols of his royal status. He wore a metal band around his head, called a diadem by the Greeks, adapted from the band that the Persian kings wore, the *kitaris* or tiara; and his cloak was partially made up of purple cloth, another adaptation from Persian royal style. See n. 4.7.4b and n. 4.7.4c, and Appendix K, §4.
7.9.9b Whatever Arrian thought of these claims, they are belied by information found in other sources. A passage quoted from the *Ephemerides* (Aelian, *Varia Historia* 3.23), thought by scholars to date from 324, suggests that Alexander was regularly sleeping through entire days after long drinking bouts.
7.10.2a Alexander's major wounds, as recorded by Arrian, were four: a sword wound in his thigh at 2.12.1, an arrow through his leg and a fractured fibula at 3.30.11, an arrow to the shoulder at 4.23.3, and an arrow above the breast that pierced a lung at 6.10.1. Plutarch supplies a fuller list (*Moralia* 341a–d).

[3] I have made the same marriages as you have, and the children of many of you will be related to my own. And if any of you had incurred debts, I paid them off without troubling to find out how they were incurred, though you earn a handsome wage and have had many opportunities to plunder after a siege. Most of you have golden crowns,[3a] immortal remembrances of your valor and my esteem. [4] And anyone who has died has met with a glorious end and a splendid funeral; bronze statues of most have been set up at home, and their honored parents are exempt from all public duty and tax.[4a] For none of you died fleeing the enemy while I held command.

[5] "I was now going to send back those of you who are unfit for war, to be envied by those at home.[5a] But since you all wish to go, be gone, all of you, and report, when you get home, that Alexander, your king, who conquered the Persians, Medes, Bactrians, and Sacae,[5b] [6] who subjugated the Ouxioi,[6a] Arachosians,[6b] and Zarangians, who acquired the lands of the Parthians, Khorasmians, and Hyrcanians as far as the Caspian Sea, who crossed the Caucasus beyond the Caspian Gates, and the Oxus, the Tanais,[6c] and the Indus, too, which none had ever crossed but Dionysos, and the Hydaspes, the Akesinos, and the Hydraotes, [7] and who would have crossed the Hyphasis[7a] had you not shrunk back, and who burst into the Great Sea by both outlets of the Indus, and who traversed the Gedrosian desert, which none had crossed with an army, and along the way acquired Carmania and the land of the Oreitae,[7b] the fleet having already sailed from India to Persia—tell them, why don't you, that when you returned to Susa you abandoned him and departed, turning him over to the safekeeping of the barbarians you had conquered. Such a report may win you renown from men and will, no doubt, be holy in the sight of god. Now go!"

[1] So saying, he quickly leaped down from the platform and passed into the palace, where he took no care of his physical needs[1a] and was seen by none of his Companions, even on the next day. On the third day, he called in the foremost Persians and distributed among them the commands of his battalions and directed that those men, whom he called his kinsmen, were

7.10.5–7
OPIS
As a final stratagem, Alexander dares his men to leave for home and to report to their countrymen that they abandoned their king in hostile territory.

7.11.1–4
OPIS
Alexander ends his speech and retreats in solitude to his quarters. After three days he calls in his Persian officers and appoints them to the high commands formerly held by Macedonians. Hearing of this, the Macedonians rush to the palace and beg the king to admit them, offering to surrender additional leaders of the insurrection.

7.10.3a A number of officers received golden crowns at Susa (see 7.5.4–6), but surely "most" had not been so rewarded.
7.10.4a The twenty-five Companions killed at the Granicus had been honored with bronze statues, as Arrian informs us, and the parents of all those slain there had been exempted from taxes and public duties; see 1.16.4–5. But whether these honors were extended more widely is unclear. Certainly the awarding of bronze statues could not have been a common occurrence.
7.10.5a This promise to reward those departing—later fulfilled (see 7.12.1) with a bonus of a talent per man—supports the version of the text adopted at 7.8.1.
7.10.5b The following locations can be found on Map 7.2: Persia, Persian Gulf inset; Media,

BY; Bactria, AY; Sacae, possible location of territory, AY.
7.10.6a Ouxioi, location of territory: Map 7.9, BY.
7.10.6b Arachosia: Map 7.2, BY.
7.10.6c The following locations can be found on Map 7.9: Zarangiane (Drangiane), BY; Parthia, AY; Khorasmia, possible location, AY; Hyrcania, BY; Caspian/Hyrcanian Sea, AY; Indian Caucasus/Paropamisos, BY; Caspian Gates, BY; Oxus River, AY; Tanais/Iaxartes River, AY.
7.10.7a Indus, Hydaspes, Akesinos, Hydraotes, and Hyphasis rivers: Map 7.2, India inset.
7.10.7b Gedrosia; Carmania; Oreitae, location of territory: Map 7.16.
7.11.1a As he did after the murder of Kleitos (see 4.9.3–4), Alexander here deliberately avoids eating, drinking, or washing to convey his extreme emotional distress.

alone permitted to kiss him.[1b] [2] As for the Macedonians, when the speech ended,[2a] they remained in stunned silence near the platform, nor did anyone follow the departing king except the Companions and Bodyguards who attended him. Most of them stayed where they were; they had no idea what to do or say, but were unwilling to leave. [3] But when they were told about the Persians and Medes,[3a] the commands being given to the Persians, the barbarian troops being drafted into companies, and the Macedonian names—a Persian *agema*, Persian infantry companions, other *asthetairoi*,[3b] a Persian battalion of Silver Shields,[3c] and the Companion cavalry with a new royal *agema*—they could no longer contain themselves. [4] They ran together to the palace, flung their weapons before the door to signal that they were the king's suppliants, and stood before it, shouting and pleading to be admitted. They said they were willing to surrender the men who were responsible for the present disturbance and those who had started the uproar, but they would not depart, day or night, unless Alexander took pity on them.

[5] When this had been reported to Alexander, he hurried out. Seeing them so downcast, and hearing most of them wailing piteously, he too shed tears. He stepped forward as if to speak, while they remained in the posture of suppliants. [6] One of them, a man named Kallines, who was distinguished both by age and by hipparchy[6a] in the Companion cavalry, said, "Sire, what grieves the Macedonians is that you have now made some of the Persians your kinsmen, and that Persians are called 'kinsmen of Alexander' and may kiss you, but none of the Macedonians has yet enjoyed that honor."[6b] [7] Alexander interrupted him and said, "But I consider all of you my kinsmen, and from now on I will call you so." At these words Kallines approached and kissed Alexander, and anyone else who wished to do so kissed him as well. They then retrieved their weapons and returned to camp, shouting and chanting their song of triumph.

[8] Alexander now performed a sacrifice to the gods to whom he customarily sacrificed, and held a public banquet. He seated all the Macedonians around him, and next to them the Persians, and next to them the other foreigners notable for rank or some other merit. Drawing wine from the same bowl, Alexander and those around him poured the same libations, after the Greek

7.11.1b The Persian king's favorites were permitted, by tradition, to greet him with a kiss on the mouth. The Macedonians had no such custom (see 7.11.6). This ritual differs from the kiss associated with *proskynesis* (see 4.12.3–5), which was given rather than received by the king.

7.11.2a Arrian has slightly disrupted the chronology here in order to keep a connected narrative of Alexander's actions. After the three days of the king's retreat into isolation have already been described, we jump back to the point in time reached at the end of 7.10, to observe the reaction of the army to Alexander's speech.

7.11.3a Arrian now returns to the point in time reached at the end of 7.11.1.

7.11.3b *Asthetairoi*: very little is known about the composition of this elite unit.

7.11.3c The Silver Shields (Argyraspides) are mentioned only here by Arrian, though they figure prominently in the years following Alexander's death. They were a select contingent of three thousand shield-bearers (*hypaspists*), specially honored after the Indian campaign with silver adornments for their weapons. Whether Silver Shields became their name during Alexander's lifetime or afterward is a matter of debate.

7.11.6a On hipparchies or cavalry squadrons, see n. 3.29.7a. Arrian here implies that the hipparchies differed in degree of distinction.

7.11.6b For this ritual, see n. 7.11.1b.

FIGURE 7.12. Alexander's administrative arrangements for his empire were promulgated on tablets like this one, found in the ruins of Priene in Asia Minor. The inscription begins, "King Alexander dedicated the temple to Athena Polias," and goes on to list the various parts of Priene and its surroundings that were either subject to or exempt from taxation. The edict cannot be securely dated; it may have been engraved after Alexander's death.

seers and the Magi[8a] had led the way. [9] Along with other requests, Alexander prayed that the Macedonians and Persians might enjoy concord and partnership in the empire.[9a] It is said that nine thousand men attended the banquet and that all of them poured the same libation and joined in a song of victory.

[1] All the Macedonians who were unfit for fighting, from either old age or some other misfortune, were now willing to leave him. There were nearly ten thousand of these men. Alexander compensated them not only for the time they had already served but also for that of their homeward journey, and paid each man a talent over and above his wages.[1a] [2] But he ordered those who had children by Asian women to leave them behind with him and not to introduce strife into Macedonia by bringing children of another race and of barbarian women to the children who had been left behind at home and to their mothers.[2a] He said he would see to it that they were raised in the Macedonian manner, particularly with regard to their military training, and he would himself bring them to Macedonia and deliver them to their fathers when they had grown to manhood. [3] The men who were departing were given these vague and uncertain promises, though Alexander also saw fit to present them with the strongest proof that he loved and needed them: he sent Krateros, the man he trusted most and considered his equal, as guard and commander of their journey. When he had personally taken leave of all the departing soldiers, on which occasion tears were shed on all sides, he dismissed them. [4] He ordered Krateros to escort them home and to take charge, thereafter, of Macedonia, Thrace, Thessaly,[4a] and the freedom of the Greeks. He sent orders for Antipatros to bring out fresh Macedonian troops as replacements for those he was sending back. As Krateros' second in command Alexander dispatched Polyperkhon,[4b] so that if any misfortune befell Krateros on the journey (as Alexander was sending him off in a weakened condition), the men would not lack a commander.

[5] A rumor was gaining currency among those who are always more eager to discuss royal affairs when they are being kept secret, and who are more inclined to credit the baser interpretation (to which they are attracted by conjecture and their own baseness) than the truth.[5a] It was said that Alexander, succumbing to his mother's slanders about Antipatros, wished to remove this man from Macedonia. [6] Perhaps Antipatros' summons was not intended to bring him into dishonor, but was issued to prevent any

7.11.8a   The Magi were a powerful priestly caste who attended the Persian king under the Achaemenid empire, interpreted dreams and signs, and presided over various state rituals.

7.11.9a   For this banquet and the content of Alexander's prayer, see Appendix K, §12.

7.12.1a   According to the going rates for military service in this period, a talent of silver would amount to about eight years of aggregate income for an ordinary enlisted man.

7.12.2a   This policy provides an interesting glimpse into the cultural tensions that Alexander's sojourn in Asia had created. His troops

could be persuaded, with some difficulty, to marry Asian women and consider mixed-race children their legitimate heirs; but such equality between the races would never be recognized by Macedonians who had not gone on the campaign.

7.12.4a   Macedonia; Thrace; Thessaly: Map 7.9, inset.

7.12.4b   Polyperkhon was later an important participant in the struggle for succession; see the Epilogue, §9, 11.

7.12.5a   This is one of several comments in which Arrian clearly speaks from his own experience of Roman imperial politics. See 4.12.6 for another.

mutual unpleasantness caused by their disagreement from becoming a breach of the kind Alexander could not heal.[6a] As it was, Antipatros and Olympias never ceased writing to him. Antipatros would describe Olympias' willfulness, quick temper, and tendency to meddle—traits by no means becoming in the mother of Alexander. Consequently, a remark was attributed to Alexander in reference to the reports he was receiving about his mother: that she was charging him heavy rent for having housed him for ten months.[6b] [7] Olympias, meanwhile, wrote that Antipatros exaggerated his dignity and demanded excessive attendance; no longer mindful of who had appointed him, he considered himself preeminent among the Macedonians and Greeks. The reports that tended to slander Antipatros appeared to carry more weight with Alexander, since they were of the kind to confirm a monarch's worst fears. Yet no obvious deed or remark on Alexander's part would have led anyone to conclude that his attitude toward Antipatros had changed. [. . .][7a]

[1] It is said that Hephaistion, humbled by this line of reasoning, was reconciled with Eumenes. Eumenes came around willingly, but Hephaistion only reluctantly. It was on that journey that Alexander is said to have seen the plain that pastures the royal horses. According to Herodotus, it is known as the Nesaian Plain,[1a] and the horses are known as the Nesaian horses. In ancient times there were nearly a hundred and fifty thousand of these horses, but Alexander found no more than fifty thousand, as most of them had been seized as plunder by brigands.

[2] They say that Atropates, the Median satrap, presented Alexander with a hundred women, claiming that they were Amazons. The women were equipped with cavalry gear except that they carried axes instead of spears and smaller, lighter shields. Some say that their right breasts were smaller and were exposed in battle.[2a] [3] It is said that Alexander dismissed them from the army lest their presence cause any turmoil by inciting the Macedonians or barbarians toward rape; he is also said to have urged them to inform their queen that he would pay a visit to beget children by her. Yet neither Aristoboulos nor Ptolemy nor any other reliable witness has

7.13.1
Summer 324
MEDIA
Eumenes and Hephaistion reconcile. Alexander views the home of the Nesaian horses.

7.13.2–6
MEDIA
Atropates, satrap of Media, presents Alexander with a company of "Amazons," though Arrian believes these are some other barbarian women equipped to look like Amazons.

7.12.6a It is not clear either to Arrian or to modern historians why Alexander summoned Antipatros to Babylon, or why Antipatros did not come but sent his son Kassandros in his stead. We need not suppose that Alexander intended to do Antipatros harm or that Antipatros assumed so, for if either were the case, Kassandros would most likely not have been sent to become a convenient hostage.

7.12.6b Since the ancient Greeks used lunar months of twenty-eight days to divide the year, they reckoned the term of pregnancy at ten months rather than nine.

7.12.7a Following this chapter, a manuscript page of Arrian's original text has become lost in the process of transmission, sometime after the tenth century C.E. The missing portion of text certainly contained an account of the return to Greece of Alexander's one-time

friend Harpalos, as we know from a summary of Arrian's text made by a medieval reader. Some have argued that the missing portion also dealt with the Exile's Decree, a highly significant episode in Alexander's reign that otherwise goes unmentioned by Arrian (see n. 7.19.1a and Appendix M, §11). The missing text also dealt with the quarrel between Hephaistion and Alexander's Greek secretary Eumenes, since when the narrative resumes, that quarrel is being patched up.

7.13.1a Nesaian Plain: location unknown. See n. 7.3.4a.

7.13.2a According to the traditional Greek understanding, the name Amazon, which could be taken to mean "lacking a breast," arose because these legendary warriors had their right breast amputated so that the bow could be drawn more easily.

recorded this incident.[3a] [4] Nor do I think the race of Amazons was still in existence at that time, or even in the period before Alexander; otherwise Xenophon would have mentioned them,[4a] since he mentioned the Phasianoi, the Colchians, and all the other barbarian tribes the Greeks met before reaching or after setting out from Trapezus,[4b] where they would indeed have encountered Amazons if they still existed. [5] Yet I find it hard to believe that this race of women never existed, seeing that it has been celebrated by many distinguished writers. Legend has it that Herakles was sent to them to fetch back to Greece a girdle belonging to Hippolyta, their queen, and that the Athenians with Theseus were the first to defeat them in battle and drive them back when they invaded Europe.[5a] And Mikon[5b] has painted the battle of the Athenians and Amazons just as he has the battle of the Athenians and Persians.

[6] Moreover, Herodotus has often mentioned these women in his writings,[6a] and all the Athenians who have eulogized the war dead have made special mention of the Athenians' action against the Amazons.[6b] But if Atropates did indeed present some mounted warrior women to Alexander, I imagine they belonged to some other barbarian tribe who had been trained to ride and who had been dressed in the traditional garb of the Amazons.

[1] At Ecbatana[1a] Alexander performed a sacrifice, as was his custom after successful ventures, and held competitions in athletics and the arts and drinking parties with his Companions. At that point Hephaistion fell ill. It is said that on the seventh day of his illness the stadium was filled with spec-

7.14.1–7
Autumn 324
ECBATANA
Hephaistion suddenly falls ill and dies. Arrian pauses to survey the varying accounts he has read of Alexander's extreme grief, some of which he finds hard to accept.

7.13.3a The vulgate sources (see the Introduction, §2.5–6) all recount such a visit during the course of Alexander's campaigns near the Caspian (Diodorus 17.77.1–3; Quintus Curtius 6.5.24–32; Justin 12.3.5; Plutarch, *Parallel Lives*, "Alexander" 46.1–2). The Amazon queen is said to have sought out Alexander and to have shared his bed for thirteen days and nights, for the express purpose of conceiving a child.
7.13.4a Xenophon (c. 450–354) served as a mercenary soldier on the military expedition led by Cyrus of Persia against his reigning brother, Artaxerxes II. After a long march inland to Cunaxa, near Babylon, Cyrus' army was successful but Cyrus himself was killed. Xenophon helped lead the Greek forces north through the heartland of Asia and ultimately back to Greece, an ordeal he recorded in his *Anabasis*.
7.13.4b Trapezus (Map 7.9, AX) was the point at which Xenophon and his men reached the sea after their long overland journey through the lands of the Phasianoi (Phasioi) and Colchians, among other nations, from the site of their battle against Artaxerxes (Xenophon, *Anabasis* 4.8.22). They were at that point close to the region where Amazons were said to dwell, so Arrian expects that, had Xenophon encountered any, he would have mentioned them in his account.

7.13.5a According to Greek myth, Herakles was directed to fetch the girdle of the Amazon queen (a task that implies sexual conquest) as one of his twelve labors, while Theseus, the first king of Athens, had to repel an invasion by Amazons (see Plutarch, *Parallel Lives*, "Theseus" 27–28). The theme of the battle between Greek heroes and Amazons was a popular subject in classical Greek art. Arrian's attitude toward mythic literature here differs markedly from the skepticism he evinced at 5.1.2.
7.13.5b Mikon was an Athenian artist of the late fifth century who helped decorate the famous Painted Stoa in the Athenian agora.
7.13.6a See Herodotus, *Histories* 4.110–117, 9.27.4.
7.13.6b At Athens a state custom required a leading citizen to deliver a public oration over the bodies of those killed in war. Usually these funeral orations center on the glorious history of the city; one highlight of that history, as Arrian notes here, was Theseus' war with the Amazons. However, our two surviving examples of funeral orations—those of Pericles in the Peloponnesian War and of Hypereides in the Lamian War—make no mention of Amazons.
7.14.1a Ecbatana: Map 7.16, Assyria inset.

tators, as it was the day of the boys' athletic competition. When it was reported to Alexander that Hephaistion's condition was grave, he rushed to his friend's side but found him no longer alive. A variety of accounts have been written about Alexander's grief. All writers agree that it was profound. As for Alexander's conduct on the occasion, reports vary depending on whether the writer was well or ill disposed to Hephaistion or to Alexander himself. [3] Among the writers who describe Alexander's unrestrained behavior, some seem to me to think that everything he did or said in his intense grief over his dearest friend was to his credit; others, however, find his conduct shameful, befitting neither a king nor Alexander. Some say that for most of that day, having flung himself onto his friend's body, Alexander moaned and wept and refused to leave until his Companions carried him off by force. [4] Others maintain that he lay prostrate on the body for the whole day and the whole night. Still others say that he hanged the doctor, Glaukias, because of a drug given by mistake, or because Glaukias, though he himself had seen Hephaistion drinking heavily, had not intervened.[4a] That Alexander cut his hair over the corpse I do not consider improbable, especially given his emulation of Achilles,[4b] whom from boyhood he had sought to emulate. [5] Some say that Alexander himself drove the chariot on which the body was borne—an implausible report, in my opinion. Others say that Alexander commanded that the temple of Asklepios in Ecbatana be razed[5a]—a barbaric act utterly out of character for Alexander, but more in keeping with Xerxes' arrogance toward the gods and the tale about the fetters he lowered into the Hellespont with the actual intention of punishing it.[5b] [6] Another story, one that strikes me as not completely implausible, has it that when Alexander marched to Babylon,[6a] many ambassadors from Greece met him on the way, including a deputation from Epidauros.[6b] When these men had obtained what they requested from Alexander, he gave them an offering to convey to Asklepios, saying that he did so "despite the fact that Asklepios has not treated me fairly; he failed to save my companion whom I valued as I do my own life." [7] Most writers have reported that Alexander gave orders that Hephaistion was to be

7.14.4a Plutarch also reports this otherwise unknown story regarding the killing of the doctor (*Parallel Lives*, "Alexander" 72.3). Both he and Diodorus (17.110.8) agree with Arrian that Hephaistion's condition was aggravated by a drinking bout (though Plutarch seems to feel that a heavy meal, rather than the wine that accompanied it, was to blame). The information that Hephaistion drank greedily at the time of his fever has encouraged speculation that his death was due to malaria, a disease that produces intense thirst.

7.14.4b The reference is to Achilles' extreme grief over the death of Patroklos (Homer, *Iliad* 23.135–153). It was common in both Greek and Roman traditions for mourners to cut their hair as a sign of grief. Some-

times the cut locks were placed on the tomb of the deceased.

7.14.5a Asklepios was the Greek god of healing and medicine, so Alexander's command would be a symbolic revenge for Hephaistion's fatal illness. He probably chose a Mesopotamian god to stand in for Asklepios.

7.14.5b This story is told by Herodotus (*Histories* 7.36). Xerxes was angry at the Hellespont because his attempt to bridge it had been defeated by a storm. By throwing iron shackles into the water, he symbolically made the Hellespont his slave.

7.14.6a Babylon: Map 7.16, Assyria inset.

7.14.6b Epidauros, on the Peloponnese, was the site of the Greek world's most important shrine of Asklepios.

considered a hero and that sacrifices were to be offered to him.[7a] Some say that Alexander also sent envoys to Ammon[7b] to ask the god whether it was permissible to sacrifice to Hephaistion as to a god, but the oracle would not allow it.

[8] All the writers agree that for the two days following Hephaistion's death Alexander neither tasted food nor took any care of his physical needs, but lay either moaning or in grief-stricken silence. He reportedly ordered a pyre[8a] to be made ready in Babylon at a cost of ten thousand talents (some say it cost even more) [9] and a period of mourning to be observed throughout the barbarian land.[9a] It is said that many of Alexander's Companions dedicated themselves and their weapons to the dead Hephaistion. Eumenes, whose quarrel with Hephaistion we mentioned a little earlier,[9b] initiated the gesture lest he appear to Alexander to be exulting over Hephaistion's death. [10] Alexander made no one else chiliarch[10a] of the Companion cavalry in Hephaistion's place, so that Hephaistion's name would not disappear from that unit; it continued to be called Hephaistion's Chiliarchy and followed the standard Hephaistion had designed. Alexander also planned to hold a competition in athletics and the arts far more distinguished than all previous competitions, in both the number of competitors and the fortune spent on it, as he provided three thousand competitors in all. It was these men, they say, who competed a little later at Alexander's funeral.

[1] Alexander's mourning lasted a long time, but at last he called himself back from it, and the Companions began to have more success in bringing this about. He then made an expedition against the Cossaeans, a warlike tribe that shared a border with the Ouxioi.[1a] [2] The Cossaeans were mountain dwellers who established their villages in mountain strongholds. Whenever a

---

7.14.8–10
Autumn 324
ECBATANA
Continuing his review of the reports of Alexander's grief, Arrian lists those on which all his sources agree. Alexander orders a lavish funeral pyre constructed in Babylon to honor Hephaistion, decrees a general period of mourning, and keeps vacant his friend's former position in the Companion cavalry.

7.15.1–3
Winter 324/3
COSSAEAN TERRITORY
Alexander at last ceases his mourning for Hephaistion and conducts a winter campaign against the Cossaeans, a tribe of mountain-dwelling raiders.

7.14.7a The term "hero" as used here denotes a superhuman being, not quite a god but an immortal spirit to whom prayers and sacrifices could be directed. Normally only figures of great antiquity, such as mythic kings from Homeric times, were worshiped as heroes, but on rare occasions a contemporary figure could be so elevated after death.

7.14.7b "Ammon" here refers to the oracle of the god Ammon at Siwa, in northwestern Egypt, the shrine visited by Alexander at 3.3–3.4.

7.14.8a Diodorus has a detailed description of this sumptuous pyre (17.115.1–5). Hephaistion's body was embalmed to prevent decomposition while the pyre was constructed. Remains of the destroyed pyre have been uncovered in the ruins of Babylon.

7.14.9a According to Plutarch (*Parallel Lives*, "Alexander" 72.3), Alexander ordered the Persians to shear the manes of their horses throughout the empire and to extinguish the sacred fire of the Zoroastrians (the Avesta), which, according to the laws of that faith, could be put out only to mark the death of a Persian king.

7.14.9b The earlier account of the quarrel between Eumenes and Hephaistion was lost from Arrian's text due to the gap just before 7.13.1.

7.14.10a Arrian's first and only reference in the *Anabasis* to a chiliarch, literally "commander of a thousand," is hard to interpret. In his *Events After Alexander* Arrian apparently claimed that Hephaistion's chiliarchy passed to Perdikkas after his death (see the Epilogue, §3), but here he says that it was kept vacant as though Hephaistion still occupied it. The office itself seems to correlate with the old Persian institution of a *hazarapatis* (the word means "commander of a thousand" in Persian) or vizier, a designated right-hand man of the king—an office reestablished by Alexander for his own court (Diodorus 18.48.5). It seems possible Arrian has confused this newly created chiliarchy with a separate office, command over the Companion cavalry, or that the two offices were in fact connected (as implied in the phrase "chiliarch of the Companion cavalry").

7.15.1a Cossaeans (Cossaei), possible location of territory; Ouxioi, location of territory: Map 7.16, Assyria inset.

hostile force approached them, they would retire to the mountain crests, either all together or however it was practicable for each tribesman, and thus escape, leaving the attacking forces at a loss. Then, as soon as their attackers departed, the Cossaeans would turn again to the plundering from which they made their living. [3] Alexander destroyed this tribe. The campaign was conducted in wintertime, but neither the season nor the difficult terrain proved a hindrance either to him or to Ptolemy son of Lagos, who led a division of the army against the Cossaeans. So it was with every military undertaking Alexander set in motion: nothing was beyond his abilities.

[4] As he was traveling down to Babylon, he was met by Libyan[4a] envoys, who presented their compliments and crowned him in honor of his sovereignty of Asia. Envoys also arrived from Italy,[4b] from the Brettians,[4c] Lucanians, and Tyrrhenians,[4d] for the same purpose. It is said that the Carthaginians[4e] sent embassies and that envoys seeking friendly relations arrived from the Ethiopians, the European Scythians,[4f] the Celts,[4g] and the Iberians.[4h] It was then that the Greeks and Macedonians first became acquainted with these tribes' names and attire.[4i] [5] It is said that some of these tribes even appealed to Alexander to settle their differences. It was then, more than ever, that Alexander appeared both to himself and to those around him to be master of every land and of the sea. Among those who have written about Alexander, Aristos and Asklepiades say that the Romans also sent an embassy and that Alexander, when he met with their envoys, spoke prophetically about the Romans' future power, as he had observed that their people were orderly, hardworking, and free, and he had also learned about their constitution.[5a] [6] I have recorded this report as neither accurate nor wholly implausible, though none of the Romans has made mention of this embassy to Alexander, nor have Ptolemy or Aristoboulos, the historians I mainly follow. Nor would it have been reasonable for the Roman state, which was then at its freest, to send an embassy to a foreign king, especially one so far from home, from whom it had nothing to fear nor could expect any benefit, given that the Romans, more than any other people, harbored a hatred of the race of tyrants and even the name of tyranny.[6a]

7.15.4–6
ASSYRIA
En route to Babylon, Alexander is met by embassies from many distant tribes, ceding him universal power or asking him to settle their disputes. Arrian deems implausible a report that the Romans also sent an embassy, and that Alexander foretold the future power of Rome.

7.15.4a Libya (North Africa): Map 7.16.
7.15.4b Italy: Map 7.16 and Italy inset.
7.15.4c The Brettians are unknown. Perhaps the Bruttians (location of territory: Map 7.16, Italy inset) are meant.
7.15.4d Lucanians; Tyrrhenians (Etruscans), location of territories: Map 7.16, Italy inset.
7.15.4e Carthage: Map 7.16 and Italy inset.
7.15.4f Ethiopia; Scythia: Map 7.16.
7.15.4g Celts, possible location of territory: Map 7.16. At 1.4.6 Alexander received an embassy from Celts dwelling in the Balkan peninsula. Probably a more distant branch of the Celtic nation is referred to here.
7.15.4h Iberia: Map 7.16.
7.15.4i It is not clear from Arrian's Greek how many of the preceding "tribes" this sentence refers to. Probably only the Celts and Iberians are meant.

7.15.5a Little is known about either Aristos or Asklepiades, except that they are later in time than the first generation of Alexander historians. The attempt to bring the Romans into the Alexander story no doubt reflects a desire common among Roman readers to see their own national glory prefigured in the achievements of Alexander, but in reality, Rome was probably still too small and provincial a place in the fourth century to have been much concerned with Alexander (or he with them).
7.15.6a According to their own historical legends, the Romans had expelled from their society the kings who once ruled it and established themselves as a republic in the sixth century. Thereafter the idea of kingship or autocracy was officially reviled by the Romans, even after the quasi-royal *principes*, "first citizens," came to power.

[1] Alexander now sent Herakleides son of Argaios to Hyrcania[1a] with shipwrights, telling him to fell trees in the Hyrcanian mountains and build warships, some with decks, some without, in the Greek manner. [2] For a desire had seized him to find out with what body of water the sea known both as the Caspian and the Hyrcanian is connected: whether it joins the Black Sea,[2a] or whether on the eastern side the Great Sea, the same body of water that surrounds the Indian regions, flows into the Caspian to form a gulf (just as, thanks to Alexander's discoveries, the Persian Gulf, also called the Red Sea,[2b] is known to be a gulf of the Great Sea).[2c] [3] The sources of the Caspian Sea had not yet been discovered, though several tribes inhabit its shores, and navigable rivers empty into it; from Bactria the Oxus, the largest of the Asian rivers except for the rivers of India,[3a] empties into that sea, as does the Iaxartes,[3b] which flows through Scythia. It is generally believed that the Araxes, too, flowing from Armenia, empties into that sea.[3c] [4] These are the largest rivers, but many others either converge with these or else have their own confluences with that sea. Some of these streams became known to Alexander and his men when they came upon the tribes in the region; the rest probably emptied into the sea on the far side of the gulf in the land of the Nomad Scythians,[4a] a region that is utterly unknown.

[5] Alexander now advanced to Babylon, and as he crossed the Tigris[5a] with his army, he was met by the Chaldaean soothsayers,[5b] who took him aside and asked him to halt his march to the city. They declared that they had received a prophecy from the god Bel[5c] to the effect that an entry into Babylon at that time boded evil for Alexander. It is said that he answered them with a verse of the poet Euripides: "The best of seers is he who guesses well."

7.16.1a Hyrcania: Map 7.16.
7.16.2a Black (ancient Euxine) Sea: Map 7.16.
7.16.2b Arrian variously uses the terms Persian Gulf (Map 7.16), Persian Sea, and Red Sea for the same body of water.
7.16.2c Thanks to the voyage of Nearkhos, Alexander knew that the Persian Gulf was connected to the waters at the Indus mouth, what we call the Arabian Sea but Alexander thought of as part of the Great Sea, or Ocean, encircling the earth (see Appendix N, §2–3). The point of his sending Herakleides to Hyrcania was to determine whether the Caspian, which Herodotus (*Histories* 1.203) had earlier declared to be landlocked, was in fact similarly connected to Ocean at its northern end, or to the Black Sea at its southern end.
7.16.3a Bactria; Oxus River; India: Map 7.16.
7.16.3b The standard Greek name for this river, Iaxartes, has been substituted in most modern editions for the manuscript's reading, Oxyartes. We cannot know what name Arrian actually wrote here for the river he elsewhere calls Tanais (Tanais/Iaxartes River: Map 7.16). At 3.30.7 Arrian indicates that local inhabi-

tants call it Orxantes, and Plutarch records the name as Orexartes (*Parallel Lives*, "Alexander" 45.6). Oxyartes, however, is the name of Rhoxane's father (Alexander's father-in-law) and hence probably crept into the text here through scribal error. See n. 3.30.7a.
7.16.3c Araxes River; Armenia: Map 7.16, Assyria inset.
7.16.4a Nomad Scythians: location unknown, despite Arrian's attempt here to situate them on the northeast shore of the Caspian Sea (here referred to as "the gulf" on the assumption that it joined the Great Sea). At 4.5.3 he placed them much farther east, perhaps because he confused the Caspian and Aral seas.
7.16.5a Babylon: Map 7.16 and Assyria inset; Tigris River: Map 7.16, Assyria inset.
7.16.5b In Greco-Roman usage the term Chaldaean refers to the Babylonian priestly caste, known for its practice of divination and astrology. See also n. 3.16.5b.
7.16.5c Bel, also known as Marduk or Bel-Marduk, was the chief god of the Babylonian pantheon and protector of the city of Babylon.

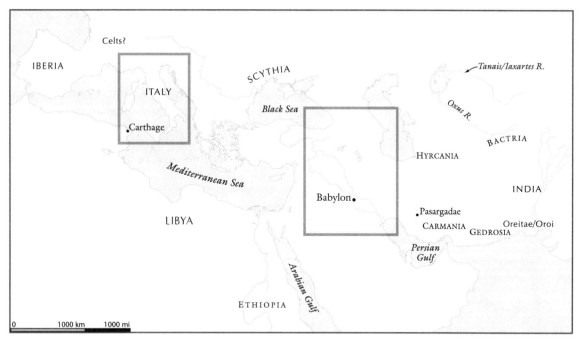

Celts?

IBERIA

SCYTHIA

ITALY

Black Sea

Carthage

Tanais/Iaxartes R.

Oxus R.

BACTRIA

HYRCANIA

INDIA

Mediterranean Sea

Babylon

Pasargadae

LIBYA

CARMANIA   Oreitae/Oroi

GEDROSIA

Persian Gulf

Arabian Gulf

ETHIOPIA

0   1000 km   1000 mi

Tyrrhenians

ITALY

Lucanians

Bruttians

Carthage

Sicily

0   250 km   250 mi

COLCHIS

Hyrcanian/Caspian Sea

ARMENIA   *Araxes R.*

Tigris R.

Ecbatana

Cossaeans?

Babylon   Susa   Ouxioi

Euphrates R.

0   400 km   400 mi

MAP 7.16

[6] In reply the Chaldaeans said, "Do not face west, sire, or lead your army into the city in that direction, but go around and enter on the east side." [7] Even that approach presented difficulties, owing to the difficult terrain; but in any case the power of the divine was leading Alexander to the point beyond which he was fated to die. And perhaps it was better for him to depart at the high point of his fame and of the world's longing for him, before any of the calamities of man's lot befell him—the kind of calamities that, in all likelihood, prompted Solon to advise Croesus to look to the end of a long life and not to declare any human being happy until then.[7a] [8] Hephaistion's death had in fact been no small misfortune for Alexander, and it seems to me he would have wanted to die first rather than live on after losing Hephaistion, in the same way that I suppose Achilles would have chosen to die before Patroklos rather than become an avenger of his death.[8a]

[1] Alexander also suspected that self-interest, rather than prophetic power, prompted the Chaldaeans to try to prevent him from marching to Babylon at that time. For the temple of Bel, a vast structure built of baked brick bound together with pitch, stood in the center of Babylon. [2] On his return from Greece, Xerxes had razed it to the ground, as he had razed all the other Babylonian shrines.[2a] According to some writers, Alexander had intended to rebuild the temple on the earlier foundation, and that was why he ordered the Babylonians to remove the mound. Others maintain that he planned to build an even larger temple. [3] Since in his absence the men to whom the project had been entrusted had not applied themselves to it with any zeal, he intended to put the entire army to work on it. Large tracts of land and an enormous amount of gold had been dedicated to the god Bel since the time when the Assyrians ruled Babylon, [4] and this fund had long ago supplied the money for temple repairs and sacrifices to the god. But at this time the Chaldaeans were administering the god's property, since there

7.17.1–6
Spring 323
NEAR BABYLON
Alexander suspects that the priests are really seeking to protect their own financial prerogatives. According to one source, he tries to heed their warnings anyway, but is prevented from moving to the city's eastern entrance by a stretch of marshy ground.

7.16.7a The reference is to a famous dialogue found in Herodotus' *Histories* (1.30), in which the Athenian wise man Solon seeks to answer the question put by Croesus, king of the Lydian empire, as to who are the happiest human beings. Solon, to Croesus' surprise, names no wealthy or powerful individuals but, rather, relative nobodies. The two men he judges second happiest in all human history are a pair of Argive brothers, Cleobis and Biton, who died suddenly at the peak of their youth, beauty, and glory, in answer to a prayer to the goddess Hera that they receive the best reward any mortal could aspire to. The lesson Solon draws from their example is that, since human life is subject to unpredictable troubles and misfortunes, the best fate one can hope for is to leave it at one's peak and not to risk a reversal of fortune. Arrian somewhat distorts this teaching by applying it to Alexander, since part of Solon's point is that the wealth and power that come with imperial rule do not

increase the sum of one's happiness.
7.16.8a Arrian here lends his support to the idea, first fostered by Alexander himself, that the bond between Alexander and Hephaistion paralleled the mythic friendship of Achilles and Patroklos (see 1.12.1 and n. 1.12.1d).
7.17.2a This attack on the Babylonian temples by Xerxes probably took place just before the Persian invasion of Greece in 480, rather than just after, as Arrian asserts. According to Herodotus (*Histories* 1.183), Xerxes plundered the golden statue of Bel associated with the great temple, probably as part of his suppression of a Babylonian revolt around 482 (though Herodotus does not say the temple was destroyed). The symbolic connections between the worship of Bel and the political control of Babylon are amply demonstrated by Alexander's own earlier rebuilding of the temple and participation in Bel's rites (see 3.16.4–5 and n. 3.16.4a).

FIGURE 7.16. Digital reconstruction of ancient Babylon (top) as seen from the north, looking down the Processional Way toward the Ishtar Gate. The ziggurat of the Temple of Bel, known to the Babylonians as Etemenanki, is here shown intact, though in Alexander's time it lay in ruins. The Ishtar Gate (bottom), rebuilt with the glazed bricks removed from Babylon, is now in the Pergamon Museum in Berlin.

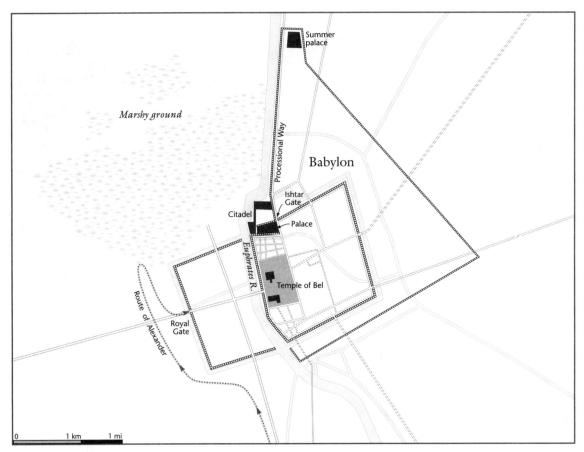

MAP 7.17. Plan of Babylon, showing the route by which Alexander attempted to enter the city from the east as the priests had advised but, stopped by the terrain, doubled back to the west entrance.

was nothing on which the revenue could be spent. Alexander suspected that this was why they were opposed to his entering Babylon, lest the swift completion of the temple deprive them of the benefits of the revenue. [5] But Aristoboulos says that Alexander was nonetheless ready to obey them, at least when it came to making a detour at the entrance to the city, and that he made camp on the first day at the bank of the Euphrates;[5a] the next day he advanced, keeping the river on his right, since he wished to pass the west-facing part of the city, turn there, and lead his forces eastward. [6] But the difficult terrain prevented such an approach, for anyone who comes up to the city from the west and then turns eastward will find the ground marshy and covered with shoal water. And thus, according to Aristoboulos, Alexander disobeyed the god partly by intention and partly not.

7.17.5a Euphrates River: Map 7.16, Assyria inset.

[1] Aristoboulos has also recorded the following story: Apollodoros of Amphipolis, one of Alexander's Companions, was commander of the army Alexander had left behind with Mazaios, the satrap of Babylon. When he met Alexander on his return from India and saw how savagely the king was punishing all the satraps who had been appointed in the various provinces, Apollodoros wrote to his brother Peithagoras, a prophet of the kind that examines the entrails of sacrificial victims, and asked him to prophesy about his own safety. [2] Peithagoras wrote back to learn why Apollodoros wished to have recourse to prophecy—who it was that he especially feared; Apollodorus replied that he feared both the king himself and Hephaistion. Peithagoras sacrificed first with reference to Hephaistion, and when a lobe of the victim's liver was missing,[2a] he wrote a note, sealed it, and sent it from Babylon to Apollodorus in Ecbatana,[2b] informing Apollodoros that he had nothing to fear from Hephaistion, for he would soon be out of the way. [3] According to Aristoboulos, Apollodoros received this letter the day before Hephaistion died. Peithagoras sacrificed a second time with reference to Alexander, and again the victim's liver lacked a lobe; he then sent Apollodoros the same message, this time about Alexander. Apollodoros did not remain silent but informed Alexander of the letter's contents, thinking that he would be showing the king more loyalty if he advised him to take precautions against impending danger. [4] Alexander thanked Apollodoros (as Aristoboulos reports) and when he arrived in Babylon asked Peithagoras what sign had prompted him to send word to his brother; Peithagoras replied that the liver of the victim had lacked a lobe. When asked what that signified, Peithagoras said it portended a grave misfortune. Alexander was so far from being angry with Peithagoras that he showed him even more respect for having spoken candidly. [5] Aristoboulos says that he learned this from Peithagoras in person. He also claims that Peithagoras later consulted sacrificial victims for Perdikkas and Antigonos, and that the same sign appeared for these two men as for Hephaistion and Alexander; indeed Perdikkas would later die while making war on Ptolemy, as would Antigonos in the battle at Ipsus against Seleukos and Lysimakhos.[5a]

[6] Along the same lines, the following story has been recorded about Kalanos the Indian sage.[6a] On his way to his own funeral pyre, Kalanos embraced all his other companions to say farewell, but refused to approach or embrace Alexander, declaring that he would do so when he met him in

7.18.1–5
Spring 323
NEAR BABYLON
A seer named Peithagoras observes another portent of Alexander's imminent death, according to the report of Aristoboulos.

7.18.6
NEAR BABYLON
A further prophecy of Alexander's death is recalled, supposedly spoken by Kalanos the Indian just before his self-immolation.

7.18.2a   The lack of a lobe in a sacrificial victim's liver was a particularly bad omen.
7.18.2b   Ecbatana: Map 7.16, Assyria inset.
7.18.5a   Perdikkas was killed by his own troops a few years later, in 321; Antigonos survived him by two decades, dying in battle in 301 in his eighties. Arrian seems oblivious to the fact that the difference in the longevity of the two men greatly diminishes the effectiveness of this anecdote in confirming Peithagoras'

prophetic powers. All of the seer's clients, after all, were fated to die eventually. The battle of Ipsus (Map 7.20, AX) pitted the armies of Antigonos and his son Demetrios against the combined forces of Lysimakhos and Seleukos, in a struggle for supremacy in Asia. See the Epilogue, §15.
7.18.6a   For a description of Kalanos' death, see 7.2.4–7.3.6.

7.19.1–2
Spring 323
BABYLON
Alexander is hailed by a
delegation from Greece.
He returns to the Greeks
the spoils taken by Xerxes
during his occupation of
Greece in 480.

7.19.3–6
BABYLON
Reunited with the fleet
under Nearkhos' command,
and joined now by a new
fleet commissioned from
the Phoenicians, Alexander
lays plans to make Babylon a
major port and to use it as a
base for a naval expedition
against the Arabians.

Babylon.[6b] This remark was ignored at the time, but was later recalled, by those who heard it, when Alexander died in Babylon, and understood in hindsight as a portent of Alexander's end.

[1] On his arrival in Babylon, Alexander was met by envoys from the Greeks. The aims of their various embassies have not been recorded,[1a] but it seems to me that most had come to crown Alexander, to celebrate all his victories and particularly those over the Indians, and to express their joy at his safe return from India. Alexander is said to have welcomed these men and to have sent them home after according them appropriate honors. [2] He also entrusted them with all the statues, ornaments, and votive offerings that Xerxes had taken from Greece and conveyed to Babylon,[2a] Pasargadae,[2b] Susa,[2c] or any other city in Asia. And the bronze statues of Harmodios and Aristogeiton are said to have thus been brought back to Athens,[2d] along with the foundation of the statue of Artemis of Kelkes.[2e]

[3] In Babylon, according to Aristoboulos, Alexander also encountered the fleet, part of which had sailed up the Euphrates from the Persian Sea[3a] under Nearkhos' command, the other part having arrived from Phoenicia,[3b] consisting of two Phoenician quinquiremes, three quadriremes, twelve triremes, and nearly thirty thirty-oared ships.[3c] These had been cut into segments and conveyed from Phoenicia to the city of Thapsacus on the Euphrates,[3d] where they were reassembled and sailed down to Babylon.

7.18.6b The remark is somewhat obscure, since in Greek belief Kalanos' soul would go to the underworld rather than accompany Alexander's army on its journey. But the general idea—that it would be at Babylon that Alexander's soul would join the spiritual realm, where Kalanos could welcome it—is clear enough.

7.19.1a In fact, the Greeks almost certainly came to see Alexander in connection with the Exiles' Decree, an edict he issued in the late summer of 324, forcing all the Greek states to take back their exiles and restore them to citizen status. Arrian's text bears no mention of this remarkable and far-reaching proclamation, though it was probably dealt with in the missing passage that followed 7.12.7. Alexander issued the decree in an effort to settle political instability in Greece and to repatriate the bands of rootless Greek mercenaries who, if paid and organized by his enemies, might someday be used against him. His unilateral action—he took it without consulting the League of Corinth, which, under the framework imposed by the Macedonians themselves, held jurisdiction over such matters—caused great disaffection and turmoil among the Greek states, and many of them sought mitigation of its terms. See Appendix M, §11.

7.19.2a Babylon: Map 7.16 and Assyria inset.
7.19.2b Pasargadae: Map 7.16.
7.19.2c Susa: Map 7.16, Assyria inset.
7.19.2d Arrian previously reported the return of these statues at 3.16.7–8, after Alexander's first entry into Babylon. This is a rare case in

which the historian has been careless in his use of multiple sources, failing to notice their different chronologies for this episode and therefore recording it in two different places.

7.19.2e Nothing is known of this statue beyond what Arrian says here, and the meaning of the epithet "of Kelkes" is obscure.

7.19.3a Persian Gulf: Map 7.16.
7.19.3b Phoenicia: Map 7.20, AX.
7.19.3c The prefixes in the terms "trireme" (*tri-* meaning "three"), "quadrireme" (*quadri-*, "four"), and "quinquireme" (*quinqui-*, "five"), are Latin numbers rather than Greek since our standard ship names come from the Romans. They seem to refer to the number of oarsmen manning each set of oars. In a trireme, rowers sat on three vertically aligned decks, one man to an oar, so that each column of oars totaled three rowers. The quadriremes and quinquiremes developed later seem to have used only two oars per column but with larger oars worked by either two or three men each, allowing for more thrust and better efficiency. The new fleet commissioned by Alexander from Phoenicia (probably in late 325 or early 324, though Arrian has not made any reference to it until now) thus exhibited the increase in the power and speed of warships that had recently become possible due to advances in naval engineering. For an illustration of a trireme, see Appendix D, Figure D.2. Also see Figure 2.21, a modern reconstruction of a trireme.

7.19.3d Thapsacus, possible location; Euphrates River: Map 7.20, AX.

[4] Aristoboulos says that the cypresses of Babylon were being cut down in order to build Alexander yet another fleet, cypress being the only tree that grows abundantly in the land of the Assyrians[4a] (the country is said to lack all other materials for shipbuilding). An enormous number of purple-fishers[4b] and seafaring men of all kinds reportedly came to Alexander from Phoenicia and the other coastal areas to man these ships and to serve in other naval offices. It is also reported that in Babylon Alexander excavated a harbor large enough to accommodate up to a thousand ships.[4c] Docks were built there as well, [5] and Mikkalos of Klazomenai was sent with five hundred talents to Phoenicia and Syria[5a] to hire, or in some cases purchase, seafaring men. For Alexander intended to colonize the coast near the Persian Gulf and the neighboring islands, as he supposed that that region would prove no less prosperous than Phoenicia. [6] He directed his naval preparations against the Arabs of the coast, offering as pretext the fact that they, alone among the barbarians of the region, had neither sent an embassy nor paid him proper attention or honor. But the truth of the matter, it seems to me at least, is that Alexander was insatiable for ever-increasing gain.[6a]

[1] A story has it that Alexander learned that the Arabs honor only two gods, Ouranos and Dionysos[1a]—Ouranos because he can be seen and because he encompasses the stars and especially the sun, from which the greatest and most conspicuous benefits have accrued to mankind, and Dionysos because of the fame of his expedition to India. Alexander did not think himself unworthy to be regarded by the Arabs as a third god, since his own exploits would be no less significant than those of Dionysos—if indeed he were to conquer the Arabs and grant them, as he had granted the Indians, the right to govern in their customary manner. [2] The prosperity of the country also urged him on, for he had heard that cassia was found in the Arabs' lakes, that their trees produced myrrh and frankincense, that cinnamon was cut from their bushes, and that spikenard grew wild in their meadows.[2a] He was also impressed by the size of the country, having been informed that Arabia's[2b] coastline was as

7.20.1–2

ARABIA

Arrian lists the motives that prompted Alexander to plan an attack on Arabia: rivalry with its native gods and desire to control its great economic resources.

7.19.4a Assyria: Map 7.20, AY.
7.19.4b "Purple-fishers" made their living gathering the murex snail, the source of the dye that was used in the manufacture of the purple cloth worn by Persian royalty.
7.19.4c Babylon was clearly intended by Alexander as the capital and center of his empire, as well as an important military base. The "thousand ships" mentioned here may be connected to the plans for a new navy—to consist of a thousand ships larger than the trireme class—that Alexander supposedly had in mind at this time for use in an expedition against Carthage; see 7.1.2 and n. 7.1.2c.
7.19.5a Syria: Map 7.20, AX.
7.19.6a Whether or not one accepts Arrian's analysis of Alexander's true motive, there were good strategic reasons for the Macedonians to embark now on the conquest of the Arabian peninsula, mainly having to do with control of sea routes between the

western center of the empire (Alexandria) and eastern ports. It seems probable that Alexander did indeed plan such an expedition for the summer of 322, though there is dispute over this, as there is over all of Alexander's so-called Last Plans.
7.20.1a Similar deities are named by Herodotus (*Histories* 3.8.1) as the objects of Arab worship, though he refers to a female deity, Ourania, and Dionysos. The Greek word *ouranos* means "sky" or "heavens," sometimes personified by the Greeks as a god, the consort of Gaia or Earth.
7.20.2a Arabia's rich stores of spices and aromatics had long been legendary in the Greek world. Herodotus reports that the Arabs paid tribute to the Persian king in the form of frankincense (*Histories* 3.97) and also records the unusual method by which cinnamon, cassia, and gum-ladanum were harvested by them (3.110–112).
7.20.2b Arabia: Map 7.20, BX.

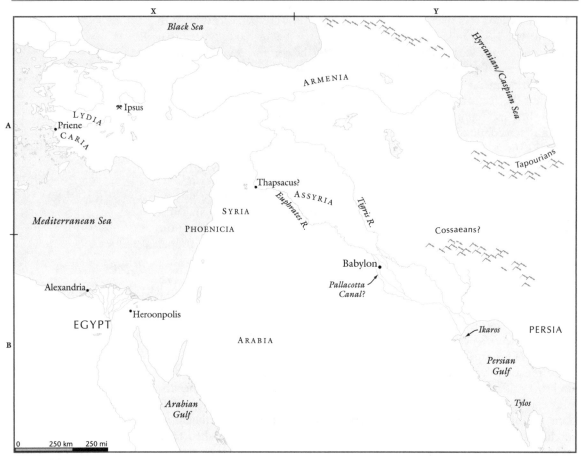

MAP 7.20

extensive as India's,[2c] that it had many islands just offshore, and that harbors were to be found everywhere that could furnish anchorages for the fleet and building sites for cities that would prosper.[2d]

[3] Alexander had been informed that two islands lay in the open sea near the mouth of the Euphrates. The first lay at no great distance from the river's outlets, roughly fifteen miles from the shore and the river's mouth. This island was the smaller of the two and was dense with all kinds of trees. It had a temple of Artemis, and the inhabitants passed their lives in its vicinity.[3a]

7.20.3–10
Spring 323
PERSIAN GULF
Several reconnaissance reports give Alexander a picture of the islands in the Persian Gulf and the size of the Arabian peninsula, which had been glimpsed by Nearkhos the previous year. It is now found to be so vast and desolate as to make circumnavigation perilous.

7.20.2c India: Map 7.16.
7.20.2d Alexander's interest in Arabia's coastline and harbors underscores the primary strategic goal of the planned invasion: to secure maritime communication between eastern and western parts of the empire.
7.20.3a This island, Ikaros (Map 7.20, BY), has been identified as the modern Failaka (off

Kuwait). It is unlikely that the native population, who were certainly non-Greek, worshiped Artemis, the Greek goddess associated with wild animals and the hunt. Alexander's troops probably identified some local deity with Artemis based on the presence of wild deer around the temple.

[4] The island pastured wild goats and deer that were consecrated to Artemis and allowed to range free. It was unlawful to hunt them unless the hunter wished to offer a sacrifice to the goddess; only for that purpose was it lawful to hunt. [5] According to Aristoboulos, Alexander ordered that the island be named Ikaros, after the island Ikaros in the Aegean Sea, to which, legend has it, Ikaros, son of Daedalus, fell when the wax that secured his wings melted. Ikaros had not kept close to the earth, as his father had instructed him to do, but in his folly flew too high and allowed the sun to melt and loosen the wax; thus he gave his name to the island of Ikaros and the Ikarian Sea.[5a] [6] The other island was reported to lie a day and a night's voyage from the mouth of the Euphrates for a ship sailing with the wind. Most of this large island, called Tylos,[6a] was neither rugged nor wooded; it produced cultivated crops and all things in season. [7] These details were reported to Alexander, in part by Arkhios, who had been sent with a thirty-oared ship to reconnoiter the coastal route to Arabia and had reached the island of Tylos but had not dared to go any farther. Androsthenes, sent with another thirty-oared ship, also sailed alongside a stretch of the Arabian peninsula. But the pilot, Hieron of Soloi, advanced the farthest of any sent off on reconnaissance. He, too, had received a thirty-oared ship from Alexander, [8] and had been ordered to sail around the entire Arabian peninsula as far as Heroonpolis, a city on the Egyptian side of the Arabian Gulf.[8a] But he did not dare to go farther, though he had sailed around most of Arabia.[8b] Turning back, he reported to Alexander that the peninsula was enormous—almost as large as India—and that its tip extended far out into the Great Sea.[8c] [9] Nearkhos' men, sailing from India, had noticed it jutting out not far from where they were before they turned into the Persian Gulf,[9a] and were just about to cross over to it, on the advice of Onesikritos the pilot. But Nearkhos says that he prevented them, arguing that, having sailed around the Persian Gulf, he was obliged to report to Alexander about the business on which Alexander had dispatched him— [10] not to sail the Great Sea but to obtain intelligence about the coastal region and the tribes who inhabited it, its anchorages, sources of water, and its people's customs, and to learn which regions were fertile and which were not;[10a] and that this was why Alexander's forces got safely away, since they would not have survived had they sailed alongside the desert regions of Arabia. For the same reason Hieron, too, is said to have turned back.

[1] While his triremes were being built and the harbor at Babylon[1a] was being excavated, Alexander sailed down the Euphrates from Babylon to the

7.20.5a Ikarian Sea was the Greek name for the southeast portion of the Aegean, roughly between Chios and the Anatolian peninsula.
7.20.6a Tylos: Map 7.20, BY. Thought to be the main island of modern Bahrain.
7.20.8a Heroonpolis; Egypt; Arabian Gulf (modern Red Sea): Map 7.20, BX.
7.20.8b There is no further information on this voyage.
7.20.8c The "tip" glimpsed by Hieron was the modern Musandam peninsula in Oman, astride the Strait of Hormuz.
7.20.9a Persian Gulf: Map 7.20, BY.
7.20.10a Arrian retells this episode in his *Indika* as well (32.6–12), in very similar language.
7.21.1a Babylon: Map 7.20, BY.

7.21.1–5
Spring 323
PALLACOTTA CANAL
Alexander goes down the Euphrates and examines the Pallacotta Canal, built to drain off the river in the spring and prevent floods.

river known as the Pallacotta,[1b] which lies roughly a hundred miles from Babylon. The Pallacotta is a canal cut from the Euphrates, not a river rising from springs. [2] For the Euphrates, which has its source in the Armenian[2a] mountains, flows within its own banks during the winter when its volume is small; but when spring comes, and especially at the time of the summer solstice, the river becomes enormous and overflows its banks, flooding the land of Assyria. [3] For at that time of year the melting snow in the Armenian mountains raises the water level greatly. As the river rises it floods the country, unless it is allowed to flow along the Pallacotta into the marshes and lakes that begin at that canal and extend as far as the land bordering on Arabia. From there the water empties mainly into shallows, and then into the sea at many unseen mouths. [4] When the melting of the snow comes to an end, near the time of the setting of the Pleiades,[4a] the Euphrates' water level drops, though most of its water continues to empty into the lakes by way of the Pallacotta. Indeed, if the Pallacotta were not dammed each year in order to seal it off from the Euphrates, it would drain the Euphrates into itself and prevent it from irrigating the Assyrian land. [5] But the satrap of Babylon used to go to great trouble to dam the outlets of the Euphrates into the Pallacotta. It was easier to open them than to close them, since the local soil, which is muddy and composed mainly of clay, is the kind that lets the water through and makes it hard to erect a barrier. But for nearly three months, more than ten thousand Assyrians were engaged in that toil.

[6] When these matters were reported to him, Alexander was prompted to benefit the land of Assyria.[6a] At the point where the Euphrates is diverted into the Pallacotta, he decided to close the outlet securely. But when he had advanced nearly four miles, he found that the soil looked quite stony, and he supposed that if a cut were made through it to connect with the old canal along the Pallacotta, the hardness of the soil would effectively prevent the water from seeping through, and at the appointed time would easily divert its flow. [7] With this in mind he sailed to the Pallacotta and down it to the lakes, heading toward Arabia. There, having noticed a fine site, he built and fortified a city, in which he settled those Greek mercenaries who volunteered or who through age or injury were unfit for battle.[7a]

7.21.6–7
Spring 323
PALLACOTTA CANAL
Alexander undertakes to overhaul the old, inefficient water-management system by cutting a new juncture between the Euphrates and the Pallacotta. He founds a new city in southern Mesopotamia.

7.21.1b Pallacotta (Pallaconta) Canal, possible location: Map 7.20, BY. The variant spelling found in the manuscripts, Pallacopas, has been changed by most editors based on an adaptation of this passage by another ancient historian, Appian.
7.21.2a Armenia: Map 7.20, AY.
7.21.4a The Pleiades are one of the most prominent constellations seen from the Mediterranean. The Greeks gauged the seasons by the changing path of this constellation. They judged that winter began when it was seen setting below the western horizon in the early morning hours (late October by our calendar).

7.21.6a Reflecting his sources' bias, Arrian attributes the engineering projects that Alexander planned to his beneficence, ignoring the military advantages that accrued from them. If the harbor of Babylon was to be the base for his 1,000-ship flotilla and the staging area for his invasion of Arabia, Alexander had to secure his route to the Persian Gulf and his ability to bring warships into the artificial lakes of southern Mesopotamia. The voyage "toward Arabia" described at 7.21.7 hints at the probable goal of these operations.
7.21.7a The name and site of this city, the last Alexander was to found, are unknown.

[1] Thinking he had proved the Chaldaeans' prophecy false, since he had suffered none of the unpleasantness in Babylon they had prophesied but had marched from the city before meeting with any misfortune, Alexander sailed boldly back inland over the marshes, keeping Babylon on his right. A part of his fleet drifted into the narrows for lack of a pilot, until he himself sent them a pilot and brought them back to the channel.

[2] The following story is told: The tombs of the Assyrian kings were mostly built in the lakes and marshes. When Alexander was sailing over the marshes—the story has it that he was steering the trireme himself—a strong gust of wind caught up his *kausia*[2a] and the diadem attached to it. The *kausia*, being heavier, fell into the water, while the diadem, carried away by the gust, lodged in a reed that had grown up from one of the tombs of the ancient kings. [3] That, in and of itself, signaled what was to come, as did the fact that one of the sailors, after swimming out to the diadem and taking it from the reed, did not carry it in his hand lest it get wet as he swam but placed it around his own head and thus carried it across. [4] Most writers have related that Alexander rewarded the sailor with a talent for his zeal but ordered him beheaded, since the prophets had warned Alexander not to let the head that wore the royal diadem get safely away. Aristoboulos, however, agrees that the sailor received the talent, but says he was only whipped for putting on the diadem. [5] Aristoboulos actually says that one of the Phoenician sailors brought the diadem to Alexander, though there are some who say that Seleukos brought it, and that this foreshadowed both Alexander's death and Seleukos' great empire. (That Seleukos was the greatest of the kings who succeeded Alexander, and that he possessed, in the highest degree, a kingly spirit and ruled a domain second in extent only to Alexander's, does not seem to me to admit of doubt.)[5a]

[1] On his return to Babylon, Alexander found that Peukestas had arrived from Persia[1a] with some twenty thousand Persian troops and a large number of Cossaeans and Tapourians[1b] (the tribes reported to be the most warlike of those whose lands bordered on Persia). Philoxenos[1c] also arrived with an army from Caria,[1d] Menandros[1e] with other troops from Lydia, and Menidas in command of the horsemen who had been assigned to him. [2] Embassies from Greece also arrived at that time. The ambassadors, wearing golden crowns, approached Alexander and placed golden crowns

7.22.1

BABYLON
Alexander returns by ship to Babylon, thinking the prophecies that warned him away from there have been proven wrong.

7.22.2–5

BABYLON
According to legend, during the voyage a gust of wind blows Alexander's royal diadem off his head. A crewman bringing it back to him places the diadem on his own head to keep it dry, and this act is seen by onlookers as another omen of the king's imminent fall.

7.23.1–2

BABYLON
In Babylon Alexander finds new recruits awaiting him. Another Greek delegation visits Alexander and accords him the honors due to a god.

7.22.2a *Kausia*: a distinctively Macedonian broad-brimmed hat.
7.22.5a Seleukos served only as a midlevel officer under Alexander, but he gradually rose to prominence in the decades after Alexander's death until he controlled virtually all of Alexander's Asian holdings. See the Epilogue, §12–16.
7.23.1a Persia: Map 7.20, BY.
7.23.1b Cossaeans (Cossaei), possible location of territory: Map 7.20, BY. Tapourians

(Tapouroi), location of territory: Map 7.20, AY. Alexander's forces had subdued these two mountain-dwelling tribes at, respectively, 7.15.1–3 and 3.23.1–2.
7.23.1c This may be the same Philoxenos whom, at 3.6.4, Alexander appointed to collect taxes from Asia Minor.
7.23.1d Caria: Map 7.20, AX.
7.23.1e Alexander had appointed Menandros satrap of Lydia (Map 7.20, AX).

on his head as well, really as though they had come to pay honor to a god.[2a] But as it turned out, Alexander's end was not far off.

[3] Alexander then commended the Persians for their zeal, since they obeyed Peukestas in everything, and praised Peukestas himself for governing his men in an orderly manner. He enrolled these men in the Macedonian units, appointing a Macedonian as commander of each company of ten,[3a] and with him a Macedonian double-pay man and a ten-stater man[3b] (so named for the amount of his wage: he was paid less than a double-pay man but more than a soldier of the lowest rank). [4] He also enrolled twelve Persians,[4a] and, as the last of a company of ten, a Macedonian (another ten-stater man). Thus each company of ten included four Macedonians (three earning higher pay and the company commander) and twelve Persians. The Macedonians were equipped with their traditional weapons; the Persians carried bows or thonged javelins.[4b]

[5] Meanwhile, Alexander was frequently putting his fleet to the test. There were many contests between his triremes and any quadriremes they could find on the river. There were also competitions among the rowers and steersmen, and crowns for the victors.

[6] The envoys from Ammon, whom Alexander had sent to ask how he might appropriately honor Hephaistion, also arrived. They reported that Ammon had declared it appropriate to sacrifice to Hephaistion as to a hero.[6a] Alexander was pleased with the response, and from then on honored Hephaistion with a hero's rites. He also sent a letter to Kleomenes, a despi-

7.23.2a This sentence has provoked much debate and touches on the hotly contested issue of whether, at the time he issued the Exile's Decree, Alexander requested that the Greeks worship him as a god. There is no evidence in any of our sources for Alexander's life that he made such a request, though it is clear that the Greeks were debating the question of divine honors for Alexander by 323 and that many were hostile to it (see Appendix C, §17). Arrian here reports that the Greek ambassadors visiting Alexander were treating him as a god, but attaches a Greek word, *dethen* (translated "really"), to show an ironic detachment from this reverential attitude. It is impossible to tell whether Arrian is attributing this detachment to the Greeks, who in this reading would be shamming worship in order to please a deluded monarch, or is expressing it in his own voice, to show that he at least knows Alexander to be mortal.

7.23.3a The term "company of ten" (*dekad*) is a holdover, since these companies, as the next sentence makes clear, would in the new dispensations contain sixteen men.

7.23.3b The term "ten-stater man" probably refers to the amount of monthly pay, but it is unclear whether a gold or silver stater is the unit of currency referred to. If the former, then these midlevel infantrymen were receiving the equivalent of two

hundred drachmas a month, several times the amount that common soldiers were paid at the outset of the campaign. It seems clear that in the new mixed-race army Alexander was creating, Macedonian troops were highly paid, both because they bore increased responsibility and because they found their conditions of service less appealing. For more on soldiers' pay, see Appendix F, §4.

7.23.4a The reorganization of the infantry units would have resulted in a phalanx (heavy infantry) made up of three front lines of Macedonians armed with *sarisas* (long spears), then a large interior of bow-wielding Persian troops, and finally a rear guard composed of a single line of Macedonians. The resulting phalanx would have been less effective militarily than the old one, but it had the important political function of integrating Macedonian and Persian troops.

7.23.4b Thonged javelins were thrown by the whip-like motion of a leather strap, which increased their distance and accuracy.

7.23.6a For more on Alexander's efforts to honor Hephaistion, see 7.14.7, n. 7.14.7a, and n. 7.14.7b. At 7.14.7 Arrian reported only that "some say" such envoys were sent; here he regards the mission as a certainty. A variant report by Diodorus (17.115.6) has the oracle agreeing to the request for a god's honors.

cable man who had committed many crimes in Egypt.[6b] I do not fault the letter for its fond remembrance of the dead Hephaistion, but I do fault much of its other content. [7] For the letter said that hero shrines were to be built in Egyptian Alexandria,[7a] in the city itself and on the island of Pharos near the lighthouse,[7b] that were to be unsurpassed in grandeur and extravagance. It instructed Kleomenes to see to it that the shrines be named after Hephaistion and that the name Hephaistion be inscribed on all contracts drawn up between merchants. [8] This I cannot fault, except insofar as Alexander was wasting effort on trivial matters, but what follows I utterly deplore. "If I find," ran the letter, "that the temples in Egypt and the shrines of Hephaistion are well built, I will pardon you for any wrong you have done thus far, and if you misbehave in the future, you will meet with no punishment from me." This message, directed from a great king to a man who held sway over a large and well-populated region, I cannot approve, especially as the man was a villain.

[1] But Alexander's end was near. Aristoboulos says that the following incident foreshadowed what was to come: Alexander was distributing into the Macedonian battalions the troops who had arrived from Persia with Peukestas and from the coast with Philoxenos and Menandros. Feeling thirsty, Alexander departed the council, leaving the royal throne unoccupied. [2] On either side of the throne stood silver-footed couches on which the Companions who attended him had been sitting. Now some obscure fellow, a criminal on parole according to some, saw the throne and couches unoccupied and the eunuchs standing near the throne (the Companions having risen with the king when he went out); and, passing through the group of eunuchs, he went up and sat on the throne. [3] The eunuchs, in obedience to a Persian custom, did not remove him but tore their clothes and beat their chests and faces as if at some calamity. When the incident was reported to Alexander, he gave orders that the culprit be tortured on the rack to learn whether his action had been part of a plot. But the man maintained that he had only acted on an impulse.[3a] This actually strengthened the seers' impression that nothing good lay in store for Alexander.

[4] Not many days later, having made his customary offerings for good fortune as well as others that had been suggested by prophecy, Alexander feasted with his friends and drank far into the night. He is also said to have

7.24.1–3
Summer 323
BABYLON
Yet another portent of Alexander's imminent doom is seen.

7.24.4
BABYLON
Alexander attends a drinking party, then (according to some) continues drinking at the home of a Companion, Medios.

7.23.6b   At 3.5.4 Alexander had appointed Kleomenes finance minister of Egypt (Map 7.20, BX) in 331, and he since had either been promoted to satrap or had usurped the powers of one. He had been using his position to enrich himself by exploiting his control over grain shipments to Greece and by extorting bribes from Egyptian priests.
7.23.7a   Alexandria: Map 7.20, BX.
7.23.7b   The island was at the entrance to the harbor of Alexandria, where entering ships would see the monument.
7.24.3a   Diodorus (17.116.2–4) and Plutarch (*Parallel Lives*, "Alexander" 73.6–74.1)

give different accounts of this episode. In Plutarch's version the interloper was a criminal who was motivated by a divine voice to do what he did. In that of Diodorus, he gives no explanation for his act. In both versions Alexander had the man put to death. There seems to be a connection with a Babylonian religious ritual in which a condemned criminal was briefly put on the throne as a substitute king, then led away to execution, as a magical way to avert real threats to the king's life; but the exact relationship of the rite to the three differing narratives is obscure.

distributed animal sacrifices and wine throughout the army's regiments and companies. Some have written that when he left the drinking bout and wished to go to bed, he encountered Medios, the Companion he trusted most at the time,[4a] and that Medios asked Alexander to be his guest at a party, promising him that he would enjoy himself.

[1] The *Royal Journals*[1a] give the following account: Alexander drank and caroused with Medios; then, after rising and bathing, he slept, dined again with Medios, and again drank far into the night. On leaving the drinking party, he bathed. After his bath he took a little food and slept where he was, since he was already in a fever. [2] He was carried out on a couch to make his customary daily sacrifice; after sacrificing, he lay down in the men's quarters until dark. At that time he gave his officers instructions about the march and voyage;[2a] the infantry were to depart in three days, and those who were accompanying him by sea were to set sail in four. [3] He was then carried on his couch to the river; he boarded a vessel there and sailed across to his private pleasure ground,[3a] where he again bathed and rested. The next day he again bathed and made his customary offerings. Going to his canopy bed, he lay down and talked with Medios. He also instructed his officers to meet him early the next morning. [4] He then took a little food. Carried again to his canopy bed, he spent the whole night in a fever.

The next day he bathed and sacrificed. He informed Nearkhos and the other officers that the voyage would start in two days' time.[4a] The next day he again bathed and performed the appointed sacrifices; thereafter his fever never left him. Even so, he called in his officers and instructed them to prepare for the voyage. He bathed in the evening, and afterward was already very ill. [5] The next day he was carried to the building near the bathing pool,[5a] where he performed the appointed sacrifices. Though very ill, he called in his most important officers and again instructed them about the voyage. The next day he managed to be carried out to the sacrifices,

7.25.1–6
Summer 323
BABYLON
Taking his information from a detailed log called the *Royal Journals*, Arrian traces the progress of Alexander's illness over the course of ten days. Despite his worsening condition, Alexander attempts to continue his normal activities during this time and to lay out plans for the imminent invasion of Arabia.

7.24.4a This is a curious statement, given that Arrian has not mentioned Medios before and he has held no major military commands. In the *Indika* (18.7) he is listed as a trierarch (commander of a trireme) on the Hydaspes River.

7.25.1a See Appendices O and P for two widely varying views of the *Journals*. This document purports to be part of an official record maintained either by Eumenes, Alexander's chief scribe, or his successor. But there is no good account of how such a document would have come into Arrian's hands (at 7.26.3 he seems to indicate that he did not find it in the works of his two main sources, Ptolemy and Aristoboulos, but there is dispute concerning his language). Complicating the issue is the fact that Plutarch also cites the *Royal Journals* for an account of Alexander's death, but there are several distinct differences from Arrian's account. It seems likely the document circulated as an independent

text in multiple versions, but who initially published it or why remains a mystery. If, as is widely believed, one of Alexander's generals published it in the years after Alexander's death, to refute the charge that the king was poisoned, then it may well have been doctored or even forged outright.

7.25.2a Meaning the campaign against the Arabians.

7.25.3a Presumably this was the summer palace in northern Babylon (see Map 7.17), a cooler spot than the southern palace, where Alexander's principal residence and throne room were located.

7.25.4a According to Plutarch's version, the final conference with Nearkhos was not about the upcoming voyage to Arabia but Nearkhos' journey on the Indian Ocean and the Persian Gulf along the coast from the Indus River to the mouth of the Tigris River.

7.25.5a The location of the building and bathing pool is unknown. Plutarch (*Parallel Lives*, "Alexander" 76.5) also mentions the bathing pool.

made his offerings, and in spite of his condition continued to instruct his officers about the voyage. [6] The next day, though ill, he still performed the appointed sacrifices. He instructed the generals to wait in the court, the brigade and division commanders outside his door.[6a] Now, desperately ill, he was carried from the pleasure ground to the palace. When his officers entered, he recognized them but said nothing; his voice was gone. He was gravely ill with fever that night and day, and his condition remained unchanged throughout the next night and day.

[1] These events have been recorded in the *Royal Journals*, where we also read that the soldiers longed to visit him, some in hopes of seeing him still alive, others because word was being passed that he was already dead, and I imagine they suspected that his death was being concealed by his Bodyguards.[1a] But most of his men forced their way in to see Alexander out of grief and longing for their king. They say that he had already lost his voice by the time the men moved past him, but that he greeted each of them, raising his head with difficulty and making a sign with his eyes. [2] The *Royal Journals* say that Peithon, Attalos, Demophon, and Peukestas, together with Kleomenes, Menidas, and Seleukos, passed the night in the temple of Sarapis[2a] and asked the god whether it would be better for Alexander to be brought to the temple as a suppliant and be cared for by the god. The god's response was that he should not be brought to the temple, as it would be better for him to remain where he was. [3] His Companions reported the response, and shortly thereafter Alexander died, since that, after all, was now "better."

Aristoboulos and Ptolemy have nothing more to add.[3a] Others have recorded that when his Companions asked Alexander to whom he was leaving the kingdom, he answered, "To the strongest."[3b] He is also said to

7.26.1–3

BABYLON

After gazing weakly on the many soldiers who file past his bedside, Alexander dies. In two comments he is reported to have made shortly before his death, he foresees the turmoil that will result from the absence of a successor.

7.25.6a The significance of these orders is unclear. Perhaps Alexander sensed that his end was near and wanted all the leadership present to ensure a smooth transfer of power, or perhaps he hoped to launch the Arabian campaign the following morning.

7.26.1a This mistrust of their commanders by the rank and file, also seen in India after Alexander had been gravely wounded (see 6.12.3), boded ill for the cohesion of the army once Alexander was dead. The day after his demise, the infantry and cavalry would be fighting each other over the designation of a successor; see the Epilogue, §4.

7.26.2a This detail has occasioned much comment. It was long supposed that the Serapis/ Sarapis cult was invented by Ptolemy in the years after Alexander's death, so that mention here of this deity would be an anachronism condemning the *Royal Journals* as a fake. But there have been various solutions proposed to the problem, including the idea that Serapis was actually imported, not invented, by Ptolemy, based on a cult he had encountered in Mesopotamia.

7.26.3a This sentence can be interpreted to mean

either that Arrian's two main sources contained the *Royal Journals* he reports on above, or that those two sources are not in disagreement with the *Journals*, implying that those existed separately. There is much at stake for our understanding of whether the *Journals* are authentic, but Arrian is almost entirely ambiguous.

7.26.3b The words can also be translated "to the best." The anecdote, also found in the vulgate sources (see the Introduction, §2.5–6), is clearly at odds with the record of the *Journals*, according to which Alexander had become unable to speak in his last days. The idea that Alexander expressed no preference in the matter of succession is also at odds with a report, found not in Arrian but in other sources, that he handed his signet ring to Perdikkas, thereby entrusting to him the management of the empire (see Appendix E, §9). While some scholars challenge the authenticity of this story, most accept it. If the transfer of the ring did take place, then Arrian's main source, Ptolemy, may have deliberately omitted it so as to rob his chief rival, Perdikkas, of an important prop to his authority.

have added that he saw that he would be the object of a great funeral competition.[3c]

[1] I am aware that many other versions of Alexander's death have been recorded; for example, that Antipatros sent Alexander a drug that caused his death, and that the drug was concocted for Antipatros by Aristotle, who was now afraid of Alexander on account of Kallisthenes,[1a] and carried by Kassandros, Antipatros's son.[1b] Some have even written that the poison was carried by Kassandros in a mule's hoof [2] and given to Alexander by Iollas, Kassandros' younger brother, since Iollas was a royal wine pourer and had been offended by Alexander shortly before his death.[2a] Others say that Medios, who was Iollas' lover, took a hand in the affair, seeing that it was Medios who suggested the drinking party to Alexander and also seeing that Alexander felt a sharp pain on taking a drink and left the party for that reason.[2b] [3] One writer is even shameless enough to report that Alexander, sensing that his end was near, went to throw himself into the Euphrates[3a] so that he might disappear and thereby make it seem more credible to posterity that he had sprung from a god at birth and now had returned to the gods at death; but his wife Rhoxane noticed him going out and stopped him, at which point he moaned and said that she was actually begrudging him the eternal renown of having been born a god.[3b] I set down these stories more so I may not be thought ignorant of them than because they are credible.

[1] Alexander died in the hundred and fourteenth Olympiad, during the

7.26.3c "To be the object of a great funeral competition" has an elegant and untranslatable pun in the Greek: the phrase *epitaphion agōna* can mean either a set of athletic games held in honor of the dead king, or a struggle shortly after his burial for the right to succeed him.

7.27.1a See 4.10 and following for the falling-out between Alexander and Kallisthenes, Aristotle's nephew. Arrian's wording perhaps implies that Aristotle considered himself a target of assassination after one of his kinsmen had been charged with conspiracy against Alexander. A more detailed version of this legend records that Aristotle collected the poison from the waters of the River Styx. For more on the rumors of Alexander's poisoning, see Appendix P, Alexander's Death: The Poisoning Rumors.

7.27.1b See 7.12.4–7 for Alexander's orders that Antipatros come to him from Macedonia. He sent his son Kassandros in his place, and Kassandros had recently arrived in Babylon at the time of Alexander's death (though Arrian does not mention him prior to this passage). According to a story found in Plutarch (*Parallel Lives*, "Alexander" 74), Kassandros laughed mockingly when he first witnessed the rites of adoration lavished on Alexander by his Asian subjects, for which Alexander grabbed him

by the hair and beat his head against a wall. See Appendix E, §15, and Appendix P, §1–2.

7.27.2a The source of the offense is unknown. Iollas (or Iolaos) was so widely believed to be involved in the death of Alexander that Hypereides, an Athenian orator who staunchly opposed the Macedonians, proposed in the assembly that Iollas be awarded state honors. After Iollas' death, Alexander's mother, Olympias, had his remains exhumed and his ashes scattered to the winds. The *Liber de Morte* (see Appendix P, §3) not only makes Iollas responsible for administering the initial poison to Alexander at Medios' banquet but claims that when the king asked for a feather to induce vomiting, Iollas gave him one that had been dipped in poison.

7.27.2b The sharp, stabbing pain following a draft of wine is part of the vulgate tradition that supports the idea of poisoning; see Appendix O, Alexander's Death: A Medical Analysis, §4, 7.

7.27.3a Euphrates River: Map 7.20, AX.

7.27.3b Alexander's purpose had been to drown himself in the Euphrates so that his body would disappear, thus erasing the evidence of his mortality. The strange tale is known to us from only one other source, the *Alexander Romance* (3.32).

FIGURE 7.28. The text of this Babylonian astronomical tablet supplies our most accurate date for the death of Alexander. In a log entry designed to permit a correlation of political and astronomical events, an anonymous scribe wrote in cuneiform, for the date corresponding to June 11 of the Julian calendar, "The king died."

archonship[1a] of Hegesias at Athens. According to Aristoboulos he lived thirty-two years and eight months,[1b] and reigned for twelve years and those same eight months.[1c] He had an extraordinary physical beauty and hardihood and an exceedingly shrewd and courageous spirit; he was unsurpassed in his love of honor, his zest for danger, and his scrupulous attention to the rites of the gods. [2] With regard to bodily pleasures, he enjoyed perfect self-control; where pleasures of the mind were concerned, he was insatiable only for men's praise. He was extremely adept at seeing immediately what had to be done when it was not yet obvious, and was exceptionally good at guessing what was likely to happen based on the available evidence; he showed outstanding talent for drawing up, arming, and equipping an army. In raising his soldiers' morale, filling them with good hopes, and dispelling their fear in times of danger by his own fearlessness, he showed himself supremely gifted. [3] All that needed to be done openly he did with the utmost courage, while in situations requiring stealth and speed he also excelled at getting the jump on his enemies before they suspected what was coming. He was utterly reli-

7.28.1a   The date of Alexander's death has been fixed at June 11 thanks to a notation in a Babylonian astronomical record preserved on a cuneiform tablet (see Figure 7.28). The archonship of Hegesias ended in June. Ancient historians, who had no universal system for numbering years, routinely used the names of Athenian archons or Roman consuls—officials who served one-year terms—to identify points in historical time.

7.28.1b   Aristoboulos' reckoning of Alexander's lifespan would put his birth in October of 356, in contrast to Plutarch, who places it in July (*Parallel Lives*, "Alexander" 3.5). There is no agreement among historians about the exact date.

7.28.1c   On this reckoning Alexander assumed the throne in October 336, at around the time of his twentieth birthday.

313

able in honoring promises and agreements, and no one was less likely to be taken in by deceivers. Uncommonly sparing in the use of money for his own pleasures, he spent ungrudgingly for the benefit of others.

[1] If any offense was given by Alexander's sharpness or anger, or if he carried to an extreme his taste for barbarian pomp, I do not myself regard it as a serious matter. One might reasonably take into account Alexander's youth, his uninterrupted good fortune, and the influence of royal counselors who consider what will please, not what will be for the best, and who harm and always will harm the kings they attend. But Alexander is the only ancient king I know of whose nobility moved him to feel remorse for his misdeeds.[1a] [2] Most men, if they recognize that they have erred, defend what they have done as if it were perfectly proper, hoping, in their poor judgment, to conceal their error. In my view, the only remedy for a misdeed is for the guilty party to acknowledge his error and show clearly that he repents it. Those he has hurt get some relief when he admits he has acted improperly, and since he himself is dismayed by what he has done, he can hope he will never again commit the same offense.

[3] The fact that Alexander traced his birth to a god does not impress me as a serious fault; it may merely have been a clever means of inspiring awe in his subjects. He does not seem to me to have been any less illustrious a king than Minos or Aiakos or Rhadamanthys,[3a] whose births were traced by the ancients to Zeus himself without any taint of hubris, or than Theseus son of Poseidon, or Ion son of Apollo. [4] As to his donning Persian dress, this also strikes me as an expedient, adopted for the barbarians, so that their king might not seem entirely foreign to them, and, with regard to the Macedonians, so that he might have some refuge from their native harshness and arrogance.[4a] It seems to me he had the same end in view when he included the Persian Apple Bearers[4b] in the Macedonian squadrons and the Persian nobles in the *agemas*.[4c] As for Alexander's drinking parties, they were prolonged not because he cared for wine—Alexander did not drink much wine[4d]—but out of friendship for the Companions.

[1] Anyone who reproaches Alexander should not simply cite those deeds that deserve to be reproached. Instead, after collecting in one place all of Alexander's qualities, let his critic then consider who he is and what sort of fortune he has had that he reproaches Alexander, a man who became

---

7.29.1a   Arrian here seems principally to be thinking of Alexander's self-isolation after the murder of Kleitos. He gave much credit to the king's remorse in his narrative of that episode (4.9.2–4).

7.29.3a   The three mythical kings Arrian mentions here are sons of Zeus by mortal women. Minos and Rhadamanthys supposedly ruled in Crete, while Aiakos ruled the island of Aegina. All three were believed to have been honored after death with the role of judges of souls in the underworld.

7.29.4a   Arrian here weighs in on one of the prin-

cipal disputes regarding Alexander's character; see Appendix K, §4–6.

7.29.4b   The Persian Apple Bearers were an elite corps of royal bodyguards whose spears were fitted with golden ornaments shaped like apples at the butt end.

7.29.4c   For Alexander's creation of hybrid elite units, see 7.8.2 and 7.11.3, and Appendix K, §8, 10.

7.29.4d   For Arrian's rejection of reports that Alexander drank to excess, based on the convictions of his source Aristoboulos, see n. 4.13.6a.

so great and attained such a peak of human success as the undisputed king of both continents whose name reached every land—whereas he is a lesser man, toiling at lesser things and not even handling them with any ability.

[2] I suppose there was no race of men, no city at that time, no single person whom Alexander's name did not reach. I therefore assume that a man unlike any other in the world would not have been born without the intervention of the gods. Oracles are said to have indicated this at Alexander's death, as did various apparitions that were seen and dreams that were dreamt, the honor in which Alexander has to this day been held by mankind, and the memory of him, which surpasses the merely human. Even today, after so much time has passed, other oracles in his honor have been proclaimed for the people of Macedonia.[2a]

[3] Though I have myself had occasion to find fault with some of Alexander's deeds in the course of my history of them, I am not ashamed to admire Alexander himself. If I have condemned certain acts of his, I did so out of my own regard for truth and also for the benefit of mankind. That, after all, was my purpose in embarking on this history, and I, too, have been favored with help from god.

7.30.2
Arrian finds grounds to believe that Alexander's birth was indeed, in some way, divine.

7.30.3
"I am not ashamed to admire Alexander."

7.30.2a   It is unclear what Arrian refers to here, though a set of Greek "prophecies" (concocted after the events they describe), known as the *Sibylline Oracles*, set down in Arrian's time and later, contain several veiled references to Alexander.

EPILOGUE

The Breakup and Decline of Alexander's Empire

§1. The decades following Alexander's death were eventful and turbulent, at times even chaotic. The struggles of Alexander's former generals—dubbed the Diadochoi, or Successors, by Diodorus (18.42) and so termed by many modern historians—to increase power and enlarge territory, or to dominate the entire empire Alexander had left behind, went on almost continuously over a vast portion of the globe. The complexity of the era can be judged by the length and detail of the historical treatises that chronicled it. Arrian, whose account of Alexander's reign (the *Anabasis Alexandrou*) occupied seven books, required ten books to record only four years in his *Events After Alexander*. That work is almost totally lost, but its principal plot points were summarized in the ninth century C.E. by Photius, a Byzantine cleric, and that summary remains one of our best sources for the first years of this period. The same years and those that follow are documented by both Diodorus and Justin, and some of Plutarch's *Parallel Lives* deal with the figures who dominated this power struggle. The second half of Book 10 of Quintus Curtius' *Historia Alexandri Magni* supplies an extremely detailed, but often unreliable, account of the week that followed Alexander's death; he seems to have regarded the events in Babylon of mid-June 323 as a crucial, and deeply tragic, denouement to the story of Alexander's life. These five ancient sources do not always agree with one another and are often maddeningly vague; but, taken together, they furnish a fairly clear picture of how Alexander's empire came apart at the seams.

§2. The period following Alexander's death was dominated by the need to fill two interrelated power vacuums: the Macedonian throne and leadership of the highly trained but geographically dispersed armed forces. In Alexander the roles of monarch and commander in chief had been fused, but it became clear immediately after his death that there was no other individual who could similarly combine them. Kingship and generalship would part ways, and the question of which held

note: Most locations mentioned in the Epilogue and appendices can be found in the Reference Maps section. Also, the authors of the appendices may have used their own or other translations.

317

greater power remained to be settled. Moreover, there were too few candidates for the first office but all too many for the second. Alexander had trained and promoted a first-rate officer corps, carefully dividing responsibilities among a half-dozen highly skilled leaders; each was qualified to assume overall command, and each coveted the opportunity. On his deathbed Alexander bequeathed his power "to the strongest," according to a legend recounted by Arrian (7.26.3; the Greek can also be translated "to the best"), and foretold that a long series of funeral games would be held over his tomb. Most likely the words are spurious, but they accurately reflect the crisis the army found itself in at that moment. The top generals were intensely ambitious and evenly matched; the years to come, almost inevitably, would see a Darwinian struggle for supremacy among them.

§3. Whoever emerged as top general also appeared likely to serve as surrogate king, for any of the three potential heirs to Alexander's throne would need to be governed by a regent. Alexander had fathered a son named Herakles by his mistress Barsine, an illegitimate child perhaps five years old in 323; and one of his three wives, Rhoxane, was in the last trimester of pregnancy at the time of his death. In addition, Alexander had a half-brother named Arrhidaios who suffered from some sort of mental incapacity. One of these three blood relations had to occupy the throne, but the Macedonians had no clear-cut protocols for making the choice. Responsibility for resolving the matter rested chiefly on Perdikkas, one of Alexander's seven Bodyguards, whom Alexander had elevated to chiliarch—a kind of right-hand man to the king—after Hephaistion's death and (if the legend can be trusted) given the signet ring he used to seal executive orders. But trusted though Perdikkas was by the king, he commanded little reverence among the troops and his fellow officers. Krateros was far more popular and respected, but when Alexander died, he was off leading the ten thousand veterans sent home from Opis back through western Asia. Similarly Antipatros—in his late seventies the grand old man of Macedonian politics—had more seniority and the greatest natural authority but was weeks away from Babylon, in Pella, the Macedonian capital. Perdikkas had to make a go of wielding executive power in a situation that almost guaranteed his failure.

§4. According to Quintus Curtius (10.6–7), at a council meeting held in the throne room of a Babylon palace, Perdikkas proposed waiting for Rhoxane's baby to be born and designating that child as king, should it be a boy. Ptolemy—another Bodyguard, already apparently estranged from Perdikkas—wanted to eliminate the monarchy altogether and form a junta of leading generals. An infantry officer named Meleagros voiced the preference of the phalanx troops for Arrhidaios, who was not competent to rule but was at least viable as a figurehead. Perdikkas managed to get his plan adopted by the cavalry officers present at the council; but Meleagros, backed by the ever more headstrong infantrymen, refused to go along. Their two factions nearly came to blows before a compromise was reached in which

Arrhidaios, now renamed Philip III, and Rhoxane's unborn child would *share* the throne, provided the child was male. Perdikkas and Meleagros agreed to collaborate on regency in Asia over the two monarchs, while Antipatros and Krateros were given executive powers in Europe. Ptolemy was left out of the power-sharing arrangement, a slight by Perdikkas that was to have grave repercussions in the years ahead. The cavalry and infantry were reunited, though Perdikkas took precautions against further dissension by executing Meleagros, his putative partner in rule, and the chief supporters of the infantry mutiny. Rhoxane gave birth to a boy, Alexander IV, and Alexander's only legitimate child and only male sibling became co-rulers.

§5. Perdikkas conducted two important administrative tasks in the months following Alexander's death. First, according to Diodorus (18.4.1–4), he announced to the army the so-called Last Plans of Alexander, found in a document in the king's chambers, and asked for their judgment. These plans were grandiose in scope: A huge navy was to be built for a campaign against Carthage and other North African cities; roads and harbors were to be constructed across North Africa to the Strait of Gibraltar; vast temples were to be erected at key religious centers, along with a tomb for Alexander's father that would rival the biggest Egyptian pyramid; and populations were to be transplanted from Europe to Asia and vice versa, so that the two continents would in effect become intermarried.[5a] As Perdikkas no doubt hoped and expected, the army rejected any notion of carrying out these plans. Perdikkas' second task was to enlist the support of the leading Companions by conducting a distribution of satrapies, assigning the choicest and most important posts to the highest-ranking officers. Ptolemy received Egypt, the wealthiest and most peaceful of the provinces, while the important regions astride the Hellespont (modern Dardanelles), Hellespontine Phrygia and Thrace, went to two other members of Alexander's Bodyguard, Leonnatos and Lysimakhos. The province of Cappadocia, not yet fully pacified, went to Alexander's former secretary, Eumenes, a Greek who had little leadership experience but was soon to gain much more.

§6. The new satraps departed for their assignments in the autumn of 323, and Perdikkas, with the joint kings by his side, set about trying to run the empire. He met defiance right away from Antigonos One-Eye (so named after he lost an eye while fighting under Alexander's father), the long-serving satrap of Phrygia. Antigonos, an older man accustomed to doing things his own way, stubbornly refused to obey Perdikkas' order to reinforce Eumenes in Cappadocia. Leonnatos, who had been given similar orders, soon followed suit. Meanwhile, in Egypt, Ptolemy declared his own obstinacy by executing a Greek official there, Kleomenes, who had been appointed by Perdikkas as Ptolemy's watchdog. The western Asian and African provinces were thus starting to come unglued from the center at Babylon, and further trouble soon arose in the east, where the Greek troops left to garrison Bactria and Sogdiana deserted their posts and headed for the

---

Epi.5a   See Appendix K, Alexander's Policy of Perso-
         Macedonian Fusion, §13.

Aegean. Perdikkas dispatched an army under Peithon, another former Bodyguard, to meet them, and a huge number of the Greeks were treacherously slaughtered after their offer of surrender had been accepted. According to Diodorus, Perdikkas ordered the slaughter to prevent Peithon from absorbing the Greek army into his own and mounting yet another challenge to central authority.

§7. Meanwhile in Europe, Antipatros, too, was facing problems. The Athenians, long resentful of Macedonian hegemony in Greece, launched a revolt as soon as they learned of Alexander's death; the Macedonian army sent against them found itself outmatched and retreated into the fortified town of Lamia. There it might easily have been starved into submission, but two relief forces came to Asia to help, the first led by Leonnatos, the second by Krateros. Macedonian hegemony in Europe was saved by their intervention, and Krateros married one of Antipatros' daughters to become his close ally. No sooner had Krateros and Antipatros settled affairs in Greece, though, than they were summoned to Asia to take up arms against Perdikkas' regime. Antigonos One-Eye had reported to them that Perdikkas was planning to marry Kleopatra, Alexander's sister—clearly an attempt to make himself eligible for the throne, an ambition that these other generals could not allow to go unopposed. The First Diadoch War, as it is sometimes called, broke out in 321 when Antipatros and Krateros crossed the Hellespont with their armies to unseat Perdikkas.

§8. Ptolemy in Egypt was in league with this anti-Perdikkas alliance and had made yet another declaration of independence from the Babylon regime by hijacking Alexander's funeral cortege as it made its way toward Europe. The king's mummified body was brought to Memphis, Ptolemy's temporary home, and was soon thereafter installed in Alexandria, the newly built imperial capital, as a talisman of Ptolemy's power and legitimacy. Perdikkas invaded Egypt to punish Ptolemy, leaving his deputy Eumenes behind in Asia to deal with Krateros and Antipatros. After several failed attempts to ford the Nile, the last a debacle in which two thousand men were drowned, Perdikkas lost the allegiance of his own troops and was murdered by a cabal of officers led by Seleukos, his former head of staff, and Antigenes, commander of an elite infantry unit known as the Silver Shields. The army of invasion he had brought into Egypt chose new leaders and went off to join the forces of Antipatros and Krateros in Asia. But they soon learned that Krateros had been killed in a battle against Eumenes. Distraught over the loss of a much-loved officer, they condemned Eumenes to death in absentia along with all other known supporters of Perdikkas' regime.

§9. The army returning from Egypt met the forces that had arrived from Europe at Triparadeisos, in what is now Lebanon, and Antipatros took control. He arranged a new distribution of satrapies and a new regency, giving his ally Antigonos One-Eye control of the kings and a commission to hunt down the former leaders of Perdikkas' now discredited government. Soon, though, he became mistrustful of Antigonos and took the kings under his own guardianship, returning them to Macedonia in

FIGURE EPI.1. This superb bronze portrait bust is generally thought to depict Seleukos, the general who in the late fourth century came to control the greatest portion of Alexander's fragmenting empire. It was recovered from Herculaneum, a Roman city buried along with Pompeii in the volcanic eruption of 79 C.E.

319. Alexander's experiment in intercontinental rule, whereby a European monarch was to hold sway from an Asian imperial capital, was coming to an end. Shortly after his return to Macedonia, Antipatros died of old age, leaving the regency not to his son Kassandros but to an undistinguished Alexander veteran named Polyperkhon. Kassandros rejected his father's unorthodox choice of successor and gathered allies to his cause. Civil war thus arrived in Europe, after Asia and Africa had been riven by factional fighting for two years.

§10. In Asia, Antigonos One-Eye succeeded in killing or imprisoning Perdikkas' former officers and attaching their armies to his own. The last to go was Eumenes, who had shown remarkable pluck and talent as a general but finally was betrayed by the Silver Shields, his invincible infantry cohort, after Antigonos coerced them by capturing their families and fortunes. The one-eyed commander seemed poised to rule all of Asia and perhaps invade Europe as well, but he alienated Seleukos, at that time satrap of Babylon, and pushed him into making common cause with Ptolemy in Egypt. A pattern had begun to emerge among the Successors in which any one general who grew strong enough to unite and rule the empire quickly aroused the opposition of all the others. A rough balance of power was created by the mutual rivalries of these men, ensuring that conflict would continue throughout their lifetimes and that no dominant figure would emerge. Breakaway provinces, like Ptolemy's Egypt and (increasingly) Lysimakhos' Thrace, could not be brought back into the empire, because no central figure was powerful enough to control them.

§11. Europe, meanwhile, became factionalized by the civil war between Polyperkhon and Kassandros, and the joint kings ended up on opposing sides of the conflict. Alexander IV, now championed by his grandmother Olympias, backed Polyperkhon against Philip III and his wife Eurydike, partisans of Kassandros. First one side, then the other, got control of Macedon, each in turn executing the other's leaders, so that Philip, Eurydike, and Olympias all came to bloody ends in 317–316. Alexander IV survived the turmoil but was imprisoned by Kassandros in Amphipolis along with his mother, Rhoxane. The boy was now seven or eight and nominally the heir to the throne, but Kassandros, who at this point had sole power in Europe, was determined not to let him rule. Alexander IV was secretly executed in 309 or 308, bringing the Argead dynasty to an end. (Kassandros had meanwhile fathered three sons by an Argead princess, Thessalonike, but these boys are not generally considered part of the royal line.) An effort shortly thereafter to install Herakles, Alexander the Great's illegitimate son, on the throne was aborted when the boy was killed by treachery. The throne that officially conferred command over the empire now stood empty. Leadership henceforth would arise not from a royal title but from the ability to amass and deploy huge armies, and from the wealth to outfit them with increasingly exotic, expensive weapons of war.[11a]

§12. Alexander's former generals were supremely well suited to this new model of leadership, especially Ptolemy, Seleukos, Lysimakhos, and Antigonos. Kassandros, who had never served under Alexander, seems nonetheless to have absorbed his lessons at second hand. These men squandered huge amounts of cash, and used up the lives of most of Alexander's surviving veterans, in endless struggles with one another, alliances always shifting to offset the power of whoever seemed to be on top. Antigonos had the grandest ambitions and seemed the most able to reunite the fragmenting empire, especially with the help of his extremely talented son, Demetrios. But the bravado and grandeur of these two inevitably united the others against them, and they were stymied. No one now held the royal prerogative to stand above the others, to provide a center around which all could rally.

§13. The political situation changed in 306 when Antigonos, following an impressive naval victory over Ptolemy, had himself and Demetrios crowned kings. It was not clear to anyone what they were kings of—certainly not Macedonia, nor of the old Persian empire—or what gave them the right to their new status, but the title stuck. In the next two years Ptolemy, Seleukos, and Lysimakhos followed Antigonos' lead and had themselves crowned as well, with Kassandros perhaps following last (the evidence in his case is unclear). Monarchy had been reinvented to give the Successors an office and a set of protocols, where officially they were only former satraps of a defunct imperial regime. In terms of the global balance of power, nothing had

Epi.11a   The story of the years following Alexander's death, up to the assassination of Alexander IV, is told in more detail in my forthcoming *Ghost on the Throne: The Death of Alexander the Great and the War for Crown and Empire* (New York: Alfred A. Knopf, 2011). A somewhat longer span of the post-Alexander period is chronicled by Robin Waterfield in the forthcoming *Dividing the Spoils: The War for Alexander the Great's Empire* (New York: Oxford University Press, 2011).

changed. The endless round of wars and shifting alliances went on as before, with no one able either to win a decisive victory or to knock anyone else out of the contest.

§14. Refinements in technology and tactics made warfare more expensive and bigger in scale. In 305 Demetrios mounted a siege of Rhodes (an island that had allied with Ptolemy) that included vast siege engines and towers; it was said that a thousand men were required to operate a single battering ram. For this operation Demetrios earned the nickname by which he has been known ever since, Poliorketes ("City-Besieger"), but all his efforts resulted in failure, and the Rhodians later melted down the scrap from his machines to build the famous Colossus at the entrance to their harbor. Indian elephants, only just coming into use by the Macedonians in Alexander's lifetime, became a weapon of choice in the era of the Successors. Seleukos bargained away rights to India, briefly a Macedonian holding, to the new Mauryan emperor, Chandragupta, in return for five hundred trained elephants and their mahouts. Troop counts increased as more and more men found there was good money to be made fighting for the wealthy and generous Successors.

§15. The long struggle for Asia, chiefly pitting Antigonos and Demetrios against Seleukos, finally came to resolution in 301 at the battle of Ipsus. Here in Phrygia, in the biggest engagement the western world had yet seen, Lysimakhos and Kassandros brought their forces to bear to support Seleukos, who was newly strengthened by his elephant herd. The combination was too much for Antigonos and his son. Antigonos was killed in the battle and Demetrios was driven out of what had become his home base. But this remarkable family refused to give up its ambitions. Demetrios somehow got into power in Macedonia after the collapse of Kassandros' dynasty and in the 290s began a buildup of weapons and troops in preparation for an invasion of Asia—a second *anabasis*, seemingly planned on the model of Alexander's four decades earlier. Once again, the other generals joined forces to stop him. In 286 he was captured and imprisoned by Seleukos, and three years later he drank himself to death. Seleukos and his son Antiokhos now controlled nearly all of Asia, the start of a long dynasty that modern historians call the Seleucid empire.

§16. Lysimakhos gained territory in western Asia as a result of his support of Seleukos at Ipsus, and after helping to drive Demetrios out of Macedonia in 288, he got control there as well. Though now in his seventies, he seemed very much on the upsurge, but domestic troubles roiled his court and led him to kill his son, Agathokles. Agathokles' widow took refuge with Seleukos and inflamed opinion against Lysimakhos. The two greatest of the surviving Successors went to war, and in 281, at the battle of Corupedium in western Asia Minor, Lysimakhos was killed. Seleukos enjoyed his victory for only a year before he was assassinated by one of Ptolemy's sons, Ptolemy Keraunos ("the Thunderbolt").

§17. Ptolemy himself (now known by the epithet Soter, or "Savior") died of old age in 283, not quite the last of Alexander's generals but certainly the most successful. Egypt remained his stable and secure power base throughout the half century of war and turmoil that afflicted the rest of the former empire. His dynasty, called Ptolemaic because every heir to the throne invariably took the name Ptolemy, endured for almost three hundred years, until its last monarch, Cleopatra VII, surrendered it to the Roman conqueror Julius Caesar. The other provinces of what was once Alexander's empire, including Macedonia itself, had gradually succumbed to Rome or to internal conflict during the second century B.C.E.

James Romm
James H. Ottaway Jr. Professor of Classics
Bard College
Annandale-on-Hudson, New York

APPENDIX A
Arrian's Sources and Reliability

§1. Since the nineteenth century Arrian has been consistently perceived as "the best" and the "most reliable" of all our extant Alexander sources; among modern scholars only Georges Radet openly preferred the so-called Alexander vulgate (Diodorus Siculus, Quintus Curtius, and Justin's summary of Pompeius Trogus).[1a] Arrian's high estimation in modern opinion has rested largely on his choice of eye-witness sources and his understanding of military (3.10.3–4) and engineering (5.7.2–5) logistics. But does his history deserve its reputation?

§2. In Alexander studies over the past forty or so years, Arrian's history has been exposed to careful and detailed analysis and has been the subject of one of the most penetrating modern commentaries (by A. B. Bosworth) in classical scholarship. In his very first volume, Bosworth (I.33) raised concerns about Arrian's worth: "Arrian's qualities as a historian can be called into question both in his selection of sources and his use of them." Now, after a lifetime of intensive study of Arrian's works, Bosworth has formed a less negative opinion, and admires Arrian's sheer sophistication as a writer.[2a]

§3. But before we can address the issue of Arrian's sources or his historical methods, it is helpful to have some appreciation of his life and times. He was writing during the reign of the emperor Hadrian[3a] (r. 117–138 C.E.), at the height of Roman imperial power, and he faced challenges that were different from but no less daunting than those of his models, Herodotus, Thucydides, and Xenophon. First, he stood at a remove of more than four hundred years from his subject; and although the differences in mind-set between an educated Greek of the second century C.E. and his counterpart in the fourth century B.C.E. probably would not have been as great as between our own time and the seventeenth century, they would certainly have been significant. Arrian was a citizen and high official of a wide-ranging, multicultural, stable, and organized empire,[3b] rather than a member of a small, autonomous Greek city-state. He spent much of his career in the military and

A.1a For more on the vulgate historians and Arrian's other sources, see the Introduction, §2.
A.2a Bosworth in Marincola (2007), 452.
A.3a The date of the *Anabasis* is uncertain, but Bosworth (1995, 2–6) has argued convincingly for a Hadrianic date.

A.3b Arrian's full name, Lucius Flavius Arrianus, suggests that his family most likely received Roman citizenship after Vespasian's triumph in the civil wars (69–70 C.E.).

administrative leadership of that empire, most prominently as the governor of Cappadocia, the Roman province that included much of modern-day Turkey, in the 130s. He was closely connected to Hadrian and shows a deep and automatic respect for authority,[3c] which at times (as with his notoriously brief account of Philotas' fall at 3.26) almost certainly affected his interpretation of historical events. As a military man who fended off a threatened invasion of his province by a nomadic tribe dwelling in what is now Armenia, the Alanoi, Arrian also had a high regard for great generalship and tactical success, as is evident throughout his *Anabasis Alexandrou*.

§4. A second challenge Arrian faced in undertaking his history was that Alexander, already a legend, was arguably the most famous and instantly recognizable personage in the ancient world.[4a] His story had been told in multiple histories and literary works, and his image was widely disseminated in sculpture, painting, coinage, mosaic, pottery, and jewelry. It is also important to remember that the Alexander tradition was inconsistent; the plethora of accounts (remarked on by Arrian at Preface.2) was often contradictory, and the persona of the Macedonian conqueror himself was elusive and ambiguous. By the time that Arrian wrote, representations of Alexander were colored by Roman prejudices, particularly rhetorical depictions of the king's excesses. Greek writers, moreover, could be just as negative about Alexander as Roman. Kleitarkhos' history, which was probably the main source for the vulgate historians, appears to have contained both favorable and unfavorable material, while other accounts, like the pamphlets that sensationalized the king's drinking and attributed his death to it, were downright hostile. Arrian's knowledge of Latin is a matter of dispute, but it is certain in any case that he was more steeped in Greek literature than in Roman.

§5. Arrian's chief literary role models and rivals were Greek. His emulation of canonical giants like Homer, Herodotus, Thucydides, and Xenophon is well known, and such was his admiration for the last of these that he even styled himself "the New Xenophon."[5a] There is every reason to think that there were also contemporary writers whom Arrian could regard as rivals. Plutarch is a clear case. He wrote in the reign of Trajan (r. 98–117 C.E.) and was an older contemporary of Arrian's. In certain passages in his life of Alexander the wording is so close that one suspects they are borrowing from each other, as in those relating to two philosophers, Diogenes the Cynic[5b] and Kallisthenes of Olynthos.[5c] It is impossible, however, to know for certain whether either of them read or used the work of the other.

§6. There is no denying that Arrian was deeply interested in the philosophers at Alexander's court, particularly the interplay between Kallisthenes and Anaxarkhos of Abdera (and again Plutarch and Arrian deal with the same material in the same wording). However, if we look for philosophical influence on Arrian's work, which we would expect to find, given his studies with Epictetus,[6a] we are disappointed. Yet he gives occasional glimpses of philosophic thought, most impressively at the beginning of Book 7. There Arrian surprisingly rejects the notion of world empire. In

A.3c See 4.12.6; see also 4.8.5 and 4.9.1.

A.4a The high recognition rate of Alexander continues in modern times; see Borza (2007), 413.

A.5a See the Introduction, §1.1, 1.3.

A.5b Plutarch, *Parallel Lives*, "Alexander" 14; Arrian,

Anabasis Alexandrou 7.2.1.

A.5c Plutarch, "Alexander" 54.4–6; Arrian, *Anabasis* 7.2.1).

A.6a See Appendix R, Arrian's Life and Works, §2.

Stoic vein he dismisses military glory as inessential and insists on the primacy of moral virtue. Interestingly the models for behavior are given by the Indian ascetics and Diogenes himself. The counterpart is the behavior of Alexander, caught in the toils of unlimited aggrandizement. Arrian here faintly echoes Epictetus, but he cannot disguise his admiration for Alexander's unparalleled military achievement. He condemns Alexander on moral grounds, but the criticism is overridden by the king's awe-inspiring success.

§7. Bosworth's studies have argued that Arrian's text operates on several levels: his selection and arrangement of his primary material, his engagement with past and contemporary writers, and his play on his audience's knowledge and erudition (evident when he breaks into Homeric meter at an appropriate moment, as at 4.24.5).[7a] Even his use of a word like *eris* ("rivalry" or "strife"), which appears on only three occasions (2.27.6, 6.24.3, and 7.23.5), can carry pointed significance.[7b]

§8. Although Bosworth's assessment of Arrian's intertextual pyrotechnics might be a little overstated for some critics, he is surely right to stress that Arrian belonged to a highly sophisticated, intellectual milieu that valued not only reliability in historiography but also supreme stylistic elegance. Arrian knew he was a great writer—among the masters of Greek letters, as he reminds us (1.12.5). His confidence in his own literary ability has been endorsed by history: he is quoted extensively by later writers, and the great Byzantine patriarch Photios, who was responsible for epitomizing some of Arrian's major histories, lavishly praises his style.

§9. If Arrian wanted his version of the Alexander story to stand out from the rest, he could not simply present another recycled history, synthesized and packaged from mediocre accounts. He needed to catch his audience's attention from the outset. However, it is clear that he was not after hype; as we have seen, sensationalism had already been tried, and he probably could have pulled out any number of examples of overly dramatic and exaggerated accounts from the scrolls on his library shelves.

§10. Instead Arrian, in a sober and methodical fashion, and uniquely among our extant authors on Alexander, begins the *Anabasis Alexandrou* by naming his principal authorities: Ptolemy son of Lagos and Aristoboulos son of Aristoboulos. In his preface he states that wherever these two writers agree, he has accepted their testimony "as in every way true" (*pante alethe*). If these sources diverge, he has selected the version that he has judged the "more trustworthy" (*pistotera*) and "more worthy of narration" (*axiaphegetotera*), thereby highlighting his own role as an editor and stylistic arbiter. He then establishes the credentials of each of his main authorities. Ptolemy and Aristoboulos accompanied Alexander, and both wrote after the king's death, when there was neither danger of repression nor hope of profit. Moreover, Ptolemy was a king and it was more shameful (*aischroteron*) for a king to be caught in a lie. Veracity is Arrian's first priority; this principle is repeatedly endorsed in his eagerness to correct past historical errors and misconceptions (see, for example, 6.11.4–6 and 6.11.7–8). Arrian then acknowledges that he has included other

A.7a   Bosworth (1996), 46.
A.7b   Bosworth (forthcoming), 7.23.5. My thanks to
       Professor Bosworth for giving me access to the
       manuscript of the third volume of his Arrian
       commentary.

sources he has deemed both plausible and worth mentioning, but only as *logoi* ("tales"). The implication is that these stories are outside his main authorities, and the reader should not accept them with the same degree of confidence—although on occasion he affirms the value of a logos (2.12.8). He finishes by emphasizing the challenge he has faced in writing yet another history of Alexander, and issues a challenge of his own: the reader should judge him only after having read everything else (which again suggests the extent of Arrian's research).

§11. As an introduction, Arrian's preface is extremely clever and succinct, but whether his claims are justified or consistently realized is another matter. On one level, his choice of Ptolemy and Aristoboulos is commendable, as both were eyewitnesses, the former a trusted friend, the latter most likely a midlevel officer with technical expertise. Yet each of these accounts is not without its flaws. Several recent studies of the earliest Alexander histories offer far more detail and analysis than is possible in this appendix,[11a] but some observations highlighting the main questions relating to these sources may help.

§12. Aristoboulos of Kassandria was possibly an interior decorator; whether he was also an architect or an engineer (as is often claimed) is debatable.[12a] He was clearly interested in Cyrus' tomb and its contents (6.29.4–11), but although he mentions Indian river patterns,[12b] he was strangely silent on how Alexander crossed the Indus—a problem that intrigued Arrian (5.7.1). According to one tradition,[12c] Aristoboulos was well over the age of eighty when he began his history, and although long-term memory can still be very vivid at that age, and he could have worked from a diary or notes, it is unlikely that he would have had many comrades left with whom he could have checked details. Aristoboulos' history was apparently readily available in the ancient world and used by several writers, including Strabo, Quintus Curtius, Plutarch, and Athenaios. It appears to have consistently played down the darker side of Alexander's nature. According to Aristoboulos, Alexander solved the puzzle of the Gordian knot using his brains, rather than resorting to brute force (2.3.7); Kleitos was not an innocent victim of Alexander's drunken rage but was responsible for his own death (4.8.9); Kallisthenes was not hanged by Alexander but was placed under arrest and eventually died of sickness (4.14.3). Arrian seems to have found Aristoboulos' approach congenial to his own views; he, too, downplays Alexander's drinking habits, as Aristoboulos seems to have done (see 4.13.6 and n. 4.13.6a), refraining from any reference to the infamous bacchanal before the burning of Persepolis (3.18.11–12) and describing the prolonged drinking bout that preceded Kleitos' murder as a new development in Alexander's behavior (4.8.2).

§13. Ptolemy Soter is an even more complex and problematic source. It has been rightly emphasized that Arrian considered him the more important of his two principal authorities;[13a] he is named first in the preface, and because he became one of Alexander's elite Bodyguards (3.27.5), Arrian would have been well aware that Ptolemy was a close friend, who was no doubt privy to sensitive information and

A.11a See Baynham (2003), 3–29; Zambrini in Marincola (2007), 210–220.
A.12a Stadter (1980), 69; compare Bosworth (1988), 47–55.

A.12b See Strabo 15.17–19.
A.12c See Lucian "Macrobii" 22.
A.13a See Arrian 6.2.4; but *contra* Stadter (1980), 71.

confidences. Of course, what Ptolemy chose to record and what to omit was entirely up to him. Arrian's opinion that Ptolemy's regal status would have encouraged him to tell the truth is often seen as naive, but Arrian is not saying that Ptolemy would never lie, merely that as a high-profile public figure he would be all the more embarrassed if his mendacity were publicly exposed. Arrian has Alexander emphasize the virtue of truthfulness in monarchs at 7.5.2; and although, in view of his extensive military and civil administrative experience, he was probably as realistic as the rest of us about any ruling authority's use of "truth," he would nevertheless tend to endorse the official line. Ptolemy's bias has often been noted by modern scholars; he denigrates rivals like Perdikkas (1.8.1),[13b] and he seems to have been particularly tight-lipped about the military laurels of Lysimakhos, a fellow Bodyguard and later ruler of Thrace, and Seleukos, a former *hypaspist* (shield-bearer) commander who became one of the greatest of those who followed Alexander, as Arrian himself openly acknowledges (7.22.5).[13c] Ptolemy's history was evidently not without color; for example, contrary to other traditions, Ptolemy stated (3.3.5) that Alexander's expedition to the oracle of Zeus Ammon at Siwa was guided by two hissing snakes, animals that are sacred to the god.

§14. Ptolemy probably gained considerable publicity from writing his history, regardless of when he published it; the date of publication is unknown but certainly falls within the four decades of Ptolemy's rule over Egypt after Alexander's death. Quintus Curtius (9.5.21) stated that Ptolemy was "not one to detract from his own glory," and detailed studies have shown that he shaped his history to enhance his own achievements. His success as a master of propaganda seems to have been spectacular; he was the first of Alexander's generals to issue brilliantly innovative coinage that stressed not only Alexander's divinity but his own links with the king. He hijacked Alexander's body, eventually housing it in a golden sarcophagus in the heart of his capital, Alexandria—the most famous of the cities Alexander founded, which both Ptolemy and his successor, Ptolemy Philadelphus, developed into one of the great cultural centers of the ancient world. Ptolemy may have also been behind the circulation of fictitious documents like the *Liber de Morte*, a pamphlet on Alexander's death and last testament—under whose terms Ptolemy is clearly favored as the king's most loyal supporter and true heir.[14a]

§15. As noted earlier, Arrian explicitly states that he uses alternative traditions to Ptolemy and Aristoboulos, which he usually indicates by using varying formulaic phrases—"it is said," "they say," "people say," "the following story is"—but he rarely notes a specific source for the colorful legends and stories that are thus introduced. Arrian also used other eyewitness sources like Nearkhos, Alexander's admiral, whose writings inform Arrian's account of the Indian campaign in Books 5 and 6. He also mentions Onesikritos, Alexander's helmsman, as a source at 6.2.3. In this instance Arrian is critical, although he used Onesikritos more extensively in the *Indika*, his monograph on India and Nearkhos' westward voyage from there. He also refers (at 5.51) to later writers like Megasthenes and Eratosthenes, whom he

A.13b   See Diodorus 17.12.3.
A.13c   Bosworth in Bosworth and Baynham (2000),
        15–26, with n. 48.
A.14a   Ibid., 207–241.

calls "men of repute," and (at 7.15.5) even to very obscure Alexander historians, Aristos and Asklepiades—the latter is not attested elsewhere. In doing so, Arrian underscores a rather curious omission. He cites Aristos and Asklepiades as his authorities for the story that the Romans sent an embassy to Alexander in 323, a story he personally doubts. But Kleitarkhos, who, as we noted earlier, was the main source for three of our extant histories, also recorded the Roman embassy,[15a] and for Arrian to have overlooked this account perhaps weakens the reliability of his work. Kleitarkhos was a well-known author, and even though he was criticized in ancient times for embellishment and inaccuracy, his history probably offered a more balanced account than the blatantly pro-Alexander tradition of Ptolemy and Aristoboulos. It is possible that he did not fit Arrian's preference for a truly primary source, and most modern experts accept that he probably did not go on the campaign.[15b] My own feeling is that Kleitarkhos' great popularity among later historians could well have been one reason why Arrian avoided him.

§16. One problematic issue is Arrian's use of the *Ephemerides*, or *Royal Journals*, which he refers to in his account of Alexander's last illness (7.25.1). According to Athenaios (*Deipnosophistae* 10.44), the journal was a daily record of Alexander's activities that was kept by his secretaries, Eumenes of Kardia and Diodotus of Erythrai. Considerable importance has been placed on the *Royal Journals* in modern times, because apart from Arrian's possible access to the document, it is still widely believed (thanks to Droysen, Tarn, Hammond, and other modern scholars) that official records underpinned Ptolemy's history.[16a] Although it is hard to know, it seems unlikely that Arrian used the *Journals* firsthand; it is more likely that he used the writings of Ptolemy and Aristoboulos—who in turn had used an edited document circulated after Alexander's death, which claimed to be based on the *Journals*. We cannot be sure that a complete text of the *Journals* even existed; according to Plutarch,[16b] a considerable number of papers in Eumenes' tent were destroyed by fire, and although Alexander ordered his satraps to send replacement copies of correspondence, we cannot tell what was lost. It is just possible that Ptolemy may have secured the *Journals* (or parts of it) from among Perdikkas' papers in the aftermath of the latter's invasion of Egypt and assassination by Peithon and Seleukos. But even if this were so, it seems highly unlikely that Aristoboulos ever got the full text.

§17. Regardless of his sources, it is Arrian's history that we possess—his synthesis, his thought, and his voice. His history is a brilliantly skillful piece of writing. It is also clear that Arrian's main objective was to record Alexander's deeds, and so his

A.15a Pliny, *Natural History* 3.57.8.
A.15b The dates of Kleitarkhos' life are unknown. Until very recently most scholars would have conceded that he was a contemporary of Alexander's (mainly on the testimony of Pliny the Elder) and therefore in a position to talk to eyewitnesses. There would have been plenty of surviving veterans in Ptolemy's pay, who no doubt frequented the bars of Alexandria. However, new evidence has once again made Kleitarkhos' date very controversial. According to a papyrus fragment from Oxyrhynchus in Egypt (*Oxyrhynchus Papyri* 4808, P. A. Parsons, ed.), which mentions several early Hellenistic historians, including Khares, Hieronymus of Kardia, and Polybius. Kleitarkhos was

"pretentious" (*kompodes*), but he was also possibly "the keeper of records," presumably in the great library; moreover, he was the tutor of the young Ptolemy Philopator, the grandson of Ptolemy Soter. If the papyrus is right, Kleitarkhos would be placed in the 260s—much later than the usual date of 310. However, the text is very fragmentary, and its interpretation is difficult and uncertain. I am grateful to Professor Robin Lane Fox for drawing my attention to this papyrus shortly after its publication.
A.16a See Appendix P, Alexander's Death: The Poisoning Rumors, §4.
A.16b Plutarch, *Parallel Lives*, "Eumenes" 2.2–3.

focus is necessarily military.[17a] He begins his account with Alexander's accession and mentions details about Alexander's parents or the king's early life only when they are pertinent to his main narrative.

§18. Is Arrian's history also the most reliable? The *Anabasis Alexandrou* is detailed and informative. However, given that the first two books of Quintus Curtius' ten-book history have been lost, Plutarch's life of Alexander is selective, and Diodorus' and Justin's accounts do not cover events in as much detail as Arrian's, it is hard to find alternative extended narratives for many episodes in the very early part of Alexander's reign. Arrian also occasionally makes mistakes,[18a] and he can manipulate his audience by his placement of certain episodes or the particular emphasis he might give to aspects of Alexander's behavior. For example, he places the story of Alexander's heroic refusal of water during the horrendous crossing of the Gedrosian desert (6.26.1–3), even though he was well aware that other versions of the episode located it elsewhere. By concentrating on Alexander's self-denial, Arrian diverts the reader's attention away from the king's self-aggrandizing motives for choosing the disastrous route in the first place.

§19. Arrian constructs his portrait of Alexander most freely in the speeches he assigns to the king, principally the two long speeches delivered to his mutinous troops at the Hyphasis River (5.25.3–5.26.8) and again at Opis (7.9.1–7.10.7). There is much dispute about the authenticity of these speeches, as well as about the long speech given to Kallisthenes in the debate over *proskynesis* (4.11). Did Arrian find the substance of these speeches in his primary sources and only alter the wording (for he certainly at the least put them into his own words), or did he invent them out of whole cloth? There is no hard evidence either way; scholars must instead assess the likelihood that statements attributed to the speaker were actually made, or gauge the degree to which a speech seems conventionally rhetorical in content, or, when possible, compare the version of a speech reported by Arrian with those found in other sources. On all these counts, the two long speeches of Alexander seem to this author largely invented by Arrian, though probably based on at least a nucleus of reported content he found in the works of Ptolemy and Aristoboulos. Both are highly rhetorical, drawing on stock themes familiar in Arrian's day, and both contain anachronisms or improbabilities that indict them as fiction. (For example, would Alexander have really spoken to his war-weary and recalcitrant troops at the Hyphasis about his plans for a further campaign in Africa, as Arrian has him do at 5.26.2?) The long speech of Kallisthenes, by contrast, seems more suited to its setting and therefore more likely to have been based rather closely on a reported original. Other scholars, however, have taken very different positions on all three speeches, and no certainty is possible. The shorter, prebattle speeches assigned to Alexander by Arrian seem largely authentic.

§20. But understanding Arrian's portrayal of Alexander is also the key to understanding his history. There are four passages where Arrian identifies very strongly with his subject and states what his aims are in his history: the preface, the so-called second preface (1.12.2–5), the beginning of Book 7, and the conclusion of the book, known as the peroration (7.28–30). As we have seen, Arrian is quite open in his admiration

A.17a Bosworth (1980); compare Baynham (1998), 39.   A.18a Stadter (1980), 71.

for his subject (7.30.3); Alexander was an exceptional individual, perhaps even something more than human (7.30.2). But Arrian goes even further—he links his own glory to Alexander's (1.12.5) and claims that, like Alexander, he has had divine help (7.30.3).

§21. It could be argued that if Arrian's history were the only ancient source we possessed, we would be left with a badly tilted picture. But such a view underestimates Arrian. Although he undoubtedly glorifies Alexander, his characterization is now regarded as more balanced and ambivalent than it formerly was, particularly in Book 7, where he elaborates the theme that was raised earlier: that glory and imperialism can be ruinous.[21a]

§22. There is no indication that Arrian thought the *Anabasis Alexandrou* would erase other Alexander histories. In fact, he indicates in his preface that he is more or less expecting the continuing existence of other accounts. But he also assumes his history's superiority and its place in posterity: a great subject and a great literary work immortalize each other (1.12.5). This is the same supreme self-confidence that we see in Thucydides, Horace, and Shakespeare—and, as in their cases, time has proven Arrian right.

Elizabeth Baynham
Senior Lecturer
School of Humanities and Social Science
Faculty of Education and Arts
University of Newcastle
Newcastle, Australia

A.21a Bosworth in Marincola (2007).

Bibliography

Baynham, E. J. *Alexander the Great. The Unique History of Quintus Curtius.* Ann Arbor: University of Michigan Press, 1998.

_____. "The Ancient Evidence for Alexander the Great." In Joseph Roisman (ed.), *Brill's Companion to Alexander the Great.* Leiden: Brill Academic Publishers, 2003, 3–30.

Borza, E. N. "Alexander the Great: History and Cultural Politics." *Journal of the Historical Society* 7 (2007): 411–442.

Bosworth, A. B. *A Historical Commentary on Arrian's History of Alexander.* Oxford: Oxford University Press, 1980. Vol. I, 1980. Vol. II, 1995. Vol. III, forthcoming.

_____. *From Arrian to Alexander.* Oxford: Oxford University Press, 1988.

_____. *Alexander and the East.* Oxford: Oxford University Press, 1996.

_____. "Arrian, Alexander and the Pursuit of Glory." In John Marincola (ed.), *A Companion to Greek and Roman Historiography.* Vol. 2. Oxford: Blackwell, 2007, 447–453.

_____ and E. J. Baynham (eds.). *Alexander the Great in Fact and Fiction.* Oxford: Oxford University Press, 2000.

Brunt, P. A. *Arrian: History of Alexander and Indica.* Loeb Classical Library. I–II. Cambridge, MA: Harvard University Press, 1976–83.

Oxyrhynchus Papyri. London, 1898–.

Stadter, P. A. *Arrian of Nicomedia.* Chapel Hill: University of North Carolina Press, 1980.

Zambrini, A. "The Historians of Alexander the Great." In John Marincola (ed.), *A Companion to Greek and Roman Historiography.* Vol. 2. Oxford: Blackwell, 2007, 210–220.

APPENDIX B

Greek and Macedonian Ethnicity

§1. At the northwest corner of the Aegean Sea rises a landmass that provides a transition between the warm, bright, and dry climes of the Mediterranean and the more somber and extreme character of the Balkans. Blessed with abundant timber and rainfall, ever-flowing rivers, and rich veins of precious and other metals, Macedonia is a land well endowed with natural resources, capable of sustaining a large population on farmland, mountain pastures, and lowland grazing areas. With the exception of that odd, three-fingered peninsula called Chalcidice—which was settled by Greek colonists who arrived by sea and felt comfortable in its Mediterranean aura—Macedonia looks mainly inward toward the Balkans. The early history of the region, known primarily from archaeological investigations, is dominated by unnamed and unknowable peoples who form an enigmatic chapter in ancient Balkan history. It is an era still in the hands of the archaeologists who study prehistory.

§2. The origins of the historical Macedonians as a people are obscured partly by ancient Greek myth and partly by an archaeological record that is both scanty and uncertain. Indeed, we cannot even be confident that a phrase like "origins of the historical Macedonians" is appropriate, because it suggests the beginnings of an ethnicity ("Macedonian") as something distinct from other peoples in the Balkan region, including the Greeks, who lived mainly to the south, and the many non-Greek peoples who lived west, north, and east of the Macedonian heartland. At best we can speak only in general terms of the peoples who inhabited the region, but without any evidence of the kind used to define ethnicity, such as language, cultural habits, self-ascription, and external opinions. One matter, however, is certain: modern scholarship no longer adheres to the anthropological question that dominated so much of mid-twentieth-century thought: Where does a people come from? Unless there is a clear archaeological and/or literary tradition describing the migration of a people from one place to another, modern scholars are increasingly inclined to ask: How and when does a people emerge? That is, by what process and under what influences does it acquire a character that makes its constituent members appear to be different and distinct from others, and to those around them, for these are the ways that ethnicity is characterized.

§3. The old view that the ancient Macedonians had their origin as a Greek people has been largely discredited, except by those for whom Greek origins for the Macedonians is a necessary component of modern Balkan politics. The theory of the Hellenic origins of the Macedonians is rooted largely in early Greek legends. Hesiod[3a] relates that Makedon, the mythical progenitor of the Macedonians, was the son of Zeus and Thyia, daughter of Deukalion. In an account of the origins of the Macedonian royal house, the historian Herodotus[3b] tells of three brothers, refugees from the Greek city of Argos, one of whom, Perdikkas, came to rule over the local people in Macedonia and thereby established the Argead dynasty that would rule over the Macedonians until the death of Alexander IV, the son of Alexander the Great, in the late fourth century. Moreover, in describing several Peloponnesian peoples, Herodotus[3c] connects the Macedonians with the Greek Dorians. But recent scholarship has shown that the connection of the early Macedonians and their royal house with Dorians and Argives is probably part of a process of mythmaking, and has also called into question the Hellenic origins of the mythic progenitor Makedon. Like other ancient peoples, the Macedonians (or their ruling house) created a foundation mythology designed to suit contemporary needs—in this case, to forge closer political and cultural links with the Greeks, as opposed to the Balkan tribes.

§4. If the Macedonians had shared the same prehistory as the Greeks, one would expect to find material evidence of that common ancestry. But the most recent studies have shown that Macedonia was not part of the Mycenaean—that is, early Greek—world. While Mycenaean artifacts have been excavated at many sites in Macedonia, they are either imported or local imitations, not evidence of Mycenaean settlement. Thus we are driven to ask: If Macedonia was not Greek in the late Bronze Age, when and under what circumstances did it become Greek? It is true that Greeks colonized the coastal periphery of Macedonia, but these settlements seem to have remained isolated from Macedonian development. By the time the fully formed Greek city-states (*poleis*) appeared in the north, in the late sixth and early fifth centuries, the kingdom of the Macedonians had already emerged as a separate, independent entity. Thus we cannot escape the conclusion that, to whatever extent Greek culture gradually permeated Macedonian life, it is the result of a long-term process of Hellenization and not of a shared Hellenic ancestry.

§5. Modern ethnic studies have used techniques for defining ethnicity that borrow from linguistics, social anthropology, political science, and a variety of other academic disciplines. One begins with a basic understanding of ethnicity as that which distinguishes "us" from "them." Those who allege that the Macedonians were a tribe of Greeks offer two basic arguments to support their view: the Macedonians spoke a dialect of Greek, and they worshiped the same gods as the Greeks. But what language did the Macedonians use? Was it Greek? Was there a difference between their spoken language and their system of writing? In fact, we know virtually nothing about the native spoken language of the Macedonians. We do know that as late as the age of Alexander the Great, interpreters were needed at the Mac-

B.3a   Hesiod, *Catalogue of Women* fr. 3.
B.3b   Herodotus, *Histories* 8.137–139.
B.3c   Ibid., 8.43.

334

edonian court to translate between Greek and the native language, whatever it was. We also know that literate Macedonians used Greek as their written language system, as evidenced by surviving official documents, funerary monuments, and the occasional inscription on personal objects. But the use of written Greek no more identifies the Macedonians as ethnic Greeks than does the use of written Greek by another Balkan people, the Thracians, who, to the best of our knowledge, never had a written language and who were never considered to be ethnic Greeks by their contemporaries in antiquity. As for religion, the fact that the Macedonians appear to have worshiped many of the same gods as the Greeks is irrelevant, as considerable borrowing and syncretism of religious forms took place among ancient peoples. Indeed, Thracian gods were worshiped in ancient Athens, correspondences existed between Egyptian and Greek gods, and the pantheon of the Romans was not much different from that of the Greeks aside from the names. To use a modern analogy, one cannot claim any ethnic similarity based solely on religion between, say, the neighboring French and the Italians, even though they both adhere to the same forms of Roman Catholicism.

§6. One could recite a litany of cultural similarities between Greeks and Macedonians, especially in art and architecture, as some Macedonians gradually absorbed more and more components of what they probably believed was an attractive higher Hellenic culture. Macedonian kings adopted a Panhellenic pose beginning with Alexander I, known as the Philhellene (c. 498–c. 454). He assisted the Athenians in their defense against the Persian invasion by supplying timber for their fleet, and he may have been responsible for informing Herodotus about the purported Argive origins of the Macedonian royal family, even though his own participation in the Olympic Games was protested by the other athletes on the grounds that he was not a Greek! During the last years of the fifth century King Arkhelaos imported Greek artists, architects, and intellectuals into the Macedonian court; and Alexander the Great, himself a pupil of Aristotle, was said to have kept close at hand his own copies of Euripides and Homer. There is no doubt that over a long period of time the Macedonian royal family demonstrated their desire for a close cultural relationship with their Greek neighbors, even though the Greeks denied any ethnic affinity. The extent to which this Hellenic attraction permeated the consciousness of ordinary Macedonians, however, is difficult to gauge. And one must recognize what modern ethnic studies have shown clearly: that what constituted Greek ethnicity changed over time even among the ancient Greeks themselves, who variously defined it as common ancestry or common religious belief or common political associations or common language. We have come to recognize that the perception of one's own ethnicity is mutable (and occasionally capricious), depending upon the necessities of survival and success in the contemporary world.

§7. The differences between Greeks and Macedonians makes the historical relationship between these two peoples one of the more interesting ethnic phenomena of Classical antiquity, of a northern people much influenced by aspects of Hellenic culture yet distinct in many ways, not least in their political systems. Probably the best evidence concerning the perceptions of Greek and Macedonian ethnicity comes from the ancients themselves, as it is unencumbered by modern theories and prejudices. Greek and Roman writers over several centuries down to the period of the early Roman empire believed that the Greeks and the Macedonians in the Classical era were two distinct peoples. Arrian himself, for example, is able to refer at 2.10.7 to an ethnic rivalry between Greek and Macedonian forces at the battle of Issus, and he regularly refers to the two peoples as distinct (see 3.22.2, 4.11.8, 5.26.6, 7.9.4–5). We are reminded that the early period of Roman rule in that part of the world made a clear distinction between the provinces of Achaea (Greece) and Macedonia, and the early Roman coins of the occupation of Macedonia reveal an unusual Roman tolerance for the symbols and traditions of the old Macedonian state that is not found in the completely romanized coinage that marked the advent of Roman rule over the Greek city-states. In time, however, any remaining distinctions between Greeks and Macedonians would become blurred and would lose most of their significance as a result of the new political divisions the Romans imposed on the Balkan peninsula. But in the Classical world that marked the centuries leading up to the reign of Alexander the Great, and even shortly afterward, the Macedonians made their mark as a separate people, not as a tribe of Greeks.

Eugene N. Borza
Professor Emeritus of Ancient History
The Pennsylvania State University

APPENDIX C
Alexander the Man (and God?)

§1. It is a hard thing to reconstruct the personality of a man who has been dead for more than two thousand years. To recover the nature of someone who died even a generation ago can bring biographers into dispute, despite the wealth of evidence they have to draw on. It is important to remember what we lack in approaching the personality of Alexander. First, we have nothing that he wrote himself. We know from frequent references in Plutarch's life of Alexander[1a] that he wrote a great many letters. Plutarch speaks as if he had access to these, or a collection of them, but many spurious Alexander letters circulated (some are preserved in the medieval French *Alexander Romance*[1b] and in the Greek *Letter of Alexander to Aristotle About India*), and we cannot be sure that Plutarch could always distinguish the genuine from the spurious. Second, we have almost no contemporary writings about Alexander: the "fragments" we do have are quotations in later writers who generally had a particular case to argue. Thus Athenaios selects anecdotes about heavy drinking, Cicero has some about liberality, and Seneca concentrates on those that illustrate Alexander's "tyranny." All these were no doubt traits of the historical Alexander, but the way they are presented reminds us of the "aggregating" method of ancient character analysis, which is more prone to collect examples of particular traits as exemplars to support moral points than to penetrate psychology. Thus the moralists can tell us a good deal about Alexander's behavior but little about his psychology.

§2. The two authors who provide the most help in tabulating Alexander's personality traits are Plutarch, who inserts discussions of character throughout his "Alexander," and Arrian. Besides scattered comments, Arrian provides a short summary obituary (7.28–30), but it is notably defensive of the hero against the moralizing critics:

> Anyone who reproaches Alexander should not simply cite those deeds that deserve to be reproached. Instead, after collecting in one place all of Alexander's qualities, let his critic then consider who he is and what sort of fortune he has had that he reproaches Alexander, a man who became so great and attained such a peak of human success as the undisputed king of both continents whose name reached every land. (7.30.1)

C.1a Plutarch, *Parallel Lives* "Alexander" 27.8, 39.7, 41.4,
       60, and especially 42.
C.1b See Appendix L, The *Alexander Romance*.

Both Arrian and Plutarch moreover wrote almost five hundred years after Alexander's death and interpreted their sources by their own lights: they were admirers of Alexander, which was certainly not the universal view in the second century C.E.

§3. Arrian's listing of physical traits provides a starting point in evaluating Alexander the man. He mentions, first, physical beauty (7.28.1). Other sources, including Plutarch, tell us that Alexander was notably short but had a leonine countenance that undoubtedly radiated charisma. His distant gaze, which is reproduced in contemporary and later sculpture (see the Frontispiece), may have been the result of an affliction known as ocular torticollis, a palsy of the eye that causes the sufferer to twist his neck. The curling lip and look of cold command on some coins, most notably a recently discovered but suspect gold decadrachm from Afghanistan (see Figure 5.11), convey a character that could cause enemies to tremble.

§4. Arrian then speaks of Alexander's clarity of mind and self-control (7.28.1–2), qualities that could have been enhanced by the education he received at the hands of Aristotle; and of his gift for strategic thinking and daring (*tharsos*; later moralists would describe this as *tolma*, a kind of impetuosity bordering on recklessness). Arrian regards Alexander's qualities of haste and anger as unimportant and emphasizes his capacity for remorse, which is one of the few internal traits Arrian mentions. Other traits relate to his drinking, his use of Persian dress, and his claims to be the son of a god, or even to be a god himself.

§5. Arrian's portrait is not much, but it provides some headings on which we may expand to investigate the ways in which Alexander's actions expressed his inner motivations and passions. We may begin with education.

§6. Plutarch describes Alexander's education by Aristotle and calls him a "lover of learning and a lover of reading."[6a] He carried with him everywhere a copy of Homer's *Iliad*, the Bible of the Greeks. It provided him with a role model, as a member of a society of aristocratic peers, in the character of Achilles, whom he often explicitly emulated. At Troy, Arrian tells us, Alexander made it a priority to honor the tomb of Achilles (1.12.1); his tactic when the army was resistant to his desires was to retire to his tent (7.11.1), as Achilles did in the *Iliad* when he felt disrespected by his fellow Greeks; and Alexander's mourning for his best friend, Hephaistion (7.14.4), was like Achilles' for Patroklos in style and proportion. Another influence of Aristotle was surely on the scientific aspects of Alexander's expedition: it seems possible that, as the Roman writer Pliny[6b] reports, Alexander was under commission from the philosopher to send back information.

§7. Alexander's intellectual curiosity is related to another trait, which was isolated in a classic article by Victor Ehrenberg:[7a] his *pothos*, or "longing"—in Alexander's case, a thirst for knowledge and conquest that assumes an almost erotic dimension. Arrian refers to it many times (3.1.5, the desire to found Alexandria; 5.25.2 and 5.26.1, to travel farther into India; 7.1.1, to sail down the Tigris and Euphrates to the

C.6a "Alexander" 7–8. All quotations from "Alexander" in this appendix are from Plutarch, *Lives*, trans. Bernadotte Perrin, vol. 7 (Cambridge: Harvard University Press, Loeb Classical Library, 1919).

C.6b Pliny, *Natural History* 8.17.44.

C.7a "Pothos," reprinted in English translation as chapter 2 of G. T. Griffith (ed.), *Alexander the Great: The Main Problems* (Cambridge, MA: Heffer, 1966).

sea; 7.2.2, to see the Indian sages). The word is so persistent that it seems to go back to Arrian's source Ptolemy, who marched with Alexander; it may thus be a record of a word actually used by the king. This intense longing to go further is one of Alexander's defining characteristics and an important part of his unique psychology.

§8. The consuming nature of this desire may bear comparison with the milder passions Alexander showed in relation to sexual matters. Plutarch, in the course of a long discussion of his temperance and self-control, devoted more than a full chapter to Alexander's sexual restraint.[8a] It was customary for Greeks living in aristocratic societies to have sexual relations with both men (often younger men or teenagers) and women, and the Macedonians emulated this practice. Alexander seems to have followed this pattern, though evidence is thin and far from clear. Certainly he had sexual relations with women; besides his wife Rhoxane, who bore him an heir, we know that he married two Persian princesses, Stateira and Parysatis, and also had a child with a half-Persian, half-Greek mistress named Barsine. His relations with men are harder to characterize. Hephaistion was an intimate friend and close confidant, but only twice in the whole ancient record is he referred to as a lover, and both times by sources who seem not to have had any privileged information.[8b] Quintus Curtius (7.9.19) names a different male figure, whose name varies in the manuscripts but may be Excipinus, as someone beloved of Alexander due to his youth and bodily beauty. Then there is the complex evidence surrounding Bagoas, a Persian eunuch from Darius' court who surrendered himself to Alexander in 330.[8c] Arrian does not mention him (the Bagoas at 2.14.5 is a different person, also a royal eunuch), and some historians consider him a fiction. Plutarch, however, calls Bagoas Alexander's *eromenos*, his "beloved" in a sexual sense, and reports a lurid scene in which the king publicly kisses and fondles the eunuch in a moment of infatuation.[8d] This relationship is still very much a matter of debate, though most modern historians believe it was real and sexual. But it may be fair to deduce that the drive that in many men is sexual was turned in Alexander's case to ambition.

§9. Another factor in his relations with the opposite sex is his evident fondness for mother figures. His own mother, Olympias, was never out of his thoughts, and he wrote letters to her until the end of his life. But he obviously hit it off with the exiled queen of Caria, Ada, who Arrian says adopted Alexander as her son (1.23.8). Her eagerness to send him little treats to eat was countered by him in one of his most famous statements of temperance: that to give him an appetite for his breakfast, he needed simply a night march, and for supper, a light breakfast.[9a] The respect he showed to Darius' mother, Sisygambis,[9b] is in keeping with this striking and, to some, attractive trait.

§10. These personal characteristics need to be seen in a context of the expected behavior of a Macedonian king, the first among equals of an aristocratic society, whose claim to military leadership must rest on both ability and charisma. Of Alexander's

C.8a "Alexander" 21.4–22.3.
C.8b Aelian, a Roman collector of anecdotes who lived in the second and third centuries C.E., implies a sexual bond between Alexander and Hephaistion in his *Varia Historia* (12.7). The Stoic sage Epictetus refers to Alexander's *eromenos* (sexual love object), in a context in which Hephaistion is clearly meant, at 2.22.17–18 of the *Discourses*.
C.8c Quintus Curtius 6.5.23.
C.8d "Alexander" 67.7–8. See also Athenaios 603b; Quintus Curtius 10.1.22–38.
C.9a "Alexander" 22.7–10.
C.9b Diodorus 17.37.6.

ability as a general there can be no doubt. It is the reason he has become a figure of history. Nor can his charisma be doubted, since he persuaded an army to follow him to the ends of the earth in pursuit of a dream of universal conquest. It was expressed, too, in his famed liberality,[10a] which became one of his dominant traits in the *Alexander Romance.* The great wealth he had won enjoined equally great munificence.

§11. One corollary of his position as a Macedonian aristocrat is his indulgence in heavy drinking of wine. This was absolutely customary at the Macedonian court, and instances of the practice abound in all the sources. Plutarch stated that Alexander was "less addicted to wine than is generally believed"[11a] and spent long hours talking over a single cup. Some of the great binges were the result of specific motives: the riotous procession, emulating the god Dionysos, through Carmania;[11b] his attempt to drown his sorrow at the death of Hephaistion.[11c] It would be going too far to see, as some scholars have done, the demon drink as the cause of Alexander's "failure," but it undoubtedly was the cause of at least one great crime: the murder of Kleitos. In his telling of the story (4.8–9), Arrian criticizes Alexander for being overcome by anger and drunkenness on this occasion, but even here he commends the king's remorse.

§12. Arrian's defense may seem specious, and certainly the moralists and philosophers who dealt with Alexander singled out this act as a prime example of the king's anger, tyranny, and cruelty. Another stain on his reputation was his treatment (perhaps execution: the sources Arrian cites at 4.14.3 leave it uncertain) of the philosopher Kallisthenes; it is not surprising that later philosophers would unite in hostility to such an attack on one of their own.

§13. The picture that seems to emerge is of Alexander's progressive loss of control over his impulses as his power grew. What had begun as impetuousness (*tolma*) in such actions as the cutting of the Gordian knot became something less admirable in, for example, the burning of Persepolis (3.18.11–12) or even his hurling himself into the fray at the battle of the Mallian town (6.9–10), from which he had to be rescued by his friends. His mass executions in India were called by Plutarch a "stain on his career,"[13a] while his suppression of the conspiracy of Philotas made him "an object of fear to many of his friends."[13b] Later, Kassandros, who was sent as an emissary to Alexander at Babylon, reportedly received a roughing-up at the king's hands and could never afterward pass an image of Alexander without a shudder.[13c] Alexander's single-mindedness and belief in his own rightness and power had turned him into a bully.

§14. One motivation for anger may have been fear. There are good grounds for supposing that the conspiracy of Philotas (3.26–27) was not really a conspiracy at all and that both he and his father, Parmenion, were unjustly executed. Equally, Kallisthenes, even if he criticized Alexander, was probably not involved in the Pages' Conspiracy and did not deserve his fate. The historical sources present Alexander as absolutely in the right in both instances, but a later, fictional source may penetrate to the heart of Alexander's psychology at this point. The *Life of the Brahmans,* attributed to Palladios, the basis of which is a Cynic diatribe that was current a century or two after Alexander's death, has Alexander explaining himself to the Indian

C.10a "Alexander" 39, 41.
C.11a Ibid., 23
C.11b Ibid., 67; Quintus Curtius 9.10.24–25.
C.11c "Alexander" 75.

C.13a Ibid., 59.7.
C.13b Ibid., 49.14.
C.13c Ibid., 74.

FIGURE C.1. Whether or not Alexander thought himself a god, his generals often found it useful after his death to depict him as one. In this spectacular coin portrait minted by Lysimakhos, a member of Alexander's Bodyguard who later took control of Thrace, Alexander is shown wearing ram's horns, symbolizing a spiritual link to the Egyptian god Ammon (who was sometimes portrayed as a ram).

philosopher Dandamis: "What shall I do, seeing that I live with incessant fears? . . . How far must I fear those who protect me even more than my enemy? . . . By day I torment the nations, but when night comes on I am tormented by my own reflections, my fear that someone may come at me with a sword."[14a] The loneliness of absolute power, and the corruption it brings, could not be more clearly expressed. Plutarch describes this fear in a different aspect: "Alexander, since he had now become sensitive to indications of the divine will and perturbed and apprehensive in his mind, converted every unusual and strange occurrence, were it never so insignificant, into a prodigy and portent."[14b]

§15. Alexander's extraordinary military success led to debates as to whether his conquests were really the result of his own genius or whether he had been aided by Fortune (in the sense either of chance or of a guiding deity who loomed large in the Hellenistic world). Plutarch speaks of "heaven-sent fortune" causing the sea to withdraw to allow Alexander's passage along the coast of Pamphylia,[15a] and even Arrian (1.26.2) regards this as the result of "divine intervention." Quintus Curtius (3.16.17–20) saw the corrupting influence of Fortune as the mainspring of Alexander's career; Livy[15b] attributed the king's success to Fortune and suggested that if he had encountered Romans, he would not have been so lucky: "and no man was less able to bear good fortune than Alexander."

§16. Alexander's own answer to such criticisms would undoubtedly have been that he owed his success to the gods; indeed, his successes had been so great that he had become godlike himself. The Cynic philosopher Teles, in a list of unreasonable desires, included that of his contemporary Alexander to become immortal. If Alexander had indeed developed immortal longings, it was the result of his perceived relationship with the gods. As a Macedonian king he claimed descent from Herakles, a hero who had become a god; he was also the son of Zeus or Ammon, according to rumors related by Plutarch[16a] and to the response Arrian (3.3–4) reports that Alexander received from the oracle at the shrine of Ammon in Siwa, Egypt (though we shall never know what it really said). His devotion to Ammon

C.14a Palladios, *Life of the Brahmans* II.32–34.
C.14b "Alexander" 75.1–2.
C.15a Ibid., 17.6.
C.15b Livy, *Ab Urbe Condita* 9.18.1.

C.16a "Alexander" 1–3.

was unchanging, and the word must have got about that he saw himself as the god's son, for, as Arrian reports (7.8.2), the soldiers taunted him about this belief when they were incensed by his edicts at Opis. Plutarch recounts several anecdotes in which Alexander is invited by admirers to declare himself a god (he declines), and concludes, "It is clear that Alexander himself was not foolishly affected or puffed up by the belief in his divinity, but used it for the subjugation of others."[16b]

§17. It seems certain that Alexander was regarded by others as a god in his lifetime. But did he demand to be treated as a god? He certainly behaved like one in issuing the Exiles' Decree,[17a] promulgated at the Olympic Games of 324, ordering the restoration of the exiles to the notionally free cities that belonged to the League of Corinth.[17b] Officially Alexander had no basis for rule over the free cities of Greece. His authority, then, had to be superhuman, and he may perhaps (the evidence is incomplete) have requested at this moment that the Greeks institute cult worship of him. It may have been in reference to this that Aristotle wrote that "the good king" could not be ruled, "for that would be like ruling over Zeus himself."[17c] The idea that Alexander might be worshiped prompted several ironic bon mots from Greek statesmen. Demosthenes the Athenian declared that Alexander could, for all he cared, become a son of Zeus—and of Poseidon too, if he wanted.[17d] The Athenian orator Hypereides complained, apropos of the heroic honors paid to Hephaistion, that the Greeks were being compelled to honor rulers as gods, and their servants as heroes; in the same speech[17e] he refers to a cult at Athens. And Arrian adds that the embassies to Alexander at Babylon came to him "in the manner of sacred envoys" (7.23.2). But whether they did so of their own accord or because Alexander asked them to is unclear.

§18. Though Alexander's psychology on this matter cannot be penetrated, it seems likely that he did, at this stage of his career—when he had gone so far beyond what any man had achieved before—regard himself as having joined the company of the gods. Yet it was not this that gave the moralists and historians a stick to beat him with, for they concentrated on his human failings, and sometimes his virtues. But the clash of Alexander's godlike achievements with his unexpectedly early death made him a figure of legend. His vices and his virtues were both magnified by his power, and the young man with a dream of universal conquest disappeared beneath the lonely autocrat. He was a victim of his own success.

Richard Stoneman
Honorary Fellow
Department of Classics and Ancient History
University of Exeter
Exeter, Devon, UK

C.16b   Ibid., 28.
C.17a   See Appendix M, Alexander and the Greeks, §11.
C.17b   See Appendix M, §3.
C.17c   Aristotle, *Politics* 1286a 30.
C.17d   Hypereides, *Speeches* 5.31.
C.17e   Hypereides, *Epitaphios* 21 and 20, respectively.

APPENDIX D
Alexander's Army and Military Leadership

§1. Perhaps the only thing all scholars of Alexander are agreed on is the brilliance of his generalship and the devastating effectiveness of his army. In his thirteen years as king and commander, he led this army to victories over forces many times its size, overcame a huge range of strategic challenges and perils, marched at astounding rates through rough or unfamiliar terrain, and almost never ran short of supplies (until he met with a set of logistical failures on his last great march, see §14). These phenomenal achievements were only in part the result of Alexander's own prodigious talents, however. The groundwork for them was laid by his father and predecessor, Philip, who, with a series of profound innovations in the 350s B.C.E., changed the face of organized land warfare forever. Alexander's brilliance is beyond dispute, but his success was in large part determined by the remarkable inheritance he received from Philip.

§2. Before Philip's time the Macedonians had always been strong in cavalry, the corps dominated by the horse-owning nobility, but had lacked an effective infantry. On coming to power in 360, Philip quickly built up his infantry by recruiting strong, vigorous youths from the lower classes and equipping them with a new kind of spear, the *sarisa*, sixteen or more feet in length. The advantage of this long spear in an infantry clash, where two phalanxes jabbed at each other at close range, was obvious; the downside was that, since the fifteen-pound weapon had to be held with both hands, the heavy, arm-mounted shield that protected most Greek infantry soldiers had to be abandoned. Thus Philip's new infantryman—generally referred to by modern historians as a "phalangite" to distinguish him from the Greek hoplite, with his shorter spear and larger shield—had greatly increased offensive power but almost no defense. He had some kind of protective armor but carried only a small, light shield that could be slung around the neck. The infantry corps as a whole was given (probably by Philip) the collective name "infantry companions" (*pezetairoi*) as a parallel with the terms used to describe the king's aristocratic inner circle, the Companions (*hetairoi*), and the elite cavalry unit in which many served, the Companion cavalry.

§3. It may also have been Philip who created a new corps of infantry soldier, the *hypaspists*, or shield-bearers, to help cover the phalanx's flank and keep a connection between it and the faster-moving cavalry. Unfortunately our evidence as to how these shield-bearers were armed is very scant, but it seems likely they were more lightly outfitted than the phalangites, given their great need for mobility. Certainly they were an elite corps chosen for their speed, strength, and stamina, for under Alexander various segments of the three-thousand-man corps were almost always the first selected for fast-moving pursuits or taxing physical challenges. They were also elite in terms of their loyalty to the king, since a subdivision of them, the thousand-man *agema* ("royal squadron"), formed his personal bodyguard and security brigade. (Under Alexander there was also a cavalry *agema*, made up of elite horsemen; one unit or the other would accompany the king into battle, depending on whether he was fighting on foot or on horseback.)

§4. The drilling and training of these new infantry forces was Philip's next order of business. Following a model he had seen in use at Thebes, where he resided for several years before his ascent to the throne, he made his new recruits into a standing army, paying them enough of a wage that they could remain in service year-round. Constantly in action, either on the battlefields of the Balkan region or on the parade grounds of Pella, the infantry companions attained a high degree of cohesion and proficiency in a short space of time, mastering rapid movements or changes of formation in response to commands. Many would remain in service throughout Philip's reign, attaining more than twenty years of seasoning and expertise before Alexander took over as their commander. By that time they had surpassed the legendary Spartans in their ability to hold formation and execute coordinated movements even under the stress of combat.

§5. Having developed his phalanx to such a pitch of reliability, Philip could exploit the potential of his cavalry in new and untried ways. Prior to his time, horsemen had mainly been used to fight other horsemen, or to pursue disorganized infantrymen in flight from the battlefield; their ability to penetrate a front-facing phalanx, even in full charge, was very limited. But in a long confrontation between two phalanxes, one of the two was bound to lose cohesion, and Philip could be virtually certain that it would be his enemy who would be first to do so. At that point his heavy-armed Companion cavalry, stationed on the far right wing of the line of battle, could hurl themselves at the weak point in the opponent's line and smash it open. Newly devised wedge-shaped and rhomboid formations made this cavalry devastatingly effective at achieving such penetrations. Philip's great victory at Chaeronea, where the Macedonians faced the highly trained Theban hoplites and their Athenian allies, was won by just such a charge, led by crown prince Alexander in the vanguard; later, as king, Alexander used a similar strategy in all his set battles, relying on the Companion cavalry as his principal striking arm.

§6. As Philip's army won more and more territory it took on new units and new capabilities. After their absorption into the Macedonian empire, the Thessalian Greeks contributed an expert cavalry corps that became the counterweight to the

FIGURE D.1. A drawing based on a wall painting from a Macedonian tomb near Lefkadia, Greece, preserves an image of a Macedonian cavalryman charging a Persian. The Persian's shield bears the Macedonian star emblem, leading some interpreters to suppose that this is a scene of target practice. The rider sits on an animal-skin saddle and wields what looks like a cavalry *sarisa*, about the same length as the infantry *sarisa* but light enough to be held in one hand. The original frescoes were destroyed when the tomb—probably dating to a few decades after Alexander's time—was damaged during construction of a nearby railway line.

Companions, fighting from the far left wing in nearly every set battle. An allied Balkan people, the Agrianians, contributed an elite infantry corps useful for special operations. Greek hoplites, clad in heavy armor and carrying a shield on the left arm and a seven-foot spear in the right hand, augmented Philip's infantry phalanx, serving either as paid mercenaries or, later, as recruits levied from the cities subjugated by the victory at Chaeronea. Missile units—slingers, archers, and javelin throwers—were added from the various tribes and nations reputed for these styles of combat. Of great importance also was the engineering and artillery corps, led by Greek experts hired by Philip with his new sources of tribute and income. The new generation of torsion weapons they developed (see Figure 2.27)—catapults and other artillery driven by power of tightly wound ropes and fibers—enabled Philip, and later Alexander, to breach city walls that had been considered invulnerable for centuries. Vast improvements were made to siege towers, which conveyed troops and battering rams up to the base of a wall in relative safety.

§7. By the time of his assassination, in 336, Philip had amassed not only the largest but the most complex and expert fighting force ever fielded by a European power. This was a truly multinational force, with Macedonians numerically in the minority, though occupying nearly all the leadership roles and the front-line stations in battle. Among the allied or contributing peoples, the Greeks were by far the most numerous, followed by a loose assortment of Balkan tribes and then by Thracians, Odrysians, and Paionians. Eventually, in the last days of Alexander, Persians and Bactrians came to predominate in the army of the Asian campaign, much to the dismay of the Macedonian veterans, who now were asked to fight alongside their former enemies (see 7.6.3–5).

§8. Readers of Arrian's history can observe at close range how these diverse units were marshaled for battle, because Arrian, a front-line general himself, follows Alexander's dispositions in detail before each confrontation. (Map D.1 illustrates the wealth of information Arrian supplies about the arrangement of forces at Gaugamela.) The king's first step was to learn about his enemy's deployments and the terrain of the battlefield, for which information he relied on his mounted Prodromoi, or Scouts. His own deployments had to counter the tactical strengths of his opponent—in the case of the Persians, an overwhelming superiority in cavalry—and to make allowances for uneven ground or obstructions that might impede the steady progress of his forces. Once he had formed an idea of how the action might unfold, he laid out his order of battle, always starting from the time-tested template that put the infantry phalanx at the center of the line. This phalanx was divided into segments called *taxeis*, here translated "battalions," each led by a different taxiarch. Stationed on one or both sides of the phalanx were other infantry units, including the shield-bearers, with the two principal cavalry units, the Companions and the Thessalians, stationed on either wing. Sometimes, as at Gaugamela (see Map D.1), special flank and rear guards were put in place to prevent encirclement.

§9. Alexander rode in the vanguard of the Companion cavalry in every major battle. Though ancient generals and commanders usually fought in the front lines of their armies, Alexander took the custom to an unprecedented extreme, again and again placing himself where he could do most harm to the enemy but where his life was most at risk. With his distinctive clothing and helmet, he was clearly visible both to his own troops and to the enemy, inspiring the former and terrifying the latter with his willingness to defy death. His bravado turned the tide of battle at both Issus and Gaugamela, when he led the Companion cavalry straight at the chariot of Darius in the Persian center. The contrast between his own conduct in battle and that of Darius speaks volumes about the energy and aggression that enabled the Macedonian army to defeat far larger Persian forces. Darius occupied a fixed position, hoping to motivate his troops by his mere presence while staying safe behind elite infantry units or a defensive palisade (2.10.1) or protecting himself with a wall of slow-moving elephants (see Map D.1). Alexander by contrast was constantly in motion, out in front of his infantry, inspiring by force of example rather than by pomp or regal pageantry. When the two styles of leadership collided

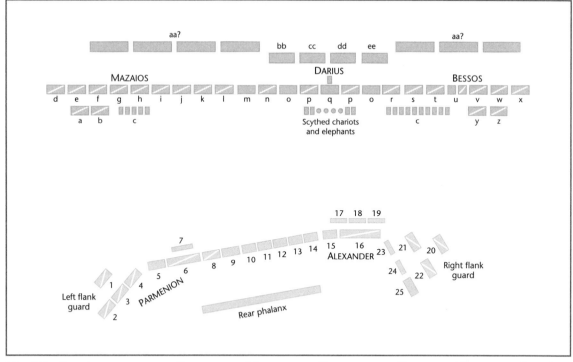

MAP D.1. THE ARRANGEMENT OF PERSIAN AND MACEDONIAN FORCES AT THE BATTLE OF GAUGAMELA (based on 3.11.3–3.12.5).

Order of Battle Listing Commander and Unit

Macedonian army

LEFT FLANK GUARD
1   Andromakhos: mercenary cavalry
2   Agathon: Odrysian cavalry
3   Koiranos: allied cavalry
4   Sitalkes: Thracian cavalry

LEFT WING
5   Achaean mercenary cavalry
6   Philip: Thessalian cavalry
7   Klearkhos: Cretan archers
8   Eriguios: allied cavalry

INFANTRY PHALANX
9   Krateros
10 Simmias
11 Polyperkhon
12 Meleagros
13 Perdikkas
14 Koinos

RIGHT WING
15 Nikanor: shield-bearers
16 Philotas: Companion cavalry
17 Half of Agrianians

18 Half of archers
19 Balakros: javelin men

RIGHT FLANK GUARD
20 Menidas: mercenary cavalry
21 Aretes: Scouts
22 Ariston: Paionian cavalry
23 Attalos: half of Agrianians
24 Brison: half of archers
25 Kleandros: "old" mercenaries

Persian army

RIGHT WING
a   Ariakes: Cappadocian cavalry
b   Orontes and Mithraustes: Armenian cavalry
c   Scythed chariots
d   Mazaios: Hollow Syrian cavalry
e   Mazaios: Mesopotamian cavalry
f   Atropates: Median cavalry
g   Phrataphernes: Parthian cavalry
h   Mauakes: Sacae cavalry
i   Phrataphernes: Tapourian cavalry
j   Phrataphernes: Hyrcanian cavalry
k   Atropates: Albanoi cavalry
l   Atropates: Sakesenai cavalry

CENTER
m   Mardian archers
n   Indian cavalry
o   Greek mercenaries
p   Darius' kinsmen
q   Apple Bearers
r   Displaced Carians

LEFT WING
s   Atropates: Kadousian cavalry
t   Oxathres: Susian cavalry
u   Mixed Persian cavalry and infantry
v   Barsaentes: Arachosian cavalry
w   Dahae cavalry
x   Bessos: Bactrian cavalry
y   Scythian cavalry
z   Bactrian cavalry

REAR
aa Massed infantry
bb Ouxioi
cc Boupares: Babylonians
dd Red Sea tribes
ee Sittacenians

347

at Issus and Gaugamela, Darius felt himself entirely outmatched and turned to flee, drawing much of his army's leadership away with him.

§10. The downside to Alexander's constant risk-taking was that a single sword stroke or arrow could have ended the Macedonian campaign in an instant, as very nearly happened at the Granicus (1.15.8) and again in India (6.10–6.11.2). Members of his seven-man Bodyguard were charged with protecting his person in battle, but if Alexander became reckless or heedless of danger, as he did in India by trying to fight virtually alone against a town filled with Mallian archers, there was little these forces could do. After he incurred his near-fatal arrow wound in this operation, escaping death only through the efforts of two fellow officers who shielded his fallen body with their own, his senior generals remonstrated with him for taking too many chances with his own life (6.13.4). Their cautions may have come too late, for many scholars believe that Alexander's punctured lung was a secondary factor contributing to his death, and some even regard it as the main cause.[10a]

§11. In line with Alexander's aggression in open battle was the tenacity of his siege operations. In Alexander's time, sieges were protracted and laborious operations, which often proved too expensive and time-consuming for attackers to see through to their end. But the new artillery weapons developed under Philip swung the strategic balance in siege warfare to the offense for the first time. Relying on these new weapons, and on a crack team of engineers whose task was to overcome physical and natural obstacles, Alexander succeeded in taking a number of towns and strongholds that, to contemporary observers, appeared impregnable. The siege of Tyre, described in great detail by Arrian, illustrates the way that technological innovation, massive commitment of human labor, and unwavering determination finally yielded victory after more than half a year of stymied effort and four hundred lives lost.

§12. Such demonstrations of tenacity and drive, and of cruelty as well—for many thousands of Tyre's inhabitants, civilians and soldiers alike, were massacred in the aftermath of the town's fall (2.24.3–5)—became increasingly important propaganda weapons to Alexander as his campaign progressed. Resisters came to believe that, once the king had committed to a confrontation, he would never relent or agree to negotiation; many cities and peoples that could have opposed him did not, or else submitted as soon as Alexander arrived with his army. In Bactria and Sogdiana, Scythian guerrilla fighters betrayed their most potent leader, Spitamenes, to Alexander, after seeing that the king was about to invade their territory in pursuit of him (4.17.4–7). In the last phase of the eastward march, in India, Alexander seems to have resorted to deliberate terror tactics as a way to subdue entrenched resistance, for example by sanctioning several mass killings in which no mercy was accorded to noncombatants (for example, 6.6.6, 6.8.3). By this time many of his troops had become exhausted and disaffected from the goals of the campaign and may have turned to cruelty out of sheer frustration. Also, Alexander may have judged that

D.10a See Appendix O, Alexander's Death: A Medical
       Analysis, §9.

FIGURE D.2.
Cross-sectional diagram of
a trireme, showing place-
ment of rowing stations.

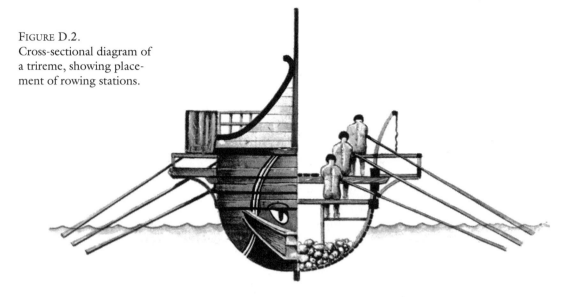

there was no way he could conquer or hold such distant territory without instilling high levels of fear in the population.

§13. At the siege of Tyre, Alexander and his officers fought from shipboard and commanded a navy for the first time. Macedonians of this day had little experience of naval warfare and tended to subcontract their operations at sea to their more nautical Greek allies, especially the Athenians. A large contingent of Greek triremes, warships powered by three banks of rowers, initially accompanied Alexander into Asia, but he soon dismissed it on the grounds that it was both expensive and unreliable (1.20.1). Most of the Asian campaign entailed land warfare exclusively, but in India Alexander again had need of a fleet and commissioned his Greek friend Nearkhos to command it. In the last year of his life Alexander became increasingly interested in naval warfare, ordering the construction of new ships, including many that were larger than the standard Greek trireme (7.19.3–5), and the deepening and expansion of Asian harbors and waterways. He had foreseen by this time that control of the sea would be vital in unifying and policing his empire as well as in expanding it toward the west, into the Mediterranean regions then dominated by Carthage, a naval power.

§14. Among the most astonishing of Alexander's talents as a commander was his management of food and supplies throughout the Asian campaign. An expert on Macedonian logistics has estimated that Alexander's army required 255 tons of food and 160,000 gallons of water every day, plus fodder for his many horses, pack animals, and, eventually, elephants.[14a] Much of the territory through which he passed

D.14a The number is cited in Frank L. Holt, *Into the Land of Bones: Alexander the Great in Afghanistan* (Berkeley: University of California Press, 2005), 32, based on the calculations of Donald Engels in *Alexander the Great and the Logistics of the Macedonian Army* (Berkeley: University of California Press, 1978), Appendix 1, 5.

did not produce nearly enough for a large force to live off the land, and some regions, including the two high-altitude passes he crossed in the Hindu Kush range, were nearly devoid of life. Yet provisions rarely ran short. The one great exception was the march through the desert of Gedrosia in southern Iran in 325 (6.23–26), a disaster sometimes compared to Napoleon's retreat from Moscow, though the loss of life among the Macedonians was probably not nearly so great as in that modern debacle. Nonetheless, the shortages were severe enough that Alexander lashed out, upon his emergence from the desert, at nearby officials he believed had deliberately withheld supplies. Whatever the truth of this charge, the primary responsibility for the disaster undoubtedly lay with Alexander, who had chosen the route of march despite its obvious uncertainties and perils. It is possible, though hardly subject to proof, that the king's judgment was at this time becoming impaired by alcoholism or delusions of godhead, or that he was so angered by the rebellion of his troops in India that he deliberately subjected them to the extreme hardships of Gedrosia.

§15. Perhaps Alexander's best asset as a military leader was the confidence he inspired in his troops and the amount of effort and exertion he could elicit from them. On his very first campaign as king, if Arrian's account can be believed, he persuaded his men, who were advancing against Thracians rolling heavy carts down from a high hilltop, to lie still on the ground under their shields and let the carts roll over them (1.1.9). Soon thereafter he led thousands of them across the broad and fast-moving Danube (ancient Istros) River, at night, bobbing in the water on makeshift floats, with a hostile force stationed on the opposite bank (1.3.5–6). The rate of march he was able to attain in strategic emergencies, such as the unexpected revolt of Thebes, could approach twenty miles a day, a speed considered strenuous for even a modern mechanized army. Alexander's two elite light-armed infantry units, the shield-bearers and the Agrianians, were especially adept at rapid marches, even over rough terrain or in poor weather conditions. By feats of stamina and fortitude such as these, Alexander was able to surprise or preempt his enemies time and time again, suddenly appearing with his army in places he was thought unable to reach. His arrival at Thebes in Boeotia, after a 250-mile march from rugged Balkan territories in only thirteen days, came so unexpectedly that the Thebans could not believe it was Alexander's army at their gates and thought a different force must have come from Macedonia instead (1.7.6). On this and many subsequent occasions, the shock caused by Alexander's rapid movements demoralized and intimidated his opponents, inflicting a psychological defeat before any weapon had been drawn.

§16. The last phase of Alexander's campaign, in India, brought him into extensive contact with trained war elephants, then unfamiliar to his troops and hence greatly intimidating. Guided by driver-trainers called mahouts, these elephants were used as a defensive screen to ward off cavalry (since horses were afraid to approach them), as an offensive weapon to trample and gore infantrymen and penetrate phalanx formations, and even as a battering ram to pound down city walls. Alexander first faced a large elephant corps in the battle of the Hydaspes, in 326, and was forced to devise innovative weapons and tactics to counter it (5.16.2, 5.17.3–6). Thereafter he incorporated an elephant troop into his own army and brought some two hundred of the beasts back from India to the central satrapies, but he died before ever employing them in battle. The elephant would, however, become an essential part of the arsenal of Alexander's Hellenistic imitators and followers.

§17. Even Alexander's admirers recognize that his prowess as a leader was waning in the last year of his life, perhaps dulled by frequent drunkenness. His men had by then become less tractable and harder to manage, and at Opis in 324 Alexander had to resort to summary executions to keep them in line (7.8.3). Nonetheless, he continued to plan major campaigns that would extend his empire into Arabia and, if we believe the evidence of the Last Plans,[17a] across North Africa as far as the Strait of Gibraltar. His death from illness, in June 323, saved him from the errors and embarrassments that almost certainly would have followed had he tried to drive his overtaxed troops into these forbidding new regions.

§18. Alexander's death did not end the style of warfare his father had initiated, but it did destroy the cohesion of his army. Veterans toughened by the Asian campaign remained the world's most highly prized warriors even into their sixties and seventies, but they splintered into small units attached to the various Successors who struggled to control portions of the empire (see the Epilogue). It is a sad testimony to Alexander's effectiveness as leader that virtually all his immediate subordinates imitated him in their tactics and methods, as well as in the scope of their ambitions. The result was an unstable fifty-year period of recurrent warfare across three continents, with several cloned versions of Alexander's grand army turning their well-honed tactics on one another.

James Romm
James H. Ottaway Jr. Professor of Classics
Bard College
Annandale-on-Hudson, New York

D.17a   A document known as the *Hypomnemata*, or Last Plans of Alexander, found among the king's papers at the time of his death, according to Diodorus Siculus (18.4.2–6), called for a campaign that would spread Macedonian territory to the Strait of Gibraltar and the construction of a road all along the North African coast, though without specifically mentioning Carthage as an objective. These plans also called for construction of an enormous fleet, perhaps with the ultimate goal of challenging Carthage for control of the western Mediterranean. Some scholars doubt the authenticity of all or part of these Last Plans.

APPENDIX E

Alexander's Inner Circle

§1. When at the age of eighteen Alexander succeeded his father, Philip II, who had been assassinated in the theater at Aigeai, support for his kingship was far from secure. Philip's recent marriage to Cleopatra (whom Arrian calls Eurydike at 3.6.5), the niece of his general Attalos, had called Alexander's right to succeed into question, as there might now be a full-Macedonian heir (Alexander's mother, Olympias, was a Greek princess from Epirus). A faction at court clearly favored the claims of Amyntas son of Perdikkas (III), whose kingship Philip had set aside in the tumultuous events that followed Perdikkas' death. Plutarch[1a] reports that at the time of Philip's assassination, Amyntas was promoted as a candidate for the throne by many Macedonians hoping to turn back the clock and reassert the claims of Perdikkas' line.

§2. Thus it was that Alexander owed his position to the support of the powerful factions around Antipatros, the senior statesman of dynastic politics, and the willingness of Philip's senior general Parmenion and his adherents to sacrifice the interests of Attalos and his niece. A purge of contenders eliminated the immediate threat.[2a] Nevertheless, Alexander had no choice but to reach an agreement with the aristocratic power brokers of the kingdom. He had indeed become king, but he was yet to establish himself as his own man.

§3. Power at court and in the army—and for the duration of Alexander's reign the two were synonymous—was based on family, faction, military leadership, and the goodwill of the troops. And although blood ties remained constant, family and faction could be shaped by intermarriage. Securing military office was the prerogative of the local aristocracy in certain areas—such as the command of the infantry battalions—but in others, influence played no small part. The greatest threat to the aristocratic elite's power, however, resulted from a practice that may have been instituted by Philip. This involved the education of the sons of the Macedonian nobility, who resided at the court, where they were indoctrinated in the values of the kingdom (with a view to breaking down their regional loyalties) while also serving as hostages for the good conduct of their fathers. As *paides basilikoi*, or pages, as they are often called, they grew up and were trained along with the young men of the royal house: Amyntas, Alexander, and even (one imagines) the mentally deficient Arrhidaios, son of Philip and Philina of Larisa.

E.1a   *Moralia* 327c.
E.2a   See Diodorus 17.2.3–6, 5.1–2; Quintus Curtius
         7.1.3; Justin 12.6.14.

§4. The friendships young noblemen developed during this educational process provided the networks upon which future careers would be built. As the political developments of Alexander's reign were to show, the most powerful individuals (and the most threatening to others) were those who could claim to have been "foster brothers" (*syntrophoi*) of the king. Another reason for this is that career progress led from membership in the page corps as a youth to later ranking in the Companions—a group of nobles who had the privilege of dining and hunting with the king, offering political and military advice, as well as leading troops on special missions, normally on an ad hoc basis—or even for a select few to the circle of seven Bodyguards,[4a] who shared the king's most private quarters and closest confidence.

§5. Alexander's Macedon was not simply a rigid aristocracy of birth but also to some degree a meritocracy.[5a] Competition led to promotion in many cases, but often this created rivalries that led to the destruction of factions and the ruin, if not the deaths, of individuals. Hence, the executions that followed conspiracy trials invariably resulted in changes of command, though determining who benefited from these changes may or may not bring us closer to the truth. Indeed, many who favored and encouraged the elimination of individuals thought guilty of "treasonous activity" did so without having contributed to their entrapment.

§6. By far the most significant shakeup of the Macedonian power structure resulted from the execution of Philotas, one of Alexander's more powerful but least popular young officers, on charges of conspiracy, and the murder of his father, Parmenion. The so-called Philotas affair is given extremely brief treatment by Arrian (3.26.1–3.27.3), in part because of the apologetic nature of Arrian's history but also perhaps because its most unsavory aspects were omitted by Aristoboulos and Ptolemy. Ptolemy clearly benefited from the demise of one of the conspirators, replacing Demetrios as a member of the Bodyguards. When one compares the extant sources, it becomes clear that the existence of the actual conspiracy, which involved an otherwise obscure Companion named Dimnos and Demetrios the Bodyguard, cannot be doubted. It is only the extent of Philotas' guilt in not reporting the news of it to Alexander and the severity of the punishment that are open to interpretation.[6a]

§7. In the wake of the Philotas affair, Alexander took steps to decentralize the powers held by his subordinates—dividing command of the Companion cavalry in two, for example (3.27.4)—and also began to rely more heavily on his *syntrophoi*, men of his own generation whom he had known a long time and whose character he

E.4a See N. G. L. Hammond, *The Macedonian State: Origins, Institutions, and History* (Oxford: Clarendon Press, 1989), esp. 140–142. Membership in the Bodyguards may, at least in Philip's time, have been restricted to certain families.

E.5a See Waldemar Heckel, "*Somatophylakia*: A Macedonian *cursus honorum*," *Phoenix* 40 (1986): 279–294, reiterated in *The Marshals of Alexander's Empire* (London: Routledge, 1992), 237–259. For the political factions, see W. Heckel, "King and 'Companions': Observations on the nature of power during the reign of Alexander," in Joseph Roisman (ed.), *Brill's Companion to Alexander the Great* (Leiden: Brill, 2003), 197–225. Of particular value for the study of the politics of Alexander's reign is Sabine Müller, *Massnahmen der Herrschaftssicherung gegenüber der makedonischen Opposition bei Alexan-*

der dem Grossen (Frankfurt am Main: Lang, 2003).

E.6a The view that Philotas was framed by Alexander was put forward by E. Badian, "The Death of Parmenio," *Transactions and Proceedings of the American Philological Association* 91 (1960): 324–338. For less extreme views see Z. Rubinsohn, "The 'Philotas Affair'—A Reconsideration," *Ancient Macedonia* 2 (1977), 403–420; W. Heckel, "The Conspiracy Against Philotas," *Phoenix* 31 (1977): 9–21; W. L. Adams, "The Episode of Philotas: An Insight," in W. Heckel and L. Tritle (eds.), *Crossroads of History: The Age of Alexander* (Claremont, CA: Regina Books, 2003), 113–126. For the individuals involved in the conspiracy see H. Berve, *Das Alexanderreich auf prosopographischer Grundlage* (Munich, 1926), vol. 2, and W. Heckel, *Who's Who in the Age of Alexander the Great* (Oxford: Blackwell, 2006) s.vv.

felt certain of. The elevation of Ptolemy to Bodyguard in late 330 is a revealing example. Ptolemy was at this point an undistinguished midlevel officer who had held no important commands; he was hardly suited by training or experience for the responsibilities of his new post. But he had a long history with Alexander, dating back many years; by 336 he was already close enough to the young prince to collude with him in a surreptitious marriage scheme (the so-called Pixodaros affair).[7a] Alexander now wanted such old friends, men of proven loyalty, as his high-ranking officers. Ptolemy began receiving important commands in India and executed them with distinction, but Alexander had no way to be certain of his capabilities at the time of his promotion. He was putting trustworthiness first, talent and training second.

§8. The same may be said of the important commands Alexander bestowed on Hephaistion, a boyhood friend almost exactly the king's age but, to judge by his lack of independent commands, only a mediocre military officer. It is unclear at what point Hephaistion became a Bodyguard, but in late 330, again following the execution of Philotas, Alexander put him at the head of half of the army's most prestigious unit, the Companion cavalry (3.27.4). Such preferments made Hephaistion resented by other, more soldierly members of Alexander's inner circle.[8a] Of all Alexander's top staff, Perdikkas (see §9) seems to have been most well-disposed toward Hephaistion, so it is no accident that these two were often paired on missions—for example, to subdue the region of Peukelaotis (4.22.7–8) and to bridge the Indus (4.28.5). Alexander's fondness for Hephaistion was deeply personal and, in some reckonings, sexual (see Appendix C, §8), but on the latter point there is no reliable ancient evidence; nothing more than strong emotional attachment need be read into Alexander's intense grief at Hephaistion's death (7.14). In the marriages Alexander arranged at Susa in 324, Hephaistion was given Drypetis, a Persian princess and a sister of Alexander's own bride Stateira (whom Arrian calls Barsine), in the hope that the two men would become related through their children (7.4.5). At some point in the later stages of the campaign, Alexander made Hephaistion "chiliarch" (see 7.14.10 and n. 7.14.10a), apparently a newly devised office based on that of the Persian vizier, the special counselor and right-hand man to the king.

§9. Perdikkas was a *syntrophos* Alexander had promoted to Bodyguard well before the Philotas episode. Unlike Ptolemy or Hephaistion, Perdikkas was a natural leader and a talented soldier, distinguished before Alexander's accession by his membership in Philip's honor guard. Arrian's account of the siege of Thebes depicts Perdikkas as impetuously launching an attack without orders (1.8.1), but this is contradicted by other sources and does not seem accurate, given Perdikkas' steady, professional conduct in other commands. In India, where Alexander often sent his officers on independent missions, Perdikkas served with distinction and assumed de facto command of military operations after Alexander was wounded in the Malloi town (at 6.15.1 he is apparently leading the campaign to subdue the Indus valley). Only Arrian, of all the ancient sources, reports the possibility that Perdikkas extracted the arrow from Alexander's chest after that wounding (6.11.1). Plutarch supplies testimony, omitted by Arrian, that Perdikkas took over Hephaistion's honorary position as chiliarch.[9a] All three of the vulgate

E.7a Plutarch, *Parallel Lives* "Alexander" 10.
E.8a Ibid., 47.9–11.

E.9a Plutarch, *Parallel Lives,* "Eumenes" 1.

sources[9b] recount that Alexander on his deathbed passed his signet ring to Perdikkas, designating him as the next steward of the empire. This important event is totally absent from Arrian's narrative and its veracity is doubted by some scholars. But Perdikkas would have been the logical choice for this honor, and the narrative of Ptolemy, on which Arrian largely based his *Anabasis Alexandrou*, is known to have deliberately obscured Perdikkas' role on Alexander's staff.[9c]

§10. Standing apart from the *syntrophoi* and peers who made up most of Alexander's inner circle, but equally central to the command structure, was Krateros. Perhaps fifteen years Alexander's senior, Krateros was already a trusted leader in the first stages of the campaign, apparently third in rank next to Parmenion and Alexander himself at the battle of Issus (2.8.4). After Parmenion's elimination (see §13), Krateros was often second in command, leading the main body of the army on occasions when Alexander was absent on special missions (3.21.2, for example). He was fiercely loyal to Alexander—Diodorus (17.114.2) calls him *philobasilea*, "king-loving"—but, as a cultural conservative, disliked the king's fusion policies and even challenged him openly on this score.[10a] For this reason, as well as for his sober, steady leadership, Krateros was beloved of the rank-and-file soldiery, but Alexander held him at arm's length. Krateros was the only top general not to be admitted to the Bodyguard, and in 324 he was sent back to Europe on Alexander's orders to take over Antipatros' home-guard duties (7.12.4). The appointment was at one level an honor, but it also removed from the king's Asian court the man who was least comfortable with its new international style. After Alexander's death Krateros was as well positioned as Perdikkas to take control of the empire, and considerably better qualified, but the turbulence of the post-Alexander years consumed the lives of both men at virtually the same moment (see the Epilogue, §8).

§11. Two Greeks were also part of Alexander's inner circle, at least in the late stages of the campaign, despite the fact that Greeks generally were excluded from the highest levels of Macedonian power. Nearkhos of Crete was an old friend of the king's who, like Ptolemy, had taken part in the failed arranged-marriage caper of 336 and had been exiled by Philip. In 334 Alexander appointed Nearkhos to a satrapal post in western Asia (3.6.6), but in 328 he was summoned to the east to rejoin the army (4.7.2). His naval expertise—a talent more natural to a Greek than to a Macedonian—proved invaluable in India (6.2.3) and on the voyage of the fleet along the Gedrosian coast, a harrowing journey Nearkhos later described in a memoir. Both Plutarch[11a] and Arrian (7.25.4) depict Alexander as conferring closely with Nearkhos in his final days of life, though for different reasons.

§12. The other Greek in the inner circle, Eumenes of Kardia, also brought a uniquely Hellenic set of skills to Alexander's court. He had been recruited as state secretary and bookkeeper under Philip and served Alexander in the same capacity for many years, supposedly recording the daily events of the campaign in the *Ephemerides*, or *Royal Journals*. Late in the campaign, in India, this longtime secretary began taking on military commands (5.24.6); Arrian gives no explanation for the shift, but Alexander presumably saw some hint of the talent for generalship that would, in the years

---

E.9b See Diodorus 17.117.3, Quintus Curtius 10.5.4, Justin 12.15.12.

E.9c See Appendix A, Arrian's Sources and Reliability, §13.

E.10a See Plutarch, "Eumenes" 6.3, and Appendix K, Alexander's Policy of Perso-Macedonian Fusion, §4, 11.

E.11a "Alexander" 76.3.

after his death, make Eumenes an important factor in the battles for control of the empire (see the Epilogue, §5, 8, 10). Both Eumenes and Nearkhos were married at Susa to relatives of Barsine, the mother of Alexander's son, Herakles, perhaps signifying that he wanted to make them, like Hephaistion, members of his extended family.

§13. As these younger men and outsiders rose through the ranks to become Alexander's senior staff, older, more established Companions were pushed aside, sometimes violently. Parmenion, a man almost half a century older than Alexander, served as second in command at all of the major battles against the Persians, the stalwart anchor of the Macedonian left wing. His military record was a long and glorious one, but by age and temperament he was a more cautious general than Alexander; Arrian relates several occasions when the king ignored Parmenion's counsels of restraint (1.13.2–7, 2.25.2, 3.18.11) or of stealth (3.10.1–2). These episodes may well have been invented by Alexander's partisans to blacken Parmenion's reputation, for the old general and the king would not stay allies forever. Left behind in Ecbatana for reasons left unexplained by Arrian, Parmenion was killed in 330, on Alexander's orders, directly following the execution in Bactria of his son, Philotas (see §6 and the Introduction, §7.2–3). Scholars are divided as to whether Alexander had intended for some time to get rid of Parmenion—perhaps even framing Philotas so as to gain a pretext—or came to regard the old man's murder as necessary only after Philotas' execution. Arrian inclines toward the latter view at 3.26.4, but it is inevitable he would do so, given his admiration of Alexander.

§14. Another older Companion, Kleitos the Black, a man twenty years Alexander's senior, was also destined for a bad end. Kleitos had single-handedly saved Alexander's life at the battle of the Granicus (1.15.7–8), and at Gaugamela he had the command of the elite royal squadron of the Companion cavalry. He still stood in high favor in late 330; in the wake of Philotas' death he received, along with Hephaistion, cocommand of the Companion cavalry. But that was the last occasion when Alexander appointed a man of Philip's generation to high office. According to Arrian, Kleitos, to an even greater degree than Krateros, could not conceal his dislike of Alexander's cultural fusion policies (4.8.4). Alexander sidelined him by appointing him as satrap of Bactria and Sogdiana,[14a] a post that would get the older man out of his hair and out of active service. Kleitos, no doubt sensing he was being forced into a kind of retirement, turned surly at a drunken banquet just before his departure, and Alexander, stung to fury, stabbed him to death with a *sarisa* (4.8.4–9). Alexander's remorse following the murder was no doubt genuine but may have been tinged with a measure of relief.

§15. Antipatros, the senior general left behind to oversee Europe when the invasion army crossed into Asia in 334, was the only member of the old guard to survive Alexander's reign, and even he barely made it. The grand old man of Macedonian politics, a top general for decades before Alexander came to the throne, Antipatros was the ideal guardian of the home front; he was expert at both military and diplomatic undertakings and unswervingly loyal to the Argead royal house. He must have been intelligent as well, to judge by the firm friendship he formed with Aristotle during the philospher's years in Macedon. Alexander relied on Antipatros for shipments of new

E.14a   See Quintus Curtius 8.1.19.

recruits and weapons; but he also sent cash and troops back to Macedonia when he sensed they were needed, for example in the war against the army of Sparta's King Agis (3.16.10).[15a] Antipatros aroused the jealousy and ire of Alexander's mother, Olympias, and each wrote letters to Alexander complaining about the other (7.12.6–7), but it is not clear how seriously Alexander took these. In 324 Alexander sent Krateros back to Macedonia to relieve Antipatros and send the old man to his court in Babylon, but there is no consensus as to what prompted the move or what he had in mind for Antipatros. The old man was sufficiently wary not to heed the summons but to send his son, Kassandros, in his place. After Alexander's death there were widespread rumors, reported by Arrian but not credited by him (7.27.1–3), that Antipatros had conspired to have Alexander poisoned, sending a lethal drink to Babylon by way of his son.

§16. The least typical but in many ways most intriguing member of Alexander's inner circle was Harpalos, mentioned by Arrian only at 3.6.4–7 and 3.19.7 of the extant *Anabasis* but also a significant figure in the portion of the text lost after 7.12 (as we know from a summary made by a medieval reader). One of Alexander's close friends since boyhood, Harpalos was unfit for combat duty due to an unspecified birth defect. Alexander assigned him an important nonmilitary post as supervisor of the treasury, but in 333 Harpalos fled to Greece with some of the treasury funds (3.6.4–7), evidently under the influence of the otherwise-unknown Tauriskos. Through emissaries Alexander cajoled Harpalos into returning to Asia, where, remarkably, he reinstated him to his old post without punishment. Left in the rear as satrap of Babylon when Alexander headed east, Harpalos debauched himself and spent vast amounts of money;[16a] when Alexander returned from India in 325, Harpalos fled to Greece a second time, knowing there were no further pardons to be had. The tangled tale of his misadventures in Europe, which resulted in his assassination in 323, are beyond the scope of this essay.[16b] For our purposes, the friendship between Alexander and Harpalos prior to 325 underscores once again the value to the king of his *syntrophoi*, his old friends and age-mates, even when they were not skilled soldiers. Alexander's bond with Harpalos, and to a lesser degree with Hephaistion as well, stood outside the military hierarchy that tended to make his most dependable generals his closest associates and friends.

Waldemar Heckel
Professor of Greek and Roman Studies
University of Calgary
Ontario, Canada

James Romm
James H. Ottaway Jr. Professor of Classics
Bard College
Annandale-on-Hudson, New York

E.15a See Appendix M, Alexander and the Greeks, §9.
E.16a Diodorus 17.108.4–5, Plutarch, *Parallel Lives* "Alexander" 35.15.

E.16b But see Diodorus 17.108.6–8, Quintus Curtius 10.2.1, Plutarch, *Parallel Lives* "Demosthenes" 25.

APPENDIX F
Money and Finance in the Campaigns of Alexander

§1. The subject of money and finance may seem unheroically mundane in a consideration of Alexander's momentous career. We naturally think of the young king as a fighter, not a financier. Yet, as Cicero famously remarked, "Great sums of money are the sinews of war,"[1a] and few leaders have had such strong sinews as did Alexander the Great. He amassed prodigious amounts of wealth through plunder and tribute, which furthered (if not motivated) his extensive campaigns and fueled the wars of his successors. The details of this process are unfortunately lost to us; our sources tend to focus on the king's battles and bravado rather than the day-to-day business of imperial finances. In Arrian's *Anabasis*, we find an occasional reference to taxes and tribute;[1b] the sale of prisoners;[1c] the recruitment of troops;[1d] gifts, bribes, and bonuses;[1e] plunder;[1f] and lavish displays,[1g] but no consistent treatment of Alexander's fiscal policies, military budget, or tax system. Elsewhere, Plutarch reports gifts of 10,000 gold coins to the poet Pyrrho of Elis,[1h] ten talents to the comic actor Lykon of Scarpheia,[1i] one talent to the victor of a drinking bout,[1j] and a gold cup to an officer for bringing in the head of a slain enemy.[1k] Quintus Curtius records individual payments of 30 and 80 talents each to two informants,[1l] plus an outlay of 9,870 talents to cover the debts of his soldiers.[1m] Athenaios (9.398e) famously cites a grant of 800 talents for animal research given by Alexander to his teacher Aristotle. Most of the written evidence at our disposal is therefore anecdotal rather than archival, leaving us an incomplete and often contradictory impression of just a few of Alexander's assets and expenditures. That information may be supplemented by other sources, however, most notably the vast quantities of coinage minted by the king.

§2. Although the sinews of war cannot easily be seen working beneath the skin of our ancient narratives, the basic cash flow of Alexander's campaigns may be inferred. Arrian and other writers suggest that Alexander began his reign in financial difficulties

F.1a   Cicero, *Philippics* 5.5.
F.1b   Taxes and tribute: 1.16.5, 1.17.7, 3.16.4, 5.29.5.
F.1c   Sale of prisoners or enslavement for later sale: 2.24.5, 2.27.7, 6.17.1.
F.1d   Dispatch of money for recruitment of troops: 3.16.10, 7.19.5.
F.1e   Gifts, bribes, and bonuses: 2.12.1, 2.18.4, 3.19.5, 4.18.7, 7.22.4.
F.1f   Plunder: 1.2.1, 2.11.10, 3.16.7, 6.16.2.
F.1g   Arrian gives only one example (7.14.8), but other authors indicate there were many (see Athenaios 12.53.5).
F.1h   Plutarch, *Moralia* 331E.
F.1i   Plutarch, *Parallel Lives*, "Alexander" 29.6.
F.1j   Ibid., 70.1–2.
F.1k   Ibid., 39.2.
F.1l   Quintus Curtius 5.7.12 and 8.11.3–4.
F.1m   Ibid., 10.2.10–11.

(7.9.6),[2a] due in part to Philip's poor management of Macedonia's resources and the financial strains of preparing the expedition against Persia.[2b] This may be true, but we must be aware that Alexander's initial poverty provided a "rags to riches" story that most writers (Arrian included; see 7.9.7–9) could not resist embellishing.[2c] Plutarch even alleges that Alexander hoped as a child to inherit a humble throne in order to prove his mettle. This tradition enhanced the moral contrast between virtuous poverty and vain opulence; between Alexander, who earned his wealth, and Darius, who wasted his. To underscore this notion, Plutarch tells the tale of an admiring Persian envoy who declares of the adolescent Alexander: "This boy is the great king; ours is only rich."[2d]

§3. In the first years of Alexander's reign, Darius' possessions duly became Alexander's as the spoils of war.[3a] Alexander's financial problems therefore disappeared under a mountain of plundered Persian gold and silver (3.16.7, 3.18.10). The sums are so high that our written sources usually express them by weight in silver, using a unit of accounting called the talent (56.88 pounds). Arrian, for example, reckons in talents almost exclusively; rare exceptions occur at 4.18.7 and 7.23.3–4, where he mentions darics and staters. In the period down to 330, our sources credit Alexander with the capture of some 200,000 talents, equivalent to nearly 6,000 tons of silver. Efforts to convert these spoils into modern equivalents such as dollars are essentially useless, but it has been calculated that this sum was sufficient by the standards of Alexander's day to support a million men for ten years. (A talent equaled 6,000 drachmas, which was a great deal of money. One talent could cover the monthly wages of a 200-man warship.)

§4. During the next phase of Alexander's campaigns (329–327), the financial picture changed dramatically. Gone were the heady days of hauling away on the backs of thousands of beasts the stockpiled treasures of Persia. Arrian records no significant financial rewards for the long and costly war in Bactria and Sogdiana, beyond the capture of some cattle. This coincides with another noteworthy development: the growing discontent among Alexander's troops, exacerbated perhaps by the decreased cash flow. Matters improved somewhat in India (326–325), where we again find references in Arrian (5.29.5, 6.16) and others to plunder and tribute, albeit far from the levels experienced in the Persian heartland. Finally, the last years of the reign (324–323) witnessed a reckoning of sorts, wherein the king (back among his treasuries) rewarded his soldiers with gifts, covered their debts, and issued their back pay (7.5, 7.12). The various rates of pay for Alexander's Macedonians, mercenaries, and allies are not easily reconstructed. In one instance (7.23), however, some interesting pay scales are cited: "double-pay men," "ten-stater men," and "rank-and-file men." It has been conjectured that the first group earned sixty drachmas per month, the second earned forty, and the average soldier received thirty. In spite of his wealth, there is evidence that Alexander had not met all of his financial obligations at the time of his death, leaving his successors the task of paying some arrears to the troops.[4a] Furthermore, Alexander's chief financial officer, named Harpalos (3.19.7), had disgraced himself by spending foolishly and twice running away with embezzled

F.2a   See also Quintus Curtius 10.2.24; Plutarch,   F.2d   Plutarch, *Moralia* 342c.
   "Alexander" 15.   F.3a   See also Plutarch, "Alexander" 20.10–13;
F.2b   Theopompus F224.   Herodotus, *Histories* 1.88.
F.2c   "Alexander" 5.6.   F.4a   See the Epilogue, §9.

fortunes. Some scholars believe that Alexander ended his reign just as broke as he began it, completing the morality tale of "rags to riches to rags again."

§5. In the end, our haphazard information cannot really prove how or how well Alexander managed his money. What we do know, thanks to the survival and study of thousands of Alexander's royal coins, is that the king indeed had a lot of money to be managed, more perhaps than any other conqueror in history. In whatever fashion Alexander dispersed these funds, they circulated for generations and transformed the ancient economy. In fact, many modern authorities liken this phenomenon to the later economic repercussions arising from the discovery and despoliation of the New World.[5a] At the time of Alexander's accession, trade in the eastern Mediterranean was dominated by Athenian tetradrachms, called "owls," struck on the so-called Attic weight standard (approximately 17.25 grams). Macedonia under Philip had issued silver coins on a lighter standard of 3.62 grams for drachmas and 14.48 grams for tetradrachms, plus gold staters on the Attic standard (8.60 grams). Alexander chose to adopt the Attic standard for both his silver and his gold issues,[5b] and eventually his voluminous imperial currency replaced Athenian money in most markets.

§6. Alexander also introduced new coin designs, called types, that were widely imitated. On the obverse ("heads") of his silver coinage, he placed a bust of Herakles, while on the reverse ("tails") he showed Zeus enthroned (see Figure 3.3). On gold issues he stamped an image of helmeted Athena, with winged Victory (Nike) on the reverse. These coins were all stamped "Alexander's [coinage]"; near the end of his reign, Alexander added the title "king" to his name. Most coins also bore a symbol or monogram identifying the issuing mint, of which Alexander operated dozens, from Macedonia to Babylonia. Many millions of coins poured from these mints. The king also struck a series of elephant medallions that commemorated his "superhuman" victory over Poros at the Hydaspes River. Serving as military awards (*aristeia*), these silver medallions depict various stages of the battle and accentuate the king's mastery of the monsoonal weather that contributed to the defeat of the Indians (see Figures 5.16 and J.1). In addition to a variety of bronze fiduciary coins, some local coinages were allowed to circulate, particularly in the western part of the old Persian empire. The eastern regions were slow to monetize until well into the Hellenistic period.

At the moment, our only hope for reconstructing an accurate economic picture of any portion of Alexander's empire rests on the testimony of coins and some newly emerging archival data from Babylonian texts. This may allow us to move beyond Arrian and other writers and to study such important things as consumption levels, commodity prices, wages, labor supply, and so forth. Mundane as it may seem at first, economic rather than military history may someday constitute the true measure of Alexander's life and legacy.

Frank L. Holt
Professor of History
University of Houston
Houston, Texas

F.5a Discussed in F. Holt, "Alexander the Great and the Spoils of War," *Ancient Macedonia* 6.1 (1999): 499–506.

F.5b See Appendix Q, The Royal Macedonian Tombs at Aigeai, §8.

APPENDIX G
The Persian Empire and Alexander

§1. The Persian empire was founded by Cyrus II, known as Cyrus the Great, who became king of the region of Persis[1a] in 559. With assistance from the king of Babylon, Cyrus conquered the more northerly region of Media in 550 and created the kingdom of the Medes and Persians. The conquests of Sardis in 547 and Babylon in 539 transformed the kingdom into an empire, and its rulers were known as the Achaemenid dynasty after their legendary ancestor Achaemenes. By the time of Darius I (r. 522–486) the empire comprised thirty subject peoples, which are listed in an inscription from Susa:

> My law held them firm. Media, Elam, Parthia, Aria, Bactria, Sogdiana, Khorasmia, Zarangiane, Arachosia, Sattagydia, Gandara, Sind, Amyrgian Scythians, Scythians with pointed caps, Babylonia, Assyria, Arabia, Egypt, Armenia, Cappadocia, Sardis, Ionia, Scythians from across the [Black Sea], Skudra, *petasos*-wearing Ionians, Libyans, Ethiopians, men from Maka, Carians.[1b]

This proud claim describes an empire that stretches from the steppes of southern Russia and Ukraine almost to the equator in Africa, and from the shores of the Aegean to Afghanistan and the Indus valley. The subject peoples are portrayed with their characteristic clothing and offerings paying tribute to Darius on a relief in the audience hall of the king's palace in Persepolis (see Figures 4.10 and G.1).

§2. This vast empire was ruled from the king's several capitals: at Persepolis (ceremonial), Susa (winter), and Ecbatana (summer), the former Median capital. But it was not a highly centralized empire; the key to its functioning was the local governors, whom the Greeks called satraps. Cyrus the Great had left the administration of each conquered region intact but with the imposition of a governor. Satraps were often Persian but equally often local men who were recruited for their local expertise. Despite the occasionally problematic question of their loyalty, this system generally worked well (and Alexander adopted it when he conquered Persia). But there

---

G.1a The satrapy called Persis here and at §6, §14, and §15 is referred to elsewhere in this volume by its more familiar name, Persia (see Ref. Map 1).

G.1b Cited in Maria Brosius, *The Persians* (New York: Routledge, 2006), 49. The *petasos* was a kind of wide-brimmed hat worn especially by Thessalian Greeks.

FIGURE G.1. The walls and stairways of the Apadana palace at Persepolis, the Persian king's main reception hall, were adorned with elaborate reliefs of subject peoples bringing tribute from all corners of the empire. The group shown here, however, seems to be made up of priests, since they are bringing an animal for sacrifice, some other unidentified offering, and two censers for burning incense. The vast sculptural program of the palace was begun by Darius I in the late sixth century and completed by his son Xerxes in the early fifth.

was no route to higher posts for the local elite: central control remained in the hands of Persians.

§3. The Great King was the dominant figure of this highly centralized empire. While he was not a divine king in the fashion of the pharaohs of Egypt, his special relationship with the gods put him on a higher plane than the rest of his people. The special nature of the King was reinforced by the efforts made to keep the dynastic line pure, at least in theory. When the King died, his eldest son succeeded him; if he died, his brothers succeeded in turn; and if there was no male heir, it was open to a collateral branch of the family to seize the throne. Thus when Artaxerxes IV (r. 338–336) was assassinated, his cousin Darius III seized the throne in a coup and reaffirmed the royal line by marrying his own sister. The King maintained the splendor of his position by surrounding himself with an aristocracy with whom he engaged in royal sports, notably hunting, and great banquets on the occasion of major festivals, including his birthday, the anniversary of his investiture, and probably the new year. The royal women had considerable power and financial independence.

§4. The main responsibility of the subject peoples was the payment of tribute. The yearly embassies to Persepolis were facilitated by the excellent road systems through the empire. The Persians extended the existing systems to connect the main cities and satrapal centers. The best known of these was the Royal Road, described by Herodotus (*Histories* 5.52–53), which led from Persepolis to Susa and Babylon; from Babylon a northern branch led through Cappadocia and a southern one extended all the way to Sardis, fifty miles inland from the Aegean shore. Another trunk route linked the Persian center to Damascus, branching off from there to Egypt via Jerusalem, and to Asia Minor. There were 111 stages from Sardis to Susa, each marked by an inn or hostelry of some kind, and Herodotus computed that it was a journey of ninety days. These routes were also the basis of what was in effect the first postal system in history.

§5. It has been argued that the empire became moribund and stagnated because of the "greed" of the King. In this view, the empire simply sucked wealth out of the subject peoples and stored it up in the treasuries of Persepolis and Susa. In fact, the redistribution of this wealth is plain to be seen, as the empire was a main employer of labor. Most of the distribution took the form of rations rather than coined pay. In addition, the empire invested, in the homeland at least, in such major operations as securing the water supply: the creation of the *qanats* (underground water channels) of Iran goes back at least to Achaemenid times. It seems likely, however, that there was no comparable economic development of the regions, as suggested by the notable absence of anything recognizable as Persian building in Asia Minor.

§6. The languages of the empire were as various as its peoples. The lingua franca that was adopted for administrative purpose was not Old Persian but Aramaic, a language previously disseminated by the Babylonian empire, though the major inscriptions of the Persian kings, found in Persis itself, are trilingual: Old Persian, Elamite, and Babylonian. Religion, too, was left to the local traditions. The Persians themselves followed Mazdaism (which later became defined as Zoroastrianism), the essentials of which were the belief in the good god Ahura-Mazda and his evil counterpart, Ahriman; a morality based on truth-telling (with the lie regarded as the ultimate sin); and the worship of the gods at fire altars, where an eternal flame was tended by the Mazdaean priests. But foreign gods were normally respected.

§7. There was thus no empirewide "Achaemenid identity." The responsibilities of the subject peoples began and ended with loyalty and tribute: they were not expected to identify ideologically with their rulers, nor could they expect ever to join the empire's elite. A corollary of this was that it might be straightforward for a conqueror to detach the sympathies of individual peoples, which Alexander was able to do easily at Sardis (1.17.3), Magnesia and Tralles (1.18.1–2), and Babylon (3.16.3) but with great difficulty at, for example, Miletus (1.18.3–1.19.6), Myndos (1.20.5–7), and Tyre (2.18–2.24).

§8. Control of the empire was in the hands of the army. The Persian army was based on cavalry, for the Iranian peoples were skilled horsemen: there were perhaps twenty thousand cavalry in the Achaemenid army in Artaxerxes II's reign.[8a] (However, all such figures must be treated with caution, and the reports in the classical authors give contradictory information on troop numbers.) The infantry may have numbered as many as one hundred thousand. The most famous unit in the army was the Ten Thousand Immortals, so called because any who were killed were immediately replaced to keep the number constant. One division of the Immortals served as the King's bodyguard. The army also included Scythian bowmen, Bactrians fighting from camels, and Greek hoplites.

§9. The role of mercenaries was very important, and as early as the sixth century we hear of Greeks fighting in the Persian army. Large numbers of Greeks were available throughout the fourth century as a result of the economic hardships and displacements caused by the Peloponnesian War. One of the best known is Xenophon, who took part in the rebellion of Cyrus the Younger in 401. However, the Persian army included mercenaries from many other parts of the empire, with large contingents in 334 from Armenia, Chaldaea, and other eastern satrapies. Classical authors often give the impression that the Greek troops constituted the elite of the Persian army and that they were frequently placed at the forefront in an engagement, but this may be special pleading. The mercenary general Memnon was of undoubted importance in the initial resistance to Alexander's invasion. Having been exiled from 352 to 342 for his part in a revolt against Artaxerxes III, he was restored to favor thereafter and, until his death in 333, proved a formidable opponent to Alexander.

§10. Defense of the empire was handled by the satrapal armies except for major conflicts, when the Persian army would be called out. The King accompanied it when it went out in force but would not head a satrapal army of the kind that was initially entrusted with the resistance to Alexander. In fact, Alexander's invasion represented the first external onslaught on the whole empire since its foundation, which is one reason the deployment of the Persian army seems to have been somewhat slow and no attempt was made to prevent Alexander's army from crossing the Hellespont (see Diodorus 17.18.2; Arrian 1.11 does not refer to this surprising circumstance).

§11. Because of the relative abundance of Greek sources, the Greek world's relations with Persia are better known than those of other parts of the empire. Greek disaffection from Persian rule had begun with the Ionian revolt in 499, while the Persian invasions of Greece in 490 and 480/79 ensured the Greeks' hostility to their superpower neighbor. In the Peloponnesian War the Persian satraps of western Asia Minor came to play an important role, as directed by the ruling regime, which saw in Sparta's attack on Athens an opportunity to recover the cities of Asia Minor. In 393 the satrap Pharnabazos brought a fleet to Greece, prompting hasty negotiations between Sparta and the King that culminated in the Peace of Antalkidas, or "King's Peace," of 387/6. This was reaffirmed in 375 in the Com-

G.8a Cornelius Nepos, *Datames* 1–2, cited in Pierre
    Briant, *From Cyrus to Alexander* (Winona Lake,
    IN: Eisenbrauns, 2002), 796.

mon Peace, as the King wished to be able to secure Greek support for the suppression of rebellion in Egypt.

§12. The long reign of Artaxerxes II from 404 to 359 saw a revolt by his brother Cyrus in 401, repeated campaigns against Egypt, and the so-called Satraps' Revolt (366–360), which led to the creation of relatively independent subordinate dynasties, including that of Mausolus in Caria. Artaxerxes III (r. 359–338) and Artaxerxes IV (r. 338–336) came into conflict with the expansionist plans of Philip II of Macedon, who sent Attalos and Parmenion on a mission to Asia, but the negotiations ended with Philip's assassination in 336. Also in 336 Artaxerxes IV was assassinated and his cousin Darius III (whose grandfather had been the brother of Artaxerxes II), then satrap of Armenia, came to the throne with the help of the vizier Bagoas. The two opponents, Darius III and Alexander III, thus became king in the same year, and in similar circumstances.

§13. Why did the Persian empire fall to Alexander's army? It had been a stable institution for more than two hundred years. A traditional interpretation goes back to the great historian Johann Gustav Droysen, who attributed it to overtaxation and resultant stagnation: "When Alexander liberated these riches that had been sequestered . . . the economic life of the peoples, from whom Persian dominion had sucked the life force like a vampire, had to recover and prosper."[13a] This interpretation will not stand. Though the wealth of the Persian empire was enormous, and Alexander funded his campaign from the resources seized at Sardis and Persepolis, the Persian king was regarded even by Greeks as a good manager of his empire's wealth. Xenophon, in his *Education of Cyrus*, makes this clear. Some anecdotes tell of people having difficulty paying the tax that was due, but this should not be extrapolated into a picture of a top-heavy system supporting a decadent elite. Arguing against that picture is the fact that there were no tribute revolts during the Achaemenid period.

§14. Resistance to the empire, which there certainly was, was based, rather, on cultural and political considerations. In Egypt the people resented the impieties that had been shown (uncharacteristically) to their gods and temples, while in both Babylon and Greece the destruction of temples by Xerxes had not been forgiven. In fact, the Greek invasion, which must have looked from Persis like another provincial revolt, is good evidence for the main concerns of subject peoples, which are generally political (the slogan "Freedom for the Greeks") and cultural (the expedition was originally put forward as revenge for the destruction of Athens' temples by Xerxes' army in 479). Alexander did indeed abolish the tribute to Persia in the Greek cities of Asia, but he replaced it with "contributions" to the new ruler—a distinction that may have required some ingenuity to substantiate.

§15. The cause of the fall of the empire was, in the end, a simple military one. The army, strategy, and tactics of the brilliant general Alexander were superior at every stage, and the conqueror was quick to place new administrators in position to hold his conquests as he marched on to the east. He did not disturb the satrapal

---

G.13a   Cited in Briant, *From Cyrus to Alexander*, 801.

structure of government. To begin with, in Asia Minor, Alexander installed Greek or Macedonian military governors, while in Cappadocia a local man was appointed satrap. In the Levant local kings were in some cases retained, in others (Sidon) replaced. A military commander was frequently placed alongside a local ruler as a control. After the battle of Gaugamela, Alexander, seeing himself now as de facto ruler of the empire, began to appoint satraps in the Persian heartlands from the defeated Persian nobility, though Macedonians were in charge of the garrisons and financial affairs. The policy worked for a time, though in 325/4 Alexander had to carry out a purge of disloyal satraps on his return to Persis from the East. Alexander increasingly took on the role and accouterments of the Great King and attempted to create a mixed ruling elite through a mass marriage in which he and other members of his court wed Persian noblewomen in 324 (7.4.4–8). While W. W. Tarn's view that these actions bespoke a belief by Alexander in the "brotherhood of man"[15a] commands no adherence today, it is clear that he envisaged the continuance of the Persian empire in its new form.

Richard Stoneman
Honorary Fellow
Department of Classics and Ancient History
University of Exeter
Exeter, Devon, UK

G.15a　W. W. Tarn, *Alexander the Great* (Cambridge: Cambridge University Press, 2003), Appendix 25, 399–434.

APPENDIX H
Alexander at Persepolis

§1. There is no episode of the Alexander history about which Arrian's account is more at variance with the other sources than the burning of the palace at Persepolis in the spring of 330 (3.18.11–12), and few episodes are as consequential for our understanding of Alexander's methods and motives. This appendix deals with some of the complex factors that figure into an analysis of the episode.

§2. In 331, flush with his victory over Darius III on the plains of Gaugamela, Alexander headed south toward the fabled urban centers of the ancient Near East. The Achaemenid ruling dynasty of the Persian empire had not designated a single imperial capital in the sense that the city of Rome later would serve the Roman empire. Rather, the Persians developed a number of imperial centers that had specific functions. Consistent with their ethnically diverse empire and with the decentralized satrapal administration that characterized Achaemenid rule, the Persians retained royal residences at their three principal cities, Persepolis, Susa, and Pasargadae, and also established regional centers for Persian rule at former national capitals, such as Sardis and Memphis.

§3. Persepolis fell easily to Alexander, and while the town was turned over to the army, the king kept the royal buildings secure for his own purposes. Alexander lingered four months at Persepolis. He may have been awaiting word of the defeat of the Spartan king Agis III, leader of a rebellion back in Greece that Alexander had ordered suppressed. He may also have been rewarding his troops for their recent exertions. But two additional factors help to explain the delay at Persepolis. Alexander was awaiting intelligence about Darius' whereabouts: he could not risk an advance toward the north and have Darius move west and cut him off. Moreover, it was winter, and the passes north of Persepolis were snowbound.

§4. During the stay at Persepolis, the royal complex was systematically and thoroughly looted by Alexander's men, according to Diodorus (17.70.2–17.71.2), (apparently confirmed by the lack of precious objects still in the palaces when they burned; see §5). The amount of loot was enormous. Diodorus 17.71.1 mentions a sum of 120,000 talents of gold and silver—nearly 3,500 tons of precious metal, if measured according to the Attic-Euboic standard (a talent on the Attic standard was about 57 pounds). Other sources provide both higher and lower numbers. What is certain is that thousands of pack animals were used to transport the bulk of the treasure back to Mesopotamia (it is likely that Alexander kept some resources with him to help meet the army's road expenses). It is the continuing task of scholars to understand the impact of such a release of gold and silver on the economy of the eastern Mediterranean world.

§5. Not only was the treasury emptied, but in the complex as a whole, excavations by American and Iranian archaeologists have revealed an almost complete absence of small objects of the type normally associated with such a wealthy site. While the remains of smashed pottery and glass vases and cups were excavated, not a single gold or silver object was recovered. What is more, excavators found that statues and relief sculpture had been defaced and works of art demolished. The vandalism doubtless performed by the Macedonians may have been part of Alexander's plan to exact vengeance for the Persian destruction of the Athenian temples a century and a half earlier; that is, both the vandalism and the looting may have been planned as acts of policy.

§6. The same may be true of the fire that completely destroyed the palace complex. Although the Persepolis monuments were constructed of stone, their roofs and supporting superstructures were of wood, and the buildings' interior decorations and furnishings were almost entirely of flammable materials, all sufficient to generate intense heat as the fire began to feed on itself. At one stage in the conflagration, the stone itself became vulnerable to the flames and heat. Given that many of the stone blocks show substantial cracks, it is possible that the Macedonians threw large amounts of liquid on the superheated stones in a determined effort to destroy them (the rapid expansion of water as it turns to steam will crack porous stone). The intensity of the destruction suggests that what occurred at Persepolis was not only the demolition of a defeated enemy's headquarters but also an act of revenge and a sign to the contemporary world that Persian rule had come to an end.

§7. An unintended result of the fire has proved fortunate for posterity: hundreds of clay tablets trapped amid the debris were baked, thereby preserving their inscriptions—a priceless source of information about Persian administration that would likely have been lost otherwise when the unfired clay inevitably turned to dust.

§8. One of the curiosities of the historical record is that, among our major ancient sources for these events, Arrian has the least to say. Indeed, he provides no details about the destruction of Persepolis beyond Parmenion's advice not to destroy it, Alexander's reply that his policy was an act of revenge, and Arrian's own disapproval. In contrast to this lean account (and fragmentary references in other ancient writers) are the extensive treatments in Plutarch (*Parallel Lives* "Alexander" 37.2–38), Quintus Curtius (5.6.1–5.7.11), and Diodorus Siculus (17.70.1–17.73.2).

Although some of the details vary, these three tell a nearly unified story that clearly represents the prevailing belief of their day, which is as follows: Toward the end of the Macedonian sojourn at Persepolis there was a banquet marked by wild celebration and drunkenness. One of the revelers was the Athenian courtesan Thais, who made an impassioned speech urging that a great victory procession be formed to set fire to the palaces, thereby enabling a single Athenian woman to act as the instrument of revenge for what it took the whole Persian army to accomplish in Athens a century and a half earlier. Alexander was invited to join in, and, with the king leading the way, the revelers wound their way through the buildings hurling firebrands everywhere. Alexander is said to have repented his actions almost immediately.[8a] (Arrian, too, describes Alexander's remorse, at 6.30.1, but puts it at a later time, during the return from India.)

§9. Modern scholars have puzzled over Arrian's omission of this tale. Some have suggested that Arrian or his sources—among whom was Ptolemy, the future ruler of Egypt—suppressed the story of Thais, who at the time of the fire was Ptolemy's mistress. While one may accept that Ptolemy concealed Thais' role, it is hard to believe that Arrian was unaware of such a famous story. He may have wished to avoid indirectly implicating Ptolemy, whom he admired, for an act of destruction of which Arrian disapproved. But the crux of the matter is whether the fire was accidental or premeditated. If we accept Arrian's abbreviated account, the conclusion is inescapable: the destruction of Persepolis was an act of policy that Alexander eventually came to regret. Our other major sources, however, all of whom relish telling the story of Thais and Alexander leading a drunken procession of arsonists through the fabled Persian palaces, would have us believe that the arson was spontaneous and unpremeditated. In the end, the resolution of this conflict is a matter of judging Alexander's personality: Was he capable of such a violent act of destruction when not in the heat of battle, or even in a drunken rage such as the one that marked his murder of Kleitos?

§10. While drunkenness may have played a role in the events at Persepolis, it is not unreasonable to believe that the decision to destroy the royal complex was premeditated, and that Thais either emerged during the procession as a fitting symbol of revenge or had been chosen in advance to initiate the conflagration with the dramatic grand gesture of her speech. If the decision to set the fire was indeed Alexander's, it may have been a difficult one to make: By destroying Persepolis in order to promote the idea that his campaign had been undertaken on the Greeks' behalf, for revenge against Persia, he risked giving up his legitimacy as the successor to the Achaemenids, just as Parmenion (in Arrian's account) had warned. For reasons we can only guess at, Alexander apparently chose revenge over legitimacy, and later, perhaps, regretted the decision (see 6.30.1 and n. 6.30.1b). Indeed, in the end, Parmenion's advice proved sound: Whether or not Alexander aspired to become a successor to the Achaemenids—and we cannot be certain that he ever did—he had

H.8a Quintus Curtius 5.7.11; Plutarch, *Parallel Lives* "Alexander" 38.4. Whenever Alexander's change of heart occurred, he eventually recognized the value of Parmenion's advice. Arrian reports (3.22.1) that Alexander ordered that Darius III be buried in a royal tomb at Persepolis. Both Persepolis and Parsargadae retained their traditional roles as centers of Persian ideology until at least the end of the fourth century B.C.E.

committed an act of vandalism that would greatly strengthen the Asian resistance soon to be mobilized against him. He would spend the next few years in military campaigns against peoples, many of whom had previously accepted Achaemenid sovereignty, who after the torching of Persepolis had to be forced back into the fold.

Eugene N. Borza
Professor Emeritus of Ancient History
The Pennsylvania State University

APPENDIX I
Alexander in Central Asia

§1. A fourth-century Greek playing a game of Where in the World Is King Alexander? would have sensed right away that something was wrong. In the winter following the 112th Olympic Games (332/1), Alexander had bivouacked in balmy Egypt; just one year later he occupied Persepolis, beyond Mesopotamia. The following winter (330/29) found the king far to the east, in the vicinity of modern-day Kabul, Afghanistan. In giant strides the conqueror had stormed across the map from the Mediterranean to the mountains of the Indian Caucasus (modern Hindu Kush). Then it happened: Alexander spent the next three winters still camped within a few hundred miles of Kabul. The campaign of conquest had plainly stalled, and not just for weeks or months but for years. A keen observer might notice more than a loss of momentum. Gone were the glowing dispatches from Kallisthenes about Alexander's latest deeds; the author had offended the king and forfeited his life, a fate recently shared by some of the army's best generals. The string of spectacular set-battle victories (Granicus, Issus, Gaugamela) interspersed with notable coastal sieges (Miletus, Halicarnassus, Tyre, Gaza) had been broken, replaced by interminable marches and countermeasures against resourceful local warlords. Great cities, palaces, and treasuries no longer were falling into the hands of Alexander's Greeks and Macedonians; plunder now provided barely enough cattle and grain to keep the invaders alive. The mercifully low casualty rates of the early years suddenly soared, and the king himself was wounded more often—and more seriously—than ever before. The hero and his glorious adventure had obviously changed in Central Asia, a fact no contemporary could ignore.

§2. Centuries later, Arrian drew attention to this same fact when crafting his history of Alexander's reign. When describing the invasion of Bactria-Sogdiana at the exact midpoint of his text (4.7.4), Arrian signaled his own concerns. He abandoned his narrative in favor of a lengthy moral excursus about the transformation of the king and his court as they tarried in the east. From various parts of the long Bactrian-Sogdian campaign, Arrian pulled together the "shocking" episodes that best illustrated the unfortunate drift of events: the mutilation of Bessos, the murder of Kleitos, the disgrace and death of Kallisthenes, and the Pages' Conspiracy. While

Arrian's thematic approach effectively highlights the downward spiral in Central Asia, it does so at the expense of his normally full and straightforward record of events. The resulting confusion can be ameliorated by consulting our other ancient sources, primarily Quintus Curtius (since Diodorus Siculus suffers a long lacuna here). Even so, readers will find that Arrian and Curtius present very different versions, marked by unusually discordant renderings of names, geography, and chronology. A brief chronological summary of events might therefore be useful for those trying to sort through Arrian's account of Alexander's campaigns in Central Asia.

§3. Early in the spring of 329, long before the mountain passes had sufficiently cleared of snow and ice, Alexander led his troops north across the Hindu Kush into Bactria. A logistical crisis soon developed, compelling the invaders to eat the uncooked carcasses of their baggage animals. This was but the first of several such disasters brought on by the exceptionally harsh weather and rugged terrain of the area. Weeks later, as Alexander pursued Bessos (now calling himself King Artaxerxes V) across the desert from Bactra to the Oxus River, the dehydrated Greeks and Macedonians endured even heavier losses. Their recent sufferings from cold and hunger, heat and thirst, eased somewhat with the news that Bessos had been betrayed by some of his last followers. Instead of a battle beyond the Oxus, the invaders needed only to take custody of a criminal. Arrian records at length (3.30.1–3) Ptolemy's role in the arrest of Bessos (no doubt drawing from Ptolemy's own written history) but omits other episodes such as Alexander's massacre of the Branchidae (described by Quintus Curtius at 7.5.28–35 but not confirmed by other sources and doubted by some modern scholars).

§4. A momentary lull in the war soon gave way to a growing insurgency across Sogdiana, led in part by Spitamenes. The tipping point may have been Alexander's decision to fortify the Sogdian-Scythian frontier by founding a new city (Alexandria Eschate) on the banks of the Iaxartes River. Alexander's plan backfired, bringing the nomadic trans-Iaxartes tribes into the conflict on the side of the Sogdians and Bactrians. The fighting escalated rapidly, with heavy casualties. Though twice wounded and for a time unable to walk, ride, speak, or see, Alexander systematically sacked the towns of the region and defended the emerging fortress of Alexandria Eschate by launching an attack across the Iaxartes. Meanwhile, Spitamenes and some Scythian allies threatened Alexander's garrison and supply line back at Marakanda. The large relief force sent there by the king was lured into an ambush and thoroughly defeated, the worst military setback of Alexander's career. In person, the beleaguered king rescued Marakanda and ordered devastating reprisals against all nearby settlements.

§5. During the winter of 329/8, Spitamenes and other warlords remained on the loose as Alexander regrouped at Bactra. There he punished the captive Bessos in the savage fashion that so troubled Arrian. Large numbers of reinforcements, most of them Greek mercenaries, arrived in Bactria and were soon put to use as soldiers and permanent settlers. In the spring of 328, fighting resumed as Alexander divided his forces in order to meet the demands of a widespread guerrilla war. Five commanders

FIGURE I.1. The Greek city known as Ai Khanoum (after the Afghan village nearest its locale) was discovered by chance in 1961, when an Afghan king on a hunting expedition stumbled upon some half-buried remains. Now partly excavated, it gives us our best information to date on the lives of Greek settlers in Bactria, though not on those of Alexander's garrison troops, who dwelt in much smaller and poorer settlements. Once identified as a city founded by Alexander, Alexandria on the Oxus, Ai Khanoum is today thought to date from somewhat later times, when Bactria was part of the empire of one of Alexander's former officers, Seleukos, and his descendants. The name it bore in ancient times is still unknown.

operated in Bactria, while another five (including Alexander) crossed the Oxus and swept across Sogdiana. The mountain stronghold of Ariamazes fell to the king, who scourged and crucified the enemy leader. But as the Sogdian wing of Alexander's army completed its missions, Spitamenes boldly raided Bactria. This was another attempt to disrupt Alexander's exposed logistical network, and it succeeded. The king abandoned Bactra as his headquarters for the coming winter of 328/7; he instead quartered his troops among various Sogdian districts and allowed them to raid a protected Persian game park for food. Alexander also replaced his Persian satrap of Bactria, Artabazos, with a prominent Macedonian, Kleitos. At a raucous banquet in Maracanda, however, Alexander quarreled with Kleitos and killed him (4.8.4–9). This is another of the episodes that troubled Arrian, and it may indicate the growing crisis of post-traumatic stress disorder within the army. Another Macedonian, Amyntas, took the post of satrap.

§6. Dispersed units of Alexander's army continued to move about the region, flushing out rebels and subsisting on the hoarded provisions of native settlements. In one notable engagement, Koinos finally managed to defeat Spitamenes. The warlord lost the confidence of his Scythian allies, who delivered his severed head to Alexander (Curtius [8.3.1–15] claims that Spitamenes' wife did the deed). Meanwhile, Alexander successfully besieged the so-called Rock of Sisimithres, another mountain redoubt, using battering rams and long-range missiles. Unlike Ariamazes, the rebel Sisimithres received a pardon and was even permitted to retain his power. Clearly, Alexander had decided upon a new, less punitive policy toward the remaining tribal leaders.

§7. Another beneficiary of this policy was Oxyartes, whose daughter Rhoxane Alexander precipitously married in Sogdiana. The twenty-eight-year-old king had never taken a wife (his father, Philip, had had seven), and it vexed many Macedonians that Alexander so honored a warlord's family from this distant and difficult land. Yet that very difficulty probably explains Alexander's nuptials. Rather than for love or lust, the union served the king's immediate political, social, and military interests as he contemplated how best to extricate himself from Bactria-Sogdiana. At the same time, Alexander set in motion the training of large numbers of local boys to serve in his army (rather than have them recruited into the lingering insurgency). By siphoning away these natives, marrying one of their sisters, and settling among their towns and villages a huge number of Macedonian veterans and mercenary Greeks, Alexander hoped that Central Asia would be reasonably secure as he advanced into India.

§8. After one more weather-related disaster in Sogdiana (a crippling blizzard during an early spring march; see n. 4.18.4a), Alexander assembled his forces at Bactra. There he attempted to introduce the Persian practice of *proskynesis* among his countrymen, but the objections of Kallisthenes spoiled the staged event. Soon thereafter, Kallisthenes found himself under suspicion when a plot against Alexander's life was uncovered among the royal pages. As the tutor for these highborn teens, Kallisthenes was to some degree held accountable for their actions. The downfall of Kallisthenes completed, in Arrian's eyes, the chain of unhappy events that befell Alexander and his companions in Bactria-Sogdiana. Arrian expresses no sympathy for the victims of Alexander's wrath (Bessos, Kleitos, Kallisthenes), but he does attribute to Alexander's moral deterioration some of the blame for these episodes.

§9. In 327, the king left in Bactria an army of 13,500 troops plus as many as 10,000 settlers. Alexander had spent more time trying to pacify Bactria than any other satrapy of the old Persian empire, and he garrisoned/colonized the region more thoroughly than any other. In spite of these costly efforts, Central Asia remained turbulent, and twice Alexander's unhappy settlers and soldiers tried to leave. The king and his successors responded vigorously and forced the survivors to stay. For these long-suffering men, Where in the World Is King Alexander? had been anything but a game.

Frank L. Holt
Professor of History
University of Houston
Houston, Texas

APPENDIX J
The Indian Campaign

§1. Arrian devotes almost a quarter of the *Anabasis* (4.22.3–6.20) to his account of Alexander's Indian campaign, which lasted from spring 327 to late summer 325. In addition, he wrote the *Indika,* comprising both an ethnographic and a geographic account of India and a narrative of the sea voyage from the Indus' mouth to Babylon undertaken at Alexander's behest by his admiral Nearkhos. Arrian's concentration on this brief portion of the campaign is remarkable. It can be explained in part by the exotic nature of the material, but the Indian campaign was particularly important for other reasons. It took Alexander for the first time beyond the limits of the Persian empire (at least those of his day; see §4) and raised in his mind the possibility of world domination. Probably, too, it aroused the scientific ambitions once fostered in him by his tutor Aristotle: Alexander's scientific staff were numerous, and several of them, including the philosopher Onesikritos and his admiral Nearkhos, wrote much about the conditions in India.[1a] Yet, despite the quantities of blood shed in the conquest, Alexander ultimately made little attempt to retain his Indian possessions, and they began to slip from his grasp even before he had left the country.

§2. The conquest of the Persian empire had occupied eight years and was not complete until the suppression of the Sogdian rebel leader Spitamenes in late 328. At this point it might have been expected that the expedition would be over. But Alexander had made it clear to the Khorasmian king Pharasmanes that "by subduing India, he would at once be in possession of Asia as a whole, and with Asia in his possession he would return to Greece" (4.15.6). So in mid-327 he began the yearlong march into "India" (4.22.3). This term as used by Arrian encompasses the area from eastern Afghanistan and Pakistan to the eastern regions of the Indus valley. Alexander did not enter any part of the modern state of India.

§3. Alexander sent heralds ahead to the native rulers on the west side of the Indus and divided his army in two. Hephaistion led one part, probably down the Khyber Pass (4.22.7). Alexander took the remaining troops on a more northerly

J.1a Nearkhos' narrative of the voyage was the major
    source for Arrian's *Indika.*

route, in the process of which he razed several cities; fought a battle at Massaka (4.26.1), which turned into a massacre; and conducted the attack on Aornos Rock (4.28.1–4.30.4), which became one of his best-remembered exploits. It was also somewhere in this region that he visited a city called Nysa, which was supposed to have been founded by the god Dionysos, India's only previous conqueror. Now Alexander must have felt he was treading in the footsteps of the gods. After crossing the Indus, he was welcomed by the native ruler of the city of Taxila, whom Arrian knows as Taxiles,[3a] and other allies (5.8.2–3). In Taxila he had time to take an interest in the local philosophers (7.2.2), but the breathing space was brief. Onesikritos was sent to interview the ascetics about their way of life and beliefs but found the conversation difficult, as he had to use three different interpreters (as Strabo 15.1.64 tells us; the episode is not in Arrian); but Alexander was sufficiently impressed by the results to adopt one of the philosophers, Kalanos, as a member of his court (another philosopher, Dandamis, refused to come; see 7.2.2–4). The episode is emblematic of the increasing difficulty of communications in the region.

§4. Arrian calls the native rulers "hyparchs" (4.22.6, 5.8.2, 5.20.6), usually translated "governors" but literally meaning "subrulers." The name implies that they were once subject to a Persian ruler, presumably a satrap; but if this had ever been so, the arrangement must have lapsed, for no satraps are recorded in these regions. When Alexander reached the Malloi and Oxydrakai in 325, they claimed that they had always enjoyed "freedom and autonomy" (6.14.2). If these peoples had been in the ambit of the Persian empire, they had not, it appears, been its subjects. Ambhi and his peers can most accurately be described as Indian rajahs. So the advance into India really took Alexander beyond his original stated objective, revenge on Persia for its invasions of the Greek world, and into a new phase of the war.

§5. The first opponent he faced was Poros, a local ruler who is introduced without explanation by Arrian (5.8.4); in the unreliable *Alexander Romance*[5a] he is a long-standing ally of Darius, but no other author suggests this. He and Taxiles were longtime enemies, and the latter surely saw in Alexander's arrival an opportunity to settle old scores and to increase his power through Poros' defeat.

§6. The battle on the River Hydaspes is the final large-scale conflict of Alexander's campaign. Arrian's account (5.9–5.18.3) is fuller than any other and is no doubt reliable. The conditions taxed Alexander's strategic genius. The armies met in June, when the monsoon rains had begun, and it was the first time Alexander's army had faced elephants in battle. The massive army of perhaps fifty thousand infantry and three to four thousand cavalry was daunting to the Macedonians, and Alexander concentrated on confusing the enemy. He lit fires at different points on the west bank of the Hydaspes to give the impression that that was where his army was camped, then brought a large body of troops across the river some seventeen miles upstream, under cover of darkness (5.8.4–5.13.4). Once these troops had attacked, Krateros brought the main army across, opposite the Indian troops. Poros' chariots,

---

J.3a   Taxiles was known as Ambhi or Omphis in his native Persian; the Macedonians called him Taxiles because he was from Taxila.

J.5a   See Appendix L, The *Alexander Romance.*

FIGURE J.1. These two faces of a medallion minted by Alexander, found in very small quantities, contain images from the Indian campaign. The tall bow wielded by the archer seems to be of the same type Poros' troops used at the battle of the Hydaspes, and one theory about these medallions is that they, like the so-called elephant medallions (see Figure 5.16), may have been struck by Alexander to commemorate his victory there. The markings on the medallion's two faces—the letters AB beside the leg of the archer and an unknown symbol beneath the elephant—are not as yet well understood but may indicate the satrapy in which it was minted.

which looked formidable, proved useless in the muddy terrain, and conditions were made worse by a violent thunderstorm. Once the chariots were disposed of, the Indians were caught in a pincer movement; Poros beat a retreat but was captured by Alexander's troops before he got far. Evidently seeing qualities he valued in Poros, and certainly running short of competent commanders he could spare from his own army, Alexander restored his former enemy to power in exchange for promises of loyalty, and even extended his rule after reconciling him with Taxiles (5.20.4).

§7. One result of the defeat of Poros was the surrender of his former ally Abisares and the submission of another hyparch, also called Poros. (Alexander's men came to refer to them as "good Poros" and "bad Poros," and Arrian follows their usage.) This initial military and diplomatic success must have encouraged Alexander. From here on, every people the army encountered was ordered to submit, and most did so; those that did not were subject to massacre, as the people of Sangala were (5.24.5).

§8. According to Diodorus (17.93.2), Alexander had reports that the Ganges was within twelve days' march and that this river would lead him to a presumed Outer Ocean (what Arrian has him call the Eastern Sea at 5.26.1). Were he to reach that mythical body of water, he could consider that he had conquered the world as far as its eastern limit. But now the army began to feel they had had enough. Their clothing and arms were worn out,[8a] and even extensive raiding did not satisfy all their wants. The soldiers wanted to go west and reap the rewards of their labors; the objective for which they had taken up arms was long since achieved. One of the

J.8a   See Diodorus 17.94.1–3, Quintus Curtius 9.2.6–11.

generals, Koinos, made an eloquent speech (reported by Arrian at 5.27), recalling the king to his duty to his men and to the responsibilities of rule at home: "Nothing is so honorable as self-restraint in the midst of good fortune" (5.27.9). If Arrian's record of the speech at all resembles what was really said,[8b] then Koinos played on the theme that Alexander had been blessed by fortune, a leitmotif of later treatments of the king's career. In Koinos' eyes, Alexander was pushing his luck; ambition was taking precedence over policy. At first Alexander insisted he would go on alone if need be, but the united resistance of his companions prevailed. After three days of ominous silence, he announced to the army—to their great delight—that they were turning back.

§9. Alexander had altars erected to commemorate the conquest and the turning point (5.29.1); a later writer, Philostratos[9a] tells us that these were dedicated to "Father Ammon and Brother Herakles, Athena of Foresight, Olympian Zeus, the Kabeiroi of Samothrace, the Sun of India, and Apollo of Delphi"—a group so odd that it may well be true. The "Altars of Alexander" later became a standard feature of medieval world maps, but no trace of them has ever been found. The army then prepared to set sail down the Indus.

§10. But this was no leisurely cruise home. There was fighting all the way, as Alexander continued to demand submission of all he encountered. The first peoples he met were the Malloi and the Oxydrakai, known to modern scholars from their appearances in the *Mahabharata* as the Malavas and Kshudrakas. Among these, Arrian tells us, was "a city of the Brahmans" (6.7.4). In this initial reference, Arrian writes as if these Brahmans were a people; neither he nor the later writer Pliny the Elder properly grasped the Indian system of caste or understood that the Brahmans were a segment of society. But Arrian's source Aristoboulos and Alexander's admiral Nearkhos, as well as the later Greek writer Megasthenes (who did almost grasp the Indian caste system), understood that the Brahmans were royal advisers, in part owing to their status as "philosophers," and Arrian later (6.16.5) refers to them as "sages." His reference to a "city of the Brahmans" may indicate that the Brahmans had concentrated their numbers in this particular town of the Malloi: no king is mentioned among them, and since, as discussed above, they lay claim to self-government (like the "autonomous Indians" of 5.20.6), perhaps the Brahmans held particular power here. Whatever the truth of the matter, the inhabitants of the "city of the Brahmans" were massacred (6.7.6). This must have been particularly horrifying to the Indians, for whom it was sacrilege to kill a Brahman.

§11. Brahmans were at the fore also in the next places attacked. In the Kingdom of Sambos, a "self-appointed satrap of the mountain Indians" (6.16.3), Alexander's forces killed "as many of the Brahmans . . . as were responsible for the revolt." After subduing another rajah, Mousikanos, Alexander ordered him hanged (or perhaps crucified: the Greek could mean either) along with, once again, "the Brahmans who were responsible for the revolt" (6.17.1–2).[11a] Following this campaign of terror,

J.8b   See Appendix A, Arrian's Sources and Reliability, §19.

J.9a   Philostratos, *Life of Apollonios of Tyana* 2.43.

J.11a   According to Kleitarkhos (repeated in Diodorus 17.102.7 and Quintus Curtius 9.8.15), 80,000 were killed.

directed against a religious caste that had evidently become leaders of the local insurgency, the remaining peoples offered submission. The last Brahman city to be subdued was Harmatelia, a place not mentioned by Arrian, which surrendered after a short battle.[11b] Alexander conquered the Indians and then just sailed away—no commanders were left to maintain his authority, apart from Poros many hundreds of miles to the north (and he soon made himself independent again)—leaving behind nothing but a legacy of hatred among the Indian population.

§12. The Indian campaign is hard to interpret satisfactorily. The impression given is one of indiscriminate massacre with no political end in view, but this is surely not the whole story. The relative difficulty of communication with the Indian peoples, who lay outside the realm in which the Persian lingua franca of Aramaic could be used, isolated the army from its surroundings—a situation A. B. Bosworth[12a] has compared to that of the conquistadors in Mexico. In addition, Alexander's own "intellectual isolation" (the phrase is Bosworth's) divided him from the practical soldiers and commanders who surrounded him. The conspiracies he had suppressed in 330 and 328—if indeed they really existed—had perhaps led to a kind of paranoia. But ultimately the reign of terror was an admission by Alexander that he had no better way of retaining the loyalty of the peoples he had subdued. He bludgeoned them into submission and then headed back toward the West.

Richard Stoneman
Honorary Fellow
Department of Classics and Ancient History
University of Exeter
Exeter, Devon, UK

J.11b See Diodorus 17.103.
J.12a "A Tale of Two Empires: Hernán Cortés and
       Alexander the Great," in *Alexander the Great in*
       Fact and Fiction, eds. A. B. Bosworth and E. J.
       Baynham (Oxford: Oxford University Press,
       2000), 23–49.

APPENDIX K
Alexander's Policy of Perso-Macedonian Fusion

§1. The war between Alexander's forces and those of the Persians was a war between two monarchies. That made it fundamentally different from the Greek struggles with Persia over the preceding two centuries. The Greeks of Classical times had largely rejected hereditary kingship as a political institution; even the Spartans, who retained it, had two kings serving simultaneously and therefore checking each other's power. The Greeks could thus portray their wars against Achaemenid Persia as a political, even an ideological, struggle.[1a] Observers of Alexander's invasion of Asia, however, could not draw nearly as stark a contrast, nor could writers like Arrian who chronicled it. This was a clash of like against like, involving two overwhelmingly powerful rulers, each the heir of a centuries-old royal family, the Achaemenids of Persia and the Argeads of Macedonia.

§2. That said, monarchy was a very different institution in Macedonia than in the Persian empire. In Greek descriptions of the Persian court, we see the Achaemenid kings kept at an awesome remove from their subjects, their persons sanctified by solemn rites of greeting, attendance, and burial. The Argeads of Macedonia enjoyed a more equal fellowship with their Companions, the nobles who were admitted to their inner circle to share meals, drinking parties, and hunting outings. The bow of prostration known as *proskynesis*, a central ritual at the Persian court but, up to the time of Alexander, utterly rejected by the Macedonians and Greeks, provides a telling measure of these different levels of royal elevation. To bow down before a monarch was, among the Persians, obligatory, to the point that Spartan visitors to the Persian court in 480 were forced to do it against their will.[2a] By contrast, the Macedonians following Alexander in Asia, when first beholding the sight of Persians performing *proskynesis*, were sometimes moved to bewilderment or scorn (4.12.2).[2b]

§3. Alexander's upbringing and early reign accustomed him and his subjects to one model of monarchy, but his conquest of the Persian empire forced them to confront a very different one. The clash of monarchic cultures produced a political dilemma that dominated the second half of Alexander's reign, from 330 up to the time of his death. Now ruler of both a European army and an Asian imperial bureaucracy, attended both by Macedonian Companions and by Persian courtiers,

K.1a See, for example, Herodotus, *Histories* 7.101–104.   K.2b Also see Plutarch, *Parallel Lives*, "Alexander" 74.2.
K.2a Ibid., 7.136.

Alexander had to invent a new style of monarchy by blending elements of the two existing ones. It was a delicate balancing act, in which any step too far in one direction risked alienating the subjects who preferred the other. Our sources for the Alexander period, being Greek in either nationality or outlook, tend to stress the failures of Alexander's attempt at fusing monarchic styles and mixing ruling elites, though one Greek writer, Plutarch, was more enthusiastic about the successes. Modern historians are similarly divided, with many inclined to see Alexander's adoption of Persian rituals as a descent into vainglory, despotism, or even delusions of godhead.

§4. There were many graduated steps in the project, begun by late 330 if not earlier, that has been variously called medism, orientalism, Persification, or (a less weighted term) fusion. It is unclear at what stage this project took shape as a formal state policy, though it certainly had become that by the time of Alexander's return from India in 325. Its first manifestation was Alexander's donning of some elements of Persian royal garb (4.7.4 and n. 4.7.4c)—including probably a purple-and-white striped tunic, a golden belt, and a diadem or circlet around the head—in place of plainer, less sumptuous Macedonian clothing. According to Plutarch,[4a] the king avoided the more extravagant trappings worn by the Medes (Arrian apparently uses the terms Medes and Median in error at 4.7.4 and 7.6.2) and introduced his new dress style gradually, at first only allowing close friends to see it in private settings. This interesting detail suggests that Alexander tried to build support for his new brand of monarchy, first enlisting a circle of close associates he could count on to give it public endorsement. Indeed, in years to come, his favors would be largely bestowed on those among his staff who embraced his fusion policy; those who did, such as Ptolemy, Peukestas, Nearkhos, and Hephaistion, gained promotions, while Krateros and Meleagros, who did not, saw their careers languish. Kleitos the Black, the first known opponent of the program, was killed by Alexander after a drunken rant that played in part (in Plutarch's account,[4b] at least) on fusion themes.

§5. It is difficult to disentangle Alexander's policy choices regarding Persian royal style from matters of personal taste or habit. Indulgence in wine, fine food, and opulent dress and furnishings might be assigned to the latter category, but in the Greek view they were also characteristic of the Asian royal model, with its predilection for extravagant displays of wealth. Arrian, for example, says that Alexander's drinking patterns "had taken on a more barbarian character" by 328 (4.8.2), using the word "barbarian" to signify, largely, "Asiatic." Similarly, Arrian describes the cruelty practiced by Alexander in the mutilation of Bessos as "barbarian" (4.7.4) and moves from that topic to "the luxuriousness of the Medes and Persians and the differences of status the barbarian kings maintained between themselves and their subjects"—as though these were linearly connected to the mutilation. Lopping off ears and noses was a form of punishment associated with the Asian autocracies. Did Alexander choose it for that reason, in deliberate emulation of his Persian counterparts, as Arrian implies? Or had he simply learned a new way to gratify his innate desire to humiliate his enemies?

§6. Equally difficult to unravel is the question of whether Alexander's fusion pol-

K.4a   Ibid., 45.
K.4b   Ibid., 51.2.

FIGURE K.1. The two long panels of the so-called Alexander sarcophagus eloquently attest to the aspirations of Alexander's fusion program. On one panel (a detail of which is shown above), Alexander and his army are shown defeating the Persians in a vigorous battle, while on the other (opposite), the two peoples join together in a shared heroic enterprise, a lion hunt. Deliberate parallels and echoes bind the two scenes closely together. The message seems to be that the conquered Persians would share in Alexander's new empire so long as

icy was driven more by his own inclinations and vision or by the practical needs of governing a diverse, multicontinental empire. Alexander was keenly aware of the cultural expectations of his Asian subjects and tried to meet them when he could, for example by sacrificing to the Apis bull in Egypt (3.1.4) and to Bel-Marduk in Babylon (3.16.5). Arrian ends his *Anabasis* with a eulogy of Alexander in which he explains the donning of Persian royal garb as "an expedient, adopted for the barbarians, so that their king might not seem entirely foreign to them" (7.29.4). Doubtless there is some truth in this, though Arrian introduces the idea only as an afterthought, and in so doing contradicts his own earlier assessment. A similar late-stage reevaluation is applied to Alexander's drinking habits, disparaged in the main narrative as a "barbarian" habit (4.8.2) but excused in the eulogy merely as good politics (7.29.4). Arrian's evident ambivalence about the fusion policy stems from his lack of insight into Alexander's motives (a problem that bedevils modern scholarship as well). At some moments, particularly in Book 4, Arrian sees a man lured by success into surrendering to his baser appetites and drives; at others he sees a supremely rational and self-controlled ruler, crafting an image that will keep his subjects in thrall.

they recognized his ultimate supremacy. This gorgeous sarcophagus, one of the best-preserved art objects from the Greek world, was found at Sidon in the nineteenth century and is now housed in the Istanbul Archaeological Museum. It seems to have been intended for a high Persian official, perhaps Mazaios (satrap of Babylon under both Darius and Alexander), and, according to the most recent analyses, was quite possibly created during Alexander's lifetime.

§7. Late in 328, Alexander tried a new step in his fusion program, introducing the idea that he would receive *proskynesis*, the Persian ritual bow, from even his European subjects. As with the adoption of Persian dress, his initial moves were tentative; the suggestion was floated by his agents at a banquet, as though it had come from them, while he himself stayed out of the room and listened from behind a screen (as implied at 4.12.1, confirmed by Quintus Curtius 8.5.21). It was at this banquet that a second opponent to the fusion policy declared himself: the Greek philosopher Kallisthenes, to whom Arrian attributes a long and fervent speech in defense of European-style limited monarchy (4.11). Kallisthenes came to no better end than did Kleitos, though it is unclear whether Alexander had him executed or only imprisoned him for trial, indirectly causing his death from disease. Significantly, though, Alexander withdrew the attempt to institute *proskynesis* on a formal basis and never returned to it. He was as yet responsive enough to the sensibilities of his countrymen to spare them such an ideologically loaded rite. His Persian subjects, however, bowed to him as a matter of choice, creating the bifurcated court Kallisthenes had described satirically in his speech, with the king "honored by the Greeks and Macedonians in the human and Greek manner, while receiving barbarian honors only from the barbarians" (4.11.8).

§8. Though *proskynesis* was abandoned as official policy, Alexander continued to advance the fusion program in the last years of his life. Integration of the armed forces became part of his agenda even before his invasion of India. Perhaps in 327, he ordered the thirty thousand Asian boys called the Epigonoi, or Offspring, to be trained in Macedonian-style warfare and outfitted with Macedonian clothing and arms. (Arrian mentions them only at 7.6.1, when, in 324, their training is complete.) Again, the motivations behind this move are complex and hard to discern. Diodorus Siculus (17.108.3) regards the Epigonoi as Alexander's hedge against another mutiny by his native troops, like the one at the Hyphasis River, whereas Plutarch ("Alexander" 47.6) asserts that the boys were taught to speak Greek, the empire's new lingua franca, as though being prepared for participation in governance. Quintus Curtius (8.5.1) says the boys were enlisted as hostages, also no doubt partly true, for even in Macedonia the Argead kings kept a suite of high-born children as pages to check their fathers' ambitions. Finally, it is not unlikely, given later developments, that Alexander wanted his largely European army internationalized, as testimony to the shared goals and ambitions of the Macedonian and Persian elites.

§9. The fusion policy took on a very different dimension in Alexander's selection of wives for himself and his highest-ranking officers. In a courtly milieu where marriages were invariably contracted with political ends in mind, it is startling to observe that Alexander never contemplated a liaison with a European woman. His first known involvement was with Barsine, daughter of the formidable Persian warlord Artabazos, with whom he had an illegitimate child, Herakles, probably in 327. Late in that same year he married Rhoxane, a teenager from Sogdiana, as a means of securing an alliance with her father, Oxyartes, a chieftain with wide influence in that troublesome region. Rhoxane became pregnant shortly afterward, but their child died in infancy during the Indian campaign. By this time Alexander's Companions recognized that the next heir to the Macedonian throne would likely have an Asian mother, a completely new phenomenon in their dynastic history. Doubtless many disapproved, but Alexander, undaunted, in 324 arranged marriages for some eighty of them with high-ranking Persian and Bactrian women, while he himself wed Parysatis and Stateira (whom Arrian, following Aristoboulos, calls Barsine, 7.4.6), daughters of the two most recent Persian kings. Like the Epigonoi, these princesses had been tutored in Greek at Alexander's behest;[9a] they were to be no mere concubines but queens, and matriarchs of a mixed-race royal family, had Alexander lived long enough to have children by them.

§10. Following this mass intermarriage at Susa of the Macedonian and Persian ruling classes, Alexander presided over a much larger wedding ceremony, solemnizing the unions of some ten thousand soldiers with their common-law Asian wives and giving a cash bequest to each. His gifts were clearly coercive, for the rank and file were unsympathetic to his fusion project, certainly more so than the noble Companions (who at Alexander's court consorted with Persian officers on a regular

K.9a   See Diodorus 17.67.1.

basis). Indeed, the common soldier's resentment of Alexander's persianizing moves was coming to a head at Susa in the spring of 324, as Arrian reports in the much-debated sixth chapter of Book 7. According to this chapter, Alexander had by this time, or else *at* this time—either reading is possible—introduced elite Asian horsemen into his highest-ranked unit, the Companion cavalry; created a special hipparchy, or squadron, of that unit that was largely Asian in composition; and even placed the sons of some very distinguished Persians and Bactrians (men important enough to be listed in a kind of roll call at 7.6.4–5) in the cavalry *agema*, the honor guard that fought alongside the king in battle. Historians have varying opinions as to when this integration of the cavalry took place, since Arrian tells us all we know of it, and he gives no chronological clues. What is clear is that Alexander had by this time undertaken a sweeping restructuring of his army, from the highest ranks to the lowest. His intentions have been variously assessed: to give his most powerful Asian subjects a share in the honor, and spoils, that came with service under him; to keep sons as hostages ensuring the obedience of their fathers; to remove respected leaders from their power bases, where they might otherwise mount rebellions; and to supplement native Macedonian levies, now running thin after years of continual drawdowns.

§11. The resentment of the rank and file at the integration of the army was stoked into fury a few months later, at Opis, when Alexander announced the decommissioning of ten thousand old or wounded veterans and their replacement by Asian recruits. Incredulous and insulted, emboldened by their victory over him at the Hyphasis two years earlier, the troops began taunting Alexander, suggesting that he go on campaign alone or with only his "father," the god Ammon—who, according to some sources, had claimed him as a son during his visit to the oracular shrine in the Egyptian desert—to help him. Alexander shocked them into silence by ordering the summary arrest of thirteen ringleaders; then, after a long harangue, he retired to his quarters and barred the door. For the next three days, Alexander played his fusion card with a vengeance, assigning all the high commands in his army to his new Asian subjects and admitting only them to his private chambers. If he had indeed created the Epigonoi as a hedge against mutiny, as Diodorus (17.108.3) claims, his strategy had succeeded. Realizing that they could easily be made obsolete, the Macedonian troops threw themselves on Alexander's mercy and begged to be taken back into favor. The king acceded but dismissed the ten thousand veterans as planned, detailing Krateros—not coincidentally, the staunchest remaining opponent of the fusion project among his inner circle—to lead them back to Europe. Significantly, Alexander ordered that their Asian wives and children be left behind, recognizing that his native land was not yet ready to be globalized, but he promised to raise the mixed-race boys along traditional Macedonian lines and someday reunite them with their fathers (7.12.2).

§12. Alexander staged an enormous banquet at Opis to celebrate the restoration of unity in his army and invited thousands of Asians to take part. As described by Arrian, the guests were seated concentrically, with Macedonians nearest to Alexander, Persians next to them, and the nobility of other races farthest away (7.11.8). The arrangement provides a good image of how Alexander conceived his new international regime: mixed and inclusive, with all peoples represented, but with Macedonians occupying the first positions, Persians second. Power and wealth were to be shared with the Asian races, the Persians in particular, but shared on Alexander's terms. Libations were poured to the gods by both Greek and Persian priests, and Alexander uttered a prayer that famously included a request "that the Macedonians and Persians might enjoy concord and partnership in the empire" (7.11.9). W. W. Tarn, one of Alexander's staunchest modern defenders, hailed this prayer as an assertion of the unity of all humankind;[12a] other historians have seen it, more cynically, as shrewd propaganda cloaking an exploitative imperial hierarchy. However we regard it, we must acknowledge that Alexander was attempting a radical revision of the relationship between his own Greco-Macedonian culture and what was formerly the world superpower, the Achaemenid Persian empire. A conflict stretching back almost two hundred years had been laid to rest, immolated in the fires that destroyed the palaces of Persepolis. The future, so Alexander might hope, was to be marked by cooperation and mutual trust. The imperial capital, Alexander clearly intended, would be in the homeland of neither Persians nor Macedonians, but in a city that had served as a friendly base to both, Babylon.

§13. Alexander's fusion project included one further, and vastly more far-reaching, step, if we accept (as most historians do) the authenticity of a document known to historians as the Last Plans. Reported only by Diodorus, supposedly recovered from Alexander's personal papers, the Last Plans described the goals Alexander had in mind at the time of his death; they were read out posthumously to the assembled army by Alexander's highest-ranking officer, Perdikkas, in the summer of 323. Apparently the king had intended, to quote Diodorus, "the joining together and transplantation of peoples from Asia into Europe and vice versa, from Europe into Asia, so that he might bring the greatest continents into harmony and filial affection by means of marriage and bonds of kinship" (Diodorus 18.4.4). Apparently Alexander intended to end the conflict of the continents forever, by expanding to vast scale the plan that had given rise to the Susa weddings. How, or whether, this global intermarriage and relocation scheme would have been carried out, had Alexander lived longer, is a subject only for speculation. The rank-and-file soldiers, mistrustful of Alexander's fusion policies from the beginning, bullied into cooperation only by the king's unyielding will, had their way at last: they rejected the Last Plans and set Europe and Asia back onto their separate historical courses.

§14. Alexander's fusion policy had varying fortunes among the generals who survived him and went on to control segments of his empire. Its greatest adherent, Peukestas, who won Alexander's admiration for adopting Persian dress and learning to speak Persian (6.30.2–3, 7.6.3), achieved great popularity and power as satrap of Persia using fusion-based methods, and even staged an extravagant multirace banquet in imitation of Alexander's grand feast at Opis (Diodorus 19.21.2–19.23.1). Seleukos, an obscure midlevel officer in Alexander's lifetime, who later came to control nearly all of Alexander's Asian holdings, stayed married to the wife assigned to

K.12a W. W. Tarn, *Alexander the Great and the Unity of
        Mankind* (London: Milford, 1933).

him at the Susa weddings, the Bactrian noblewoman Apame, and with her begot a son, Antiochus, who went on to succeed him. So the Seleucid dynasty, which ruled in Asia for more than 250 years, was made up of mixed European and Asian blood lines, just as Alexander had planned for his own royal house (as far as is known, the other Companions repudiated their Asian wives soon after Alexander's death). In Egypt, Ptolemy followed a policy of cultural fusion to some degree, for example by fostering the cult of a newly imported deity, Serapis, whose image was carefully crafted to appeal to both Greco-Macedonian and Egyptian populations. But on the whole, the rulers who followed Alexander were less inclined than he was to share power with subject peoples or to attempt the monumental task of merging European and Asian populations.

James Romm
James H. Ottaway Jr. Professor of Classics
Bard College
Annadale-on-Hudson, New York

APPENDIX L

The *Alexander Romance*

§1. Alexander was always intensely conscious of the ruler's need for an "image." He was careful in his choice of artists, allowing no painter but Apelles and no sculptor but Lysippos to represent him. "Both Alexander's daring and his looks Lysippos caught," wrote the poet Asklepiades,[1a] and Plutarch[1b] wrote that only Lysippos had captured the distinctive upward gaze, which may have been the result of a paralysis of one eye but became the symbol of the king's aspirations. Alexander knew when to reject a proposal, though, like the architect Deinokrates' idea of carving the whole of Mount Athos into a statue of the king.[1c]

§2. Alexander also kept a careful eye on what was written about him in his lifetime. His court writers were generally adulatory, like Kallisthenes, whose history of the king may have been an encomium in form but whose flatteries did not save him from a gruesome execution when he was implicated in a plot against Alexander (4.13–14). A famous story tells how the king rejected the proposal of the poet Khoirilos to write an epic about him: "I would rather be Thersites in Homer than Achilles in your poetry"—meaning that the basest, most unappealing character could be immortalized by a great poet more easily than a demigod by a hack.

§3. Soon after his death, Alexander's life story was written up by an anonymous author connected to the court of the Ptolemies at Alexandria, whom some manuscripts identify, impossibly, as Kallisthenes (he has thus been given the surrogate name Pseudo-Kallisthenes). This work, known as the *Alexander Romance*, emphasized the fabulous elements of Alexander's story and added many new fables that, in late antiquity and the Middle Ages, came to define the memory of the conqueror far more tellingly than the historical sources. This work seems, however, not to have been known to the Romans until it was translated by Julius Valerius in the fourth century C.E.; this has led to the mistaken view, still shared by many, that the Greek original was not written until shortly before that date. Probably it arose much earlier, perhaps in the early third century B.C.E.

§4. The *Alexander Romance* is a fictional biography that starts from the premise that Alexander was the son of the exiled pharaoh Nectanebo, who tricked his way

L.1a   *Anthologia Palatina* 16.120.
L.1b   *Moralia*, "Fortune of Alexander" 2.2.
L.1c   Plutarch, *Parallel Lives*, "Alexander" 72.5, in which

the would-be sculptor is mistakenly called Stasikrates.

388

into Alexander's mother's bed disguised as a dragon. The story of the conquest of Persia forms a relatively small part of this narrative (and the order of events is strangely mangled), while the bulk of it concerns such adventures as Alexander's visit to the Ethiopian queen Kandake, his encounters with monstrous beasts in India, and his construction of a diving bell to explore the bottom of the ocean and of a flying machine powered by griffins to explore the heavens. He also meets the Indian philosophers in person and has a long discussion with them about their respective ways of life. The Alexander of the *Romance* is preoccupied with the prospect of death, about which he consults the god Sarapis in Alexandria, the dead king Sesonchosis in the Cave of the Gods, and finally the oracular Trees of the Sun and Moon in India. His search for the Water of Life is unsuccessful when his cook gets there first, discovering it when he tries to cook in it a dried fish, which promptly comes to life. For this author, Alexander's death in Babylon was the result of poison, and the installation of his body in Alexandria the fulfilment of the destiny of that great city. It is of interest as indicating the way that the memory of Alexander was shaped a generation or two after his death.

§5. As the *Alexander Romance* developed, in both the Hellenistic Greek and later the Roman worlds, it took on new layers of material, and some of these came from the realm of moral philosophy, in which Alexander had begun to loom large as an exemplar (whether good or bad). The anarchic Cynics, for example, known for their renunciation of all conventional marks of status and power, concocted dialogues between Alexander and ascetic figures like the gymnosophists, or "naked wise men," of India. In these dramatizations of encounters that no doubt really occurred—Arrian recounts two fairly plausible ones at 7.1.5–6 and 7.2.2–4—Alexander receives his comeuppance from self-reliant sages like the Indian Dandamis (also called Mandanis or Dindymos), who neither fear his power nor covet any prize he can bestow. Several versions of such encounters made their way into the *Alexander Romance*, and some went on to become models for Christian writers of the early Middle Ages. A homegrown anecdote based on the same Cynic themes, recounted by Arrian at 7.2.1, puts Alexander into a confrontation with the famously unflappable Diogenes, who tells the king that the greatest favor he can grant is to stand aside and stop blocking the sunlight.

§6. The *Alexander Romance* continued to grow in popularity, displacing other, less fanciful texts. Early Byzantine chroniclers were more familiar with the narrative of the *Romance* than with the works of the Alexander historians. The *Romance* was rewritten several times in the Greek world: one version dates from the eighth century and was combined with a later one into a new, overblown composite not long afterward. In 1388 the second version was recomposed in verse (the *politikos stichos* of medieval Greece), and another verse version (the *Rimada*) was published in Venice in 1529. Several prose versions were also written in medieval Greek and formed the basis of the immensely popular *Phyllada tou Megalexandrou*, which was first published in 1680 and has been through innumerable editions up to the present day.

FIGURE L.1. A Kashmiri manuscript of Nizami's *Iskandarnameh*, a Persian epic poem based on the legend of Alexander, shows an episode unknown to the Greco-Roman traditions. Iskandar (Alexander) is received by a seated Dara (Darius), who gives him a gift of a bag of sesame seeds. Iskandar throws the seeds to the ground and they are immediately devoured by a flock of birds. The incident is then interpreted as an ill omen for Dara, whose empire will be swiftly "devoured" by the ravages of Iskandar's army.

§7. The Greek *Romance* was translated into Syriac, the language of the Syriac church, in the sixth century C.E.; thus it became well known in the Arab world following the Arab conquest of Syria and also in Persia, where knowledge of the story probably descended through oral tradition until it was written up in the tenth century in the "national epic," the *Shahnameh,* or *Book of Kings,* of Firdausi. The narrative follows the same form as the *Romance,* except that Alexander is made a legitimate king of Persia by being the son of the Persian king and ousting his half-brother Dara. The *Shahnameh,* following the Syriac version, also describes Alexander's dealings with the emperor of China. The same narrative forms the basis of the *Iskandarnameh* of Nizami (twelfth century), which treats Alexander as an Ideal King. Several other Persian narratives also take Alexander as their hero: some diverge very widely from the Greek *Romance.*

FIGURE L.2. In this fourteenth-century carving on a misericord in the cathedral of Glouces-
ter, England, King Alexander is shown being borne aloft by griffins as he tries to investigate
the upper atmosphere. This episode from the *Alexander Romance* was one of the most popular Alexander legends in medieval European art.

§8. The Arabs drew on the Persian writers in composing a number of long narratives about Alexander from the seventh century onward. But they also took as their
starting point his appearance in Sura 18 of the Qur'an, where he seeks the Water of
Life and builds a wall to keep out the tribes Gog and Magog (the "unclean nations"
that threatened to wreak apocalyptic havoc on the civilized world). In these narratives Alexander becomes a Prophet of God and a warrior for Islam. He is referred to
in the Qu'ran as Dhul-Quarnayn, "the two-horned one," an epithet probably based
on his depiction on some coins with curling ram's horns on the sides of his head (see
Figure C.1), signifying descent from the god Ammon. The Arabs brought the legends to Spain, where they influenced some of the Hebrew books about Alexander.

§9. In western Europe the spread of Alexander's legend follows an equally
remarkable trajectory. The Latin translation of the *Romance* by Julius Valerius was
not well known in the Dark Ages, but in the tenth century a new translation was
made by Leo the Archpriest of Naples, who had brought back a manuscript of the
Greek text from a diplomatic mission to Constantinople. This in turn was rewritten
three times in Latin, in variant versions with additional material, between the
eleventh and thirteenth centuries: these are known (from the title in one of the
manuscripts) as versions of the *Historia de Proeliis* (the *History of Alexander's
Battles*). The second of these adds a story of Alexander's visit to Jerusalem and his
conversion to Judaism; the third adds an account of the sayings of the sages at the

tomb of Alexander, which originated in sixth-century Syria and had become popular in Arab writings about Alexander.

§10. These versions of the *Romance* became enormously popular and by the fifteenth century had been translated into every language of medieval Europe, from Icelandic and Swedish to Italian and Romanian, from Hebrew (five times) and Irish to Italian, German, and English (four main versions, plus some in Scots). The Serbian, Russian, and other Slavic versions mainly derive from Greek originals. The French and Spanish adaptations, in particular, are masterpieces of their own literatures. In all, the *Alexander Romance* was translated more frequently in the Middle Ages than any other work except the Gospels. In addition, it was inserted into the German and Dutch "History Bibles" of the fifteenth century to fill the gap between Maccabees and the New Testament. Thus Alexander became a virtually scriptural figure.

§11. Alexander's image adorns cathedrals throughout Europe, usually in depictions of his aerial flight, a perennially fascinating theme for the medieval Christian world. Another twelfth-century Latin work, *Alexander's Journey to Paradise*, based on a Hebrew original, tells how Alexander arrived at the gates of paradise but was sent away to learn the limits of mortal possibilities. So the obsession of the Alexander of the *Romance* with early death is the key to his function as another type of the medieval Everyman.

Richard Stoneman
Honorary Fellow
Department of Classics and Ancient History
University of Exeter
Exeter, Devon, UK

APPENDIX M

Alexander and the Greeks

§1. In 336, at the time Alexander the Great became king, only three Greek city-states still possessed significant military strength: Sparta, Athens, and Thebes. For a century before that, these states had struggled for supremacy within the Greek world in a series of inconclusive wars. All three had been greatly weakened, with the Spartans, whose population had entered a steady decline, weakest of all. Their endlessly shifting alliances had bred a mutual enmity and mistrust that served them ill in the period of Macedonian hegemony, for all eventually would challenge Alexander's regime singly, without help from the others, and all would fail.

§2. Alexander's relations with these three leading states, and with the Greek world generally, initially followed the lines laid down by his father, Philip. In 338, two years before his death, Philip decisively defeated a combined Athenian and Theban army on the battlefield of Chaeronea, ending any illusions that a Greek hoplite phalanx could stand up to the new tactics and weapons of the Macedonians. In the wake of his victory, which was spearheaded by a cavalry charge led by Alexander, Philip treated his two Greek opponents very differently: at Thebes he installed a garrison force on the high ground called the Kadmeia, but Athens he left ungarrisoned, preferring to win hearts and minds there by deference rather than a show of force. There were many in Athens who supported Philip's cause, including Isocrates, a leading essayist and intellectual, who regarded the king and his planned invasion of Asia as the salvation of the war-torn Greek world. Philip was also sensitive to Greek public opinion, which would regard any rough handling of revered Athens—the "school of Hellas," as Pericles reportedly had called it—with dismay. Sparta, which had taken no part in the battle at Chaeronea and posed no immediate threat, he simply ignored.

§3. Philip enrolled all the mainland Greek states, excluding Sparta, into a security organization called the League, dubbed League of Corinth by modern historians after its meeting place. In effect, this was a Greek United Nations, whose members swore to resolve disputes amicably and to vote on matters of common concern. Philip officially took the role of the League's enforcement arm, pledged to execute its decrees rather than initiate them, but in practice he was very much its moving force and guide. League members were bound by treaty not to change governments or accept the return of exiles, since Philip had by this time ensured that politicians opposed to his hegemony had been kicked out of their home cities (except at Athens, where Demosthenes and Hypereides were cowed but hardly silenced as leaders of the anti-Macedonian faction). Among its first orders of business after its founding in 337, the League became the official sponsor of the invasion of Asia Philip had already planned and prepared, assigning contributions of troops by various member states and appointing Philip himself *strategos,* or commanding general. Greek mercenary soldiers were forbidden by the League from fighting on the Persian side in the upcoming conflict.

§4. Alexander inherited leadership of the League, along with his throne, when Philip was killed by an assassin's dagger in the summer of 336. The Greeks momentarily celebrated Philip's death as a liberation—in Athens, state honors were awarded to his murderer—but quickly lost their cheer when Alexander entered Greece with his army to restore his father's political order. The Athenians belatedly sent an embassy to hail him, and the League voted to affirm him as its leader and as *strategos* of the Asian expedition. It was clear to Alexander from the rapid about-face that the Greek cities, Athens in particular, could be easily intimidated but not won over in any lasting sense to the Macedonian cause. His Greek opponents would always be lurking, waiting to take advantage of any lapse or weakness. Nonetheless, he continued his father's laissez-faire policy toward Athens, leaving the city ungarrisoned and its democratic constitution unaltered. Perhaps he felt reverence for the city that had once been home to his boyhood tutor, Aristotle, and so many other great writers and thinkers; without doubt he foresaw that its navy, the strongest by far in the Aegean, might be needed to support his invasion of Asia.

§5. Alexander took his army north in 335 to quell revolts in the Balkans, and rumors soon reached Athens that he had been killed in battle. Demosthenes had an extensive network of contacts with anti-Macedonian agents, including both exiled Theban politicians and Persian satraps in Asia Minor, and he alerted both that the time for rebellion was at hand. Thebes, which had been subjected to the humiliation of a Macedonian garrison, eagerly heeded the call, and the Persians sent cash by way of Demosthenes to help finance the revolt. In Athens, opinion was divided, but after a tense showdown between rival speakers in the Assembly, the citizens voted not to send troops to aid the Thebans. Demosthenes was disappointed, then appalled as he watched Alexander, still very much alive, wreak a terrible vengeance on Thebes. After virtually annihilating that city, Alexander made his first intervention in Athenian politics, demanding that Demosthenes and his partisans be surrendered to him to pay the price for fomenting revolt. It was a stern challenge to Athenian autonomy, and the Athenians were again torn as to how to meet it, but a compromise solution saved them from making an agonizing choice: Alexander was persuaded by his Athenian supporters to let the city punish its own citizens. Demosthenes was spared, but his party was in disrepute, while the moderates who had brokered the deal exercised new influence over policy toward Macedon.

§6. The shock waves from the destruction of Thebes meanwhile continued to spread throughout the Greek world. Our sources are divided as to whether Alexander ordered the butchering of the city or, as Arrian believes (1.8.8), merely stood back and allowed Thebes' Greek neighbors to avenge past wrongs. In either case, Alexander must have intended the fate of Thebes to be an object lesson for the other Greek states, designed to deter any further rebellions while his army was away on the Asian campaign. He could not leave enough troops behind with Antipatros, his designated surrogate in Macedonia, to overcome determined Greek resistance. He made the policy choice, as he would do again on several occasions in Asia, to let his subjects hate him so long as they feared him. This policy succeeded, in the sense that the Athenians, now his principal European threat, never challenged Macedonian power while he was alive. It was instead from Sparta, as yet an independent state that had never joined the League or submitted to Macedonian power, that his next European challenge would come.

§7. As he campaigned through Asia Minor, meanwhile, Alexander confronted the problem of Greeks who supported the Persians against him. The Greek cities of Asia Minor were divided in their sympathies; some regarded him as a liberator, while others, notably Miletus and Halicarnassus, forced him to mount sieges before submitting. Their resistance derived from complex motives, but chief among these must have been the calculation that Alexander would fail and the Persians would, as they had done in the past, punish severely any cities that had aided their enemy. A different problem was posed by Greek hoplite soldiers fighting in the employ of the western Persian satraps, despite the League prohibition on such service. At the battle of the Granicus, Alexander confronted a sizeable force of such mercenaries and, despite what some sources (but not Arrian, see 1.16.2) report as their request for quarter, ordered the cavalry to attack them. Many thousands were killed where they stood, and two thousand more were taken prisoner and sent back to Macedon as slaves. Alexander once again, as at Thebes, displayed signal cruelty to the Greeks as a way to deter future defiance. In this case his strategy was less effective, in that Greek mercenaries continued to fight for the Persians throughout the next several years, and Alexander treated them more humanely in future encounters.

§8. The Macedonian invasion of Asia was presented to the Greeks as a retribution for the Persian attacks on their cities, Athens in particular, 150 years earlier. Alexander made several moves to underscore that his campaign was on their behalf, though he probably did not persuade many (Arrian shows his own skepticism at 3.18.12). After his victory at the Granicus River, he sent back to Athens three hundred dedicatory suits of captured armor, together with an inscription making clear that allied Greek armies (with the pointed exception of the Spartans) had participated in the winning of the spoils. An even shrewder move was the return to Athens of statuary plundered by Xerxes in 480, recaptured in Susa (3.16.7–8). This was an act of repatriation, framing his conquest of Persia as a true and fair retribution for Xerxes' invasion; and it helped that the returned statues included portraits of Harmodios and Aristogeiton, tyrannicides celebrated as freedom fighters in Athenian legend. The question of whether, or to what degree, the burning of the palace at

Persepolis had a similar intention—surrogate vengeance on behalf of the Athenians, who had seen their acropolis temples burned by Xerxes' troops—is hard to answer due to the uncertainties surrounding this episode.[8a] Whatever we make of the Persepolis fire, and the curious legend in the vulgate sources that an Athenian courtesan had suggested it, it is clear that Alexander valued the good opinion of the European Greeks, and especially the Athenians, enough to court it with politically meaningful gestures. He made a further attempt to conciliate the Athenians in the spring of 331, when he granted their request—which had already been deferred for two years—for return of their countrymen captured at the Granicus (1.29.5–6, 3.6.2).

§9. Alexander's clemency toward the Athenians in 331 was partly an effort to keep them out of a revolt that had by then begun in Greece, led by King Agis of Sparta. Recruiting troops from the Peloponnesian states and hiring mercenaries with Persian money, Agis fielded an army of about twenty-two thousand; the Athenians declined to join him, not wanting to lose the favor Alexander had shown them (at least according to Diodorus 17.62.7). The revolt is almost entirely ignored by Arrian, who notes only its inception (2.13.4–6) and Alexander's dispatch of money to Antipatros to help combat it (3.16.10). From Diodorus (17.62–3), Quintus Curtius (6.1), and Justin (21.1), however, we know that the Spartan-led army won an initial battle against the Macedonians and then attacked Megalopolis, a lone Peloponnesian holdout from the rebellion, while Antipatros, Alexander's designated home guard, invaded Greece with an army of some forty thousand Macedonians and allies. The two forces met in a bloody battle near Megalopolis in the autumn of 331, around the time Alexander was at Gaugamela, and the rebels were crushed. Antipatros then installed regimes loyal to Macedonia in the cities of the Peloponnese and returned home. The fate of the defeated Spartans was submitted to the League of Corinth for adjudication, and that body referred the matter to Alexander; the king showed magnanimity by pardoning his now-irrelevant foes.

§10. Only Athens remained as a potential threat to Macedonian hegemony in Europe, and the city was politically divided. Demosthenes' oppositional policies had been discredited, yet he was still the most popular leader Athens had, and an effort by his rival Aeschines to embarrass him publicly failed badly in 330. The upper classes had prospered during the Alexander years and were not eager to endanger the benefits they received under the Pax Macedonica. But the city's loss of autonomy and the forced garrisoning of allied Greek states still rankled. The deep split in the Athenian body politic was revealed in 324 when Harpalos, a renegade Macedonian satrap fleeing Asia to escape punishment, sailed up to Athens' harbor with a large mercenary force and a huge hoard of stolen cash. To admit him would be an act of rebellion from Macedon, yet with the money and troops he had brought, the rebellion might well succeed. Our extant text of Arrian does not deal with these events, due to the loss of a manuscript page after 7.12 (see n. 7.12.7a; the flight of Harpalos discussed by Arrian at 3.6.4–7 is an earlier episode), but we know from other sources that Harpalos was refused admission to the city, largely at the urging

M.8a The burning of the palace is dealt with at greater
      length in Appendix H, Alexander at Persepolis,
      §8–10.

of Demosthenes. The great opponent of Philip and Alexander had turned cautious, fearing that the Macedonians might destroy Athens as they had once destroyed Thebes. Harpalos eventually found refuge in Athens, but only after depositing most of his money and troops in the Peloponnese.

§11. It was only a matter of weeks before Athens, and the Greeks, had a huge new problem to deal with in their relations with Alexander. In the summer of 324, at the athletic festival in Olympia, a letter was read aloud to the assembled Greeks containing what has become known as the Exiles' Decree. Speaking in his own voice, Alexander declared that all Greek cities had to resettle citizens who had been sent into exile, and threatened that Antipatros would intervene to ensure compliance (Diodorus 17.109, 18.8.2–7). Arrian makes no mention of this important moment in Greco-Macedonian relations, though it is possible the missing text that once followed 7.12 contained a discussion of it. There is much debate as to why Alexander undertook this measure, but his principal goals seem to have been strategic: with his Asian enemies completely subdued, his primary threat came from rootless Greek mercenaries who could be collected by rebellious satraps into powerful armies; resettlement of exiles would restore homes and occupations to many of these mercenaries. This was a vast new arrogation of power by Alexander. Legally he was supposed to submit such policy changes to the League of Corinth for approval, but he now dispensed with that sham institution; he had declared himself the ruler of the Greeks, not merely their leader. The reaction from Athens, he knew, would be adverse, especially since Athens stood to lose a huge colonial possession, the island of Samos, whose expelled inhabitants would be forcibly returned under the decree. But the Athenians, once again guided by a cautious Demosthenes, elected to try negotiation first, sending an embassy to Alexander in Babylon to ask for exemption from the decree's terms.

§12. Events in the Greek world in 324 and 323 are complex and poorly documented; Arrian takes no note of them at all. Several Greek cities at this time were debating measures to give Alexander divine honors, as though he were a god, but it is not known whether this proposal came from Alexander. Demosthenes acceded to such a measure at Athens, perhaps hoping to use divinization as a bargaining chip in the coming negotiations over Samos. But Demosthenes fell from power shortly afterward, accused of pocketing some of the money brought to the city by Harpalos. Hypereides, a long-standing war hawk, stepped into the political breach and began secretly recruiting mercenaries to be used in a revolt. Athens had steadily built up its economic and military power during the Alexander years, and there are signs that Alexander, in the last year of his life, considered it a threat he would soon need to confront. But in June 323 Alexander died, and the Athenians seized the opportunity to launch their long-deferred rebellion. Rallying other Greek cities behind what they termed the Hellenic War, the Athenians marched out to meet Antipatros in northern Greece and defeated him, forcing him to take refuge behind the walls of the fortress of Lamia. They had good hopes of starving him into submission there, but forces from Alexander's Asian army arrived the next year and broke the siege. The Athenian-led army was defeated by the combined forces of Antipatros and Krateros at the battle of Krannon in August 322, and Athens was forced to give up its democratic constitution and at last accept a Macedonian garrison.

§13. Because his interests were primarily military rather than political or cultural, Arrian does little to explore the relationship between Alexander and the Greek world, even omitting several significant episodes (as noted above). Himself a Greek who had embraced Roman power and served as a high official under the emperors Trajan and Hadrian, Arrian seems to have had little sympathy for the perennial Greek yearning after autonomy; at 1.7.2 for example he seems to mock the Thebans' effort to use *eleutheria*, "liberty," as a rallying cry to defy Alexander. The *Anabasis* therefore sheds little light on one of the more consequential aspects of Alexander's reign: the end of the era dominated by independent Greek city-states, and the end of the Athenian democracy. The European Greek cities were hereafter forged together into a loose federation sharing common political goals, no longer in continual conflict with one another, but also lacking the dynamism and vitality that had characterized the Classical age.

James Romm
James H. Ottaway Jr. Professor of Classics
Bard College
Annandale-on-Hudson, New York

APPENDIX N
Alexander's Geographic Notions

§1. Before he invaded Asia, Alexander learned what the Greeks knew of it primarily through the writings of Herodotus, Ktesias, and Hekataios of Miletus and through the lessons taught to him by Aristotle. He may also have gained geographic information from the Persian diplomats visiting the Macedonian court at Pella, whom Plutarch represents the young Alexander asking questions about the distances involved in traveling through their empire.[1a] The regions west of the Hindu Kush, a mountain range he called the Paropamisos, were reasonably well known to the educated Greeks of his day, but what lay beyond was much less clear. "India," a name initially derived from the Indus River but then applied by the Greeks to all territory east of the Hindu Kush, stretched eastward for an unknown distance. Herodotus[1b] frankly admitted ignorance of what lay beyond the known portions of India, whereas Aristotle, in his writings[1c] and perhaps also in the lessons he taught to the young Alexander, asserted that an "outer sea" could be glimpsed by an observer from the top of the Hindu Kush.

§2. Most Greeks (Herodotus excepted) assumed that the *oikoumene* (the "inhabited world" or known world) was surrounded by water on all sides, a continuous band of sea they named Ocean. (Arrian prefers the terms Great Sea or Outer Sea.) They had direct knowledge of it only in the west, however, by way of trading voyages through the Strait of Gibraltar and into the Atlantic. But they assumed that other bodies of water to the south and east were connected to it. Herodotus reports a theory advanced in his day that the Nile had its source in Ocean (2.21), and another, which he rejects, that the Caspian Sea was a gulf of Ocean (1.202.4–1.203.1). Alexander was uncertain enough about the Caspian Gulf theory that, in the last year of his life, he sent an exploratory mission to investigate it (7.16.1–2; a connection between the Black Sea and the Caspian was also sought), though Arrian represents him, in his address to his army at the Hyphasis River, as asserting confidently that the Caspian and Eastern seas "will turn out to be joined" (5.26.1). It was in the king's interest to believe in such interconnections and to defend them to his troops, to demonstrate that a journey homeward by sea from the fringes of the empire could be easily managed. This also helps explain Alexander's

N.1a *Parallel Lives,* "Alexander" 5.2.
N.1b Herodotus, *Histories* 1.203, 4.40.

N.1c Aristotle, *Meteorologica* 350a, 22–23.

insistence, again in the speech Arrian gives him at the Hyphasis, on the link between the Persian Gulf and the "Indian Gulf" (our Arabian Sea)—the truth of which was later demonstrated by Nearkhos' voyage from the Indus to the Euphrates—and the connection of both to Ocean (see Ref. Map 8a for an illustration). We cannot know whether Alexander advanced such notions himself or whether Arrian, who still entertained them, created a fictional speech out of them based on what he thought Alexander ought to have said;[2a] but they are wholly consistent with Greek geographic orthodoxy in Alexander's day. Alexander certainly thought of the sea by the Indus mouth, our Arabian Sea, as part of Ocean, and this in part explains his determination to sail into it (6.19.5).

§3. In the speech at the Hyphasis, Arrian represents Alexander as telling his men that "we are not far from the Ganges and the Eastern Sea" (5.26.1). There can be little doubt, given the access Alexander had to information, that he indeed knew about the Ganges valley and the powerful Nanda kingdom centered there.[3a] Whether he thought the "Eastern Sea" (Pacific Ocean or Bay of Bengal) was in more or less the same locale is difficult to determine. Aristotle, as mentioned above, may have taught him that India was not very broad in extent, but his own admiral Nearkhos seems to have known better; Arrian quotes him in the *Indika* (3.6), his more detailed treatise on India and on the voyage west from there of Nearkhos' fleet, as claiming that it would require four months to cross it. Perhaps Alexander concealed his doubts for the sake of inspiring his troops, as he seems also to have done in the case of the Caspian "Gulf." It seems likely that the same informants who described the Ganges to Alexander would also have told him about the Bay of Bengal, into which it empties, a body of water Alexander would almost certainly have understood as a part of Ocean. Reaching that Eastern Sea must have held strong appeal to him, in that it would mean reaching the end of Asia; Arrian represents him as strongly motivated by the goal of subduing an entire continent (5.26.2). But it was Arrian's Roman readers, rather than Alexander's Macedonian troops, who were deeply interested in the question of whether their empire could be coterminous with the *oikoumene*. Arrian may well have imported this theme into the speech he gave Alexander at the Hyphasis, as leading Alexander scholar Brian Bosworth (II.345) suggests, just as other Roman writers spun fictions about Alexander's supposed quest for new worlds to conquer.[3b] At 7.1.1–4 Arrian speculates in his own voice about what further conquests Alexander had in mind but does not there mention the distant east; his hero has by that time turned his attention toward the west (see §9).

§4. It was not only toward the east but also toward the north that Alexander faced the question of how far his conquests should go. In the end he fixed on the Iaxartes (modern Syr Darya) River, which Arrian calls the Tanais, as the limit of his empire on the Sogdian frontier. Though he was willing to cross this river even in the face of discouraging omens (4.4.3) and won concessions from the Scythian king on the other side (4.5.1), he elected to build his "Farthest" Alexandria (Alexandria Eschate) on the south bank. The significance of this river and its curiously misas-

N.2a See Appendix A, Arrian's Sources and Reliability, §19.

N.3a See Diodorus 17.93.2–3.
N.3b See, for example, Seneca the Elder, *Suasoria* 1.

signed name—for the Tanais, properly speaking, was a river far to the west, the modern-day Don, flowing into the Sea of Azov—needs further explanation, for it involves questions of Greek continental geography that were hardly clear to Alexander and his men, never mind to us.

§5. By Herodotus' time, the Greeks were using the real Tanais to mark the boundary between Europe (west) and Asia (east), much as we today use the Ural mountain chain. But Herodotus himself has an alternate scheme, using the Araxes (modern Aras) River, which flows east into the Caspian Sea, to delimit the continents, defining them essentially as the north and south, rather than the west and east, of the *oikoumene*. Aristotle tried to combine the two schemes in the *Meteorologica* (1.13), asserting that the Tanais was a side stream of the Araxes—a doctrine he may have taught to Alexander when tutoring him in the 340s. So Alexander may have been predisposed to think of these two rivers as connected, and also to situate the source of the Araxes farther east than Herodotus did, for Aristotle believed it flowed out of the Paropamisos. More important, Alexander certainly thought of both as being markers of the limits of Asia, and therefore logical places for the "king of Asia" to adopt as his frontier.

§6. The Iaxartes and the Araxes are two very different rivers, but their names, when pronounced in the strange dialects of native inhabitants, may have sounded alike to European ears. (Indeed, the name of the Iaxartes was heard and pronounced differently by different reporters: Plutarch ["Alexander" 46.5] calls it the Orexartes, and Arrian [3.30.7] says the local population called it the Orxantes.) Thus the Macedonians may have thought the Iaxartes was the same river as the Araxes and hence connected, as Aristotle postulated, with the Tanais. Alternatively, Alexander and his officers may have deliberately fostered the idea that the Iaxartes was part of the Tanais, as Strabo (11.7.4) believed they had done, so as to win the renown of having reached the limits of Asia. Perhaps too they were influenced by a different geographic misconception by which the Indian Caucasus or Hindu Kush came to be identified as the Caucasus (see §8), for the true Tanais has its headwaters near the true Caucasus, while the Iaxartes was thought to rise in the Hindu Kush (3.30.7; in fact, its source is in the Kirgiz Range). Probably all three factors were at work at the same time, combining to produce a conviction in the minds of Alexander's men that the Iaxartes was the Tanais.[6a] Arrian's two main sources, Aristoboulos and Ptolemy, both called the Iaxartes the Tanais in their narratives, and Arrian (much to our frustration) follows their usage, even though he knew the difference between the two rivers and perhaps even knew the Iaxartes by that name (see n. 7.16.3b).

§7. A related set of ideas led Alexander himself to identify the Indus as part of the Nile, as Arrian tells us in some detail at 6.1.2–5. At first glance this confusion may seem utterly delusional, but Greek geography often posited an uninhabited, unknown land bridge linking southwestern Asia with eastern Africa, so that the two continents were merged and the Red Sea was an enclosed body of water. Alexander clearly accepted the possibility of such a bridge, based on Arrian's report at 6.1.3 that he thought the Nile/Indus flowed through it.[7a] Then, too, he was influenced

N.6a See Ref. Map 8b.
N.7a For an illustration, see Ref. Map 8b.

by the similarity of flora and fauna in the two rivers, in particular the presence of crocodiles in both (6.1.2; Arrian does not mention the coincidence of elephants, but that must have also played a part, for the distinction between African and Indian elephants had not yet been discovered). Last, he was once again, as at the Iaxartes, influenced by the desire to reach continental boundaries, for the Nile was considered by the Greeks the border between Africa and Asia, just as the Tanais, or Araxes, delimited Asia and Europe. If Alexander had conquered all the way to the Nile in the south of India and to the Tanais in the north of Sogdiana, then he had well and truly become king of Asia, with the exception of the small eastern segment beyond the Hyphasis.

§8. The third great geographic misconception of the Alexander campaign was the identification of the Hindu Kush, or Paropamisos as Aristotle called it, with the Caucasus, or at least the use of the name Caucasus to refer to the Hindu Kush. The true Caucasus, which Arrian once calls the Scythian Caucasus to distinguish it (5.5.3), is the range still known as the Caucasus today, stretching between the Black and Caspian seas in southern Russia and Georgia. The archaic Greeks thought of it as the northeastern edge of the *oikoumene*; Aeschylus, for example, spoke of it as such in his plays *Prometheus Bound* and (now lost) *Prometheus Unbound*, which took these mountains as the setting for the binding of the rebel god Prometheus and his liberation by Herakles. The name Caucasus thus came to have powerful mythic resonance, denoting a place only divine beings could reach. As Alexander moved farther east and beyond the limits of the world formerly known to the Greeks, his journeys were often compared to those of gods and heroes, especially Herakles, so the association of the Hindu Kush with the place of Prometheus' punishment must have been tempting. Arrian, drawing on the work of the Hellenistic geographer Eratosthenes, discusses how this association might have arisen: perhaps the sight of a mountain cave, or a legend told by a local guide, first suggested a link to the Prometheus myth (5.3.1–4), and then the impulse to assimilate Alexander to his mythic ancestor Herakles quickly reinforced it (5.5.3). Uncertainties about where, or whether, the true Caucasus reached an eastern endpoint contributed to the fallacy; even Arrian, with access to much greater geographic knowledge, speculated that the true Caucasus and the Paropamisos might in fact be part of the same chain (5.5.3).[8a] So the Macedonians under Alexander came to call the Hindu Kush by the name Caucasus, and Arrian once again, as with the Tanais/Iaxartes, faithfully replicates their confused terminology.

§9. At two points in his narrative, 4.7.5 and 5.26.2, Arrian says that Alexander, at the end of his life, intended to circumnavigate Africa from east to west. The second of these passages is part of Alexander's speech to his troops at the Hyphasis, and as we have seen above, this speech contains several inauthentic passages woven by Arrian out of Roman-era rhetorical themes. At 4.7.5, by contrast, Arrian speculates in his own voice that Alexander planned to sail around "Libya" (our Africa) in order to attach it to his empire. At 7.1.2 he claims to have read in the works of earlier writers that "Alexander was planning to circumnavigate most of Arabia, Ethiopia, Libya

N.8a   See Ref. Maps 8a and 8b.

. . . and thus sail to Gadeira and on into the Mediterranean; then, after subjugating Libya and Carthage, he would indeed have earned the right to call himself king of all of Asia." Plutarch may have read the same writers Arrian drew on here, for he attributes exactly the same intention to Alexander;[9a] Quintus Curtius (10.1.17–19), by contrast, speaks of a campaign directed at Carthage and the western Mediterranean that did not entail a circumnavigation of Africa. The Last Plans recorded by Diodorus (18.4.4), a document of disputed authenticity supposedly reporting Alexander's intentions at the time of his death, envision a campaign against Carthage conducted solely within the Mediterranean, with a road to be built along the North African coast as far as the Pillars of Herakles (our Strait of Gibraltar). The idea that Africa could be circumnavigated had been raised by Herodotus,[9b] but in his account the journey took more than two years. It is unlikely that Alexander, even if he believed Africa to be circumnavigable, would have contemplated a long and perilous journey around its southern perimeter, especially when his principal objective was Carthage, readily accessible by way of known sea routes. Arrian seems once again to be projecting back onto Alexander the fantasy of his own Roman-dominated era: that a single world-state could be made coterminous with the boundaries of the *oikoumene*.

James Romm
James H. Ottaway Jr. Professor of Classics
Bard College
Annandale-on-Hudson, New York

N.9a   "Alexander" 68.1.
N.8a   Herodotus, *Histories* 4.42–43.

APPENDIX O
Alexander's Death: A Medical Analysis

§1. In late May or early June 323, while Alexander was in Babylon, he fell ill with fever, fatigue, and generalized pain. For several days he continued his daily regimen of work, bathing in cool water, and drinking wine during the evening. As the days wore on, his fever and fatigue increased and he became virtually comatose. Sensing that the end was near, he ordered a final review of his officers but was so weak that he was barely able to nod in recognition of his old comrades. On June 11, he appeared to have died (but may not have done so; see §4). The sources on Alexander's final days[1a] have been exhaustively examined by scholars. While there are a number of discrepancies among sources regarding details, there is general agreement among them about the course of Alexander's illness. The accounts of Arrian and Plutarch provide us with the greatest wealth of detail, and both of these, as the authors themselves write, were based on the *Ephemerides* (*Royal Journals*). However, the versions they consulted must have been different, as their summaries of it diverge; and there is some doubt as to the authenticity of what purported to be the *Ephemerides.*[1b]

§2. The evidence concerning Alexander's death is problematic, to say the least, and it may be impossible to pinpoint accurately the cause of his death. We cannot apply to the case the exacting methods of modern diagnostic medicine, both because ancient medical accounts do not describe illness precisely enough for such methods and because the surviving accounts of the king's final illness may be corrupted by misunderstanding and propaganda. We are dealing with the death of a remote historical figure, and there is simply no expert medical testimony regarding his final illness. Yet it is possible that modern medical analysis can determine whether the ancient accounts of Alexander's last days are consistent with any known illness or medical condition.

§3. Each year the University of Maryland School of Medicine sponsors a clinico-pathological conference whose subject is the death of a person, or a medical prob-

O.1a See Arrian, *Anabasis Alexandrou* 7.24.4–27.3;
      Plutarch, *Parallel Lives* "Alexander" 75.2–77.3;
      Diodorus 17.117.1–4; Justin 12.13.7–16.1; and
      Athenaios 10.434a–b.
O.1b The question of the authenticity of the
      Ephemerides is discussed in Appendix A, Arrian's
      Sources and Reliability, §16, and Appendix P,

Alexander's Death: The Poisoning Rumors,
§4–10.

lem, of historical significance. This annual exercise has examined, for example, the deaths of Ludwig van Beethoven, the Roman emperor Claudius, Gen. George Armstrong Custer, and the plague that struck Athens during the early years of the Peloponnesian War. In 1996 I took part in that annual conference, whose subject was the death of Alexander. Some of what follows derives from the conclusions reached by those associated with that conference.[3a]

§4. Three issues relating to Alexander's illness may be subjected to modern medical analysis. The first is the progressive decline of the king's health over the final eleven days (in Arrian's account; the duration varies in other sources) of his life. This slow decline is consistent with a number of known diseases. The second is the possibility, if we trust a report in the vulgate sources that is rejected by Plutarch and doubted by Arrian,[4a] that Alexander drank a huge goblet of wine and felt a stabbing pain that made him cry out just before the onset of his other symptoms. Finally, the ancient sources agree that Alexander's body did not decay for several days following his death, even in the heat of the Babylonian summer. While this may at first appear to be a fiction—an example of Alexander hagiography—it may have a basis in fact: some terminal diseases, including typhoid fever, are marked by an ascending paralysis that results in the impression that death has occurred before it becomes a clinical fact. The neurological response to such a disease moves upward from the feet, resulting in muscle paralysis and slowed breathing and heartbeat.

§5. Some causes of death can be eliminated—for example, very heavy drinking and alcohol poisoning. Ethanol toxicity can produce the type of gradual weakening experienced by Alexander, and the conversion of some natural substances found in wine into formaldehyde could explain the delay in putrefaction, but extreme fever and abdominal pain are not associated with large doses of alcohol. And while abdominal pain is consistent with a perforated ulcer, it cannot be connected with other symptoms of the king's fatal illness. Lead poisoning, caused by contact with the lead found in the glazes of ceramic containers, can be eliminated as well, both because no correlation between lead toxicity and these glazes has been established and because fever is not associated with lead poisoning.

§6. Two of the most popular theories offered to explain the king's illness are deliberate poisoning and malaria. All our ancient sources report a rumor that Alexander was poisoned,[6a] but the story tests credulity. If the poison were strongly lethal, one wonders why Alexander lingered for so many days. Administering the drug in weaker doses over a longer period of time would have required a sophisticated and well-coordinated conspiracy at court, and there is no evidence for such a conspiracy. From a clinical point of view, moreover, the symptoms of Alexander's final illness are not consistent with known poisons. It may be possible that some poison unknown to us was used. But ancient poisons were for the most part or entirely derived from organic sources, and as those sources are known to us and are

---

O.3a See the reports by David W. Oldach, M.D., et al. "A Mysterious Death," *New England Journal of Medicine* 338, no. 24 (June 11, 1998): 1764–1769; and E. N. Borza and J. Reames-Zimmerman, "Some New Thoughts on the Death of Alexander the Great," *Ancient World* 31.1 (2000): 22–30.

O.4a See Diodorus 17.117.1–2 and Justin 12.13.8–9;

Quintus Curtius' text is broken by a gap at this point. Arrian reports the stabbing pain among the versions of Alexander's death he does not credit (7.27.2), while Plutarch condemns the story as an operatic fiction ("Alexander" 75.5).

O.6a See Appendix P.

often used in the preparation of modern poisons, we are reasonably confident that we have knowledge about most ancient poisons.

§7. As for the attribution of Alexander's death to malaria: Alexander and his Macedonian troops hailed from a Balkan region that saw severe endemic malaria in antiquity, and it is likely that they continued to be exposed to the disease in the regions of Asia Minor, the Levant, Egypt, Mesopotamia, and perhaps even the Indian frontier. Malaria is an infectious disease, and while the fever and fatigue experienced by the king are typical symptoms of malaria attacks, severe abdominal pain is not normally associated with the most common form of the disease, caused by the parasite *Plasmodium falciparum*.

§8. The Maryland clinicopathological conference and its report in *The New England Journal of Medicine* concluded that, since poisoning and chronic malaria can be eliminated, the cause of Alexander's death must have been an infectious disease; and that, while there can be no certainty, the symptoms related by the ancient sources are consistent with typhoid fever, caused by the bacterium *Salmonella typhi*. This disease may have been complicated by bowel perforation, which would have resulted in the abdominal pain reported by the vulgate sources, and perhaps also ascending paralysis, which would account for the delay in putrefaction.

§9. Several of the physicians attending the Maryland conference suggested that multiple factors might have contributed to the deterioration of Alexander's health. These include fatigue, the stress of campaigning and administration, endemic malaria, occasional heavy drinking, and multiple wounds, the most serious of which occurred during the Macedonian attack on the Malloi town in India more than two years earlier (6.10.1–6.11.8). Alexander's chest was penetrated by a great Indian arrow, and the wound nearly killed him. According to Arrian, "air came hissing out from the wound, along with spurts of blood" (6.10.1)—a medical complication of a pierced lung, or hemopneumothorax. Although Alexander recovered from the injury, there may have been a lingering secondary infection that eventually weakened him and made him more susceptibile to typhoid fever, or even worked together with the typhoid infection to cause his demise.

§10. One further factor may have played a role in Alexander's decline. His closest longtime companion, Hephaistion, died of a febrile illness, perhaps in October 324. Our sources agree[10a] that Alexander underwent a prolonged period of intense grief. Numerous recent studies have demonstrated a clear link between bereavement and a weakening of the immune system. Thus, if Alexander fell victim to an infectious disease at Babylon, he may have been unable to stand against it for this reason.

Eugene N. Borza
Professor Emeritus of Ancient History
The Pennsylvania State University

O.10a See Arrian, *Anabasis Alexandrou* 7.14.1–7.15.1;
       Plutarch, "Alexander" 72.2–4; Diodorus
       17.114–115.

APPENDIX P

Alexander's Death:
The Poisoning Rumors

§1. The most complex tradition in Alexander historiography concerns the king's death. Within a few years of his demise, a story had taken shape that he did not die from natural causes. This story identified an evil genius—namely, Antipatros, the regent in Macedonia—who was summoned to Babylon by Alexander regarding a dispute with the queen mother, Olympias, but instead sent his eldest son, Kassandros, bearing a poison of exceptional virulence. Antipatros' younger son, Iollas, happened to be the royal wine pourer; as such he occupied a unique position, ideal for administering the poison but also exposing him to suspicion. He would need accomplices to share the guilt. A famous banquet took place, hosted by the Thessalian noble Medios of Larisa (Iollas' lover, according to a story Arrian reports but does not credit, at 7.27.2). In the course of it Alexander consumed a prodigious amount of undiluted wine. As he drank he was taken ill with a sharp pain in the back and left the revels.[1a] The pain continued and intensified, and Alexander's condition gradually deteriorated until he died.

§2. This is a composite narrative. No source gives us a full account with all the details; on the other hand, there is no internal contradiction among the various accounts. The story can be reconstructed out of some half-dozen derivative authorities, and it is sensational material even now. In the years immediately following Alexander's death, it became something of a political football. Practically any member of Alexander's staff who had been present in Babylon could be accused of his murder. Rumor and innuendo would have played their part, and it is not surprising that Antipatros and Kassandros, who by 316 had got control of the Macedonian throne (see the Epilogue, §11), attempted to quash them. According to Quintus Curtius (10.10.18–19), Antipatros and Kassandros teamed up to squelch the allegations against them; Diodorus Siculus (17.118.2) says that many historians did not dare to write about the poisoning during the time Kassandros was in power. There

---

P.1a   The sharp pain recurs in Diodorus (17.117.1–2),
Justin (12.13.9–10), and *Liber de Morte* (99) but is
rejected by Arrian (7.27.2) and Plutarch (*Parallel
Lives*, "Alexander" 75.5).

is a tradition that the Athenian orator Hypereides, a long-standing foe of Macedonia's hegemony in Greece, proposed a motion conferring honors on Iollas, which is no doubt why Antipatros inflicted such an atrocious death on him: according to Hermippos, the third-century B.C.E. biographer, Antipatros had Hypereides' tongue cut out and his body left unburied.[2a] It was an object lesson that one should be very wary of speaking about poison. Silence was the best policy.

§3. There is, however, a more revealing narrative, conventionally termed the *Liber de Morte,* or *Book About the Death [of Alexander].* Originally published in a Greek version that has since been lost, it is known through a later Latin translation (the second half of the summary history of Alexander called the *Metz Epitome*) and through some excerpts that found their way into versions of the Greek novelistic biography the *Alexander Romance.*[3a] To judge by these two surviving witnesses, the *Liber de Morte* provided the lengthiest, most detailed version of the conspiracy story known from any ancient text. It affirmed the allegations of poisoning previously spread in a memoir published by Onesikritos, one of Alexander's Greek officers, and even named the names Onesikritos had kept hush: after listing twenty-three high-ranking Macedonians present at Medios' banquet, the *Liber* exculpated six, claiming that the rest were complicit in Iollas' plot. While only Kassandros and Iollas administered the poison, according to the *Liber,* seventeen others stood by and did nothing, including some of the king's Bodyguards and long-standing friends. The motives behind this lost document are hard to access, given the odd assortment of names that are accused and exculpated. But, as I have argued at length elsewhere,[3b] it is possible that Ptolemy had a hand in its creation, during his struggles for power against other former Alexander generals in the last decade of the fourth century. In any case, its testimony is deeply suspect, especially given that it went on to record a last will and testament of Alexander that is quite clearly a fiction.

§4. Another important document that relates to the allegations of poisoning is the so-called *Ephemerides* (*Royal Journals*). What exactly they were remains a mystery, but the traditional view is that they were a court journal, documenting the activities of the king and constituting an official record of state business. That record, according to this view, was in the hands of Ptolemy, who made it the basis of his account of Alexander, since lost but used by Arrian as one of two sources for the *Anabasis.* Ptolemy's record was therefore privileged, based on material from the immediate entourage of his king, collected and edited by the royal secretary, Eumenes of Kardia. This traditional view, however, is too simplistic. The material that has come down to us in Arrian's summary (7.25–26) bears no similarity to any archival record from antiquity. There are no pronouncements by the king, no edicts, no royal correspondence. Instead we find in Arrian's summary a day-by-day record of Alexander's terminal illness, focused only on his symptoms and routine. Moreover, the version of Alexander's last days presented by Arrian contains a number of

P.2a   As related in Plutarch, *Moralia* 849 b–c, f.
P.3a   *Alexander Romance* (A recension) 3.31. See
       Appendix L, The *Alexander Romance.*
P.3b   "Ptolemy and the Will of Alexander," in A. B.
       Bosworth and E. J. Baynham (eds.), *Alexander the*

Great in Fact and Fiction (New York: Oxford University Press, 2000).

inconsistencies and contradictions with Plutarch's "Alexander" 76–77.1, which also purports to represent the *Ephemerides*.[4a]

§5. As with the *Liber de Morte*, the testimony about Alexander's death contained in the *Ephemerides* can best be explained through the motives of its author. According to the third-century C.E. Greek grammarian Athenaios (10.434b), the *Ephemerides* were written by Eumenes of Kardia and Diodotos of Erythrai. The latter is unknown, but the first name is significant. Eumenes was the chief secretary for Alexander and his father, and he was in an ideal position to access archival material—*if* his intention was to put on record his king's mundane daily activities. But from what is preserved of them, those activities were drinking, sleeping, and carrying out the mandatory sacrifices. It might be argued that the record was meant to be mundane. It was business as usual at the court, with the king sacrificing and briefing his senior officers in anticipation of the forthcoming campaign against the marsh Arabs.[5a] The emphasis was on the fatal fever that first appeared at a banquet, then slowly intensified and finally resulted in death. No one reading this account would suspect that Alexander had been poisoned. Eumenes' account of Alexander's last days seems highly apologetic, conveying the impression that the king died a natural death.

§6. The original *Ephemerides* on which Arrian and Plutarch later drew is impossible to date: it could have been written at any time between Alexander's demise, in 323, and Eumenes', in 316. The later date seems more likely in that it helps explain why an excerpt from the document was apparently published, and in particular the portion that dealt with Alexander's death from fever. In the *Liber de Morte* Eumenes is named as one of the guests at Medios' party; he himself was perhaps vulnerable to allegations of poisoning, just as Antipatros and Kassandros were. That might have given Eumenes motive to publish a diary that excluded any suspicion of poison, thereby saving his credit with his troops, since shortly after Alexander's death he became a general and a major competitor in the imperial power grab (see the Epilogue, §8, 10).

§7. The *Liber de Morte* and the *Ephemerides* represent two traditions regarding Alexander's death. The first states categorically that Alexander was murdered by Antipatros and his sons; the second suggests that his death came about through natural causes. We cannot go further. Alexander's death will always be shrouded in mystery, and much of the tradition is systematically misleading. The daily record of the *Ephemerides* can be interpreted either as a meticulous description of actual symptoms or an attempt to quash damaging suspicions of poisoning. We do not have enough information to choose between the two traditions on medical grounds. As for the idea of a poisoning conspiracy, much depends on the degree to which Antipatros and his family were threatened by Alexander in the last months of the king's life. Antipatros had been ordered to step down from his post in Macedonia

P.4a Plutarch presents for the most part a verbatim record, arranged by the Macedonian calendar, beginning on 18th Daisios and ending on the 28th (June 10). Arrian ignores the Macedonian month and gives a simple day count. By and large, his account coheres with Plutarch's, but among the inconsistencies are two extra days in the count.

P.5a Arrian, *Anabasis Alexandrou* 7.25.3–5; Plutarch, "Alexander" 76.5.

and to report to Alexander in Babylon, but even if hostility and mistrust between the king and regent were growing, we cannot assume that Antipatros resorted to poison. The evidence is simply too thin; and, as always, it can be interpreted in different, often contradictory ways.

A. B. Bosworth
Professor of Ancient History
Macquarie University
Ryde, North Sydney
New South Wales, Australia

APPENDIX Q

The Royal Macedonian Tombs at Aigeai

§1. The heartland of Macedonia is a flat central plain, long ago an inlet of the sea and, more recently, a swamp. Modern reclamation has transformed it into one of the most fertile agricultural regions in the southern Balkans. The periphery of this area, however, is marked by a number of ancient sites, including tumuli, that are at odds with the natural features of this otherwise level landscape. Modern archaeological excavation has revealed that these tumuli are artificial earth mounds designed to protect burials. Grave robbers through the centuries have understood their purpose, and most of the burials have been looted.

§2. The Greek village of Vergina lies along the southern edge of the plain, roughly opposite Pella, the Macedonian political and administrative center. The village was founded from two existing hamlets for the resettlement of Greeks displaced from Asia Minor in the 1920s. At its center was a large tumulus that for years had drawn the interest of archaeologists until in 1977 excavation commenced under the directorship of Manolis Andronikos, a professor of archaeology at the Aristotle University of Thessaloniki. Two years of digging yielded some important finds, including ancient inscriptions and several small buildings. The most important of these structures included three tombs—one a small cist tomb, the other two larger chamber tombs.

§3. The cist tomb (Tomb I) was, simply put, a box 11.5 feet long by 6.5 feet wide and 10 feet in height, made of fitted stones covered with a stone-slab roof. It had been looted in antiquity, but its interior walls were adorned with well-preserved paintings of excellent quality, including a depiction of one of the most famous incidents of ancient mythology, the Rape of Persephone. Scattered on the floor were the remains of a middle-aged male, a female aged eighteen to twenty, and an infant. (The question of their identity and that of the other tombs' inhabitants is discussed in §13.) Tomb II was unlooted. It was constructed of two chambers covered by a barrel vault, and its interior area was nearly five times larger than that of Tomb I. In the main chamber was the untouched burial of a middle-aged male, in the antechamber that of a female perhaps eighteen to twenty. Both burials contained lavish grave goods, including bronze and iron weapons, silver vessels, gold jewelry, and regal paraphernalia. Clearly the deceased were wealthy royal persons. The somewhat smaller Tomb III was also an unlooted chamber tomb, marked by a single burial in the main chamber. Here too were found a rich assortment of grave goods fabricated from precious metals and finely executed ceramics. An analysis of the human remains revealed that the deceased was a teenager, perhaps thirteen to sixteen, likely a male because of the character of the grave goods.

§4. British Alexander historian Nicholas Hammond had identified Vergina in 1968 as the site of ancient Aigeai, a major ancient Macedonian center and, as we know from literary sources (for example, Justin 7.2.2–5), the burial place of Macedonian royalty. The discovery of the rich tombs in 1977–78 instantly produced speculation about whether the excavations had in fact revealed the remains of famous kings. It was clear on archaeological grounds that the tombs dated to the last half of the fourth century B.C.E., and there are only a limited number of candidates for royal burials at this place during that era. In 336 Philip II—king since 359, conqueror of the Greek city-states, and father of Alexander the Great—was assassinated by a bodyguard during ceremonies at Aigeai marking his daughter's wedding. Shortly thereafter his young wife Cleopatra and their infant were killed by Philip's estranged wife (and Alexander's mother), Olympias. Thus we have three candidates for interment at Vergina whose deaths occurred in 336. A generation later, in 317, Alexander's half brother and successor, King Philip III (called Arrhidaios before his accession), and his wife Eurydike (formerly Adea) were killed by Olympias during the civil war that followed Alexander's death (see the Epilogue, §11). Olympias herself was killed by Kassandros, the son of the former regent Antipatros, shortly thereafter, and in the following year Kassandros, intent on honoring the fallen royalty as a way of legitimizing his own ambition to rule, reinterred at Aigeai the remains of Philip III and Eurydike.[4a] Thus, there are two candidates for the tomb's occupants from the year 316. Finally, the teenage son of Alexander the Great and the sole surviving member of the royal family, Alexander IV, who had held joint rule over the Macedonians with Philip III (see the Epilogue, §4), was dispatched by Kassandros sometime in the period 311–309. The royal family was no more, and Kassandros emerged from the Macedonian civil wars as king of the Macedonians.

§5. Immediately following his discoveries of the tombs, Andronikos announced that Tomb II contained the remains of the legendary Philip II, Alexander's father. His identification was based on a correspondence between the richness of the grave goods and the importance of Philip, and every effort was made to interpret the dating of the tomb's architecture and grave goods in accord with the chronology of Philip's death. Yet, as more information was released about the tomb and more scholars who were independent of the excavation team began to study the data, it became apparent that matters were not as clear as they had first seemed. Indeed, as time went on, no new arguments and no new evidence were presented reaffirming the Philip II connection, while a number of serious studies began to offer an alternative chronology that favored Philip III as the occupant of the tomb's main chamber.

§6. There are clues that help establish the date of Tomb II, among them its

Q.4a Diodorus 19.52.5; Athenaeus 4.155A.

FIGURE Q.1. A larnax, or chest, made of gold and weighing 24 pounds, found in Tomb II at Aigeai (modern Vergina). When opened, it was found to contain the cremated remains of a male adult, first thought to be Philip II, Alexander's father, but now more commonly identified as Philip III, Alexander's half brother. The sunburst on the lid, often called the Star of Vergina, usually with sixteen points but sometimes with fewer, seems to have been an emblem of the Macedonian royal house.

barrel-vaulted roof. The earliest barrel vault in the European world of the Greeks and Macedonians that can be securely dated is found at the Peloponnesian site of Nemea. There, a barrel-vaulted tunnel connects the athletes' preparation area with the stadium, and that passageway is dated to about 320 B.C.E. on the basis of both epigraphic and numismatic evidence. Moreover, there is no archaeological record of the development of the barrel vault in Greece and Macedonia. It seems to have arrived rather suddenly and fully developed, and at sites associated with the Macedonians— strongly suggesting that those who accompanied Alexander to Asia, where barrel vaults had been in use for some time, introduced them to the west. That is, we have a chronology for the introduction of the barrel vault that is independent of the Vergina excavations, and the use of this architectural device in Tomb II suggests that the tomb was built at least fifteen years after the death of Philip II, during the reign of Philip III or shortly after.

§7. Another interesting feature of these chambered Macedonian tombs is that their exterior façades give the appearance of Doric or Ionic architecture, yet their components are not structural or supportive but purely decorative, little more than plaster or stucco attached to the front of a stone building. As with the barrel vault, the origin of this kind of decoration lies in western Asia, where it had been in use for some time, and its appearance in the Balkans looks to be another import resulting from Alexander's invasion, again supporting the later dating of the tomb.

§8. Among the most beautiful of the silver objects found in the main chamber of Tomb II was a device used for straining wine. It was perforated (like a modern tea strainer) and designed to fit over a cup, into which wine was poured through it. The strainer bore an inscription, giving us the name of the Macedonian artisan who produced it and also its ancient weight. It is a simple matter to determine what ancient system of weights and measures was used to mark such an object, and this wine strainer had been evaluated according to the system devised at Athens and adopted by much of the Greek world, as they were by Macedonia in the time of Alexander.[8a] Two other silver objects from Tomb II also bear inscribed ancient weights that were calculated according to the Athenian system. If they were made in Macedonia and not imported from Greece, these objects must date from the reign of Alexander or later and could not possibly have found their way into a tomb closed in 336, the date of Philip II's death.

§9. Tomb II also yielded several small black-glazed salt cellars, spool-shaped ceramic objects used as tableware. Their origin is Athens, where they have been firmly dated, based on parallel examples from other datable archaeological contexts, to the period 325–295.[9a] Assuming that these parallels are correct, the salt cellars cannot be dated earlier than the last quarter of the fourth century, so the tomb in which they were found cannot be that of Philip II.

§10. As a final piece of evidence, the human remains from Tomb II have undergone three separate forensic examinations, and the most recent study concludes that both the osteological evidence and the manner of burials is far more consistent with what we know of the interment of Philip III and Eurydike than of the burial of Philip II and Cleopatra.[10a]

§11. Turning to Tomb III, the main chamber here yielded a silver vessel (*hydria*) containing the cremated remains of a teenager. Fixing the age of the deceased is made possible in part by an examination of the hip bones. In all teenagers, a gradual fusion of three separate bones into a single adult hip bone takes place. That process was under way in the remains in Tomb III and therefore dates the deceased to thirteen to sixteen years of age. Determining gender from the osteological evidence is

Q.8a   On Alexander's metrological reform, putting the Macedonians on the Athenian standard, see Martin J. Price, *The Coinage in the Name of Alexander the Great and Philip Arrhidaeus* (Zurich and London, 1991), 27ff. and 38ff.

Q.9a   The evidence for the dating of the salt cellars is cited and summarized in Eugene N. Borza and Olga Palagia, "The Chronology of the Macedonian Royal Tombs at Vergina," *Jahrbuch des Deutsches Archäologischen Institut* 122 (2007): 105 and n. 147. The chronology is based on the work of Susan Rotroff, "Royal Salt Cellars from the Athenian Agora," *American Journal of Archaeology* 86 (1982): 283, and "Spool Salt Cellars in the Athenian Agora," *Hesperia* 53 (1984): 343–354.

Q.10a The original osteological study of the Tomb II bones was done at the request of the excavator, Manolis Andronikos: see N. I. Xirotiris and F. Langenscheidt, "The Cremation from the Royal Macedonian Tombs at Vergina," *Archaiologike Ephemeris* (1981): 142–160. They concluded that the bone fragments did not support Andronikos' theory that the burial was that of Philip II. Lacking forensic support, Andronikos turned the matter over to a different team, which published its analysis in a prestigious British journal: see A. J. N. W. Prag, J. H. Musgrave, and R. A. H. Neave, "The

Skull from Tomb II at Vergina: King Philip II of Macedon," *Journal of Hellenic Studies* 104 (1984): 60–78. The British team argued that the bone fragments were those of Philip II. There the matter stood for several years. In 2000 a Greek physical anthropologist, Antonis Bartsiokas, using advanced forensic techniques including macrophotography, published the results of his study of the bones, "The Eye Injury of King Philip II and the Skeletal Evidence from the Royal Tomb II at Vergina," *Science* 288 (21 April): 511–514. Bartsiokas argued that the skull fragments did not reveal the head wounds that Philip had suffered during his siege of the Greek city of Methone in 354 (an arrow shot had destroyed one of the king's eyes). Moreover, an examination of the long bones suggested that the cremation of the deceased occurred sometime after his death, which is consistent with the disposition of the remains of Philip III, not Philip II. Additional information and more extensive bibliography about the human remains in Tomb II can be found in Borza and Palagia, 81–125 (see n. Q.9a). The most complete study of Philip II's several injuries is by A. S. Rigonos, "The Wounding of Philip II of Macedon: Fact and Fabrication," *Journal of Hellenic Studies* 94 (1994): 103–119.

difficult, but the grave goods attending the burial suggest a male. There is only one possible candidate for the Tomb III interment—assuming, of course, that this is the Macedonian royal necropolis—and that is the son of Alexander the Great and his Bactrian wife Rhoxane, born in 323 shortly after the conqueror's death. The young Alexander had been proclaimed joint ruler with his uncle Philip III and would have been twelve to fourteen at the time of his death, in 311–309. Tomb III must therefore be Alexander IV's burial place.

§12. It is thus possible to establish a chronology for the three major tombs along the following lines: Tomb III contains an adolescent male who is most likely Alexander IV, dispatched by Kassandros between 311 and 309. Tomb II appears to be the resting place of Philip III and his queen Eurydike, killed by Olympias in 317 and, following Olympias' own death, given an elaborate burial by Kassandros in 316. Some scholars, however, question the chronological evidence discussed above and continue to defend the original verdict of Andronikos, that Tomb II contained Philip II and Cleopatra.[12a] The museum at the site in Vergina also holds to Andronikos' theory.

§13. If the attribution of Tomb II to Philip III is correct, then by a process of elimination and by forensic evidence, the remains in Tomb I should be those of Philip II, his wife Cleopatra, and their infant, killed in 336. To those who might object that such a famous and powerful ruler as Philip could be interred in such a modest cist tomb, it need only be pointed out that Philip's burial occurred prior to the introduction into Macedonia of the monumental barrel-vaulted chamber tombs that characterized the later royal funeral venues, and prior to the vast influx of wealth that accompanied Alexander's conquests.

§14. Following this chronology of the tombs and identification of their occupants, it becomes possible to interpret much of the decoration and many of the grave goods of Tombs II and III as dating from the age of Alexander and his successors, Philip III and Alexander IV. For example, the exterior façade of Tomb II is decorated with an elaborate hunting frieze (for a detail of the frieze, see Figure 4.13). Recent analysis strongly points to an Asian source, in particular the art of the Persian empire, as the inspiration for the depiction of multiple-quarry hunts. Moreover, if, as has been suggested, the huntsmen shown in the frieze are royal personages and their train, they may well include Alexander himself and his half brother Arrhidaios, later Philip III (indeed, Alexander was known to have engaged in such hunts while in Asia).

§15. Of perhaps more interest are an assortment of unique items from Tomb II that appear to be Alexander's own paraphernalia, to judge by the ancient evidence[15a] regarding his tokens of authority and what happened to them after his death. Quintus Curtius (10.6.4) informs us that, on the day after Alexander's death, Perdikkas, in order to awe the other generals, set up a council furnished with Alexander's robe and several items of the deceased king's regalia, including his royal diadem (*diadema*) and a set of armor (*hopla*). It may thus be significant that Tomb II

Q.12a See, most recently, Ian Worthington, *Philip II of Macedonia* (New Haven: Yale University Press, 2009), Appendix 6.

Q.15a Diodorus 18.60.3–61.3, 19.15.3–4; Quintus

Curtius 10.6.4, 10.7.13; Plutarch, *Parallel Lives,* "Eumenes" 13.3–4; Cornelius Nepos, *Eumenes* 7.2–3; Polyaenus 4.8.2.

yielded a gilded silver diadem—a unique item—and a variety of weapons and armor (see Figures 1.4, 6.12), including an iron helmet that seems to match descriptions of the famous one worn by the king in battle (see Figure 1.15). These items may indeed be relics deriving from Alexander's reign, presumably used by Philip III to solidify his rule and interred with his remains in Tomb II.[15b]

§16. Thus, in summary, several categories of evidence—including the dating of some of the grave goods, an analysis of the style of these tombs' architecture and decoration, and the forensic examination of the skeletal material—suggest the following chronology of the royal Macedonian tombs at Vergina: Tomb I dates to 336 and contains the remains of Philip II, Cleopatra, and their infant. Tomb II dates to 316 and contains the remains of Philip III and Eurydike. Tomb III dates to 311 or shortly after and is the resting place of Alexander IV.

§17. In the more than three decades that have elapsed since the opening of the Vergina tombs, no credible new argument has been offered to support the notion that Philip II is buried in Tomb II, while the evidence continues to mount suggesting that he cannot be. Though challenges have been raised to some of the arguments presented here for the late dating of the tomb and the identification of the remains it contained,[17a] none has been convincing, and the consensus of scholarly opinion increasingly favors the attribution of the tomb to Philip III and Eurydike.

Eugene N. Borza
Professor Emeritus of Ancient History
The Pennsylvania State University

Q.15b   In addition, one of several ivory heads found in the tomb (see the Frontispiece) has usually been identified as a portrait of Alexander, done by an artist who presumably knew the king in life.

Q.17a   Summarized most recently by Ian Worthington, *Philip II of Macedonia* (see n. Q.12a), Appendix 6, "The Vergina Royal Tombs," 234–41.

APPENDIX R

Arrian's Life and Works

§1. Arrian's birth can be dated only by inference, but it must have been sometime in the 80s C.E. He was born into a wealthy Greek family in the city of Nicomedia, in what is now north-central Turkey, where he eventually received an official appointment as a priest of the goddesses Demeter and Kore. His full name, Lucius Flavius Arrianus, contains two Latin elements before the final Greek one, showing that his family was already in favor among the Roman elite before his birth; they may commemorate some otherwise unknown Roman official serving in Arrian's home province, who had conferred Roman citizenship, a high honor for Greeks at this time, on one of his ancestors.[1a] Arrian himself was to rise in the Roman political world, eventually holding some of its highest offices under the first two Antonine emperors, Trajan (r. 96–117) and Hadrian (r. 117–138).

§2. Arrian, however, did not start off on a career track typical of political and military aspirants. He studied during the first years of the second century under a philosopher, the Stoic sage Epictetus, who was then teaching at Nikopolis in Epirus, Greece. The four books we possess of the *Discourses* and the short treatise called the *Encheiridion* (often translated *Handbook*) ascribed to Epictetus are actually the work of Arrian, who did not want the oral lessons of his teacher to go unrecorded. These volumes show us what Arrian was taught in his youth—Epictetus stressed moral virtue and self-reliance as the keys to happiness and scorned wealth and power—but tell us little about Arrian himself. Presumably he admired Epictetus greatly and considered himself a second Xenophon sitting before a second Socrates (see the Introduction, §1), but it has been justly asserted by scholars that his later works, in particular the *Anabasis Alexandrou* (here translated as *The Campaigns of Alexander*), bear few traces of his philosophic education.

§3. Arrian began his Roman political career under Trajan, an emperor who styled himself a warrior and conqueror very much in the mold of Alexander the Great, and it is possible that Arrian became interested in Alexander's life as a result. Almost certainly he began writing a work entitled *Parthika* (now lost), a history of the Parthians, because of a series of aggressive campaigns Trajan led against this

R.1a Stadter, Philip A. *Arrian of Nicomedia*. Chapel Hill:
University of North Carolina Press, 1980, 2.

417

nation from 113 to his death, in 117, and it is possible that Arrian served as an officer on one or all of those campaigns.[3a] By the time of Trajan's death, at any rate, Arrian had advanced far in Roman political circles, and in the late 120s he became a consul at Rome, the highest elected office to which a Roman citizen could aspire. Shortly thereafter, Hadrian appointed him governor of the province of Cappadocia, on what was then the northeastern frontier of the Roman empire, where his term of office can be securely dated by way of documents and inscriptions to 132–137.

§4. Arrian's service in the east led to the composition of two of his shorter works, both still extant. Ordered by Hadrian to inspect the Roman forts that dotted the Black Sea coast, Arrian took the opportunity to compose a *Periplous* ["tour by ship"] *of the Black Sea*, a Greek-style geographic excursus designed to please his famously philhellenic emperor. Also while in Cappadocia, Arrian had to confront the threat of an invasion by the Alanoi, a nomadic tribe moving west from the steppes of what is now Armenia. His disposition of his troops at the frontier deterred the invaders from encroaching, and he subsequently wrote a detailed description of that arrangement titled *Ektaxis* ["arrangement of forces"] *Against the Alanoi*. This tract, written in a clipped style that captures the wording of a general's orders to his troops, is of great interest to military historians, as is another technical treatise called *Tactics*, which Arrian composed probably at the end of his term in Cappadocia.

§5. Our only evidence about Arrian's later life comes from a list of archons (chief civic officials) in Athens, which shows that he held one of those largely ceremonial offices in the year 148/9 (archonships began and ended in the summer). By that time Arrian was probably in his sixties, presumably retired from military life and service to Rome. It is possible he wrote his most famous surviving work, the *Anabasis*, during this late phase of his life, but there are no internal clues as to its date; it may have been composed under Trajan, when interest in imperial expansion was much stronger at Rome than under Hadrian.[5a]

§6. Presumably at some point after the *Anabasis* was finished, Arrian wrote another historical chronicle, titled *Events After Alexander*, a richly detailed treatment of the struggles to fill the power vacuum in Alexander's empire during the years 323 to 319. This long work would have been a major contribution to historiography, to judge by a few fragments that have been recovered in modern times,[6a] but it became lost sometime after the ninth century C.E. (when a Byzantine cleric, Photius, read the work and summarized it in his reader's log). His *Indika*, an account of Nearkhos' harrowing voyage through the Arabian Sea from the Indus to the Euphrates under Alexander, was also subsequent to the *Anabasis*, as is clear from a prospective reference to it at 6.28.6.

§7. Remarkably for a military and political leader, Arrian was accounted a major writer by his contemporaries; the essayist and satirist Lucian,[7a] who lived a genera-

R.3a See Philip Stadter's speculation in Stadter, 9.
R.5a A. B. Bosworth's point in "Arrian's Literary Development," 163–172, restated in "Arrian and Rome" (II.257); but Stadter (178–187) believes that the *Anabasis* came later in Arrian's career.
R.6a One whole page of text is currently being recovered from a medieval palimpsest by way of digital imaging technologies; see Boris Dreyer, "The Arrian Parchment in Gothenburg: New Digital Processing Methods and Initial Results," in W. Heckel, L. Tritle, and P. Wheatley (eds.), *Alexander's Empire: Formulation to Decay* (Claremont, CA: Regina Books, 2007), 245–264.
R.7a Lucian, *Life of Alexander* 2.

FIGURE R.1. An inscribed statue base found in Athens and pieced together in the 1960s attests to Arrian's varied and illustrious career. The Greek text appears to read L PHL ARRI-ANON UPATIKON PHILOSOPHON, using common abbreviations to give Arrian's full name as Lucius Flavius Arrianos, though there is a small possibility that the first letter is a Greek alpha, or A, instead of lambda, or L. The two epithets attached to his name indicate he was both a philosopher and a former consul (in Greek, *hupatos*) at Rome. At one time a portrait statue of Arrian stood on this base, a posthumous tribute by the city of Athens to one of its distinguished honorary citizens.

tion later than Arrian, refers to him as a man celebrated for his *paideia*, a Greek word that combines ideas of education and literary sophistication. Among his shorter works were several lost biographies, including one intriguingly focused on a robber chieftain named Tilloboros, and a treatise that survives entitled *Cynegeticus* (*On Hunting*), modeled on a work of the same name by Xenophon. A historical survey of Arrian's home region, Bithynia, entitled *Bythiniaka*, survives, like the *Events After Alexander*, only in small fragments and in a summary by Photius. Like Xenophon, whom he considered his foremost literary model, Arrian seems to have delighted in trying out a variety of literary genres. He even went beyond Xenophon in attempting different styles, composing the *Indika*, for example, in an Ionic Greek dialect rather than in the Attic standard for high Greek literature in his day. He took great pride in the mastery he had achieved as a writer, to judge by the tone of his self-assertion in the second prologue to the *Anabasis* (1.12.5).

§8. The date of Arrian's death is not known, but he is reputed to have had a long life. Perhaps he lived into the reign of Marcus Aurelius, which began in 161 C.E. Sometime after his death the Athenians erected a statue of him as a mark of his distinction, the base of which still survives (see Figure R.1). In the inscription on that base, the Athenians awarded Arrian perhaps the greatest honorary title they could bestow, dubbing him, among other things, a philosopher.

> James Romm
> James H. Ottaway Jr. Professor of Classics
> Bard College
> Annandale-on-Hudson, New York

Bibliography

Bosworth, A. B. "Arrian's Literary Development." *Classical Quarterly*, n.s. 22 (1972): 162–185.
_____. "Arrian and Rome: The Minor Works." In *Aufstieg und Niedergang der römischen Welt* II.34.1. Berlin: Walter de Gruyter, 1993, 226–275.

Stadter, Philip A. *Arrian of Nicomedia*. Chapel Hill: University of North Carolina Press, 1980.
Syme, Ronald. "The Career of Arrian." *Harvard Studies in Classical Philology* 86 (1982): 181–211.

ANCIENT SOURCES

Cited in This Edition of Arrian's *Anabasis Alexandrou*

Aelian (c. 170–235 C.E.): Roman author and teacher of rhetoric, author of *Varia Historia*, a collection of anecdotes.

Aristoboulos (c. 380–301), a Greek who accompanied Alexander's campaign as an engineer or technical expert of some kind. It is not clear what became of him after Alexander's death or what prompted him to write his historical narrative, now lost but regarded by Arrian as one of the two best sources (the other was Ptolemy). Aristoboulos is known to have admired Alexander and to have defended him against criticisms, especially regarding alcohol consumption.

Aristotle (384–322), philosopher, pupil of Plato, teacher of Alexander the Great, and founder of the Lyceum (Lykeion) at Athens c. 335. Much of his work survives, on subjects including logic, natural sciences, politics, and poetics.

Arrian (c. 85–c. 160 C.E.), a Greek from Bithynia and a Roman citizen who rose to high office in both the Greek and Roman political worlds. His literary output was huge and varied, including principally the *Anabasis Alexandrou*, his sole surviving long work and the subject of this volume. He based his account of Alexander on the writings of Ptolemy and Aristoboulos, with anecdotes selected from other sources.

Athenaios (fl. beginning of the third century C.E.), Greek writer from Naukratis, Egypt. His only extant work, *Deipnosophistae* (*Banquet of the Sophists*), a collection of excerpts from some eight hundred ancient authors (many of whose works are now lost) provides information on many aspects of the ancient world.

Diodorus Siculus (first century), Greek author of a universal history, of which large sections survive. His Book 17, concerned almost entirely with Alexander, is broken in places but nearly complete. Diodorus based his account of Alexander largely on the writings of Kleitarchos, and so is considered one of the vulgate sources.

Eratosthenes (c. 276–195), librarian of Alexandria, geographer, scientist, and literary critic. He was known for debunking mythic accounts of distant travels, including those of the Alexander historians.

Eumenes (c. 360–319), a Greek from Kardia, employed by both Philip and Alexander as court secretary, and finally by Alexander as a minor military officer. After Alexander's death he became a major rival for power in the fragmenting empire. He supposedly wrote most of the *Ephemerides*, or *Royal Journals*, perhaps including the portion Arrian supposedly relied on in his account of Alexander's final illness (7.25–26). But there is no certainty about whether this document survived Alexander's death, or if it did, which later authors had access to it.

Euripides (c. 485–406), great Athenian tragedian. Eighteen (possibly nineteen) of his plays survive.

Hekataios, author of geographical and historical accounts of Asia Minor and the East, late sixth century, and a source both used and criticized by Herodotus.

Herodotus (c. 485–425), Greek historian originally from Halicarnassus, Asia Minor. Traveled extensively. Wrote a history of the Persian War of 480–479, which survives today.

Hesiod (flourished c. 700), poet and author of two works that have come down to us: *Works and Days* and *Theogony*.

Homer, poet who the Greeks believed to be the author of the epic poems *Iliad* and *Odyssey*, which are thought to have been composed and compiled in the late eighth or early seventh century.

Hypereides (390–322), Athenian politician and public speaker, a lifelong foe of Macedonian hegemony in Europe. His speeches survive in part.

Isocrates, Athenian speechwriter and pamphleteer of the fourth century. He encouraged Greeks to unite and attack Persia, even under Macedonian leadership.

Justin (third century C.E.?), Roman writer about whom very little is known. He summarized the *Historiae Philippicae* of Pompeius Trogus in a terse epitome that somehow survived when the original work perished. Books 11 and 12 relate the Alexander story. He derived most of his information from Kleitarkhos by way of Trogus.

Kallisthenes (c. 360–328), a Greek from Olynthos, a distant relation and student of Aristotle. Kallisthenes accompanied Alexander's campaign as an officially recognized historian, and produced an encomiastic account of which only a few fragments survive. His decision to speak out against Alexander's adoption of *proskynesis* (4.11) cost him his life, though it is not clear whether he was executed or died in prison.

Khares (fourth century), a Greek from Mytilene who accompanied Alexander's campaign and came eventually to serve as chief butler to the king. He later wrote a memoir of which very little survives except a few fragments that focus on scandals and unseemly behavior at court.

Kleitarkhos, a Greek writer living at Alexandria in the late fourth or early third century. His history of Alexander has completely perished but was the principal source for Diodorus, Pompeius Trogus, and Quintus Curtius. He dramatized the Alexander story with lots of scandal, anecdote and rhetorical declamation, much of it unreliable, but also preserved much primary information not known to other writers. It is not clear at what date he wrote his history, or whether he had himself been part of Alexander's campaign.

Ktesias (late fifth century), Greek who spent many years as physician to the Persian court and wrote a book derived from his experiences and researches there, as well as an account of India called the *Indika*. Only fragments of this work survive.

Lucian (second century C.E.), Greek satirist and traveling lecturer. His surviving dialogues include *How to Write History*.

Megasthenes, a Greek of unknown origin, author of an *Indika* that gave an account of India in the time of Chandragupta (some years after Alexander's death). He visited Chandragupta's court as an ambassador, probably representing Seleukos. The work is lost but substantial fragments survive.

Nearkhos (c. 360–c. 300), a Greek from Crete, a boyhood friend of Alexander who served as the chief admiral of the Indus river fleet. His account of the voyage from India to the Persian Gulf is lost, but Arrian based his *Indika* substantially on it.

Onesikritos (c. 360–c. 290), a Greek who accompanied Alexander's army in India and later wrote a memoir, now lost except for a few fragments. As a philosopher of the Cynic school, Onesikritos had a strong interest in the Brahman ascetics he encountered near Taxila.

Pausanias (c. 150 C.E.), geographer who, in his work *Periegesis of Greece* wrote detailed travel descriptions of topography, monuments, art, history, customs, and more. Archaeological work has revealed that many of his descriptions were accurate.

Photios (c. 810–c. 890 C.E.), Byzantine Greek cleric who became Patriarch of Constantinople. An avid reader and intellectual, Photios compiled summaries of the many works he had read, and these in some cases preserve outlines of ancient texts otherwise lost, including Arrian's *Events After Alexander*.

Pliny the Elder (23–79 C.E.), Roman writer who compiled the encyclopedic *Natural History*, which survives. He died while observing the eruption of Mount Vesuvius in 79 C.E.

Plutarch (46–120 C.E.), prolific writer from Chaeronea, Boeotia, many of whose biographies and essays survive. Plutarch's life of Alexander, one of his fifty *Parallel Lives* designed to show correlations between Greeks and Romans, was based on a variety of primary sources, not all of them identifiable.

Pompeius Trogus (first century), Roman historian who produced a 44-book *Historiae Philippicae* tracing the rise and fall of the Macedonian empire. The work is entirely lost but an outline survives in the work later compiled by Justin. The material on Alexander was almost wholly derived from Kleitarkhos.

Pseudo-Kallisthenes, the name conventionally given to the author who first published the *Alexander Romance* under the name Kallisthenes. It is not known who this author was but presumably he lived in Egypt in the third century. He relied on oral legends and fables about Alexander as well as some written sources, including a collection of fictionalized letters. Much of the material in surviving versions of the *Romance* were added later by other anonymous authors.

Ptolemy (c. 365–283), boyhood friend of Alexander who rose to become one of the chief generals of the Asian campaign. After Alexander's death Ptolemy controlled Egypt, at first as a satrap of the Macedonian empire but later, after 306, as a self-crowned king. It is not known at what point in his long reign he composed his historical narrative of Alexander, a work that has entirely perished but served as the principal source for Arrian's *Anabasis Alexandrou*.

Quintus Curtius (first century C.E.), Roman statesman and author who served in the high office of consul, possibly in 43 C.E. His *Historia Alexandri Magni* in ten books survives largely intact, though the first two books are missing and there are gaps in the others. His account of Alexander was largely based on that of Kleitarkhos, though he amplifies speeches and political machinations that resonated most strongly with his Roman readers. Sometimes he is known by his full name, Quintus Curtius Rufus.

Strabo (64 or 63 B.C.E.–c. 21 C.E.), Greek geographer, historian, and traveler. His *Geography* is a series of sketches, based on his travels and the works of predecessors, describing the known world of his day. Book 15, concerning India, contains much information from Onesikritos and other Alexander veterans.

Thucydides (c. 460–390s), Athenian historian of and general in the Peloponnesian War.

Xenophon (c. 430–late 350s), Greek historian, author of several surviving works, including the *Anabasis,* an account of Cyrus the Younger's expedition against his brother Artaxerxes, in which Xenophon participated.

BIBLIOGRAPHY

for the General Reader

BACKGROUND WORKS AND GENERAL HISTORIES

Adcock, Frank. *The Greek and Macedonian Art of War.* Berkeley and Los Angeles: University of California Press, 1957.

Billows, R. *Kings and Colonists: Aspects of Macedonian Imperialism.* Leiden: Brill, 1995.

Borza, Eugene N. *In the Shadow of Olympus: The Emergence of Macedon.* Princeton: Princeton University Press, 1990.

Briant, Pierre. *From Cyrus to Alexander: A History of the Persian Empire.* Translated by Peter Daniels. Winona Lake, Indiana: Eisenbrauns, 2002.

The Cambridge Ancient History, 2nd ed. Vol. 6, *The Fourth Century* B.C. Cambridge: Cambridge University Press, 1994.

Errington, R. Malcolm. *A History of Macedonia.* Translated by Catherine Errington. Berkeley and Los Angeles: University of California Press, 1990.

Hammond, N. G. L. *The Macedonian State: Origins, Institutions, and History.* Oxford: Clarendon Press, 1989.

———— and F. W. Walbank. *A History of Macedonia.* Vol. 3, 336–167 B.C. Oxford: Clarendon Press, 1988.

ALEXANDER BIOGRAPHIES AND STUDIES

Bosworth, A. B. *Conquest and Empire: The Reign of Alexander the Great.* Cambridge: Cambridge University Press, 1988.

Carney, Elizabeth. *Olympias: Mother of Alexander the Great.* New York and London: Routledge, 2006.

Cartledge, Paul. *Alexander the Great: The Hunt for a New Past.* Woodstock, NY: Overlook Press, 2004.

Cawkwell, G. L. *Philip of Macedon.* London and Boston: Faber and Faber, 1978.

Green, Peter. *Alexander of Macedon, 356–323 B.C.: A Historical Biography.* Berkeley and Los Angeles: University of California Press, 1991.

Hammond, N. G. L. *Alexander the Great: King, Commander, and Statesman.* Park Ridge, NJ: Noyes Press, 1980.

Lane Fox, Robin. *Alexander the Great.* London: Allen Lane in association with Longman, 1974.

Mossé, Claude. *Alexander: Destiny and Myth.* Translated by Janet Lloyd. Baltimore, MD: Johns Hopkins University Press, 2004.

Stoneman, Richard. *Alexander the Great.* New York and London: Routledge, 2004.

Tarn, W. W. *Alexander the Great.* 2 vols. Cambridge: Cambridge University Press, 1948.

Wilcken, Ulrich. *Alexander the Great.* Translated by G. C. Richards, with Introduction by Eugene N. Borza. New York: Norton, 1967.

———— and Eugene N. Borza. *Alexander the Great.* New York: Norton, 1967.

Worthington, Ian. *Alexander the Great: Man and God.* Harlow, England: Pearson Longman, 2004.

————. *Philip II of Macedonia.* New Haven: Yale University Press, 2008.

COMMENTARIES ON ARRIAN AND RELATED AUTHORS

Bosworth, A. B. *A Historical Commentary on Arrian's History of Alexander*. Oxford: Oxford University Press. Vol. 1, 1980. Vol. 2, 1995. Vol. 3, forthcoming.

Brunt, P. A. *Arrian: History of Alexander and Indica*. Loeb Classical Library. Cambridge, MA: Harvard University Press. Vol. 1, 1976. Vol. 2, 1983.

Hamilton, J. R. *Plutarch: Alexander; A Commentary*. Oxford: Clarendon Press, 1969.

Heckel, W. *Justin: Epitome of the Philippic History of Pompeius Trogus*. 1, *Books 11–12: Alexander the Great*. Translated (and appendices) by J. C. Yardley. Oxford: Clarendon Press, 1997.

Sisti, Francesco, ed. *Arriano: Anabasi di Alessandro*, Vol. 1. Milan: Fondazione Lorenzo Valla, 2001.

——— and A. Zambrini, eds. *Arriano: Anabasi di Alessandro*, Vol. 2. Milan: Fondazione Lorenzo Valla, 2004.

STUDIES ON SPECIAL TOPICS

Arnold-Biucchi, C. *Alexander's Coins and Alexander's Image*. Cambridge, MA: Harvard University Art Museums, 2006.

Baynham, Elizabeth. *Alexander the Great: The Unique History of Quintus Curtius*. Ann Arbor: University of Michigan Press, 1998.

Bosworth, A. B. *From Arrian to Alexander: Studies in Historical Interpretation*. Oxford: Clarendon Press, 1988.

———. *Alexander and the East*. Oxford: Oxford University Press, 1996.

Engels, Donald. *Alexander the Great and the Logistics of the Macedonian Army*. Berkeley: University of California Press, 1978.

Fuller, J. F. C. *The Generalship of Alexander the Great*. New Brunswick, NJ: Rutgers University Press, 1960.

Heckel, Waldemar. *The Marshals of Alexander's Empire*. London: Routledge, 1992.

Holt, Frank Lee. *Alexander the Great and the Mystery of the Elephant Medallions*. Berkeley: University of California Press, 2003.

———. *Into the Land of Bones: Alexander the Great in Afghanistan*. Berkeley: University of California Press, 2005.

Romm, James. *Ghost on the Throne: The Death of Alexander the Great and the War for Crown and Empire*. New York: Alfred A. Knopf, forthcoming (2011).

Stadter, Philip A. *Arrian of Nicomedia*. Chapel Hill: University of North Carolina Press, 1980.

Stewart, A. *Faces of Power: Alexander's Images and Hellenistic Politics*. Berkeley; Los Angeles; Oxford: University of California Press, 1993.

ANTHOLOGIES AND REFERENCE WORKS

Badian, E., ed. *Alexandre Le Grand: Image et Réalité*. Geneva: Fondation Hardt, 1976.

Bosworth, A. B., and Elizabeth Baynham, eds. *Alexander the Great in Fact and Fiction*. Oxford: Oxford University Press, 2000.

Griffith, G. T., ed. *Alexander the Great: The Main Problems*. Cambridge: Heffer, New York: Barnes & Noble, 1966.

Heckel, Waldemar. *Who's Who in the Age of Alexander the Great*. Malden, MA, Oxford: Blackwell Publishing, 2006.

——— and Lawrence A. Tritle, eds. *Alexander the Great: A New History*. Malden, MA: Wiley-Blackwell, 2009.

——— and J. C. Yardley, eds. *Alexander the Great: Historical Sources in Translation*. Oxford: Blackwell, 2003.

Roisman, J., ed. *Brill's Companion to Alexander the Great*. Leiden: Brill, 2003.

Talbert, Richard J., ed. *Barrington Atlas of the Greek and Roman World*. Princeton: Princeton University Press, 2000.

Figure Credits

Frontispiece, 6.12 — The Art Archive/Archaeological Museum Salonica/Gianni Dagli Orti

Pref. 1, 3.3, 5.18 (left) — The Museum of Fine Arts, Boston

1.4, 1.11 1.15, 2.14, 4.13 — 17th Ephorate of Antiquities © Hellenic Ministry of Culture and Tourism, Archaeological Receipts Fund

1.13 — Robert Harding World Imagery

1.16 — © Jastrow/Wikimedia Commons

1.18 — Bildarchiv Preussischer Kulturbesitz/Art Resource, NY

1.20 — Valery Shanin, 2010, used under license from Shutterstock.com

1.26 — Tom Brosnahan

2.4 — New York State Archives Digital Collection

2.7 — 16th Ephorate of Antiquities © Hellenic Ministry of Culture and Tourism, Archaeological Receipts Fund

2.21 — The Trireme Trust USA, photo: Paul Lipke

2.23 — A. Poidebard, *Un Grand Port Disparu* (Paris: Librairie Orientaliste, Paul Geuthner, 1939)

2.27, 3.14 — akg Images/Peter Connolly

3.5, 5.7, 3.18b — The Art Archive/Gianni Dagli Orti

3.12 — The Art Archive/Musée Archéologique Naples/Alfredo Dagli Orti

3.13 — DeA Picture Library/Art Resource, NY

3.15, 5.11, 7.12, 7.28 — © Trustees of The British Museum

3.18a — The Art Archive/Alfredo Dagli Orti

3.19 — Oriental Institute, University of Chicago

3.28 — top: V. Waldron; bottom: © The Trustees of The British Museum/Art Resource, NY

4.10 (top) — Oriental Institute, University of Chicago

4.10 (bottom), 5.8, 7.3, C.1, G.1 — Wikimedia Commons, GNU Free Documentation License

4.22, 4.28, 6.23 — Michael Wood

4.29 — Hulton Archive/Getty Images

4.30 — Time & Life Pictures/Getty Images

5.5 — Bunbury, E. H., *A History of Ancient Geography Among the Greeks and Romans from the Earliest Ages Till the Fall of the Roman Empire* (London: John Murray, 1883).

5.6 — Pierre-Jean Durieu, 2010, used under license from Shutterstock.com

5.18 (center, right), I.1, J.1 — Courtesy of Frank L. Holt

5.26 — M. Tsibidou-Avloniti, *The Macedonian Tombs at Phoinikas and Ayios Athanasios in the Area of Thessaloniki*, Athens 2005, Pl. 31, 16th Ephorate of Antiquities © Hellenic Ministry of Culture and Tourism, Archaeological Receipts Fund

6.28 — C. Vita-Finzi

7.16 — © Curt-Engelhorn-Stiftung für die Reiss-Engelhorn-Museen/FaberCourtial (top); Bildarchiv Preussischer Kulturbesitz/Art Resource, NY (bottom)

Epi.1 — Doreio, Creative Commons Attribution-Share Alike 2.0 Generic License, 2008

L.1, L.2 — Courtesy of Richard Stoneman

D.1 — Kinch, K. F. 1920. "Le tombeau de Niausta. Tombeau Macedonien." *Mémoires de l'Académie Royale des Sciences et des Lettres de Danemark*, Copenhague, 7me Serie Section des Lettres. Vol. IV. No. 3.: 285–288.

D.2 — John Gibson Warry, *Warfare in the Classical World: An Illustrated Encyclopedia of Weapons, Warriors, and Warfare in the Ancient Civilizations of Greece and Rome*. New York: St. Martin's Press, 1981.

K.1 — The Art Archive/Archaeological Museum Istanbul/Gianni Dagli Orti

K.2 — Murat Besler, used under license from Shutterstock.com

Q.1 — HIP/Art Resource, NY

R.1 — Courtesy of Eugene N. Borza

INDEX

In cases where Arrian does not distinguish clearly between different people with the same name, the index of names compiled by Francesco Sisti and Andrea Zambrini has been used as a guide (*Arriano: Anabasi di Alessandro*, Vol. 2 [Milan: Fondazione Lorenzo Valla, 2004], 673–699).

Abastanes, subdued by Alexander on voyage to Indus River, 6.15.1

Abdera, on his route to Asia, Alexander passes through, 1.11.4

Abii, Alexander receives envoys from, 4.1.1–2

Abisares, reportedly sends forces to Ora, 4.27.7; Indians flee to, 4.30.7; sends envoys to Alexander in Taxila, 5.8.3; sends envoys to Alexander east of Hydaspes River, ordered to present himself to Alexander, 5.20.5, 5.20.6; unable to subdue autonomous Indians in Sangala region, 5.22.2; sends representatives to Alexander at Akesinos River, is appointed satrap of his own country, 5.29.4–5

Aboulites, appointed satrap of Susiana, 3.16.9; executed by Alexander for abuses of power in Susa, 7.4.1

Abreas, follows Alexander in scaling of wall at Mallian city, 6.9.3; jumps inside Mallian wall, struck in face by arrow, 6.10.1, 6.11.7

Achaean harbor, Alexander performs rituals on arrival at, 1.11.6–7

Achilles (mythic hero), Alexander places wreath on tomb of, 1.12.1; Homer's preservation of fame of, 1.12.1–2; Alexander's emulation of, 7.14.4; and Patroklos, 7.16.8

Achilles (Athenian ambassador), sent to Alexander in Tyre, 3.6.2

acropolis, Athenian, Alexander sends Persian armor as dedicatory offering to Athena on, 1.16.7; statues recovered from Susa stand near, 3.16.8

Ada, installed as satrap of Caria after surrendering Alinda to Alexander and making him her adopted son, 1.23.7–8

Adaios, defenders at Triple Gate of Halicarnassus defeated by battalions of Timandros and, 1.22.4; perishes at Halicarnassus, 1.22.7

Admetos, serves on ship sent to lay gangway across breach in Tyrian wall, 2.23.2, 2.23.4; death of, 2.23.5, 2.24.4

Adrestae, Alexander comes to terms in Pimprama with, 5.22.3–4

Aegean Sea, as boundary of Asia, 5.6.2; island of Ikaros in, 7.20.5

Aegyptus River, as ancient name for Nile River, 5.6.5; as Homer's term for Nile River, 6.1.3; *see also* **Nile River**

Aeolis, Alexander establishes democracy in, 1.18.1; Darius' loss of, 3.22.3; Smyrna as city in, 5.6.4; Alexander reminds Macedonians at Opis of conquest of, 7.9.7

Aeschylus, appointed overseer of Companions in Egypt, 3.5.3

Aetolians, Alexander fears joining of Theban revolt by, 1.7.4; Alexander's forgiveness for revolt, 1.10.2

Africa, *see* **Libya**

Agamemnon, in Trojan War, 1.11.5

Agathon (son of Tyrimmas), commands Thracians at the Granicus, 1.14.3; in command of Odrysian cavalry at Gaugamela, 3.12.4

agema, infantry, in Mount Haemus battle against the Thracians, 1.1.11; kept outside the palisade in Thebes, 1.8.3; archers at Thebes flee back to, 1.8.4; arrayed for battle at Issus, 2.8.3; in Macedonian phalanx at Gaugamela, 3.11.9; accompanies Alexander on visit to Dionysian sites on Mount Meros, 5.2.5; accompanies Alexander on voyage from Susa to Persian Sea, 7.7.1

agema, cavalry, Alexander advances through western India with cavalry, 4.24.1; Companion, accompanies Alexander on crossing of Hydaspes River, 5.12.2; arrayed for battle after crossing Hydaspes River, 5.13.4; posted on Alexander's right wing at Sangala, 5.22.6; under Alexander's command for voyage to Great Sea, 6.2.2; accompanies Alexander on well-digging expedition and attack on Oreitae, 6.21.3; accompanies Alexander on march from Oreitae territory to Gedrosia, 6.22.1; Macedonians upset at Alexander's inclusion of foreigners in, 7.6.4–5

agema, royal, arrayed for battle after crossing Hydaspes River, 5.13.4; Macedonians upset by inclusion of Persians in, 7.11.3, 7.29.4; *see also* **bodyguard(s)**

Agesilaos, receives money and ships obtained from Persians by Agis, 2.13.6

Agis (Spartan king), requests money and military support from Persians at Siphnos, joins Autophradates at Halicarnassus, 2.13.4–6

Agis (of Argos), flatterer of Alexander, 4.9.9

Agrianians, in Mount Haemus battle against the Thracians, 1.1.11; Alexander receives support from, 1.5.1–2; Autariatae attacked by, 1.5.3–4; in rescue of Philotas, 1.5.10; occupy hill near Pelion, 1.6.6; cross the Eordaikos, 1.6.7; in night raid on the poorly defended camp of the Taulantians and Illyrians, 1.6.9–11; sent inside the Theban palisade, 1.8.3; stationed alongside Alexander on the right wing at the Granicus River, 1.14.1; start for Miletus with

Agrianians *(cont'd)*
Alexander, 1.18.3; posted in front of the right wing in Sagalassos, 1.28.4; stand their ground as the Macedonian phalanx approaches Sagalassos, 1.28.5–6;

advance with Alexander to Cilician Gates, 2.4.3; Alexander marches against Cilicians with, 2.5.6; praised by Alexander for their battleworthiness, 2.7.5; deployed for battle at Issus, 2.9.2, 2.9.4; accompany Alexander from Tyre to Sidon, 2.19.6; accompany Alexander to Arabia, 2.20.4;

accompany Alexander from Memphis to Alexandria, 3.1.4–5; posted in front line and reserve at Gaugamela, 3.12.2, 3.12.3; attack Persian chariots at Gaugamela, 3.13.5; accompany Alexander to Persian Gates, 3.18.2; accompany Alexander on alternate route to Persian Gates, 3.18.5; accompany Alexander toward Parthia in pursuit of Darius, 3.20.1–2; Attalos as commander of, 3.21.8; in skirmish in Tapourian Mountains, 3.23.5; advance against Mardians with Alexander, 3.24.1; accompany Alexander in suppression of Areian revolt, 3.25.6; dispatched with Ptolemy to help Spitamenes and Dataphernes seize Bessos, 3.29.7;

enter Cyropolis through breach in wall, 4.3.2–3; led by Alexander against Scythians at Tanais River, 4.4.6; accompany Alexander in pursuit of Spitamenes, 4.6.3–5; accompany Alexander through western India, 4.23.1, 4.24.1; in Ptolemy's division of army in western India, 4.24.10; led by Alexander through Assakanian territory, 4.25.6; charge Indians at Massaka, 4.26.3–4; prepare for assault on Aornos Rock, 4.28.8; under Ptolemy's command at Aornos Rock, 4.29.1–3; sent with Nearkhos to pursue Assakanians, 4.30.6;

accompany Alexander on crossing of Hydaspes River, 5.12.2; arrayed for battle after crossing Hydaspes River, 5.13.4; accompany Alexander on advance against Indians east of Hydaspes River, 5.20.3; posted on Alexander's right wing at Sangala, 5.22.6; posted with Ptolemy son of Lagos to prevent Indians' second escape attempt from Sangala, 5.23.7;

under Alexander's command for voyage to Great Sea, 6.2.2; accompany Alexander in march against Malloi, 6.6.1; sent to second Mallian city with Perdikkas, 6.6.4; meet Alexander at Hydraotes River, 6.8.7; accompany Alexander in attack on Oxikanos' territory, 6.16.1; in Peithon's force for march to Patala, 6.17.4; accompany Alexander on march from Oreitae territory to Gedrosia, 6.22.1; left among Oroi with Leonnatos to assist Apollophanes, 6.22.1

Aiakid clan, Neoptolemos as member of, 2.27.6

Aiakos, as kin to Alexander, 4.11.6; as descendant of Zeus, 7.29.3

Aigeai, Alexander celebrates Olympic Games at, 1.11.1

Aigobares, included in Alexander's cavalry *agema*, 7.6.5

Aigospotamoi, Athens' defeat at, 1.9.3

Akesinos River, size of, 5.4.2, 5.20.8, 5.20.10, 5.21.4; southward flow of, 5.5.5; Alexander makes treacherous crossing of, 5.20.8–10, 5.21.6; Alexander leaves to pursue rebel Poros from, 5.21.1; at Hyphasis River, Alexander recalls success at, 5.25.5; Alexander makes return journey to, prepares for voyage to Great Sea from, 5.29.2–5;

Alexander mistakes connection between Nile River and, 6.1.2, 6.1.5; invoked by Alexander at start of voyage to Great Sea, 6.3.1; Philip sent ahead from Hydaspes River to, 6.4.1; Alexander reaches juncture of Hydaspes River and, 6.4.4–5; Macedonian fleet brought to anchor for repairs at, 6.5.4; Alexander divides his army, plans to reunite it at juncture of Hydraotes River and, 6.5.5–7; Alexander marches against Malloi from, 6.6.1–2; Macedonian army camped at juncture of Hydraotes River and, 6.13.1; Alexander sails from Hydraotes River to Indus River via, 6.14.4; route to Indus River of, 6.14.5; Alexander waits for Perdikkas, makes administrative and military arrangements at juncture of Indus River and, 6.15.1–2; as border of Philip's and Peithon's satrapies, 6.15.2, 6.15.4;

Alexander thought unable to return from, 7.4.2; Alexander reminds Macedonians at Opis of his crossing of, 7.10.6

Akouphis, entreats Alexander to spare Nysa out of respect for Dionysos, 5.1.3–6; convinces Alexander not to take hostages from Nysa, 5.2.2–4

Albanoi, in Darius' force at Gaugamela, 3.8.4, 3.11.4, 3.13.1

Aleion Plain, Philotas leads Alexander's cavalry across, 2.5.8

Alexander, succession to throne of, 1.1.1; visits Peloponnese to ask Greeks for leadership of Persian campaign, 1.1.1–3; returns to Macedonia, 1.1.3, 1.11.1–2; marches against the Triballoi, 1.1.4, 1.2.6–7, 1.3.1–6; launches campaign against Thrace, but is checked by free Thracians occupying Mount Haemus, 1.1.4–7; devises strategy to counter free Thracians, 1.1.8–10; orders the archers to shoot at the Thracians and forms left wing with himself in command, 1.1.11–12; Danube reached by, 1.2.1–3; crosses the Danube, 1.2.5–6, 1.4.1, 1.4.2, 1.4.5; plunder sent to coastal cities by, 1.3.1; reaches Lyginus, 1.3.1; advances against Getae, and seizes their city, 1.4.1–5; envoys from the Danube tribes, Syrmos, and the Celts pay visits to, 1.4.6–8; approaches Agrianians and Paionians, 1.5.1; Langaros as well disposed toward, 1.5.2; Langaros attacks Autariatae and is rewarded by, 1.5.3–4; advances on Pelion, 1.5.5; besieges Pelion, but is stopped by arrival of Taulantian army, 1.5.7–9; Philotas rescued by, 1.5.10–11; maneuvered into a difficult position by the forces of Kleitos and Glaukias, 1.5.11–12; seeks a way out of position between two enemy armies at Pelion, and succeeds in driving off Taulantians, 1.6.1–4; seizes the high ground, crosses the Eordaikos, 1.6.5–8; in night raid on the poorly defended camp of the Taulantians and Illyrians, 1.6.9–11; Thebans incite revolt against, 1.7.1–3; rumors about death in Illyria of, 1.7.2–3, 1.7.6; moves swiftly to counter Theban revolt, 1.7.4–6; arrives in Thebes, but avoids full-scale attack to allow an opportunity for negotiations, 1.7.7–11; drawn into attacking Thebes by his own officers, 1.8.1–4; Thebans routed by, 1.8.5; makes final dispositions for Thebes, saves house of poet Pindar, 1.9.9–10; Greek states that supported Theban revolt seek to regain favor of, 1.10.1–3, 1.10.6; demands surrender of nine anti-Macedonian politicians in Athens but later relents, 1.10.4–6; Kharidemos ordered into exile by, 1.10.6; omen regarding, 1.11.2; marches to the Hellespont, 1.11.3–5; crosses the Hellespont, 1.11.6–8, 1.12.9, 1.13.6; reaches Troy, 1.11.7–8, 1.12.1; continues Asian march, receives

for completing difficult ascent up Sogdian Rock, 4.18.5, 4.18.7; Sogdian Rock ascended by climbers from, 4.19.1–4; makes preparations to assault Rock of Khorienes, 4.21.3–6; Khorienes supplies provisions to, 4.21.10; advances to India from Bactra, 4.22.3; Alexander sends Hephaistion and Perdikkas to subdue Peukelaotis with force from, 4.22.7–8; attacks western Indian cities, 4.23.4–5; divided by Alexander in preparation for attack on western Indian force, 4.24.9–10; defeats large rebel force in western India, 4.25.1–4; Krateros rejoins Alexander in Assakanian territory with his forces from, 4.25.5; makes initial attack on Indians at Massaka, 4.26.1–4; besieges Massaka, attacked by defenders, 4.26.5–7, 4.27.1; Indian mercenaries at Massaka slaughtered after breaking agreement to join, 4.27.3–4; sends forces to additional western Indian cities following capture of Massaka, 4.27.5–6; in battle against Bazirans, 4.27.7–8; secures western Indian cities, prepares for siege of Aornos Rock, 4.28.4–8; suffers setback in initial assault on Aornos Rock, 4.29.1–3; reunited at Ptolemy's position at Aornos Rock, 4.29.4–6; builds mound from which to attack Aornos Rock, 4.29.7, 4.30.1–2; advances to Indus River, captures elephants along the way, 4.30.7–9;

Alexander sees chance to rival Dionysos' exploits as motivation for, 5.2.1; crosses Indus River, 5.4.3; advances to Hydaspes River from Taxila, 5.8.5; performs maneuvers intended to confuse Poros at Hydaspes River, 5.9.1–3; prepares for secret crossing of Hydaspes River, 5.11.1–2; arrayed for battle, led forward by Alexander at Hydaspes River, 5.13.4, 5.14.1–2; differing accounts of crossing of Hydaspes River by, 5.14.3–6; Poros prepares for battle at Hydaspes River against, 5.15.4–7; drives Poros' less-experienced army back a second time, attacks Poros' men and elephants at Hydaspes River, 5.17.4–6; surrounds Poros' force at Hydaspes River, cuts them to pieces, 5.17.7, 5.18.1; losses at Hydaspes River in, 5.18.3; Krateros left to fortify Alexander's cities at Hydaspes River with portion of, 5.20.2; Philip and Tyriespis sent to subdue revolt in Assakania with force from, 5.20.7; makes treacherous crossing of Akesinos River, 5.20.8–9; Koinos left at Akesinos River to oversee crossing of supplies for, 5.21.1; proceeds with Alexander to Sangala to subdue Indian revolt, 5.21.1–4; Hephaistion sent to subdue land of rebel Poros with force from, 5.21.5; arrayed for battle at Sangala, 5.22.5–7; undermines Sangala's wall, takes city by storm, 5.24.4–5; captures and kills Indians attempting to flee rebel cities after fall of Sangala, 5.24.7; advances from Sangala to Hyphasis River, 5.24.8; dissents against Alexander's plans to advance further into India, 5.25.2; Koinos responds to Alexander's address at Hyphasis River on behalf of, 5.27.1–9; Koinos reminds Alexander of losses and hardships suffered during Alexander's campaigns by, 5.27.4–6; Koinos urges Alexander to return home to get fresh recruits for, 5.27.8; Koinos urges Alexander to show restraint for the benefit of, 5.27.9; Alexander says he will not force unwilling men to continue campaigning with him, continues to sense reluctance from, 5.28.2–4; rejoices at news of Alexander's decision to turn back from Hyphasis River, 5.29.1; ships prepared for voyage to Great Sea of, 6.1.1, 6.1.6;

divided by Alexander prior to start of voyage to Great Sea, 6.2.2–3; embarks on voyage to Great Sea, 6.3.1; continues along Hydaspes River, 6.4.1; caught in violent currents at juncture of Hydaspes and Akesinos rivers, 6.4.5, 6.5.1–3; divided again at Akesinos River, to be reunited at juncture of Akesinos and Hydraotes rivers, 6.5.5–7; marches across desert to Malloi city, 6.6.1–3; attacks Mallian cities, 6.6.4–6; attacks Brahman city, 6.7.4–6; in continued pursuit of Malloi, 6.8.1–3; assaults wall at Mallian city, 6.9.1–3; attempts to aid Alexander under attack in Malloi city, breaks through city gate, 6.10.3–4; distressed by reports of Alexander's wounding in Malloi city, 6.12.1–3; rejoices when Alexander appears in person at Hydraotes River following his wounding in Malloi city, 6.13.1–3; Alexander criticized by his friends for putting himself in danger in front of, 6.13.4; led along left bank of Indus River by Krateros, 6.15.4, 6.15.5; receives plunder from Oxikanos' territory, 6.16.2; marches to Sambos' territory, captures Brahman city, 6.16.3–5; divided for marches to Carmania and Patala, and for shipboard voyage to Patala, 6.17.3–4; returns fugitives to Patala, 6.17.6; attacked by local Indians while digging wells in desert near Patala, 6.18.1; Leonnatos ordered to march down Indus River alongside fleet with portion of, 6.18.3; occupies Cilluta near Great Sea, 6.19.3; Peithon arrives in Patala with his division of, 6.20.1; Leonnatos left at lake in Indus River with troops from, 6.20.3; makes preparations for voyage of fleet along Great Sea coast, 6.20.5; marches from Patala to continue to create water supplies for fleet along coast, crosses Arabis River to attack Oreitae, 6.21.3–5; advances to Gedrosia with Alexander, 6.22.3; encounters unusual plants in Gedrosian desert, 6.22.4–5; continues difficult march through Gedrosia in search of water supplies, 6.23.1–3; consumes supplies meant for fleet until Alexander properly provisions them in Gedrosia, 6.23.4–6; march through Gedrosian desert as most difficult undertaking in Asia of, 6.24.1; suffers greatly from heat and lack of water in march across Gedrosian desert, 6.24.4–6, 6.25.3; kills and eats its own pack animals, leaves behind the sick and exhausted in march through Gedrosian desert, 6.25.1–3; caught up in sudden flood of nearly dry stream in Gedrosian desert, 6.25.4–5; encounters further difficulties in march through Gedrosian desert when it comes across abundant supplies of water, 6.25.6; Alexander refuses water brought to him in Gedrosian desert in solidarity with, 6.26.1–3; becomes lost in Gedrosian desert, led by Alexander to the sea, 6.26.4–5; rested in capital of Gedrosia, 6.27.1; joined by additional forces in Carmania, executes those accused of despoiling shrines in Alexander's territories, 6.27.3–6; in Carmania, Alexander celebrates escape from Gedrosian desert of, 6.28.3; Hephaistion sent along coast from Carmania to Persia with largest division of, 6.28.7;

Indian sages unimpressed by, 7.1.5–6; at Kalanos' funeral pyre, 7.3.5, 7.3.6; Alexander pays debts of soldiers in, 7.5.1–3; distressed at Alexander's assimilation of Persians and adoption of Persian ways, 7.6.1–5, 7.8.2–3, 7.11.3; led from Susa to Persian Gulf by Hephaistion, 7.7.1; Alexander sails to camp on Tigris River of, 7.7.6; Alexander announces honorable discharges from, is

7.19.6; disapproves of Alexander's letter to Kleomenes, 7.23.6–8; assesses Alexander's character, 7.28.1–3, 7.29.1–4, 7.30.1; discusses renown of Alexander, 7.30.1–3

arrow(s), fired at Alexander's men outside Halicarnassus, 1.20.4;

abundance of Persian, 2.6.6; Macedonians use screens to protect men working on siege engines from, 2.18.6; fired by Tyrians at burning Macedonian towers to prevent Macedonians from approaching, 2.19.4; fired by Tyrians at Macedonian war engines, 2.21.3;

Alexander captures Darius', 3.15.5; Amyntas (son of Andromenes) killed by, 3.27.3; Alexander wounded near Tanais River by, 3.30.11;

wounds Krateros at Cyropolis, 4.3.3; fired by Asian Scythians into Tanais River to provoke Alexander, 4.4.2; Spitamenes assaults Macedonians in Sogdiana with, 4.4.4, 4.5.6, 4.5.9; fired at attacking Macedonians at Tanais River by Scythians, 4.4.6; fired at Rock of Khorienes by Macedonians, 4.21.6; Alexander wounded in western India by, 4.23.3; fired at Macedonians by Indians at Massaka, 4.26.3, 4.26.7; Alexander wounded at Massaka by, 4.26.4; mound at Aornos Rock to enable use of, 4.29.7;

fired at defenders of Brahman city by Macedonians, 6.7.4; strike Abreas and Alexander in Malloi city, 6.10.1, 6.11.7; removed from Alexander in Malloi city, 6.11.1–2; *see also* **archers**

Arsakes (Persian official), appointed satrap of Areia, 3.25.7; replaced as satrap of Areia, 3.29.5; brought to Alexander in Zariaspa, 4.7.1

Arsakes (governor in India), visits Alexander at Akesinos River, given appointment by him, 5.29.4, 5.29.5

Arsames (Persian officer), at Persian commanders' council to discuss how to meet Alexander's advance, 1.12.8–10; forced to abandon Tarsus without plundering it, 2.4.5–6; killed at Issus, 2.11.8

Arsames (son of Artabazos), surrenders to Alexander in Zadrakarta, 3.23.7

Arses, Darius accuses Philip II of unjustly injuring, 2.14.2; Darius usurps throne of, 2.14.5

Arsimas, sent as envoy from Darius, 2.14.3

Arsites, rejects scorched earth policy at Persian commanders' council, 1.12.8–10; kills himself after being blamed for defeat at Granicus, 1.16.3; Kalas appointed satrap of former territory of, 1.17.1

Artabazos, refuses to participate in coup against Darius, 3.21.4; surrenders to Alexander in Zadrakarta, 3.23.7; sent to escort surrendered Greek mercenaries to Alexander, 3.23.9; sent by Alexander to suppress second Areian revolt, 3.28.2; appointed satrap of the Bactrians, 3.29.1, 4.15.5; Alexander commends Pharasmanes to, 4.15.5; assigned division of army with Koinos in Sogdiana, 4.16.2; sent with Koinos to pursue Spitamenes in Scythia, 4.16.3; request to be relieved as satrap of Bactria, 4.17.3; Perdikkas and Eumenes marry daughters of, 7.4.6

Artacama, Perdikkas marries, 7.4.6

Artakoana, Satibarzanes musters Areians in, 3.25.5; Alexander reaches, 3.25.6

Artaxerxes, Bessos calling himself, 3.25.3

Artaxerxes (II), King, expedition of Cyrus' Ten Thousand against, 1.12.3, 2.7.9, 4.11.9

Artaxerxes (III), King, Darius recalls alliance between Philip II and, 2.14.2; daughter of wed by Alexander, 7.4.4; *see also* **Okhos**

Artemis, despoiling of Ephesus temple of, 1.17.11; Alexander's Ephesus sacrifice to, 1.18.2; island in Persian Gulf dedicated to, 7.20.3–4

Artemis of Kelkes, Alexander sends Athenians foundation of statue of, 7.19.2

Artiboles (son of Mazaios), included in Alexander's cavalry *agema*, 7.6.4

artillery, Macedonians drive Gazan defenders back with, 2.27.4

Artonis, Eumenes marries, 7.4.6

arts competition(s), held by Alexander in Memphis, 3.1.4, 3.5.2; held by Alexander in Tyre, 3.6.1; held by Alexander in Ecbatana, 7.14.1; planned by Alexander in honor of Hephaistion, 7.14.10

Asandros (son of Philotas), appointed ruler of Lydia and the rest of Spithridates' domain, 1.17.7; and Ptolemy defeat Orontobates in great battle, 2.5.7; joins Alexander in Zariaspa, 4.7.2

Asia, Protesilaos' crossing into, 1.11.5; Alexander disembarks, builds altar in, 1.11.7; as home of those plundered by Alexander, 1.16.7; Alexander's infantry in control of, 1.20.1;

prophecy of Gordian knot to predict ruler of, 2.3.6; transference of power in, 2.6.7; Alexander explains inferiority of troops from, 2.7.5; Alexander sees victory over Darius as key to Macedonian control of, 2.7.6; Alexander sees war with Darius as lawful struggle for sovereignty of, 2.12.5; Darius explains his actions against Macedonians as defense of, 2.14.2; Alexander explains his desire to avenge Macedonia by attacking Persians in, 2.14.4; Alexander asserts his supremacy over, 2.14.8–9;

Alexander makes administrative arrangements in, 3.6.4, 3.6.7–8; Darius' force at Gaugamela drawn from all across, 3.8.3–6; Alexander sees battle at Gaugamela as decisive for sovereignty of, 3.9.6; Parmenion concerned for Alexander's reputation in, 3.18.11; Bessos claiming to be king of, 3.25.3; Caucasus as one of largest mountain ranges in, 3.28.5; rivers in, 3.29.2, 4.4.6, 5.4.1, 5.4.2, 5.5.4–5, 5.6.4, 5.6.7–8, 7.16.3–4; Tanais River in Scythia considered by some to be boundary between Europe and, 3.30.8–9; Libya separated by Nile River from, 3.30.9;

Scythian tribes in, 4.1.1; Alexander concerned for his reputation in, 4.4.3; Alexander's intentions in, 4.7.5; Kallisthenes reminds Alexander of his original intent to subjugate, 4.11.7; Alexander believes submission of India will lead to control over, 4.15.6; Alexander makes administrative changes in, 4.18.1–3; Darius' wife as most beautiful woman in, 4.19.5–6;

great warriors of, 5.4.4–5; mountain ranges in, 5.5.2–4, 5.6.1, 5.6.3; major regions of, 5.6.1–3; at Hyphasis River, Alexander expresses his wish to conquer, 5.26.2, 5.26.6; Koinos reminds Alexander of hardships suffered by Macedonian army in, 5.27.5;

march through Gedrosian desert as most difficult undertaking of Macedonian army in, 6.24.1; reportedly traversed by Dionysos after subjugating the Indians, 6.28.2;

cavalry, Scythian, posted in front of left wing of Darius'
force at Gaugamela, 3.11.6; makes contact with troops in
front of Alexander's line at Gaugamela, 3.13.2; routs
Alexander's mercenary cavalry in initial attack at
Gaugamela, 3.13.3; gives strong resistance to Paionians
and mercenaries of Alexander at Gaugamela, 3.13.4; in
battle with Macedonians at Tanais River, 4.4.6–7; ally
with Spitamenes to assault Macedonian force, 4.5.4–5;
routs Macedonians at Polytimetos River, 4.5.8–9; in Spitamenes' force defeated by Macedonians in Sogdiana,
4.17.4–6; accompanies Alexander on crossing of Hydaspes
River, 5.12.2
cavalry, Sogdian, accompanies Bessos to Nautaka, 3.28.10;
accompanies Alexander on crossing of Hydaspes River,
5.12.2
cavalry, Thessalian, commanded by Kalas son of Harpalos at
Granicus, 1.14.3; Parmenion sent to Sardis with, 1.24.3;
Alexander son of Aeropos in command of, 1.25.1, 1.25.2,
1.25.5; advance to Syrian Gates with Parmenion, 2.5.1;
Alexander praises, 2.7.8; deployed for battle at Issus, 2.8.9;
moved to support left wing at Issus, 2.9.1; inflicts heavy
casualties on Persian forces at Issus, 2.10.2–3; on Alexander's left wing at Gaugamela, 3.11.10; in battle against Persian right wing at Gaugamela, 3.15.3; sent to Persepolis
with Parmenion, 3.18.1; given choice at Ecbatana of staying with Alexander or returning home, 3.19.5–6
cavalry, Thracian, in march to Miletus, 1.18.3; in new Macedonian army at Gordion, 1.29.4; Alexander praises, 2.7.8;
sent to Alexander in Memphis, 3.5.1
Cayster River, plain formed by, 5.6.4
Celtic Rhine, Romans' bridging of, 5.7.2
Celts, territory beyond the Danube controlled by, 1.3.1; show
no fear of Alexander, make alliance with him, 1.4.6–8;
send envoys to Alexander, 7.15.4
Chaeronea, Athenian disaster at, 1.10.5
Chalcedonians, Alexander releases envoy of, 3.24.5
Chalcis, Proteas' warships depart from, 2.2.4
Chaldaeans, advise Alexander on Babylonian temples, 3.16.5;
Alexander advised not to enter Babylon by, 7.16.5–6,
7.22.1; to be deprived of revenue should Alexander reconstruct temple of Bel in Babylon, 7.17.1, 7.17.4
chariot(s), Alexander captures Darius', 2.11.5–6, 2.12.5,
3.15.5; captured by Macedonians at Gaugamela, 3.15.6;
Poros' son arrives at Hydaspes River with, 5.14.3,
5.14.5–6; captured by Alexander at Hydaspes River,
5.15.2; in Poros' force at Hydaspes River, 5.15.4; arrayed
for battle by Poros at Hydaspes River, 5.15.7; of Poros'
army destroyed at Hydaspes River, 5.18.2; taken by Macedonians at Sangala, 5.24.5; given to Alexander by Malloi,
6.14.3; carrying Hephaistion's body reportedly driven by
Alexander, 7.14.5
chariot(s), scythe-bearing, in Darius' force at Gaugamela,
3.8.6, 3.11.6, 3.11.7; Alexander stations Agrianians,
archers, and javelin men at Gaugamela opposite, 3.12.4;
unsuccessfully sent into action at Gaugamela, 3.13.5–6
children, capture of Thracian, 1.1.13; sent to Peuke Island by
Triballoi, 1.2.2; taken up on horseback by the Getae,
1.4.4; slaughtered indiscriminately in fall of Thebes, 1.8.8;
enslaved in Thebes, 1.9.9; of Granicus dead exempted
from land taxes and duties, 1.16.5;

of Darius captured at Issus, 2.11.9, 2.12.3–5, 3.22.4;
Darius pleads for release of, 2.14.1, 2.14.3; of Darius to
be returned upon recognition of Alexander's rule over
Asia, 2.14.8; Darius offers Alexander money in exchange
for, 2.25.1; Alexander enslaves Gazan, 2.27.7;
of Darius raised and educated by Alexander, 3.22.6;
taken by Macedonians from Gaza near Tanais River,
4.2.4; Athenians' war with Eurystheus on behalf of
Herakles', 4.10.4; taken prisoner at Sogdian Rock,
4.19.4;
of Akouphis sent to Alexander at Nysa, 5.2.4; Koinos
reminds Alexander of soldiers' longing to see, 5.27.6;
of Malloi and Oxydrakai sent to strongest cities in
preparation for battle against Alexander, 6.4.3; slaughtered by Macedonians in Malloi city, 6.11.1; killed by sudden flood in Macedonian camp in Gedrosian desert,
6.25.5;
of Alexander as relatives of other Macedonians' children, 7.10.3; of Macedonians leaving Asia ordered to be
left behind, 7.12.2; Alexander reportedly plans to have
Amazon queen bear his, 7.13.3; *see also* **daughter(s)**
Chios, surrendered by treachery to Memnon, 2.1.1; Persian
fleet stops trading vessels to Lesbos from, 2.1.2; following
army's defeat at Issus, Persian fleet seeks to prevent revolt
in, 2.13.4–5; revolts against Persians, 3.2.3–6; Alexander
receives prisoners from, 3.2.5, 3.2.7
Choes River, Alexander advances through western India
along, 4.23.2
Cilicia/Cilicians, Alexander enters, 2.4.4–5; Parmenion
sent to border between Assyria and, 2.5.1; Alexander
launches mountain attack on, 2.5.6, 2.6.4; Balakros son
of Nikanor appointed satrap of, 2.12.2; Persian force in,
3.7.4; Menes appointed governor of, 3.16.9; Darius' loss
of, 3.22.4; Taurus Mountains as boundary of, 3.28.5,
5.5.2
Cilician Gates, Alexander frightens defenders away from,
2.4.2–5
Cilluta, Alexander occupies, sacrifices at, sails into Great Sea
from, 6.19.3–4
cinnamon, found in Arabia, 7.20.2
Colchians, Khorasmians propose alliance with Alexander
against, 4.15.4; mentioned in Xenophon, 7.13.4
common people, prevented from seeking revenge in Ephesus, 1.17.11
Companions, in operations against Taulantians, 1.6.5–6;
sent ahead of the army to accept surrender of Priapus,
1.12.7; stationed alongside Alexander at the Granicus
River, 1.14.1; Alexander commissions commemorative
statues following Granicus River deaths of, 1.16.4;
sent with Parmenion to receive Magnesia and Tralles,
1.18.1; in start for Miletus, 1.18.3; in failed attack on
Myndos, 1.20.5; sent to Sardis with Parmenion, 1.24.3;
express distrust of Alexander son of Aeropos, 1.25.5;
unnerved by omen indicating plot against Alexander,
1.25.6–8;
urge Alexander to lead army from Mallos against Darius,
2.6.1; dispatched by Alexander to report on Darius' position, 2.7.2; Leonnatos as one of, 2.12.5; assembled by
Alexander following Tyrians' declaration of neutrality,
2.16.7; capture Tyrian wall with Alexander, 2.23.6; hear

Macedonian army prepares to set out for Great Sea from, 6.2.2–4; Alexander sacrifices to, sets out on voyage down, 6.3.1–5; Macedonian fleet creates tremendous spectacle as it sails down, 6.3.3–5; Alexander continues voyage down, comes to terms with or subdues Indians along, 6.4.1–3; Alexander reaches juncture of Akesinos River and, 6.4.4–5; Alexander's forces transported across, 6.5.5; route to Indus River of, 6.14.5; ships prepared for Alexander's voyage to Great Sea down, 6.1.1, 6.1.5–6;

Alexander reminds Macedonians at Opis of his crossing of, 7.10.6

Hydraotes River, size of, 5.4.2, 5.21.4; southward flow of, 5.5.5; Alexander reaches, 5.21.4; Alexander secures allegiance of Indians near, 5.21.5–6; Alexander marches toward Sangala from, 5.22.3; at Hyphasis River, Alexander recalls success at, 5.25.5; Alexander makes return journey to, 5.29.2; Alexander plans to reunite his army at juncture of Akesinos River and, 6.5.7; Alexander reaches, pursues Malloi fugitives across, 6.7.1–3; Alexander follows Malloi across, causes them to flee when his infantry arrives at, 6.8.4–8; Alexander reassures Macedonian army following his wounding in Malloi city by traveling in person to camp at, 6.13.1–3; Alexander comes to terms with Malloi and Oxydrakai, orders building of many new ships at, 6.14.1–4; route to Indus River of, 6.14.5; Alexander reminds Macedonians at Opis of his crossing of, 7.10.6

hymns, as honoring gods, 4.11.2

Hyparna, Alexander captures, 1.24.4

Hypereides, Alexander demands surrender of, 1.10.4–6

Hyphasis River, size of, 5.4.2; southward flow of, 5.5.5; Alexander advances to, 5.24.8; country surrounding, 5.25.1; Alexander addresses battle-weary officers at, 5.25.2–6, 5.26.1–8; Alexander emphasizes importance of advancing beyond, 5.25.5, 5.26.3; Alexander celebrates his achievements, grants territory to Poros at, begins return journey from, 5.29.1–2; route to Indus River of, 6.14.5; Alexander speaks at Opis of Macedonians' reluctance to cross, 7.10.7

Hyrcania/Hyrcanians, in Darius' force at Gaugamela, 3.8.4, 3.11.4; Darius plans to head toward, 3.19.1; Parmenion ordered to march to, 3.19.7; Amminapes appointed satrap of, 3.22.1; Alexander advances into, 3.23.1–2; Alexander receives surrender of satrap of, 3.23.4; Alexander advances to Zadrakarta in, 3.23.6; Alexander returns to Zadrakarta in, 3.25.1; Oxus River empties into Great Sea in, 3.29.2; Phrataphernes as satrap of, 5.20.7, 7.6.4; at Hyphasis River, Alexander recalls success in, 5.25.5; Pharismanes as satrap of, 6.27.3; Alexander reminds Macedonians at Opis of his victory over, 7.10.6; Alexander orders ships to be used in exploration of Caspian Sea built in, 7.16.1–2

Hyrcanian Sea, *see* **Caspian/Hyrcanian Sea**

Hystaspes the Bactrian, appointed commander of foreigners in Macedonian cavalry, 7.6.5

Iakkhos, sung by Athenians to Dionysos, 2.16.3

Iapygia, speculation about Alexander's future plans in, 7.1.3

Iasians, captured from Persian fleet in Miletus, 1.19.11

Iaxartes River, empties into Caspian Sea, 7.16.3; *see also* **Tanais/Iaxartes River**

Iberians, Herakles as worshiped by, 2.16.4; and story of Argive Herakles, 2.16.5–6; send envoys to Alexander, 7.15.4

Ida, Mount, source of river Praktios on, 1.12.6

Ikarian Sea, named for Ikaros, 7.20.5

Ikaros, Alexander names island in Persian Gulf for, 7.20.5

Illyrians, Alexander marches against, 1.1.4, 1.5.5–6; revolt against Alexander begun by, 1.5.1; abandon the heights around Pelion, 1.5.7; take refuge in Pelion, 1.5.8, 1.5.11–12; rumor of Alexander's death in land of, 1.7.2–3, 1.7.6; praised by Alexander for their battleworthiness, 2.7.5; in address at Hyphasis River, Alexander minimizes victory over, 5.26.6; Alexander speaks at Opis of early Macedonian troubles with, 7.9.2; *see also* **Taulantians**

India

rivers in: Oxus, 3.29.2; Arrian lists all the major ones, 5.5.5; Indus, 5.6.3; Ganges compared to other rivers, 5.6.6–8; Indian rivers in different seasons 5.9.4; Indus, Hydaspes, Akesinos, Hydraotes, and Hyphasis flow into each other, 6.14.5; Oxus, Iaxartes, Araxes, 7.16.3;

Alexander announces intention to conquer, 4.15.6; Alexander revisits Alexandria in the Caucasus on his advance to, 4.22.3; Arrian questions truth of stories about Herakles in, 4.28.1–2;

Dionysos in, *see under* **Dionysos**; Nysa as only source of ivy in, 5.1.6, 5.2.6; Macedonian stories of Alexander's exploits as confusing geography of, 5.3.3–4; Arrian discusses legends about, 5.4.3–5; Arrian promises to write more complete account of, 5.5.1, 6.16.5; Caucasus Mountains in, 5.5.3–4, 5.6.3; as largest region of Asia, 5.6.2–3; Great Sea as boundary of, 5.6.3, 7.16.2; Taurus Mountains in, 5.6.3; Alexander brings provisions across Akesinos River for further excursions into, 5.21.1;

Alexander believes he has found source of Nile River in, 6.1.3–5; Alexander accepts surrender of autonomous tribes, plans further wars in, 6.14.1–3; territory of Mousikanos as most prosperous in, 6.15.5; Alexander reaches Great Sea beyond, 6.19.5; Semiramis' and Cyrus' marches through Gedrosian desert in conquest of, 6.24.2–3; Alexander learns of rebellion against Philip in, 6.27.2; in Carmania, Alexander celebrates his victory in, 6.28.3;

Alexander encounters sages in, 7.1.5–6, 7.2.2–4; Macedonian officials commit offenses in other territories during Alexander's expedition to, 7.4.2; Alexander presents gifts in recognition of valor during campaign in, 7.5.4–6; Alexander reminds Macedonians at Opis of their acquisition of treasure in, 7.9.8; Alexander reminds Macedonians at Opis of voyage of Macedonian fleet to Persia from, 7.10.7; Apollodoros fears punishment by Alexander on his return from, 7.18.1; Greeks send envoys to Alexander to celebrate his return from, 7.19.1; Arabian peninsula reportedly as large as, 7.20.2, 7.20.8; Nearkhos encounters Arabian peninsula on voyage to Persian Gulf from, 7.20.9

India, eastern, Koinos imagines future campaign of Alexander in, 5.27.7

India, western, Alexander advances through, 4.23.1–3; Alexander takes cities in, 4.23.4–5; Alexander pursues fugitives in, 4.24.1–2; Alexander prepares to attack large rebel force in, 4.24.7–10; Alexander defeats large rebel force in, 4.25.1–4; Alexander makes military and administrative arrangements in, 4.28.4–7

as warriors under Cyrus son of Cambyses, 5.4.5; at Hyphasis River, Alexander recalls success against, 5.25.5; Alexander's intention to appoint Peukestas as satrap of, 6.28.3; Hephaistion ordered to lead largest division of army along coast from Carmania to, 6.28.7; Alexander travels to Pasargadae, deals with rebels in, 6.29.1–3; Alexander visits Cyrus son of Cambyses' tomb as ruler of, 6.29.9; Alexander visits previously burned palaces in, appoints Peukestas as satrap of, 6.30.1–3; Orxines put to death for acts against, 6.30.2; Peukestas adopts language and manner of, 6.30.3, 7.6.3;

as rulers over only a small part of Asia, 7.1.3; death of Kalanos in, 7.3.1–6; during Alexander's expedition to India, Macedonian officials commit offenses in, 7.4.3; Alexander's Companions marry daughters of distinguished, 7.4.5–6; Alexander's weddings in Susa held in manner of, 7.4.6–7; Alexander destroys weirs on Tigris River built by, 7.7.7; Alexander reminds Macedonians at Opis of their victories over, 7.9.6–7, 7.10.5; Alexander reminds Macedonians at Opis of their acquisition of treasure in, 7.9.8; Alexander reminds Macedonians at Opis of voyage of Macedonian fleet from India to, 7.10.7; given commands by Alexander following his rebuke of Macedonians at Opis, 7.11.1, 7.11.3, 7.29.4; Kallines explains Macedonians' distress at Alexander's favoring of, 7.11.6; Alexander holds banquet in Opis for Macedonians and, 7.11.8–9; battle between Athenians and, 7.13.5; Peukestas joins Alexander in Babylon with additional troops from, 7.23.1; enrolled in Macedonian army in Babylon, 7.23.3–4, 7.24.1, 7.29.4; *see also* **army, Persian**; **fleet, Persian**; *specific cities*

Persian campaign, Alexander asks Greeks for leadership of, 1.1.2–3; *see also* **Asian campaign**; **Aspendos**; **Caria/Carians**; **Ephesus**; **Granicus River**; **Halicarnassus**; **Lycia**; **Miletus**; **Perge**; **Phaselis**; **Phrygia/Phrygians**; **Sardis**; **Side/Sidetans**

Persian Gates, Alexander encounters Ariobarzanes at, 3.18.2–3; Alexander finds alternate route to, 3.18.4–5; Alexander routs Ariobarzanes' force at, 3.18.6–9

Persian Gulf, Alexander expresses his wish to advance to, 5.26.2; Alexander plans to send Nearkhos with Macedonian fleet to, 6.19.5; Alexander orders Hephaistion to lead army from Susa to, 7.7.1; Tigris River emptying into, 7.7.3; Alexander's discovery of connection of Great Sea to, 7.16.2; Alexander intends to colonize coast near, 7.19.5; Macedonians' reconnaissance of, 7.20.3–10

Persian Sea, Arrian promises future account of Nearkhos' voyage from Indus River to, 6.28.6; Alexander plans to sail down Euphrates and Tigris to, 7.1.1; Macedonian fleet sails to Babylon from, 7.19.3

Persian Wars, Theban betrayal of the Greeks in, 1.9.7

Petenes, at Persian commanders' council to discuss best way to meet Alexander's advance, 1.12.8–10; death at Granicus of, 1.16.3

Petisis, appointed governor of Egypt by Alexander, 3.5.2

Peuke Island, Triballoi wives and children sent to, 1.2.2; Syrmos flees to, 1.2.3

Peukelaotis (region of Indian Caucasus), Alexander sends force to subdue, 4.22.7–8

Peukelaotis (city near Indus River), brought to terms by Alexander, 4.28.6

Peukestas (Companion), follows Alexander in scaling of wall at Mallian city, 6.9.3; jumps inside Mallian wall, protects Alexander with sacred shield from Troy, 6.10.1, 6.10.2, 6.11.7, 6.11.8; enrolled as bodyguard during celebrations in Carmania, 6.28.3–4; appointed satrap of Persia, adopts Persian manner, 6.30.2–3, 7.6.3; awarded golden crown by Alexander, 7.5.4; joins Alexander in Babylon with additional troops from Persia, 7.23.1, 7.24.1; praised by Alexander in Babylon, 7.23.3; spends Alexander's final night in temple of Sarapis, 7.26.2

Peukestas (son of Makartatos), appointed general of Alexander's force in Egypt, 3.5.5

phalanx, Macedonian, Thracians plan to send wagons down Mount Haemus at, 1.1.7; unhurt by Thracian wagons, drives Thracians from mountain, 1.1.10–12; led against Triballoi at Lyginus River, 1.2.4, 1.2.6; Getae flee at approach of, 1.4.1–4; performs series of drills in view of Taulantians, 1.6.1–3; in close formation at Eordaikos River, raises war cry against Taulantians, 1.6.6–7; drives Thebans inside city, 1.8.5; arrayed in two rows at Granicus River, 1.13.1; led against foreign mercenaries at Granicus River, 1.16.2; attempts to undermine wall at Myndos, 1.20.6; arrayed for battle at Sagalassos, 1.28.3; led by Alexander in attack on Pisidians, 1.28.6;

on favorable terrain for battle at Issus, 2.7.3; rolled out during advance prior to battle at Issus, 2.8.2; Darius posts Greek mercenaries opposite, 2.8.6, 3.11.7; Thessalian cavalry movement at Issus screened by, 2.9.1; at Issus, Alexander seeks to strengthen, 2.9.3–4; surges forward at Issus, 2.10.3; attacked by Greek mercenaries in Persian army at Issus, 2.10.4–7, 2.11.7; decimates Greek mercenaries in Persian army at Issus, 2.11.2; advances on Gaza, 2.27.5;

marshaled for battle at Gaugamela, 3.11.9–10; at Gaugamela, Alexander creates double-fronted, 3.12.1–5, 13.14.5–6; Persians at Gaugamela send scythe-bearing chariots against, 3.13.5–6; counterattacks Persians in force at Gaugamela, 3.14.1–3; suffers break in left wing at Gaugamela, is aided by reserves, 3.14.4–6; accompanies Alexander toward Parthia in pursuit of Darius, 3.20.1–2; with Alexander in Tapourian Mountains, 3.23.3;

assaulted by Spitamenes and Scythian cavalry, 4.4.4–5; crosses Tanais River, 4.4.5; Alexander pursues Spitamenes with nimblest of, 4.6.3–5; charges Indians at Massaka, 4.26.3–4; in siege of Massaka, 4.26.6; Alexander selects men for assault on Aornos Rock from, 4.28.8;

Krateros left on bank of Hydaspes River with battalions from, 5.11.3; Alexander accompanied on crossing of Hydaspes River by units from, 5.12.2; arrayed for battle at Hydaspes River, 5.13.4, 5.16.3; Poros arrays elephants at Hydaspes River opposite, 5.15.5–6; reaches Alexander's cavalry force at Hydaspes River, 5.16.1; in battle against Poros' elephants at Hydaspes River, 5.17.3; routs Poros' force at Hydaspes River, 5.17.7; strengthened with additional infantry at Sangala, 5.22.7; forces Indians at Sangala to take refuge inside city, 5.23.1–3;

led by Alexander to wall of Brahman city, 6.7.4; *see also* **army, Macedonian**; **infantry, Macedonian**

REFERENCE MAPS
Directory

Sites that are listed in this directory but, due to inappropriate scale or crowding of map labels, could not be placed on the Reference Maps are identified as located on the text map on which they appear.

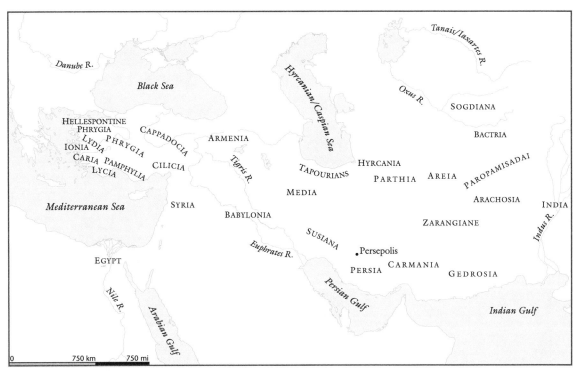

REF. MAP 1. PERSIAN SATRAPIES MENTIONED BY ARRIAN IN THE *ANABASIS*

491

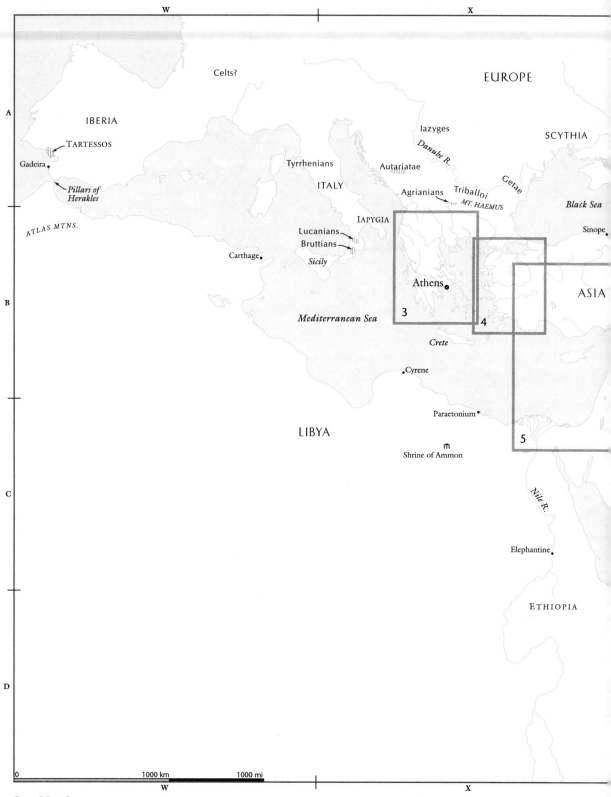

W   X

Celts?   EUROPE

IBERIA   SCYTHIA
A   Iazyges

TARTESSOS   *Danube R.*
Gadeira•   Tyrrhenians   Autariatae   Getae
Pillars of   ITALY   Triballoi   *Black Sea*
Herakles   Agrianians   MT. HAEMUS
                                                                      Sinope•
ATLAS MTNS.   IAPYGIA
                      Lucanians   ASIA
                      Bruttians
                  Carthage•   *Sicily*
                                        Athens•
B   3   4
                        Mediterranean Sea

                                        Crete

                                   •Cyrene

                            Paraetonium•   5

                 LIBYA   m̂
                          Shrine of Ammon

C
                                                  Nile R.

                                          Elephantine•

                                                  ETHIOPIA

D

0   1000 km   1000 mi
W   X

REF. MAP 2

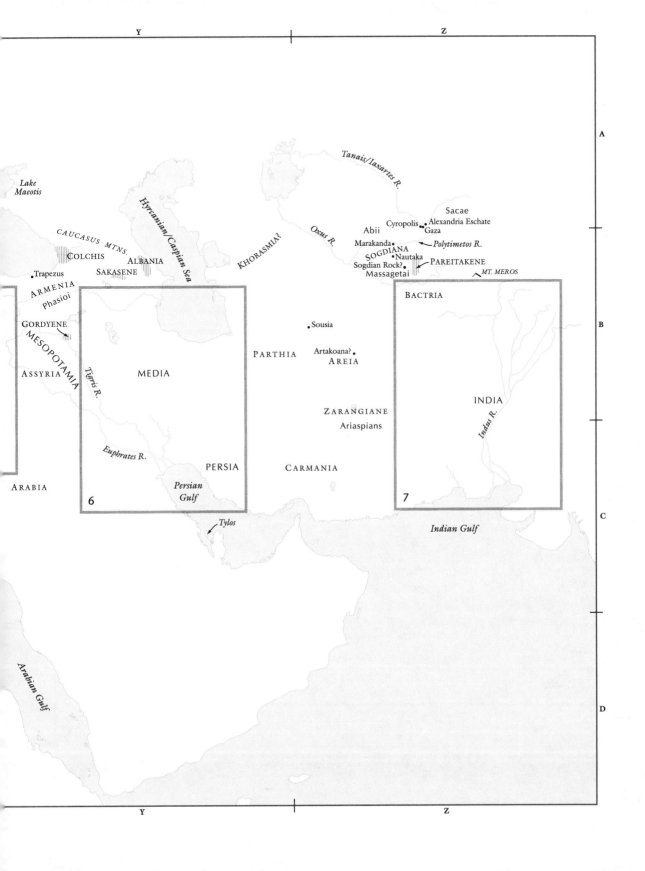

Y   Z   A

Lake
Maeotis

Tanais/Iaxartes R.

Hyrcanian/Caspian Sea

Oxus R.

Sacae

CAUCASUS MTNS.

COLCHIS

ALBANIA

SAKASENE

•Trapezus

ARMENIA

Phasioi

GORDYENE

MESOPOTAMIA

ASSYRIA

KHORASMIA?

Abii   Cyropolis •• Alexandria Eschate
                         Gaza

Marakanda•
          SOGDIANA   ← *Polytimetos R.*
             •Nautaka
Sogdian Rock?•   ← PAREITAKENE
Massagetai •

∧ *MT. MEROS*

BACTRIA

•Sousia   B

Artakoana? •
      A R E I A

PARTHIA

Tigris R.

MEDIA

INDIA

Indus R.

ZARANGIANE
Ariaspians

Euphrates R.

PERSIA

CARMANIA

ARABIA

*Persian
Gulf*

6   7   C

Tylos ↙

Indian Gulf

Arabian Gulf

D

Y   Z

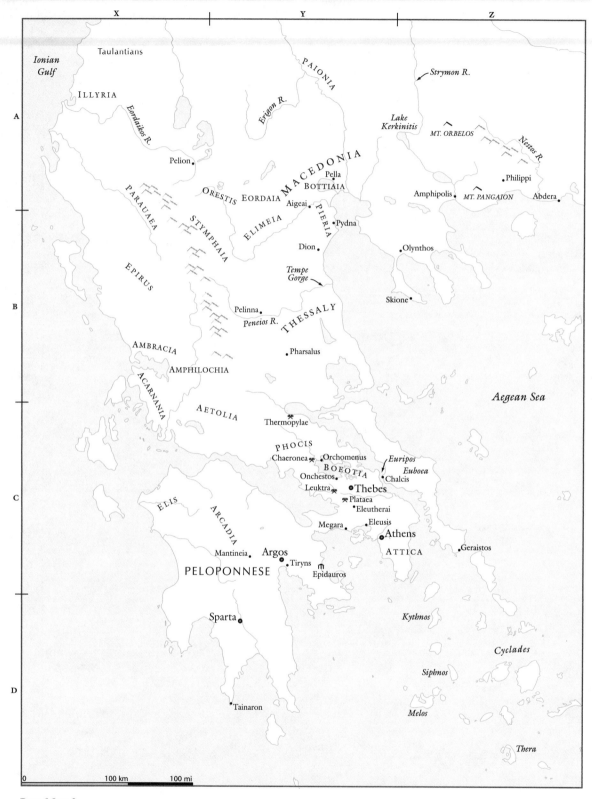

X   Y   Z

Ionian Gulf

Taulantians

ILLYRIA

Eordaikos R.

Erigon R.

PAIONIA

Strymon R.

Lake Kerkinitis

MT. ORBELOS

Nestos R.

Pelion

ORESTIS EORDAIA MACEDONIA

Pella

BOTTIAIA

Philippi

Amphipolis

MT. PANGAION

Abdera

PARAUAEA

STYMPHAIA

Aigeai

PIERIA

Pydna

EPIRUS

ELIMEIA

Dion

Olynthos

Tempe Gorge

Skione

Pelinna

Peneios R.

THESSALY

AMBRACIA

AMPHILOCHIA

Pharsalus

ACARNANIA

Aegean Sea

AETOLIA

Thermopylae

PHOCIS

Chaeronea

Orchomenus

Euripos

Euboea

BOEOTIA

Onchestos

Chalcis

ELIS

Leuktra

Thebes

ARCADIA

Plataea

Eleutherai

Megara

Eleusis

Mantineia

Argos

Athens

Tiryns

ATTICA

Geraistos

PELOPONNESE

Epidauros

Kythnos

Sparta

Cyclades

Siphnos

Melos

Tainaron

Thera

0   100 km   100 mi

REF. MAP 3

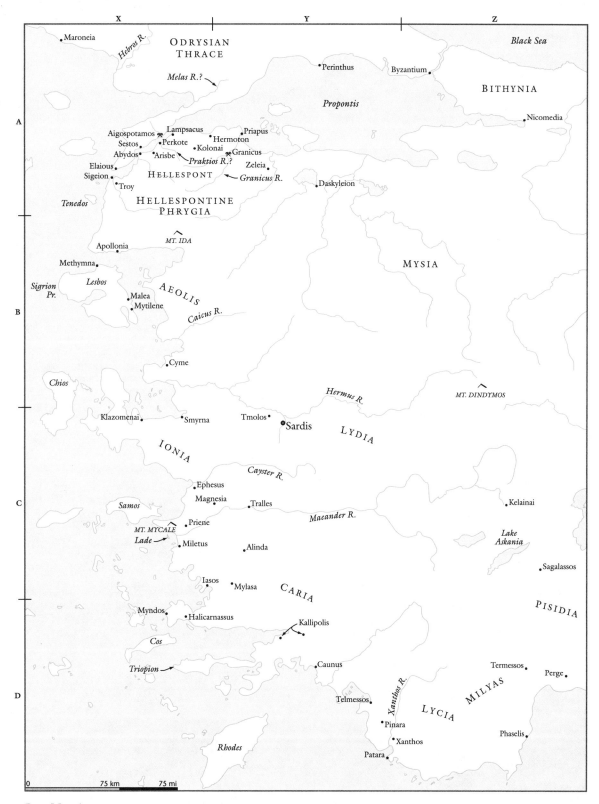

X Y Z

Maroneia

Hebros R.

ODRYSIAN
THRACE

Melas R.?

Propontis

Perinthus

Byzantium

Black Sea

BITHYNIA

Nicomedia

A

Aigospotamos
Sestos
Abydos
Elaious
Sigeion
Troy

Lampsacus
Perkote
Arisbe

Priapus
Hermoton
Kolonai
Granicus

Praktios R.?
Zeleia

HELLESPONT

Granicus R.

Daskyleion

Tenedos

HELLESPONTINE
PHRYGIA

MT. IDA

MYSIA

Apollonia

Methymna

*Sigrion
Pr.*

Lesbos

AEOLIS

Malea
Mytilene

Caicus R.

B

Cyme

Chios

Hermus R.

MT. DINDYMOS

Klazomenai

Smyrna

Tmolos

Sardis

LYDIA

IONIA

Cayster R.

Ephesus
Magnesia

Tralles

Macander R.

Kelainai

C

Samos

MT. MYCALE
Lade

Priene

Miletus

Alinda

*Lake
Askania*

Sagalassos

Iasos
Mylasa

CARIA

PISIDIA

Myndos
Halicarnassus

Kallipolis

Cos

Termessos
Perge

Triopion

Caunus

Xanthos R.

MILYAS

D

Telmessos

LYCIA

Pinara
Xanthos

Phaselis

Rhodes

Patara

0 75 km 75 mi

REF. MAP 4

495

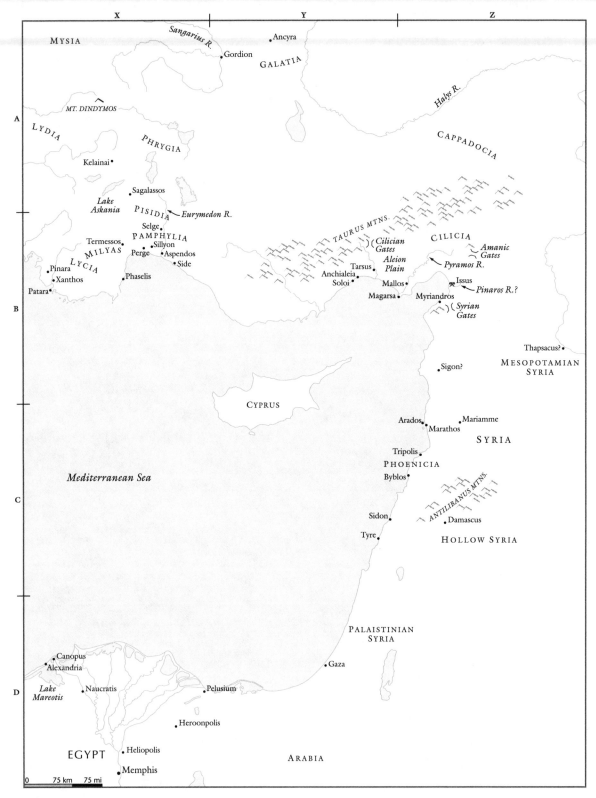

MYSIA

Sangarius R.

Ancyra

Gordion

GALATIA

Halys R.

MT. DINDYMOS

LYDIA

PHRYGIA

CAPPADOCIA

Kelainai

Sagalassos

Lake Askania

PISIDIA

Eurymedon R.

TAURUS MTNS.

CILICIA

Selge

Amanic Gates

Termessos

PAMPHYLIA

Sillyon

(Cilician Gates

MILYAS

Perge

Aspendos

Aleion Plain

Pyramos R.

LYCIA

Side

Pinara

Xanthos

Phaselis

Anchialeia

Tarsus

Soloi

Mallos

Issus

Pinaros R.?

Patara

Magarsa

Myriandros

(Syrian Gates

Thapsacus?

MESOPOTAMIAN SYRIA

Sigon?

CYPRUS

Arados

Mariamme

Marathos

SYRIA

Tripolis

PHOENICIA

Byblos

Mediterranean Sea

ANTILIBANUS MTNS.

Sidon

Damascus

Tyre

HOLLOW SYRIA

PALAISTINIAN SYRIA

Canopus

Alexandria

Gaza

Lake Mareotis

Naucratis

Pelusium

Heroonpolis

Heliopolis

EGYPT

ARABIA

Memphis

0   75 km   75 mi

REF. MAP 5

X   Y   Z

A

B

C

D

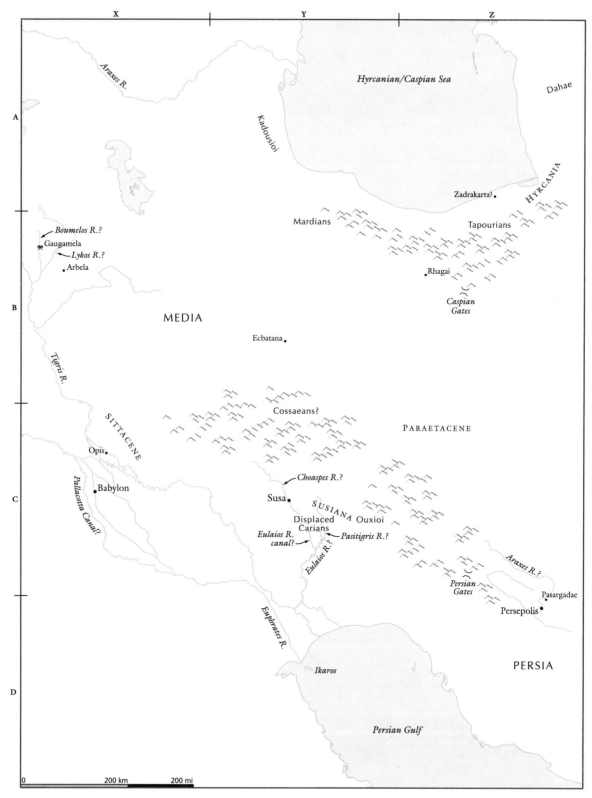

X   Y   Z

Araxes R.

Hyrcanian/Caspian Sea

Dahae

Kadousioi

A

HYRCANIA

Zadrakarta?

Boumelos R.?

Mardians   Tapourians

Gaugamela

Lykos R.?

Arbela

Rhagai

B   MEDIA

Caspian Gates

Ecbatana

Tigris R.

SITTACENE   Cossaeans?   PARAETACENE

Opis

Pallacotta Canal?   *Choaspes R.?*

Babylon   Susa

C   SUSIANA   Ouxioi

Displaced Carians

Eulaios R. canal?   *Pasitigris R.?*

Eulaios R.?   *Araxes R.?*

Persian Gates   Pasargadae

Persepolis

Euphrates R.

PERSIA

Ikaros

D

Persian Gulf

0   200 km   200 mi

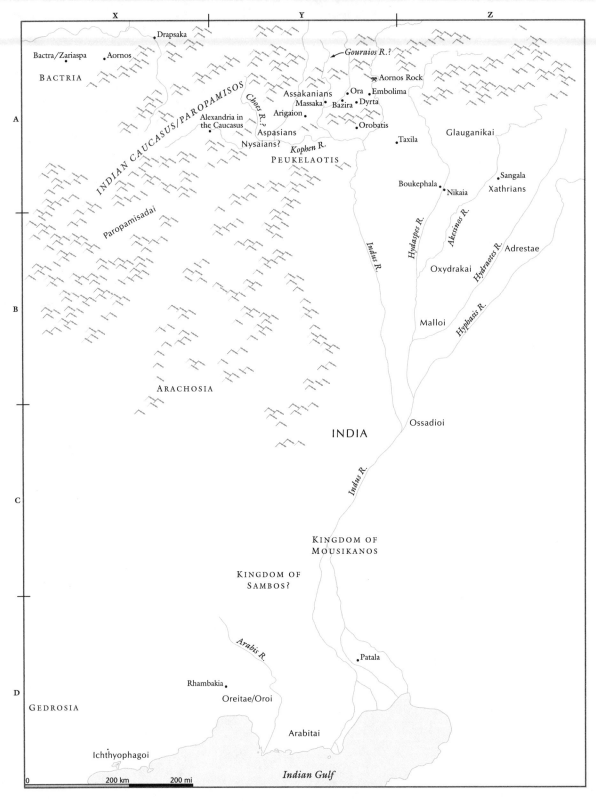

X   Y   Z

• Drapsaka

Bactra/Zariaspa   • Aornos

B A C T R I A

Gouraios R.?

✠ Aornos Rock

Assakanians   • Ora   • Embolima

Massaka •   • Dyrta

• Alexandria in   Arigaion •   Bazira •
the Caucasus

A   • Orobatis

Aspasians   Glauganikai

Nysaians?   *Kophen R.*   • Taxila

P E U K E L A O T I S

Boukephala •   • Sangala

• Nikaia   Xathrians

I N D I A N   C A U C A S U S / P A R O P A M I S O S

Choes R.?

Paropamisadai

Oxydrakai   Adrestae

B

Indus R.   Malloi   *Hyphasis R.*

A R A C H O S I A

Ossadioi

I N D I A

C

K I N G D O M   O F
M O U S I K A N O S

K I N G D O M   O F
S A M B O S ?

Indus R.

Arabis R.

• Patala

Rhambakia •

D   Oreitae/Oroi

G E D R O S I A

Arabitai

Ichthyophagoi

Indian Gulf

0   200 km   200 mi

REF. MAP 7

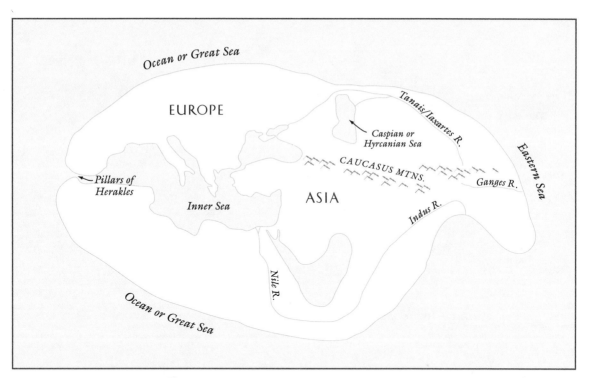

A. The Connections Between Rivers

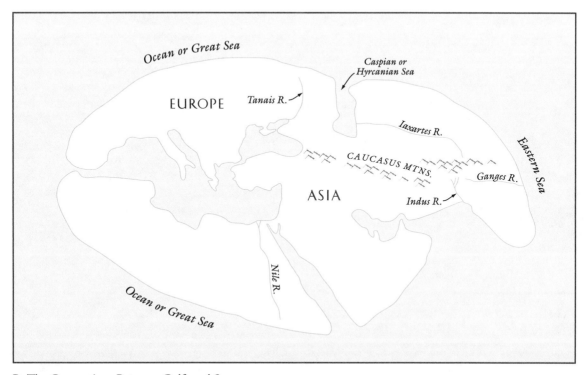

B. The Connections Between Gulfs and Seas

REF. MAP 8. ALEXANDER'S GEOGRAPHIC NOTIONS

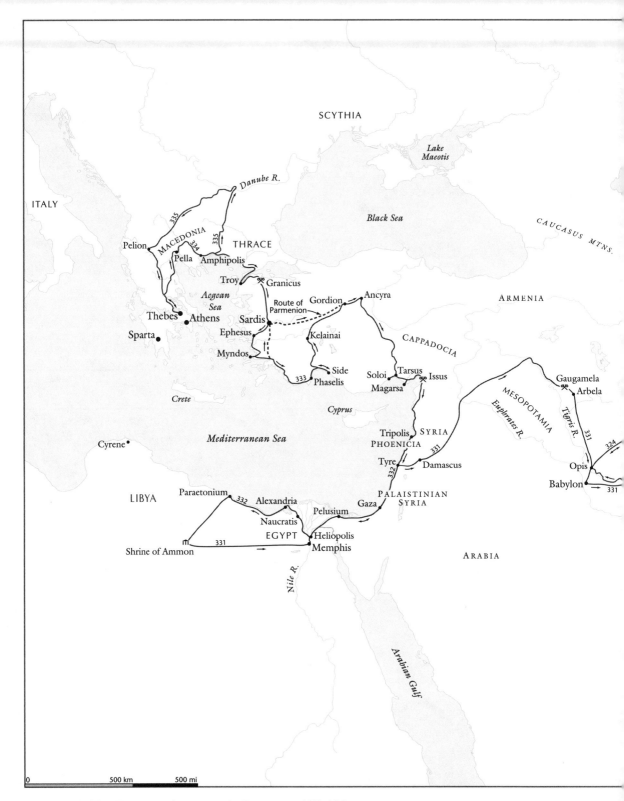

SCYTHIA

Lake Maeotis

ITALY

Danube R.

MACEDONIA

THRACE

Black Sea

CAUCASUS MTNS.

335
334
335

Pelion
Pella
Amphipolis

Troy
Granicus

Route of Parmenion

Gordion

Ancyra

ARMENIA

Aegean Sea

Thebes
Athens

Sardis

Sparta

Ephesus

Kelainai

CAPPADOCIA

Myndos

333

Side
Phaselis

Soloi
Magarsa

Tarsus
Issus

Gaugamela
Arbela

MESOPOTAMIA

Euphrates R.

Tigris R.

331

324

Crete

Cyprus

Mediterranean Sea

Tripolis
PHOENICIA

SYRIA

Cyrene

Tyre

Damascus

331

Opis

Babylon

331

332

LIBYA

Paraetonium

332

Alexandria

Naucratis

EGYPT

Pelusium

Gaza

PALAISTINIAN
SYRIA

Heliopolis
Memphis

Shrine of Ammon

331

ARABIA

Nile R.

Arabian Gulf

0   500 km   500 mi

REF. MAP 9. THE ROUTE OF ALEXANDER'S CAMPAIGNS 335–323

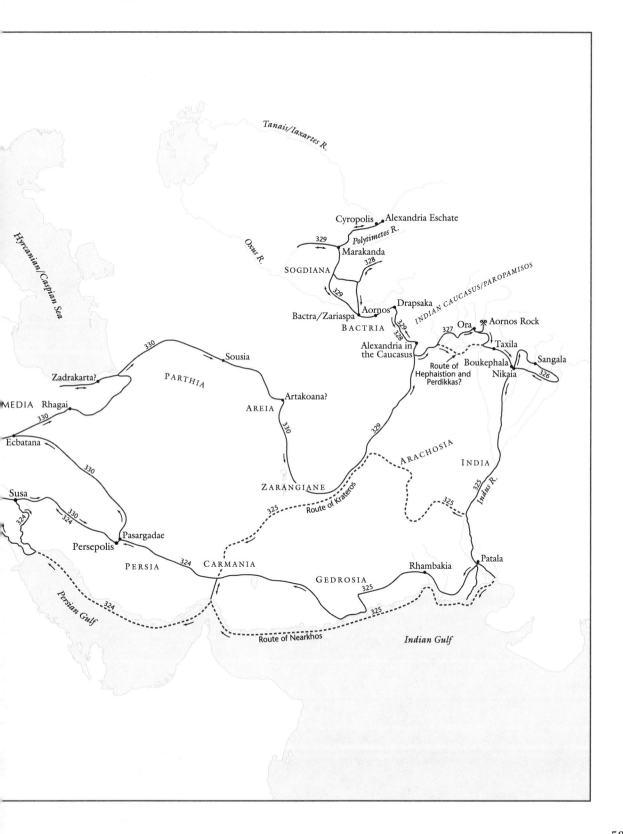

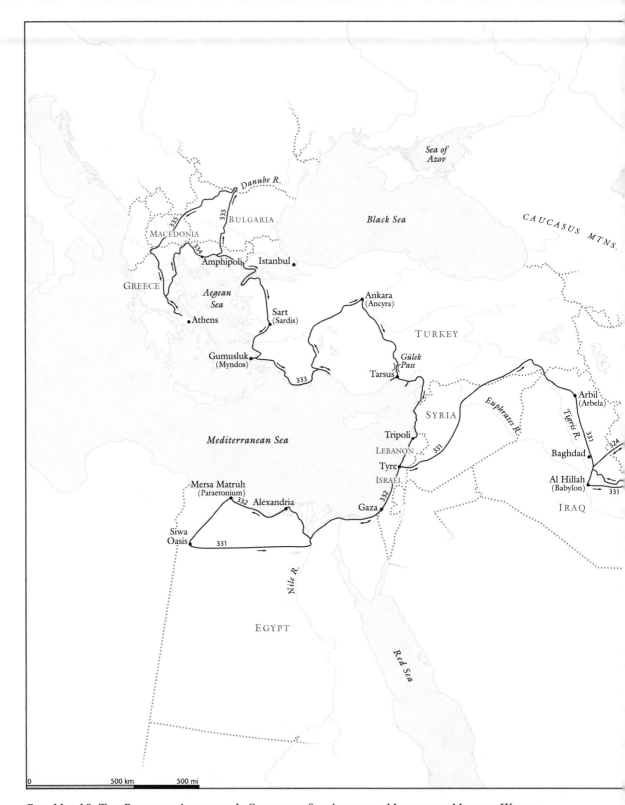

Sea of
Azov

CAUCASUS MTNS.

Black Sea

Danube R.

BULGARIA

MACEDONIA

Amphipoli   Istanbul

GREECE

Aegean
Sea

Ankara
(Ancyra)

TURKEY

Athens

Sart
(Sardis)

Gülek
Pass

Gumusluk
(Myndos)

333

Tarsus

Arbil
(Arbela)

SYRIA

Euphrates R.

Tigris R.

331

324

Mediterranean Sea

Tripoli

LEBANON

331

Baghdad

Tyre

ISRAEL

Mersa Matruh
(Paraetonium)

332   Alexandria

332

Gaza

Al Hillah
(Babylon)

331

IRAQ

Siwa
Oasis

331

Nile R.

Red Sea

EGYPT

0   500 km   500 mi

Ref. Map 10. The Route of Alexander's Campaigns Set Against a Map of the Modern World

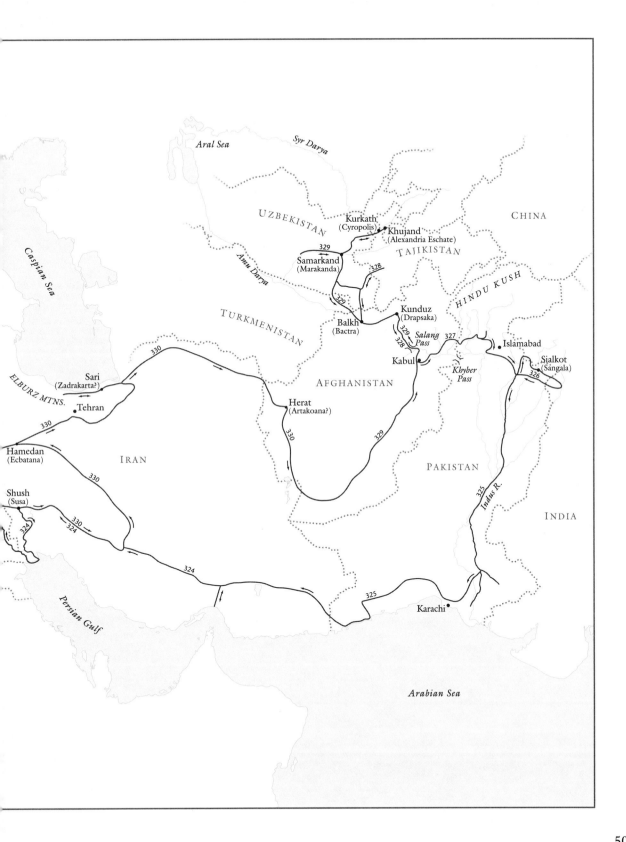

503

HIRCANUM

Marginia
Bazaria
Bocara

Massagetæ
Zaweh
tha
Dahæ Scy
Derbiccæ

Duæ Urbes ad
austrū Marginiæ
ab Alexandro Conditæ

S
OG

Branc

MARGIANA

Mardi

Pays de Marou

Roy

Cadusii
Zadracarta
Hyrc. Caput
Ferabad
Tapuri
Barcani
SAN
Zariaspe Seu
HYRCANIA
Astrabad
Arvas
ORIA
BACT

Tabristan
Thoberis
Dara Sive
Darathe
Hecatompylos

Caucasus
ROY
me

Rhages
Rhey ruine
Susia Suse ou
Zeuzen
HERAT

Tabas Sava
Portæ
Caspiæ
Parthiene

MI
PARTHIA
Artacoana
Sive Chortacana
Alexandria
Ariæ
Herat

IA
Choroane
M
A

Paretacene
Tabiene
E

Prophtasia
Drangarū
I
P
R

Zarangæorū seu
Drangarum Regia
Zarang ou Segestan

Aspadana
Ispahan
Arimaspi
Seu Ariaspa postea
Evergetæ

Uxiorum Montes
Hatichæ
Yesd

Uxii
Persidis Deserta
Caramania
deserta
DRANGIA

SIANA
SEGEST
SISTAN
PERSIS
D

FARSISTAN
ARI

Mardi
Persepolis
Chelminar
Carmana metropolis
Kerman

Chiras

Pasargada
Passa
CARAMANIA

KERMAN

GEDROS

Myrrha et Aromatibus ab

Bassora R.
MECI

SINUS
Armuzia seu
Harmatia emporium

Salmunte
Sermion
Ortus
Mons
Semiramidis
Pura
Gedrosiæ Metropolis
I. de Z. Quesmo
Ichthiophag

PERSICUS
Deserta inaquo

RUBR
Sive
ERYTHRÆ